RICHARD B. RUSSELL, JR., SENATOR FROM GEORGIA

RICHARD B. RUSSELL, JR.,

SENATOR FROM GEORGIA

BY   GILBERT   C.   FITE

THE FRED W. MORRISON SERIES IN SOUTHERN STUDIES

The University of North Carolina Press   *Chapel Hill & London*

Publication of this book was assisted by a generous grant from the Richard B. Russell Foundation, Inc., of Atlanta, Georgia. The views expressed in the book are the author's alone and are not intended to reflect the opinions of the Russell Foundation or its trustees.

MANUFACTURED IN THE UNITED STATES OF AMERICA

THE PAPER USED IN THIS BOOK MEETS THE GUIDELINES FOR PERMANENCE AND DURABILITY OF THE COMMITTEE ON PRODUCTION GUIDELINES FOR BOOK LONGEVITY OF THE COUNCIL ON LIBRARY RESOURCES.

95 94 93 92 91   5 4 3 2 1

ISBN 0-8078-1937-9

LIBRARY OF CONGRESS CATALOGING-IN-PUBLICATION DATA APPEAR ON THE LAST PRINTED PAGE OF THIS BOOK.

To June,
WHOSE LOVE AND SUPPORT I
CAN NEVER PROPERLY REPAY

Contents

Illustrations

═══

Preface

===

riting a biography of "Richard Brevard Russell, Democrat, of Winder, Ga.," as he liked to be known, has been
a challenging but rewarding adventure. Russell's contemporaries found him a difficult man to understand, and the
passage of time since his death in 1971 has not done much to clarify his
enigmatic character. Indeed, Russell was in many ways a complex and
contradictory figure. A quiet, reserved, and modest man, he relished the
frequent praise heaped upon him; although he never married, he believed deeply in family values; he had many admirers in Georgia and
throughout the nation but very few close personal friends; and he held
no personal ill will toward blacks, but he was largely responsible for
delaying effective civil rights legislation for nearly twenty years. These
and other seeming inconsistencies and contradictions may make it difficult to understand Russell the man, but they in no way cloud his long
career of distinguished public service. It is my hope that this biography
will help explain Russell's thought, his strength of character, and his
contributions to his state and nation. Because of his penchant for secrecy on some matters, not all of Russell's actions can be adequately
explained. This was especially true in regard to aspects of national defense and his oversight of the Central Intelligence Agency.

Born on November 2, 1897, and reared in an elite southern family,
Russell grew up in a highly stratified and class-conscious society. No
other factor made such a deep impression on him as his upbringing and
residence in the South and his understanding of the region's history. The
Russell family planned that Richard, Jr., the oldest son, would pursue a
political career, and that he did. He served in public life from 1921 to
1971, a period that witnessed some of the most dramatic and far-reaching changes of any half century in American history. After ten years in
the Georgia General Assembly, the last four as Speaker of the House, he
was elected governor in 1930. He served in that office from 1931 to

January 1933, when he began his thirty-eight years in the U.S. Senate. Russell spent more than two-thirds of his life in elective office and more than half of it in the Senate. He worked with six presidents from Franklin D. Roosevelt to Richard M. Nixon.

During his long public career, Russell lived through a virtual revolution in American life and society. From the 1920s until his death, the United States experienced the stock market crash of 1929, the Great Depression, World War II, the cold war, the beginning of the nuclear age, the exploration of space, a great expansion of the welfare state, a vast increase in the nation's international responsibilities, the civil rights movement, and a host of other changes. Russell was a key participant in many of these revolutionary developments and adjusted to much of the rapid change that characterized the twentieth century. But he could never abandon his dedication to the South's traditional social values. The issue on which his ideas and attitudes could not be modified was racial equality and integration. Because of his unwillingness to adjust to, or compromise on, this matter, and his masterminding of the anti–civil rights forces, he had to remain content with regional rather than true national leadership.

This did not mean that Russell failed to achieve national recognition. He did and for very good reasons. He became one of the nation's strongest supporters of economic equality for American farmers. He fathered the school lunch program and supported the distribution of surplus food to the needy. Russell served on the Senate Appropriations Committee from the time he arrived in Washington until his death, the last two years as chairman. As a member of that committee, there was little major legislation that he did not affect in some way. He calmed the national hysteria that surrounded the dismissal of General Douglas MacArthur in 1951 by conducting hearings on the issue with integrity and fairness, and a year later, he ran a respectable campaign for the Democratic presidential nomination. Perhaps his greatest contribution was his determination to maintain a strong national defense during the cold war era. As chairman of the Armed Services Committee from 1951 to 1953 and from 1955 to 1969, Russell emerged as the acknowledged leader in Congress on defense matters. Also of great importance was his legislative skill and knowledge of Senate rules, which permitted him to get many bills through the Senate that might have died in legislative logjams. In January 1969, as the senior member of the Senate and as one who commanded the admiration and respect of his colleagues, he was elected president pro tem. While no major legislation bears Russell's name, he was very influential in the legislative process over an entire

Senate generation. Despite his opposition to civil rights legislation, by the end of his career he had become in many eyes nothing less than the "Georgia Giant," a "Senator's Senator," and, as Richard Nixon said, a "President's Senator."

This is an old-fashioned biography because Richard B. Russell, Jr., was an old-fashioned man. He personified the ancient values of integrity, reliability, fairness, and kindness, and he viewed women in a special light. These were values that were losing ground in American life and politics. In some ways, his values extended back well into the nineteenth century when life was simpler and seemed more genuine. To give the reader a feel for what Dick Russell was really like, I have permitted him to speak for himself in many cases. I hope this book will at least partially express the depth of his character and help the reader to better understand one of the South's, and the nation's, leading statesmen of the twentieth century.

Many individuals and institutions have provided valuable assistance in the preparation of this book. First, I want to express my thanks to the Board of Trustees of the Richard B. Russell Foundation for funding the Russell Chair in American History at the University of Georgia. I also appreciate the fact that the Department of History and the University of Georgia appointed me the first holder of that chair in 1976 and gave me time and support during the next ten years for a wide range of research, including this biography. Underlying all of this university support was that given by President Fred C. Davison, who understood and promoted research and scholarship during his years of leadership.

This book could not have been written without the resources provided by the Russell Memorial Library at the University of Georgia, with its huge Russell Collection, including correspondence, reports, memos, oral histories, and other materials. The Dwight D. Eisenhower presidential library at Abilene, Kansas, and the Lyndon B. Johnson presidential library at Austin, Texas, also contain valuable material on Russell. The papers of former senator J. William Fulbright at the University of Arkansas library at Fayetteville were among a number of additional personal collections that were most useful in this study.

Among the people who have been very helpful are Sheryl Vogt, archivist at the Russell Memorial Library, members of the Russell family, and individuals who worked in Russell's Senate office. A number of my graduate students at the University of Georgia, especially David D. Potenziani and Edward Nagy, helped with many aspects of the research on Russell. Paula Wald did a splendid job of copyediting the manuscript for the University of North Carolina Press. I am especially grateful to my colleague Numan V. Bartley, whose knowledge of southern history far exceeds my own, for reading the manuscript and making many helpful suggestions. While Professor Bartley saved me from numerous errors, any mistakes are my responsibility and mine alone. Without the secretarial assistance of Edna Fisher, Nancy Heaton, and Sheila Trembley, this book would never have been finished. Finally, while my wife, June, is no history fan, she has never failed to make the way clear and easy at home so I could pursue Clio, a mistress who has competed for her love and attention for nearly half a century. To her, no amount of thanks can be sufficient.

RICHARD B. RUSSELL, JR., SENATOR FROM GEORGIA

1

A Rich Heritage

===

November 2, 1897, was a cold, blustery day in North Georgia. Richard B. Russell of Winder was in court in Jefferson some thirteen miles away. When word reached him in the early morning hours that his son had been born, he hurried toward Winder as fast as a team and buggy could take him. Arriving at his home on Park Street, he rushed into the house to greet his wife Ina and Dr. C. B. Almond, who was holding the new baby boy. Exuberant over finally having a son after fathering three daughters, Russell clapped Dr. Almond so hard on the back that the doctor stumbled across the room and nearly dropped the infant. Family tradition has it that Russell then rushed out into the backyard and fired both barrels of his shotgun into the air to celebrate the grand event. Russell wrote years later that he could scarcely contain his joy when he learned that the baby was a boy. Of course, the first son and newest member of the family was named Richard Brevard Russell, Jr.[1]

Richard B. Russell, Jr., was born into a successful and accomplished family whose roots sank deep in American history. As one admirer said of young Russell's father, "He had descended from the oldest and choicest American stock."[2] Of English background, the Russells had lived in South Carolina and Georgia since colonial times. John Russell, Richard, Sr.'s, great-great-grandfather, was a businessman who lived near Charleston, South Carolina. Because of his sympathies with the British during the American Revolution, he was forced to flee the country and settle in the Bahamas. John's oldest son, Edward William, returned to the United States, first to Florida and then to Glynn County on the Georgia coast, where he established a successful plantation in the 1820s. In 1824 Edward William married Susan Sarah Way, the daughter of a prominent Liberty County family. Their oldest son, William John, lived in the home community until 1845, when he moved to Marietta in North Georgia. In the 1850s, in partnership with Charles James Mc-

Donald, a former governor of Georgia, William Russell established a successful cotton cloth and yarn mill not far from Marietta.

William Russell married Rebecca Harriette Brumby in December 1859. Harriette's father, Richard Trapier Brumby, the son of a prominent South Carolina planter, had married Mary Martha Brevard, a daughter of one of North Carolina's wealthiest and best-known families. After their marriage, Mary and Richard Brumby lived in Alabama, where Richard taught science at the University of Alabama. In 1849 he accepted a position at the University of South Carolina in Columbia, where the Brumbys lived for six years. Because of Richard's emphysema, they moved to Marietta where he taught at the Georgia Military Academy. It was after the Brumbys moved to Marietta that their daughter Harriette met and married William Russell. The first son to this union, Richard Brumby Russell, was born April 27, 1861.

Things went well for the Russell family as the cloth factory prospered during the late 1850s. Demand was even greater during the Civil War. But in 1864 General William T. Sherman's troops approached the area. William Russell joined the militia to try to halt Sherman's advance, and his family fled. But the Yankees overran the community and burned the Russell factory. After the war ended, the Russells settled at Princeton, a small community in Clarke County not far from Athens and the University of Georgia. He again entered the textile business, managing the Princeton Manufacturing Company.[3]

The Russells' oldest son, Richard, turned out to be a remarkable young man who soon launched a highly successful legal career. He was extremely intelligent and extraordinarily ambitious. In 1876, at age fifteen, he enrolled at the University of Georgia as a sophomore after passing special examinations. He excelled in debate and public speaking. During his senior year, he was president of the Phi Kappa Literary Society and the champion debater. In 1879 he graduated fourth in his class with two degrees, a Bachelor of Arts and a Bachelor of Philosophy. By that time, Russell reputedly could read five languages, including Greek and Latin.

Russell continued his formal education by enrolling in the university's Law School, and he completed the one-year course in 1880. Shortly afterward, he changed his middle name from "Brumby" to "Brevard." Family tradition holds that, being a politically ambitious young man, he did not want to be too closely associated with the Brumby name because two Brumby uncles were known in parts of Georgia as being heavy drinkers.[4]

After completing law school, Russell began to practice law in Athens. A law practice, however, was not enough to satisfy or fulfill this restless and energetic young man. In 1882 he ran successfully for the Georgia House of Representatives. When he took his seat in the House in 1883, he was only twenty-two and the youngest man in the General Assembly.

Russell was a tall, well-built man with sharp facial features and a full head of dark hair. He had a large mustache, which was sometimes stained with tobacco juice since he was an inveterate tobacco chewer, a devotee of R & W (Rich and Waxy). He also smoked cigars. One writer recalled that Russell was the only man he ever knew "who could chew tobacco and make a speech and never miss a lick at chewing or speaking."[5] He was also a joiner, becoming a member of the Odd Fellows, the Knights of Pythias, and the Masons. Filled with nervous energy, Russell was always looking for larger fields to conquer.

Education was one of Russell's major legislative interests. In his first term, he was appointed to a committee to investigate the question of establishing a school of technology in Georgia. He traveled with the legislative committee to visit the Massachusetts Institute of Technology and other institutions and was a strong supporter of the bill that provided for setting up the Georgia Institute of Technology in 1887. Besides being concerned about technological education, Russell was deeply interested in education for women. In April 1887, he introduced a bill to establish an Industrial Institute and College for white women at Milledgeville. This bill did not pass until 1889, by which time Russell was no longer in the legislature, but he deserves much of the credit for the founding of the Normal and Industrial College for Women. As a member of the legislature, Russell also worked hard to increase appropriations for the University of Georgia, and in 1887 he was elected to the university's board of trustees. He was distressed that students from poor farm families had little or no chance to attend the university, stating that it should be possible "for the poorest students to have an equal chance with the richest."[6]

In 1888 Russell passed up running for the legislature and sought election as solicitor general of the Superior Court for the Western Judicial Circuit of Georgia. The Western Circuit contained six counties in addition to Clarke and was the largest in the state at the time. Russell was elected to the post and during his eight years as solicitor general was, as one authority noted, "an able, fearless and vigorous prosecutor."[7]

Besides practicing law and serving in the legislature in the 1880s, Russell was active in business and publishing. From 1880 to 1882, he was associate editor of the *Athens Chronicle*; in 1884–85 he owned half interest in, and wrote for, the *Athens Banner*; and from 1890 to 1893, he was editor of the *Athens Daily Ledger*. In 1886 he was one of the organizers of the Athens Street Railway Company, and the following year, he participated in setting up the Athens Savings Bank. He also helped to organize the North Georgia Telephone Company in 1894. Russell was elected to the first Athens Board of Education in 1885, where he served until 1894 when he moved from the city.[8]

On May 12, 1883, this busy young lawyer married Minnie L. Tyler of Barnesville. Their marriage was short and tragic. After two children died in infancy, Minnie herself succumbed in childbirth on January 6, 1886. Some five years later, on June 24, 1891, Russell married Blandina Dillard. Ina, as she was known, descended from George Dillard who had arrived in America from England in 1660. After the Revolution, some of the Dillards migrated to Georgia. Ina's parents, Fielding and Frances Chaffin Dillard, lived in Oglethorpe County. She was the last of thirteen children and a great favorite of her father. She attended school at Emory College in Oxford, Georgia, and later studied at Lucy Cobb Academy, a girls' school in Athens. She then began teaching in the Athens public schools. As a member of the Board of Education, Russell met this pretty, petite teacher and later recalled that he had wanted to marry her after noticing that "she was so sweet that she left honey in her footprints everywhere she went."[9]

If Ina Russell believed that she would settle down to a quiet family life in Athens after her marriage, she was badly mistaken. Her husband was already considering a move to Winder, a small farm town some twenty miles northwest of Athens. Ina was distraught. Why, she asked, would anyone want to move there? But Russell believed that residence in Winder, which was located at a point where the boundaries of three counties—Jackson, Gwinnett, and Walton—met, would be politically advantageous. It was closer to the center of the seven-county Western Judicial Circuit, and from that point, it would be easier to make contacts and develop political friends and supporters—or so he believed. He was also interested in serving as solicitor of the City Court of Jefferson, which would require that he reside in Jackson County.

Ina still resisted the move to Winder. Besides being at home in a town only a dozen miles from where she was born, Ina enjoyed the cultural and intellectual atmosphere of the university community. The Russells' first baby, Mary Willie, had been born March 1, 1893, and in 1894 Ina was expecting her second child. She wanted to have the baby

House in Winder, Georgia, where Richard B. Russell, Jr., was born, November 2, 1897. Young Russell is standing on the steps in front of the woman second from left. (Photo courtesy of Russell Memorial Library, University of Georgia, Athens.)

in Athens where there was better medical service. Ina Dillard, the second daughter, arrived on June 22, 1894, as plans for moving were underway.

Exactly when the Russells left Athens for Winder is not clear. As early as September 12, 1893, C. D. Flanigan, secretary of the School Board, notified the Athens City Council that Russell had moved from Athens and that a replacement should be selected. However, the council ignored this advice because there was "doubt as to whether or not Mr. Russell had removed from the city."[10] On November 7, 1893, Russell attended the City Council meeting and offered his resignation, which became official August 6, 1894. It was probably two or three weeks earlier that the Russell family actually moved to their comfortable nine-room house at 107 Park Street in Winder. For a short time before they located a house, the Russells had lived in the Bush Hotel.[11]

At the time the Russells moved to Winder, it was a sleepy farm village of about a thousand people. Originally called Jug Tavern, it was first settled in 1872. By the 1890s, it was becoming a railroad center, and in 1893 the town's name was changed to Winder in honor of John H. Winder, general manager of the Seaboard Air Line Railroad.[12]

Winder rested in the midst of small farms tilled mainly by tenants and sharecroppers. The average size of farms in the three counties that converged on the town was about seventy-eight acres. Although the region was on the northern edge of the Plantation Belt, blacks operated 26 percent of the farms in Jackson County and 33 percent of those in Walton County. The vast majority of black farmers were sharecroppers or tenants. Out of 925 black farmers in Walton County in 1900, only 36 owned their farms; in Jefferson County, only 67 black farmers out of a total of 1,107 were owners. A higher percentage of whites owned their farms, but a majority were not landowners. In the three-county area, only 31 percent of all farmers owned their farms in 1900. Whether white or black, farmers raised little besides cotton and corn, and poverty stalked most of the farm homes. Annual incomes for many families were less than $250.[13]

Shortly after he moved to Winder, Russell began to buy land. He had a Jeffersonian love for land and believed that it was a good investment. It did not burn up or blow away, he often said. One of his daughters speculated that Russell might have been a typical plantation owner if he had been born a generation or two earlier. By the early twentieth century, Russell owned several hundred acres of farmland, plus a number of city lots. He bought some of the property at public auction on the court house steps as it was being sold because of debt. Also, his wife later inherited some farmland in Oglethorpe County.[14]

Russell arranged to have his farmlands operated by sharecroppers or tenants and had a typical paternalistic attitude toward his black tenants. At one time, he had one white and five black tenants and maintained a small commissary from which they could draw their supplies. Despite being the owner of several hundred acres of land, Russell found it difficult to squeeze any profit out of his farms. He experienced a good deal of frustration as he dealt with his tenants.[15]

The Russell family continued to increase rapidly. Frances Marguerite, a third daughter, arrived in April 1896, and the next year, Richard, Jr., was born. By 1900 two more children were born to Richard and Ina Russell: Harriette Brumby in 1899 and Robert Lee in 1900. Another daughter, Patience Elizabeth, was born in 1902, and a third son, Walter Brown, in 1903.

Meanwhile, Russell quit his solicitor's job at the end of 1896 and began practicing law in Winder. In 1898, however, the General Assembly elected him to a four-year term as judge of the Superior Court for the Western Judicial Circuit of Georgia. He assumed his duties in January 1899 and heard his first case in Watkinsville on January 23.[16]

Despite the rural nature of Winder, Judge Russell wanted to move his family to a more farmlike environment where the children would have plenty of room to play and roam about. Yet he wanted to be in an incorporated place near a railroad line. With the support of state senator L. G. Hardman of Jackson County, who later became governor, the General Assembly chartered the town of Russell in December 1902. This newly incorporated town was located about a mile southeast of Winder's business district.

In December 1903, the Russells moved to what was known as the Gresham House just inside the Russell city limits on Hog Mountain Road. The tracks of the Seaboard Railroad ran about three hundred feet behind the house. Some years later, a small frame flag stop was built along the track just a few hundred feet from Russell's back door. There Judge Russell could flag the train for trips to Atlanta or elsewhere. It was said that one of the main reasons for chartering the village of Russell was to enable Judge Russell to commute easily and conveniently to Atlanta. In any event, one or more of the children would watch for the train, and when they saw it coming around the curve about a mile away, they would call their father. The judge would then dash for the train, sometimes with a cup of hot coffee still in hand.

Since Judge Russell was often absent from home holding court, the responsibility for raising the rapidly growing family rested mainly with Ina. Mrs. Russell usually had a black cook and sometimes other household help as well. But she still had a great deal of work with such a large family. Between 1903 and 1912, five additional children were born—twins William John and Fielding Dillard in 1907, Henry Edward in 1909, Alexander Brevard in 1910, and Carolyn Lewis in 1912—making a total of thirteen, seven boys and six girls. Two other children died in infancy. Thus, much of the time between 1892 and 1912, Ina Russell was pregnant. Nevertheless, she was up to the task of managing her large family. In contrast to her husband who was full of nervous energy, Ina was a calm, stable woman who ran her household with a firm but loving hand. When discipline was required, she administered it with firmness and impartiality. Judge Russell left this aspect of family life almost entirely to his wife. On one occasion when several of the children went to an "old negro house" and picked up a metal hoop to roll, Ina Russell, according to Richard, Jr., put them to bed "without any supper except 1 cracker, 2 pieces of dried toast and 1 dipper of water."[17] Ina spent such long hours with family matters that Russell later wondered when and if his mother ever slept. After the children left home, she usually found time to write each one once a week but often commented understandably that she was tired and sleepy.

While the Russells did not live on a farm, they had enough land for a large garden and kept two or three milk cows, a few pigs, and some chickens. The Russell boys had the same kinds of chores as the sons of actual farmers. R. B. milked cows, worked in the garden, cut wood, and tended chickens. As a boy, he raised some special roosters of which he was very proud. All the boys hauled dirt when they became big enough. Filling wheelbarrows and wagons with dirt was one of their most common tasks. Judge Russell always seemed to be digging. He built flower beds, reshaped the yard, improved soil drainage, and planted trees, for which the children also had to haul water. The judge thought such work cleared his mind for difficult law cases, but the Russell boys could find no virtue in such labor. Richard, Jr., once recalled that he had three degrees before he ever went to college: DMC (Doctor of Milking Cows), DDD (Doctor of Dirt Digging), and DWC (Doctor of Wood Chopping).[18]

Ina Russell was deeply concerned about the intellectual, cultural, and religious training of her children. She played the piano and encouraged her daughters who had musical talent to take music lessons. The family also had a Victrola. Ina read to her small children and provided the older ones with plenty of reading material. The Russells had a good library and subscribed to such popular magazines as the *Saturday Evening Post* and *Colliers*, as well as several religious journals. Ina Russell had a deep religious faith based on Methodism, and she instilled strong religious principles in her children. Grace was always said at the table before eating, by Judge Russell himself when he was home. The family regularly attended the Winder Methodist Church.

Education was among the highest priorities in the Russell family. Although Judge Russell served on the Winder Board of Education from 1895 to 1897, he did not believe that the public school was adequate for his children. He had a house moved in across the street from his residence on Hog Mountain Road, installed school desks, and employed Miss Anita Stroud to maintain a private school for the Russell children. While R. B. was not her best student by any means, she had faith in him and confidence that he had a bright future.[19]

There was a strong emphasis on morality and uprightness in the Russell home. Both Judge and Ina Russell wanted their children to be "good." They stressed honesty, virtue, decency, responsibility, fairness, and respect for others. Their son Richard, Jr., felt the impact of this concern early. In his 1907 school book, he copied such ideas as "life is real, life is earnest," "I live for those who love me," and "the good that I can do." He wrote that he planned to learn the speech, "Don't give up the ship," because he "liked that speech very much." Bible reading and memorization were common among the Russell children. On Sunday evening, August 23, 1908, for example, Richard, Jr., and his sister Patience sang religious songs and read a chapter of the Bible.[20]

R. B.'s boyhood experiences and the kind of life he enjoyed are best revealed in his diary, which he began keeping on January 9, 1907, when he was nine years old and in the fourth grade. He recorded both important events and insignificant incidents that reveal a full and happy childhood. He told about working in the garden, about going fishing and catching tadpoles, about killing a twenty-five-inch water moccasin, and about his many trips to town to buy candy and ice cream. Most of his pennies and nickels were spent on sweets. He wrestled with other boys and had occasional fights. On April 11, 1907, he wrote that he got into a fight with two older boys and "very nearly whipped them." The teacher then kept them all after school.

Friends such as Warren Toole, William Henry Quarterman, and other boys often visited R. B., and they played soldier, police, train and robbers, baseball, and other games. He particularly liked to play soldier and built a fort in the pasture. In the true Confederate spirit, he named it Fort Lee. R. B. developed an early love for hunting. After dinner on Thanksgiving Day in 1907, he wanted to go hunting but did not because, as he wrote, "Mama did not want me to for fear of being killed." By the time he was twelve, however, he had his own shotgun and often hunted in nearby fields and woods.

As he got a little older, R. B. played third base on the Russell baseball team. On March 5, 1910, he recorded that Winder beat Russell 8 to 7. Even though he hit a home run in a game with Winder on March 12, Winder won again. The day before, he had gone to Atlanta to buy a good baseball glove and bat.

R. B. also played with girlfriends. "I think I am catching a new girl. Her name is Anna," he wrote on February 2, 1907. He bought Anna a valentine on February 13 for only a penny but wrote that it was very pretty. With the quarter he had received from his parents for getting a score of 100 on a spelling test, he wrote, he planned to get a nickel's worth of candy for Anna. Apparently Anna's attractions did not last. On March 10, he wrote that he rambled through the woods and carved "Ruth Hale and R. B. Russell on a tree."

Even at nine and ten years old, young Russell earned small sums

Young Russell, barefoot, ca. 1909, enjoying one of his favorite pastimes—reading. (Photo courtesy of Russell Memorial Library, University of Georgia, Athens.)

of money. He received twenty-five cents from his mother on May 20, 1907, for churning the family butter, and a few days later, he made twenty-one cents working at the Winder Lumber Company. He wrote that "the work is hard," but he returned the next day and made another quarter. He sometimes got as much as $5 for scoring 100 on spelling tests. While R. B. loved candy and other sweets, he did not spend all of his money for such things. He had a stamp collection and carried on a regular correspondence with dealers concerning stamp orders. Moreover, he saved money. His later penchant for thrift and economy developed early. On April 20, 1907, he had $11.42 in the Winder Savings Bank, and the amount grew steadily in later months.

The Methodist Church in Winder was an important part of young Russell's life. He was baptized in June 1898, when he was about eight months old. By age nine, he was going to Sunday school and church quite regularly. As he grew older, he continued to attend, but less frequently. On May 10, 1907, he went to a special church revival and "went up to the altar." "There were hundreds of people there. I am glad I went up there. I am going to always try to be right with God," he wrote. Two days later, he recorded that he went to Sunday school and while there resolved not to read history, his favorite pastime, on Sundays. That evening he went to a special religious service at the city hall with his father. According to the young Russell, several people were converted, and he added, "I gave my heart to God tonight." He actually joined the Methodist church on May 26, a membership that he retained until his death some sixty-five years later.

While many southern families had poor diets, the Russell family had plenty to eat and a good variety of food. Years later, trying to convince a constituent that he had not been raised "on the fat of the land," Russell wrote that in his youth, "grits and gravy were a standard article of diet twice a day" in the Russell household. This statement, however, represented a myth of memory rather than a fact. The large family garden produced an abundant supply of vegetables, and fruits were available from nearby orchards. The Russells had chickens and butchered hogs. On January 21, 1907, R. B. wrote that they had just butchered their "black hog." The big meal was usually dinner, served at noon, and often the table was laden with good food. On January 26, R. B. wrote that for dinner they had croquettes, chicken, potatoes, rice and gravy, cake, and sliced bananas topped with milk.

Holidays were gay times for the Russells. Often friends and relatives joined the family for food and fellowship. However, at Christmas Ina Russell preferred to have just her own children at home. There were presents, big meals, and much playing and visiting. The children hung up their stockings on Christmas Eve, and on Christmas morning they would find them filled with candy, apples, oranges, and, for the boys, fireworks. Before the gifts were distributed, Judge Russell would stand in front of the decorated tree and explain the meaning of Christmas.

There were many things for a boy to do in the rural farm environment in which young Russell lived, but best of all, he liked to read. His mother taught him to read before he started school, and by the time he was in the fourth grade, he was reading an unbelievable number and variety of books. January 22, 1907, he wrote in his diary that he was reading *Little Women*. He had almost completed it by February 3. A little later, his mother brought him five books from Atlanta by the English author George A. Henty, including *With Wolfe in Canada* and *With Clive in India*. They were all good books, he wrote. R. B. greatly admired the manly characters in the Henty volumes. He also read the writings of Horatio Alger, James Fenimore Cooper, and other popular authors of the day.

Most of all, however, young Russell liked to read history. On April 22, 1907, he mentioned that he did not go to school but read U.S. history at home. A week later he wrote, "I read all morning." He recorded in his diary that he read English history, French history, and also a book on the recent war between Russia and Japan. Only nine years old, he wrote, "I like to read histories of all countries." It was probably R. B.'s extensive reading that permitted him to skip the fifth grade and go directly to the sixth in the fall of 1908. Moreover, it is not difficult to understand, even in those early years, why Judge and Ina Russell believed their oldest son was someone special. He had a keen and inquisitive mind, he retained what he read, he was mature beyond his age, and his interests involved things not customarily of concern to children of his age.[21]

R. B. also got to travel more than most early twentieth-century youth in the South. Judge Russell traveled extensively in his legal work, and he attended various professional meetings outside of Georgia. He was gone so much that his homecoming was worthy of special mention. "Papa came home tonight" was a common entry in R. B.'s diary. So it was not unusual for the Russell children to make trips. It was easy and convenient to catch the train to Atlanta, Athens, and other towns. Young Russell often visited his grandmother in Athens, and on one trip in 1908, he went to the place "where Grandpa's slaves were buried." Even as a small boy, he was interested in his family's history. One summer R. B. spent several weeks with relatives in Washington, Georgia, and the Russell children often went to Atlanta by train to shop or to see sporting events.

The children took longer and out-of-state trips as well. In March 1908, Judge Russell took R. B. and his daughter, Ina, to Savannah. They traveled by train overnight from Atlanta, and R. B. was surprised when he awoke the next morning and looked out of the train window at the flat Coastal Plain. How different from the rolling hills of his home community. Judge Russell and his children stayed at the DeSoto Hotel, Savannah's finest. They visited the area's historic sites, including the forts and gun emplacements, which R. B. enjoyed the most. They took a trip on a boat that had a bedroom, dining room, and sitting room, which greatly impressed young Russell. Sending a postcard to "Dear mama," R. B. wrote that he was having a fine time and wished that she were with them. He told his mother that they were saving their fruit to bring home, "I mean [the fruit] that we get off the table at dinner."[22]

One of his most memorable boyhood trips was to Atlanta on March 25, 1907, to visit Governor Joseph M. Terrell. He went with his father, mother, and brother Rob. After they arrived in Atlanta, R. B. wrote that "papa took me to the Governor's office." Governor Terrell invited young Russell to sit in his chair, which, R. B. said, "I did for about 3 minutes." Then, he wrote: "I went all about the capitol looking at pictures of great men which were life size. At 1 o'clock I went to the [governor's] mansion and ate dinner. Until half past 2 I walked about the house." Later R. B. went to a small store and bought some candy, ice cream, and chewing gum, after which the judge's secretary took him to the movies.

But the trip's highlight was staying all night at the governor's mansion. The next morning, he got up before either the governor or Mrs. Terrell and walked around the yard a while. His only problem was that he could not tie his shoelaces. Although his sister Marguerite had helped him learn this art some two months earlier in preparation for his trip, the skill now failed him. But one of the governor's maids came to his rescue. After the Terrells arose and they all had breakfast, he and the governor walked to the capitol together. He stayed at the governor's office until about one o'clock when he went to his father's chambers and reunited with his family. Later in the day, Mrs. Russell took the boys to Grant Park before taking the train home to Winder. It was an experience that Russell never forgot.[23]

In May 1910, when R. B. was twelve, he accompanied his father, mother, two brothers, and some friends on a trip to Montreal, Canada. Arriving by train in Washington, D.C., in the morning, the Russell family spent the day looking around the nation's capital. They saw the House and Senate in session, visited several Georgia congressmen and senators, and went to the Library of Congress. It was "the most beautiful building in the world," R. B. wrote. After having dinner, the family reboarded the train and continued to Montreal through Philadelphia and New York City. Young Russell did not write about his stay in Montreal, but it is safe to assume that he enjoyed it and learned much from his experience.[24] By the time R. B. had finished grade school, his education and knowledge had been greatly expanded through travel.

Even though the Russells lived in a community that was about 25 percent black, R. B. seldom referred to blacks in his boyhood diary or letters. He once mentioned that he had seen a "nigger" house on fire and on another occasion told about a dog that had attacked a black man who was crossing a Winder street. It is not surprising that R. B. seldom mentioned blacks. He grew up in a strictly segregated neighborhood where blacks were designated positions of social and economic inferiority. The blacks that he had any association with were servants or farm tenants. Adults had established the norm in race relations, and he accepted them as did other young whites. It seemed as though things would always be as they were. The Russells were fond of their black servants, but they related to them, as was the custom, only as servants.

R. B. enjoyed a happy, active, and contented boyhood. He was a member of a family that frequently and openly expressed love for one another. In writing to his mother, he usually signed his letters "your loving son," and Mrs. Russell generally closed her letters to him by writing, "With a heart of love, Mother." The Russells were a fairly typical late-Victorian family that expressed sentiment and affection openly. As the first son, R. B. was a favorite of both his parents. Ina Russell declared years later that Richard, Jr.'s, birth was one of the happiest occasions of her life, as it had been for her husband, because he "came after we had three girls."[25] On R. B.'s fifteenth birthday, Judge Russell wrote his son recalling the day of his birth. When he knew he had a baby boy, he explained, "my own R. B. Russell Jr.—I was crazy with happiness." As he had said many times of his namesake, "That is me living over again."[26]

This closely knit and loving family had many happy times together. Dinners, the arrival of company, parties, and trips were all very much a part of family life. In the early 1900s, the *Winder News* carried a column each week on activities in the village of Russell. It was filled with accounts of social events held by the Russells. The paper reported on July 9, 1908: "We have had a pleasant time in Russell this week. The town has been filled with boys and girls attending the house party at the home of Judge Russell." R. B.'s sisters had frequent parties for their friends, some of whom often came from out of town. The Russells quickly became identified with Winder's leading families, although their upper middle-class position was based more on the judge's public recognition than on wealth or property. In fact, the judge's salary was only enough for a modest but comfortable living, and rent from his farms brought in only a little additional income.

Young Russell, then, enjoyed a pleasant and stable family atmosphere during his most formative years. It was an environment where children were respected and where they could have their say. Judge and Mrs. Russell inculcated Christian virtues in their children and emphasized morality, hard work, and individual responsibility as marks of good character. Their eldest son was lucky to have been born into such a family and reared in such an environment.

2

In School, 1911–1918

═══

After R. B. finished primary school in 1911, the Russells faced the question of where to send him for his secondary education. There was a high school in Winder, but Judge Russell did not consider it adequate for his eldest son. He wanted R. B. to attend an institution with stronger academic credentials. The school that met this requirement was Gordon Military Institute in Barnesville, Georgia. Many Georgians considered Gordon Institute to be one of the best preparatory schools in the South.

The curriculum at Gordon matched that of some of the best schools in the country. The institute offered courses in algebra, geometry, and trigonometry; in science there were classes in botany, chemistry, physics, geography, and geology. Foreign languages included Latin, Greek, French, and German. Work was also offered in history, English, literature, and other subjects. It was from among these solid academic courses that students fulfilled the requirements for the so-called classical course.[1]

Gordon Military Institute also had a strong faculty. In 1912 Edward T. Holmes became president. A native of Augusta, Georgia, Holmes had graduated from Gordon in 1888 and later attended Mercer University, Harvard University, and the University of Chicago. He taught Latin at Mercer for seventeen years before assuming the Gordon presidency. The vice president, L. D. Watson, was also a native Georgian who had solid academic training. After graduating from the University of Georgia with a major in mathematics in 1897, Watson pursued advanced studies at Harvard and the University of Chicago. Other members of the faculty also had strong academic backgrounds, many holding master's degrees. The institute offered an impressive group of teachers who demanded high standards and hard work from the boys and girls, most of whom came from the state's best families.

The quality of the faculty and the rigorous academic program were good enough reasons for sending R. B. to Gordon Institute. But to Judge Russell there was an even more important factor. Although R. B. was only thirteen years old, his father was already planning that he should have a distinguished political career. The judge believed that at Gordon, R. B. would meet boys from leading families who might later help his son politically. Russell once said that a person never developed better or closer friends than those made in school.

In September 1911, R. B. left home for Barnesville, some seventy miles south and a little west of Winder. He found a place to room and board with Mrs. C. H. Humphrey for $20 a month. He enrolled in Latin, algebra, arithmetic, history, and English. Now that R. B. was out from under the parental roof, he received a steady stream of advice and suggestions through the frequent letters sent to him by both his mother and father. From the time he left home in 1911 until he completed law school at the University of Georgia nearly seven years later, R. B.'s parents put strong pressure on him to be a good person and to have a strong academic record. Young Russell had hardly settled at Gordon before letters began arriving from his mother urging him to concentrate on his studies and to do well. She also expressed concern about his conduct. "Always have a *good* time," she wrote, "but be a gentleman."[2] Ina Russell wanted her son to grow large and strong and warned him against eating too much candy and drinking soft drinks. She strongly objected to his consumption of Coca Cola. In one letter, she told R. B. that he could not be a "strong man and indulge in these things." She frequently sent him boxes of fruit and other foods that she considered more healthy.[3]

The family reputation was a matter of vital concern to Judge and Ina Russell. They both urged their son not to sully the family's good name in any way. In one of her first letters to R. B. after he arrived in Barnesville, Ina Russell mentioned this matter. Even the other children referred to it. Rob, his younger brother, wrote him on October 20, 1911, that there were still six Russell boys at home, and they did not want their oldest brother to make "any bad record." Mary Willie, then in school at Milledgeville, wrote her brother that she hoped he was behaving himself "becomingly." She added that she could never do anything bad if she just stopped "long enough to think whose child I am, and think of my dear father and mother, who have their hopes set on us, and who want to do the right thing always."[4]

It was Judge Russell, however, who pushed his son the hardest. His letters were filled with urgent admonitions to R. B. to work hard and do well in his studies. On November 5, three days after R. B.'s fourteenth birthday, Russell wrote his son: "Do *your very level best*. Work is what counts my boy so don't fail to study every *spare moment*." A few weeks later, the judge wrote again on the same subject and included a grammar lesson at the same time. "Do study *hard, harder hardest* my dear boy," he wrote. He even brought up the possibility of his own death, which would prevent the family from helping R. B. continue his education. In a letter written on October 16, 1911, Judge Russell told his son to learn all that he could "this *year*" in case something should happen to make it impossible for him to send R. B. to school another year. Moreover, by 1911 Judge Russell was beginning to see his own unfulfilled dreams in a more distinguished career for his oldest son. He frequently reminded R. B. that he was his father's namesake. Urging the boy to gain as high a class standing as possible, Judge Russell stated, "You bear my name, and I want you to carry it higher than I have done or can do in my few remaining days."[5]

R. B. received the constant parental pressure to excel with surprising good spirits. If he ever resented the advice, warnings, and admonitions, he never mentioned it. He simply ignored them. He did well enough in his studies the first term, except for algebra and Latin. These two subjects were difficult for R. B., partly because he had no liking for them. Nor did he care for the military aspects of the Gordon program. "I just despise drilling," he wrote his mother. This may have been because he was a small thirteen-year-old, and the guns weighed eighteen pounds. The students had to drill an hour and a half daily and two hours on Saturdays, so it is easy to understand why young Russell objected to military exercises.[6]

He spent a good deal of time visiting with friends, talking with girls, and going to entertainments. Russell and other boys went to the circus in Barnesville and also to band concerts. These distractions undoubtedly were partly responsible for his low grades. Despite R. B.'s failure to fulfill his father's wish for higher marks, it was not until the second term early in 1912 that his poor grades in algebra and Latin caused his parents great worry. Judge Russell became almost frantic at the possibility that his son might not achieve greatness in some yet undefined way.

To some extent, R. B. was the teenage victim of a frustrated father who was dissatisfied with his own career. Judge Russell was a greatly ambitious man whose main goals and aspirations had eluded him. While he had won success on the bench, he had a strong desire for high political office. In 1904 he had run for chief justice of the Georgia Supreme Court. Although Chief Justice T. J. Simmons had held the office for some twenty-five years, Russell claimed that in a democratic society there should be no life tenure. Russell carried on a statewide campaign, but he was overwhelmingly defeated by a county unit vote of 232 to 98.[7]

Rather than discouraging his driving ambition, the campaign of 1904 seemed to whet his desire for political office even more. In 1906 he resigned from his superior court position to make a run for the governorship. Russell presented himself as an "anti-ringer" and one who would work for the common people. He pushed the image of "plain Dick Russell" against the special interests. Russell advocated tax reform and proposed local option as a way to handle the growing controversy over the liquor question.

It was Russell's position on the liquor issue that produced some strain within the family and eventually caused the Russells to leave the Methodist church. Mrs. Russell's brother, Miles Dillard, was a Methodist minister, and his wife, known to the Russell children as Aunt Lella, was a leader in the state Woman's Christian Temperance Union. She was a strong prohibitionist and during the campaign went about the state attacking the judge's stand on local option. She even advised people to vote against her brother-in-law. Russell was furious. Some years later, Judge and Ina Russell joined the Presbyterian Church in Winder as a kind of slap in the face of the prohibitionist Methodists. For the judge, this was a return to his church home because he had been a Presbyterian before he married.

R. B. and his sister, Ina, however, did not leave the Methodist church. Mrs. Russell was distressed over the fact that the entire family did not settle on one denomination, and she wrote R. B. some years later, asking if he objected to leaving the Methodist church and joining the Presbyterians. Besides wanting the family to be members of one church home, Mrs. Russell believed that if R. B. became a Presbyterian, "papa" would again become active in the church. But Mrs. Russell told R. B. that as far as his father was concerned, "You can do as you please." R. B. decided to remain a member of the Winder Methodist Church.[8]

The family differences over how to deal with the liquor issue in 1906 had no influence on the outcome of the election. Russell's opponents were Hoke Smith, who had been President Grover Cleveland's secretary of interior, and Clark Howell, an experienced legislator and state politician. While Russell made a strong statewide race, he did not even get into the runoff.[9] When news of the judge's defeat reached the Russell home, his wife Ina cried with disappointment. Observing his mother's distress, young R. B. reputedly tried to comfort her by saying, "Don't cry mother, when I get to be a man I'll be governor and you will be the first lady of Georgia."[10] The story is probably apocryphal, but it represents the essence of fact.

The Russell household was filled with political ambition; if Judge Russell could not obtain high office himself, perhaps his eldest son could achieve that goal. Russell used every opportunity to expose his son to political leaders and the affairs of state. He took R. B. to visit Governor Terrell in 1906, as mentioned earlier, and to see President Theodore Roosevelt when he visited Atlanta in 1908.

Although Russell had resigned his superior court judgeship and had lost his bid for the governorship, he was soon back on the bench. In 1906 the General Assembly created the Georgia Court of Appeals and selected Russell to serve on that court.[11] In 1913 he became chief justice of the Court of Appeals. Meanwhile, unable to resist the political bug, Russell ran for governor again in 1911. During R. B.'s first term at Gordon, the judge was canvasing the state for votes. R. B. followed his father's campaign with great interest and wrote to his mother in November that he was getting excited over the forthcoming election.[12] But victory again eluded Judge Russell in his third statewide race.

Gloom and disappointment pervaded the Russell household as it had after the judge's earlier defeats. Ina Russell wrote R. B. on December 9, 1911, saying that she was struggling hard to accept the results, and although "dad" was being brave, "oh how it hurt." Judge Russell wrote R. B. the "sad sad news" that he had lost everything except his "manhood and . . . manly honor." Then he poured out his soul to his namesake. He had sought the governorship, he said, so that R. B. could have a better chance in life than he had experienced. Since he had failed, "you must fight for yourself." At one point in the letter, he told R. B. that he could never be governor but later remarked, "Be *a man* and you can be a governor, but if you never are a governor be a man dear boy." The judge wanted his son to carry on the fight "after I am dead and gone" against "dirty and hypocritical politicians and unchristian churchmen," referring to those who opposed his position on local option. "*Keep this letter* and read it often after I am dead," he concluded. The same day, R. B. wrote to his father about the results of the election. He was more philosophical about the loss than his father. The fourteen-year-old simply wrote, "It is too bad we got beat but we will try again."[13]

The campaign for governor had placed additional financial pressure on the Russell family, and during the fall of 1911, Judge Russell felt the pinch of hard times. Maintaining several children away at school was a further drain on family finances. R. B. wrote home often, and a major topic of his letters was need for more money. Writing his mother on October 13, he urged her to send funds quickly because he only had twenty cents. Both his father and mother sent him money, sometimes without knowing what the other had done. When they did send him a small amount, they warned him to be economical. They also asked for frequent accountings of his expenditures.[14]

Writing that he was "crazy to get home" for Christmas in 1911, R. B. enjoyed a happy holiday season in Winder. All the children were home, and Ina Russell thoroughly enjoyed having her "chicks," as she sometimes called them, close around her. Early in January 1912, R. B. returned to Gordon for the second term. He got along fairly well in his studies but did not meet his parents' hopes and expectations. He was late for drill on one occasion and received demerits. There were some class fights, and his grades were still weak in Latin and algebra. His letters home were optimistic about his progress, but the actual results were less than encouraging.

On February 9, 1912, Judge Russell wrote R. B. a long letter after receiving his grade report. The judge was pleased with his son's progress but said he hoped for even more improvement. R. B. had plenty of brains to stand high in his class, Judge Russell wrote, "if he would just apply himself diligently." A few days later, Ina Russell urged her son to write "a better hand and a better letter" and to pay attention to his paragraphs. She added that "your poor daddy grieves" about his son's less than superior work. By March R. B.'s grades had improved, and his parents were ecstatic. Judge Russell wrote that he was proud of this progress and happy because "my darling boy and namesake is building his life upon broad foundations." Despite being "real hard run," an expression indicating poor financial circumstances, the judge sent R. B. $10 as a reward for his improved marks.[15]

By April, however, R. B.'s grades had slipped again, and Ina Russell wrote her son that "I dread for papa to see your report." R. B. realized that he might be in a precarious position with his father and asked his mother how best to approach "papa" for the money he needed to attend the annual encampment. Just ask for it, his mother advised. Judge Russell sent him $15, but when R. B. did not attend the encampment, the judge asked him to account for the funds. Meanwhile, Ina Russell urged him to study hard. She wrote in late May advising him to concentrate on studying for final examinations and encouraging him to do well. "I'm always expecting my R. B. Russell, Jr., never to fail in anything," she said.[16]

R. B. had not given a stalwart performance in his first year at Gordon, but his work was good enough so that he could return in September 1912. He enrolled in Latin, English, mathematics, history, algebra, geology, and botany. He was also promoted to corporal, which made his father extremely proud. But Judge Russell continued to pressure his son to do even better. "I yearn for you to be a great success," he wrote on September 28, a few days after the youth returned to Barnesville. The judge did not confine his advice to academic matters. "Make every friend you possibly can," he wrote, because the friends made in school "will stick much closer to you than any you make after you and they are 30 years old."[17]

On November 2, R. B.'s fifteenth birthday, his father wrote to "My dear, dear boy," wishing him honor, fame, wealth, happiness, and above all a long life. But the judge took this opportunity to counsel his son. Work hard, be responsible, and achieve the goals that had eluded him, Judge Russell wrote. "You must carve out your own destiny and be at it *now* every day," he said. He again admonished his son to carry the name of R. B. Russell "higher than I will ever be able to carry it." Judge Russell said that he would die, but "son I swear you to carry on my work and fulfill what I leave undone." Russell wrote that R. B. could make the name of R. B. Russell "live long after I die and thus you will help to keep me alive." He hoped that his son would make "a mark for mankind and human happiness," so that future generations would celebrate November 2 "as a day blessed in history."[18] The idea that young Russell should become famous and enhance the family name had become almost an obsession with the elder Russell.

Later in the fall term, R. B. again experienced grade trouble. He received a grade of 45 on a scale of 100 in Latin, a situation that caused President Holmes to write Judge Russell about his son's problem. Ina Russell could not understand why R. B. had so much trouble in that subject. Study harder, she urged. By early December, R. B.'s mother had become temporarily disgusted with her son's poor grades. He was not a "blockhead," she wrote, but perhaps he would have to repeat the freshman year because he did not study hard enough. "Go to work at once," she pleaded in a letter of December 8. Mrs. Russell said that she would never consent to his quitting school. To motivate her son, she asked him to think of all the good things in life that he might want. Then he had to realize that to get them he must be "educated and competent." "Will for yourself fame and money," she wrote. Think of what you would like to be ten or twenty years from now, Mrs. Russell advised, and then grit "your teeth and resolve that your *dream* shall come true." Education was the key to opening up and fulfilling dreams, Ina Russell continued. Finally, she told her son that she had not brought him into the world "to be a failure or to ever *fail* in anything you might undertake."[19]

Young Russell made no excuses for his poor grades. He usually just ignored his parents' pleadings. The most common topic of his letters home was his need for money. By 1912 Judge Russell was struggling to support his large family. In letter after letter, he reported how hard up he was. He was inundated with bills. Late in the year, he wrote that he had never seen "money as tight in my life." Since he depended on his farms for part of his income, when agriculture was depressed, things were difficult around the Russell household. He reported that the 1912 cotton crop had not even paid for the fertilizer on three farms and barely made expenses on two more. These conditions made it very hard for Judge Russell to send his son money for school expenses. On some occasions, he asked R. B. to hold the check for his board until the very last day it was due.[20]

Part of the family's financial problems stemmed from Judge Russell's decision to build a new house. On May 11, 1912, Mrs. Russell wrote her son to "hold your breath. Papa has sold our house and promised to give possession in 3 months." They intended to begin construction "on our big new house at once," she said. The financial pinch came when Russell did not sell his current house for cash but took in other property for it. In any event, by the end of the summer, the Russells had completed a large, two-story frame house with a broad front porch. The family moved in during August. The youngest Russell child, Carolyn, was born there on August 19.

The new house was still close to the Seaboard Railroad but on the other side of the tracks. The downstairs rooms had fireplaces, and Ina's "Majestic" range was in the kitchen. The builders also installed gaslights. At the time of construction, the house sat in the midst of one of Russell's cotton fields, but soon it was surrounded by trees, shrubs, and flowers. Much of Judge Russell's dirt moving had to do with improving the immediate landscape around the new house. It was not long before what the *Winder News* called "Judge Russell's elegant home" was a center for parties.[21]

R. B. arrived from Barnesville as the family prepared for the Christmas festivities. Despite constant parental pressure to do better school work, his love for his parents and his desire to be at home did not diminish. Judge Russell had bought a barrel of apples, a box of oranges, and other good things for the Christmas season. All the children were home, and it was a loving and festive occasion.

Russell family home in Winder, Georgia, built in 1912. (Photo courtesy of Russell Memorial Library, University of Georgia, Athens.)

Vacation from school was all too brief. In early January 1913, R. B. returned to Gordon to face academic problems that seemed to be worsening. He made new boarding arrangements with Mrs. White Jordan, which he seemed to like. He also enjoyed his friends and the nonacademic activities such as sports, parties, and other social functions. But the pressure of class work continued to plague him. President Holmes again wrote Judge Russell about R. B.'s poor grades, saying that he could do better in all of his subjects, except possibly Latin.

R. B. was so discouraged that he even discussed dropping out of school and taking a job. Reversing a stand taken some months earlier, Ina Russell told him that he could quit school but that he would have to work. She explained that he could cut wood and ship it to Atlanta until planting time when he could plow, plant, and chop cotton. Adding a postscript to his wife's letter, Judge Russell insisted that if R. B. quit school there would be no "loafing or learning idle habits because that would ruin you." Then he again reminded R. B. that "you are my oldest son and you carry my full name. You can have—and *you must have,*—a future of usefulness and distinction in Georgia or it will break my heart." The prospect of working in a cotton field quickly caused R. B. to abandon any thoughts of dropping out of school.[22]

His grades, however, sank even lower. His March report gave him only 20 percent in Latin, 55 percent in geometry, and 60 percent in algebra. He did well in English and spelling but dropped to 83 in history, his favorite subject. "This is awful," his mother wrote, and it was a "disgrace to R. B. Russell Sr. and Jr. I'm thoroughly disgusted."[23]

Young Russell simply did not study very much. In his diary, he wrote about his interest in girls, although early in 1913, he said, "Thank goodness I am not in love at present writing." But he corresponded with several young ladies. He spent a lot of time in town, eating, smoking, drinking those soft drinks his mother hated so much, and just killing time. He not only smoked cigarettes at age fourteen, he occasionally puffed on cigars, which he got from his father's liberal supply or from schoolmates.[24] He played tennis, went to a masquerade ball, and made a trip to Atlanta to obtain advertisements for the school yearbook. He even attended church. Some of the pages in his workbooks were filled with nothing but names of big-league baseball players. All of these activities kept him from concentrating on studying, something he badly needed to do to get decent grades.

His critically low marks in March may have resulted from leaving school for several days to attend the inauguration of President Woodrow Wilson. The family had discussed the possibility of such a trip, but it was only a week before the event that R. B. got permission from his father, who was already in Washington, to attend. After a telephone call from the judge, he borrowed some clothes from his roommate, Marion Wilson, and $25 from his landlord and prepared to leave. On March 2, he arose at 3:30 A.M. and took the train for Atlanta. There he bought a ticket for an upper berth in the sleeping car, and at 11:25 the train pulled out of Atlanta for Washington. He ate dinner in the dining car and had company in his travels when he met his cousin James Dillard. No breakfast was served the next morning, but he bought two sandwiches to eat before arriving at the Washington station about nine o'clock.

Getting off the train, R. B. was "momentarily bewildered by the tremendous inauguration crowds." Pushing his way through the mass of people, he asked a policeman how to get to 1811 R Street N.W. where his Uncle Rob lived. The officer directed him to the right streetcar, and young Russell was soon at his uncle's home, where he met his father and other relatives. That evening they all went out for an oyster dinner, after which R. B. and Judge Russell walked around Washington. These were times of great pleasure for both father and son. They discussed history, government, and politics, and Judge Russell dreamed of the day when his namesake would hold high political office.

The next day, R. B., his father, and other relatives stood outside the Capitol with tens of thousands of other Americans to see the first Democrat inaugurated as president in twenty years. Better yet, Woodrow Wilson, who once lived in Augusta, Georgia, was considered a southerner. Later the Russell party watched the four-hour parade from the Continental Hotel, where an Athens friend had rooms.

Early on March 5, the Russells took a boat down the Potomac to visit Mount Vernon, and before they returned home, they visited the National Museum, toured the Smithsonian Institution, and saw Georgia's congressmen and senators. Although R. B. had visited Washington once before, the entire trip was an impressive and memorable experience for a fifteen-year-old boy from Winder, Georgia.[25]

Back at Gordon, young Russell continued to struggle with his grades. His parents even became concerned over whether he would do well enough to be promoted to the junior class. Judge Russell offered to provide tutoring or anything else that might help. To make matters worse, R. B. seemed to be spending more money than necessary and not always for the right purposes. Funds sent for books were apparently used for other things. When he wrote home for money to buy a botany book in April, near midterm, Ina Russell chastised him for not having purchased the book with money sent for that purpose earlier. After lecturing her son on economy and the careful use of money, she said that it was a pity J. P. Morgan did not leave him "a million or two." R. B. seemed to have abandoned his earlier conservatism in handling his finances. On one occasion when he telephoned home for money, his mother responded sharply and told him not to be so impatient. A telephone call, she explained, cost sixty to eighty cents, and that expenditure was unnecessary.[26] Despite continued hard times, Judge Russell usually managed to send his son the money requested.

By the end of the term, R. B.'s grades had improved some, but the final examinations in May 1913 were a real challenge. Fortunately, he passed all of his courses except one. President Holmes wrote him in August, some two months after school was dismissed, informing him that he would be promoted in all subjects except Latin, which he had failed. His final grade was only 42 percent.[27] Judge Russell seemed to be getting a little more tolerant of his son's lack of initiative. Writing from Quebec, Canada, where he was on a trip in late May, Russell told his son to do his very best on the final exams, but "if you fail you are still *my boy.*"[28]

The failure of R. B. to achieve a strong academic record at Gordon Institute caused Judge Russell to reassess the future of his son's education. Sometime during the summer of 1913, the family decided that R.

B. would not return to Gordon but attend the Seventh District Agricultural and Mechanical (A & M) School at Powder Springs. This was one of several such institutions in Georgia that provided a three-year high school education for young people and permitted them to work for part of their expenses. The cost of board and room was only $6.40 a month, less than half what it had been in Barnesville. From Judge Russell's point of view, the school at Powder Springs had several advantages. Besides costing less at a time when Russell was pressed for cash, it was closer to home and the curriculum was less rigorous than at Gordon. Also the judge knew Professor H. R. Hunt, previously superintendent of the Winder school, and hoped that he might give R. B. special attention if he needed it. Finally, Judge Russell foresaw his son making an additional set of friends at the Seventh District A & M School. "Make all the friends you can every day," Judge Russell urged his son. "I am trying to pave the way for you someday to be governor though I could not be."[29]

So, in September 1913, Dick, as he was now beginning to be called, made his way to the Seventh District A & M School. He disliked it from the start. Located some three miles outside of Powder Springs northwest of Atlanta, the school was isolated and dull for a young man of Russell's social background. Moreover, he had to work nine hours a week at what was essentially farm labor. He probably did not enjoy the joshing letter that he received from a friend who said, "Dick, while you are milking, picking cotton, racking up hay etc.," do not worry since some great men had come out of the A & M school.[30] Most of the young people there probably came from less well-known and prestigious families than the Russells, thus making it more difficult for Russell to fit in.

Dick was not accustomed to the routine and bleak surroundings at the Powder Springs school. He told his parents that the furniture in his room consisted of a cheap iron bed and an unpainted pine table. The only way to take a bath, he said, was to put water in a small ten-inch tin pan. The boys got together and each put up twenty-five cents to hire a black person to clean the rooms so that they would not have "to bring up water, wood and empty slop and sweep." The food was terrible, according to Russell. The bread, syrup, bacon, and vegetables were not good, and the fish was so salty that he could hardly eat it. Since most of the students had rural backgrounds, they wore overalls and blue shirts. Only a few dressed in a way that Russell considered "nice." The school had one advantage, though: R. B. was given full senior status, and he would get a diploma if he passed the year's work.[31]

The isolation and routine at A & M sometimes bored Russell. Late in September, he and a friend struck out for Marietta, nine and a half miles away, on foot. They enjoyed a big supper, ate four ice cream sodas, and went to the movies. They had expected to get back to Powder Springs by car but after missing their ride found themselves with only a little money and no way to get back to school. They decided to stay all night in Marietta, but they did not have money for a hotel room. They stayed in the pool hall until 10:30 P.M., and around 11:00 they set out for the school on foot. After walking awhile, they lay down on the wet ground and tried to sleep. At 3:00 A.M. they decided it would be better to be arrested for vagrancy than to freeze. They returned to town, and a kindly policeman let them stay in the courthouse until later in the morning when they caught a ride to Powder Springs.[32]

Russell's grades did improve at A & M. By the spring term of 1914, he seemed to be studying harder with encouraging results. "Bully for you for passing trigonometry," his father wrote on May 21, 1914. Dick even showed a flash of excellence now and then. He surprised and gratified his parents when he won the school spelling contest. "Bravo!! Bully!! as T. R. would say," his father wrote.[33] Next Dick represented A & M at a district spelling meet in Cedartown. He did not win at Cedartown, but his father expressed deep pride that he had at least earned the right to compete at that level.

During the year at Powder Springs, Dick began to practice public speaking. Associating this talent with personal and political leadership, his parents urged him to speak and debate whenever he got a chance. Judge Russell wrote that he hoped his son would learn to speak better than his father—something, he added immodestly, "not many of the present time can do." The judge wrote on another occasion that Dick should not "refuse a single invitation" to speak; "Practice makes perfect," he concluded.[34]

Although Dick's grades were poor in the fall of 1913, before the end of the school year there were signs that he was beginning to meet some of the high expectations of his parents. Besides achieving a degree of excellence in spelling and public speaking, his overall grades were better. Also he was elected president of the literary society, and he made the basketball team. Perhaps he achieved more because there were fewer opportunities in the rural Powder Springs environment to do anything but school work. In any event, in May 1914, he was graduated from the three-year high school course.

During the school year, Judge Russell had discussed with his son the prospect of returning to Gordon Institute to graduate there in 1915. If he was going to return to Gordon, however, it would be necessary to somehow complete the Latin course that he had failed in 1912–13. They found the solution to that problem by sending Dick to the University of Georgia for a summer term in 1914. In early July, Dick moved to a room at 573 Hill Street in Athens and enrolled in Latin (Caesar), French, elementary German, and physiology classes. Back in a livelier town, Russell found plenty to do besides study. On July 13, his mother wrote that she was "horrified" to learn that he had not been in before midnight for some time. She insisted that he could not do good class work if "you dissipate all night." She was afraid that he might get into trouble, and surely such careless habits would make it hard for him ever to "knuckle down." It seemed that Mrs. Russell was right. Out of twenty-three days of classes in Latin, Dick missed four, and he was absent from French class nearly a third of the time. Nevertheless, he somehow managed to pass Latin, which qualified him to return to Gordon.[35]

However, in the fall term of 1914–15, Dick did not attend school. The reason for his absence is not clear. Arriving back at Gordon in January 1915, he enrolled in senior Latin, mathematics, English, and physics. To help him make up work that he had missed the previous fall, Dick engaged a tutor. On February 8, he wrote his father that he had made up the work in both physics and chemistry and had caught up with the rest of his class.

Judge Russell constantly harangued his son about doing well in school but at the same time urged him to get in the public eye as much as possible. When the time came to publish the school yearbook, Russell wanted Dick to get his picture included in as many places as possible. Despite being very short of money, the judge said he would "cheerfully pay for that." "The thing that will benefit you in the future," he wrote his son, "is being brought prominently before those of your school-mates who are careful enough to keep their copies of the annual."[36]

The elder Russell continued his obsession with the idea of Dick becoming a great man and achieving objectives that the judge had missed. The thought that Dick could make the Russell name famous and honor both father and son was an ever-present theme in the judge's letters. He wrote, "My son—my namesake—*never* let this thought leave your mind and may it influence your every act": he had nothing to live for except to see his children, especially Dick, succeed.

Hard times haunted the Russells during 1915. The judge had struggled to improve his financial position, but to no avail. Reporting on a visit to the farms that his wife had inherited in Oglethorpe County, Judge Russell said that he was filled with gloom. His tenants were heavily in debt to him, and he had to extend them even more credit to put in the 1915 crops. The situation was so bad that he was unable to send Dick money for school expenses in April until he obtained a loan. As he wrote, he "was sick at heart." Nevertheless, Russell somehow managed to respond to his son's frequent requests for money.[37]

Despite parental pressures, there was some doubt whether Dick would graduate with his class at Gordon in May 1915. He struggled with his old enemies, Latin and algebra, and it appeared for a time that he would lose the battle. In April, a little more than a month before the term's end, Russell received a very low grade in Latin. His mother wrote that "papa threw a fit over your Latin mark." He did his best work in physics, getting a grade of 85. He also had a respectable grade of 77 in English. But in Latin, he received only 62 and in mathematics a barely passing grade of 60 percent. It was the lowest grade one could get and still pass. Years later when Russell was speaking at Barnesville, he fondly recalled his days at Gordon Institute and referred to Professor Watson as one who, "more through grace and pity than through knowledge," had finally given him a "passing mark in Calculus." He evidently had taken seriously the statement that appeared beside his picture in Taps, the school's 1915 yearbook, which said, "Much study is a weariness to the flesh."[38]

During his last term at Gordon, Russell was fairly active in extracurricular affairs. He made corporal his sophomore year and was still a corporal at graduation. As one of the "Senior Bucks," he was known as the "wise buck." He was a member of the North Georgia Club and of the Euphradean Society, a debating and speaking group. Russell was listed as one of the students who made an enthusiastic speech at the society's meeting on January 8, 1915.[39] Dick also engaged in several school debates. Despite these activities, it could not be said that Russell was a student leader at Gordon.[40]

After graduating with Gordon's largest class up to that time on May 26, 1915, Dick returned home. He now was ready for college or professional school. He never seriously considered any career other than law and politics. Moreover, the Russells always assumed that he would attend the University of Georgia. His father had not only graduated there but had later served on the board of trustees. So in September 1915, Dick went to Athens and enrolled in the university's Lumpkin School of Law. Law had been only a one-year course in 1880 when his father attended, but it was now a two-year program.

Dick moved into Room 2 in Old College dormitory with his boyhood friend from Winder, William H. Quarterman. First built in 1806, Old College did not offer very comfortable quarters. Years later, in recalling his days at the university, Russell told the venerable Dean William Tate how he carried coal up the stairs to the fireplace in his room. The bathing and toilet facilities were in the basement.

Entering the junior class, Russell joined forty-five other beginning students, all of whom were residents of Georgia except two. He studied Blackstone, criminal and institutional law, contracts, sales, bailments, public corporations, and agency and insurance law. Most of his grades were around 80 percent, but he received 94 in torts and a high 98 in Blackstone, book one. As had been true at Gordon, Russell did enough work to get by, but he did not extend himself. He joined the Gordon Club on campus, which had thirty-nine members in 1915–16, indicating that the university received a healthy number of transfer students from Gordon Institute.[41]

One of Dick's main interests was the Sigma Alpha Epsilon (SAE) fraternity. His father had joined the SAEs back in the late 1870s and had always been a strong booster of his fraternity. The SAE group was the largest, and probably the most prestigious, fraternity on a campus that had a large number of social fraternities. Years later Russell wrote to a friend whose son had joined the SAEs, saying that he was glad that at least one member of the family "was truly discriminating in his choice of a fraternity."[42] Russell was also a member of the Phi Kappa literary society.

Just before Christmas 1915, Dick became seriously ill with pneumonia. He got such a high fever that on December 27 he was admitted to the Atlanta Registered Nurses Club by the Russell family physician, Dr. Almond. During the next few days, his temperature rose as high as 103 degrees. He also complained of pains over his heart. The doctors treated him with strychnine, cough syrup, castor oil, and occasional shots of whiskey. He coughed up blood, and his back and legs ached. Nurses rubbed his chest and limbs with turpentine, camphor, and lard and quinine. Russell talked in his sleep and at times was delirious. For over a month, he remained in the hospital, and it was not until mid-February that he was well enough to return home.[43]

Too weak to resume his studies at the university, Dick left for Sea Breeze, Florida, on March 30, 1916, where he recuperated at the home of an aunt. During his illness, he received letters from many of his male and female friends. William Quarterman, his former roommate, wrote from the university that "lots of fellows ask about you every day," and Rebecca Hill wrote from National Park Seminary in Forest Glen, Maryland, saying how sorry she was that Dick was ill. Russell soon recovered in the Florida sunshine and returned home in May. The letters and invitations that he received testified to his popularity among his peers. Melissa Hood of Commerce, Georgia, invited him to a party in June and said that every girl who planned to attend wanted to meet Dick.[44]

Russell did not return to the university to continue his law studies until January 1917, when he moved into the Sigma Alpha Epsilon fraternity house at 357 Pulaski Street. Writing his mother on January 5, he complained of the cold, praised the food served by the SAEs, and reported that he was doing well in his classes. He believed that he would pass all of his courses. February 18 he wrote his mother, "the sweetest mother in the world," a birthday letter. After wishing her a happy birthday, Dick wrote about the big SAE dance and the need to get his Ford car fixed up. He failed to mention his school work. He told his mother that he could do the one-step and had not missed a single dance, but he had a mortal fear when the band played a waltz or fox-trot since he simply could not do those dances.[45]

Young Russell greatly enjoyed the social life at the university and in Athens. When his father dropped in to the fraternity house on a surprise visit to Athens on February 1, 1917, Dick's fraternity brothers told the judge that Dick was not in but he might find his son at the Cue Club, a frequent haunt of Dick and his friends. Much to his disappointment, however, Judge Russell could not locate Dick on or off campus. Dick always seemed to have plenty of time for socializing.

No amount of activity in Athens, however, could keep Dick away from Winder for very long. He frequently took the train home for weekend visits, something that greatly pleased both Judge and Ina Russell. During his law school days, Dick continued his very close relationship with his mother. For a young man of twenty, the age when many young people break close family ties and strain to gain independence, Russell seemed happy and content to remain in the family fold. There was no streak of rebellion in Dick Russell. Ina doted over her oldest son and never made any move to push him out of the family nest. Dick reciprocated his mother's love and affection. From the time he was a small boy, he often referred to her as "dear." It is interesting to note that, in registering later for military service, when he was asked to list his nearest relative, he wrote, "Mrs. R. B. Russell, Sr., Winder, Georgia." There was no mention of his father.

On those occasions when Dick returned home for a weekend, Judge Russell talked to his son about doing well in his classes and striving for greatness—the same themes that filled the parental letters. After one such visit, Ina Russell was greatly distressed to find evidence that Dick had been chewing tobacco. She could not have felt worse, she

wrote, if she had found a flask of whiskey in the closet. Smoking cigarettes and cigars was bad enough, his mother wrote, but to chew—
"your mother can't stand it." She added that chewing tobacco had been
a "hindrance to papa," and she could not understand why Dick would
want to "form this filthy habit." Ina did not forbid her son to chew.
That was not her way. She did insist, however, that he *think good*
before you do." Dick explained that he just put a little tobacco in his
mouth when he stopped smoking temporarily, and he promised that he
would not do it again.[46]

A much more important issue that haunted Ina Russell and her
oldest son early in 1917 was the possibility of the United States becoming involved in war. In a letter to his mother on January 5, Dick said
there was not the slightest chance that "they" could get him to go to
war. Mrs. Russell often wrote about how awful the prospect of war
appeared. By late March, Ina wrote that she was "so depressed" over
the war question that she scarcely knew what to do. On April 3, the day
after President Wilson asked Congress to declare war against Germany,
Dick wrote his mother that if the United States entered the war, he
might be in a training camp in three months. He hoped, however, that
he could finish out the school year. Trying to reassure his mother, Dick
added that U.S. troops probably would only be used to protect the
country's bridges, railroad terminals, and other public facilities. "None
of our troops will ever get to Europe," he naively concluded.[47]

Neither Dick nor his parents wanted him to be taken into military
service. Judge Russell wrote on April 5 that he was so glad that "the
first call will not take you in." No one under twenty had been called,
permitting Dick to complete his first year of law school—consisting of
the first semester of 1915–16 through the second semester of 1916–17.
A few days later, Dick told his father that he was relieved at not having
to go, at least until August, but he again expressed the optimistic view
that not many Americans would ever get to the battle front. He admitted to being "a coward" and said that when he did have to serve
he would join the navy. Things were much different than in 1861, he
wrote, when everyone seemed eager to join the army and fight. He had
not met a single "boy" who wanted to go to war. Indeed, the war news
had "nearly demoralized" the entire college campus. Then Dick added
that "this generation" was not as brave as preceding ones.[48]

In June 1917, Dick completed all of his spring term courses with no
grade under 75 percent. After spending the summer at home, he returned to Athens in September ready to complete his senior year of law.
His courses included common law pleading, Georgia procedure, federal

procedure, equity, private corporations, domestic relations, wills, evidence, and realty. But he found plenty of time for extracurricular activities. Besides being active in his fraternity and a member of the Phi Kappa Literary Society, Dick joined the Jefferson Law Society and the Gridiron Club. Other than the fraternity, Dick was not very active in the clubs and societies to which he belonged. He did not hold any student offices, although in 1917–18 he did represent the SAEs on the Pan-Hellenic Council. Dick was a friendly, outgoing young man who liked to visit with friends, sit around talking, and have frequent dates. Since women had not been generally admitted to the university at the time Russell was in school, dates had to be arranged with girls from Lucy Cobb Academy or elsewhere. Russell had one serious relationship with a young woman during his university years, which he broke off just before graduation. In an undated letter, she wrote Dick that she would always care for him but would respect his wish to break up. "Goodbye Dick darling," she sadly concluded, "luck to you and happiness always." It was clear that although Dick had many dates, he shied away from serious relationships.[49]

In his senior year of law school, Russell's grades improved slightly. They were good but not outstanding. Indeed, there was nothing in his academic record that reflected his sharp intelligence or that forecast the understanding and grasp of politics for which he later became so well known. In the *Pandora*, the university's yearbook for 1918, the editor wrote about Dick: "When Mr. Nix brings out his absence blanks [Russell] is one of the most paramount students we have. 'Dick' reads the book through occasionally and always knocks up the weight to the seventy-five mark or better, which is going quite some [distance]." Russell was not a campus leader in any sense. Even though he was a great baseball and football fan, he never took part in these sports at the university.

In June 1918, Dick completed his law studies. The *Pandora* editor wrote that he was one of the most popular students in the class and predicted "a bright future in his practice with his father." However, the grave problem of military service hung over him. Just before classes ended, Dick wrote his mother a long letter describing how "blue" he was because so many of his friends were leaving for military duty. As these friends, some of whom had been in school with him for six or seven years, left for war, he "began to feel like I ought to go into some branch of the service for a family as large as ours certainly ought to have someone to fight for them." The only reason that he had not signed up for the navy in June was because he wanted to help his father, who "has

Russell in his navy uniform, late 1918. (Photo courtesy of Russell Memorial Library, University of Georgia, Athens.)

been so sweet and longsuffering with me." He was still interested in joining the navy but thought it would be hard for him to endure the discipline "after the easy life I have led." Besides writing about military service, Dick discussed friendships made in school and the problems of facing the "real world." He concluded by saying that he hoped he had not bored his mother, but "I felt just like I was a child again and just wanted to confide in you."[50]

After spending the summer of 1918 at home, the time arrived when Dick had to respond to his nation's call. On September 12, less than two months before the armistice and shortly before his twenty-first birthday, he signed up for service in the U.S. Navy. During the seventy-nine days that Russell served as an apprentice seaman, he stayed in Athens. Since he was quite distant from the sea, he jokingly acquired the name, "Admiral of the Oconee River."[51]

Russell found little to enjoy in his navy experience. The courses in mathematics, physics, and navigation were hard for him, and he had to spend hours in study hall. Also the environment was dull for a young man who had just left the university where he enjoyed rich social activities. The general confinement, drilling, guard duty, and scrubbing of barracks floors had no redeeming value for Dick. Although Russell wanted to become an ensign, he did not like the work and effort needed to achieve that end. He told his mother during one of his depressed periods that he had made "an awful mistake by going into the Navy."[52]

So it was with great relief and much happiness that Russell received his discharge papers around December 1, 1918. He immediately returned home to enjoy the Christmas season with his family. While Russell's military service was minimal, he was always proud to call himself a veteran. He soon became active in the American Legion and stayed in the Naval Reserves until 1923.

3

Political Apprenticeship

hen Dick Russell returned to Winder in December 1918, he had just recently turned twenty-one. He was a young man ready to take his position in the world. He was tall, about six feet, and weighed between 170 and 180 pounds. His high forehead suggested early baldness, and his rather large ears did not detract from his attractiveness. The quizzical expression of his blue eyes, his slightly drawn smile, and his prominent nose all seemed to blend into a face of interest and character. His upright posture, conservative blue suit, neatly groomed dark hair, and a cigarette between his fingers gave the appearance of someone on his way to success.

Dick moved into his parents' big white house almost as if he had never been gone. Although he had been away attending school most of the time during the previous seven years, he had returned home frequently. Now that he was an adult and ready to begin practicing law, it never occurred to him that he might get a house or apartment of his own. That also would have been unthinkable to Ina and Judge Russell who were happy to have their "boy" with them again. Judge Russell had longed for the day when he and his namesake would practice law together. His office in the Peoples' Bank building was now ready to include another Russell.

Winder had experienced a great deal of change since Dick was growing up in the fields and forests of nearby Russell. Winder was no longer split among three counties but had become the county seat of Barrow County, which had been formed in 1914. By 1920 the population of Winder had reached 3,335, an increase of over 2,000 in twenty years. About 80 percent of the people in Winder were white and about 20 percent were black. Barrow County had a black population of 30 percent, but most of the blacks lived on the county's small farms. The community was strictly segregated, and the color barrier between whites and blacks was firm.[1]

The change of Winder from small rural village to thriving town was evident in many ways. While it still depended on the surrounding farms and remained a center of the cotton trade, a number of factories employed several hundred people. There were five financial institutions, specialty stores, a lumber company, a hardware store, and an increasing number of professionals. Automobiles were common on Winder streets; both Judge Russell and Dick owned cars. Services had also improved. The telephone company that Judge Russell had helped to organize in 1900 provided service throughout the town and beyond. More people were receiving water and electricity from the town-operated utility works. There was a movie theater and an opera house. It was no longer necessary to walk in the mud, since block after block now had paved sidewalks. When the Granite Hotel with forty rooms opened in 1919, some local citizens viewed their town as an emerging urban center.[2]

Dick Russell felt very comfortable and at home in this environment. He had a strong sense of place and an emotional attachment to the community. Although he had traveled a great deal for a young man raised in the South during the first two decades of the twentieth century, he had seen nothing that surpassed the place of his birth. He loved the family home, the neighbors, and the pace of life. As he grew to manhood in a large family, he developed an increasing love and affection for his six brothers and six sisters and for his father and mother. Although he was the fourth child, as the oldest son he gradually assumed the leading role among the Russell children. His father and mother eagerly pushed him into that position, and just as enthusiastically he accepted it.

As emphasized earlier, there was a strong family expectation that Dick would have a distinguished political career. His father hoped fervently that he would become governor, an office that the voters had denied Judge Russell. Dick's father left nothing undone in his effort to push Dick toward politics. Judge Russell hoped that his son would benefit from being a member of a family whose name he had made well known statewide as a result of his own extensive but unsuccessful political campaigns. The many friends Dick had made at the three schools he had attended could certainly become useful politically, as Judge Russell had planned. Dick's involvement in groups could also benefit him in the political world. Besides belonging to the American Legion, he held memberships in the Georgia and American bar associations, the Odd Fellows, the Elks, the Masons, the Forty-and-Eight, and the Burns Club in Atlanta, and he kept up his contacts with the SAE fraternity. He also continued his membership in the Winder Methodist Church.

Dick was not insensible of the ambitions that his father and other members of the family had for him. Indeed, he was keenly aware of his membership in a distinguished upper middle-class family, and he recognized that this accident of birth was a great asset. He knew that his family was special and that he held a distinctive place in it. His father would never let him forget who he was or what was expected of him. Some young men might have resented such family pressures to succeed and left home to escape the parental advice that through Russell's university years bordered on nagging. But if Dick Russell ever had such thoughts, he never expressed them. Rather, he seemed to take it for granted that he would achieve the greatness that his father hoped for him.

After Dick completed his short tour with the navy, he had at least two opportunities to join other law firms. But none of the offers attracted him away from Winder. He believed that he could establish a successful practice there with his father. However, he was concerned that, since he had been gone from Winder for much of seven years, he did not know as many people as he considered desirable. He thought it was important that he become acquainted with people who might sit on juries. One way to do this was to run for public office and campaign throughout the county.[3]

On July 8, 1920, Dick announced that he was a candidate from Barrow County in the Democratic primary for the Georgia House of Representatives. In a small statement that appeared in the *Winder News*, Russell said, "I will appreciate the support and influence of every white voter and, if elected, I pledge my best efforts to serve you acceptably." That was all. There was no platform, no statement of principles, no stated goals. Indeed, when he announced his candidacy, Russell had no expectations of winning a House seat. The idea was to get known in order to help his law business. Next to the announcement, the editor of the paper added his view of Russell, writing, "He is a fine young man, a rising attorney and has many friends who will loyally back him in his laudable ambition." Concluding that Russell was "ambitious, energetic, educated and popular," the editor said that he would be "a strong contender for this honor."

Russell's reference to seeking the support of all "white" voters was typical of the time and place in which he lived. The Democratic primary was only open to white voters, and victory there was tantamount to election. Of course, everyone knew that blacks could not vote in the primary, but to appeal specifically to white voters emphasized a candidate's southernness and firmness on racial segregation. Russell was well within the established pattern of southern politics.

Two weeks after Dick became a candidate, Albert G. Lamar, the elderly editor of the *Barrow Times*, announced that he would seek the state House of Representatives seat. Competition from a well-known and respected older man did not frighten Dick Russell. While both he and his opponent advertised weekly in the *Winder News*, Russell also launched an intense personal campaign. During the next two months, he went from house to house and person to person soliciting votes. He stated years later that he "saw every voter I could find." Before the primary in early September, he had talked to hundreds of voters and had concluded that he could win.[4]

Russell's hard campaigning paid off handsomely. When the returns were reported on September 9, they showed that Russell had defeated Lamar by a vote of 1,315 to 644. "Little Dick" carried every district in the county by strong margins. Reviewing the campaign and the candidates, a writer for the *Winder News* said that Lamar was a "pleasant, kind and affable Christian gentleman," but that he was a product of the political past. Russell, on the other hand, represented youth, vim, vigor, and ability. "The interests of Barrow County will not suffer in his hands," the front-page story concluded.[5]

When Dick arrived in Atlanta in June 1921 to take up his seat in the House of Representatives, a position his father had held forty years earlier, he was twenty-three, making him one of the youngest members of that 198-person body. He quickly became a part of a group of "young turks" in the General Assembly who looked forward to wresting power from the old Bourbons who controlled state government. These young men hoped to improve the image of Georgia politics and to solve some of the state's pressing problems. There were around forty younger representatives and senators, many of whom had seen other parts of the United States and the world during the recent war. Also, many of them were college educated, mostly recent graduates of the University of Georgia, and were embarrassed by Georgia's "redneck" image. Five of these House members, including William S. Tyson from McIntosh County, who served from 1921 to 1928, had been classmates of Russell at the university. University graduates Roy V. Harris of Jefferson County and Hugh Peterson of Ailey, who were both elected in 1922, and others soon became part of this younger, ambitious legislative group. Besides being graduates of the university, several of these young lawmakers had another important connection—membership in the SAE fraternity. Russell felt completely at home among this group of legislators who gradually and subtly brought major changes to Georgia politics and governmental administration. Russell helped to create a new politics that carried him to the governorship and beyond.

Russell received good committee assignments for a young new-comer. He was appointed to the committees on rules, constitutional amendments, public property, and the University of Georgia and its branches. He was named vice-chairman of the latter committee. In 1923 he was given additional assignments on the committees on agriculture, labor, the judiciary, and public highways.[6] Of his first committee assignments, the *Winder News* wrote, "We congratulate 'Dick' on his good fortune and feel sure that the interests of Barrow county will be well taken care of."[7]

There is abundant evidence in Russell's early legislative career that his ambitions went far beyond serving in the Georgia General Assembly. With this in mind, he consciously and carefully planned his political strategy and adopted a special style. He left nothing to chance. His first step was to get to know as many legislators and political leaders as possible. He already had a wide set of friends and acquaintances. Judge Russell's hope that, by sending his son to three schools, Dick would make more friends had paid off. Everywhere Russell turned he saw friends from his days at Gordon Institute, the Seventh District A & M, or the university. Being a friendly, gregarious young man, Russell also soon met those colleagues in the House he did not already know. At the outset of his public career, Russell considered personal contact as the first rule of politics. Then he quietly identified the power centers in the legislature and made sure that those people knew him. The Russell name was a great help and made contacts fairly easy because many legislators, or their fathers, knew Judge Russell. In his early political career, the newspapers usually identified Dick as the son of a famous state jurist. Russell was careful to identify himself with the highway and education issues and was an especially strong backer of the University of Georgia. There was no risk here to his advancement since the legislature was filled with enthusiastic Georgia Bulldogs.

As Russell advanced politically, he carefully followed the principle of not getting involved in other legislators' political fights. This was almost an article of faith with him. He knew that in every election and legislative battle there were winners and losers. Becoming involved, he reasoned, only aroused animosity from one side or the other against him. Russell tried to avoid controversies that would alienate colleagues and sought instead to operate quietly behind the scenes to work out compromises and settle disputes. Moreover, he did not often create issues. He was careful not to jump out in front on a political question, because he knew the point man always took flak and made enemies. Rather he tended to observe and study an issue until he saw which direction it was taking and then to identify himself with the popular side. This is not to say that he was an opportunist—in later years, he took some strong stands on major state and national issues. It demonstrates, however, that as he built a political base in the legislature, he was careful not to place himself in a position where he would be attacked or held responsible for unpopular results.[8] As Roy V. Harris recalled years later, Russell made a strong speech in support of education and Confederate pensions early in his legislative career and "you couldn't get in trouble doing that."

Russell won the admiration and respect of his colleagues for two important qualities—integrity and fairness. Fellow legislators soon learned that they could always count on Russell's word. A commitment was a commitment, not something to renege on or squirm out of. This point is well illustrated by the campaign for the Speaker of the House in 1921, Russell's first legislative session. W. Cecil Neill of Columbus and several of his friends had asked Russell to support Neill for the Speakership, and Russell had agreed. Then J. H. Ennis, a close friend of Dick's father, urged Russell to back his candidacy. Ennis not only wanted Russell's vote but hoped that Dick would help him among alumni of the University of Georgia. In some ways, Russell would have preferred to back Ennis instead of Neill, and he admitted that he was in a quandary. But in reply to Senator Thomas E. Watson who supported Ennis, Russell said that he had promised to vote for Neill and must keep his word.[9]

Russell might change his mind or adjust a position, but he was always open and honest about it. Furthermore, in dealing with House members in committee or on the floor, Russell always maintained a scrupulous fairness. Whenever he was in a position to hear arguments on an issue, he was open and fair to both sides. By the mid-1920s, his reputation for fairness was widely recognized in the House of Representatives and had much to do with his ultimate election as Speaker. Finally, Russell made a special effort to learn the rules and procedures of the House. He prepared carefully on every issue and was always very well informed. Dick believed that knowledge was power, and he did his homework on every major question.

Georgia legislators faced many problems in the early 1920s. Agriculture, the state's main industry, was badly depressed, the state was heavily in debt, highways were poor or nonexistent, and education at all levels was weak or worse.[10] Education and highways were emerging as the two main issues confronting Georgia legislators. Obtaining enough revenue to fund a better educational system and improved roads was a constant challenge, but the voters were looking for immediate results.

Russell was among those who believed that better public education, including a stronger university system, and more highways would stimulate the state's economic development. Legislative controversies in the 1920s did not center around the ends that should be achieved but around the means to reach desired goals. The question was how to finance education and highways. The political jockeying occurred between one group of legislators who wanted to float bonds to finance highways and one who wanted to adopt a pay-as-you-go plan. Russell joined the latter group.

During his first terms in the legislature, Russell worked quietly and without fanfare. He introduced some minor amendments to the general tax bill, served on a committee to investigate the A & M schools, and established his credentials as a fiscal conservative by voting against deficiency appropriations. At the same time, he supported education and highway legislation. In August 1921, the General Assembly passed a measure requiring that each county have at least one consolidated high school. Lawmakers also passed legislation providing state funds for highways.[11] Russell avoided inflammatory and emotional issues such as lynching and the Ku Klux Klan. Retiring Governor Hugh M. Dorsey told the legislators that violence against blacks must be ended. It was a shameful fact, he said, that there had been fifty-eight lynchings in Georgia since he became governor in 1917. While Dorsey talked at length about the horrors and injustices of lynchings, the General Assembly ignored the issue. This was an issue that Russell and his colleagues did not want to confront.[12]

By the end of his first legislative session in the late summer of 1921, Russell had gained some public attention. Writing his "legislative personals" in the *Macon News*, John T. Boifeuillet referred to Dick as "the talented namesake of a distinguished Georgian" and noted that he was "sparkling and fervent." Boifeuillet mentioned that Dick was single but added that "he has the persuasive charm which few women can resist."[13] It was true that he had always been popular with women, but he seemed much more interested in politics than courtship. Dick liked to sit around hotel rooms in the evening talking, making friends, and discussing political questions and strategy.

Russell's performance in Atlanta clearly pleased the home folks as he had no opposition for reelection in 1922. Referring to him as Colonel R. B. Russell, the editor of the *Winder News* said that he had "made Barrow a fine representative." Later the editor called him a "splendid young lawyer, sane, safe, progressive, always on the job." Meanwhile, Dick received local acclaim when he gave the Confederate Memorial

Day address in April 1922. The *Winder News* reported that it was a "masterful oration." His talk, one writer said, was "replete with noble thoughts and splendid diction throughout. His tribute to noble women of the lost cause was great, while he did not forget the private soldier who on the bloody fields of the South so nobly illustrated the courage and chivalry of these great people."[14]

The big event for the Russell family in 1922, however, was not Dick's reelection to the General Assembly but his father's election as chief justice of the Georgia Supreme Court. Dick played a prominent role in his father's campaign and wrote to scores of his friends soliciting support. He also contacted many people he did not know and made several talks throughout the state on behalf of his father's candidacy. The hard campaigning of the Russell family and a host of friends finally brought victory to Judge Russell in a statewide race.[15] His election as chief justice lessened much of the judge's earlier disappointment and frustration, but it did not diminish the hopes and ambitions that he had for Dick, or, as it turned out, for himself.

Political conditions in the legislature were already shaping up in a way that would benefit Dick Russell. The 1922 session achieved very little, but during the summer, a number of younger members began discussing how they might elect one of their members as Speaker pro tem. W. Cecil Neill of Muscogee County was Speaker. He was one of the older members of the House and had strong support. There was no desire to oust Neill, and, besides, the "young turks" did not have the votes. They did have a chance, though, to place one of their own men in the position of Speaker pro tem. It was for this post that Russell's name emerged.

One of the leaders behind this move was Roy V. Harris of Louisville. In June 1923, he corresponded with a number of House members, urging them to support Russell. He wrote to Hugh Peterson of Ailey, who had been elected to the House in 1922 and would be attending his first session within a few days, that the younger lawmakers should stick together and elect Russell. Harris explained that Dick had been "at Georgia along about our day," and they had been good friends ever since their university days. Harris explained that Dick was a member of that group called "the younger element in the Legislature" and that all the "younger crowd of the last House are behind Dick, and pushing his candidacy." These legislators, Harris continued, had agreed a year ago to put one of their members forward. He said they had been sticking together to force some recognition from the "powers that be." They had achieved some success, Harris wrote, and they hoped to continue during the next two years. Peterson replied that he could not support Russell because he had promised to vote for J. Herman Milner of nearby Dodge County.[16]

Despite the initial reluctance of some House members, by the time the session opened in late June 1923, Russell and his friends had developed overwhelming support for his election. On June 27, Lawrence S. Camp of Campbell County, a close friend of Russell, nominated him for Speaker pro tem, and the motion was seconded by several members. Russell received 195 votes, all that were cast. Everything had been arranged ahead of time: members like Peterson who at first had refused to support Russell saw the light and jumped on the bandwagon when Milner withdrew his candidacy.

Now Russell had a platform from which he could enhance his visibility and prestige. With an opportunity to preside over the House from time to time, he could demonstrate his fairness and impartiality. His vigor, youth, and knowledge and his school and university connections, along with his skillful political maneuvering, were beginning to pay off. Already, at age twenty-five, Dick was marked as a political comer in Atlanta and to some extent throughout the state.[17]

Outside of politics, things were not going so well for Dick Russell. The returns from a law practice in a depressed farming community in the early 1920s were too meager to give him the standard of living that he enjoyed. Consequently, he was in debt to all kinds of vendors who hounded him for payment of overdue bills. He was frequently threatened with lawsuits to collect unpaid accounts. At one time, Russell even had trouble paying for some law books. On October 10, 1922, a representative of Callaghan and Company, sellers of law books in Chicago, wrote Dick that the firm had exhausted every means of obtaining an "amicable adjustment of your account," which had a balance of $80. If Russell did not remit within fifteen days, the company would employ "one of your brother attorneys" to sue for payment.

Demands to pay unsettled accounts came from every direction. On January 16, 1923, the superintendent of the Winder Water and Light Company wrote Russell that if his bill was not paid in three days, service would be disconnected. At about the same time, the Bernstein Brothers, home furnishers in Athens, demanded a check on their account by return mail. Even his dentist in Athens kept pressing Russell for payment without success. He apparently could not pay for a typewriter purchased at McGregor's in Athens, and management threatened him with a lawsuit. His Winder banker did not have much better success than his other creditors. The demand that Russell pay off a note of

$100.72 went unanswered. Dick's problems continued throughout the 1920s. In June 1927, just before he was elected Speaker of the House, an Atlanta banker reminded him that a loan installment of $39.05 was overdue and asked him to remit at once. Some creditors were pressing him for payment as late as 1929.[18]

The Georgia General Assembly continued to struggle with a host of problems at the 1923 session. Governor Clifford M. Walker, elected in 1922, urged lawmakers to improve education at all levels, including the provision of free textbooks. He also recommended the construction of more and better hard surface roads, which could be paid for by selling state bonds and by levying an income tax. The legislators refused to act on the governor's main proposals. In 1924, however, they did pass a constitutional amendment providing for biennial, rather than annual, legislative sessions limited to sixty days, all in the name of economy.[19]

Russell, like most of his colleagues, made no genuine effort to tackle the huge problems facing the state. Rather, he continued to make friends and to build a network of support. He ran again unopposed in 1924, and it was rumored even at that time that he might seek the Speakership. " 'Dick' Russell is unquestionably one of the most popular members of the present House," his hometown paper reported in March.[20] Shortly afterward the Athens Banner-Herald referred to him as "one of the leading members of the House," who had frequently presided over that body in a way that brought credit to him and to the House. The writer said that he was "a mixer and a friendmaker, the equal of his illustrious father." The Athens paper ventured that it would not be many years before Russell would "aspire to be governor," at which time the "chair will be waiting for him."[21]

By the mid-1920s, Governor Walker was pushing hard for a more progressive legislative program in Georgia. In his second inaugural address on June 27, 1925, he again emphasized that education and roads were the big issues facing the state. They should have top priority with lawmakers, he said. He also insisted that the tax system be revised to reduce the burden on tangible property. Walker argued that universal education and more consolidated high schools were needed to drive "ignorance, superstition and prejudice" out of Georgia society. Good roads, he added, would "revolutionize the social and civic life of the state" and stimulate the economy.[22]

Although the General Assembly, meeting in its first biennial session since the 1890s, passed a few minor tax reforms in 1925, the major issues as seen by Governor Walker remained unsolved. Consequently, he felt there was a need for a special session. Walker wrote lawmakers that

Georgia had been "in a rut" for several years. He warned that other southern states would surpass Georgia if the state did not "NOW adopt an active and progressive highway and school and college program." He proposed calling a special session in February 1926. Most legislators, however, including Hugh Peterson, to whom he wrote, opposed the governor's idea of bond financing for highways. Calling a special session unwise, Peterson urged the governor to drop the matter. In regard to floating highway bonds, Peterson said that debt bondage was "the worst of all kinds of bondage," because it would require greater taxes. Despite this kind of advice from a number of legislators, Walker proceeded to call the special session.[23]

Here was a governor who had graduated from the University of Georgia in 1897, about the time Russell and a number of other younger legislators were born, pushing a progressive program that met strong resistance from the younger group. The opposition to Walker's program was clearly spearheaded by the young lawmakers with whom Russell worked closely. Raymond W. Martin from LaGrange wrote on February 8, 1926, that the younger House members had agreed to meet prior to the special session to organize their opposition to the "bond crew." Martin blamed Walker and "a few saphead professors who are ancient landmarks at the University" for pushing the idea of bond financing for highways. Hugh Peterson, Jud P. Wilhoit, J. S. Burgin, and other younger members vigorously attacked the idea of a special session and the passage of laws for what they called special interests "that were not beneficial to the people."[24]

Russell remained in the background during the special session and let his friends defeat the governor's program. Russell was being cautious since he was planning his campaign to become Speaker. Editor John S. Cohen of the *Atlanta Journal* reported on February 26, 1926, only two days after Governor Walker addressed the special legislative session, that Russell was a "full-fledged candidate for the Speakership of the next House of Representatives." The *Journal* editor claimed that Russell already had received "many assurances of support." The *Winder News* carried an article on March 4 with the headline, "Rep. Richard B. Russell Candidate for Speaker." Since W. Cecil Neill had indicated that he would not seek reelection, the time seemed right for Russell to make his move.

It was not until the summer and early fall of 1926, however, that Russell made a final commitment to seek the post. Sometime in August, he visited in Atlanta with three of his closest political friends—Jud Wilhoit, Frank A. Hooper, Jr., and James C. Davis. They urged him to run. As a result of those conversations, Russell told Hugh Peterson, "I have definitely decided to make the race for Speaker." He added that he was counting heavily on Peterson, because "you are one of the fellows who entered into this conspiracy at its inception." Russell further explained that he was not "devoid of ambition, as you well know, and am very susceptible to flattery." While his private affairs were at a stage where he did "not care about making the fight," he said that Jud Wilhoit had talked him into it. Of course, he added, he wanted to win "not only for my sake but for the friends who support me." Then he asked Peterson to write new legislators "setting forth as strongly as you can, without stultifying yourself," reasons why they should back Russell. Congratulating Peterson on his reelection, Russell said he was pleased that they would be working together in the next session. "We are going to have a real chance to do something for Georgia," Dick concluded.[25]

Roy V. Harris also considered making the race for Speaker. The relationship between Harris and Russell had cooled since 1923 when Harris pushed Dick for Speaker pro tem. It is not clear just what came between them, but they were both among the young legislators jockeying for political position. The Russell group needed to move fast to turn Harris aside. They did not want a division among the younger House members, which would reduce their influence. Jud Wilhoit, head of the Russell forces, spared nothing. He wrote Peterson on September 16, 1926, asking for the names of House members in his part of the state who might be for Harris instead of Russell. Wilhoit said, "We will take their names and write them and see if they cannot be showed their error." The strategy was to make House members think that "Dick is already elected, or rather has enough pledges to elect him, and advise that they 'get on the bandwagon' and enjoy the music." Wilhoit concluded: "Get busy for Dick and keep in touch with me."[26] One of the main arguments for Russell's election was that he would make good committee appointments. Both Peterson and Wilhoit wrote that these appointments were very important and that it was essential to have a "fair, competent and impartial Speaker." Russell would be such a leader.[27]

On September 21, Marion H. Allen of Milledgeville wrote to Frank A. Hooper that he believed Dick's race for Speaker was in good shape. Allen said he thought all the young men in the House were for Russell. An unnamed correspondent wrote Allen that he believed many older members of the House were also for him. The person who wrote to Allen thought it wise that wavering legislators back Russell before he won the position. "A man appreciates help most when he needs it," according to this writer. The veiled suggestion was that it would not be prudent to wait too long to throw in with Dick.[28]

As his friends were gearing up his campaign for Speaker in 1927, Dick had to undergo the embarrassment and sadness of his father making another unsuccessful, some said foolish, campaign, this time for the U.S. Senate. In June 1926, without resigning from the Supreme Court, Judge Russell launched his campaign against incumbent senator Walter George, one of Georgia's most beloved political figures. Judge Russell campaigned against the League of Nations, the World Court, and all policies that might involve the United States in European affairs. Because George had voted for joining the World Court, Russell portrayed him as a dangerous internationalist. He said that the "overwhelming majority of the people" opposed meddling in European matters. He also tried to appeal to the farm vote by promising to help agriculture if he were elected.[29]

Seeking election to the U.S. Senate in Georgia in 1926 on a platform opposing the World Court revealed a bewildering political naïveté on the part of Judge Russell. The politicians knew that it was a phony issue, and the people could hardly have been less interested. Although Dick, too, knew that his father's effort was hopeless, he directed the campaign and worked hard for his father's election. But prospects were discouraging. Press comment on the judge and his campaign was critical, sarcastic, and sometimes almost brutal. Newspapers did not provide pleasant reading for members of the Russell family. The *Thomasville Times* of June 25, 1926, called the judge an "old stager and some stump artist," while the *Macon Telegraph* said he was a "misfit" and as a senator would be a "tragedy."[30] The *Greensboro Herald* remarked that the judge "had been feeding at the public trough during his entire life," and he had not contributed a single constructive thing.[31] Some editors presented him as a kind of laughingstock. On July 1, the *Columbus News* wrote that there was no better way to emphasize Senator George's talents than to compare him with Russell. The voters fully agreed, and again the judge suffered a crashing defeat in a vote of 128,179 to 61,911.[32]

Dick's political fortunes, however, were faring much better. By the time the legislature met on June 23, 1927, the Russell forces had everything under control for his election as Speaker. Dick set up campaign headquarters in Rooms 108–110 of the Kimball Hotel in Atlanta on June 18. As the House members arrived for the coming session, Russell and his friends visited and socialized with them. Although Harris was still in the running, his friends had said that he would not make a fight for the post. As Harris recalled the situation later, when he set out to line up support, he found that the Russell forces had already obtained most representatives' pledges. Once he saw the political realities, Harris announced on the evening of June 21 that he would not be a candidate for Speaker. Now everything was clear sailing for Russell.

Russell had asked Hugh Peterson on June 10 if he would place his name in nomination. Peterson gladly accepted.[33] When the House went into session, Peterson made a strong speech for Russell, not so much to win votes—that had already been settled—but to give Dick publicity and press coverage. Peterson said that the Speaker should be a man who would preside with "wisdom and decorum." He should have a thorough knowledge of the duties of the office, treat all members equally and with respect, and strictly enforce the principles of honesty and fairness. Peterson claimed that there was a man of "superior abilities" in their midst who could lead the House most effectively. He continued, "Though young in years, his previous demeanor has shown him to be a leader—judicious, conservative and fair." Russell, he concluded, would make a presiding officer of "unsurpassed excellence."[34] His colleagues agreed, and all members present voted for Russell. C. E. Gregory, a writer for the *Atlanta Journal*, wrote that Russell was "one of the most able and popular young legislators in Georgia's history." The editor of the *Winder News* observed that his election as Speaker was "a splendid recognition of the commanding ability of Dick Russell."[35]

The General Assembly was now led by young, vigorous legislators. Russell was twenty-nine, and E. B. Dykes, president of the Senate, was thirty-three. The contrast between the legislative leadership and incoming governor L. G. Hardman was easy to see. Hardman, a native of Commerce, was seventy-one years old and a medical doctor who had extensive business interests. As the legislative leaders sat on the platform of the capitol grounds Saturday afternoon, June 25, for Hardman's inauguration, their youth was obvious. Most of the leaders were less than half as old as the governor. The *Atlanta Journal* congratulated Russell and Dykes, saying that they were both seasoned legislators who had many friends and acquaintances. The *Journal* editor believed that the forthcoming session would be a fortunate one for the state.[36]

Russell immediately presented himself as a consensus leader. Upon taking his post as Speaker, he called on his colleagues to give "careful consideration of all legislative proposals" presented by the governor, "regardless of our past political affiliations." He reminded the House members that they had a great responsibility to take care of the state's business in a short sixty-day session. He concluded by saying that if he made mistakes, they would "be of the head and not of the heart." Then he moved quickly to get the House committees organized and working. He named his close friend, Jud Wilhoit, vice-chairman of the Rules Committee. Russell himself was the ex officio chairman. He then appointed Paul H. Doyal of Floyd County, an early Russell supporter for Speaker, chairman of the Appropriations Committee.[37]

Russell quickly and firmly established his authority in the House. It had been customary for years for certain special interests to use their influence to get friendly legislators on key committees. The story was told that Russell was approached by a prominent citizen who handed the new Speaker a list of names. "These are the persons we would like to see appointed to committees," the citizen said. Dick replied that if the gentleman hoped to have any of the individuals on his list named to a committee, he should never let Russell see it. Russell reputedly said that even if he had already planned to appoint someone, once he saw that person's name on the list, he could not appoint him. The citizen declared that this must be a new day. Russell replied, "Yes, sir."[38]

The editor of the *Atlanta Journal* missed the mark badly when he suggested that the 1927 session would be a good one because of the new and younger House and Senate leadership. Instead, strife and controversy characterized the session. The issues were the same as during the previous sessions—education, highways, and how to find money for these major needs. Acrimony reached such heights that one House member recommended an additional appropriation of $10,000 to add quarters at the state mental hospital to house legislators because it was not in "the best interests of the state for them to be at the state capitol."[39]

Governor Hardman, who had served in the General Assembly from 1902 to 1910, recommended a full legislative agenda. First of all, he told the legislators that his would be a "business administration." He said that the people wanted full value in return for every dollar of tax money spent on government services. He recommended reorganization of the state departments and boards to achieve greater governmental efficiency and suggested equalizing tax burdens, reorganizing the state highway department by creating a State Highway Commission, and improving education at all levels.[40]

One of the main problems in Georgia government over recent years had been that appropriations regularly exceeded tax revenues. Lawmakers wanted to spend but not to tax. For that reason, some debts could not be paid. Hardman told members of the legislature that such deficits in state agencies threatened the finances of the state. Income and expenditures should be balanced, the governor insisted. Part of the problem rested with school supporters who wanted more money for all levels of education but no major new taxes. Rural legislators were also insistent on increasing so-called equalization funds to help poor school districts with low tax bases.

As the 1927 session got underway, tax measures quickly made center stage. Jud Wilhoit, a close associate of Russell, introduced a bill to raise the gasoline tax from four to five cents a gallon to provide more money for roads, but it was defeated. Paul Doyal, another Russell man, pushed for an income tax. It passed the House but was blocked in the Senate. The House defeated the sales tax twice after portraying it as a tax on the poor.[41]

As the lawmakers in both houses struggled over the budget, Russell strove toward fiscal responsibility, at least in the House. He declared that it was dangerous to make appropriations before knowing what revenues would be. That, of course, depended on whether there would be any new tax legislation. On August 10, Russell expressed strong opposition to the appropriation bill that was $5.5 million over the previous budget and some $3 million above projected revenues. After trying unsuccessfully to get the House to reduce a proposed increase of $500,000 for the educational equalization fund, he reluctantly had to break a tie vote. He voted for the deficit-laden measure but explained to his colleagues that such a vote demanded new taxes.[42] But the legislators were not convinced.

During the session, Russell pushed members hard to get their work completed. August 20, the last day of the session, was approaching rapidly. He called Saturday and night sessions and even started work an hour earlier in the morning. Despite such efforts, the hard decisions were postponed. Saturday, August 20, was nothing short of bedlam in the General Assembly. There were charges and countercharges about where responsibility lay. Russell did not excuse the House, but he said the Senate had been even more negligent by refusing to vote taxes to raise enough money to cover appropriations. "They have voted appropriations with an even freer hand than we," he said. No agreement could be reached on revenue bills, and wrangling within and between the legislative branches continued into Saturday night. When it became apparent that the necessary bills could not be passed by midnight, officials covered the clocks so business could proceed. It was not until six o'clock Sunday morning, August 21, that the lawmakers agreed to the necessary compromises and adjourned.[43]

Russell breathed a sigh of relief as his first session as Speaker ended. His problem did not rest so much with the House as with the inability of the House and Senate to agree on tax measures. Russell's men had done yeoman service in trying to get revenue bills to the governor's desk, but they had been foiled by the Senate. The two key bills had been Doyal's income tax amendment and the sales tax proposal pushed by Charles J. Bloch of Macon, also a close friend of the Speaker. Nevertheless, Russell came out of the session with an enhanced reputation. He had stressed fiscal responsibility and at the same time emerged as a strong supporter of better education and improved highways. He appeared as a responsible, capable leader who was trying to get the lawmakers to face up to the state's major problems. He also supported Governor Hardman's proposal for reorganizing state agencies and boards.[44]

The affairs of state were not in good shape as Russell went back home in late August to get some rest and to resume his law practice. The *Atlanta Constitution* said legislators had left Georgia in a state of chaos with looming deficits totaling millions of dollars. Not only was there insufficient prospective revenue to meet the appropriations of $13,122,000 for 1928 and slightly more for 1929, but the state still owed over $8 million on 1927 appropriations. While some taxes were still due, it took unreal optimism to believe that the state would be able to pay all of its bills during the coming biennium.[45]

Back home in Winder, Russell left these problems behind. It was time to take things a little easier after the hectic pace in Atlanta. He took a hunting trip with friends on Hugh Peterson's plantation near Ailey. Russell greatly enjoyed these outings, for there was a great deal of camaraderie among this group of young friends. While quail and deer might be the subject of evening conversations around the fire, the hunters usually came back to a discussion of politics before the night was over. He had been unable to visit Peterson earlier in the year because he could not afford to leave Winder and "lose two . . . handsome fees." Russell explained that he was "in pretty bad shape financially" after losing "practically all of last year from my practice." This had been caused by his father's campaign for the U.S. Senate and his own race for the Speakership.[46]

On September 10, 1927, Russell left on the *Leviathan* for France to attend a meeting of the American Legion in Paris. He took great pride in his American Legion membership, and he once served as commander of the Winder unit. He often spoke at veterans' affairs. The convention gave him his first opportunity to see Europe. After visiting the Louvre, Versailles, Napoleon's tomb, and other sights in and around Paris, Russell visited the principal cities in Italy. In Venice he got in an argument with a gondolier over the fare. One report on the incident said that Russell won the "street trial." Dick also visited Vienna and Prague before going on to Scotland, Ireland, and England. He spent his last five days in London. Russell greatly admired the British people and their traditions.

In viewing conditions in Europe, Russell observed that he was surprised at how fast the countries had recovered from the war. Yet he perceived a great deal of distrust among the nations and predicted that, although perhaps not in this generation, another war was sure to come. He concluded that the European nations were maintaining excessively large armies.[47]

After he returned home, Russell made several talks about his European trip. By this time, too, he was becoming a popular commencement speaker. In May 1928, he talked to the graduating classes at Middle Georgia Junior College and at Georgia Middle College. He was also rapidly gaining a reputation as a speaker on public and patriotic occasions, at least locally. The editor of the *Winder News* said that Russell was "considered one of the most powerful orators in the state."[48]

Besides practicing law in 1928, Russell had to think about his reelection to the House of Representatives. When he announced his candidacy for a fifth term, the editor of the *Winder News* wrote that he was "one of the recognized leaders in the legislature, a young man of splendid ability," and declared that Russell's friends would gladly support him. Russell announced that the main issues that would receive his attention in the legislature were education, protection of farmers from inferior fertilizer, lowering or eliminating property taxes, and payment of Confederate veterans' pensions.[49] He defeated George Thompson by a vote of 1,553 to 449. No local candidate with opposition had ever won such a massive majority, he told his friend Hugh Peterson.[50]

As Speaker, Russell had to deal with some problems in making appointments. In handling these matters, he revealed his attitude toward women and his view of their place in society. Like most cultivated southern gentlemen of his time, he believed that women were the guardians of family and community morals and that they should be an uplifting influence in society. Russell acknowledged that women might work outside the home—one of his sisters was a lawyer and others were teachers—but he thought they should enter only a limited number of professions.

This attitude was well illustrated when Hugh Peterson urged Russell to appoint a woman to a job in the House of Representatives for the 1927 session. Russell replied "that the places [in the House] which can be filled by a young lady are very limited in number." The jobs of postmistress and two assistant messengers were the only ones for which women could qualify, he asserted. Earlier he had sought to help a former female resident of Winder obtain employment in the House by appealing to the then Speaker, Cecil Neill. He told Neill that she had "exceptional mental qualities" and "a wonderful personality." "In her is combined all of the charm and modesty known to the womanhood of the Old South with the business ability and initiative of the new," he claimed, "and there can be no question as to her fitness."[51] Both Judge Russell and Dick looked to Ina Russell as the womanly ideal. She was educated and taught school for a short time but then devoted her life to raising a large family. Her main influence was on her children. Ina ran the home while the judge was free to pursue his career. To Dick that was the proper role for most women.

Dick's social life included frequent dates, parties, and dances after he left college and returned home to Winder. The *Winder News* reported on September 4, 1919, for example, that he attended a dance given by Thelma Woodruff in honor of out-of-town friends. He had a number of different girlfriends in the 1920s, but he did not date any of them regularly or become a serious candidate for marriage. Perhaps he could not make up his mind among the many girls who pursued him. At one time, he had the names and addresses of fourteen women in Atlanta alone in his "little black book."

Through the 1920s, Russell frequently received letters from women who were interested in him. These letters usually expressed regret at not having heard from him or seen him recently. Such letters came from women in Winder, Athens, Elberton, Atlanta, and even Florida. One wrote in 1924, "Precious . . . when may I see you?" Another wrote that she wished Dick would not tell her about his redheaded friend because she was already "dead with jealousy." Still another woman reminded Russell that he had promised to visit her but had not done so. She asked him to make the trip to her place "P.D.Q." But as had been his custom since he was in secondary school, when a woman became serious, Russell broke off the relationship.[52] After he became Speaker, he accompanied Josephine Hardman, the governor's daughter, to several social functions. Russell later told a close friend that he felt sorry for Josephine because she did not really care for him but went out with him because he was Speaker and later governor-elect.[53] The press often portrayed Dick as a highly desirable bachelor, who would be a good catch for some lucky girl. But Russell would not be caught.

By the mid-1920s, Russell had stopped driving Fords and had an

Oldsmobile. He traded his first Oldsmobile for a new model at the Olds Motor Works in Atlanta in August 1929. This new Olds coupe cost $990. He received $575 for his old car on the trade, leaving a balance of $415. He paid $25 cash on the deal and financed the remainder at $37 a month.[54] Russell was then receiving $10 a day as Speaker of the House while the General Assembly was in session, plus mileage between Winder and Atlanta. His main income, though, came from his law practice. This, as mentioned earlier, was very modest in a depression-ridden farm community like Winder. But Russell did not need a large income to live quite comfortably. Since he was single and lived with his parents when he was not in Atlanta, his expenses were small compared to those of a married man with a family. In the early 1920s, despite his small income, he began investing in land, and between 1923 and 1930, he acquired about 250 acres of farmland and several town lots. By 1930, however, he was borrowing against some of his land.[55]

As Speaker of the House, Russell was in the midst of the growing controversies that gripped the legislature in 1929. Governor Hardman said that the state's most pressing problem was how to pay off the deficits created by overspending. Actually, the state had been able to pay only about 70 percent of the appropriations for 1928 and 1929, and deficits had reached about $3.8 million.[56] What kind of a tax program could produce the needed revenue, particularly for highways and education? Governor Hardman also pushed for government reorganization, which he claimed would save the state $800,000 to $1 million a year. On April 2, 1929, Hardman had appointed a commission to study this problem, but nothing could be done without legislative approval.

Russell, too, had his agenda. He saw his first task as trying to achieve a degree of unity in the House so that a responsible fiscal program could be approved. When he was escorted to the rostrum on June 26 after his unanimous reelection as Speaker, Russell told his colleagues that the forthcoming session promised to be the most important for many years. The "varied and momentous problems," he said, "will arise to challenge the ability and patriotism of every member here." He insisted that "Georgia must move forward along progressive lines." He urged all members to do their best to solve the state's problems, to work hard, and "to lay aside personal bickering and factionalism." Russell was already beginning to develop dislike for what he called "factionalism" and special interest politics.[57]

The hottest issue before lawmakers was how to finance needed paved highways. At the opening of the session, a resolution was introduced to sell $100 million worth of highway bonds to fund a statewide road-building program. Bond supporters argued that this was the only practical way to build a highway system within any reasonable time. Russell immediately announced that he opposed selling highway bonds. As presiding officer in the House, he said, he would give bond and all other legislation a "fair hearing," but as a representative of Barrow County, he had always "openly opposed bonds for highways." Russell warned that the bond proposal could not get a majority vote, to say nothing of the two-thirds vote that was required. Some critics accused Russell of not stating his position on highway bonds until after he had won the Speakership. However, Russell had opposed bonds at least since 1925. In any event, Russell declared that he believed it would be better public policy to raise the gasoline tax.[58]

In keeping with his pay-as-you-go philosophy, Russell introduced a bill to raise the gasoline tax from four to six cents a gallon. One-half of one cent of the tax would go for schools. He argued that the gasoline tax was the best way to finance highways and that, if his proposal passed, there would be $20 million available for highway construction by January 1, 1931, some eighteen months in the future. Russell then coordinated his six-cent gasoline tax bill with the growing sentiment against selling bonds.[59]

Contractors and others who would benefit by building roads strongly supported the bond program, as did legislators who believed it was the best and quickest way to get the needed roads built. The pro-bond forces hired four full-time people to help publicize the campaign. Rumors circulated around the capitol that big corporations were trying to influence the legislation. R. W. Martin, representative from Troup County, denounced the "insidious corporate influence" that threatened the integrity of House members. But no amount of lobbying could push the bond program through against Russell and his supporters. The anti-bond forces and those wanting more money for common schools combined to pass the six-cent gasoline tax in both houses of the General Assembly. Before the legislature adjourned, lawmakers passed a limited sales tax bill and an income tax measure. These measures, too, created a good deal of controversy, but they provided the state a responsible way to meet the funding needs for vital services.[60]

The question of government reorganization was less emotional than tax and spending measures, but to many legislators, it was very important for the state's long-range welfare. In February, several months before the General Assembly met, Hugh Peterson had told Russell that nothing was more urgent or vital than the reorganization of the state departments. He said that the governor could not really lead the fight because he was restrained by the "officers in the capitol." Because of Russell's knowledge of government and legislative affairs, Peterson said, he could develop a reorganization program and push it through the forthcoming legislature. According to Peterson, Russell was equal to the task, which would be a great opportunity for him to "render valuable work in your chosen field as a public servant." "Do not," he concluded, "fail to take advantage of the opportunity."[61]

Although Russell supported the reorganization principle of achieving greater efficiency in government, he did not make it a major issue in the 1929 session. Russell's keen political sense warned him that the time for reorganization had not quite arrived. Making unnecessary enemies over this question when it was not going to pass anyway was contrary to Russell's political nature. He always tried to operate within the possible. Thus he did not work hard for Peterson's reorganization bill, which failed to receive nearly enough votes to pass the House.[62] Russell accepted the 1929 session as one that would prepare the way for government reorganization. He would wisely wait his time. Moreover, if he were to seek the governorship, this might be a good political issue.

By the end of the 1929 session, Richard B. Russell, Jr., was one of the best-known young politicians in the state. He had carefully nurtured the image of a hard-working, responsible public servant who was interested in the welfare of people rather than being identified with any special interests. He was seen as progressive in his support of education and in his belief in government efficiency. He was considered credible and conservative in his insistence on fiscal responsibility.

Despite his youth, Russell had established a reputation for effective leadership. However, his style was to lead without being very far in the forefront and without making much fuss. He liked to work things out in private and never made any effort to push himself into the spotlight. As Isaac S. Peeples, an Augusta attorney and former state senator, said, Russell was the kind of "leader who leads without one's consciousness of his leadership." He supported ideas, made suggestions, and quietly urged his position but always made others feel that they had helped to shape the policies.[63] Russell seldom expressed pride in authorship of policies but gave credit to others. Peeples said that members of the legislature "love him and trust him." This trust had grown out of the fact that, as Speaker, Russell had treated everyone fairly and with consideration.

Russell tended to shun political labels. He was primarily interested in the results of governmental action, and, as he often said, he wanted those actions to help the people. The editor of his hometown paper described him as one who had "sufficient imagination, emotion and sentiment to be human, and enough insight, fortitude and personal force to be safe."[64] A growing number of Georgia citizens were looking to him to give the state better and more constructive leadership.

4

The Campaign for Governor

===

No one who knew Dick Russell well in the 1920s ever doubted that he had his eye on the governorship. His position on legislative matters, the care he took to avoid alienating or angering any important faction in the House of Representatives, and the personal contacts he sought were all aimed at enhancing his political image and statewide voter strength. He also had the full support and encouragement of his large family.

Russell had a unique sense of political timing. By 1930 he believed the time had come for him to enter the race for governor. Conditions seemed just right. He sensed that the people were ready to follow a new leader who was free from the old politics and factional alignments. On Saturday, April 5, Russell made the formal announcement that he would be a candidate for governor.[1]

The next day, the *Atlanta Constitution* carried Russell's platform statement in full. His statement set the tone and outlined the principles on which he intended to seek the state's highest office. He first sought to establish his independence and disassociate himself from any of the state's political machines or factions. He was undertaking the race, he wrote, without consulting any political groups that might "have favors to seek or political debts to pay." Russell claimed that he was beholden to no one except the people, who were tired of "personal and factional politics." Georgia citizens, he said, wanted a governor "independent of past alignments and existing factions, who represents no clique or interest with a political axe to grind," and who holds himself answerable only "to the whole people alone." He added that voters wanted "an honest and economical administration" and that government must be "remodeled and placed on a strictly business basis."

After presenting himself as an independent candidate free from all political debts and deals, Russell offered a ten-point program. He first insisted that the state needed a governor who could work closely with the legislature. His experience as Speaker, he declared, would make him such a governor. Russell emphasized the need for a better educational system that would serve "all of our people." A nine-month term should be the goal in all common schools, and he declared that more help should be given to schools in poor counties. Russell urged that the state provide cheaper textbooks by printing them and furnishing the books to pupils at cost. He argued that free public schools were "an empty promise" when some students could not afford textbooks. He also advocated more support for higher education.

Moreover, Russell recommended revising the tax system so that the cost of government would be more equitably distributed. This meant lowering ad valorem taxes. Directing a blow at Governor Hardman, he promised that, as governor, he would veto any appropriation bill that caused state expenditures to exceed potential revenues. In other words, Russell made a strong pitch for fiscal responsibility. At the same time, he recommended a statewide modern, paved highway system, which he believed was crucial to future economic progress. He argued that this could be accomplished without going into debt.

The reorganization of state government now had Russell's full and enthusiastic support. There were too many departments and agencies that were duplicative and wasteful, he said. Russell claimed that Georgia government was "top heavy, cumbersome, inefficient and far too expensive" and that reorganization and coordination of agencies would result in greater governmental efficiency and save money. Despite the fact that farmers had been having a tough time, Russell did not propose any immediate relief for them. He declared that the state might help with marketing and excessive freight rates but that only the national government could solve the basic problems of debt and low prices facing agriculture.

Russell delineated three main focuses of his campaign. He advocated leadership free from the influence of deals, factions, and special interests. Secondly, he sought to meet what he considered the major needs of the state—tax reform and fiscal responsibility, better education at all levels, paved highways, and government reorganization. Finally, he presented himself as a young, vigorous leader, "active and energetic and experienced in affairs of government." Russell reminded his readers that he was "a sixth generation Georgian" who was thoroughly familiar with the "state's history and tradition." He assured people that, if elected, he would take the state forward on the road to "conservative progress."

Russell's campaign strategy emerged quickly. He set out to organize a grass roots campaign that would bring him in contact with thousands of voters on the farms and in the small towns. Russell would present himself as the peoples' candidate. To portray this image, he must distance himself from Atlanta and the large corporate interests there. Consequently, he established his campaign headquarters in Winder. This broke a long-standing precedent whereby Georgia politicians centered their political operations in the state capital.[2]

The announcement of Russell's candidacy did not arouse much public comment. Indeed, some observers believed that Russell did not expect to win and was just making a trial run in order to become better known for a future campaign.[3] This was a common practice in Georgia, and one of his initial problems was to convince people that he was really serious. Those who believed that he was only sampling his strength, however, did not know the real Dick Russell. When he entered a race, it was to win.[4]

Immediately after his announcement, Russell borrowed $1,000 on an insurance policy and set out on an extensive speaking tour of the state. On April 9, the *Savannah Press* reported that Russell was traveling widely "throughout the state getting acquainted." The editor added that it would take "a lively opponent to keep up with Richard." Dick's early campaigning is well illustrated by his activity in Savannah in late April. He arrived in town and announced that he would be staying with his sister and her husband, Mr. and Mrs. J. H. Bowden, who, incidentally, had many friends in the community. Russell began his visit with good friends like Spence Grayson and Columbus E. Alexander. They took him to the courthouse to meet officeholders and organized small groups of other influential citizens to visit with Russell. He gave optimistic interviews to the press, saying that he expected to win and predicting that labor, among other groups, would support him because of his record in the General Assembly. At the end of two days, Russell had cemented a stronger relationship with his friends, had made tentative plans for a political organization in Chatham County, and had won numerous additional supporters. People were impressed with Russell's energy, his clear explanation of the issues, his sincerity, and his friendly personality.[5]

One of Russell's greatest strengths was his memory and effective recall. If he had once met a person, he was likely not only to remember him or her but to remember the circumstances under which they met. This was a tremendous asset to someone who was staging a person-to-person campaign and who had met hundreds of individuals during his school and legislative years.

During April and May, Russell kept up a busy speaking schedule. As he traveled throughout the state, he met and talked with hundreds of people. He got mechanics out from under cars, stopped farmers along the roadsides in their fields, and went up and down the main streets of small towns introducing himself and asking for support. He was even known to have stopped at farmhouses at night, awakening the residents and soliciting their votes. He demonstrated the qualities he claimed to have—energy and concern for the plain people.

Russell had no difficulty making arrangements to appear in different towns or drawing crowds. In virtually every town and community in Georgia, Dick or his father had friends or acquaintances who were willing, even anxious, to organize and arrange a Russell meeting. This foundation of support had worked out just as Judge Russell had hoped since 1911 when Dick first went to Gordon Military Institute. Russell had a kind of personal network throughout the state that included former schoolmates at three institutions, legislators, friends who had campaigned for his father, and even members of his family. There were Russells and Dillards, and the families of their spouses, scattered throughout the state. The thirteen Russell children had made many friends and acquaintances throughout Georgia who now rallied to Dick's support.[6]

Russell was an excellent speaker. The speaking and debating skills that he began to develop at Powder Springs and Gordon Military Institute some fifteen years earlier had been fine-tuned and sharpened over time. He spoke clearly, he was informed on the issues under discussion, and he could lace his remarks with humor or irony depending on what the occasion required.

Moreover, Russell had a keen ability to relate to almost any kind of audience. He was equally at home talking to a group of farmers on the courthouse steps or to a meeting of lawyers or bankers in the finest hotel. He usually stuck to the issues and avoided personal attacks in his talks, but if the situation called for it, Russell could devastate an opponent. One of his chief critics turned out to be W. T. Anderson, editor of the *Macon Telegraph*. Having received many barbs from the *Telegraph*'s editorial page, Russell finally responded by saying that he felt sorry for anyone who had to depend on the *Telegraph* for information and that Anderson made "Ananias look like a man of great integrity and character."[7]

In 1930 it was important in Georgia politics to be able to relate effectively to farmers. They made up more than half of the state's voters. At first blush, it did not appear that Russell would have any special

Russell gubernatorial campaign poster, 1930. (Photo courtesy of Russell Memorial Library, University of Georgia, Athens.)

appeal to farmers. He did not look or act like a farmer, and he made no pretense to do so. Dick Russell did not have a straw in his mouth or manure on his shoes. He always dressed well while campaigning, usually wearing a white shirt and tie, and he generally wore his suit coat unless it was especially hot. He was educated at the state's best schools, and the Russells represented Georgia's upper middle-class nonfarm families. Russell never used poor English or engaged in emotional tirades against purported enemies of agriculture as did Eugene Talmadge, who was running for his third term as Georgia's commissioner of agriculture.

Despite some apparent handicaps, Russell actually was a hit with farmers. By talking about hoeing and picking cotton and working for fifty cents a day under the hot Georgia sun in his youth, Dick gave the impression that he had a true farm background. It had not been important in American history for a politician to be an actual farmer, but it was a great advantage to have had some farm experience. Russell had enough of that to give him legitimacy among farmers. Moreover, Russell sincerely believed that farming was a superior way of life, and he talked about this to both farm and nonfarm groups. A true Jeffersonian, he emphasized that farmers were the backbone of America and that the nation's political purity and stability, and its economic strength, depended on its farmers. His country listeners liked such talk.

But more important, farmers seemed to appreciate his direct, honest approach to their problems. In his platform, he did not promise to do things for them that were impossible. Unlike many of his contemporaries, he refused to make unrealistic promises. Farmers responded to his friendly but somewhat reserved manner, his realism, and his integrity.

By the time the campaign really got underway, there were five politicians, including Russell, in the race. Conventional political wisdom held that George H. Carswell and John N. Holder were the strongest contenders. Born in 1874, Carswell was a native of Wilkinson County. After graduating from the Mercer Law School in Macon, he practiced law and later entered politics. He served in both the state House and Senate and in 1928 became secretary of state. He appeared to be especially strong in middle Georgia, where he had the backing of the *Macon Telegraph* and its editor, W. T. Anderson. John N. Holder was one of the most familiar and controversial political figures in the state. As chairman of the State Highway Commission, Holder had become a political power through the effective use of patronage. He had strong support from many legislators who sought highways in their districts.

A fourth candidate was E. D. Rivers, a forty-five-year-old lawyer and politician from Lanier County in South Georgia. He was elected to the state House in 1924 and two years later to the Senate. Rivers was initially aligned with Eugene Talmadge's political forces, and he had made an earlier run for governor in 1928. A final candidate, but a man with little prospect among a group of seasoned and successful politicians, was James A. Perry, head of the Public Service Commission.

With five candidates in the field, Russell had one clear advantage. It was not likely that anyone would win a clear majority in the primary election. Russell believed that he had a good chance to get more votes than any of the older candidates, but if he failed to emerge as the leader, he could surely take second place. In either case, he would be in the runoff election.

As the campaign heated up, Russell redoubled his efforts to meet voters in individual and group settings. On many days, Dick saw numerous individuals, made three or four talks at different localities, and concluded the day with a major address at a county seat town. Russell used a microphone to make himself heard and to save his voice.[8] Mark Donahoo, a friend and neighbor in Winder, drove Russell's car so Russell could rest between speeches. As he traveled from community to community, he found an increasing number of people at crossroads stores and roadside farms who supported him. On one occasion, he walked into a country store in South Georgia and, without introducing himself, asked the elderly storekeeper how the campaign was going in the area. The old gentleman replied that some people were going to vote for Carswell and others for Holder. But he hastily added that he planned to vote for Russell. Delighted at this prospect, Russell asked why. "Well," the storekeeper said, "I'm for Mr. Russell because he's running against a crowd of lawyers, and I don't want to elect a lawyer Governor of Georgia." Russell quietly left without revealing his identity.[9]

On May 18, the *Atlanta Constitution* reported a rumor that Holder, Russell, Rivers, and Perry might meet in Atlanta to decide which one of them would drop out of the race. Russell reacted sharply to the article. He implied that the other candidates wanted him to withdraw but that "nothing save death" could take him out of the campaign.[10]

While Russell was out on the road, Lewis C. Russell, his uncle, ran the campaign headquarters in Winder. He was ably assisted by Dick's closest brother, Robert. Workers at the headquarters received mail, wrote letters, published and distributed fliers and posters, and assisted county organizations. While the *Savannah Press* may have been right in describing Russell's campaign as being conducted in "a small town way" from an out-of-the-way office, Uncle Lewis, brother Rob, and a few other volunteers were very effective.[11] Russell took every opportunity to play up his poor-boy image, and he used his campaign office in Winder to make the point. In late July, he remarked that much of his mail was being sent to Atlanta and reminded his friends that he had no office there. Since, he said, his campaign was not financed by "any trust or selfish interest," he could not afford "an expensive and elaborate" campaign headquarters in Atlanta.[12]

Russell's campaign literature stressed his personality and character much more than issues. One flier advertised him as being "young, active, able, clean, honest, progressive, experienced," and in smaller type, "A Christian Gentleman." His advertisements also played up his freedom and independence from special interests and emphasized that his election would end factional political struggles in the state. Supporters scattered these fliers from an airplane.[13]

Russell also used the radio to advance his candidacy. He gave his first talk over radio station WRHA in Rome, Georgia. Years later Russell wrote that he would never forget "the sensation of standing up and speaking into a microphone without having any audience." It was most frightening, he recalled. Later in the campaign, a friend said that he had listened to the broadcast and that it had come in so clearly that he could hear Russell shuffling his notes. Those noises, Russell replied, did not come from notes being shuffled but from his "knees knocking."[14]

Russell saw early in his campaign that voters were especially responsive to his attacks on special interests, which, he claimed, had controlled Georgia politics for years. In talk after talk, he pitted the plain people, for whom he claimed to speak, against contractors, the schoolbook trust, powerful utility companies, and other representatives of big business.[15] This was classic progressive rhetoric.

One of the main issues that emerged during the campaign was how to pay off the state's debts. This had been a matter of growing concern for several years as the legislature appropriated more money than tax revenues could cover. The legislature had been spending without taxing. Russell had favored a conservative approach to state financing, but as Speaker he had not fought hard to reduce spending. Moreover, the state's governors had not tried to block excessive expenditures by vetoing appropriations bills. In any event, the result was that educational commitments, Confederate pensions, and other claims on state revenues had gone partially unpaid. As the *Atlanta Constitution* described the situation, millions of dollars of schoolteachers' warrants were being "hawked over the state at usurious discounts," institutions did not have enough money with which to operate properly, and Confederate veterans were "hungering for their pitiful doles."[16]

The financial issue had not raised much interest until Carswell recommended that the state take $5 million from the license tag income and gasoline taxes that normally went to the highway department and pay off other obligations. This would be only a temporary diversion of funds, and he stated that there would still be some $14 million left for highway construction in 1931.[17] Here was a concrete proposal that some Georgians thought might solve the state's most pressing financial problems until the legislature could find a solution to permanent funding of the state's needs. The other candidates, however, immediately blasted Carswell's proposal.

Russell became an especially sharp critic of Carswell on this issue. He claimed that it was not necessary to take money from the highway department to meet state obligations. He insisted that the state could rent out some of its facilities and cut useless jobs through government reorganization and save enough money to pay state debts. Russell's proposals actually were not very realistic. Critics pointed out that the money derived from state properties was already committed up through 1936.[18] Scoffing at Russell's idea, the editor of the *Macon Telegraph* computed that it would take 750 years to pay off the state debt through rentals according to Russell's proposal.[19]

Indeed, Russell's challengers argued that he was largely responsible for the state debt. Governor Hardman criticized both Russell and Rivers for the state's financial plight. Russell was Speaker of the House and Rivers was chairman of the Senate Appropriations Committee in 1927 when the legislature had passed excessive appropriations and defeated necessary tax legislation. Russell, as presiding officer, had provided the one vote that was required to pass the spending bill in the House. Hardman said that Russell then had opposed new taxes.

The record was clear on Russell's vote. But he explained that he had voted for the appropriation bill with "the express understanding that Governor Hardman would veto it" if he found there was not enough projected income to cover it. It was "poor grace," Russell said, for Hardman to criticize appropriations bills when he did not have the gumption to veto them.[20]

To blame the governor for the fiscal failure of the legislature may not have been very statesmanlike, but through this tactic, Russell successfully diffused the charges of his own fiscal irresponsibility as Speaker. In an effort to keep the financial issue from tarnishing his image as a responsible fiscal conservative, Russell concentrated on such matters as clean, honest, and efficient government. His record of leadership on spending and taxing was not something he could boast about. The best strategy was to divert attention away from the issue. Consequently, he also stepped up his personal attacks on Carswell and Holder and kept hammering away at their purported irresponsibility and backing from special interests. He told a group at Royston on August 2 that if Holder's "promises were pavement the highway system of Georgia would be the modern wonder of the world." When Carswell charged that Russell had helped Holder, who had many critics, keep his job as chairman of the State Highway Commission, Russell let go with a stinging rebuke. Such a charge, he said, was "despicable" even by Georgia political standards, and if Carswell would agree to a debate, he would expose him "before the people as a scandal-monger and falsifier."[21]

At the beginning of the campaign, Russell had purposely avoided getting into personalities. But as the primary got closer, he did not hesitate to attack his main opponents personally. He declared that old-line political leaders such as Holder and Carswell would never reorganize the government, a move needed to improve efficiency and to reduce unnecessary jobs and fat payrolls. No one could expect these politicians to support such a reform, he said, because their power depended on jobs handed out to their cronies and maintained at the taxpayers' expense. As an independent, committed leader, Russell argued that he could implement the needed changes. His hands, he said, were not bound by jobholders and political factions.[22]

Although Russell carried on a demanding speaking schedule as he looked forward to the primary election on September 10, he also relied heavily on backers throughout the state. Russell did not have in 1930, or ever, anything that resembled the usual political organization held together by favors and jobs. What some observers called a political organization was more a loose federation of friends and supporters. Most of these individuals were only interested in a single candidate—Russell. They avoided becoming involved with candidates for other races because they did not want to risk losing the support for Russell of local individuals who did not agree with the positions taken in support of other candidates. Russell himself refused to endorse candidates for other offices for the same reason. Thus there was a special political single-mindedness about Russell and his friends as they concentrated on his election.

Russell had one clear advantage. He had the backing of a large number of state House and Senate members.[23] Russell could appear in

almost any county in the state and be met by a member of the legislature
who was a personal friend and political backer. These individuals introduced Russell up and down main street and presented him at political
rallies. When a fellow House member introduced Russell to an audience
in Decatur, he said that Russell was "clean, honest and entirely above
reproach."[24] Dick claimed that three-fourths of the House and Senate
members were for him, while one enthusiastic supporter put the number
as high as 90 percent.[25] Such support proved, Russell said, that the
people who knew him best and worked closest with him were among his
most avid backers. Under the county unit system in which each county
had two votes, personal contacts of this kind were highly beneficial to a
candidate. Most Georgia counties were small in area and population,
and the support of legislators and local officials among the relatively
few whites who voted was usually a great asset. Russell had the contacts
in most counties to enable him to use the system very effectively.[26]

Many of the state's counties and cities formed Russell clubs. Friends
from Barrow County organized one of the first such groups. Walter C.
Hartridge headed the Russell Club in Savannah, which had the backing
of numerous prominent businessmen and attorneys. There was also an
active Russell Club in Atlanta. The promoters included such outstanding leaders as Frank Hooper, a former member of the state House of
Representatives and close associate of Russell, Hughes Spalding, one of
Atlanta's most prominent attorneys, and John B. McCallum, president
of the Atlanta Lawyers Club.[27]

These county and city Russell clubs held meetings, arranged talks,
placed advertisements in local newspapers, and generally solicited support for their candidate. The Savannah Russell Club ran a half-page
statement in the *Savannah Press* on September 9 charging that previous
governors had done nothing for the city except "give her a small Negro
College which probably no other place wanted." But Russell, the advertisement claimed, was a friend of Savannah. He had helped to make the
city a state port in 1922, which had won him the support of cotton
dealers, and he had pushed for a road to Tybee Island. If Russell were
elected governor, his friends claimed, Savannah would receive additional benefits.[28]

Dick was also able to get special support from women's groups in
some cities. In Savannah attorney Stella Akin was vice president of the
Chatham County Russell-for-Governor Club. According to Akin, this
was the first time since women had won the right to vote in Georgia
that they had a "real opportunity" to vote for a strong progressive
candidate. Without mentioning specifics, Akin said that Russell stood

for "the principles which the women believe in" and that his legislative record should "appeal to every woman voter." Many of the fliers and posters advertising Russell meetings proclaimed, "Ladies are welcome."[29]

Friends of Russell also organized people who could speak in support of Russell in places where they had special influence. Lawrence Camp had from ten to twenty supporters who could hold talks wherever the need arose. These friends included such people as Jud P. Wilhoit, Frank A. Hooper, Jr., Paul H. Doyal, Cliff Hatcher, and others. Hugh Peterson, who married Russell's sister Patience in 1930, was an effective campaigner when time permitted. He also edited a newspaper, the *Montgomery Monitor* in Mount Vernon, that kept the drums sounding for his former colleague in the House and his new brother-in-law.[30]

Russell's strategy was to keep on the offensive, but at times he was forced to defend himself. Some of his critics charged that the Russells were trying to build a political dynasty in the state. The *Dallas New Era* said that no doubt "Dick's daddy" thought his son should become governor, but "we haven't come to the place where we are dependent on one family to run the affairs of our state." The *Butler Herald* declared that Judge Russell had been feeding at the public trough for fifty years and that now some Georgians seemed to feel that Richard B. Russell, Jr., should be supported "out of the state's treasury." The editor ventured that there were plenty of people besides the Russells who were competent to hold public office.[31]

Dick responded harshly to the charge of nepotism. He said that his opponents were introducing "irrelevancies" into the campaign and that any relationship between his father being chief justice of the state Supreme Court and his running for governor was a false issue. If the children of successful fathers could not hold public office, he explained, it would condemn them to oblivion. He believed the voters would recognize this accusation as unfair and senseless. Dick said that he was proud of his father and that he hoped his father was equally proud of him.[32]

Some of Russell's opponents also tried to convince voters that he was too young to be governor. At thirty-two, Russell was sometimes pictured by critics as the "school boy" candidate. Opponents also presented his bachelorhood as a handicap for the governorship. Russell replied rather philosophically to these contentions. It was clear that in trying to discredit him because he was young and single, his opponents were grasping at straws to save their campaigns, Russell declared. Russell said that voters were much more interested in his qualifications than in his age or marital status. He explained that he met the constitutional age requirement and that twelve years earlier he had served his term in the navy. Half humorously, he added, "While I did not win the war, I was old enough to enlist for service and I did it." He was proud that he was "young, active and energetic, and experienced in affairs of government." Russell told one audience that he did not know whether his opponents called him the "school boy" candidate because he was fighting for cheaper textbooks or because the "leaders of political rings and the representatives of special and selfish interests" had found that he would not bow "to their dictates and commands." The action that most effectively silenced the age issue was Russell's invitation to engage his opponents in public debate. They all backed away quickly from such a challenge. None of the candidates wanted to meet Russell on the platform. They knew they would be no match for his sharp mind, his skill in turning a phrase, his store of facts, or his effective sarcasm.[33]

On the question of being unmarried, Dick remained coy. When the subject arose, he usually explained with a twinkle in his eye that "when the people of Georgia come to the executive mansion, Mrs. Russell will be there with me to greet you." While some people thought that possibly Russell was contemplating marriage, his closer friends knew full well that the Mrs. Russell he referred to would be his mother.[34]

During the last month of the primary campaign, the Russell forces issued regular statements claiming that Russell was well ahead. Russell joked that Carswell's campaign should be referred to with reverence, "as one should do in speaking of the dead." More objective observers did not agree with that assessment, but they did admit that Russell was running strong. The *Atlanta Constitution* reported on August 17 that he was either first or second in the race at that point. Russell flatly declared on September 6, four days before the primary, that he would win.[35]

As the candidates entered the final days of the race, Russell intensified his claim that he was the only candidate not "tied hand and foot" to special interests or not a complete "tool" of the factions that had controlled the state for years. In a statement to the people of Georgia, Russell declared that his campaign had been the most unusual ever waged in the state. Without a big Atlanta headquarters, without support of any state agency, and without "a campaign slush fund contributed by special interests," he had through personal effort and the help of friends and others interested in good government carried the issues to the voters. He had presented a "conservative and constructive" program, he said. On election eve, Russell again reviewed his campaign and his position on the issues in a fifteen-minute radio address.[36] He then left Atlanta for Winder to await the voters' decision.

On September 10, white Georgians from Rabun Gap to Tybee Island flocked to the polls to nominate a governor. With five candidates in the field, the vote was bound to be widely split, but Russell was right when he predicted that he would have more votes than any other man in the race. He received 132 county unit votes, while Carswell came in second with 126. E. D. Rivers was third. Russell carried 49 counties and Carswell won 47. His popular vote was 56,177 to Carswell's 51,851.[37]

Dick was especially pleased with the results in light of the small amount of money he had spent campaigning. His expenditures had only been $3,848. He had furnished all of the funds himself except about $600 that had been provided, for the most part, by relatives. Both Carswell and Rivers had spent a good deal more.[38]

There were just three weeks between the primary and the runoff election on October 1. The primary votes were hardly counted before speculation arose over just what political alignments might develop for the general election. Russell declared immediately that he would make "no trades or combinations" and solicited support from all of the people who wanted "clean, honest and progressive government."[39]

Three days after the primary, E. D. Rivers announced that he was urging his supporters to vote for Carswell. Rivers explained that Holder had decided to back Russell and that he and Carswell had agreed to fight "the Holder-Russell factions." Rivers charged that road contractors and highway machinery representatives were flocking to support Russell and that Holder would continue to exert an unhealthy influence in the highway department and even extend his power to other state agencies if Russell were elected. There could be no "clean government" in a Russell-Holder administration, Rivers insisted. Carswell was jubilant at this endorsement and claimed that his election was now assured.[40]

Although it was true that Holder said he planned to support Russell, Dick heatedly denied that he was aligned with Holder or that any deal had been struck. He launched such a caustic attack on Carswell and Rivers that Carswell may have regretted ever mentioning any Russell-Holder connection. The charge of a deal with Holder, Russell said, was a "willful and malicious" lie, and the idea that he was connected in any way with road contractors could only be the "figment of a disordered brain." Continuing his offensive, Russell said that the Carswell-Rivers alliance would fail because the people of Georgia wanted to elect a governor who was free from "rings and machines." For a decade, he charged, the governorship had been "traded like a pocket knife," and people were tired of it.[41]

Russell opened his runoff campaign in Valdosta on Saturday night,

September 13. This had been Rivers territory, but it soon became clear that Russell had a lot of support in South Georgia. Moreover, it was doubtful that Rivers could deliver his backers to Carswell. The *Valdosta Daily Times*, which had backed Rivers, now switched to Russell and predicted his victory. Many individuals who had been for Rivers in the primary now said they were joining the Russell forces. In an attempt to hold support, Carswell claimed that the election was a kind of sectional fight. There had not been a governor from South Georgia for decades, he said, and he urged people to vote for him instead of another North Georgian. But the sectional issue did not deter support in the southern part of the state from shifting over to Russell.[42]

One endorsement that Russell did not appreciate was that of Benjamin Davis, the editor of the black *Atlanta Independent*. Davis wrote that votes for Russell in the primary indicated that "the Democrats of Georgia are breaking away from their suicidal policy of factionalism and race prejudice." Davis declared that Russell was the best candidate and predicted his victory. On September 18, in an editorial entitled, "The Gang versus Little Dick," Davis argued that the "ringsters, factional leaders, and special interests" were organizing against Russell. Nevertheless, he said, the people were backing Russell. Similar comments had been made by many white editors. Indeed, Russell himself had emphasized the same points. But such an endorsement from a black was dangerous to a white candidate in racist Georgia.

The Carswell people immediately began to distribute copies of the *Atlanta Independent* at political rallies in an effort to discredit Russell among white voters. This was an attempt to raise doubts among whites about Russell's position on race relations. Russell reacted quickly. He angrily denied that he had sought any black support and charged that "Carswell's crowd" had hired "this negro" to come out for him in order to "prejudice the voters," a charge that R. N. Hardeman, Carswell's campaign manager, called a "deliberate lie."[43] For several days, the two candidates sparred over this matter, but it turned out to be unimportant.[44]

While Russell was a dedicated white supremacist, he was not a rabid racist. He was careful not to use the term "nigger," he did not play whites against blacks for political purposes, and he strongly opposed lynching and physical violence toward blacks. He held the elitist, paternalistic view of blacks so common among upper-class whites in the South during that period. Russell did not wish blacks any misfortune, and he even hoped that they would make economic gains and achieve better lives. But he believed that white and black societies must be strictly segregated and that blacks should make progress within their own social, economic, and political communities. He vigorously opposed any kind of integration, which he saw as a step toward mongrelization of the races. Social and educational contacts with each other, he believed, would ruin both races. Russell's attitudes and beliefs came more from inheritance and southern tradition than from any rational examination of race relations. His contact with blacks was entirely with servants or with those blacks who were not pressing for equality and held basically a second-class position in society. Russell was comfortable with, and willing to be helpful to, black ministers and educators who lived with segregation without public complaint. He was a more restrained white supremacist than Tom Watson or Eugene Talmadge, but his commitment to segregation and keeping blacks in an unequal position was no less firm. However, he believed that it was inappropriate and unbecoming for elite southern leaders to raise the race issue for political gain. Thus he wanted to quiet the question of Davis's support and the subsequent controversy as quickly as possible.

During the last few days before the election, the Russell forces worked as though the race was extremely close. Russell held rallies two or three times a day, and his friends made talks in communities where it seemed their candidate might need help. Lewis Russell blanketed the state with campaign literature and urged some supporters to attend Carswell meetings and circulate among the crowd in an effort to undermine Carswell's impact.[45] As more and more newspapers came out for Russell, it was clear that Carswell was fighting a losing battle. Moreover, representatives of interest groups proclaimed their support for Russell. For example, George L. Googe, president of the Savannah Trades and Labor Assembly, announced for Russell in late September, as did a representative of the Federation of Labor in Brunswick. T. L. Hawkins of Washington County, former organizer for the Georgia Farmers' Union, said he was supporting "Young Dick," as he became known in the 1920s, because of his effort to bring good government to Georgia.[46] Other endorsements poured in.

Carswell found that trying to counteract this Russell groundswell was a hopeless task. His main mouthpiece, the *Macon Telegraph*, criticized Russell almost daily, accusing him of legislative failures and blaming him for the state debt. Carswell also tried to picture Russell as a man who was insensitive to the needs of schoolchildren and veterans and a tool of special interests. But Carswell could not tarnish Russell with the special interest charge—Russell had preempted that issue months earlier. Carswell also expressed resentment for the University of Georgia alumni who were backing Russell. He claimed to be one of the state's citizens who "couldn't afford to get one of those long-winded diplomas."[47]

Days before the election on October 1, every knowledgeable political observer realized that Russell would be the victor. Even the *Macon Telegraph* later admitted that the possibility of Carswell winning "had been swept away."[48] How true it was. On October 2, the *Atlanta Constitution* carried the two-inch headline, "Russell Wins by Landslide." It was more than a landslide, it was a political earthquake. The voters gave Russell the largest majority in any gubernatorial race in the state's history. He carried 126 of the 161 counties and 330 of the 414 county unit votes. Of the popular vote, Russell received 99,505 votes, while Carswell received 47,157. The *Vienna News* editorialized simply, "And Little Dick Becomes Governor Dick."[49]

Russell spent election day in Winder. Cameramen were there to take pictures as he chopped wood, listened to the radio, held his nephew Richard III on his lap, and sat near his mother on the broad veranda. He was the epitome of a happy, devoted family man, his family being the extended Russell clan.

In the evening, Russell returned to Atlanta to be with his friends at the Ansley Hotel to receive the election results. About 10 P.M. Carswell made a concession statement. Then Dick delivered a short message of appreciation to all his supporters over radio station WSB in Atlanta, at which time he credited his victory to the work of his friends. As the returns continued to arrive and his votes piled up, Dick said little. He broke into a broad smile, however, when the vote arrived from Barrow County. His majority was 1,773 to 15, better than 100 to 1. The scriptural injunction that a man is not without honor except in his own country surely did not apply to Dick Russell. He was a conquering hero to the home folks.[50]

What explains Russell's unprecedented victory? There is no doubt that his personal contacts played a key role in his first statewide race. His University of Georgia and other school friends had been very helpful. Harold Gilbert of Augusta wrote, "I knew you well as we went to college together," and that he had done all he could for Russell. Even more important was the nucleus of former and current friends in the legislature who were effective organizers for Russell in county after county. Many of his father's political friends easily shifted their loyalty and support to Dick. Russell also had contacts through organizations to which he belonged. As a Kiwanian, an Odd Fellow, a Mason, a Methodist, a loyal member of the SAE social fraternity, and a member of the

American Legion, he had contacts in a host of civil, social, and political groups.[51]

Russell also drew support because of his positions on principal issues. His stand against diverting license tag and gasoline tax money away from the highway department, his call for reorganizing state government to achieve efficiency and economy, and his enthusiastic support for better schools and good roads all won favor with voters. These were old issues that did not originate with Russell's campaign, but people seemed to believe that he was the best candidate to solve the problems facing the state. The *Columbus Enquirer-Sun* claimed that Russell was elected because people believed he would get the state out of its old political rut and take Georgia into a new progressive era. Also, he represented what the *Valdosta Daily Times* referred to as a "newer generation" of politicians, one of youth and vitality.[52]

But the issues were less important to Russell's victory than the perceptions he established among voters. These perceptions were influenced more by the personality of the candidate and the tone he could bring to state government than by how he could solve problems. People really came to believe that Russell would bring clean, honest, and more efficient government to Georgia. It seemed that a new era was about to dawn. As the *Atlanta Journal* editorialized, Russell had taken the high ground and called for "a day of better feeling, clearer thinking and broader cooperation."[53] People cheered as he scourged special interests, political bargains, back room deals, and insider manipulations. Russell had taken at least three principles from the early twentieth-century progressives. He insisted on honest government and governmental efficiency, and he fought against favors to, and the growing power of, special interests.

As the campaign advanced and Russell met more and more people, his personality began to play a vital role in his growing strength. People just liked Dick Russell. Editors increasingly referred to his personal qualities and characteristics. The editor of the *Augusta Chronicle* called him "charming and talented," "a companionable, lovable delightful chap." There was something romantic about this nearly thirty-three-year-old legislator, the editor continued. Russell was presented as having great ability, as well as being honest and sincere. He was credited with having a constructive mind and imagination and being aboveboard and straightforward. In short, it was his personality and character more than anything else that Georgia voters had come to admire.[54]

Once "Young Dick" had been elected, the people of Winder organized a mammoth victory celebration to honor the governor-elect. Between five thousand and ten thousand people, the largest crowd in the town's history, were on hand the evening of October 3. Admirers and supporters came from all over the state. Flags decorated the Winder streets and "Welcome Governor" and "Welcome Dick" banners filled store windows. Four bands, one from the University of Georgia, paraded through the streets lighted with torchlights. The crowd cheered wildly when the university band played "Glory, Glory to Old Georgia." Writing in the *Atlanta Journal*, C. E. Gregory observed that Russell's welcome home rivaled "the acclaim of a Roman conqueror."[55]

Gathering in front of the courthouse steps for the evening program at eight o'clock, the crowd packed in to see their hero and listen to an array of speakers. Several leading Russell men, including Dick's father, spoke to the crowd and outdid one another in their use of superlatives as they described Dick and his victory. The chairman of the celebration, Clifford Pratt, then escorted Russell and his mother to the microphone. There were calls for Ina Russell to speak, but Pratt said she was too modest to talk before such a throng. Holding his mother's hand, Russell said: "Someone has asked to see Mrs. Russell. Here is the best sweetheart I ever had." Mrs. Russell then sat down and Dick, dressed in dark suit and black bow tie, began addressing the attentive audience.

Russell did not talk about issues on this emotional and thrilling occasion. He thanked his supporters and again expressed appreciation for such great friends. He said it was "mighty sweet" to come back to the old red hills of Barrow County and be welcomed by so many of his boyhood chums and a host of other friends. In a spirit of deep humility, he said that he hoped God would give him the power to serve the people and justify the confidence of his friends. Russell declared that he recognized the great responsibility that accompanied the happiness of the moment but that now that government had been restored to the people, the challenges could be met. After a few other general remarks, he thanked the people from the bottom of his heart for their friendship and support. That ended the formal celebration, but Russell stepped down in front of the platform and greeted and shook hands with hundreds of people.[56] Several hours passed before the euphoria faded and Dick finally got home and to bed. Had a new era in Georgia politics really begun, as Russell and his enthusiastic backers claimed, or was this election just the launching of a new national political career?

5

Governor Russell

===

On October 5, 1930, only four days after Dick Russell's overwhelming election in the Democratic primary, the rotogravure section of the *Atlanta Journal* carried a large picture of the Russell family at home in Winder. It showed Judge and Ina Russell surrounded by their six daughters and seven sons, with Dick standing in the center directly behind his parents. This picture in a way symbolized the central place that Dick had come to hold in the Russell clan. Despite the long career of his father, and the achievements of his brothers and sisters, Dick had become the number one Russell. He was also, at not quite thirty-three, Georgia's leading citizen.

It is not known just what Judge Russell was thinking or feeling as his family clustered around him on that Saturday. It is safe to assume, though, that he was at last content and at peace with himself. The goal that he had set for his oldest son and namesake some twenty years earlier had now been achieved. Whether he felt his own unrealized ambitions fulfilled in Dick, as he so often said would be the case, is not known, but there was no mistaking his pride and satisfaction. A Russell had been elected governor, and his name was Richard B., Jr.

Nearly nine months would elapse between Russell's election in the white Democratic primary and his inauguration (he had no opposition in the November 4 election). The Georgia constitution called for swearing in a new governor on the last Saturday in June following his election. This did not mean, however, that in the meantime Russell had nothing to do but rest and practice law.

Governor Hardman called a special session of the General Assembly for January 6, 1931, to deal with the state's worsening financial plight. By the end of 1930, the Great Depression was creating havoc in a state where hard times and poverty were already a way of life for many people. Tens of thousands of poor farmers were suffering from the boll weevil infestation and were trying to eke out an existence on six-cent cotton. Closed businesses in Atlanta, Savannah, Augusta, Macon, and other cities created long lines of the unemployed. Tax revenues fell sharply, and the state was unable to meet its obligations to the schools, eleemosynary institutions, and to pay veterans' pensions in full. Hardman explained to the assembled lawmakers on January 6 that the state had $7,458,545 of excessive and unpaid appropriations.[1]

The General Assembly and the governor could not agree on how best to meet the financial crisis. The sixty-day session that ended on March 27 was noted mostly for the acrimony that developed between the governor and the legislature. As Speaker of the House, Russell played essentially a neutral role in the legislative-executive conflict. He wanted to begin his governorship in June without having been muddied by the political waters stirred up by a lame duck governor.[2]

It was fortunate that plans had been made to inaugurate the new governor outdoors. Saturday, June 27, 1931, was hot and uncomfortable in Atlanta. By eleven o'clock the temperature hovered around 95 degrees. Nevertheless, some five thousand people gathered near the capitol building to watch the inauguration of Richard B. Russell, Jr., their new governor. The House and Senate members attended as a group. Outgoing governor Hardman was not present because of illness. A select group of National Guard officers escorted Russell, accompanied by his mother, to the platform. The 122d Infantry band played the national anthem, and the Reverend Taylor Morton, a former Russell pastor, gave the invocation. Then, dressed in a dark suit and with his hand on his mother's Bible, Russell was sworn in by his father, chief justice of the Georgia Supreme Court. Following some other routine matters, Russell gave his inaugural address, which concluded the formal ceremonies.

After his talk, Russell went to his office for about an hour where he welcomed close friends and supporters. Shortly before 3:30, the governor, his parents, and a few others left for the governor's mansion, a huge two-story stone structure located at 205 Prado, to prepare for a reception. Russell had invited hundreds of people to the occasion by hand-written notes on Speaker of the House stationery. After he changed into light trousers and dark coat, Russell, his parents, and other special guests stood in front of the large fireplace in the main reception room to welcome the throng of visitors. Reporters estimated that about a thousand people an hour went through the receiving line to greet Russell and shake his hand. The crowd was so large that the reception had to be extended beyond the 5:30 termination time. It was well past six o'clock before the Russells could relax a bit in their new home.[3]

As Dick and other members of the family adjusted to the governor's

Richard B. Russell, Jr., being sworn in as governor of Georgia by his father, Richard B. Russell, chief justice of the Georgia Supreme Court, June 27, 1931. (Photo courtesy of Russell Memorial Library, University of Georgia, Athens.)

mansion, many Georgians were discussing Russell's inaugural talk. He began by expressing humility and calling for citizens' support and divine guidance. Always realistic, he did not try to paint an optimistic picture of the state's affairs. He said that people were "hopelessly disheartened" and engulfed in "a tide of pessimism" because of the depressed condition of agriculture, business, and labor. The hard facts, he said, were that working men could scarcely obtain the bare necessities of life. Russell declared that he did not describe the harsh economic conditions to spread gloom or discouragement, but because he wanted to lay out the challenges to which the state's citizens must respond.

The conditions facing Georgians, the governor explained, called for courage and self-sacrifice. He urged people to forget selfishness, "petty prejudices and personal ambitions." Under current conditions, Russell warned, there was "no place in the government or the political life of our state for petty factional or partisan politics." He said that, despite terribly hard times, the people of Georgia had not welcomed communism or socialism. They had held firm to "the ideals and institutions which have ever guided the Anglo-Saxon in government."

On the issues, Russell insisted that it was absolutely essential for the state to practice the strictest economy. The crowd's largest cheers echoed across the capitol grounds when he promised to balance state expenditures and income. There would be $8.9 million of unpaid appropriations by the end of 1931, he explained, but savings could be made through reorganization of state departments and agencies and by practicing strict economy. He told the people that the state's obligations had to be paid and the debt liquidated.

Education and highways, Russell claimed, were the "twin pathways to progress." Spending for these purposes was really an investment on which the returns would be high to the state as a whole. Russell declared that educational opportunity must be equalized. There is no "aristocracy in education," he said, and he called for the same quality of education for rural youth as for those who lived in towns and cities. This meant providing more state equalization funds to improve the poorer schools. He did not, however, say anything about the deplorable conditions of black schools, although most black students were in rural areas. In regard to roads, Russell said that Georgia must have a truly state highway system that did not depend on county funds. He had no encouraging words for depression-ridden farmers. His main advice was to produce as much of their own food and feed as possible. He called this the live-at-home movement. This advice, of course, was not new. People in the agricultural college, the experiment stations, and the cooperative extension, as well as farm journalists and state agriculture department officials, had been offering similar advice for years with only modest success.

Russell's inaugural talk combined a realistic assessment of conditions with a call to people to unite behind his program and work for "a greater and more progressive Georgia." By drawing on the state's heritage and its "courageous past," Russell hoped to gradually put the state on a solid financial basis and solve some of the most pressing problems in education and highway construction. He did not advance any new philosophy of government or propose any new political directions. Everything he dealt with had been around the legislative halls for years— government reorganization, deficit financing, and the need for improved education and a genuine state highway system. Russell often talked about a progressive Georgia or a progressive program. However, his progressivism was mainly confined to efficiency and white democratic participation.[4]

The response to Russell's approach to state problems was encouraging, even flattering in many cases. The *Atlanta Journal* editorialized that Russell had the courage "to face things as they are" and the "will to make them more nearly what they ought to be." The writer predicted that the new governor would lead a "stable and progressive administration." The *Atlanta Constitution* declared that Russell had ushered in a new day for Georgia, one of "safety and prosperity," while the *Griffin Daily News* believed that Georgia would be much better off at the end of Russell's term.[5]

Russell, said the *Augusta Chronicle*, typified the "young manhood of Georgia" and those "forward looking Georgians" who were determined to solve state problems. "The signs are fair," editorialized the *Savannah Evening Press*, that Russell could handle the challenges ahead. Still unable to forget Dick's relative youth, the editor concluded, "Good luck to the boy!" Even the *New York Times* carried editorial comment on Russell. The writer said that it would be interesting to watch "Young Dick" Russell's career in a part of the country "where white beards were long considered the indispensible equipment of a judge or governor."[6]

Russell's success as governor, however, would not depend on popular acclaim as much as on the response of the General Assembly. The legislature had met on June 24 to organize for the forthcoming session, and the signs were good for a close working relationship between the governor and the lawmakers. Russell's good friend for a decade, W. Cecil Neill of Muscogee County, was selected president of the Senate, and another friend, Arlie D. Tucker of Berrien, became Speaker of the House.

On Monday, June 29, when Russell appeared before a joint meeting of the House and Senate to deliver his annual message, he faced a friendly and cooperative audience. Scores of legislators looked upon the governor as "one of us." And Russell did everything possible to strengthen that perception. He made it clear that he had no intention of infringing on legislative turf. He emphasized that the three branches of government must always remain separate and distinct and that he had no desire "to dictate or direct your deliberations." Any recommendations he made, Russell said, stemmed only from a desire to be of service and to offer any help growing out of his experience as a member of the House. Russell assured the legislators that he would cooperate and help them in any way he could "in every progressive endeavor." He talked about compromising, listening to all viewpoints, and operating "in a spirit of give and take." If better ideas were advanced than those he presented, he would support them. Russell had a knack for making other people feel important, and he was always willing to distribute credit for any achievement. This was part of his strategy.

Having indicated his desire to work cooperatively and constructively with the General Assembly, Russell outlined his specific recommendations. He shocked some lawmakers when he suggested reducing all salaries for state employees by 5 to 10 percent as a concrete way to cut government expenses. While his own salary and those of some judges could not be reduced by legislative action, he promised to turn back from his salary whatever percent reduction the House and Senate agreed on for other employees. Russell was serious about economy.

He then turned to what he considered the most important issue before the legislature—"a complete and thorough overhauling and rebuilding of our present structure of State Government." Georgia, he said, must reduce the cost of government and greatly increase its efficiency. While admitting that some people would lose their jobs as a result of reorganization, he reminded the lawmakers that it was not the duty of the government to support the citizens but the responsibility of the people to maintain the government.

The governor then made a number of other recommendations, most of which had been before the legislature for some years. He recommended tax reform, improving education, especially continuing the equalization fund to help poor schools, restructuring the governance of the university system, providing textbooks at cost, creating a truly state highway system by eliminating county financial contributions, and a number of other proposals. One of his most important suggestions was the passage of a constitutional amendment permitting the governor to be inaugurated and the legislature to meet in January instead of June following a fall election. If such an amendment was passed, Russell said, his term would be reduced by six months, but he thought such a reform was essential to good government.

Russell's address to the legislature clearly illustrated his leadership style. He reminded the lawmakers that they had the responsibility to legislate but that he stood ready to assist in the process in any possible way. As he put it, if he could be of the "slightest aid to any one of you," they should call on him. Indeed, he hoped members would feel free to drop by his office "for conferences on the people's business."[7] Always holding out the olive branch of fairness and cooperation, Russell was the epitome of reasonableness. This was the public Russell. In a private setting, he had an opportunity to use personal persuasion, work out compromises, call up any political debts, and finally to get action. Much

Governor Russell at work in his office, 1931. (Photo courtesy of the Bettmann Archive.)

of his leadership was through others. And, as explained earlier, he led without people realizing that the action was his rather than their own.

Russell had his office team in place and ready to go to work by the time of his inauguration. Leeman Anderson became his private secretary and main assistant in the office. Thirty years old, Anderson was a native of Pike County who had been chief clerk in the State Department of Agriculture before resigning to join the Russell campaign. He was a good judge of people, he had sound common sense, he met the public well, and he was fiercely loyal to Russell.[8] I. K. Hay of Covington was named executive secretary. He was a twenty-six-year-old lawyer and a graduate of the University of Georgia. There were also seven clerks in the governor's office to help handle mail and perform other duties.

The Russells quickly settled in at the governor's mansion. Besides the governor and his parents, Dick's sister Carolyn, a student at Agnes Scott College, also lived at the mansion. Ina Russell served as the first lady for all social functions. As Russell had often said, there would be a Mrs. Russell in the governor's mansion, and there was!

One of the emoluments of office was a new Packard sedan that was always ready for the governor. The vehicle had cost the state $3,160. James "January" Smith served as the governor's porter. An elderly black, Smith had been around the capitol for forty years or more—no one knew quite how long. He had worked for a variety of different officials and reputedly knew most of Henry Grady's speeches from memory. He told a reporter that he would see to the governor's slightest need.[9]

Russell's salary as governor was $650 a month or $7,800 annually. This was a substantial increase over the $800 a year that he had received in per diem compensation as Speaker of the House. For 1931 his income from government service amounted to $4,622.92. He also collected $380 from 1929 legal cases, giving him a total income of $5,002.92. After deducting interest, Barrow County school taxes, office expenses in Winder, and $75 in contributions, he had a net income of $3,773. This was a good depression income. Also, he did not have to pay state income tax on his salary. His father received $583.33 a month, the same as the other justices of the Supreme Court.[10] Together Dick and his father were doing well in the hands of the state. Besides, they had free housing in the governor's mansion, although Judge Russell did maintain a separate apartment where he lived part of the time.

While the General Assembly began dealing with issues that Russell had laid before the lawmakers, he found himself flooded with job seekers. The depression had left thousands of Georgians in dire straits. On many days, distraught men came by the governor's office begging for any kind of a job. Russell also received pitiful letters asking for direct help. One Georgian wrote the governor asking for a loan of $10. "I need the money for my kids school clothes and books," she wrote. The woman said that her husband was ill and asked, "For the kids' sake and God's sake let me have it." In reply Russell usually explained that he was in no position to assist individuals. But these situations of stark tragedy greatly moved Russell, and, as he said later, seeing them "was a very agonizing experience." While he had no solution to the problems of want and starvation, he began to look to the federal government for help.[11]

In the minds of many people, the most important question in the Russell administration was government reorganization. Russell did not think that greater government efficiency would solve depression problems in Georgia, but he did believe that improved management of state agencies could cut costs and relieve hard-pressed taxpayers. One scholar has described this belief as a kind of "business progressivism."[12]

The idea of reorganizing the state government had been around since before Russell went to the legislature in 1921. Governor Hugh Dorsey had recommended reorganization in 1919, and in the early 1920s, Governor Thomas Hardwick had urged the legislature to make changes in the "board ridden and trustee ridden" state government. At that time, there were 102 departments, commissions, and boards. While Hardwick's suggestions got nowhere, the issue would not go away. L. G. Hardman made reorganization a major plank in his successful campaign for governor in 1926. A legislative committee studied the issue in 1927, the year Russell became Speaker, but nothing was done. Russell, like many other legislators, skirted the question. The decade before 1929 might best be described as the period of legislative gestation.

When the legislature failed to act, Governor Hardman appointed a new commission in April 1929 to study the matter. Ivan Allen, a prominent Atlanta businessman, headed the group, which consisted of both legislators and citizens at large. One of the most important members of the commission, and the person closest to Russell, was Hugh Peterson, his future brother-in-law.[13] This commission drafted a plan of consolidating the 102 departments, boards, and commissions into 14 state agencies. It was finally brought to a vote in the House in 1929, where it was defeated by a sizable margin.

By the time Russell decided to run for governor, government reorganization had become a major issue. While he sincerely believed in this reform, he had not been a strong public spokesman for the cause up to that time.[14] It was not until he decided to run for governor that he fully embraced reorganization and began to work hard for its adoption. He then made it the cornerstone of his gubernatorial campaign. His large victory in the fall of 1930 seemed to confirm that many voters considered government reorganization a high priority. Although Governor Hardman recommended that the legislature deal with reorganization in the special session, lawmakers refused to act. But the House did authorize a committee to study the matter. Here Russell had a crucial role. As Speaker, he appointed the committee, which was chaired by Gus Huddleston. Hugh Peterson, a member of the committee, was again Russell's main link to the committee. He told Peterson that he intended to "get squarely behind the plan of reorganization that you finally decide on." Then Russell revealed his usual style of operating. While this was a big job, he explained, "you are equal to it and when it is completed you will have rendered a real service to your state." Flatter, cajole, encourage, and support others to get out in front to achieve a desired goal. That was the Russell way.[15]

The Huddleston committee met in April 1931 to develop a reorganization plan. Russell suggested that the committee begin with the Searle-Miller study on reorganization done in 1930 and then produce something that would be known as a committee bill. A plan with the committee's stamp of approval, which would be ready to submit to the legislature in June, would have a better chance of passing the House and Senate, Russell claimed.

The governor-elect also advised against investigating the various departments. James T. Colson, another member of the committee and a Russell leader in the House from Brunswick, explained the reason for this. Anything that appeared to be an attack on the departments and agencies, Colson warned, would arouse such opposition that "we might as well forget the whole matter." Colson said that he and Peterson knew and "Dick knows that the combined influence of all of those departments is a stronger influence with the General Assembly than a governor." The goal should not be to get a perfect bill but to get one that could be passed. Colson added that Russell's administration would stand or fall on reorganization and "working the state out of debt."[16]

On April 28, Governor-elect Russell appeared before the Reorganization Committee. He emphasized that the people demanded reform and that Georgia's government must be simplified and made more efficient. He told the committee that few states had "a more unwieldly, haphazard and complicated department system" than Georgia. In his characteristic manner, Russell said that he had no idea of trying to dictate to the committee. He said that he had "entire confidence" in its ability and integrity and that he would support whatever plan it developed.[17]

The House committee headed by Hugh Peterson supported the Huddleston committee's recommendations. In August, after relatively little controversy, the legislature passed the Reorganization Act of 1931. It was to become effective January 1, 1932. While Russell's leadership in the legislature had not been obvious, he had kept up the needed political pressure behind the scenes. He realized that the reputation of his administration depended to a considerable degree on the passage of such legislation.

The Reorganization Act consolidated all of the old administrative agencies into eighteen new departments, boards, and commissions. One of the most important results of the law was the abolition of twenty-five boards of trustees that had governed the various institutions in the university system. They were replaced by an eleven-person board of regents. The goal of consolidating all tax collections, something that

Russell had strongly supported, was achieved by establishing a tax commission. State purchasing was also centralized, and a board of control was set up to administer the charitable and correctional agencies. Although the law was a compromise, it was a vast improvement over the previous governmental structure. Russell took great pride in the accomplishment.

As reorganization began to take shape, many people pressured Russell concerning appointments to the various boards and commissions. Especially strong demands arose regarding membership on the Board of Regents. Hugh Peterson urged Russell to appoint Philip Weltner, an Atlanta attorney, to the regents. Weltner had been active in pushing reorganization and, according to Peterson, his work had greatly improved the final bill. Weltner clearly wanted the appointment, but he told Peterson that he probably would not campaign for it. Peterson assured Weltner that Russell would appoint him and "give you an opportunity to help really build a good University System in this state." Weltner became the first vice-chancellor of the University System. Russell also appointed Hughes Spalding and other prominent citizens who were committed to improving higher education in Georgia. Indeed, making strong appointments to the Board of Regents was one of Russell's main achievements as governor.[18]

The 1931 legislature, the only session that met during Russell's governorship, also dealt favorably with the governor's other recommendations. Lawmakers passed a constitutional amendment to classify property for tax purposes. They also provided for a uniform school textbook code and arranged for the state to buy textbooks and distribute them at cost. In addition, they passed a constitutional amendment that would permit the state to pay counties for expenditures on state highways. Legislators went along with Russell's suggestion that the date of the governor's inauguration be in January following election rather than in June. The General Assembly, however, refused to reduce the salaries of public employees by 5 to 10 percent as Russell had asked.[19]

Russell was able to balance the budget without cutting salaries. The Budget Act passed at the special session in March 1931 made this easier since that law established a budget bureau and named the governor as director. Under the new system, the departments of government submitted their requests to the budget bureau, controlled by the governor, which would recommend an overall budget to the legislature. The General Assembly could not amend the budget if it created a deficit. To balance outgo with income, Russell squeezed the state agencies and saved some funds through reorganization. With utmost economy, he was able to pay the Confederate veterans' pensions, although not always on time, keep all the schools open, and maintain a highway building program. At the end of his eighteen months as governor, the state had not only met its current requirements but had paid about $2.8 million on the old unpaid appropriations. No previous governor had ever exerted such tight control over the state budget.[20]

Russell's record began to attract some national attention by the end of the summer. The *New York Times* editorialized on September 6, 1931, that little was being heard in Georgia of "corn pone, or scuppernong wine, or turtle eggs." "Young Dick Russell," the writer said, had acted fast and done much. While Russell had not reformed Georgia as far as New York and Virginia in the writer's opinion, he had done much to "restore Georgia's political and financial solvency." The implication was that Russell had greatly improved the state's image as well.

Because of dwindling state income, Russell was unable to do as much for education as he would have liked. The same was true for highways, the other twin "pathway" to economic development. Nevertheless a number of major highway improvements occurred during his governorship. On August 29, 1931, Russell attended a big affair in Neptune Park on St. Simons Island where a large group gathered to celebrate the completion of a hard-surfaced road from Waycross to Brunswick. This was the last leg of a highway linking Atlanta with Brunswick, a development, Russell said, that was of great importance to the state's growth.

That evening Russell attended an all-male dinner at The Cloister, one of the nation's finest hostelries. Those in attendance heaped praise on the governor. James Colson said that Russell had provided leadership for "the most progressive and constructive" legislative session since the Civil War. Following the dinner, the guests danced at the Sea Island Beach Casino. Russell, who always enjoyed the company of young women, socialized with Willodeen Colson and other attractive women during the evening.[21]

In January 1932, Russell was on hand to celebrate the opening of the highway that connected Savannah to the rest of the state "with a ribbon of concrete." Besides helping Georgia's economy, Russell said, road building was important because it created jobs for the unemployed. As the depression became worse, Russell looked more and more to the federal government for relief of some kind. He declared that the best unemployment relief was "an enlarged program of public works." He had already written to Georgia's representatives in Washington urging them to support an appropriation of $200 million for highway construction. Opposition to relief for people who desperately needed help was "indefensible, if not un-American," he charged. Russell said he could not understand how the Hoover administration could support $2 billion for business loans through the Reconstruction Finance Corporation and the postponement of war debts and yet oppose creating jobs for "those who are hungry and almost naked." People did not want a dole, he continued, they wanted work.

Although Russell observed that there had been much discussion about the rise of communism and socialism, he had no fear of these ideologies. "The only communism to fear in this country," he declared, "is the communism of empty stomachs and naked backs. The heart of the masses of America is as sound and devoted to our country as it has ever been," he added, "but it is difficult for this heart to beat fast and true when the body is hungry and unsheltered."[22]

Among those suffering the most were Georgia farmers. Prices of cotton, tobacco, and other farm commodities had dropped to disastrous levels, and average incomes per farm family in the state had declined to less than $200 a year. Russell had never held out any hope that the state could do much to assist farmers. However, by the late summer of 1931, as cotton picking commenced, he joined those who were saying that Congress must deal with the growing problems of low prices, crushing debts, foreclosure, and stark poverty in agriculture.[23]

Meanwhile, Governor Huey P. Long of Louisiana had announced his own plan to help cotton farmers. Suggesting the complete prohibition of cotton planting in 1932, Long argued that only such a dramatic move would raise cotton prices to profitable levels. Long called a meeting of governors of the cotton states to meet in New Orleans on August 21, 1931, to consider his proposal. Russell did not attend, but Eugene Talmadge, commissioner of agriculture, represented Georgia. Two approaches were discussed. One was the Long drop-a-crop scheme, and the other a plan to reduce cotton planting in 1932 by about one-third. J. E. McDonald, Texas commissioner of agriculture, offered the latter idea. After some discussion, the delegates overwhelmingly supported the Long proposal. They added a protective clause, however, that released any state that passed a law forbidding the planting of cotton from the agreement if states producing three-fourths of the total cotton crop in the South did not also pass restrictive legislation. If such a plan were to work, most of the cotton states would have to agree, otherwise farmers in states that might pass such a law would be penalized.[24]

Commissioner Talmadge strongly backed the Long plan. Returning from New Orleans, he recommended that Russell call a special session of the legislature to enact a measure forbidding cotton planting in Georgia in 1932. Russell reacted cautiously. He sent a telegram to Hugh Peterson on September 1 soliciting his reaction to the Long plan and asking him to obtain the views of cotton planters in the area around Ailey. He also asked for opinions from others. While Peterson did not offer a clear recommendation, many others, including Talmadge, urged Russell to call the lawmakers to Atlanta in special session.[25]

Russell, however, remained noncommittal. Two factors influenced his thinking. In the first place, the Long plan could only work if the Texas legislature agreed to cooperate. Since Texas produced about one-third of the South's total cotton crop, unless farmers there did not plant cotton, the whole scheme would fail. In order to gain firsthand knowledge of the Texas situation, Russell sent Leeman Anderson to Austin on September 11. By that time, it was clear that neither the Texas legislature nor Governor Ross S. Sterling favored a law forbidding all cotton planting. Anderson reported this situation to Russell when he returned home.[26]

Furthermore, there was strong opposition to the Long plan from business interests that depended on cotton. J. Emory Wood, a member of the state House of Representatives, wrote to all members on September 9 saying that the Long proposal would not only be a "calamity to the farmers themselves," but it would ruin merchants, bankers, railroads, and insurance companies. Wood believed that "our gins would rust out, our oil mills and fertilizer factories would close down, [and] our railroads would suffer additional losses."[27]

While Russell moved cautiously and waited to see what Texas would do, Talmadge urged the state's farmers to pressure the governor by gathering in Atlanta on September 16 for a mass protest. About a thousand farmers showed up for a big parade and meeting on the capitol grounds. There was no question about it—the Long plan had caught the imagination of farmers. They passed a resolution calling for a special session and passage of a law forbidding cotton planting in the state. One placard on a parade car read: "To hell with cotton in 1932." A farmer from Warrenton later wrote Hugh Peterson that he thought 95 percent of the cotton farmers in his area favored the Long plan.[28]

Just before noon, Russell spoke to the restless farmers who had gathered on the capitol lawn. As he began to speak, the crowd shouted, "Give us what we want," and, "Don't turn us down." While admitting that the Long plan was popular among farmers, Russell said he would not call a special session unless the Texas legislature acted first. The scheme could not succeed without Texas participation, he said, and to

call the lawmakers into session before Texas passed legislation to restrict cotton planting would simply be a waste of taxpayer money. A
special session, he explained, would cost $2,500 a day. Then Russell
went to lunch. But the farmers did not disperse. They milled around
inside the capitol building until Russell returned, and then a small delegation visited him in his office in an effort to change his mind. But
Russell held his ground. A few days later, the *Atlanta Constitution*
praised him for his "wisdom and caution."[29]

When the committee of farmers met with Russell on the afternoon
of September 16, they asked him if he would call a special session if
members of the legislature would serve without pay. If it was the cost
that caused Russell to oppose the session, the farmers hoped that this
suggestion might eliminate his objections.[30] He agreed to this idea,
knowing full well that the lawmakers would never be so magnanimous
in public service.

Russell continued to seek advice and to study the problem through
the rest of 1931. However, he refused to take any action that he considered nonproductive and useless. He was greatly concerned about the
plight of farmers, but he did not want to create any false hopes among
them. On January 22, 1932, he published a leaflet that reviewed the
situation and summarized his position on the whole matter. Russell
explained that several states had passed restrictive laws on cotton planting but that most of these laws had been repealed or were under attack
in the courts, as was the Texas law cutting the amount of acreage permitted for cotton production by 30 percent. He wrote that he had studied not only the Long plan but a number of other proposals. After
extensive review, he had concluded that the "price of cotton is beyond
the control of the Georgia legislature." Russell ended by saying that he
could not answer the cry for "the bread of relief with the stone of heavy
expense of a useless legislative session, nor seek political benefit at the
expense of human misery and create false hopes merely to serve political
expediency." As it turned out, Russell's lack of action in this instance
was not only good statesmanship but good politics as well.

Not all of Russell's responsibilities as governor dealt with the depression and legislation. In late 1932, he found himself in the midst of a
national controversy over Georgia's penal and criminal justice system
that brought a wave of criticism from northern opinion makers. The
case involved Robert E. Burns, a black who some years earlier, after
committing a theft in Atlanta, was sentenced to serve time on a chain
gang. He escaped, was returned, and escaped again. During his absence
from Georgia, he wrote *I Am a Fugitive from a Georgia Chain Gang*, a

book that portrayed the Georgia penal system as extremely inhumane. Burns also sold movie rights to his story.

When in late 1932 Georgia authorities located Burns in New Jersey, they requested that Governor Arthur H. Moore extradite him to Georgia to complete his sentence. Judging from newspaper response in the North, northern opinion strongly opposed returning Burns to Georgia. It was rumored that if Burns ever came under the control of Georgia law officers, he would probably be killed. The state's penal system was pictured as inhumane, uncivilized, and reminiscent of medieval times. Following a hearing in Trenton in December 1932, hundreds of local citizens cheered Governor Moore when he rejected Georgia's plea for extradition.

The attack on the southern justice system and Moore's refusal to return Burns made Russell boiling mad. He accused Moore of violating the Constitution and acting contrary to U.S. "custom and comity." He criticized the New Jersey governor for acting as judge and jury in the case of a felon who had committed a robbery at gunpoint. Russell also said that Moore had been misled by Burns's book and that criticisms of the Georgia penal system were absolutely false. The state did not coddle criminals, he said, but they were treated decently. Russell argued that neither the governor of New Jersey nor anyone else had the right to "deliberately insult the State of Georgia and her people by declining to honor an extradition for a convict on the ground that our state is uncivilized and backward—inhumane to her prisoners and barbarous in her punishment."[31]

While this issue soon faded away, it gave Russell an opportunity to attract additional support at home and to speak out for his state. Any attack on Georgia, her institutions, or the South always struck a raw nerve in Russell. He never let slurs or insults against his beloved South go unanswered. As far as he was concerned, southern society might not have been perfect, but it was the best in the nation. Anyone who thought otherwise had better be ready to do battle with Dick Russell.

A more pleasant task for Russell was promoting plans for economic development. The conservation and wise use of the state's natural resources had always been important to him. From boyhood, Russell had been interested in the outdoors. He enjoyed the beauty of the state's landscapes, and he liked to hunt the birds and animals that found homes in the forests, plains, and mountains. Russell developed a deep interest in the conservation of water, soil, and timber so that these resources could be used in the best interests of a growing society.

As farmers looked for additional sources of income during the depression, Georgia's millions of pine trees offered an opportunity for a money crop. The market for lumber, however, was severely depressed. Another possible use was in manufacturing pulp for making paper. But the technology available to pulp manufacturers did not permit the use of pine trees because of the presence of gum. Dr. Charles H. Herty of Savannah proposed to Russell that the state fund an experimental laboratory to develop a process to solve the gum problem and open up a new market for pine trees. Russell was enthusiastic about Herty's ideas, and in 1931 the legislature appropriated $20,000 for research on this project. The state also obtained $50,000 from the Chemical Foundation for the research. The Herty project was highly successful, and within a few years, thousands of Georgia farmers had an additional market for their pine trees. Russell was proud of the part he played in this project, and it represented at least one successful effort to encourage economic growth.[32]

Russell was also interested in other research projects that might assist farmers. He was concerned about exploring alternative crops that had not yet proved successful in Georgia. For example, he made money from the governor's contingency fund available to the state entomologist to experiment with developing a tomato plant industry in South Georgia. These projects reflected an interest by Russell in agricultural research that grew stronger with passing years.

State issues occupied only part of Russell's busy schedule. Routine matters in the office took up hours each day, and the pressure for jobs did not abate. It seemed as though almost all of Russell's friends wanted positions either for themselves or for their friends. Dick may well have felt like Grover Cleveland who, after becoming president, talked about the everlasting clamor for office. Russell often recommended several friends for a position in a department or agency and then left it to the department head to make the choice. For example, he told Peterson in early October 1931 that while he had recommended several "of my good friends" to the head of the banking department, he would suggest that Peterson's nominee be considered.[33]

Russell did find positions for many of his friends. For example, he supported Lawrence S. Camp for chairman of the State Democratic Committee, and he named Jud Wilhoit to the highway board. While he always insisted on appointing qualified persons to office, Russell told Frank A. Hooper that somehow he had always been able to find friends and supporters who qualified for positions.[34]

The office work, too, was extremely heavy. During the first months in the governorship, Russell developed a schedule and routine that he followed quite closely over the rest of his public career. He usually arrived at his office around 9 A.M. and began seeing people who had appointments and some who did not. Although Russell had an open office policy, his staff guarded it with some care. He usually had a late lunch, saw a few additional people, and then about 4 P.M. closed his private office door and began what he considered his real work of reading and answering his mail. Members of his staff handled routine correspondence, but Russell took great pride in reading most letters on substantive matters and answering them personally.

His determination to give personal attention to much of his mail required him to spend many evenings in the office. Leeman Anderson reported on November 24, 1931, that in one recent week the governor had received 763 letters. The office was sending out an average of 113 letters daily. It was no wonder, Tom Arnold wrote in the *Atlanta Georgian*, that "the lights glow at midnight through the windows of the Governor's office."[35]

All was not work, however. Russell had always liked to have a good time, and becoming governor had not lessened that desire. He enjoyed reading history, he had frequent dates, he was much interested in sports, and he liked to hunt. Russell usually spent several days every fall hunting in southeast Georgia. For example, on November 13, 1932, he and a group of friends left for Sea Island to hunt on the preserve of Howard Coffin. The friends included Lawrence Camp, Jud Wilhoit, Frank M. Scarlett, and others. The first day they fished but then concentrated on hunting turkey, quail, and deer. Later in the week, the governor joined another hunting party on the Paulk game preserve near Brunswick. There Russell shot a twenty-two-pound gobbler, and the party killed four deer, although the account did not mention whether Russell shot one of the four.[36]

In the spring and summer, Russell frequently attended sporting events, especially baseball games. During the fall months, he attended the University of Georgia football games whenever possible. He had been present at the famous game in 1929 when Georgia beat Yale, and he regularly tried to make the University of Georgia–Georgia Tech game.[37] He was a good friend of two of Georgia's best-known professional athletes, baseball player Ty Cobb and golfer Bobby Jones. Russell and Jones were frequently together, but Dick did not play much golf because it took so much time. The House had presented him with a set of left-handed clubs when he was Speaker. Although he was right-handed, he golfed from the left side.

During his year and a half as governor, Russell received numerous

Governor Russell, third from left, and friends on a hunting trip in southeast Georgia, 1933. (Photo courtesy of Russell Memorial Library, University of Georgia, Athens.)

awards and honors. In 1931 the national Junior Chamber of Commerce named him the outstanding young man in the United States. He also attended the National Convention of the American Legion in September 1931, where he tried to help elect his friend, Edgar B. Dunlap of Gainesville, as national commander. Early in December 1931, he was initiated into the Atlanta chapter of the Elks Club. The Atlanta Junior Chamber of Commerce honored him for his work in reorganizing state government at a banquet on March 18, 1932, where George Olmstead, president of the U.S. Chamber of Commerce, presented him with a Distinguished Service medal. In accepting the medal, Russell said that reorganization had not been achieved by any single individual but "by the activity of the militant young men of Georgia of whom I am but a symbol." He received a congratulatory telegram from his fellow governor Franklin D. Roosevelt, who was a part-time resident of Georgia, which read, "I am constantly proud of the fact that Dick Russell is my governor as well as yours."[38]

Russell dated regularly, but he continued to avoid any serious rela-

Governor Russell dressed for an evening of leisure, 1931. (Photo courtesy of Russell Memorial Library, University of Georgia, Athens.)

tionships. In February 1932, members at the Druid Hills Baptist Church in Atlanta thought they would have some fun with Russell by holding a mock trial and charging the governor with "malicious celibacy." Although Russell denied charges that he had remained single in the face of several good opportunities to marry, he was convicted in Cupid's court.[39] Later in the year when his staff gave him a surprise birthday party, one reporter wrote that Russell was "very eligible for matrimony," but "since college days Governor Russell has been too busy with affairs of state to develop a taking romance."

In 1932, a leap year, some observers wondered if the governor would be able to defend himself against proposals from young women. When asked by a writer for the *Atlanta Georgian* how he would protect his bachelorhood, Russell replied that it would not be a problem. Asserting that there would be no new first lady in the mansion in 1932, Russell explained that he had "lived through several leap years, and not once have I received a proposal." Then he added: "I am not immune, because I am always attracted when I see a pretty girl—but I have been pretty brave in the past. I promise to give every proposal, if any, my earnest consideration," he jokingly concluded. There were commonly "bits of gossip" about Russell and possible matrimony, but that was all it was—gossip. It was probably true that Russell was too occupied with other things to want to make a commitment to marriage.[40]

Russell's success in state politics brought him increasing attention from national Democratic leaders. During the fall of 1931, he met with Franklin D. Roosevelt several times. He was an early supporter of Roosevelt for president, stating in September 1931 that, of all the candidates mentioned, he favored the New York governor. Russell added that he thought the country would be "fortunate to have him as its Chief Executive."[41] On October 4, he and John S. Cohen, publisher of the *Atlanta Journal* and a member of the Democratic National Committee, called on Roosevelt at Warm Springs. During lunch at the cottage, they told the New York governor that he would be nominated on the first ballot.[42] Two months later, J. E. Whitley of LaGrange sponsored a possum dinner for Roosevelt. Russell, Hugh Peterson, and a number of other leading Georgia politicians attended. Indicating Roosevelt, Russell said that he was pleased to have a favorite son to "present to the next Democratic convention." A few days later, Roosevelt drove up to Atlanta from Warm Springs to have dinner with Russell at the mansion. According to Russell, the two governors talked about unemployment, prison reform, highway construction, taxation, and budgets. But, he said, they did not discuss Roosevelt's possible candidacy for president. It was purely a social visit, Russell told skeptical reporters.[43]

At the beginning of 1932, Russell could take a good deal of pride in his accomplishments as governor. After only a little more than six months of Russell's term, government reorganization was being implemented, the state was operating within its income, and state agencies were meeting minimum demands. Russell was popular among most citizens, and every serious political observer realized that a second term was his for the asking. The great majority of Georgians expected that he would run for governor. Then suddenly an act of fate dramatically changed what was perceived as the normal course of political events.

6

Election to the United States Senate

===

Georgians were shocked and saddened when they received the news that U.S. Senator William J. Harris had died of a heart attack on April 18, 1932. Even though Harris had suffered spells of illness after his reelection in 1930, his death came as a surprise. Prominent in state and national politics for more than twenty years, Harris left an unexpected void in the higher echelons of Georgia politics.

Governor Russell and his close associates, along with some three thousand mourners, gathered in the cemetery at Cedartown on April 21 to pay final respects to their departed senator.[1] Many who gathered around the grave site, however, had their minds more on who would succeed Harris than on the deceased senator. Indeed, speculation was already rife throughout the state about a Harris successor. This speculation actually concerned two questions. Whom would governor Russell appoint as interim senator until an election could be held, and who would seek the unexpired term of Harris, which ran until 1936? There was widespread belief that Russell himself would run for the unexpired term.[2]

Russell was flooded with inquiries and advice as to whom he should appoint as interim senator. Speculation ranged over a broad list of names from the senator's widow to the governor's father. Russell, however, said that he would make a decision only after Senator Harris's funeral.[3] On April 25, he answered both questions that had been the center of state political gossip. He selected John S. Cohen, publisher of the *Atlanta Journal* and Democratic National committeeman from Georgia, to serve as interim senator, and he announced that he would seek the unexpired senatorial term at an election set for September 14. Cohen declared that he would not seek election to the office, leaving the way clear for Russell and fueling speculation that some deal had been cut between the two men. Russell explained, however, that he appointed Cohen because the newspaperman was so well informed.[4]

It had also been widely surmised that Congressman Charles R. Crisp of Americus would run for the Senate. The next day, April 26, as many had predicted, Crisp announced that he would also seek the Senate seat. It was not accidental that Crisp made his announcement from the office of W. T. Anderson, publisher of the *Macon Telegraph* and one of Russell's severest critics. Born in 1870 and elected to the U.S. House in 1912, Crisp was the dean of Georgia's congressional delegation. The Crisp family, like the Russells, had been prominent in state affairs. His father had been Speaker of the House in the second Cleveland administration. Crisp was a well-known and respected House member. He was a fiscal conservative, a supporter of farm relief in the 1920s, and an advocate of a balanced budget. He had been a member of the House Ways and Means Committee for many years and became its acting chairman in January 1932. In the 1920s, he had served on the World War Foreign Debt Commission.[5]

These announcements settled the discussion about who would run and why. Most of Russell's friends had urged him to run believing that the time was opportune for him to move to the national political scene. Even some of his staunchest opponents agreed that it was the right time for him to make the race. The *Macon Telegraph* editorialized on April 22 that everyone knew Russell planned to seek national political office someday and that this seemed to be his best chance.

Most of those who wanted Russell to complete two terms as governor said they would back whatever decision he made. Edward L. Reagan, an attorney from McDonough, wrote Dick's brother Robert that although it would be a mistake to pass up a second term as governor, if Russell chose to run for the Senate, "his cause [is] my cause."[6] Offers to support Russell poured in. One friend wrote on the very day Harris died, "We are all standing by here ... ready to go down the line with you on whatever course of action you see fit to take."[7]

Not all Russell supporters agreed. Some of his most loyal backers sincerely believed that he still had work to complete as governor. They thought that even after serving another term in the state capital, he could be elected to the U.S. Senate. Moreover, a few friends were not certain that Russell could beat Crisp. But those who sought to dissuade him made no headway. When Crisp announced, Russell declared boldly, "He'll be the worst defeated man you ever saw."[8]

The reasons Russell decided to seek the Senate seat in 1932 are clear enough. In the first place, it had only been about eighteen months earlier that he had won a smashing political victory over a creditable opponent. This event was still fresh in peoples' minds. Moreover, much had been achieved in the one legislative session of the Russell governorship, and the public perceived these accomplishments to be a result of his leadership. Russell presented the image of a winner, both as a vote getter and as a political leader. He also had made a good many appointments, and he could expect loyal support from men like Hughes Spalding, a member of the Board of Regents, and a host of other prominent citizens. Most important of all, however, was that network of enthusiastic friends throughout the state who were ready and eager to help in another grass roots campaign. Hundreds of Georgians were just waiting for the signal to go to work in another "Young Dick" campaign. There was also a practical matter—there would not be another national senatorial election in Georgia until 1936. If he were reelected governor and served another two-year term, what political opportunities would be available from the end of his governorship until the senatorial election? The answer was, not many. The time was ripe now, and Russell grasped the opportunity.

After Crisp announced his candidacy on April 26, he boarded the train for Washington. At a brief stopover in Atlanta, he explained that his life had been devoted to public service and that he considered election to the Senate to be a "logical promotion." He expressed appreciation to those Georgians who wanted him to remain in the House because of his seniority, but, he added, "I'm going to run for the senate and I am going to win." In a rather mellow and optimistic mood, Crisp said that Russell had been "a splendid governor" but that he, Crisp, was better qualified for the Senate. Russell had no record in national affairs, Crisp continued, while his own record was an "open book." With that, Crisp stepped back on the train and headed to Washington, which had become almost as much his home as Americus. The next morning, the *Atlanta Constitution* headlined its story on the interview, "Crisp Asks 'Promotion,' Cites 36-Year Service," while the *Atlanta Georgian* carried an inch-high headline that read, "Crisp Announces for Senator Harris' Post; 'Battle of Century' against Russell Seen."[9]

The Crisp strategy quickly became apparent. By returning to Washington and his congressional duties, he hoped to give the impression that he was a hard-working and conscientious public servant. He also played up his experience in Washington and portrayed himself as a man who had dealt with large and important issues. He believed that Georgians would support a candidate with a known record. While Crisp was attending to the nation's business, he accused Russell of running around the state campaigning and neglecting his official duties.

Crisp's friends suggested that Russell should seek another term as governor to prevent a political bloodbath in the state. As the *Albany Herald* editorialized, this would spare the state "the strife and storm of a campaign" that would revive the "devastating factionalism and cheap politics which have afflicted Georgia in the past."[10] The Crisp forces also sought to convey the impression that their candidate would be an easy winner. Julian Harris wrote in the May 15 *New York Times* that "Georgia Views Crisp As Its Next Senator."[11]

Whatever Crisp's friends might think, Russell believed otherwise. As was his custom, he moved quickly and aggressively. He opened his campaign with a radio talk in Atlanta that set both the tone and strategy of his campaign. He reviewed his record as governor and said that he had tried to keep faith with the people. The only reason he wanted to be elected to the Senate, he continued, was so he could "truly speak the voice of Georgia on the floor of that body." He referred to Crisp as "an aristocratic gentleman of distinguished lineage" who was "a social asset in any gathering." But, Russell said, his record in Washington must be discussed and evaluated.

Russell set out to identify Crisp with the rich and the wellborn and to show that he was insensitive to the needs of depression-ridden people. He charged that the congressman had forgotten the masses and had become deaf to the struggles of average Georgians. Reviewing the economic situation, Russell described the pitiful conditions among his fellow citizens and said that because of the farm depression, "white women and children of the finest American blood are laboring in the cotton fields in tattered rags."

Russell then sought to connect Crisp with most of the nation's ills. He said that government waste was "shameful" and that federal expenditures had skyrocketed since Crisp had been in Congress. Tax laws that Crisp supported favored the rich, Russell said, and now he was supporting a moratorium on collecting America's foreign debts, which was fastening another $10 billion to the backs of American taxpayers. He also argued that Crisp had voted for a bill that had shifted the utility tax from the producers of electricity to the consumers. He charged, furthermore, that his opponent had supported the Hawley-Smoot Tariff Act that had raised tariffs and cost farmers dearly.

Turning to his own program, Russell called for currency inflation to create easier credit, reorganization of the national government, and stricter immigration controls. He said that it was essential to keep out "Mexican peons" who were brought into the Southwest to produce cotton at "starvation wages and to compete with the cotton produced by Georgia farmers." Striking a strong isolationist stance, Russell declared that he vigorously opposed the League of Nations and the World Court. He said that he would fight any agreement or alliance that might result in the deaths of American boys in foreign countries while "attempting to settle Asiatic riots or European squabbles."[12]

Russell was enough of a pragmatist to know that ideas alone would not bring victory. He must get out and see the people. To portray himself as representative of the common man, he had to visit the homes and communities of the average Georgian. So, shortly after his announcement, Russell hit the campaign trail. As had been true in 1930, he had no problem getting speaking dates. There were friends in every community anxious and willing to arrange a meeting and organize a crowd. He stopped at farms, crossroads stores, small villages, and county seat towns, where he mingled with people and sought their support. Approaching voters, he would say, "This is Dick Russell," and then proceed to talk about his campaign. He also handed out a card with his picture and a statement that read: "He has made a good Governor. He will serve the people as well as Senator."[13] Like his father before him, he tried to be known as "plain Dick Russell." Everywhere he went, he portrayed himself as the peoples' candidate. One of his campaign posters carried Russell's picture with the comment: "He is fresh from the people and knows their needs. His energy and ability will be devoted to their welfare." While Russell was democratic in manner, he also retained the dignity that he considered appropriate to a governor.

Russell soon learned that not all of his friends would back him. He wrote to Israel Manheim of Hawkinsville, clerk of the Superior Court, on May 2, stating that he was counting on Manheim's support. Manheim replied, however, that Crisp had been a lifelong friend and a strong leader and that he intended to vote for him. He still considered Russell a friend, but he could not support him against Crisp.[14]

While Russell was visiting and speaking throughout the state three or four days a week during May and June, Crisp was still in Washington. By late June and early July, Crisp's supporters were urging him to return to Georgia at once to begin contacting voters. Crisp replied that he realized the importance of getting back home, but it was impossible because of his responsibilities to important legislation. Then he added that apparently "the Governor does not agree with me as to the necessity of remaining at his post of duty."[15]

By the time Crisp opened his campaign with a radio address on July 12, Russell had placed his opponent clearly on the defensive. The governor's constant attacks forced Crisp to spend most of his time trying to refute Russell's charges. Crisp had the disadvantage of having a voting record, which exposed him to criticism, while Russell as governor could propose almost anything that seemed reasonable to deal with problems. Being a governor and proposing solutions without having the responsibility for decision making was much less risky than being an incumbent who had been in Congress and had to vote on issues.

In his speeches, Russell kept hammering away at Crisp's association with, and support for, special interests. He especially emphasized that Crisp and the power companies were in the same political bed. Russell illustrated his point by talking about the electrical surcharge that Congress levied on consumers in a 1932 tax bill. The Senate bill would have taxed the power companies, but the House bill, supported by Crisp, changed that provision and placed the tax on consumers. Russell charged that Crisp had aligned himself with the "power trust" at the expense of the people. He referred to Crisp as "Kilowatt Charlie." Russell pictured his opponent and the president of the Georgia Power Company meeting privately to conspire against consumers. With his skill for creating pictures with words, Russell gave his listeners mental images of Crisp and enemies of the common people wheeling and dealing in darkened back rooms. As Hughes Spalding so colorfully explained it, "Russell took a light bulb and crammed it up his ———."[16]

Russell also sharply criticized Crisp for not insisting that countries pay the war debts they owed to the United States. Crisp had been appointed to the bipartisan World War Foreign Debt Commission in 1922, which had been appointed to deal with the difficult problem of how to collect America's wartime debts totaling more than $10 billion. As the world financial situation worsened, in 1931 President Hoover suggested and implemented a one-year moratorium on the payment of war debts. Crisp favored this action. On the basis of this stance, Russell now portrayed Crisp as soft on international debtors and as a legislator who favored giving money away "when it was so badly needed at home." He presented Crisp as more interested in foreigners than in hard-pressed Americans.[17]

Russell also criticized Crisp for doing nothing to help farmers. The passage of the Agricultural Marketing Act and the creation of the Federal Farm Board had been Hoover's approach to solving farm problems. Crisp had supported the Hoover program that by 1932 had failed miserably to keep farm prices from falling to disastrous levels. Russell argued that Crisp had ignored the cries of Georgia farmers for relief. If Crisp was so experienced and effective in Washington, as he claimed, why, Russell asked, had he not been able to provide real farm relief? For his own part, Russell advocated a stiff tariff on jute, an import that competed with cotton, as a way to strengthen cotton prices. Crisp, an incumbent who had cooperated with the Hoover administration on a number of issues, now found Russell tarring him with the failures of that administration. Russell stated that Crisp and Hoover "are souls with but a single thought and hearts that beat as one."[18] To hear Russell talk, listeners might have concluded that Crisp was a Hoover Republican instead of a conservative South Georgia Democrat.

While Russell spoke extensively, he knew the importance of political organization in a successful campaign. He established his political headquarters at the Ansley Hotel in Atlanta and placed his brother Robert in charge. Although Russell named Frank M. Scarlett, a close friend and supporter from Brunswick, as his campaign manager, his brother Robert and his uncle Lewis C. Russell directed most of the day-to-day business, as they had in 1930. His brother Fielding also worked in the campaign headquarters. As usual, Dick could depend on his large family.

Russell's organization was thorough and comprehensive. His headquarters acquired lists of judges, businessmen, nurses, doctors, county officials, and others whom Russell then contacted by special letter. He usually began these letters by saying how much he would appreciate the support of such an influential person in the community. Then he would outline his principles and programs. He told the judges, for example, that "my candidacy represents the fight of the average man against big vested interests such as the power trust, the jute trust and international bankers" who were seeking to control the federal government.[19]

Russell's friends helped greatly by assessing local situations and informing the governor how particular people stood in the contest. Friends would often mark beside the names on a list of voters comments such as "for Dick," "very strong," "very enthusiastic," "might change," "for Crisp," and so forth. There were lists of people recently won over to the Russell camp who received special letters from the governor. Early in the campaign, he concentrated on county officers who were commonly referred to as "the court house crowd." In late June, all county officers received a form letter from Russell saying that he was "quite anxious to have the benefit of your valuable support and influence in my race."[20] Even though thousands of letters went out from the Russell headquarters, Dick gave careful personal attention to their content.

In order to keep up with local political situations, Robert Russell subscribed to scores of small-town newspapers during the campaign. In many papers, he took out advertisements that often looked like news stories. Russell campaigners ran a full-page newslike advertisement in the *Southern Cultivator* that included information on his record, his views on issues, and his picture. He was presented as the "champion of the masses."[21] The Russell clubs that had been so effective in many cities and counties in 1930 were revived, and they worked hard to promote the governor's candidacy.

As the election drew closer, the Russell forces called up every political debt and reminded people what the governor had done for them. Jud Wilhoit, one of Russell's most loyal friends and his appointee to the highway board, used the prospect of road building to gain support. A resident of Cochran in Bleckley County wrote Russell on August 22 that Wilhoit's promise to "grade our road as fast as possible" had certainly been helpful. Indeed, the next day, another citizen from Cochran said that he believed Crisp was beaten in Bleckley County. "When you saw Wilhoit and suggested that he help us out on our highway," he wrote, "I came home and advised my friends that you had done us a real favor."[22] Earlier, when Russell spoke at Garretta, people expressed their appreciation to him and Wilhoit for letting a paving contract on Highway 80 near Dublin.[23]

At the same time, Russell tried to convey the impression that he would never seek votes by offering favors. According to C. E. Gregory, a correspondent for the *Atlanta Journal*, when a citizen told Russell he could assure the votes of his area if the governor would "authorize a contract to pave our road," the governor replied in an indignant voice loud enough for those around to hear, "I do not trade highway contracts for votes and I do not appreciate that sort of proposition."[24] While Russell probably did not enter into any such direct agreement, his supporters surely used state favors to develop support whenever they could.

In some cases, backers asked Russell for a political appointment in exchange for help with voters. A distant relative wrote him from Gainesville saying that he could arrange support for Russell in Hall County if the governor would appoint a friend to one of the state boards. Russell replied that he knew the individual had a good deal of influence in Hall and surrounding counties, but he had "one inviolable rule" in politics. That rule was, he said, never to promise "an official appointment to obtain political support." Russell acknowledged that the practice was common, but he "preferred to attempt to take care of my friends after an election and reward their loyalty that way rather than to make a deal as a coldblooded business proposition."[25]

As had been true in 1930, Russell tried to give the impression that he was carrying on a "shoestring" campaign without any major funding. He wrote one prospective supporter that he had to depend on the general public to take up his fight. He explained that he had no elaborate organization with designated leaders who could carry his banner in the various counties.[26] Russell wanted to convey the idea that the people were rising spontaneously to his cause.

While Russell had gotten the jump on Crisp, by late July the congressman was back in Georgia campaigning hard. He drew good crowds, newspapers gave his views liberal coverage, and many observers predicted his victory. Crisp talked about his experience and his knowledge of the issues. But increasingly he had to defend himself from Russell's charges that he was in league with the power companies, that his votes on tariffs and taxes were unjustified, and that a moratorium on foreign debts was a bad mistake. Moreover, although Crisp offered some positive proposals, they aroused meager interest among poverty-stricken Georgians. Talk of controlling securities transactions, regulating power companies, revising the tariff downward, and disarmament were far removed from the concerns of an unemployed factory worker or a farmer selling cotton for a nickel a pound.

Crisp soon learned that it was difficult, if not impossible, to explain his stewardship in Washington to depression-ridden Georgians. Economic conditions were worsening, and Crisp was a part of a Congress that seemed incapable of dealing with the nation's problems. Consequently, while still talking about issues, Crisp responded to Russell's charges on a more personal basis. He attacked Russell and his shortcomings as governor with increasing frequency. Crisp accused Russell of abandoning his responsibilities in Atlanta to run around the state campaigning, of having state employees solicit votes on taxpayer time, and of using his appointees on the reorganized boards and commissions to build a political machine.[27]

Many of Crisp's supporters took up the "political machine" issue. The *Valdosta Daily Times*, for instance, editorialized that it had decided to support Crisp because Russell, who started out to destroy political machines, had built one of his own. Russell's political machine, claimed the *Savannah Morning News*, did not consist of high officeholders but of "lower appointees." Emerson H. George, a strong Crisp backer who wrote a series of articles on the campaign, accused Russell of not only organizing his appointees but gaining support from companies that held state contracts.[28]

The Crisp forces even raised the specter of Catholic influence in the Russell administration. A. C. Dorsey, judge of the Probate Court in Cleveland, wrote to the governor informing him that Russell supporters in White County were having difficulty because of the appointment of Hughes Spalding, a Catholic, to the Board of Regents. Dorsey wanted an explanation. Russell replied that Spalding was a man who had contributed liberally of his time and money to the state's higher education, and he was one of the best friends the University of Georgia and Georgia Tech ever had. He had known nothing about Spalding's religion when he appointed him, Russell wrote, and then he added: "I had never asked a man as to his religious faith in making an appointment for I have never seen anyone who had too much religion of any kind. I am frank to say that I do not think that it would have made any difference in the appointment for I had known him for years as a gentleman of character and ability and I do not believe that one Catholic on the board would be able to over-ride 10 Methodists, Baptists and Presbyterians, even if he wished to do so." When others raised the Catholic question, Russell never wavered. He told another constituent that he had indeed appointed Catholics to office, and furthermore he had supported Alfred E. Smith in 1928.[29]

Russell's appointment of some Catholics opened the way for Crisp's campaigners to appeal for support among anti-Catholic elements. The governor charged that the Crisp forces had distributed anti-Catholic fliers that suggested that Russell was in league with the Pope. Although Crisp denied any responsibility for these fliers, Russell obtained a letter from John Greer to Walter Vance written on August 25, 1932, that was very incriminating. The letter said that Crisp representatives would like to send Vance into counties where Thomas E. Watson had been politically strong to spread the word about Russell's Catholic appointments. Greer believed that this would help Crisp among people who feared any growth of Catholic influence. He added that Crisp would like to discuss this matter with Vance in the near future.[30] While the effort to portray the governor as a friend of Catholics caused some concern among the Russell forces, it had no noticeable effect on the outcome of the election.

The issue of Crisp's connection with the power companies continued to be particularly damaging. Russell continued to claim that the power trust issue was the biggest question in the campaign. Crisp and his friends tried to counteract Russell's charges by arguing that some of the governor's main supporters had close connections with the Georgia Power Company. Specifically, Crisp mentioned Hughes Spalding, whose law firm represented the company, James D. Robinson, a businessman and stockholder of the company who was supporting Russell, and Edgar Dunlap, who served as counsel for the company. These charges did not concern Russell. He admitted that some of his men had worked for Georgia Power, but he claimed that this only proved that some lawyers could represent a utility without selling their souls. The implication was that his friends were unsullied by connections with big business but that Crisp and his supporters had succumbed to evil corporate influence.[31]

Russell skillfully maneuvered to associate himself with Roosevelt and the New Yorker's presidential campaign. While Roosevelt did not endorse Russell, people who read the newspapers knew that the two men had visited on several occasions in 1931. Moreover, on May 13, about six weeks before the opening of the 1932 Democratic National Convention, Russell, Lawrence Camp, and other leading Georgia Democrats visited Roosevelt at Warm Springs where it can be assumed they discussed the forthcoming convention in Chicago. In any event, Russell received an invitation to make a seconding speech for Roosevelt.

Russell had to abandon campaigning during the last week of June in order to join other Democrats in Chicago. One of the Georgia delegation's first tasks was to spike rumors that the New York governor was not physically able to carry on a campaign. Russell and other Georgians went from delegation to delegation combating this "sly slandering" by assuring delegates that they knew Roosevelt personally and could testify to his vigor and energy. As one reporter stated, those who had gone possum hunting around Warm Springs with Roosevelt and had traveled with him over uncharted roads were in a position to testify to his physical endurance.[32]

Russell was scheduled to make his seconding speech late Friday afternoon, July 1. As the proceedings dragged on, it appeared that Russell would be making his two-minute talk to a tired, unattentive audience. But once again the Russell luck prevailed. Just before he was to speak, the convention recessed. His talk was rescheduled for 9 P.M. when the delegates reassembled after dinner. Moreover, he was given ten minutes.

When the convention reconvened, Russell was ready. Roosevelt, he claimed, was the man to lead the nation in its time of trial because he was free from "predatory interests who have long fattened at the trough of special privilege." According to Russell, Roosevelt was devoted to human rights and to the love of mankind. He said that when the news of Roosevelt's nomination spread across the country, there "would be gnashing of teeth in the temples of privilege," but it would be "glad news to the suffering masses." In a burst of his best oratory, Russell concluded that the Democracy that had served the United States under Jefferson, Jackson, Cleveland, and Wilson would be "brought to a glorious fruition under the leadership of Roosevelt."[33] The crowd cheered.

Returning home to his campaign, Russell played up his associations with the Democratic presidential nominee. He also criticized Crisp for not attending the Democratic convention. Crisp explained that he was too busy with legislative matters in Washington, but Russell said Crisp had not attended because the Georgia Power Company opposed Roosevelt's nomination.[34]

Assuring voters of Roosevelt's election, Russell explained that the new president would need support in Congress if he were to pull the country out of the depression. Accusing a reactionary Congress of passing laws that hurt the common man, he claimed that progressives like himself must be sent to Washington to help Roosevelt deal with critical national problems. "You cannot depend upon reactionary congressmen to carry out his progressive program," Russell stated.[35] Speaking at Elberton a few days before the election, Russell pulled out of his pocket a "Dear Dick" letter from Roosevelt and read it to the crowd. Roosevelt thanked Russell for making the seconding speech at Chicago and for helping in his campaign. The *Atlanta Journal* editorialized that Russell could be likened to Roosevelt in that he had "courage, initiative, sincerity, a talent for getting results [and] a true devotion to the rights and interests of the rank and file."[36] Some of the Crisp newspapers spoofed at this comparison, and the *Vienna News* stated that the *Journal* must be joking.

If Russell had listened to the national and Georgia press, he would have conceded early in the campaign. The *Atlanta Constitution*, the *Macon Telegraph*, the *Savannah Morning News*, the *Valdosta Daily Times*, and papers from smaller communities such as Vienna, Gainesville, and Albany all backed Crisp. These papers argued that Crisp was experienced, knowledgeable, and a man of excellent character. They also believed that he was sound on the issues. In short, he was presented as simply being better qualified for the U.S. Senate than Russell. Furthermore, the pro-Crisp local press took pride in the fact that many of the large national publications favored Crisp. The *Atlanta Constitution* carried a front-page story on August 1 announcing, "Papers of Nation

Urge Georgians to Elect Crisp." Among the publications favoring Crisp were the *New York Times*, the *Washington Post*, the *Washington Herald*, *Collier's*, *Time*, and many others.

A predominantly unfriendly press did not daunt Russell. He actually turned the support of Crisp by northern papers to his own advantage. He charged that these papers backed Crisp because they were under the influence of the power trust and other special interests. Georgia voters, the governor intimated, would not be told how to vote by outsiders.[37]

The editors of newspapers supporting Crisp not only related the virtues of their candidate but attacked Russell sharply. The *Macon Telegraph* accused him of "demogoguery and ignorance," of prejudice, and of carrying on a rancorous campaign. The *Greensboro Herald Journal* called Russell two-faced because he claimed to represent the common man whereas really he was aligned with the power and fertilizer corporations. As more and more editors attacked Russell, he dismissed their criticisms by saying that the newspapers had been bought by special interests.[38]

The *Augusta Chronicle*, the *Atlanta Journal*, and the *Columbus Ledger* were the only major daily papers that supported Russell. Many of the small, rural newspapers, however, backed the governor. The editors of these papers pictured Russell as a man who had kept his promises and who worked for the interests of the little man. He did not sit up all night, wrote the editor of the *Pembroke Journal* on June 24, "figuring out tax schedules with the aid of public utility magnates, fertilizer trust heads and other large corporations." Another writer stated that, while Russell might not be a "towering statesman," his heart was with the common people.[39]

Although much of the state's press was not enthusiastic about Russell, organized labor gave him its full support. George L. Googe, head of the American Federation of Labor (AFL) in Georgia, urged workers throughout the state to vote for Russell. Googe, who had backed the governor in 1930, was on a "Dear Dick" basis with Russell and campaigned hard for him. He also convinced William Green, national president of the AFL, to endorse Russell. On August 8, Green assured Googe that his organization would cooperate with unions in Georgia to push Russell's candidacy. Green sent a letter favoring Russell to the Atlanta Federation of Trades, which distributed it among labor groups.[40] The Railroad Brotherhoods also supported the governor in Macon and other railroad towns. An unsigned letter of August 3 from the Brotherhoods' office in Macon to all local unions said that Russell had "always been friendly to our interest," while Crisp was a supporter of "organized capital and capital's interest."[41]

On September 6, *Labor*, the AFL paper published in Washington, devoted a special four-page issue to Russell's election. The headline was "Georgia Voters Should Send Governor R. B. Russell Jr. to Senate." Filled with favorable articles about Russell, the paper portrayed him as a loyal friend of labor, the farmer, and the common man in general. One article emphasized that Russell favored tighter immigration restrictions, which would help domestic workers by keeping out foreign immigrants, who competed for jobs. In the days just before the election, bundles of these papers were sent by railway express to scores of towns for local distribution. Although the organized labor vote was not large in Georgia in the early 1930s, workers made up a special group that concentrated its vote for the governor.

As the campaign heated up in early August, Russell challenged Crisp to a series of debates, one in each congressional district. When Crisp refused to accept the challenge, Russell declared that the congressman was afraid he would not be able to defend his own record. Crisp's refusal to debate was undoubtedly wise. He would have been no match for Russell on the platform. However, his unwillingness to meet Russell in a public forum gave the governor further opportunity to present Crisp as a public servant who feared to face up to his own political record.[42]

Increasingly, Russell presented himself as a progressive in contrast to his reactionary opponent. On August 31, he wrote that "my candidacy represents the fight of the average man against big vested interests, who seek in every way to come into absolute control of our government." Russell kept hammering away at the special and privileged classes. He stated that it was time for new blood and progressive ideas in Washington and charged that the depression had been caused by preferential laws that helped large interests at the expense of the common man.[43]

At Ocilla on July 23, he spoke of the hungry and naked in the midst of plenty. Russell blasted those who were exploiting ordinary citizens. Turning to history, as he often did, he said that Thomas Jefferson would be distressed at a system that placed "a millstone around the necks of the masses," that George Washington would be grieved to see farmers lose their struggle against a vicious system, and that Andrew Jackson would curse taxes that supported a wasteful government. Russell's speeches were full of language made familiar by early twentieth-century progressives. His talks were salted with references to discriminatory legislation, the struggling masses, international bankers, interlocking economic interests, watered stocks, and inefficient government. He also criticized the urban press, which he believed abused and insulted the South.

If it hadn't been for Russell's good luck, his campaign could have ended suddenly and tragically on August 20. On his way to a speaking engagement near Dublin, his car had to swerve off the road to avoid hitting an approaching vehicle head-on. Russell was thrown into the windshield. He lost four front teeth and suffered from cuts and bruises. After being treated by a local dentist, he continued his speaking schedule. His friends even used this incident to attract votes. The *Augusta Chronicle* referred to the governor as "a man of destiny" who led a charmed life for a career "of even greater usefulness to this state."[44]

Another dramatic event in the campaign occurred at Savannah. A large group had gathered in the Municipal Auditorium to hear Russell speak on the evening of September 9. Walter C. Hartridge, solicitor general and president of the Chatham County Russell Club, finished his introduction of the governor and, visibly ill, walked off the stage where he dropped dead of a heart attack. Russell had started to speak, but when he was notified of the tragedy, he promptly adjourned the meeting.[45]

By the end of August, the campaign had become one of charges and countercharges. Much of the discussion by both candidates and many of their supporters had nothing to do with the issues. The Crisp newspapers blamed Russell for staging a mudslinging campaign and dragging the contest into the political mire. But neither side had a monopoly on low-level politics as the accusations flew back and forth.

Russell's backers had always tried to present him as a clean, honest, sincere young man who had only the peoples' interests at heart. Crisp's spokesmen set out to destroy that image. They accused Russell of selling the Senate seat to John Cohen in return for support of the *Atlanta Journal*. Opponents also charged that the governor had obligations to the power companies and that members of the Spalding law firm, who had handled some Georgia Power Company business, had made large contributions to the Russell campaign. Critics portrayed Russell as overly ambitious and somewhat reckless. Crisp even declared that Russell was running for the Senate in order to bail out of a failed gubernatorial administration. He was accused of establishing a "political tyranny" in the state, and one opponent called Russell a "pinhead politician."[46]

Russell had no problem holding his own in a campaign that deteriorated in some cases to the ridiculous. He charged that Crisp had abused his franking privilege, that he kept relatives on his payroll in Washington, and that he had voted against woman suffrage in 1919. Russell also skillfully turned issues against his opponent. For example, Crisp charged once again that University of Georgia alumni were lined up for their former classmate. He explained that he had been too poor to attend college, but he was willing for all the college-educated people to vote for Russell. He would be content with the support of the plain people who had never had an opportunity for higher education. Russell took this opportunity to take a sharp swipe at his opponent. Dick stated that the reason Crisp had passed up college was not because he was so poor but because "he just couldn't wait to get on the public payroll." Crisp had begun government service as a clerk in his father's congressional office.[47]

A high point in the acrimony was reached when Crisp claimed that it would be better to send a married man to Washington because, with a wife, he would be better cared for. A bachelor such as Russell, Crisp said, "without any one to look after him, will be running around loose up there."[48] Apparently Crisp believed that the attractions of Washington would distract a single man from his official senatorial duties.

Crisp hoped that his wife would be a political asset, and he arranged for Jennie, his spouse, to address the state's voters on the eve of the election. Jennie explained that she had been deeply hurt by the attacks on her husband and claimed that he would be a good senator. To prove the family's plebeian attitudes, a report circulated that Jennie would continue to do her own housework if her husband were elected.[49]

In the closing days of the campaign, the Russell organization worked very hard to contact people and to get out the vote. On September 9, Robert Russell mailed out hundreds of "Dear Friend" letters. He explained that there was not enough time or money to send personal letters to all of the governor's friends, but, he wrote, "please consider this as a direct personal message." He urged all Russell backers to use their influence right down to voting time on September 14. Campaign workers inserted a special notice in the letters announcing that Russell would speak over statewide radio from 7:00 to 7:30 P.M. on election eve. Robert Russell also advised friends to station poll watchers at the voting places and to have automobiles available to take voters to the polls. He left little or nothing to chance.

Meanwhile, John A. Sibley, one of the state's leading attorneys in Atlanta, agreed to speak for Russell on the radio on September 12. Sibley said that the governor was "able, experienced and independent," and he praised Russell's youth, vigor, and sound judgment, calling him a "master of the art of statecraft."[50] On the evening before the election, as Crisp talked to his supporters in Macon, Russell made his final appeal to voters over WSB radio in Atlanta. It was then up to the voters.

Up until the end of the campaign, Crisp supporters confidently predicted victory. The *New York Times* and other out-of-state newspapers also believed that he would win. But on September 14, Russell's vote stunned Crisp's supporters. It was another runaway victory for the governor. He received 162,745 popular votes to only 119,193 for Crisp, or a majority of 58 percent. His triumph was even greater in the county unit vote where he carried 296 compared to Crisp's 114, or about 72 percent of the total.[51]

What accounted for Russell's massive victory against such formidable opposition? In general it can be said that many of the same factors worked in his favor in 1932 that had helped him win the race for governor two years earlier. The statewide network of Russell friends was probably his most important asset. His school, university, and fraternity friends, as well as others, were especially active in his behalf. Moreover, Russell and his friends confined their efforts to only the Russell campaign. Other office seekers who solicited Russell's help were told that "the only campaign I'm interested in is that of Dick Russell for the United States Senate. All I can do is wish your campaign well."[52] This approach, which had worked so successfully in 1930, permitted Russell to concentrate on his own campaign and be viewed as entirely evenhanded by all other candidates.

Many of his most vigorous backers were members of the legislature, whose influence helped Russell carry the county unit vote. Furthermore, Robert Russell skillfully managed the campaign, which was also adequately financed. Although the governor tried to convey the idea that his was a kind of "shoestring" operation, such was not the case. He raised some $12,000 in campaign funds, much of it from Atlanta businessmen. About one-fourth of this amount came from the Spalding family, Senator John Cohen, and banker J. D. Robinson.[53] Although Russell probably had as many supporters from the business community as Crisp, the congressman's valiant efforts to tar Russell with big business connections did not succeed.

Russell also gained the upper hand on the issues, in as far as they played a decisive part in the campaign. More important, however, Russell won the battle of public perceptions. The governor was very successful in identifying Crisp with the failures of the Hoover administration and associating him with the special interests that Russell charged had pushed the country to the brink of economic ruin. As Russell kept hammering away at his opponent's purported ties to the power companies, Crisp struggled unsuccessfully to remove the big business stigma. It was not that Russell advocated more popular issues than Crisp. Russell built up an image of the congressman that caused people to view him as not only being tied to special interests but also old, tired, and reactionary. On the other hand, Russell presented himself as a young, energetic progressive and a man with new ideas who could work effectively with other progressives like Roosevelt. Much of politics is image, and Russell easily succeeded at creating the most popular image. He actually staged a kind of populist campaign that in 1932 found a warm response with a large majority of white Georgians.

Russell's personality, his speaking ability, and his hard campaigning also played an important part in his victory. The last two or three weeks of the campaign found Russell making sixteen to eighteen speeches a week, plus talking with many individuals and small groups. Crisp simply could not keep up with such a pace. He usually made eight to twelve talks a week. The *Columbus Ledger* editorialized that Russell's oratorical talent was a definite plus for the governor.[54] He also used the radio effectively.

There was another issue that was seldom mentioned but that prayed on the minds of many North Georgians. That was the sectional issue. It had been a kind of unwritten custom to elect one senator from North Georgia and one from the southern part of the state. The election of Crisp would have given South Georgia two senators, actually from adjoining counties: Crisp from Americus and Walter George from Vienna. The *Columbus Ledger* suggested as early as April 21, even before Russell announced, that the new senator should come from North Georgia. This implied that the paper would support Russell, which it did, but it also reflected a political reality for many people. The *Carroll County Times* went as far as to say that Crisp had violated a general understanding that the north and south would each have a senator.[55]

The best explanation of Russell's triumph was that, overall, he was an exceptionally skillful politician. William King Meadow, a close friend and supporter, said of him: "Dick Russell had the most sincere method of making his pitch to the public that I have ever heard. He had a note of sincerity that the average politician doesn't have. He was one of the best campaigners I have ever known."[56]

Following the election, the newspapers that had favored Crisp grumbled and complained that the best man had lost. They, nevertheless, wished Russell well. The *New York Times* editorialized that Crisp should have won and explained the result by saying there was "a southern political custom of setting up a State idol and changing him from one office to another according to his whim."[57] This was more sour grapes than realistic analysis, but it was true that Russell was closer to a political idol than anyone else in twentieth-century Georgia politics. He had carefully planned his political career over at least a dozen years, and the voters made those plans come true in a way far beyond what either Dick or his father could have hoped for.

Hundreds of congratulatory letters and telegrams poured into the governor's office after the election. Russell acknowledged these with a form letter that was individually typed and signed so that it appeared to be a personal note. He addressed his closer friends and associates by their first names, but to people he did not know very well, he was more formal. Russell never assumed a closeness to individuals by using their first names when in fact they were strangers or known only slightly. These friendly "thank you" letters did much to hold and deepen Russell's political support. Recipients were proud of their letters signed "Dick Russell."

Between his nomination and election, and his leaving for Washington some four months later, Russell dealt with the usual administration of state government. Before the November election, in which he had no opposition, he made some speeches for Roosevelt and the Democratic party. He was pleased when the voters approved the constitutional amendment permitting members of the legislature and the new governor, Eugene Talmadge, to take office in January instead of June. Late in November, he spoke to the Atlanta Woman's Club, where the ladies gave him a standing ovation. Only one woman, Ina Russell, did not rise when the governor was introduced. Not recognizing the governor's mother, a woman next to her turned in surprise and asked, "Don't you stand up for the Governor?" "No," Mrs. Russell replied, "I'm not getting up for him. I had to get up too much for him when he was a baby."[58]

The Russells had a large family Christmas at the mansion. Several of the children were home, including Ina from Washington, Henry Edward who was a student at the Columbia Theological Seminary, Alex who was in medical school at Emory, Carolyn who was a student at Agnes Scott College, Fielding and his wife, William, and the Robert Russells. It was the kind of family gathering loved so much by Judge and Ina Russell. For Dick, too, these were among the happiest times of his life.

Soon after Christmas, the Russells prepared to leave the governor's mansion so that Governor-elect Talmadge and his family could move in. They did not return immediately to Winder. Since Alex and Carolyn were both in school in Atlanta, the family moved to the apartment maintained by Judge Russell at 1198 Piedmont Avenue and remained there until school was out in June. When asked where Dick would live when he was not in Washington, Mrs. Russell replied that he would be at home in Winder "for he is happier there than anywhere else."[59] She understood her eldest son well.

Mrs. Talmadge later declared that the Russells had left the mansion in a mess. She said that the entire place, inside and out, had been permitted to deteriorate. She blamed it on the fact that Russell was a bachelor and had no one to care for the place.[60] Of course, Dick's mother supervised what went on at the mansion during his administration, but the problem was that Russell did not want to spend anything for maintenance. Ina Russell recalled later that she had to approach the Russell staff on the sly to get any money for upkeep and repairs. Since the state's finances were in such bad shape, Dick believed that such expenditures could be postponed.

Monday, January 9, was Russell's last day in the governor's office. Late in the afternoon, he walked up to the state treasurer's office to collect his nine and a half days' pay for January. It amounted to $191.62. Several legislators were also in the office collecting mileage expenses. Russell chatted with these friends and acquaintances, shook hands, and wistfully said that he "was going to miss all this." He mentioned that the forthcoming session of the state legislature would be the first one he had missed in thirteen years. It was a nostalgic time. But then looking ahead, Russell remarked that he had to buy a trunk to get ready to leave for Washington the next day. He paid $37.50 for his trunk and $45.00 for a new suit.[61]

On January 10, before leaving for Washington, Russell appeared before a joint session of the state legislature to give an account of his stewardship and to provide advice for the future. He had prepared a fairly long address. At the outset, Russell reviewed the extremely poor condition of agriculture and stressed how important farmers were to the nation's economy. There could never be any real prosperity in the United States, he said, "until the buying power of the farmer is restored and he is enabled to earn an income commensurate with his importance in our scheme of life." Having made that point, he then reviewed the accomplishments of his administration. He discussed government reorganization, the public school system, taxes, and the progress made in highway construction. His principal theme, however, was that the state must practice "rigid economy" and balance expenditures with income. Turning to other matters, he proudly declared that there had not been a single lynching in Georgia during his administration. Georgians, he concluded, had been tried by adversity and disaster, but he hoped that they could reach "into the recesses of the past and refresh and sustain ourselves with the unconquerable determination of those who overcame apparently insurmountable obstacles as they pressed forward in the building of the civilization we enjoy today." With that, Dick Russell completed his responsibilities as Georgia's sixty-third governor.[62]

7

Russell Goes to Washington

===

On Tuesday evening, January 10, 1933, Russell and a large group of his friends boarded the train in Atlanta for Washington. Among those making the trip to see the new senator sworn in were Russell's brother Robert, Jud Wilhoit, Lawrence Camp, Spence Grayson, and a number of other close personal and political friends. Waiting at the station in Washington the following morning to greet the Russell party were Senator Cohen and two of Dick's sisters, Ina D. Russell, a Washington attorney, and Mrs. Harriette Russell Sharpton. Later in the day, he was assigned to Room 439 in the Senate Office Building. Meanwhile, he had obtained living quarters in the Hamilton Hotel where he would live for the next several years.

Shortly after noon the next day, January 12, Georgia's other senator, Walter F. George, escorted Russell down the aisle for the swearing-in ceremony. Vice President Charles Curtis administered the oath of office. Several senators extended their congratulations, while friends and relatives looked on proudly from the gallery. By becoming a member of the Senate early in January, Russell gained seniority over other newly elected colleagues who would be sworn in on March 4 at the beginning of the new Congress.

Immediately after the ceremony, Senator Cohen held a luncheon for Russell, the Georgia congressional delegation, Dick's friends from Georgia, and several relatives. Senator Cohen welcomed Russell and praised his political record. Russell responded by expressing a deep feeling of humility. He stated that he had "come to the greatest deliberative body in the world, from the greatest state in the world whose people are the best . . . in the world, and I am surrounded here by many of the best friends I have in the world."[1]

Russell had his office staff in place and ready to begin work immediately. Leeman Anderson came to Washington with him from the governor's office to become his principal assistant. Harriet Taylor who had also worked for Russell in Atlanta joined his Washington staff. Russell also retained two secretaries who had worked for Cohen—Julia Harris, daughter of the deceased senator, and Edna P. Rousseau. Those were the days of small office staffs in Washington when a senator might operate with a personnel budget, including his own salary, of around $20,000 a year. Anderson's annual base salary was $3,900, but it soon fell to $3,315 when an economy-minded Congress reduced federal pay. After Congress cut federal salaries, the total payroll of Russell's staff was only $9,460 a year.[2] Senators received $10,000.

When Russell took his seat in the Senate in January 1933, he had just passed his thirty-fifth birthday and was the youngest man in that body. As the press put it, he replaced Senator Robert M. LaFollette, Jr., of Wisconsin as the "baby" of the Senate. LaFollette was thirty-eight. The *Atlanta Journal* carried a front-page picture of LaFollette shaking Russell's hand and turning his title over to the younger Georgian.

Since much of the important work in Congress was done in committees, Russell sought appointment to those that would accommodate his interests and also exert power. The Senate Appropriations Committee was perhaps the most powerful of all committees. When Senator Joseph T. Robinson of Arkansas, the majority leader, asked Russell about his committee preferences, Russell somewhat brashly replied, "Well, Senator, I want to be on the Appropriations Committee." A little surprised that a new senator would ask to be appointed to such an important committee, Robinson explained that a senator usually had to serve four or five years before he could expect to get on that committee. Russell, familiar with Senate practices, was not daunted by this explanation. He told Robinson that he would rather not be on any committee if he could not be appointed to the Appropriations Committee. Senator Harris had been on that committee, Russell said, and the people of Georgia expected him to have the same assignment. Robinson mistakenly interpreted Russell's position as reflecting a radicalism and independence that he did not possess. At that time, Senator Huey Long was raising a ruckus in Democratic ranks by pushing proposals far more radical than Roosevelt or the majority of Democrats favored. It was rumored that Robinson feared Russell might join Long. To discourage that possibility, he met Russell's request. Russell officially became a member of the committee on March 9, 1933. Out of fourteen Democrats on the Appropriations Committee, Russell was fifth from last in seniority.

Russell also received appointments to the committees on naval affairs, immigration, and manufactures. He had been interested in the navy since his brief service in 1918 and at one time had actually considered going to the U.S. Naval Academy. His uncle, Captain Robert L. Russell, had been a career naval officer, and over the years, Dick had maintained an interest in naval matters. Immigration was also an important concern to Georgia's new senator. He had favored the restrictive immigration legislation of the 1920s because he feared that the increasing numbers of southern and eastern Europeans, Latin Americans, and Orientals who had reached American shores before World War I posed a threat to the permanent dominance of Anglo-Saxon culture in the United States.[3]

During his first year in the Senate, Russell received the appointment as chairman of the subcommittee on agricultural appropriations. Carter Glass, chairman of the Appropriations Committee, named Russell to this post not only because he thought Russell was capable but also because he did not want South Carolina's cantankerous Ellison D. "Cotton Ed" Smith to have it. "Old Ed Smith thinks he's gonna get it, but he's not worth a damn and I'm not going to give it to him," Russell recalled Glass saying.[4] Russell was now in a position to cast great influence over agricultural legislation. His subcommittee held hearings on all appropriation bills for the Department of Agriculture, including agricultural research, cooperative extension, the experiment stations, soil conservation, money for the office of secretary of agriculture, and other purposes. Most senators had large agricultural constituencies in the 1930s and made many requests for funds to support local projects. It was virtually impossible to incorporate funds for these local interests into the agricultural appropriation bill without Russell's help. As a result, he built up many obligations from fellow senators by approving their requests for special appropriations. While he did not always get his way on these money matters, he gradually gained tremendous power in the area of farm legislation and services to agriculture.

Between the time he was sworn in on January 12, 1933, and Roosevelt's inauguration on March 4, Russell spent much of his time learning about the Senate. He believed that knowledge was power and set out to learn the minutest details about the Senate's rules, procedures, and traditions. Despite his relative youth and lack of experience in the federal government, he quickly gained the reputation among his colleagues of being an expert parliamentarian.

During his first weeks in Washington, Russell received scores of invitations to speak and to attend social functions. He often received tickets to events. While Russell attended a few dinners and parties, he turned down many invitations with the excuse that pressing congressional duties would not permit his attendance. He wrote his mother that he was keeping acceptances "to a minimum as I have to work late nearly everyday." It was not only a matter of time, however; Russell disliked large social affairs. He much preferred visiting with individuals or small groups where there was opportunity for relaxed conversation. So he easily found excuses for not attending social affairs, and the tickets to various special events lay unused in his files.[5]

At the outset of his long career in Washington, Russell consciously decided that he would be a workhorse rather than a showhorse. Moreover, he would do most of his work quietly and behind the scenes. One approach to being a senator was to seek influence through speaking and public activity. These senators appealed to audiences outside the institution of the Senate to achieve their personal and political goals. They hoped to influence policy by speaking to national and even international audiences. The man who best exemplified this type of senator, in a somewhat extreme form, was Huey P. Long of Louisiana. Long talked to the nation about the poor and the disadvantaged, and he hoped that popular opinion would force Congress to act on these matters. Other senators sought to increase their power and influence by working mainly within the confines of the Senate institution. They worked behind the scenes where they quietly decided on goals and strategy, and they generally controlled the actions of the Senate. They won their objectives through quiet negotiation, through building up obligations from colleagues, and by being informed on the issues at stake. Russell fell naturally into this latter group.

Russell had never been one to get out too far in advance on an issue. He had skillfully avoided that approach as a state legislator. He tended to take a firm stand on a public question only after it had been thrashed out by others and a kind of consensus had developed. What he did as governor was to crystallize and mobilize sentiment that already existed on important issues. After he went to the Senate, Russell operated as he had in the state legislature and as governor—quietly and mainly out of the public eye. His office, a committee room, the Senate cloakroom, or the dining room were the places where he usually did business, not the Senate chamber or the public press.

Russell had always held firmly to one principle—a political leader should be informed. He had little patience with colleagues who did not know the facts regarding a particular piece of legislation or the rules of the Senate. In order to be fully informed, Russell studied the bills and committee hearings, and he reputedly read the entire *Congressional Record* daily. Being free from family responsibilities and maintaining a fairly low social profile, Russell had more time for Senate work than most of his colleagues. He also had the advantage of being a rapid reader and of remembering what he read. Armed with a battery of information, Russell quickly won the reputation among his colleagues of knowing what he was talking about. When he spoke to them as individuals or in small groups, they listened.

During his first few years in Washington, Russell made few speeches on the Senate floor. He was a skilled debater, and occasionally he made a fellow senator cringe with a polite but cutting remark, but Russell relied mainly on developing personal relationships to increase his influence. He worked within the Senate establishment, or the inner circle, where he eventually earned the position of central character of that group. Writing in the middle 1950s, after Russell had been in the Senate for some twenty years, William S. White stated that he was "incomparably the truest current Senate type, and incomparably the most influential man on the inner life of the Senate." As a result, he became known among many as a real senator's senator.[6] The principles that Russell scrupulously adhered to in his relations with other people and that contributed to his successful Senate career were his integrity, his fairness, his willingness to accommodate colleagues when possible, and his practice of maintaining confidences.

When President Franklin D. Roosevelt launched his New Deal in March 1933, he had a staunch backer in the new senator from Georgia. Russell had come to know Roosevelt quite well personally as a result of visits to Warm Springs. He campaigned for him in 1932. Furthermore, Russell agreed with the president's proposals to use the federal government to solve some of the problems facing a depression-ridden nation. Russell linked his own campaign with that of Roosevelt by pointing out that both men talked about the need for a progressive program and the defeat of reactionaries and special interests.

What kind of a progressive was Richard Russell? Or was he a progressive at all? Up to the beginning of the depression in 1930, Russell's progressivism had not advanced beyond support for efficiency in government, economy, and fairness in taxation. As a state political leader, he had considered government's responsibility to be confined to promoting education, highways, and a limited amount of social services.

As the depression grew worse and human suffering increased, Russell began to advocate a greater role for the federal government. During 1931 and 1932, he urged the appropriation of federal funds for relief and road building to create needed employment. Russell, like Roosevelt, was very much a pragmatist. His attitude toward government action was determined by how he perceived the country's economic condition. "If the country is in bad shape, why I'll resort to drastic means," he said years later. "If the country's in good shape, I don't see any necessity for tinkering with the system."[7] Some politicians later expressed this idea by the attitude, "If it isn't broken, don't fix it." One thing was certain. Russell did not believe in changing the nation's basic economic system. He believed in a capitalistic economy, the profit system, and individual initiative. But in 1932 and 1933, he thought that the system had been thrown out of kilter by powerful special interests, and he supported the idea of the federal government righting wrongs inflicted on farmers, workers, bank depositors, and others who suffered from the depression.

If New Deal progressivism can be defined as an expansion of federal powers to serve the people and to regulate predatory interests without calling for fundamental institutional change, then Russell was a true and reliable progressive when he arrived in Washington. In his desire to do something to restore the economy in 1933, Russell was as much of a New Dealer as Roosevelt.

Consequently, Russell went along with most of Roosevelt's program during the famous Hundred Days during which nearly all the initial New Deal legislation was passed. He voted for the Emergency Banking Act, for relief, for the reduction of federal salaries, for the Agricultural Adjustment Act, for establishing the Tennessee Valley Authority (TVA), and for the National Industrial Recovery Act. Russell also strongly favored setting up such programs as the Civilian Conservation Corps. He did not completely agree with some measures but voted for them after considering conditions. For example, he explained to one constituent that he was not entirely satisfied with the Emergency Banking Act, but he thought it was probably the best that Congress could offer in the emergency. He confided to his mother that "there has been no time to quibble over details." Initially, Russell had some reservations about federally guaranteed bank deposits, but in the end, he supported the legislation.[8] His only vote against a major New Deal measure involved the bill to legalize and tax beer. Russell never explained his "nay" vote, but he may have agreed with Senator Tom Connally of Texas who opposed the bill because he considered beer intoxicating. Until the Eighteenth Amendment was repealed, Connally said, he could not vote for the legalization of beer. It is certain that the reason Russell voted against the legalization of beer was not because he opposed drinking. No one enjoyed a drink of whiskey more than Russell.[9]

Unlike some of his more experienced colleagues, Russell had no complaint about the speed with which legislation sailed through Congress. Senator Peter Norbeck, South Dakota's progressive Republican who was in his third term, was overwhelmed by such rapid action by the most deliberative legislative body in the world.[10] A great majority of legislators on both sides of the aisle, however, placed their faith in Roosevelt during those early hectic months and voted for the president's programs. Although Russell knew Roosevelt better than most of his colleagues, he was not a New Deal insider. He was simply there to help when he was needed, which he did in a quiet, unobtrusive manner.

Russell's lack of personal contact with Roosevelt in Washington during the early New Deal days was illustrated by the senator's story about a late evening telephone call from the president. About midnight the phone rang in Russell's room at the Hamilton Hotel. He picked up the receiver, and a voice said, "This is Frank Roosevelt." Not fully awake, Russell thought it was a joke and replied, "This is the Pope and I haven't time to talk to you," after which he hung up. Two or three minutes later, the phone rang again and a White House staffer asked, "Senator, did you realize that you hung up in the President's face?" Much embarrassed, Russell explained that he thought the call had been from a prankster. In any event, the incident shows that a call from Roosevelt was so unexpected that it was nearly unthinkable. In January 1934, after being in Washington a year, Russell wrote his mother that he had seen Roosevelt only three or four times.

The early New Deal had its share of critics who charged that the president was becoming a dictator and that his programs were radical, un-American, and even communistic. Russell considered such accusations ridiculous. He praised Roosevelt's leadership and the New Deal legislation. There was scarcely a more ardent defender of Roosevelt than Dick Russell. During 1933 and 1934, he made a number of strong speeches supporting the president and the economic changes he was bringing about.

Speaking to the Sigma Delta Kappa legal fraternity in the spring of 1933, Russell said that people could not yet appreciate the great effect of the New Deal on the "entire legal, commercial, industrial and social life of the nation." Displaying his sense and knowledge of history, he explained that it would be several decades before people would understand "how momentous and far reaching these changes have been." Then he praised farm, work relief, and other legislation designed to help the people. The "disciples of the do-nothing doctrine," he said, were crying out against the president and claiming to see approaching dictatorship in Washington. Such charges were silly. He explained that the present must be reconciled to the "requirements of the future." He insisted that "a poverty-stricken and long-suffering people have turned to their government for relief, and they are in no mood to see the arms of the liberating influences designed to relieve them bound by fine-spun [legal] technicalities." Russell may have regretted having expressed such thoughts when he got in the middle of the civil rights fight a few years later.

On September 2, 1933, he addressed an American Legion meeting in Blue Ridge, Georgia, and argued that "individualism" must be "secondary to the general welfare" during the present period of national emergency. While he did not agree with all of the details of the recovery program, he supported the president. Using language appropriate for legionnaires, Russell said that "when the great commander arranged the plan of battle," everyone "must pull together." Four days later, he spoke to a gathering of twelve hundred postal clerks in Atlanta, where he observed that criticism of Roosevelt was coming from both the left and the right. But the New Deal was not communism or socialism. The Roosevelt legislation was "a pattern of one great scheme to make a government of, by and for the people and not for privileged interests."[11] Russell was not a lukewarm New Dealer but a committed disciple. His views in 1933 or 1934 reflected some of the best in the twentieth-century liberal tradition.

Patronage was one of the most bothersome problems facing congressmen and senators during the depression. Russell received many requests for jobs, even before he went to Washington, and the number kept increasing. Writing to his mother at 7:30 P.M. after a hard day on April 22, 1933, Russell explained that if he wrote to, or visited with, everyone seeking help to get a job, he could never get to his Senate business. He despaired of getting home for a few days because he did not have the courage, he said, to face the three hundred people who had asked to see him about jobs when he returned to Winder. In another letter to his mother, he said, "This question of getting places for people is an awful one."

Many of these pleas for help came from close friends who wanted an appointment for themselves or for a friend. Russell helped when he could, but he had to deny the great majority of requests. For example, he even had to tell Hugh Peterson, his brother-in-law, that he could not support a mutual friend for assistant district attorney in Georgia's Southern District. He told Peterson that he was already committed and could "not sponsor the application of any additional friends."[12]

Russell managed quite successfully to keep demands and controversies over patronage from hurting him politically. His policy of not promising anyone a job in return for political support may not have reduced the number of requests, but it did cut commitments and gave him more flexibility in taking care of his friends. Russell usually expressed sympathy and concern to those asking for jobs and promised to keep their interests in mind. Other requests came from local and state officials to help them get support for an armory, a park, river development, or some other project. Russell worked hard to assist these groups, but he was careful not to promise more than he could deliver.[13]

Russell maintained a fairly low profile in the first session of the Seventy-third Congress. The only significant legislative matter that he tackled was the tariff on jute. For several years, he had expressed strong objections to the importation of jute, which competed with cotton. He claimed that jute imports actually replaced from two to three million bales of cotton annually, depressing the price and hurting farmers in Georgia and throughout the South. During the campaign of 1932, he sharply criticized Crisp for not halting jute imports and promised that when he went to Washington he would fight the jute interests.

On April 20, 1933, Russell introduced an amendment to the Agricultural Adjustment Act then under consideration that would grant the secretary of agriculture authority to raise the tariff on jute and its products if he found imports were creating unfair competition for any basic farm commodity. Russell explained to his colleagues that jute was a serious competitor for cotton and that it was produced by "pauper labor" in India. If jute continued to be imported duty free, Russell said, the living standards of cotton farmers would be forced down almost to the levels in India.[14]

The jute interests, however, had strong spokesmen in Congress. Northeastern manufacturers used jute for carpet backing, inner linings for furniture, and other purposes, while potato farmers in Maine and the Northwest used burlap bags for potatoes. Senator David I. Walsh of Massachusetts objected to giving the secretary of agriculture so much power and called the amendment "unsound" legislation. Senator "Cotton Ed" Smith of South Carolina argued that the main bill under consideration already had provisions to protect farmers against such imports, and, moreover, he opposed introducing the tariff question in an agriculture bill.[15] The Senate easily defeated Russell's amendment.

Not everything considered on the Senate floor was as serious to Russell as the debate over a tariff on jute. In May, during a speech in New York, Secretary of Labor Frances Perkins made a statement about the "barefoot South." She declared that if southerners would wear shoes, manufacturers of shoes would have a gold mine. Russell called this a most "ingenuous" plan to lick the depression. Then he tore into Perkins with his typical combination of wit and mild sarcasm. Declaring that he disliked "to remove any windmill on which the distinguished Secretary might splinter a lance," he wanted to assure her that southerners did wear shoes. He announced on the Senate floor that he was inviting the secretary to the South so that she could see the actual conditions. Russell said that when the secretary walked the streets in southern cities, crowds would not gather to "view her leather-clad feet as anything out of the ordinary or as a rare phenomena." She would not, according to Russell, find rural people wriggling their toes in the dirt and city residents exposing the "soles of their bare feet to hot pavements." While Russell delighted in joshing his colleagues on this issue, underneath his humor he resented anything that might be considered an insult to the South.[16]

When the question arose of how the Economy Act would affect veterans, Russell took a strong stand on behalf of servicemen and their dependents. The debate revolved around supporting either a conference report that included a provision that would limit the reduction of veterans' benefits to no more than 25 percent under the Economy Act and place thousands of widows and orphans on benefit rolls or the more generous Cutting-Steiwer amendment that would increase money for veterans by some $125 to $150 million. Russell favored generous treatment of veterans, but he supported the conference report because he believed it was the best legislation that could be obtained. He said that he had learned long ago that it was impossible to write legislation to please everyone but added, "Only through a meeting of the minds and by concessions can we legislate this evening." That was the Russell approach and one that prevailed in this case. Nevertheless, Russell hated to reduce any benefits for veterans. "They have always been my gang," he wrote.[17]

At the end of the first session of the Seventy-third Congress in June 1933, Russell returned home. This was his first chance in six months to get back in personal touch with his constituents. He opened an office in the Federal Building in Atlanta but spent much of his time at home in Winder. He also had a heavy speaking schedule throughout the state. On July 1, he opened the watermelon festival in Moultrie where some ten thousand people had gathered. He reviewed the recent session of Congress, praised Roosevelt, and crowned the watermelon queen. He talked at the state's bicentennial celebration in Savannah on November 18, as well as at a number of other places around the state.[18]

The months between sessions of Congress were not entirely free from official responsibilities. In September 1933, a joint group from the naval affairs committees in the House and Senate accepted an invitation from the secretary of navy, Claude Swanson, to inspect a number of U.S. naval bases. The group left Norfolk, Virginia, on September 9 and made stops in Haiti and the Panama Canal Zone before going on to San Diego where Russell joined his colleagues. He wrote his mother that he was terribly busy either with inspections of naval installations or being "very lavishly entertained." The highlight of the trip was witnessing the operations of the aircraft carrier, *Saratoga*. Russell wrote that the takeoff and landing of seventy-four planes on the ship was the most spectacular sight he had ever seen. Incidentally, this trip with the joint committee was the first time that Dick Russell had ever been west of the Mississippi River.

Russell definitely favored strengthening the U.S. Navy if effective limitations could not be achieved by treaty. At that time, the United States was operating under the London Naval Treaty of 1930. Russell said that when this agreement was reassessed in 1935, if world conditions continued to be unstable and if proper limitations could not be agreed to, the United States "should go right ahead and build the biggest navy in the world."

All, however, was not work on the inspection trip. He visited the Warner Brothers studios and saw several movie stars. Of much greater interest was his weekend visit to the Hearst Castle at San Simeon. Russell was awed by the buildings and furnishings. The place had an "aura of unreality," he wrote. In Seattle the SAE's at the University of Washington entertained him, and he spent a delightful evening visiting with his fraternity brothers.[19]

Russell did enjoy some vacation time both before and after the naval inspection trip. He went to St. Simons Island in July and on the 20th boarded the yacht of Julian Strickland of Valdosta for a three-day cruise with friends. In November he went deer and turkey hunting in southeast Georgia and bagged two turkeys.[20]

Shortly after Russell returned to Washington in January 1934, he was bombarded with requests for help in providing work relief. Beginning in the fall of 1933, the Civil Works Administration (CWA) had provided jobs for hundreds of thousands of people, but early in 1934, officials became frantic at the prospect that the CWA would be terminated. H. W. Nelson of Adel wrote Russell on March 1 that the number of CWA workers had already been cut, and there were then fifteen hundred unemployed in his county. In rural Bacon County, a resident wrote that there were one thousand unemployed and predicted if something were not done, "robbing, stealing and pilfering of all description would occur." Although Russell was deeply sympathetic with the problems people faced, he did not offer help that he could not deliver.[21]

During the second session of the Seventy-third Congress in 1934, Russell continued to give strong support to New Deal measures. He voted for the Gold Reserve Act, the veterans' bonus, the Bankhead Cotton Control Act, the reciprocal tariff legislation, the homeowners' loan bill, and a housing measure. The next year, he went down the line in supporting the Works Progress Administration, the Public Utility Holding Company Act, social security, and higher taxes for the wealthy.[22]

However, Russell did begin to depart from the New Deal on some labor legislation. While he viewed himself as a friend of labor and favored good wages for workers, by 1935 Russell had developed serious reservations about some of the more militant labor leaders such as John L. Lewis and Sidney Hillman. He did not vote on the National Labor Relations Act of 1935 because, as a colleague explained, he was "necessarily detained from the Senate." At the time, Russell was unusually silent on this important legislation. This may have been because he did not favor a law that would strengthen unions led by men such as Lewis and Hillman, but he did not want to weaken the president or the New Deal by open criticism. He quietly voted against the Guffey-Snyder Bituminous Coal Stabilization Act passed in August. This law gave a National Bituminous Coal Commission power to control coal prices as well as hours, wages, and conditions of work in the bituminous mines.[23]

In 1935 when Congress was considering the huge $4.8 billion work relief bill, labor leaders wanted Congress to include a provision that would require the federal government to pay workers in its work relief programs according to prevailing wage rates. These leaders feared that lower pay on government work projects would depress regular wages. Initially, Russell saw the Works Progress Administration as more of a relief effort than a work program. Thus he said that paying prevailing wage rates would not only raise work relief costs but be an insult to those millions of families who had no jobs and were receiving direct relief. The Appropriations Committee became deadlocked on the prevailing rate question.

Russell rescued the legislation by working out an amendment in the Appropriations Committee that gave the president discretionary authority over wage scales on work relief projects. The committee approved his idea by a vote of 14 to 9. Russell assured his colleagues that he did not want to depress wages. "This amendment," he said, "affords ample protection to the existing wage scale, and yet permits the President to place the greatest number in gainful employment." The president could be trusted to defend labor's interests. "He is labor's champion," Russell said. Russell explained that he wanted to protect prevailing wages but that he was "wholly content" to leave the matter in the president's hands. Not all senators had such confidence in Roosevelt, but Russell prevailed. The Senate defeated Senator Pat McCarran's prevailing rate amendment by a vote of 50 to 38 and then approved the Russell proposal 83 to 2.[24]

Describing Russell's role in breaking this legislative logjam, Arthur Krock called him the "hero of the drama" in the Senate. Krock referred to Russell as "a very unobtrusive young man" whose course was marked by independence. While Russell was friendly to the president, who also opposed the prevailing rate idea, Krock viewed him as being about a 75 percent New Dealer. The arguments and events surrounding the prevailing wage controversy provided the first opportunity for Russell to gain substantial publicity and attention for his work in the Senate.

Russell was in Europe when the Fair Labor Standards Act was passed in 1937, but he favored the law.[25] This measure, however, dealt only with wages and hours not with labor organization or power. By that time, Russell was expressing deep concern over strikes and unrest in the ranks of labor, a condition that he blamed mainly on radical labor leaders. He wrote a friend that he and others in Washington were very apprehensive over the sit-down strikes. "My sympathies have always been with the underdog and with labor generally," he wrote in June 1937, "but I am much concerned about the possibilities of labor leaders of the type of [John L.] Lewis controlling all of the labor organizations in the country."[26] There was also another factor lurking in the back of Russell's mind—the role of organized labor in pushing for black rights. He told this same constituent that he opposed violence and disturbances by labor organizations as a means to gain "the ends of minorities employed in industrial plants."

Although by the mid-1930s Russell was beginning to have some reservations about a few aspects of the New Deal, he continued to be an enthusiastic supporter of the president and most of his program. During 1934 and 1935, he spoke frequently and eloquently about the benefits resulting from New Deal legislation. Speaking before a large crowd at Trion, Georgia, on April 22, 1934, he praised the Roosevelt administration for bringing "a square deal for every citizen of the country." He talked about the help that had been offered to farmers and homeowners, about the Civil Works Administration and the Federal Emergency Relief Administration, all of which had brought some $24 million into Georgia to "prime the pump." The charge that the New Deal constituted a radical revolution, he continued, was nonsense. Roosevelt was, indeed, leading a revolution, but it was a peaceful one. The object of the New Deal, Russell stated, was to give everyone who wanted to work a job, a chance. He said that "all this talk of revolution doesn't mean anything to a man who is working and making a living." On July 4, 1934, he spoke to a big crowd at Carrollton and promised that no one would starve as long as there was a single penny in the federal treasury. In November he told an Atlanta audience that "there was no longer any question about turning back to the old order of things, the 'Old Deal.'" People were demanding that the government be used to fight for "social security in times of need" just as it had during the world war.[27]

Russell repeated these themes wherever he appeared. Speaking on June 10, 1935, at Emory University's commencement exercises at which his brother Alex was getting a medical degree, he criticized those who held narrow views of government functions and responsibilities. He attacked those who charged that the New Deal's social and economic programs were threatening individual liberty. If the president and Congress had held to this limited concept of government, he declared, "the only liberty these people would have enjoyed would have been the right to starve undisturbed."[28]

Political conditions at home required that Russell remain informed about his constituents' reaction to the New Deal. With his reelection approaching in 1936, he wanted to make sure that he judged political sentiment accurately. By 1935 Governor Talmadge, who had originally supported Roosevelt, had become one of the nation's most vociferous critics of the New Deal.

Eugene Talmadge was one of the most colorful politicians in Georgia's long history. The son of a farmer, he studied law at the University of Georgia, married a young widow who inherited several hundred acres of land near McRae in South Georgia, and then settled down to farming. In 1926, however, he was elected commissioner of agriculture, and in 1932 he easily won the governorship that Russell had given up for the U.S. Senate. During Talmadge's first term as governor and Russell's early senatorial years, the two men had a rather formal and polite relationship. Their letters on matters of federal and state business began with "My dear Governor" and "My dear Senator." There were no "Dear Gene" or "Dear Dick" salutations.

The strain between Russell and Talmadge should not be surprising because during his first days in office Talmadge had been battered by the Russell forces in state government. Just before leaving the governorship, Russell had sent a number of appointments to the state Senate for confirmation. Talmadge, who wanted to make his own appointments, asked the Senate to return the nominations. The Senate refused his request by the overwhelming vote of 42 to 1. This rebuff reflected what Talmadge's biographer called Russell's "immense" popularity. One state senator observed, "It looks like Dick Russell is still governor of Georgia."[29]

In any event, Talmadge soon convinced many Georgians that he was a Huey Long type of demagogue. Although in private conversation his English and grammar were excellent, when he spoke to farm groups he developed, as one observer wrote, the "choicest eccentricities of grammar, syntax and pronunciation."[30] His hallmark of commonality became red suspenders, which he began wearing in 1934. He fought with the legislature and ran roughshod over several state administrative agencies that refused his demands. On several occasions, he called out the national guard to enforce his will. For example, when the State Highway Department refused to fire several engineers, the governor ordered the troops to seize the department's funds and records and declared martial law. This kind of direct, forceful action, all purportedly for the good of the people, achieved results, but many Georgians were aghast at such actions. Talmadge became especially bitter about the New Deal in 1935 when officials took the administration of relief in Georgia out of his hands and appointed a federal administrator in Atlanta to handle matters. Talmadge was an open and avowed racist, and he expressed deep concern that the New Dealers were placing some blacks in high political office.

By late 1934 and 1935, Talmadge was speaking out sharply against welfare, big government, and the farm program. On October 5, 1934, when the state Democratic party met at Macon, the delegates praised Talmadge and criticized the New Deal. Pro-Talmadge forces cheered loudly when Hugh Howell mentioned that Talmadge should move into a "wider field two years hence." One observer declared that "the 1936 Talmadge-Russell race is on." Later Talmadge angered national party leaders when he tried to organize southern Democrats to block Roosevelt's renomination.[31]

Talmadge was certainly stirring the political pot in Georgia. Russell, however, was convinced that the great majority of Georgians supported the New Deal. In January 1934, he had written his mother that people seemed to have a "blind devotion to the President" that was "without parallel." Then he added that it would be "political suicide to oppose him in any way." So, besides agreeing with Roosevelt's major policies, Russell believed that to support the president was the best politics in Georgia. Therefore, he sought to identify himself as closely as possible with Roosevelt and the New Deal.

Talmadge continued his sharp attacks on the president. On May 7, 1935, he made a nationwide radio address over CBS in Washington, D.C., in which he portrayed the New Deal as an extravagant, wasteful boondoggle and "the largest dole system ever known in the world." On other occasions, he declared that states' rights were being destroyed and that the president was becoming a dictator.[32] If Talmadge became Russell's opponent in the 1936 senatorial election as was widely assumed, the contest would really boil down to a referendum on Roosevelt and the New Deal. If this were to be the case, Russell was prepared to cast his political lot with the president and his progressive economic and social reforms. When fifty thousand people turned out to hear President Roosevelt in Grant Field at Georgia Tech on November 29, 1935, Russell was on the platform.[33]

At Christmas time, he relaxed at home in Winder, and, as he wrote a friend, spent the season reflecting "on the friendships with which I have been blessed and which I warmly cherish." Henry C. Walthour of Savannah had sent him a barrel of oysters, which, Russell wrote, added a great deal to the family festivities on Christmas day. A highlight of the fall was a gift of Douglas Southall Freeman's four-volume biography of Robert E. Lee from Colonel T. L. Huston. Russell told Huston that it would be the "most prized possession in my modest library, treating as it does a subject who had held my life-long admiration and interest."[34] Any extended relaxation, however, was not possible. Besides returning to Washington for the congressional session early in 1936, he was a delegate to the Democratic National Convention in Philadelphia in late June. Mainly, however, he had to focus on his reelection.

Governor Talmadge officially launched his campaign for the U.S. Senate at McRae on July 4, 1936. He held a huge barbecue that brought thousands of people to the park where massive quantities of barbecued pork, beef, lamb, and chicken and Brunswick stew were served. It was the biggest barbecue in Georgia history. Talmadge told the roaring crowd that he would prevent any national debt, reduce the federal budget to no more than $1 billion, and defend states' rights. As he castigated the New Deal, the audience whooped and cheered. That Talmadge could stir the deep emotions of depression-ridden people there was no doubt. He was the special idol of tens of thousands of rural Georgians.[35]

President Franklin D. Roosevelt, at left, and Governor Russell in Atlanta, November 1935. Between the president and Russell are Eleanor Roosevelt and Senator Walter George. (Photo courtesy of Russell Memorial Library, University of Georgia, Athens.)

Russell recognized that he faced a tough race. The flamboyant Talmadge was a hard campaigner and drew large crowds. His anti–New Deal rhetoric struck a responsive chord among many voters. He appealed not only to common people but also to various economic interests that opposed Roosevelt. Some people undoubtedly went to Talmadge rallies out of curiosity, but "Old Gene" had a host of loyal supporters. Russell was aware of this support because he received critical letters from Talmadge backers. One voter told Russell that his mudslinging could never "turn us old farmers against our beloved governor." He added that "we dirt farmers" remain "Talmadge's worshippers 100%." Another critic called Russell a "yellow coward" who was depending on Roosevelt to pull him through the election.[36]

Russell developed a six-point strategy for his reelection campaign. First, he supported and defended Roosevelt and the New Deal. Second, he organized his friends and supporters as he had done so successfully in previous campaigns. Third, the Russell campaigners used every means of publicity to spread the views of their candidate—speeches, fliers, posters, advertisements, and form letters. Fourth, every effort would be made to "single-shot" Russell. Ed Dunlap of Atlanta advised in a July strategy memo that Russell's friends not get mixed up in other races. Fifth, Russell and his backers set out to picture Talmadge as an erratic, irresponsible demagogue. And sixth, Russell himself would carry on a whirlwind campaign in every part of the state. Marion Allen served as Russell's campaign manager, and his brother Robert Russell again played a key role in managing Dick's reelection.

Russell opened his campaign at Waycross on July 8 just a few days after the big Talmadge barbecue. He began his talk by praising Roosevelt and pointing out how much better off people were then than in 1932 and 1933, and he emphasized how important New Deal agricultural policies were to Georgia farmers. Russell told his listeners that they should vote for him if they wanted a senator who would "keep on trying to give the farmer and his family a fighting chance" in the future. Denying that he was nothing but a stooge and rubber stamp for Roosevelt, Russell said he took pride in his support of the president. He offered no apology, he added, for being "loyal to Roosevelt and the National Democratic Party." He claimed that his and Roosevelt's philosophies were the same—they believed it was "the duty of government to protect and aid the average man." Russell stated that he had worked for this objective ever since he began his public career. It took no dictation from the president, he continued, to get him to support laws that would save farmers and homeowners, insure bank deposits, and control the manipulations of Wall Street. He said that he was proud to vote for bills that told the "gang in Wall Street where to get off." A vote for Russell, he said, would be a vote for "progressive government."[37]

In speech after speech, Russell stressed what he had done for farmers, senior citizens, labor, veterans, and others. One of his most effective tactics was to find out from local officials how much federal money had been spent in their particular county and then use the information in his speeches in that community. By August Russell was making six, seven, or eight speeches and traveling hundreds of miles a week. It was a hectic pace. Most of his main talks were broadcast over the radio. His campaign headquarters sent out thousands of cards announcing when and where Russell would talk and indicating whether the speech would be broadcast on the radio. The 1936 campaign was the first political contest in Georgia in which candidates used the radio extensively.

The Russell forces also distributed fliers, mailed out thousands of mimeographed and personal letters, and printed advertisements. Some of the advertising was extremely clever. For example, on July 31, the *Franklin News and Banner* carried an article on the editorial page with the headline, "Heard County Profits through Government Projects Sponsored by Russell." The article referred to the federal help the county had received for roads, waterworks, a new auditorium, and other purposes. Roosevelt was highly praised as was Russell for helping the president. Appearing very much like an independent editorial, this article was really a paid advertisement with such an inconspicuous label that it could easily be missed by the casual reader.

Russell made every effort to portray Talmadge as a scatterbrained, unreliable, disloyal hypocrite. For a time in 1935, Talmadge had toyed with the idea of running for president on an anti–New Deal, anti-Roosevelt ticket. When support failed to materialize, he tried to get back in the good graces of the Democrats by saying he would support the president when he considered him to be right. But after the flirtation with independent politics, Talmadge was accused of being a disloyal turncoat and party troublemaker. He was also attacked for aiding the Republicans. The Russell forces said that he was aligned with "the [upper] classes, the DuPont dynasty, [and] the big eastern bankers." Moreover, Russell claimed that Talmadge was substituting glib and colorful language for a positive program. Part of a poem written by critics of Talmadge, entitled "Eugene Talmadge," went as follows:

> He's a rattler in the bushes
> A screw worm in a hog;
> Just a twisted, grainless knot
> On a burnt out rotten log.
> He turns his back on Georgia
> Where he gets his bread 'n meat
> He holds one hand on the cotton mills
> And the other on Wall Street

Anti-Talmadge jokes also made the rounds. According to one of these jokes, a Russell supporter says, "I hear that they had a big blowout down at McRae on July 4. They barbecued 150 pigs, 100 cows, 300 chickens, and had 200 bales of hay." A Talmadge supporter asks, "What was the hay for?" The Russell backer replies, "To feed all those jackasses that followed him down there." Another story went that following Talmadge's July 4 speech, a friend declares, "Well, Gene you'll git four votes at my house." Talmadge responds, "John, old boy, I thought there were five votes at your place." The friend explains,

"T'was, Gene, but Bill went to school and got some learnin' and we can't do a damn thing with him."

The Talmadge supporters responded in kind. They distributed one small booklet entitled, "What Senator R. B. Russell, Jr., Did in the United States Senate." Inside, the pages were all blank! Talmadge backers also distributed a flier that listed eight members of Russell's family on government payrolls. According to this information, the Russells had served 219 years in public office and had drawn at least $1 million from taxpayers. "It appears to us as farmers and taxpayers of Georgia that the Counties, State and Federal Governments have supported the Russell family long enough and others should be given a chance to be benefitted."[38]

Although Russell maintained an optimistic front at all times, some of the reports from around the state were not encouraging. On July 20, Thomas J. Hamilton, editor of the *Augusta Chronicle* and a strong Russell supporter, wrote to Marion Allen, Russell's campaign manager, that the "political psychology" was running in Talmadge's favor. Two weeks later, a friend from Valdosta informed Dick that things did not look good for him in that area. "Too many of the farmers fall for what Gene tells them," he wrote.[39]

Reports such as this stimulated the Russell forces to battle all the harder. As had been true in his earlier campaigns, Russell made as many personal contacts as possible. In mid-July he mailed out many letters to friends, which began, "This letter is written to earnestly solicit your very valuable support in my candidacy." Then he expressed appreciation for anything the recipient could do on his behalf. He also solicited advice and suggestions.

Russell's family members again helped with the campaign. Besides the work of Robert in the campaign headquarters, others labored in communities where they had influence. His brother-in-law James H. Bowden, who managed the Federal Reserve office in Savannah, worked among his friends and also raised money for Dick. Bowden wrote that when they got through with Talmadge, "he won't have any rubber left in those red suspenders." Miles Dillard, a cousin who lived in Birmingham, took a leave from his job and returned to his former home in Columbus to work for Russell in southwest Georgia.[40]

Federal employees also came to Russell's aid. Individuals in various U.S. Department of Agriculture offices were extremely loyal. They got useful information for Russell and sometimes made small contributions. A friend of Russell's who was an employee of the Federal Housing

Administration in New Orleans sent a substantial campaign check. Russell wrote that his friend must be clipping coupons or playing the races to make such a generous contribution. An official of the Reconstruction Finance Corporation wrote that he was urging his son in Baxley to do everything possible for Russell, while an appointee of the Security and Exchange Commission pledged his support and that of his family in Carrollton. Congressmen E. E. Cox and M. C. Tarver both campaigned hard for Russell.[41]

This was the first campaign in which Russell needed to raise any sizable amount of money from supporters. In 1930 he and his family provided practically all of his campaign funds, and in 1932 a few wealthy Atlantans supplied most of the money expended in the senatorial contest. Russell quickly discovered in 1936 that many people wanted to contribute small amounts. In early July, contributions began flowing in from all sections of the state. Most of these gifts were for less than $10, and hundreds of them were $1, $2, and $5. Occasionally a supporter would send $50 or $100. A few of his more affluent and closer friends such as Hughes Spalding gave $500. Russell or his staff promptly acknowledged these contributions and usually closed by saying that there would be a hard fight ahead but that the outcome was not in doubt.[42]

Three events occurred during the campaign that greatly helped Russell. At the Georgia Tobacco Festival in Adel on July 31, several leading Democrats gathered in a large tobacco warehouse to talk politics. Senator George strongly endorsed the president and the New Deal, saying that Roosevelt was the "greatest friend of southern agriculture" since the Civil War. While George did not refer to Russell, when he praised the president he implied support for Russell as well.[43]

Talmadge himself opened the way for Russell to skillfully turn a course of events against him. When the governor arrived in Monroe for a speech on August 5, he was accompanied by national guardsmen in plain clothes. A heckler yelled, "Hey, Gene, did you bring along your body guard to protect you in Russell territory?" Although he was only fifteen miles from Winder, Talmadge denied that he needed any protection. Rumors soon spread that the governor was traveling around the state protected by armed guardsmen, which reminded Georgians of Talmadge's summoning the national guard to break strikes and his use of the state military for other purposes. The *Atlanta Constitution* editorialized that "Dictatorship Comes High" and said that such use of the military had not occurred in Georgia since Reconstruction. The paper declared it an "outrage."[44]

Russell quickly turned this situation against his opponent. The American Legion in Winder had organized a drum and bugle corps of thirty high school girls to attend the senator's rallies. The day after Talmadge spoke at Monroe, as the newspapers were commenting on his national guard protection, Russell was campaigning at Royston. At the end of his talk, he pointed to the drum and bugle corps and said: "These girls in their red and black [University of Georgia colors] uniforms are thirty of the prettiest and talented girls in Georgia, and I'm going to make them my official body guard." This spoof made Talmadge and his national guardsmen look silly and had a devastating effect on the governor's image. As his biographer explained, it definitely placed Talmadge on the defensive.[45]

A combination of luck and political savvy gave Russell a major victory over his opponent at a large political gathering in Griffin. Officials in Griffin planned to celebrate the town's ninety-sixth anniversary on August 26 by inviting all of the major political candidates to appear at a huge rally and barbecue. The main candidates accepted the invitation and local officials developed a speaking schedule. As it turned out, Russell was to speak at 11:25 A.M., then there would be a break for the barbecue, after which Talmadge would have the platform at 1:55 P.M. This schedule greatly concerned the Russell forces. It was a given in politics and debate that the last speaker in any joint appearance had an advantage when there was no chance for rebuttal. But Russell was up to the challenge. Arriving in front of the speaker's stand, the drum and bugle corps—Russell's "body guards"—entertained the crowd of around forty thousand with several rousing tunes. Russell then mounted the platform and began to verbally work over the governor in the best Russell style. Using a combination of humor, sarcasm, and hard facts, he soon had the governor on the political ropes.

Russell tore Talmadge's platform to shreds. He insisted that there was nothing in it for the farmer and offered to read it to prove his point. But a farmer in the crowd yelled, "Wouldn't read it if you handed it down to me." Russell examined the platform and pointed out that the word "farmer" did not appear in the Talmadge document. He accused Talmadge of helping the Republicans and of hobnobbing with the rich Raskobs and DuPonts. Targeting Talmadge's disloyalty to the Democratic party, Russell said that now the governor was claiming to be loyal, but the crowd shouted back, "He isn't, he isn't." When Russell said that he still hoped to make a real Democrat out of Gene, a huge roar went up from the crowd: "Ole Republican Gene. He ain't changed. He's a liar still." According to Russell, Talmadge's rich Republican friends had taken him "up on the mountain tops and showed him the Promised Land," and he had forgotten the "people who made him." In a more serious vein, Russell said that there was nothing in Talmadge's proposals that would help farmers, workers, senior citizens, widows, and orphans or do anything of "a humanitarian nature."

Then Russell sought to prove that the governor had lied on more than one occasion. In one of his outbursts against the New Deal in 1933, Talmadge had called members of the Civilian Conservation Corps "bums and loafers." He later denied ever having made such a statement, but now Russell produced a copy of the *Statesman*, Talmadge's own newspaper, in which the statement had appeared under his signature. Also, the governor had criticized Russell for voting against measures designed to help veterans, but Russell left copies of the *Congressional Record* on the podium for Talmadge to prove that he had voted for payment of a bonus and other bills helpful to former soldiers. Talmadge had also made light of Russell's war record. Dick answered this by asking how Gene could attack anyone's military record when he had "hugged the banks of Sugar Creek so close during the whole war."

Russell then delivered his fatal punch. He announced that he was leaving fifteen questions tacked to the podium that he expected Governor Talmadge to answer when he appeared a short time later. He told the cheering crowd to demand answers. His questions included how Talmadge proposed to help farmers by cutting their federal payments, how he could reduce the national budget to $1 billion, and how government could be funded if the income tax were eliminated as Talmadge had insisted. Watching and listening, Ralph McGill, reporting for the *Atlanta Constitution*, wrote that it was the greatest campaign speech Russell had ever delivered.

As expected, when Talmadge spoke he ignored all but three of the Russell questions and then did not address them directly. In trying to utilize his usual bombastic form, his performance that hot afternoon seemed weak and disjointed. As his biographer wrote: "Gene had been drawn and quartered—his style and stomping, his demagoguery and showmanship all pared away."[46] It may well have been one of Russell's greatest political hours.

During his speech at Griffin and on other occasions, Talmadge and his friends attempted to smear Russell with the race issue. They sought to identify Russell with New Dealers who favored black rights, and they accused him of being unreliable on segregation and even of favoring social equality. One critic accused Russell of voting in the Senate to confirm "niggers" for federal jobs, and another announced that Harry Hopkins, head of the federal relief programs, had a "nigger" assistant in Atlanta. One anti-Russell woman said that Congressman Arthur Mitchell, a black from Illinois, was a "pet" of Postmaster General James Farley and "a close friend of Richard Russell."[47]

Russell, of course, was as strong a defender of segregation and white supremacy as anyone in the South, but he did not want race relations to become an issue in politics. He abhorred "nigger baiting" and had always avoided it in his campaigns. He considered it unworthy of people in his class and considered himself above such actions. Nevertheless, he felt that he must defend himself. He replied that Talmadge's charges were "absolutely false." He affirmed his faith in white supremacy and segregation and stated that "this is a white man's country, yes, and we are going to keep it that way." It was an insult to the people of Georgia, he said, "to even insinuate that I stand for political and social equality with the negro." His personal and official life in Georgia, Russell continued, refuted any such idea. Emphasizing that he had "a Deep South background, with all that implies," he declared that he had never done anything to foster racial equality. While vigorously defending his position as a "Deep South" southerner, Russell did everything he could to make race a nonissue. He accused Talmadge of taking "despicable" action by doing "what every candidate who is about to be beaten does. He comes in crying nigger."[48]

Russell again had the support of organized labor, which exerted strong efforts for the senator in the closing days of the campaign. The entire September 1 Georgia edition of *Labor*, the AFL's publication, was devoted to praising Russell and his accomplishments in the Senate. It included articles on how Russell had helped farmers, workers, veterans, and other average citizens. He also received praise for favoring higher taxes on the rich. Women, too, strongly backed Russell. Whether it was because he was young and single, because of his gracious southern manner, or because they agreed with him on the issues is not known, but many women worked hard for his election. Furthermore, veterans tended to support the senator, not only because he was one of them, but because Russell had voted for helpful legislation.[49]

The campaign aroused bitterness and hard feelings unlike anything Russell had ever experienced before. The crowds were often unruly, and fistfights between Russell and Talmadge supporters at political meetings were not uncommon. Russell recalled years later that "it tore the state to pieces; it had brothers stop speaking to brothers and partners dissolving partnerships. It was a very, very bitter campaign."[50] Russell even received threats of physical violence. He wrote his first will during the campaign!

During the last few days of the campaign, both the Russell and Talmadge forces worked frantically. Some observers believed that the vote would be very close. These pundits, however, were entirely wrong. Russell received another overwhelming endorsement, getting 256,154 popular votes to only 134,695 for Talmadge. The county unit vote was even more lopsided. Talmadge got a mere 32 county unit votes compared to 378 for Russell. The governor carried only 16 counties while Russell won 143.[51]

President Roosevelt was "perfectly delighted" with the outcome, writing to "Dear Dick" that his victory was "splendid news." He added that he wished he could have sent Russell public congratulations "at the time but as I did not do it in the cases of Joe [Robinson], Pat [Harrison] and Jimmy Byrnes, I could not break the rule!" Roosevelt was greatly pleased to have these prominent southern Democratic supporters back in the Senate.[52]

At the outset of the campaign, many people believed that Talmadge would carry enough rural counties to win the county unit vote. Presumably, he was strong among voters on the backcountry roads. But Russell showed that he was even more popular than Talmadge among the landowners and better-off tenants, about the only farmers in Georgia who voted. Russell and Roosevelt looked better and better to farmers who had come to realize what the New Deal agricultural programs meant to them. Thousands of Georgians had eaten Talmadge barbecue and then voted for Russell!

Undoubtedly, Russell's close association with, and support for, Roosevelt and the New Deal was a major factor in his victory. In all likelihood, however, he could have defeated Talmadge even if the New Deal had not been an issue. For over a decade, Russell had built up a loyal and reliable network of backers throughout the state. Moreover, he had a much better campaign organization than his opponent, and he campaigned harder than Talmadge. In many cases, Talmadge drew larger crowds, but Russell actually talked to more people. Also, he used the radio very effectively.

Russell also had more newspaper support than Talmadge. Much of the state's press had been turned off by the governor's use of the national guard to get his way and by his demagogic attacks on Roosevelt and the New Deal. Clark Howell, publisher of the *Atlanta Constitution*, had been a Talmadge supporter but had deserted the governor because of his vitriolic attacks on the New Deal and his moves to divide the state Democratic party. According to one account, in July 1935, Howell and Talmadge met with Roosevelt in the White House. Trying to make peace between Roosevelt and Talmadge, Howell said, "Gene, I want to say in the presence of the President that unless you come to your senses we're going to throw you out the window." Talmadge later toned down his criticism of the president, but the *Constitution* soon became his sharpest critic.[53] Ralph McGill, the *Constitution*'s rising star, wrote story after story attacking Talmadge. The governor's supporters became so bitter at McGill that they actually beat him up on a couple of occasions.[54]

Farmer support for Russell increased in 1936 partly because of his work to help out during the severe drought. By June farmers were writing Russell about the dire conditions. In some areas, there would be no crops at all, and gardens had dried up, threatening many farm families with starvation. Russell responded to all the farmers who contacted him promising to do what he could to help. He worked with officials of the Agricultural Adjustment Administration, the Resettlement Administration, the Soil Conservation Service, and other agencies. While the results were not dramatic, farmers felt that Russell was trying hard to assist them. He also managed to take a swipe at Talmadge in his letters to farmers. Russell said that he hoped he could get some drought relief, despite opposition from the governor!

With the support of personal friends, farmers, workers, federal employees, newspapers, individuals whom he had assisted when he was in the legislature and the governor's office, and an effective organization to bring these elements together, Russell was unbeatable. On a personal note, he also proved to be an even better stump speaker than Talmadge. Not only at Griffin but on other occasions, Russell showed that his political skill and savvy were unmatched in the state. A few days after the election, Russell and Talmadge met on the street in Atlanta. They shook hands and exchanged pleasantries. The governor then remarked that the two of them had the same political friends but that it seemed "they were just better friends of yours than mine." That may have been the best explanation of Russell's victory.[55]

Some seven thousand people braved a heavy rain and thunderstorm to help Russell celebrate his victory in Winder on the evening of September 10. The storm was so severe that some people from out of town turned back in face of the driving rain. Even though lightning knocked out the electricity for some thirty minutes, nothing could discourage the enthusiastic crowd. The girls of his drum and bugle corps escorted Russell to the platform. He introduced his mother as "the only sweetheart I ever had" and then thanked his friends for all they had done. He gave special thanks to the "good women of Georgia" who had supported him. Expressing deep humility, Russell said that his victory was a triumph for Jefferson, Cleveland, and Franklin D. Roosevelt. "Georgia is going forward with Roosevelt," he declared. To the tune of "The Old Grey Mare She Ain't What She Used to Be," the girls played and sang, "Old Gene Talmadge Ain't What He Used to Be." And the crowd slowly drifted away.[56]

8

The Later New Deal

═══

In commenting on the significance of the 1936 senatorial election in Georgia, the *New York Times* editorialized that Talmadge's defeat "is a sign that a too-familiar type of the Southern Demagogue is on its way to extinction." U.S. Secretary of Agriculture Henry A. Wallace declared that the Georgia contest was a political event in which a state election had national significance. It seemed clear that the people of Georgia wanted to send a senator back to Washington who would continue to support the president and the New Deal. Russell himself wrote shortly after the election, "I am confident . . . that under the President's matchless leadership we will be able to make great progress in the next four years, so that every right and interest of every class of our citizens will be protected and promoted."[1]

On specific measures of the New Deal, Roosevelt could usually count on Richard B. Russell, Jr. It was another matter, however, when the overall effect of the New Deal began to impose fundamental social, economic, and political change on southern society. Russell was no more prepared than Talmadge for federal action that might produce structural economic and political change in the South. Surely Russell was as sensitive as most white southerners at the time to modifications in race relations. He would soon be criticizing the New Deal administration for violating states' rights on racial matters. He used legal arguments in contrast to Talmadge's bombastic accusations of dictatorship, but the difference between the Talmadges and the Russells in the South was mainly one of degree rather than of substance.

Just how the New Deal and the administration of its programs would eventually affect the South was not clear in 1936. There were faint signs on the horizon, however, that disturbed Russell, especially in the area of race relations. But other than that, he continued to advocate and support programs that required expanded federal powers. His main interest was to do something for farmers, especially those who needed help to become landowners.

Russell was a philosophical agrarian through and through. Even as a high school student, he had debated the affirmative side of the question whether rural life was superior to living in the city. His growing up in the rural environment just outside of Winder had greatly influenced his outlook. As he wrote a friend years later, "I suppose that I was influenced very largely by my background." He said that he had worked on farms as a boy and had practiced law among farmers. "I think environment plays a tremendous part in the shaping of the thinking of all of us," he said.[2]

Like Thomas Jefferson, Russell believed that independent family farmers were among the nation's most valued citizens. He once declared that the family farm had been a great stabilizing influence and a significant "source of strength to our country through all of its history." In an interview with Edward R. Murrow in 1952 broadcast over CBS radio, he explained, "There is something about a man moving close to nature and nature's God that gives him an independence of thought and approach to public issues that those of us who live in the hurly burly of city life cannot always enjoy."[3] Russell told his CBS audience that American society had absorbed good values from its farm population.

Considering that Russell held so firmly to these agrarian beliefs, it is not surprising that helping farmers was one of his highest legislative priorities, especially during his first twenty-five years in the Senate. To him, assisting farmers brought direct and indirect benefits to the entire nation. He had been distressed by the large exodus of farmers from the land during World War I and the 1920s, and he hoped, as he put it, "to make farm life more attractive so they will stay here."[4]

Russell also thought that farmers needed special help because, in his view, they had been discriminated against and victimized by other elements in American society. Government programs for farmers were necessary to restore some semblance of fairness and balance with other economic groups. He also believed that the nation could not enjoy good times until farmers were prosperous. Finally, there was a very practical angle to Russell's concern for farmers. When he went to Washington in 1933, farmers made up the largest and most important economic group in the state. Georgia's economy, he said, "was largely predicated upon agriculture."[5] At that time, there were about 255,000 farms in Georgia, and farmers and their families made up 49 percent of the total population.

Convinced that small family-type farms were superior to large plantations or corporate operations, Russell began in 1935 to devote special attention to this group. He believed that farm ownership was essential, but he was from a section of the nation where tenant farming exceeded 50 percent. The figure was 68 percent in Georgia. The Agricultural Adjustment Act of 1933, and later versions of that legislation, offered very little aid to small, poorer operators. Larger farmers who had enough land to be able to take some of it out of production in exchange for government payments received significant assistance. But, as Congressman E. E. Cox of Georgia said of the Bankhead bill restricting cotton acreage, it "was hell on the little man."[6] The New Deal agricultural programs provided the least help to Georgia's approximately 145,000 white and black sharecroppers who owned no land. Most of these poor families eked out a living on less than $200 a year.

During his early days in Washington, Russell had supported every measure that he thought would assist farmers. Besides voting for the Agricultural Adjustment Act and the Farm Credit Administration, he supported "a sound program of inflation," he attempted to restrict jute imports, he worked for drought relief, and he interceded on behalf of individual farmers who had problems with various agricultural agencies. But these measures were not helping a large number of southern farmers who fell into the poorest category.[7]

The question was, of course, what should or could be done to help farmers who were at the bottom of the economic pyramid. In 1935 and 1936, Russell occasionally met with a group of congressmen, senators, bureaucrats, and social reformers who frequently gathered on Friday nights in an upstairs room of Hall's Restaurant in Washington. Among those present were Lyndon B. Johnson, John H. Bankhead, Brooks Hays, and Dr. Will Alexander, later deputy administrator of the Resettlement Administration. There, amidst good food and drink, these agrarians discussed southern problems, especially those relating to the poorest farmers.[8]

A provision for subsistence homesteads had been included in the National Industrial Recovery Act of 1933, and $25 million had been appropriated to help people settle on small subsistence farms while they earned money in nearby nonfarm activities. The Subsistence Division was set up in the Department of the Interior in late 1933. The division planned to buy land, build homes, and house families in collective communities. Little was accomplished, however, and by early 1935 only a few hundred families had been helped.[9] Not only had the program failed, but it was not the sort of approach favored by Russell and most others in Congress. Rejecting cooperative-type projects, Russell wanted a program that would help hard-pressed individual producers to become independent and successful commercial operators. Tens of thousands of such farmers were crying for assistance.

On March 12, 1935, a farmer from Douglasville wrote Russell that he was about to lose his 142-acre farm because he could not pay $85 he owed in interest for the previous year. His entire debt on the farm, which included a ten-room house, was only $835. He should be making a decent living, he wrote, but "I am now ragged, have three children that should be in school without shoes or clothes or books to go, and I am forced bitter as it may be to ask for charity." Such conditions greatly distressed Russell. Here was precisely the type of farmer who he believed was the foundation of the nation and deserved federal help.[10]

Russell was already working on a plan that he hoped would be helpful. When Congress had the huge $4.8 billion relief bill under consideration early in 1935, Russell decided to try to tap that program for funds to help poor farmers. He introduced an amendment to the relief bill that would provide loans to small, landless farmers to buy land and equipment. On March 10, he went to see the president to solicit support for this idea. He told Roosevelt that his proposal to provide credit for tenants, sharecroppers, and farm laborers to purchase land was one of the most important parts of the bill. It would discourage future depressions, he said, and reduce political and social unrest.[11]

After some legislative maneuvering, Russell succeeded in getting his amendment written into law. It gave the president authority to use funds from the relief appropriation for loans to purchase land and equipment to "farmers, farm tenants, croppers, or farm laborers." The president had the discretion to establish rules and regulations for administering the program. Essentially, it was designed to make loans and permit farmers to repay them over a long period.[12]

Russell told his colleagues that when this amendment was implemented it not only would help farmers but would relieve the depression as well. He explained that in the past people had gone to the frontier for a new start in life, but such a move was no longer possible. Now when a farmer went broke, he could do nothing but seek relief or starve. Credit was available to people who owned land but not to tenants and sharecroppers. His amendment, he said, was a practical approach for "social justice and security." He hoped that this legislation would help thousands of farmers to become owners and "make their living on the land."[13]

On the basis of the Russell amendment and another provision in the law that provided for rural rehabilitation, the president established the Resettlement Administration the last day of April 1935. He appointed Rexford Tugwell to head the agency, but Tugwell was more interested in rehabilitating farmers and in land-use planning than in making loans to poorer farmers to buy farms. Consequently, only a few loans were advanced to purchase land and equipment. Most of the agency's activities involved resettling residents from poor and eroded land, supporting migrant labor camps, and setting up cooperative communities.

Thus Russell's hope of helping a large number of poor tenants and sharecroppers to become self-supporting farm owners went unrealized. Congress gradually turned against the whole program as Tugwell increasingly involved the agency in land reform and social change. There was especially harsh criticism of the model communities and the resettlement work. Some conservative southern senators such as Harry F. Byrd of Virginia and Kenneth McKellar of Tennessee leveled vicious attacks against Tugwell and his programs. To reduce the controversy, Tugwell resigned in December 1936, and the agency's functions were turned over to the U.S. Department of Agriculture.[14] Although Russell was not an outspoken critic of the Resettlement Administration, he was disappointed that it had not stuck primarily to lending money to poor farmers to buy land and equipment.

Meanwhile, Senator John H. Bankhead of Alabama and Congressman Marvin Jones of Texas introduced legislation that was specifically designed to do what Russell had intended with his 1935 amendment to the work relief bill. Bankhead, like Russell, held deep agrarian ideals and had a genuine desire to help poorer farmers of whom there were so many in the South. Introduced into Congress in 1935, the Bankhead-Jones Farm Tenant Act was passed two years later. Russell worked hard behind the scenes to pass this legislation. Indeed, without his effective support, Bankhead told D. W. Brooks, a prominent farm cooperative leader in Georgia, he could not have obtained passage of the measure in the Senate.[15]

This law created the Farm Security Administration (FSA) for the purpose of making land and equipment loans to disadvantaged farmers in order to promote more independent, owner-operated family farms. Congress, however, never adequately funded the program. As chairman of the subcommittee on agricultural appropriations, Russell did everything he could to get more funds for what he considered such a good purpose, but his efforts were only partly successful. The first appropriation was for only $10 million. For the fiscal year of 1939, the House approved $15 million, but Russell insisted on $25 million. After tough bargaining in the conference committee, he succeeded. The next year, he asked for $50 million for fiscal 1940. Arguing for the larger amount, Russell said that Congress could not justify insuring billions in mortgages for city dwellers and spending millions for slum clearance and for other urban purposes and then telling tenant farmers that they could not have "a pittance" of $50 million to help them become farm owners. When asked about the program's progress using previous appropriations, Russell replied that some eleven thousand farmers had been assisted. He added that he would like to see $100 million available "to combat the rising tide of farm tenancy." He was successful in getting $50 million but not from appropriations. The FSA was authorized to borrow this amount from the Reconstruction Finance Corporation.[16]

Most of the loans went to farmers who had the best prospects of repayment, leaving hundreds of thousands of the poorest tenants and sharecroppers without any hope of ever becoming landowners. On June 26, 1939, Will W. Alexander, administrator of the FSA, wrote Russell that after nearly two years of operation up to May 31 some 5,084 Bankhead-Jones loans to buy land had been granted. However, thousands of rehabilitation loans had been given to small farmers for living and operating expenses, but these loans were not leading to farm ownership.[17]

In March 1939, Russell joined other senators to support a bill that would provide government-insured home loans to farmers. It was similar to the program in which the Federal Housing Authority insured home loans for town and city residents. The Senate passed this measure by a voice vote on July 6, 1939, but the House never considered the bill. Russell and Senator Walter George also introduced a bill in 1939 to allow the federal government to buy land and place it in the public domain. This land would then be opened for homesteading. However, this was another scheme that Congress would not buy.[18]

Believing that farmers were not faring as well as other elements in society, Russell worked to implement a provision in the 1938 Agricultural Adjustment Act that permitted direct payments to farmers who produced certain agricultural commodities. The idea was to bring the returns on particular crops up to 75 percent of parity prices. Price parity was the effort to give basic agricultural commodities the same purchasing power they had in the period 1909 to 1914. On June 1, 1938, Russell introduced an amendment to the relief appropriations bill designating $212 million for parity payments to producers of cotton, corn, wheat, tobacco, and rice. In the case of cotton, for example, the government would pay farmers two cents a pound. When some senators tried to make changes in the Russell amendment, they quickly learned that the Georgian had the votes. Senator Royal S. Copeland of New York, who opposed the idea of these direct payments, said adoption of the amendment was "inevitable," and Senator Charles McNary of Oregon, who wanted to modify Russell's amendment, admitted grudgingly that it "is going to prevail." And it did without change. Russell said that he would prefer to see farmers receive full parity prices, but in his practical approach to problems, he accepted half a loaf as better than none.[19] A writer for the *American Cotton Grower* suggested that "Parity Russell" would be an appropriate name for the Georgia senator.

Russell spent a lot of time each year getting the agricultural appropriations bill passed. He began with weeks of hearings, usually in March or April, followed by several days of discussion on the Senate floor. Meanwhile, he would be working with House leaders. After passage by the Senate, the measure would have to go to conference. There he fought hard for the parts of the bill in which he was most interested. For example, in 1939, he won an increase for parity payments to $225 million for fiscal 1940, up some $13 million, against tough House opposition. Russell's efforts involved negotiation, compromise, collecting on previous favors, and convincing colleagues that he was right on the issue.[20] Russell was at his best in this kind of give-and-take.

He often had to take unpopular stands with his colleagues as he moved agricultural appropriations bills through the Senate. On the one hand, he faced the demands of the Bureau of the Budget to keep expenditures down, and on the other, he received numerous requests from friends in the Senate to fund favorite projects here and there. In presenting the bill in May 1937, Russell said he doubted if "any Member of the Senate will speak to me after the bill shall have been finally enacted into law." The committee, he said, had eliminated many special requests for research facilities, wildlife stations, money to study animal and plant diseases, and for other purposes.[21]

As Russell dealt with agricultural matters, he never failed to take every opportunity to talk about farmers, their importance, and their problems. Speaking to a gathering of Georgia 4-H clubs in 1940, he declared that "the institutions of free government were conserved in the minds and hearts of farmers." American freedom, he said, had been won largely by the "blood and sacrifice of farmers." But, he continued, farmers had become the victims of the greed of more highly organized and selfish groups. Americans must improve farm life and revive the dignity of the farm home or the nation would decline in the same way as Greece and Rome.[22]

When the question came up of providing more funds for the Export-Import Bank that would be used to assist Finland after the Russian invasion in 1940, Russell objected with all his power. He said he could not understand how his colleagues could vote assistance to Finland but refuse to do anything for poor tenants and sharecroppers. These needy farmers were carrying on with "equal heroism," he said. Russell declared that he would not vote for any foreign aid as long as Congress denied farmers the help they deserved.[23] But his opposition could not stop the special appropriation for Finland, which passed the Senate 49 to 27.

When the Bureau of the Budget recommended cutting total agricultural appropriations from about $1.4 billion in fiscal 1940 to $864 million in 1941, a reduction of 40 percent, Russell was furious. What angered him most was the fact that the Budget Bureau recommended reducing nonagricultural appropriations by only 8 percent. He insisted that he was more familiar with needs of farmers than clerks and bureaucrats in the Budget Bureau. Russell pointed out that nonfarm prices had gone up much more rapidly than agricultural prices, creating a serious disparity. A farmer in 1913 could exchange 4.7 pounds of cotton for a work shirt, Russell said, but by 1940 the shirt cost 7.2 pounds. Everywhere one looked, Russell argued, farmers were at a disadvantage, and it was the responsibility of Congress to right these wrongs.[24]

As the United States began defense preparations in 1940 and drew closer to war, there was increasing opposition to the amount of appropriations Russell wanted for agriculture. A growing number of legislators believed that demand for agricultural commodities would soon catch up with output and drive prices upward, making subsidies and the provision of special credit to farmers unnecessary. Russell, however, disagreed and kept fighting for both parity payments and money for the FSA. He was able to get parity payments of $212 million approved, if needed, through 1943. He also managed to keep appropriations for soil conservation from being cut. From 1937 to 1941, lawmakers provided approximately $500 million a year for soil conservation.[25]

Russell, however, was unable to save the Farm Security Administration. As the country began to pull out of the depression, Congress took a new and harder look at a number of New Deal programs. The depression and reform mentality that had helped undergird these measures crumbled away in the face of the needs of war. Furthermore, growing criticism of some FSA programs, especially the rehabilitation and cooperative activities, and the charges that some FSA administrators were radicals if not Communists, weakened the agency. Russell rejected the demagogic attacks on C. B. Baldwin, administrator of the FSA, who was charged with being a Communist or Communist sympathizer. While Russell admitted to having had sharp differences with Baldwin, he told his colleagues that Baldwin was "as far from being a Communist as any man could possibly be." Rather, he was an "honest, sincere, patriotic American," Russell said.[26]

His efforts to protect the agency are illustrated by the major legislative skirmish that occurred in the spring of 1942. The House, in an effort to kill or greatly reduce the FSA, cut the agency's appropriations far below the president's budget request. The administration turned to Russell to try to salvage the situation. Harold D. Smith, director of the Budget Bureau, drafted a letter for Roosevelt to send to Russell on agricultural issues. Along with other matters, Roosevelt wrote "Dear Dick" that he was much concerned about the sizable reductions the House had made in FSA appropriations. Russell later wrote that this was the first time that the president had ever called on him personally to help with a particular piece of legislation.[27]

Under the leadership of Russell, Bankhead, and others in the Senate, and with presidential support, the Senate restored most of the House cuts for the FSA. Defending the agency on the floor of the Senate, Russell stated that the FSA programs were needed because they benefited the "most underprivileged and helpless people of this Nation."[28] That Russell again had the Senate on his side was clear when Senator Byrd, a leading FSA critic, disgustedly declared that it "was utterly futile to speak against any of the appropriations contained in this bill."[29] The conference committee, however, turned out to be the site of a battle royal. While Russell was unable to preserve the entire appropriation that the Senate had voted for the FSA, he kept the reduction to only 20 percent below what the president had recommended. Considering the vehement opposition in the House, this was a substantial victory.[30] Russell was as firm in his support of low-income farmers as he had ever been.

The president wrote a highly complimentary letter to Russell acknowledging his work on the agricultural appropriation bill, which greatly pleased Russell. Roosevelt thanked him for his "steadfastness," his "untiring efforts," and his "legislative leadership." Roosevelt flattered the senator even more by adding that his work had been a contribution to the war effort.[31]

The fight over the FSA in 1942, however, was only preliminary to its destruction a year later. Russell, Bankhead, and other backers could not convince many of their colleagues that trying to save poor farmers was a worthy wartime goal. The so-called "death appropriations" of 1943 left the agency struggling along but doing very little. Finally, Congress let the FSA die, and in 1946 lawmakers established the Farmers Home Administration (FHA) to make loans to poorer farmers.

If the FSA had confined its activities to lending money to farm purchasers, it might have avoided some of the attacks that led to its downfall. The problem, however, was that there were hundreds of thousands of farmers in the South who could not be saved or transformed into successful commercial operators. They needed advances for living expenses, guidance in business practices, some nonfarm income, improved health facilities, and other kinds of assistance. Some of them needed help in order to leave agriculture altogether. Most politicians did not want to confront the fundamental problems facing rural poverty—surplus labor in agriculture and the need for better education, improved health facilities, and nonfarm jobs. At this time, Russell only partly understood the great revolution that was occurring on American farms that would result in the need for many fewer farm workers.

Russell also continued to work for the betterment of more successful farmers. One of the things that greatly concerned him was the large cotton surpluses held in government storage under loans from the Commodity Credit Corporation. He believed that ways must be found to move the cotton into international markets. One way to do this was to establish a two-price system—one price for cotton used domestically and a lower, more competitive figure for the part of the crop shipped abroad. This system would require export subsidies. In May 1939, he introduced an amendment to the agricultural appropriations bill to pay such subsidies, but it was defeated 37 to 36.[32] Russell never lost interest in trying to do something to increase the income of cotton farmers, but he was unable to achieve much beyond price supports that were provided in the Agricultural Adjustment Act of 1938.

Another program in which Russell took great pride was that of providing lunches for schoolchildren. With huge surpluses of many farm commodities, the U.S. Department of Agriculture began to distribute food to a few schools in 1935. Russell immediately became interested in using farm surpluses to upgrade school lunches. The desperate poverty among many of his constituents and poor child nutrition throughout much of the country prompted him to give strong backing to this program. Of course, Russell was also interested in getting rid of the huge agricultural surpluses that kept depressing farm prices and could not be moved through regular market channels. Money came initially from Section 32 funds from the amended Agricultural Adjustment Act of

1935, and the Federal Surplus Commodities Corporation provided the food. The program grew slowly, but by 1940 some two million children were receiving school lunches at a cost of about $11 million.[33] As will be discussed later, during World War II, Russell sponsored, and Congress passed, permanent school lunch legislation.

He also supported the modest food stamp plan administered by the U.S. Department of Agriculture beginning in 1939. Some $4 million was being expended on this program by 1940. Russell fought hard to get $50 million for the food stamp program for fiscal 1942 but could not overcome House resistance that would not go beyond $25 million. Full employment and rising incomes prompted Congress to abandon this food stamp program in 1943.[34] While Russell favored the food distribution programs as a way to help reduce agricultural surpluses, he also believed firmly that the federal government had a role in upgrading diets and nutritional standards among the poor.

In his constant search for ways to help farmers, in 1938 Russell again attempted to get a tax of 1.2 cents per pound on jute imports. He charged that the jute trust was so powerful that it was delaying legislation that could help 300,000 textile workers and 2.5 million cotton growers in the United States. But again the Senate defeated his amendment, this time by a vote of 59 to 18. He simply could not get support outside of the cotton states.[35] Whenever the opportunity arose, he also fought for low interest rates on government farm loans. Because he thought it was unfair to farmers, Russell voted against the wartime price control act early in 1942. He objected to any bill, he explained, that would control prices and income for farmers, "the lowest income group in this Nation," while doing nothing to cap industrial wages. He was one of the fourteen senators, he stated, who went down "in the last avalanche of votes which adopted the price-control bill."[36]

As a dedicated conservationist and one looking for new sources of income for southern farmers, Russell supported a variety of proposals to plant more pine trees in the South. He also favored establishing one or more national forests in South Georgia. In 1935 he introduced his first bill to provide a research station that would concentrate on developing tung trees as a new crop in the South.[37]

Although agriculture and farm-related issues took more of Russell's time than anything else in the late 1930s, he was involved with other legislation. He supported the Robinson-Patman bill, commonly known as the anti–chain store measure, that was designed to prohibit unfair price discrimination against smaller retail establishments. In backing this measure, Russell wrote that he had always supported laws that would help the "masses of the people." He was also among those who early endorsed federal aid to education. When the Federal Emergency Relief Administration provided some money for schools, he declared that the day was not far distant "when the federal government will recognize its responsibility to the youth of our nation and provide funds to assist in the maintenance of the public schools of this country."[38]

Indeed, throughout his political career, Russell had emphasized the importance of education. Not only did he consider education especially significant for the perpetuation of democracy and free government, but he also believed it was critical to prepare a person "for the fine art of living." He told one commencement audience in 1930 that it was important to use good English and to develop refined and gentle manners, which came from "fixed habits of thought and action" acquired through education. The strength of the United States was not so much in armaments, he continued, but in the schoolhouses "where our young people are trained to think." Ignorance was "too expensive to be tolerated," he insisted. Russell always emphasized that people must study history as a vital part of any education.

Whatever others may have thought of Russell's political philosophy, he considered himself "a liberal and progressive Democrat." He said that he had always favored changing "the existing order when the general welfare demanded it" and that he had stood "shoulder to shoulder" with liberals who had tried to increase income and purchasing power for "the underprivileged people of the Nation." Russell claimed that he had worked to get a more equitable distribution of national income and to reduce the vast concentrations of wealth that had oppressed the poor and helpless. He had supported every bill for relief, he stated, because this was a way to redistribute funds to those at the bottom of the American economic scale.

Russell expressed his views early in 1939 as he fought to amend an appropriations bill for the Works Progress Administration limiting regional differentials in pay for similar jobs in the program to not more than 25 percent. He introduced evidence to show that pay was sometimes two to three times as much for the same Works Progress Administration work in such states as New York or Pennsylvania as it was in Georgia and other southern states. This, Russell argued, was gross discrimination against the South and could not be justified by differences in living costs. He said that the result was to widen the income gap throughout the country and freeze "the poor and underprivileged workers in the South" at a lower level than "American citizens had a right to expect." His extended argument, however, failed to convince his colleagues, who defeated his amendment.[39]

In 1937 and 1938, Russell found himself in the uncomfortable position of having to walk the fine line between supporting the president and following his own best judgment. The issues were the president's effort to reshape the U.S. Supreme Court and his move to purge Russell's colleague, Senator Walter George. During 1935 and 1936, the Supreme Court had declared the National Industrial Recovery Act and the Agricultural Adjustment Act, two pillars of the New Deal recovery program, unconstitutional. Other important New Deal laws had also fallen under the Court's decisions. Increasingly annoyed at what he considered obstructionism and mossback ideas, Roosevelt in February 1937 recommended a major judicial reorganization plan. It called for adding an additional justice for each justice on the Supreme Court who did not retire after reaching seventy years of age. No more than six justices could be added, limiting the total to fifteen. The idea was to get some new and younger blood on the Court.

Critics of the president immediately charged that he was seeking to "pack the court" and that he threatened a sacred American institution. Having been raised in a family of lawyers and judges, Russell found himself in a difficult position. Like Roosevelt, he believed that some of the Supreme Court's decisions had not been in the country's best interests, but he simply could not go along with any plan that would reshape the Court in such a drastic manner.[40] Moreover, he saw immediately that the president's proposal was going to widen the developing gulf within the Democratic party. This kind of issue was just what anti-Roosevelt conservatives needed to give some public credence to their charges that Roosevelt was an irresponsible dictator. Furthermore, fallout from the controversy might help the Republicans politically in the midterm elections of 1938, a possibility that greatly distressed Russell. As he was prone to do, Russell decided to work quietly in the background to develop some kind of compromise that would do the least damage to the president's reputation. Meanwhile, he told his mother that the president's proposal had "provoked more feelings here than any [other] of his administration." According to Russell, even dinner parties were being disturbed "by the heat of arguments on the subject."

Russell indicated that he would support the idea of adding two justices to the Supreme Court to help with the Court's work load. He considered this a reasonable compromise. Russell, Senator John H. Overton of Louisiana, and a number of other senators called on the president in February and told him that the addition of two justices was as far as they could go in reforming the Supreme Court. Roosevelt, however, said that he could not accept this proposal. As far as Russell was concerned, that ended the matter. He returned to his office, recognizing that the president's proposal was dead. Russell wrote his good friend Alex Lawrence in Savannah that he did not want to take any measures that would cause people to think that the Supreme Court could be affected by party politics or political pressures.[41]

From that point on, Russell said very little about the Court issue. Critics accused him of "straddling" the question, but he was really stalling for time. He still hoped that some kind of compromise might be worked out. When constituents asked his opinion of the proposal, he simply replied that he was studying the matter. He told one Georgian on June 24 that he was "wholeheartedly in agreement with the social and economic objectives" of the Roosevelt administration but did not think the president's Court reform bill would be of any help on "the high road to real progressive government."[42]

Russell had decided already how he would vote if the only choice was the measure proposed by the president. However, he did not want to appear to be caving in to pressure from the conservative anti-Roosevelt forces. He was especially critical of publisher Frank E. Gannett who was chairman of the National Committee to Uphold Constitutional Government. This organization generated a "tremendous number" of telegrams against the Roosevelt plan. Russell later wrote that "the diehards and the Liberty Leaguers seized on the difference of opinion within the Democratic Party in an effort to injure the President in the court fight," but he wanted everyone to know that the "Gannett-inspired telegrams had not carried any weight with him." In any event, Russell was one of the seventy senators who voted to recommit the bill to the Judiciary Committee on July 22, effectively killing the measure.[43]

After the vote, Russell told publisher Clark Howell of the *Atlanta Constitution*: "My whole purpose through all the Court controversy was to refrain from taking part in the bitter and acrimonious discussion in order that I might be able to assist in a compromise which would be just and equitable and to prevent anything being done which would impair the great power of the President in his efforts to carry forward his philosophy of progressive government." This was typical Russell strategy, but in this case, it failed. A few days later, he and two Senate colleagues left the heat and controversy in Washington to represent the United States in the dedication of war memorials built for American soldiers on European battlefields.[44]

Early in 1938, Russell found himself in an even more embarrassing position when President Roosevelt decided to try to defeat a number of conservative Democratic senators who had opposed his programs. One of those marked for purging was Senator Walter George. George had been an outspoken critic of the president's attempt to reorganize the Supreme Court, and, according to Russell, George and Roosevelt had other differences. As James A. Farley explained it, the president wanted to "make an object lesson of George," whose defeat would weaken a growing conservative southern bloc.[45]

Roosevelt invited Russell to the White House early in 1938 and told him of his plans to defeat Senator George. While the president claimed to like George, he feared that George's political philosophy was too much in line with such conservative senators as Republican Arthur Vandenburg of Michigan. Roosevelt said that if Russell would help George could be beaten. In exchange for Russell's support, the president offered to provide the necessary campaign funds for any candidate Russell might select to replace the Georgia senator. Roosevelt's bold proposition to become involved in Georgia politics for the purpose of defeating George caused Russell to break into a cold sweat. He was unaccustomed to such presidential arm-twisting. Nevertheless, he stood his ground and told Roosevelt that he could not participate in any purge effort.[46]

Russell never indicated whether he advised the president not to pursue his plan to purge George, but a number of prominent Democrats did give him that advice. Vice President John Nance Garner told Jim Farley that Roosevelt's involvement in state primary elections would only solidify opposition to his policies and programs. But the president was adamant. He wanted Georgia Governor E. D. Rivers to run against George, but Rivers declined. Then he sent White House Secretary Marvin H. McIntyre to Georgia to find a candidate, and McIntyre finally convinced Lawrence S. Camp to make the race. McIntyre wired Roosevelt on August 6, however, confirming that "Dick is not going to play ball."[47]

The situation now became truly painful for Russell. A U.S. district attorney in Atlanta, Camp was one of Russell's closest and most trusted political friends. They had been sworn in together as new House members in 1921. Camp had also organized Russell's campaign for Speaker pro tem in 1923 and supported him for Speaker in 1927. Camp had helped to manage aspects of Russell's campaigns for both governor and senator. He had accompanied Russell to Washington for his swearing-in ceremony in January 1933. They had been about as close as any two political friends could be. The question in everyone's mind was would Russell support his old friend? On the other hand, Senator George had gone out of his way in 1936 to praise the New Deal in Russell's presence, thereby giving Russell, who vigorously supported Roosevelt, an implied endorsement.

It soon became clear that Russell would stay as neutral as possible. In fact, he told Camp that he would remain silent. Observers referred to Russell as "lying low" and "remaining aloof." When pressed for a statement, Russell simply stated that he and Senator George had cooperated well in Washington, "but I am staying out of the primary."[48] Nevertheless, Russell was on hand when President Roosevelt visited the state on August 10 to dedicate a rural electrification project at Barnesville. Russell, who was master of ceremonies, was on the platform along with George, Camp, Governor Rivers, and other leading politicians. In addition to his general address, the president gave Camp a strong endorsement that was a bold but foolhardy attempt to excommunicate George from the Democratic party. George shook the president's hand and remarked that they would settle the matter of Georgia's senator at the polls in September. Ignoring the personal and political tensions of the moment, Russell spoke glowingly of the New Deal and called Roosevelt the "greatest exponent of liberal democracy and equality of opportunity for his generation."[49] George went on to defeat Camp by a large majority, confirming the wisdom of the advice Roosevelt had received about staying out of state primaries.

Russell had protected his own political position in Georgia by remaining neutral, but he had disappointed Camp, an old and valued friend. The president was so angry that, according to Russell, he would hardly speak to him for two years. This was an exaggeration, but it did take some time to restore their former cordiality. After Russell attended a White House reception on January 17, 1939, he wrote, "President cold."[50]

Russell's championship of the New Deal and the president continued up until World War II when, as Roosevelt said, "Doctor Win-the-War" replaced "Doctor New Deal." Prior to this, Russell saw farm, banking, tax, work relief, social security, public power, and other basic New Deal legislation as being good for the country and worthy of support. It was a progressive program, a term Russell used frequently, that he believed was spreading greater justice and opportunity in American life. The rising voices of criticism from both conservative Democrats and Republicans received no sympathy or succor from him.

There was one development in the 1930s, however, that Russell viewed with growing alarm. That was the movement for greater rights and opportunities for blacks. The signs of change that caused him concern could be seen in the operation of the new federal agencies where in some cases blacks were treated as equals to whites and in the demands of some northern politicians for national laws to protect black rights. The Roosevelt administration had appointed an increasing number of blacks to federal offices, and both President and Mrs. Roosevelt were shown in the media socializing with blacks.[51] Reports came to Russell that in some federal relief projects in Georgia whites and blacks worked together. Even worse in Russell's view were reports of blacks in supervisory positions over whites. Most such reports that reached Russell proved to be false, but he was ever alert to any weakening of racial segregation.

As mentioned earlier, Russell's views on race had been fixed by the region and culture in which he grew up. He did not wish ill for blacks, and he abhorred race baiting. He had always avoided crude and vulgar references to blacks, both in private and in his political campaigns. However, Russell believed that blacks were intellectually, morally, and socially inferior to whites and that segregation of the races was absolutely essential for the harmony and stability of southern society. He thought that blacks had made a good deal of progress since their freedom from slavery, and he hoped they would continue to make even further advances. He was pleased when blacks could move from sharecropping and tenancy to farm ownership. Their progress in education, religion, the arts and music, and the professions, however, according to Russell, must be within their own racial institutions not within the larger white-dominated society.

Russell believed that, because of their innate inferiority, blacks must always remain second-class to whites and must be content under white social, economic, and political control. He honestly believed in two societies, one white and one black, separate and unequal. He thought blacks must be satisfied with holding the lowest and most menial jobs. Russell once admitted to a critic that he had recommended a black for a federal job. Explaining the situation, he said he had done so only after the person had been supported by a number of solid white citizens, and furthermore the position had always been "considered a negro's job."[52] Above all, Russell insisted that there must be no race mixing because he believed it would lead to intermarriage and what he called mongrelization of the races. That, Russell insisted, would bring down both races. He never viewed blacks in the same way that he did other immigrants. Rather, he looked upon them as intruders who ought to be happy to live in the United States without ever being considered equal to whites. Russell believed that if blacks did not like how things were, they should return to Africa. His racism was deep and uncompromising.

An incident that occurred in the spring of 1936 illustrates just how sensitive Russell was to even appearing to support a black for a substantial middle-class job in a white-dominated agency. Thomas J. Crittenden of Atlanta wrote to him that he was applying for an administrative position with the TVA and would appreciate his recommendation. Not realizing that he was black, Russell wrote to the director of personnel at the TVA strongly endorsing Crittenden. Some six weeks later, Russell received a reply from George Slover, the personnel director, explaining that when there were clerical, educational, or administrative openings in the program for blacks, Crittenden would be given careful consideration. On May 13, probably the same day he received this letter, Russell wrote Slover that he had written the recommendation under a "misapprehension" and asked that his "endorsement of this negro" be withdrawn and his original letter returned. He got his letter back within a few days. Russell recognized just how damaging the distribution of such a recommendation could be in his forthcoming campaign for reelection if it got into the wrong hands. It never did.[53]

Russell was even willing to forego federal spending in Georgia if it promoted the image and influence of blacks. In 1936 Congress was considering a resolution to appropriate $2 million for a National Negro Exposition in Atlanta. Senator Joseph O'Mahoney of Wyoming asked Russell for his views on the matter. Russell replied that, while it would be nice to have that money spent in Georgia, the appropriation could not be justified and he would oppose it.[54]

As far as Russell was concerned, the long battle over black civil rights began with the antilynching bill introduced in 1935. Russell deplored the vile crime of lynching as much as anyone. He believed in order but order under law. Nevertheless, like most other southerners, he strongly opposed any federal intervention in race relations. Southern senators organized quickly, and after a six-day filibuster, the bill's supporters gave up. Southerners had easily won the first skirmish.[55]

The antilynching issue, however, would not disappear. In late 1937, senators Robert Wagner of New York and Frederick Van Nuys of Indiana introduced a new antilynching bill. Informal polls indicated that as many as 70 percent of the Senate members favored such legislation. Moreover, public opinion seemed to support greater federal protection of black rights. The entire situation greatly alarmed southern senators, including Russell. Senator Tom Connally of Texas, the leader of what was coming to be known as the "Southern Bloc," had the responsibility of organizing the opponents of antilynching legislation. Recognizing Russell's organizational talents, as well as his knowledge of Senate rules, Connally called on Russell to be second in command of the southern forces. Russell organized the southern senators and developed the strategy to defeat the Wagner–Van Nuys bill. Also Russell spoke at length against the measure. When he discussed the bill on January 24 and 25, 1938, more colleagues were present to listen than at most Senate sessions. Since they considered Russell something of a moderate on this issue, his colleagues had unusual interest in what he had to say and how he said it.

Russell took this opportunity to carefully argue the southern point of view in his usual refined, reasonable, and sophisticated manner. He did not resort to any rabble-rousing language or slurs on blacks as did some of his more extreme colleagues. As so often had been the case, he claimed that he held no ill will against blacks and declared that he had never been unfair to them. "There are no members of the Negro race in my State tonight," he said, "who would say that any official or personal act of mine had resulted in any unfairness to the Negroes."

Russell began his talk by trying to shame the Senate for taking up time with "unnecessary and uncalled for" antilynching legislation while ignoring the president's legislative agenda. Charging that the bill had been brought forward mainly for political reasons, he insisted that it was an unconstitutional infringement on states' rights. Moreover passage of such a law, he argued, would be "an unjust reflection on the people of the South" since it was a political bill that would "result in pillorying a great section of this country before the world as being incapable of its own self-government." Even though lynching had been nearly eliminated, this legislation was saying to the South, according to Russell, "You are a clan of barbarians. You cannot handle your own affairs unless we apply to you the lash and spur of Federal power."

Most important, however, was Russell's view of the future. He and other southern leaders saw the antilynching bill as only the opening wedge for legislation that would go much further in protecting black civil rights. As Russell put it, if the Senate passed this bill at the request of "a negro organization" (the National Association for the Advancement of Colored People [NAACP]), it would be snared into supporting other measures that would "strike vital blows at the civilization of those I seek to represent." He saw federal interference in southern customs and practices of race relations as cataclysmic. Such interference would not only destroy "the white civilization of the South" but perhaps even the "entire civilization of the United States."

Russell viewed this bill as a first step in bringing federal control of southern elections. That could result in a horrible situation, he said, where black governors, U.S. senators, congressmen, and local officials might be elected. Antilynching legislation was the beginning of a program to break down relations between whites and blacks that had developed "painfully through 70 years of trial and error, suffering and sacrifice, on the part of the races." He insisted that the South had a good record on race relations and that blacks and whites had learned that it was better for both groups to live apart.

Russell saw a fourfold program developing. First there was this antilynching bill. Then there would be federal intervention in elections in the South. Third, bills would be brought forward to enforce social equality. Measures were already being considered in the House that would abolish segregation on interstate public transportation, including eating facilities, rest rooms, and other accommodations. The "trend of the times," he said, would go further and "enforce social equality between the races" in schools, hospitals, colleges, and other public institutions. Finally, Russell foresaw perhaps what he considered the worst trend of all—the striking down of state laws that prohibited interracial marriage. He advised his colleagues that these objectives "were identical with the program of the Communist Party." He said that elements of the Communist party had been going about the South preaching such doctrines but that it was a tribute to "the colored people of the South" that they had not fallen for such propaganda. He read extensively from Communist literature that advocated breaking down "white supremacy."[56]

The arguments advanced by Russell in the 1938 antilynching Senate fight summarized very well the position of most southern senators. Unlike some of his colleagues, especially Theodore Bilbo of Mississippi, Russell did not deliver racist diatribes. His tone was moderate, and he never said anything malicious about blacks. He aimed to educate and convince northern conservatives that the South should be left alone to handle racial problems.

At the close of his talk, Senator William E. Borah of Idaho walked over to Russell and congratulated him on his presentation. Subsequently, Borah also spoke against the bill as a violation of states' rights. "The people of the South will ever revere the name of William E. Borah," Russell declared. On February 21, 1938, opponents of the bill defeated cloture, which would have shut off debate, by a vote of 58 to 22, and proponents dropped the measure. Russell felt good over the result. He inserted editorials in the *Congressional Record* from newspapers all over the country, which he believed illustrated growing sentiment against antilynching legislation and the expansion of federal powers into state affairs. He believed that his efforts to educate people had paid off. Just before the vote, George W. Norris, Nebraska's liberal senator, said that he had originally favored the bill but that after hearing the southern arguments he had decided to vote against cloture.[57] As it turned out, however, this was more of a holding action than a real victory for southern senators. White supremacy was an idea and condition coming under siege.

From the beginning of the antilynching fights in the 1930s through the passage of the civil rights acts of 1964 and 1965, Russell's attitudes and positions never changed. He was a prisoner of his understanding of history. He regularly referred to what he considered the horrible days of Reconstruction after the Civil War when blacks temporarily gained some political power under federal law and military backing. His favorite author on the subject was Claude G. Bowers who wrote in *The Tragic Era* that state governments controlled by carpetbaggers and blacks had brought disaster to the region. If the federal government guaranteed the civil rights of blacks, Russell believed that history would repeat itself.

Russell blamed much of the increasing concern over civil rights on Eleanor Roosevelt. He accused her of initiating the movement for "equality of employment" and, as he put it, compelling departments and agencies "to employ members of minority groups." Russell believed that, more than anyone else, it was she who convinced blacks that they should support Roosevelt and the Democratic party. He realized that President Roosevelt occasionally mentioned civil rights, but the president had never urged Congress to pass any civil rights measures. Russell did not hold the president responsible for the growth in demands from blacks. Rather, he blamed Eleanor Roosevelt and the heads of some federal agencies.[58]

Russell, who normally did not cave in under pressure, found that he could not risk even the appearance of compromise on the race question. The confirmation of Aubry Williams as administrator of the Rural Electrification Administration illustrates this point. Williams, a native of Alabama who had held several administrative positions in New Deal agencies, was nominated to head the administration early in 1945. Believing strongly in a truly democratic America, Williams had spoken up for blacks and poor people in the South. During his confirmation hearings, several southern senators strongly attacked Williams as being a radical "nigger lover." Senator Bilbo was particularly expressive and outspoken. Russell had originally told Williams that he would vote for his confirmation, but after the publicity about Williams hit the press, Russell backed down. He wrote Williams that the people of Georgia were "outraged" at his racial views, so it was "with deep regret" that he could not support him. "I hope that you will understand my position," Russell concluded. The *St. Louis Post-Dispatch* sharply criticized Russell and four other southern senators for voting against Williams. "Such men are the worst foes of the South today," the editor wrote.[59]

It is interesting to note that in 1942 when C. B. Baldwin was under attack as head of the Farm Security Administration, Russell defended him against charges that he was a Communist or Communist sympathizer. Although the senator could back a liberal New Dealer against accusations that he was a Communist, he could or would not support anyone accused of favoring racial integration.

While Russell and other southern senators managed to defeat a threat of federal interference in the southern way of life in 1938, it was not a pleasant year in his personal life. Two events, the abandonment of his marriage plans and the death of his father, were unhappy occasions.

For many years, Russell had regularly been queried by reporters about why he did not get married, but he never indicated that he had any interest in such a commitment. He had always been fond of women and had dated a great deal. In his earlier years, however, he had broken off relationships with any women who indicated serious intentions. During his first years in Washington, he was one of the most eligible bachelors in the city. Some of his colleagues' wives regularly tried to match him up with some woman. When one woman asked him why he had not married, he replied half in jest, "Well, I've been looking for a woman that was too proud to see her husband work and was able to prevent it." Not long afterward, the woman telephoned and told Russell that she had found such a woman. Needless to say, he never pursued the matter.[60] He continued to date, but it was not until he met Patricia Collins in 1935 that he considered marrying.

Patricia Collins was a native of Atlanta and a graduate of Agnes Scott College and the Lamar School of Law at Emory University. After finishing her study of law, she went to Washington where she obtained employment as an attorney in the Department of Justice. She and Dick first met at a Georgia Society dinner-dance given in his honor at the Mayflower Hotel. In the small talk accompanying their introduction, Patricia mentioned to the senator that she had nearly failed to get her position because Leeman Anderson had suggested to Russell that he stop the practice of giving political clearance to individuals he did not know personally. It happened that Patricia was up for appointment just as Russell implemented that policy. He relented and she got the position, but the situation was the subject of teasing and joking for years afterward.

In any event, Dick and Patricia soon began dating regularly, fell deeply in love, and by 1938 were making marriage plans. A professional in her own right, intelligent, attractive, poised, and gracious, Patricia appeared to be an ideal match for Russell. It seemed as though this would be a perfect marriage. But there was one hitch. Patricia was a devout Catholic.

While Russell was still a member of the Winder Methodist Church, the claims of formal religion bound him only loosely. He had attended church and had even taught Sunday school classes in the 1920s, but by the 1930s, he seldom attended a Sunday church service. He might drop in at the National Cathedral occasionally or go to the small Presbyterian church nearby, but those were exceptions to his usual Sunday routine. Surely Methodism had no special hold on him. When he filled out his personal information form as a student at the University of Georgia, he actually checked "Presbyterian" as his church preference. He once told his older sister, Ina Russell Stacy, that if it "weren't for political reasons, I'd get out of the Methodist church." It was not so much that he opposed Methodist doctrine; he was just indifferent to formal, institutional religion. During their courtship, Dick and Patricia had discussed their religious differences but concluded that these could be resolved.

In early July of 1938, Dick took Patricia to Winder to meet his parents and to tell them about their wedding plans. Full of love and hope for the future, everything seemed wonderful. As they discussed the approaching marriage at the Russell home, it soon became clear that Dick and members of his family expected that his brother, Henry, a Presbyterian minister, would perform the ceremony set for July 15. Patricia, however, wanted to be married according to the Catholic rites. Dick finally convinced her that the wedding ceremony should be performed by Henry. The matter seemed settled. Final plans could proceed for the wedding.

After a few days in Winder, Patricia returned to Washington to shop and to make her wedding preparations. But she was troubled. She feared that she had made the wrong decision or one that she could not live with happily. She expressed her doubts to Dick, and they discussed the matter at length. He was sympathetic to her concerns, and besides, he had problems of his own. It was clear that their religious differences had become a serious stumbling block. A major issue was how children born to the union would be raised. In a premarital conference, a Catholic priest had told Dick that he would have to sign an agreement that their children would be raised in the Catholic faith. Russell later told friends that he would want his children to make up their own minds about religious preference and that he could not be bound by the Catholic church's insistence that in a mixed marriage children be raised as Catholics.

Despite being deeply in love, Dick and Patricia finally agreed that they should not marry. If Patricia had agreed to make the needed religious compromises, Dick believed it would have been like "living with a broken arm that would not heal." For his part, he could not agree to accept Catholicism. When the wedding plans were dropped, Russell hurriedly called Ralph McGill at the *Atlanta Constitution* and asked him not to run the announcement of the forthcoming marriage, which already had been set in type. McGill was barely able to kill the story before press time.

The Catholic question also had another dimension. Marriage to a Catholic and an agreement to raise children in the Catholic faith might have damaging political consequences for Russell. Although Dick never expressed any such fear himself, Patricia believed that Russell saw this as a danger to his political future. It would have been an ideal issue for Eugene Talmadge and possibly others to exploit. In any event, it was the religious question that stilled the marriage.

The decision not to marry was deeply troubling for both Patricia and Dick, probably more so for her than for him. She wrote him on August 31, shortly after they decided against marriage, that she was trying to look at the entire experience as a dream. But, unfortunately, she had to wake up. Dick was then in Winder, and she asked him to visit her when he returned to Washington as she had many things to discuss. In closing, she again professed her love for him.

During the next several years, they continued a close friendship. He sent her roses and orchids on occasion, got her tickets for the Army-Navy football game, and arranged for special seats at Roosevelt's third inauguration in 1941. Since Patricia was a good friend of Russell's sister, Ina Stacy, they sometimes met at the Stacys' home in Washington. By 1942 they were seeing one another less frequently, but they dated as late as 1947.

In March 1948, Patricia broke the news to Dick that she was going to marry Sal Andretta, an assistant attorney general in the Justice Department. This, Russell admitted, surprised and shocked him. Russell's

Judge and Mrs. Richard B. Russell surrounded by their family, ca. 1930. The seven Russell sons are in the back row with Richard, Jr., in the center, the six daughters and one daughter-in-law are in the middle row, and two sons-in-law and six grandchildren are in the front row. (Photo courtesy of Russell Memorial Library, University of Georgia, Athens.)

scribbled notes and letters indicate that, while he had not married Patricia, he was not anxious for her to marry anyone else. Nevertheless, he wished her "full and complete" happiness and offered to do anything he could "for you and yours." Patricia replied that she would always treasure their friendship, and she hoped that Dick could visit her and her husband as soon as they got settled in their new apartment.[61] Although Patricia and Dick remained friends until his death, the relationship had some elements of an unhappy tragedy that should have worked out differently and had a happier ending.

Although Russell never married, he had a strong emotional relationship with his own family, and he believed deeply in family values. The Russells were a remarkably close-knit group, something that Ina Russell had promoted and encouraged during all of her married life. One of the highlights of each year was the Russell family reunion that was initiated in the 1920s. Usually held on the Saturday closest to Judge Russell and Ina's wedding anniversary on June 24, the reunion took place at the family home in Winder where the Russell children, grandchildren, nephews, nieces, and other relatives gathered. It was a time for reminiscing, visiting, meeting new members of the family, eating, and just having a good time. These occasions were among the happiest in

Dick Russell's life. In 1938 some forty-three family members attended the gathering on July 3. Dick and his six brothers and six sisters were all present. They always had a family photograph taken, and that year Dick sat to his mother's right holding one of his nieces.[62]

Uncle Dick was a favorite among the younger members of the family. He not only had interesting experiences to relate but was fond of each of his nephews and nieces. He was concerned about their education and encouraged them to keep up with current events. Sometimes at these reunions he arranged a reading contest for early teenagers. They would sit around the dining room table and he would have each one read a story out loud from the *Christian Science Monitor* or some other newspaper. Then he would grade them on their pronunciation, their reading ability, and their understanding of the material. He would then award a prize to the winners. For the boys, it might be a rifle, and for the girls, $100.

Exactly five months after the 1938 reunion, the sudden death of Judge Russell broke the family circle. On December 3, the seventy-seven-year-old judge had worked in his Atlanta office until about 4 P.M. when he returned home. He suddenly became very ill, and around 8:30 that evening he died in his bed of a heart attack. Ina Russell sat nearby. His body lay in state at the state capitol building before he was buried on December 6 in the family cemetery behind the Russell home. Among the hundreds of messages of condolence that Russell received, there was a telegram from President Roosevelt addressed to "Dear Dick." Roosevelt expressed his deepest sympathy and added that Georgia had lost "one of her great sons and I have lost a dear old friend." Dick was now the oldest male in the Russell family, and it was expected that he would take over the family leadership role. That he did.

In January 1939, when Russell returned to Washington, the clouds of war were rising on the European horizon. The New Deal was winding down, and President Roosevelt and Congress were giving increasing attention to international affairs. Russell still worked to get additional benefits for farmers and for other reforms, but he, too, found that the international crises were occupying an increasing amount of his time. Within eight months, Hitler's march into Poland would set off World War II. This terrible event presented some new and troublesome problems for Russell.

9

Foreign Affairs and World War II

═══

Richard B. Russell held a few basic assumptions that guided his views and actions in matters of foreign policy. These included his strong belief in the superiority of Anglo-Saxon culture, his fierce patriotism, and his conviction that the United States should always maintain a strong military defense. Long after World War II, Russell described himself as "by instinct, an isolationist" but one "who supports the flag when it is committed to any danger or trouble."[1] As a college student, state legislator, and governor and during his early years in the Senate, he held firm nationalist, isolationist attitudes, which meant in practical terms that he believed the United States should avoid trying to solve world problems except where its national interests were clearly at stake. Although as a young man he occasionally expressed some of the idealism of Woodrow Wilson, Russell considered the Founding Fathers to be more appropriate spokesmen of American foreign policy.

In a speech at Barnesville on Armistice Day, 1928, Russell discussed some of his foreign policy views. Sounding much like Wilson, he told his audience that the United States did not go to war in 1917 for national glory or to enslave others but to insure that all peoples could determine their own form of government. He saw an end to war as the "main hope of mankind" but warned against pacifist propaganda for disarmament. Russell was critical of individuals who enjoyed the blessings of the United States but who were not proud or supportive of their country. He praised the American Legion for its work in encouraging patriotism and love of country. Russell stated that he favored a strong defense and national preparedness. The fact that some people made money from war angered Russell. He declared that he never again wanted to see anyone wax fat on wartime profiteering. Ending his talk on an isolationist note, he mentioned George Washington's Farewell Address and said it was time for Americans to take care of themselves.[2]

Before going to the Senate and becoming a member of the Naval Affairs Committee, Russell had only light brushes with foreign policy issues. In Judge Russell's campaign against Senator George in 1926, the judge had opposed the World Court and the League of Nations, and, as his father's campaign manager, Dick heard numerous speeches on those topics. He also traveled extensively in Western Europe in 1927, which increased his firsthand knowledge of the area. But what he saw tended to strengthen his isolationism. The war debt question received considerable attention in Russell's first campaign for senator as he criticized Crisp for supporting Hoover's moratorium on the payment of war debts to the United States. When he arrived in the Senate, arms reduction and naval limitation were topics of national concern.

From the time he went to Washington until the end of his political career thirty-eight years later, Russell supported a strong defense. After he returned from visiting the West Coast naval bases in October 1933, he wrote that it was essential for the United States to keep its navy up to full strength as allowed by the London Naval Treaty of 1930. Russell saw aircraft carriers as an especially vital part of U.S. defense forces. He also believed that strictly controlling the munitions industry would be a great step toward peace. "Take the profit out of war," he stated, "and everyone concerned will think twice before wanting war."[3]

In January 1934, Russell was appointed to the Board of Visitors of the U.S. Naval Academy, a post that he held for three years. Through his own brief naval experiences and his contact with his Uncle Robert L. Russell, a career naval officer, he had maintained a special interest in that branch of military service. Upon accepting the appointment, he wrote, "I am tremendously interested in everything which relates to the efficient operation and maintenance of the Navy." Later on he lent support to the plan to establish a two-ocean navy that was being pushed by his fellow Georgian, Carl Vinson.[4]

Russell's first major foreign policy vote came in January 1935 when the Senate was considering the resolution that the United States adhere to the World Court. Although Russell had seldom commented on matters of foreign policy, he took this opportunity to express his strong isolationist views. Admitting that he ventured into the discussion "with some trepidation," Russell said that he owed it to his constituents and to himself to speak up. Like many other senators, Russell feared that a vote for the World Court was only a preliminary move toward joining the League of Nations. If the United States should become a member of the league, Russell envisioned American youth and wealth becoming committed to enforce sanctions against aggressors. This, Russell said, would lead the nation into "Asiatic brawls" and "European quarrels" that were of "no remote concern to us."

Declaring that joining other nations would not bring peace, Russell advised staying out of entanglements with European countries. "My views are those of a nationalist," he continued; he was for "the United States of America first." Although Russell said he desired peace and was interested in the welfare of humanity, he would not "trade the life of one American youth" in a quarrel where the United States had no stake "to save the lives of 10,000 citizens of another land." He summarized his views by saying that the country's historic policy of goodwill toward all nations but entanglements with none was still the proper policy after 150 years. He then cast one of the 36 votes against the resolution of adherence to the World Court.[5] The 52 votes for the measure were considerably short of the two-thirds needed for approval.

Later in the year, Russell voted for the Neutrality Act, but he made no comment on neutrality as a way to avoid getting involved in foreign wars. In 1936 when the Senate was discussing aspects of the Reserve Officer Training Corps (ROTC) program at land-grant colleges, Russell took a strong stand in favor of military training. "The people of my State," he said, "still have a spirit of reverence for the flag and our institutions."[6]

Between 1935 and 1939, as Mussolini invaded Ethiopia, the Japanese overran much of China, and Hitler tore up the Treaty of Versailles, American foreign policy discussion centered around how best to protect the nation from being drawn into another overseas war. By 1939 an intense debate emerged between the isolationists and the interventionists, who believed that the United States could best protect its interests by assisting countries under attack. Russell, however, did not become prominently involved in the debates and controversies about the course of American foreign policy. He voted for funds to strengthen American defenses before Hitler invaded Poland in September 1939, and after the fighting got underway, he supported the administration's request to modify the earlier neutrality legislation so that American aid could flow to England and France.

During 1940 and 1941, he voted for all of the major legislation designed to strengthen American military capabilities and to assist the victims of aggression. He supported the Selective Service Act, which the Senate passed in August 1940, and voted for the lend-lease legislation, which provided for aid to Allied forces, in March 1941. He was greatly worried over the implications of the lend-lease proposal, or the "give" bill, as he realistically put it. At the time the measure was being debated, he wrote his mother, "We can only pray that the President will so administer it that we can keep out of war and won't be left defenseless if we do go into the war." Russell also favored a plan to repeal three sections of the Neutrality Act of 1939, which passed on November 7, 1941, only a month before Pearl Harbor. In this period, he spoke up occasionally for more military hardware. During discussion in the Senate in May 1940, he said that he believed America's security depended on the "development of our aviation" and stated that the U.S. Air Force should have at least fifteen thousand planes "to make this country absolutely secure from any attack."[7]

As the momentous events of 1939, 1940, and 1941 transpired, Russell simply followed the president on foreign policy matters. In a speech in 1940 to 4-H members in Georgia, he declared that "our policy of aiding Great Britain and the democracies is now the first national policy of our government. It is too late now to debate; it is our duty to support the President in carrying out this policy." Americans must arm themselves, he stated, to protect American liberties and institutions "against the ruthless Nazi tyranny and the poisonous Nazi philosophy." Then he talked about building a two-ocean navy and manufacturing more tanks and planes. The future, Russell said, was going to be grim as people were required to pay high taxes and make other sacrifices.[8]

When the Selective Service Act was being debated in August 1940, Russell and Senator John H. Overton of Louisiana introduced an amendment to give the president authority to draft any manufacturing plant or facility that refused to accept defense contracts from the War Department. Russell argued that since the government was about to draft the nation's youth, it was only fair that all industries be forced to cooperate with the federal government's defense efforts. "To achieve complete preparedness we should make available to the national defense the wealth, the industry, and the genius of America, as well as the vitality and lives of American manhood," he said. Russell added that he hoped subsequent legislation would make certain that "no vast fortunes are created while men are drafted at a dollar a day."[9]

There was strong opposition to the Russell amendment permitting the president to take over industries that refused to cooperate with the defense effort. The *New York Times* condemned it editorially, and many politicians called it unnecessary and undesirable. The House favored milder and weaker legislation, but the Senate rejected the conference report by a vote of 37 to 33. A House-Senate conference reconvened, and the Senate won stronger authority in line with the Russell-Overton amendment.[10]

Unlike some southerners, Russell gave strong support to Roosevelt's election to a third term in 1940. He sharply criticized Wendell Willkie, the Republican candidate, labeling him "an inexperienced amateur" in foreign affairs and a source of confusion and contradictions in domestic policy. No one in the United States, Russell declared, knew as much about international affairs as Roosevelt, and the American people would never strike "the strong hand of Franklin Roosevelt from the wheel of the Ship of State as we travel these stormy and dangerous seas." He reminded people of the bread lines, closed banks, depressed markets, unemployment, and low farm prices that greeted Roosevelt in 1932 and then boasted of the "progressive measures" that the president had promoted to bring relief. Russell emphasized the main Democratic themes in the election—the Republicans were a depression party, and it would be dangerous to change horses in the middle of the political stream.[11]

A matter that greatly concerned Russell in the immediate prewar years was the question of immigration restriction and the deportation of dangerous aliens. As a member of the immigration committee since arriving in Washington, Russell was very sensitive to the possibility of disloyal aliens engaging in activity damaging to the country's security. On January 8, 1940, he told his colleagues that laws to deport certain individuals were more in need of "clarification and revision" than any legislation he could think of. The Senate passed by a voice vote his bill to deport any aliens who admitted in writing that they were guilty of espionage or who had violated U.S. narcotics laws.

On May 24, 1940, Russell again discussed this question. He argued that U.S. immigration laws were too liberal in regard to aliens and that the country could not be completely safe until Congress passed a law requiring aliens to register. Aliens, he said, were guests of the United States, and if they did not like having to comply with restrictive laws, they should leave or be deported. They did not have the same rights as citizens, Russell insisted. He supported the Smith Act of 1940 that made it illegal to teach or be a member of a group that advocated the violent overthrow of the government. In May 1941, Russell became chairman of the Senate Immigration Committee, and in that position, he opposed any liberalization of the immigration laws. The next month, the Senate passed his bill to give foreign service officers more authority to deny visas to any aliens who might endanger the public safety.[12]

Once the United States became involved in World War II, Russell grew alarmed over the prospect of the war's effect on race relations. Economic changes demanded by the conflict provided opportunities in southern industrial employment, in military service, and in government agencies previously denied to all but a very few blacks. Defense industries in the South opened up some jobs for blacks, while employment in the North drew tens of thousands of poor blacks away from southern farms and plantations. The war proved to be a kind of watershed in the drive for black rights—the beginning of revolutionary events that eventually saw great advances for blacks. Russell directed much of his energy during the war years toward blocking changes in established race relations.

One of the first issues that threatened white supremacy and racial segregation was the demand for a fair employment practices policy in all defense and war industries. Discrimination in employment on the basis of race seemed to deny the claim of American leaders that, in opposing Hitler's racism and bigotry, the United States was the guardian of democracy and freedom. Early in 1941, A. Philip Randolph, president of the Brotherhood of Sleeping Car Porters, threatened to lead ten thousand blacks in a march on Washington if something was not done to reduce discrimination in employment. Responding to this threat, on June 25, 1941, President Roosevelt issued Executive Order 8802, which established a Fair Employment Practices Committee (FEPC) and which made it illegal for defense contractors to discriminate against employees on the basis of race, color, or religion.

Viewing this as an attack on segregation, Russell bitterly objected to the FEPC. Even worse was the fact that the president had dealt with the problem of fairness in employment by executive order. He had bypassed Congress where an FEPC bill could have been defeated in the Senate. To Russell this was a scary and threatening situation. He had only one viable alternative left and that was to try to cut off funds for the agency. In this, however, he was unsuccessful. Russell viewed the FEPC as an agency that was less interested in the workers' welfare than in social reform. He believed that it was working to break down segregation, to place black employees in jobs previously reserved for whites, and to destroy the southern way of life.[13]

As if this was not bad enough, late in 1942 the House of Representatives passed a bill that would have eliminated the poll tax in eight southern states, including Georgia. Thoroughly aroused, Russell declared that this measure represented a political move "to satisfy the negro voters of the populous eastern and western states." He accused those supporting the bill of using the war to "destroy the existing relations between the races in the South."[14]

Russell had more than his usual reasons for opposing those promoting the poll tax bill. To get a quorum, Majority Leader Alben Barkley had proposed that the sergeant at arms bring in Russell and seven other senators, mostly southerners, for a Saturday session.[15] Having expressed his indignity over such action, Russell addressed the Senate on November 17 on the poll tax issue. He said that he was growing tired of having to defend the South year after year against legislation that would smear the region and its people, who outsiders seemed to believe did not have the good sense to handle their own affairs. Defending his position on the race question, he declared that never before in all human history has "an uncivilized race" made such progress as had blacks in the South during the past seventy-five years. According to Russell, his region had advanced in race relations despite "all the reformers, publicity seekers, vote hunters, and South baiters and haters who harrass us year after year by undertaking to tell us from Washington how to run our local affairs." Throwing out the challenge to integrationists, Russell said that if they expected this or other legislation "to force social equality and commingling of the races in the South, I can tell you now that you are doomed to failure."

Russell insisted that such a divisive issue should not even be raised in wartime when men were dying on foreign battlefields. Moreover, he expressed resentment at northern Democrats who were products of the Edward Kelly political machine in Chicago or the Frank Hague organization in New Jersey talking sanctimoniously about cleaning up southern elections. He was also concerned about the disunity in the Democratic party that such legislation was causing. Nothing good could come from "Democrats attempting to force down Democratic throats such legislation as this," he said.

On November 18, 1942, Russell sent a statement criticizing what he called the "Force Bill" to all Georgia newspapers. Besides charging that the poll tax bill violated states' rights, he stated that it was an unconstitutional measure supported chiefly by "professional South-haters or reformers." Referring again to Reconstruction days, he declared that neither Benjamin Wade, Charles Sumner, nor Thaddeus Stevens would have suggested such a law. Russell promised his constituents that he would fight the measure with everything at his command. On November 23, proponents of the bill to eliminate the poll tax lost a cloture vote by 37 to 41, effectively killing the measure.[16] Russell saw every move to increase black rights as producing catastrophic consequences. When the Senate defeated another poll tax bill in 1944, he wrote that if it were passed and "sustained by the courts, it will be the end of representative government in this country."[17]

Although legislative action to enhance black rights embittered Russell, he was even angrier over the threat posed by the FEPC. Here was a federal agency not directly responsible to Congress that proposed programs and implemented policies of its own making. Funding for the agency had not come from appropriations but from the president's Emergency Fund.

Russell vented much of his frustration over the FEPC during his questioning of Chairman Malcolm Ross at hearings before a subcommittee of the Appropriations Committee in June 1944. He was always polite and considerate of witnesses, but he made it clear to Ross that he strongly opposed the agency and its programs. Russell spoke sharply against an FEPC policy that had eliminated separate rest rooms for white and black workers at a plant in Maryland. He also expressed strong opposition to an FEPC order requiring that southern railroads promote conductors and engineers without regard to race or color. Negroes, Russell said, had not held such jobs in the past, and they should not be forced to in the future. He was greatly displeased by the fact that four of the eleven regional directors of the FEPC were black. It was unwise and unfair, he stated, that white businessmen should have to deal with black administrators when problems arose. Russell accused the FEPC of discriminating against whites.[18]

On June 16, Russell spoke for some two hours in support of a resolution that would deny operating funds for the FEPC. Despite Russell's strong plea, the Senate rejected his amendment to kill the FEPC by a vote of 39 to 21.[19] In August he was back on the Senate floor blasting the agency and urging that it be killed. The idea that the FEPC could require firms to hire qualified blacks in positions previously denied to them was abhorrent to him. If extended to the South, it would upset the established order of things. The agency's powers were so broad and extravagant, he said, that it could force a company to employ a black as its president. Such extreme statements were becoming increasingly common in Russell's talks on the race issue. His private correspondence reflected even deeper feelings. Claiming that the FEPC was administered "almost entirely by negroes," many of whom had been associated with the Communist party, Russell wrote that he could not conceive of a "greater menace to the future of the entire country, and especially to our Southland."[20]

Russell argued that, if the FEPC continued its "callous disregard of human nature" by trying to enforce integration on the entire nation, it would be disastrous for the war effort and the future peace and welfare of the United States. He said that he disliked discussing racial questions in a public forum and that he had never used "the Negro issue in order to secure votes." But in this case, he believed such a discussion was in the best interests of both whites and blacks because the FEPC was the "most dangerous force in existence in the United States today."[21]

The demands for copies of Russell's August 9 speech against the FEPC were overwhelming. A Philadelphia resident asked for ten thousand copies. Although his office could not meet such a request, a total of twenty thousand copies had been printed and distributed. Russell sent a copy to Margaret Mitchell, author of *Gone with the Wind*, who replied that it was a "masterly" treatment of the situation. Mitchell wrote that she was "appalled at the tide of racial bitterness" that had developed during the war. Professing to like blacks, she wanted them to get "a square deal." What worried her was that FEPC-types would alienate whites and blacks to such an extent that blacks would be "friendless in a no-man's land deliberately created by calculating radicals."[22]

Throughout 1944 Russell became frustrated and discouraged over his inability to stop or slow the trend toward greater black rights. He referred to the FEPC as "the most sickening manifestation of the trend that is now in effect to force social equality and miscegenation of the white and black races on the South." While he had fought the FEPC with all his influence, he said that "I am afraid that we are going to be licked." Considering that the Democrats in the East and West, as well as Republicans, were making a bid for the black vote, he stated that blacks outside the South were the most "powerful political group in this country."[23]

One of the things that especially bothered Russell was his belief that many southern whites did not fully realize just what was happening on the racial front. He wrote an Atlanta business friend that the determination to force both races into the same schools, hospitals, restaurants, swimming pools, and other public places was much stronger than most people realized. They were not aware, he said, because the press had almost stopped printing stories about integration. "I am sick about it," he wrote. Russell concluded that "our southern civilization" did not fall during Reconstruction but was collapsing at the present time.[24]

Russell spent an inordinate amount of time and energy during World War II trying to preserve racial segregation and white supremacy. To him, it was the most important issue on the home front. In his mind, there was no contradiction in holding blacks in a position of second-class citizenship in the United States while blacks died for their country on distant battlefields. As far as Russell was concerned, these black fighting men, whom he held in low esteem, would have to return after the war to the same system that they left in 1941 and 1942. Believing that blacks were naturally inferior, Russell did not think that valor on the battlefield or distinctive service at home could earn them a position in an integrated society. If racial barriers were destroyed, even "baseball [and] football teams would have to play negroes," he scribbled on an office note pad.[25]

Near the end of the war, a few Georgians were beginning to view the racial question in a different light. Josephine Wilkins of Atlanta wrote "Dear Dick," on June 27, 1945, that after carefully studying the FEPC she had changed her mind about it. She believed that something was needed to protect those who had nothing but their labor to sell. Whites did not have the right, she said, to tell people that they could only advance so far in a job because of race or color. Wilkins added that whether or not she or Russell liked it, the time was "not far distant when Negro people are going to vote." Russell replied that he and Wilkins could never agree on this issue and then added, "Negroes may vote in Georgia in great numbers and my unalterable opposition to this measure may result in my defeat, but I will get along somehow in private life."[26]

By World War II, Russell had developed about all of the arguments that he would ever use in his thirty-year resistance to civil rights legislation. As mentioned earlier, his actions were determined by a clear, unwavering, and uncompromising set of ideas. The first of these was his unshakable belief in white supremacy and in the absolute superiority of Anglo-Saxon culture. Since he considered blacks racially inferior, he believed that neither education nor anything else could possibly make them equal to whites. With a superior and an inferior race living side by side, it was to be expected that the superior group would work out the relationships that would govern the society. Thus southern whites had developed a system of race relations that Russell claimed was best for both races. Under that system, blacks had made great progress in the generations after slavery. To be sure, laws, social custom, and sometimes extralegal actions had been necessary to keep blacks in their inferior position and to maintain white supremacy, but Russell argued that these measures had really been in the best interests of blacks as well as whites. He admitted that there were some problems in southern race relations, but, if left alone, southerners would work them out. However, he believed that physical separation of the races was absolutely necessary for racial harmony and social stability. Race mixing, he insisted, would lead to intermarriage and the ruin of white civilization.

Perhaps most distressing of all to Russell was the fact that new and uncontrollable forces, largely generated by the war, were threatening the kind of South he understood and loved so dearly. His South of stable social relations, based mainly on an agricultural economy, was beginning to retreat before the forces of industrialization, huge federal expenditures at defense installations, and an influx of people from other regions of the country.

Russell found himself in the grasp of a great contradiction from which he was unable to escape. His very success in helping to expand old federal facilities and to bring new ones into Georgia during the war worked against the status quo in race relations. For example, during the war, Fort Benning near Columbus greatly expanded its training operations and brought in thousands of men from all over the country. A large air depot was completed south of Macon in 1942 at a place soon to be called Warner Robins, which employed some fourteen thousand people. Shipbuilding at Savannah and Brunswick required thousands of additional workers. Bell Aircraft established a huge bomber plant that opened at Marietta in 1943, and many other communities attracted various kinds of war industries.

Russell was proud of the facilities he had helped to bring to Georgia and boasted of the millions of federal dollars funneled into the state. But there was a catch. There were not enough white workers to meet all of the labor requirements. Although the white power structure resisted training blacks for skilled jobs, before the end of the war cracks were appearing in the armor of workplace segregation in Georgia and elsewhere throughout the South. Part of this resulted from increased efforts by blacks and from actions by the FEPC and the War Manpower Commission. Federal war facilities and industries such as Bell Aircraft that operated on government contracts had become by the end of the war reluctant participants in breaking down the old order.[27] Russell recognized the momentous economic changes stimulated by the war, but he could not bring himself to accept the accompanying social changes that were bound to follow. Without ever explaining how, Russell believed that the old order of race relations could be maintained in the rising industrial-urban economy—the process of modernization—encouraged by broader employment opportunities and better education.

Russell continued his keen interest in agriculture and the welfare of farmers during the war years. Wartime demand for farm commodities pushed prices up to high and profitable levels for producers, so Russell did not have to promote price supports or parity payments. However, he fought for increased appropriations for the Farm Security Administration before its virtual demise in 1943. He also supported the Rural

Electrification Administration and finally pushed through permanent school lunch legislation.

Despite full employment and good wages during World War II, Russell insisted that the school lunch program should be expanded. The money spent on school lunches and the milk program rose from about $4 million in the year ending June 30, 1941, to over $23 million in fiscal 1943. Originally the idea had been to expand markets for agricultural products as well as to provide better food and nutrition for schoolchildren. Up to 1943 when the program was taken over by the War Food Administration, it had been administered by the Federal Surplus Commodities Corporation, an agency of the U.S. Department of Agriculture that sought to eliminate farm surpluses. The Department of Agriculture provided food to schools through state welfare departments.

Because of the shortage of trucks and gasoline during the war, it became difficult to transport food to the schools. In February 1943, the program was changed so that schools could buy food locally and be reimbursed from federal funds for up to about 50 percent of the cost. Also in 1943, state departments of education received administrative authority to distribute the food in place of the welfare agencies.

As chairman of the subcommittee on agricultural appropriations, Russell kept working to increase funds for the school lunch program. In July 1943, Congress passed legislation permitting the expenditure of up to $50 million from Section 32 funds held by the Department of Agriculture out of tariff revenues. This amount was available for the fiscal year from July 1, 1943, to June 30, 1944. For the first time, Congress had made a specific appropriation for school lunches. Operating under special authority, the secretary of agriculture had earlier dispensed Section 32 funds for the program. By 1944 school lunches were being provided for about 3.8 million children. Congress appropriated another $50 million for 1944–45.

Meanwhile, Russell sought permanent school lunch legislation. In June 1943, he called for a law that would clearly define "the responsibility of the federal government, the states, and local school districts for this program." On March 28, 1944, he introduced a bill for this purpose. Discussing the matter in May, Russell declared that providing lunches to schoolchildren was "one of the finest and most beneficial programs our country has ever seen."[28] Neither the Russell bill nor bills introduced by other Senate and House members passed Congress before the war ended.

On May 7, 1945, Russell and Senator Allen J. Ellender of Louisiana introduced a bill for the purpose of assisting states with school

President Harry S Truman handing out pens to congressional leaders after sign-ing the Russell-Ellender school lunch bill, June 4, 1946. Senator Russell is third from left. (Photo courtesy of Russell Memorial Library, University of Georgia, Athens.)

lunch programs. It was not until February 26, 1946, however, after the House had acted, that the Senate passed permanent school lunch legisla-tion. Defending his measure, Russell said the bill promised to contri-bute more to the "cause of public education . . . than any other policy adopted since the creation of free public schools." When Senator Robert Taft objected to the cost, Russell indignantly replied that Congress had appropriated $2.7 billion for overseas relief "without batting an eye" and should not "split hairs" over something "to help our children." Russell then moved to substitute his bill for the House bill and asked for a conference with the House. The Senate agreed, and on May 24 the Senate approved the conference report that was essentially the Russell bill.[29] The National School Lunch Act finally established permanent legislation for the program. National policy now promised "to safe-guard the health and well-being of the Nation's children and to encour-age the domestic consumption of nutritious agricultural commodities."[30]

Russell viewed the school lunch program as one of his most impor-tant accomplishments in his thirty-eight-year career in the Senate. Usually he was indifferent to receiving public credit for legislation, but in this case, he showed an unusual jealousy regarding his authorship. In 1966, some twenty years later, William Bates, Russell's press secretary, asked Ray Schafer, who worked for the subcommittee on agricultural appropriations, to prepare a brief legislative history of the school lunch legislation. Schafer's mimeographed report traced the program's early history and, according to Bates, proved "beyond any doubt" that Russell was the key figure in developing this program. Russell wanted credit for his authorship, and he received it.[31]

Although Russell was not one to find excuses to make foreign junkets, in July 1943, he found himself at the head of a Senate committee sent to visit the United States' far-flung battlefields and military installations. For several months, senators from both the Special Committee to Investigate the National Defense Program, better known as the Truman Committee, and the Military Affairs Committee had considered sending subcommittees overseas. The idea was to extend outside of the United States the type of investigations conducted by the Truman Committee. Majority Leader Alben Barkley was not enthusiastic about such a trip, and he withheld his approval. Barkley did not think the time was right for such a junket, believing it would be inappropriate for two Senate committees to wander around overseas taking up the time of military commanders. He and Truman discussed the matter over several weeks. It was clear that the pressure was building up from some senators who favored such a trip.

On June 30, Barkley discussed the matter with the secretary of war and chief of staff who assured him that the army could provide transportation and take care of no more than five senators on an overseas investigation. Barkley then talked with Senator Robert R. Reynolds of North Carolina, chairman of the Military Affairs Committee, and Truman, and they each agreed to name two senators to make the trip. Barkley asked Russell to serve as chairman of the investigating committee. The other members were Albert B. Chandler, Democrat of Kentucky, and Henry Cabot Lodge, Jr., Republican of Massachusetts, representing the Military Affairs Committee, and James M. Mead, Democrat of New York, and Ralph O. Brewster, Republican of Maine, representing the Truman Committee.[32]

Russell did not particularly welcome this assignment. He had planned to spend the congressional recess in Winder resting and seeing friends. Nevertheless, he accepted the appointment and began making preparations for the trip. While the goals were somewhat fuzzy, the main objective seemed to be to investigate the distribution, quality, and use of war materials at various military installations overseas.

The idea of five senators galloping around the globe in wartime aroused some sharp criticism. Senator Bennett Champ Clark of Missouri said he did not think military leaders would permit the senators to see enough to "stick in their eye," while Senator Scott Lucas of Illinois declared that he would not vote a dime for such a trip.[33] Many expressed the opinion that military commanders around the world had more to do than entertain and chaperone a group of senators. An Atlanta businessman wrote Russell that such a junket was an "utter waste of taxpayer money." He suggested that it would be better to allocate the gasoline used on such a jaunt to "your Georgia people." Another constituent wrote that he could not even get "enough gasoline to take a pleasure trip to my summer home."[34] Russell ignored the criticism, but he did appreciate any kind words about the project. On July 3, Clark Howell, publisher of the *Atlanta Constitution*, wrote a favorable editorial that concluded that "Senator Russell and his committee are given an opportunity to be of tremendous service to the nation."[35]

There was much to do to prepare for departure on July 25. Russell took several vaccinations, he gathered names of Georgians at military bases whom he might visit, and he bought army clothes that the senators would wear when they visited field operations or flew over enemy territory. If they were captured, the army wanted to make sure they would be treated as prisoners of war. The senators also brought two business suits each. The smokers, including Russell, were advised to take an extra supply of cigarettes, and each senator was provided with a "dog tag," helmet, compass, knife, booklets on jungle survival, and emergency rations. Baggage weight for each was limited to fifty-five pounds.

On July 24, Russell had lunch with President Roosevelt who expressed great interest in the trip. Roosevelt also indicated that he was worried about the senators' safety. He was particularly concerned about that part of the trip from Ceylon over the Indian Ocean to Australia. However, acting Secretary of War Robert P. Patterson assured the president that the thirty-two-hundred-mile flight across water could be done easily. The plane had been tested for such distances and had three hours of fuel remaining.[36]

On the afternoon of July 25, the four-motored converted Liberator bomber with Captain Henry Myers at the controls lifted off from National Airport in Washington. Winging over Labrador, Greenland, and

Iceland, with only fuel stops, the plane, named "Guess Where II," landed in southwest England. The group spent about ten days in England, nearly half of the time with the Eighth Air Force. While there, Russell spoke to the men and assured them of support at home and the tremendous importance of their service. It was an upbeat talk, and Ira C. Eaker, the commanding general, wrote Russell a few days later thanking him for "the inspiring talk you made to our combat crews."[37] The senators also had dinner with the king and queen and visited with Churchill, and on August 2, Anthony Eden, the British foreign secretary, entertained them at the foreign office.

The next leg of the journey was from England to Morocco. Arriving on the morning of August 7, they were met by General Eisenhower's representative, General Arthur Wilson. Eisenhower had written Russell earlier that "urgent military matters" would prevent him from welcoming the senators in person.[38] The first big event was a dinner with the pasha of Marrakech. The pasha's palace, Russell stated, was something that he would never forget. He wrote his mother that at dinner he sat on the pasha's right and suffered from the Arab custom by which the host reaches into the common dish and serves the person sitting to his right. The guest was obliged to eat, he explained. "I barely got away under my own steam," he said; "I felt like a stuffed pig."

After visiting Casablanca on the Atlantic, the senators toured the important cities and military installations along North Africa's coast. General Eisenhower entertained the group at a dinner in Algiers on August 11. This gave Russell and the others a chance to ask about military matters, the delivery of supplies, the quality of arms, and other questions. Russell also made it a point to talk with ordinary soldiers in order to get their view of things. He often posed with soldiers from Georgia for photographs that were later sent to the men's hometown newspapers.

As Russell traveled in North African cities, he saw nothing good about the native populations. The polyglot mixture of races and people was a far cry from his beloved Anglo-Saxon culture. Scribbling notes to himself, he mentioned the "squalor and different races," and he wrote to his mother that the Arab cities were "indescribably filthy." He did not believe that an American could survive there for more than two or three days, even after taking "as many shots as I did."[39]

After visiting Cairo, the party went on to Basra and Abadan on the Persian Gulf, where they talked to Americans who were forwarding large quantities of lend-lease materials to the Soviet Union. Then the group flew on to Karachi, New Delhi, and Assam, in northeast India.

From there they flew to China. They visited with Generals Joseph Stilwell and Claire L. Chennault, as well as with Chiang Kai-shek and other Chinese officials. They had dinner with Madame Chiang Kai-shek and her husband. Russell had known Madame Chiang for some years, as she had once gone to school at Wesleyan College in Macon.

From China they flew back to India, stopping in Calcutta where they stayed an extra day because of engine trouble, before going on to Ceylon. Leaving Ceylon, they began their longest nonstop flight of the trip, thirty-two hundred miles, to Carnarvon on the west coast of Australia. This was the first time anyone had flown nonstop over the vast Indian Ocean in a land-based plane and was the part of the trip that President Roosevelt had been concerned about. But everything went well. The senators visited several installations in Australia and then flew to General MacArthur's headquarters in New Guinea. After some other stops, the Liberator made its way across the Pacific, returning back to Washington on Tuesday, September 28. The trip had taken sixty-five days. It had been a long, hard, tiring venture, and Russell was glad to be home. "You can not realize how glad I am to be back in the good old USA," he wrote to his old friend Marion Allen. He told a reporter that, while he would not go again for $50,000, "I wouldn't have missed this one for a million dollars."[40]

During his trip, Russell scratched down brief comments and observations about what he saw. He mentioned that morale was low among American troops in New Delhi because they did not have enough to do. He found some men napping in a hotel and others pitying themselves. He saw the job of supplying General Chennault in China as "insuperable" and wrote, "Chinese no good." He was least impressed with what he saw in India and China. His term for a black American battalion in Calcutta was "chaotic." On the other hand, he found morale high in most places he visited and believed that American military forces were doing a tremendous job.[41]

During his absence, Russell kept in close touch with his office and his mother in Winder. Since the senators were provided with secretarial assistance at each major stop, he wrote home frequently. In one letter to his mother, he described flying over the area between the Euphrates and Tigris rivers. It was in this region, he said, that the Garden of Eden had supposedly been located. If so, he judged that the region had greatly "deteriorated" since the time of Adam and Eve. However, the homesick traveler wrote that the real Garden of Eden was on the other side of the world—in northeast Georgia! Leeman Anderson in the senator's office also kept Mrs. Russell informed about her son.[42]

Senator Russell, at left, with General Douglas MacArthur, to his immediate left, in New Guinea during a visit to U.S. war zones, July–September 1943. (Photo courtesy of Russell Memorial Library, University of Georgia, Athens.)

In an interview shortly after he returned home, Russell said that the most important impression he had gained from the trip was the "enormous difficulties of transport and supply." These problems had underscored for Russell the truly global arena of American wartime efforts. He was fully confident of final victory, but he warned against the dangers of overconfidence.

Russell announced that the committee was preparing a report that would include general observations, problems encountered, and possible recommendations. The report, Russell stated, would be shared with all senators in executive session within about a week. Needless to say, he was greatly annoyed when Senator Lodge arose in the Senate on September 30, a week before the scheduled secret session and gave his account of the trip. This was a clear violation of an understanding among all members of the committee, but there was nothing Russell could do about what he considered such irresponsible deportment by a colleague. By speaking out before the committee was ready to make any official statement, Lodge upstaged Russell as he was the first to discuss a number of matters that would be included in the formal report.[43]

Russell considered this breach bad enough, but he was even angrier when some senators talked to reporters after the executive session on October 7. His colleagues even quoted him, including remarks that were purportedly not very complimentary of some U.S. allies. His supposed statements that England had large forces in India that were not being effectively used and that the Chinese were not fighting hard against the Japanese were not welcomed in either Great Britain or China. He was also quoted as saying that the British were using some lend-lease supplies for political purposes in other countries and that the Russians were not being very cooperative.[44]

In an effort to regain some control of his committee, Russell prepared a ten-point statement on the group's findings and had it inserted into the *Congressional Record* on October 11. This summary concluded that American troops were well supplied and cared for, more oil should be tapped from the Middle East so that American supplies could be conserved, the work of the War Information Agency ought to be reviewed, the achievements of American fighting men should be better publicized, consideration should be given to full integration of the different military branches after the war, the United States should gain postwar rights to airfields it had constructed throughout the world, access to international communications ought to be guaranteed to the United States after the war, a policy for rotating fighting men should be developed, and a clear postwar foreign policy should be established. Finally, the committee praised American fighting men for their skill and bravery.[45]

On October 28, Russell finally appeared before a well-filled Senate chamber to give his own personal report on the committee's trip. He emphasized that he was speaking only for himself. It was a fairly long, detailed account that filled nearly seven pages in the *Congressional Record*. He stressed that the committee had avoided giving any advice or interfering in any way with military operations. He did believe, however, that the committee had gained a good deal of valuable information on the quantity and quality of American military equipment, on some of the problems with America's allies, and on the complex issues that would emerge in the postwar years.

Russell elaborated on most of the points that he had inserted into the *Congressional Record* some two weeks earlier. He stressed the idea that the United States could not possibly provide the relief and assistance after the war that many countries were expecting. His also insisted that there must be a well-defined postwar foreign policy characterized by toughness and directness. It should be administered, he said, by some "two-fisted" American who understood national interests. "Kid-glove diplomacy" must be abandoned.

One of Russell's major interests was maintaining bases around the world that had been purchased "with the blood of American boys." He mentioned Dakar on the West Coast of Africa; New Caledonia, a French colony in the South Pacific; and Iceland as places where Americans must have control of bases or at least be granted special rights. Russell denied that this was imperialism. But "call it what you will," he told his colleagues, it was a realistic step "to prevent another generation of Americans . . . from being compelled to pay again in blood and treasure in taking these islands back." There were many important "spots on the globe which have been fortified and developed with American money and sweat, which will become increasingly important to the defense of the United States with the rapid improvement of air and sea transportation. The smaller the world becomes," Russell added, "the closer are these bases to our shores."[46]

Even before Russell spoke, there had been sharp criticism of the main views and recommendations of the five senators. A writer for the *New Republic* called comments by the world travelers "nonsense" and argued that their statements would damage relations with American allies. The idea of holding air bases in the postwar period in places where American men and money had built them was a bad idea, the writer stated, unless the United States intended to become the "greatest imperialist power of all time." The *Nation* declared it was unfortunate that the public had been treated to the "global gossip" picked up by the five lawmakers because such wrongheaded ideas might sink into the public consciousness. In England a correspondent for the *Chicago Sun* wrote in the *New Statesman and Nation* that the senatorial mission had aroused a great deal of anti-American feeling in Great Britain.[47]

These and other criticisms of the senators and their ideas did not bother Russell. He was convinced that his observations were sound and in the national interest. He believed that frank criticism of U.S. allies would not create any serious difficulties and that some good might even result. The *Washington Times-Herald* carried a cartoon on December 10, 1943, showing the Capitol Dome and the Washington Monument in the background and Uncle Sam surrounded by schoolchildren in the forefront looking at a sign that read, "In the words of Senator Russell: We have come to a pretty pass if a citizen of the United States cannot support with wholehearted devotion the cause of his own country without subjecting himself to the charge that he is anti-British or anti-Russian."

Russell raised several important issues that occupied a great deal of attention in the postwar world. One of these was relief and foreign aid. He did not oppose all foreign assistance, but he argued that it should be temporary and dispensed sparingly. He was distressed as he talked to officials in country after country who seemed to think that the United States had an inexhaustible supply of money and goods with which to help other nations. Second, Russell believed that the acquisition of military bases throughout the world was absolutely essential for American security. He thought, too, that the United States should begin negotiating for these before the war ended and its bargaining power diminished. On February 28, 1944, he wrote Secretary of State Cordell Hull, urging him to make arrangements with France for special rights in New Caledonia after the war. He argued that American military men agreed that such rights were necessary to provide security and "to enable us to discharge our responsibility in maintaining the future peace of the world." Acting Secretary of State Edward R. Stettinius replied on March 8 that commitments had already been made to restore New Caledonia to France after the war.[48] Russell would not hesitate to use lend-lease as a lever to get the cooperation of foreign governments. There is no doubt that Russell's trip strongly influenced his thinking on these and other issues. For the first time, he realized how much the world had shrunk due to modern technology, and he wanted to prepare defenses that recognized this fact.

Shortly after Germany's defeat, Russell headed another Senate committee that investigated conditions in the European and Mediterranean theaters of war. The committee consisted of members of the Military Affairs and Naval Affairs committees. As acting chairman of the Appropriations Committee for a time in May 1945, Russell recommended himself as the representative from that committee. The purpose of the trip, Russell told his colleagues, was to look into matters relating to redeploying troops in the Pacific theater, to study the question of what to do with surplus war supplies, to view battlefields and port facilities, and to consider the policy for discharging troops.[49]

The eight senators left Washington on May 25 and arrived at Orly Air Field in France the next day. After two days of official functions and relaxation in Paris, the group went to the Normandy peninsula where much hard fighting had occurred in 1944. They saw the port facilities at Cherbourg, visited Utah Beach, and flew over other invasion beaches. Then going into the heart of Germany, they viewed the destruction of

Cologne, the submarine pens in Bremen, and the underground plants where the V-2 rockets had been manufactured. They also went to Hitler's retreat at Berchtesgaden. After going to London, and flying back to Marseille, the group went on to Rome, arriving on June 10. They had an audience with the Pope and did a little sightseeing as well as visiting with several military commanders. Russell spent more time with military officers than most of his colleagues. Six of the members then flew from Rome to Algiers and Casablanca and on to Washington, where they arrived on June 14.

Russell and Senator Burnet Maybank returned to Paris in hope of being able to make a brief trip to Moscow. Russell had been notified on June 9 that the Soviet embassy in Paris had approved visas for all members of the party. By that time, however, six senators indicated that they did not wish to visit Russia and were about to return home. Russell then asked Ambassador Jefferson Caffrey in Paris if the Soviet Union would approve visas for only two senators. Caffrey talked to the Russian ambassador and received the necessary permission. A plane was sent from London to Paris to pick up Russell and Maybank who planned to leave for Moscow on the afternoon of June 16. They intended to make a "quick friendship visit" and return on the 19th. When Ambassador Caffrey sent the passports of Russell, Maybank, and members of the plane's crew to the Russian embassy in Paris on the morning of the 16th, word came back that visas could not be given to just two senators. Approval had been for eight!

This Soviet runaround deeply annoyed Russell. The Russians kept saying that the matter was still under consideration but that there would be a delay. Plainly irritated, Russell announced that he would return to the United States on June 23. In discussing the matter, Russell said that "our basic idea was to do everything possible to cement better Russo-American relations by furthering contacts between the two nations." He later wrote to Ambassador Caffrey that "our suspicious friends in Moscow were not really anxious to have any of us." On another occasion, he stated, "It is high time Russia grows up in a diplomatic sense."[50]

If the taxpayers viewed this as a useless junket, they were right. Although the senators received briefings from military leaders, viewed destroyed cities, and even visited General Eisenhower at his headquarters in Frankfurt, the observations and study were extremely impressionistic. What the senators did or saw had little or nothing to do with prospective legislation. The log of the trip shows that sightseeing and vacation-type activities, including the Folies-Bergère, received as much or more attention than hard work. In Russell's defense, it can be said that he spent more time in serious investigation than several of his colleagues, but the nation gained nothing from the trip. It is interesting that Russell never claimed that anything very constructive came out of his being in Europe nearly a month in the summer of 1945.

The thing that concerned Russell most of all at the war's end was whether the Japanese would be properly and severely punished. Unless the Japanese fully recognized their defeat, Russell believed the seeds of the next war were already planted. As a part of demonstrating to the Japanese just how badly they had been beaten, he strongly urged trying Emperor Hirohito as a war criminal. On September 18, 1945, Russell made a long speech on this subject before a fairly well-filled Senate chamber.

What Russell believed was softness toward Japan just before the end of the war seemed confirmed within a short time. In late July, while President Truman was at Potsdam, the United States and Great Britain issued the Potsdam Declaration. This was an ultimatum to Japan to get rid of its military leaders, permit an American military occupation, disarm, and agree to unconditional surrender. The Japanese rejected these demands. On August 6, the first atom bomb was dropped on Hiroshima, and the next day, Japan claimed to accept the Potsdam Declaration. However, the Japanese ignored the demand for unconditional surrender, and they retained their emperor.

Russell was resting at home in Winder as these momentous events were taking place. Fearing that Japan would escape with only a conditional surrender, he telegraphed President Truman on August 7, urging that the United States "carry the war to [the Japanese] until they beg us to accept their unconditional surrender." Then he added that Emperor Hirohito "should go." Russell was bitter. Remembering the wounded troops he had seen in his 1943 trip to parts of the Pacific war theater, and reading reports of Japanese atrocities, he urged the further destruction of Japan. If the United States did not have enough atomic bombs to do the job, he told Truman, "let us carry on with TNT and fire bombs until we can produce them." The United States should continue its attack, he said, until the Japanese "are brought groveling to their knees." Then he told the president, "The next plea for peace should come from an utterly destroyed Tokyo."

Truman replied to "Dear Dick" on August 9. While he admitted that Japan was "a terribly cruel and uncivilized nation in warfare," he could not agree that, "because they are beasts, we should ourselves act in the same manner." The president said that he would not wipe out whole populations because of the "pigheadedness" of their leaders "unless it is absolutely necessary." Then Truman added that he felt the Japanese would "fold up" very shortly after the Russians entered the war. Truman did not say that, on the very day he wrote, he had ordered an atom bomb to fall on Nagasaki. It was clear that Russell and Truman were far apart in their thinking on the Japanese issue.[51]

Despite the destruction of two atom bombs and the damage done by traditional American arms, the Japanese people did not understand the completeness of their defeat, according to Russell. Somehow, Russell argued, this must be brought home to them in a dramatic fashion. He even favored using Philippine, Korean, and Chinese forces, as well as troops from other countries that the Japanese had overrun or controlled, as a part of the occupation army. He also suggested that if Admiral William F. Halsey had ridden the emperor's white horse down the streets of Tokyo, the people might have gotten the proper message.

Russell predicted that there would be another war if Japan were permitted to keep the emperor. There could be no permanent peace, he insisted, until Hirohito had been not only dethroned but also tried as a war criminal. Holding the emperor responsible for Japanese expansionism, cruelty, and brutalities against American soldiers and prisoners of war, Russell called him a "superaggressor" who had headed a policy of "unparalleled barbarism." After a long speech that brought compliments from senators J. William Fulbright, Kenneth Wherry, John McClellan, and others, Russell concluded by introducing Senate Joint Resolution 94, which declared that it was the policy of the United States to try Emperor Hirohito as a war criminal. The joint resolution was referred to the Military Affairs Committee where it met a quiet death.[52] Russell's unsuccessful attempt to convince the Truman administration that Hirohito should be tried as a war criminal was only the first of many failures to influence the direction of American foreign policy after 1945.

10

Russell and Postwar America

B y the end of World War II, Richard Russell was an emerging
leader in the U.S. Senate. He was still Georgia's junior senator
and worked somewhat in the shadow of Senator George, but
his abilities and leadership were being increasingly recognized
both in Washington and beyond. In some instances, he was receiving
national recognition for his work, especially in agriculture, but mainly
he was considered a regional spokesman on domestic policies. Looking
at Russell's first ten years in Washington, Ralph Smith of the *Atlanta
Journal*'s Washington bureau wrote that he was one of "the abler and
more influential" members of the Senate. Since only nineteen senators
were senior to him in service, some of his colleagues viewed him as a
kind of senior statesman even though in 1945 he was only forty-seven
years old.

At middle age, Russell appeared to be everything people imagined a
southern gentleman to be. He was courteous, modest, usually even-
tempered, considerate, and charming. He commonly dressed in a blue
serge suit that sometimes looked a bit worn. His early baldness had
become pronounced by the 1940s. When he was outside, he generally
wore a felt hat. As his hair receded and gradually disappeared, his nose
appeared sharper and his ears larger. One writer thought he looked like
everybody's favorite uncle. He was usually smoking a cigarette, a habit
he had begun as an early teenager. It was not uncommon for him to
smoke two packs or more a day. Except for the health of his mother,
Russell had few worries. He was satisfied with his life and felt especially
privileged to serve in the U.S. Senate.

Although Russell had not desired the position, by 1945 he had
gradually replaced Senator Tom Connally of Texas as head of the southern caucus. Southern senators had turned to Russell more and more for
leadership in the battle against the growing campaign for civil rights.
They respected his abilities, his knowledge of Senate rules, his organiza-

tional talent, and his moderate approach to race problems. He had also become the head, as far as there was an acknowledged leader, of another powerful Senate group—the Farm Bloc. In 1941 he was appointed to the Agriculture and Forestry Committee, which added to the power he held as chairman of the subcommittee on agricultural appropriations. By the war's end, most people familiar with Russell associated his name with opposition to civil rights and support for a wide variety of farm legislation, including the school lunch program. No major legislation bore the senator's name, but he had often influenced the course of Senate business by introducing amendments to bills, through persuasion in conference committees, and through personal contact with colleagues. He had never been one to seek credit for legislation, and, except for the school lunch program, he made little effort to gain public recognition.

If Russell was not better known nationally, it was probably his own fault. He made no effort to publicize himself or to court newsmen. He had an innate suspicion of newspaper reporters, who he believed often twisted, garbled, or misstated the facts. While other senators called press conferences and pandered to reporters in order to gain headlines, Russell worked quietly with key individual senators. Not until the late 1950s did Russell finally conclude that a press secretary might be a useful addition to his office staff. Of course he regularly responded to questions on issues and gave interviews, but he did not seek publicity. Russell had the reputation of being a good listener and avoided most chitchat. A framed motto on his office wall read, "You ain't learning nothing when you are talking." He was closemouthed and always maintained confidences. His colleagues considered him absolutely trustworthy. One newsman who covered Washington in the 1950s said later that when Russell went to his grave, at least a thousand Senate secrets would die with him.[1]

Russell's personal and social life did not change much in the years after his near-marriage in 1938. He moved to the Mayflower Hotel in the late 1930s and continued to live there most of the time for the next several years, except for a period during the war when he moved in with his sister, Mrs. J. K. Stacy, whose husband was away on military duty. Despite his long working hours in the 1940s, he found time for an active social life. His attractiveness to the opposite sex that was so noticeable even in high school and college did not diminish with middle age. Women literally pursued him. Writing from California in 1947, a woman he had known years before said she might be coming east soon and would like to see him again to find out for herself if he was still the same "gay young blade" he used to be. She sent a picture in case he had forgotten "a certain redhead." Another woman wrote begging to see more of him, and another urged Dick "to call me sometime, please."[2]

While he dated a number of different women in the late 1930s and 1940s, his two most steady companions were Patricia Collins and Harriet Orr. As mentioned earlier, Dick and Patricia continued to see one another socially until 1947, shortly before her marriage. He met Harriet at a party on February 1, 1941. She was from North Carolina and was employed in Washington. After their first meeting, Dick referred to Harriet as being "very nice," and he did not permit the brief acquaintance to lapse. A week later, they spent the afternoon together and had dinner that evening. From that time onward, Dick and Harriet were together regularly but surely not exclusively. There were times when he would take Harriet out for dinner one night and Patricia the next.

Dick greatly enjoyed Harriet's company. They went for drives, watched movies, met for late-afternoon cocktails at the Mayflower and elsewhere, and often had dinner together. Sometimes Russell would send one of his office assistants out to buy steaks that he would cook on Friday or Saturday evening for Harriet and himself. Their relationship was a warm and friendly one but not intimate. They continued seeing one another for the rest of Russell's life.

Russell enjoyed his times with these special friends, but he had little interest in the parties and dinners given by members of Washington society. Around 1940 he quit going to most Washington parties unless they were given by or for Georgians. He turned down scores of dinner and cocktail invitations from women who considered him one of the most eligible bachelors in the nation's capital. Occasionally he would accept an invitation to a large formal affair, as he did when he had dinner with Pearl Mesta, Washington's premier party giver, on February 6, 1947. He called it a "nice party." Occasionally Russell partied too hard and drank what he considered "too much," a fact that he sometimes recorded in his diaries or daybooks.[3] Now and then he would quit drinking entirely for a short while and record that he was "on wagon" or "still on wagon."

Whenever possible he liked to get back to Georgia in the fall so that he could attend one or more of the university's football games. His love of football can be seen in his letter to a university official about attending the Orange Bowl game on January 1, 1942. Writing December 8, 1941, the day after the attack on Pearl Harbor, Russell declared that "unless the Japs are bombing Washington by then, I expect to see the game." As it turned out, he did not get to Miami. He spent Christmas with his mother and then returned to Washington to deal with important affairs of state. Wallace Butts, coach and later athletic director at the University of Georgia, was a Russell friend. Each fall Russell usually had several exchanges of letters with Butts about football tickets. In 1949 he wrote that if Butts knew of any more Charlie Trippis in military service he would try "to get them out for you." Trippi had been suddenly released from the air force in 1945 after a colonel came to his residence one evening and told him that he would be discharged the next day. Trippi returned to Athens in time for the 1945 football season and became one of the University of Georgia's greatest stars. Russell apparently had some part in Trippi's sudden discharge, but he never revealed precisely what.[4]

Russell also enjoyed baseball and often attended games in Washington. He almost always managed to listen to the world series over the radio, and in later years, he watched the games on television. The Senate secretary later had a television in his office and invited senators who were baseball fans to watch. Russell was usually with this group. Ty Cobb, one of baseball's most famous players and a native Georgian, and Russell had been friends for many years. Russell's friends claimed that he knew more statistical information on football and baseball players than most people would want to know.

By the early 1940s, Russell had given up some activities that he had enjoyed in earlier years. Bird hunting, he often said, was his favorite sport, and he did a great deal of it up to the mid-1930s. He owned five or six shotguns. After 1940, however, he seldom, if ever, fired a gun. Friends still invited him on hunting trips, but he found excuses not to accept. When he received an invitation to go deer hunting in southeast Georgia in 1953, he replied, "Frankly, I have no desire to kill any more deer as I have killed more than twenty in my time."[5] Also, the left-handed golf clubs given to him when he was Speaker of the House gathered dust in the family closet in Winder.

There were several other bachelors in the Senate during Russell's early years in Washington, but none of them was his special friends. One of his closest friends in the Senate was Harry F. Byrd of Virginia. Byrd and Russell had a number of things in common. They had both been governors of their respective states, and they had entered the Senate at nearly the same time. They both had strong ties to agriculture—Byrd grew apples. Fairly often Russell would drive down to Berryville, Virginia, to spend Sunday and have dinner with the Byrds. Russell also accepted dinner invitations from Senate friends in Washington. When the Fulbrights invited him to dinner Friday evening, October 5, 1945, for example, he happily accepted.[6]

More and more of Russell's life became involved with the Senate. It was his major interest and love; some said it was his mistress. He usually ate lunch in the Senate dining room, where he was often joined by colleagues who wanted to discuss business or just visit. He enjoyed that relationship, which came from being a member of the "club." His membership in the Senate was very special to him as were his personal and social relations with other senators. Many of his evenings were spent listening to the radio and reading. Always a prodigious reader, Russell read the *Congressional Record*, copies of hearings, and other official documents. This explains why he was so well informed on legislation and why colleagues increasingly looked to him for leadership and guidance on different bills. But he also read novels and, most of all, history. Russell read rapidly and had the knack of retaining not only the theme but also the details of what he read. He had many books in his own library as a result of gifts from publishers and others, but he also borrowed books from the Library of Congress. Sometimes he checked out more volumes than he could read and kept them beyond their due date. The librarian of Congress frequently had to gently remind Russell to return overdue books.

As often as possible, Russell liked to get back to Winder to spend time with his mother and to relax in the small-town environment that was so dear to him. Despite the growing international crisis during 1941, he made several trips to Winder to be at his ill mother's bedside. In October he wrote that the doctors had about given up hope that she would recover. Gradually, however, she got better. After she could travel in the fall of 1942, Ina Russell went to be with her daughter, Mary Willie Green, in Alexandria, Virginia, for several weeks. Dick then saw his mother often. Russell's deep love for his mother, and his appreciation of her efforts in raising thirteen children, grew with time. He often expressed amazement at how she had done so much. "Mother is the greatest woman I have ever known," he confided to one friend.[7]

It was somewhat more difficult to get back to Winder during the war, but Russell got enough extra gasoline for his Chrysler to make occasional trips. He used scarce gasoline with extreme care, and sometimes returned unused coupons to the rationing board. On some trips, a secretary would go along from his office to handle correspondence for the senator while he was in Winder. In making the trip back and forth from Washington, Russell often picked up military men who were hitch-hiking.[8]

Russell always received many Christmas presents from friends and admirers after he went to Washington. These included such gifts as a box of cigars, handkerchiefs, gloves, a ham, pecans, flowers, a toiletry set, or a necktie. He always acknowledged these items in a personal way. Russell sent beautifully phrased thank you letters, and in later years when he could not write all of the letters himself, his staff acquired the same talent. He wrote one couple that it was a great pleasure "to be so wonderfully remembered by two of my dearest friends," and he assured another friend who had sent him cigars that the spirit of friendship "represented by the gift added much to the pleasures of my holidays at home." Sometimes supporters were too extravagant. He wrote one couple that "you must not send me such nice gifts each year." Next year, he said, please just send a card.[9]

In one important aspect of his life, Russell did not change. That was in his careful handling of money. Some friends and acquaintances considered him tight. He would sometimes buy as little as $1 worth of gas for his Chrysler, something that seemed foolish to members of his staff. He seldom bought a new car or had the old one washed. If a senior staff member accompanied him to a local restaurant for dinner after a long day in the office, Russell did not offer to pay the bill, except for his own meal. He checked his laundry carefully to make sure a handkerchief or a pair of socks was not missing. Colleagues occasionally reported that when they entered Russell's office they found him poring "intently over a laundry list in a vain attempt to account for a missing handkerchief." On one trip to Winder, Russell picked up his clean laundry on his way out of his Washington hotel and did not open it until he reached home. Then he found five pairs of socks missing. He did not wait to get back to Washington to check on the matter. He wrote the hotel manager that if the socks were not found, "I shall expect to obtain compensation for them."[10]

There was no reason for Russell to keep such close track of expenditures. During the 1940s, his $10,000 salary, which represented practically all of his income, was enough to support a high standard of living. He also earned a few dollars from interest and sometimes made money on his farms. For example, in 1937, his interest income was $35, but he lost $141.52 on his farming operations. That year he paid $503.44 in federal income taxes. By World War II, his income had gone up very little, but tax rates had risen dramatically, something that never brought any complaints from Russell. In 1943 he paid $3,274 in federal income and victory taxes. Beginning in 1947, senators received an additional $2,500 a year that they could use for living expenses in Washington. This was nearly enough to cover his hotel bill. By the end of the 1940s, Russell had accumulated very substantial assets. Summarizing these in

1947, he calculated that his cash, U.S. bonds, stocks, and the cash value of his insurance totaled nearly $84,000.[11]

So while Russell was not required to be thrifty, it was a part of his nature. When he moved to the Potomac Plaza in 1962, he did not want the delivery boy coming to the door to collect for the *New York Times*. His staff made arrangements to send a check for a three-month subscription to the paper, but Russell insisted that the bill be sent to his apartment to save the fifty cents charged for billing to a separate address from where the paper was delivered. Russell would not tolerate any such useless expenditure.[12]

Russell was as careful with other people's money, including the government's, as with his own. In June 1942, after he spoke to the Cotton Manufacturers Association in Georgia, he submitted such a small expense account that the association's spokesman was surprised if not shocked. Russell regularly refused to take honoraria for making speeches in Georgia. In the handling of all funds, he was meticulously honest. If any campaign funds remained after an election, Russell would return the money to contributors on a pro rata basis. He would have abhorred the idea of keeping extra campaign money and spending it for promotional or other personal purposes as many congressmen and senators did in later years. That was a level of ethics and morality to which Russell would never have adjusted. For example, he said he would oppose any move to give General Eisenhower both a military and a presidential pension.[13]

Russell was also tight with staff salaries. Senators had the authority to give raises and adjustments within their office allowances, and Russell had the reputation of paying about the least of any senator. Staff members would go for years without salary increases. Rachel Styles, for example, went to work for Russell in October 1935 for $2,220 a year; she was still receiving the same salary in late 1942 shortly before leaving the office. Russell occasionally employed relatives but usually only on a temporary basis. For example, he hired his brother, Fielding, who was working on a Doctor of Philosophy degree at George Washington University from 1937 to 1939. He was careful not to pay relatives more than, or perhaps even as much as, other employees. In the late 1950s, William D. Russell, one of his nephews who had been working in his office, found that he was getting a considerably lower salary than others on Capitol Hill with less seniority and experience. He approached Uncle Dick and suggested a raise. Russell replied, "I can't pay you more because you are kin to me." As far as William was concerned, that was not the point, but it ended the discussion.[14]

While Russell guarded his money closely, he was generous in many ways. This was especially true in regard to his many relatives. He helped many nieces and nephews with educational expenses. He also made many small contributions to a wide variety of charities. Most of his gifts were in the $2 to $10 range. If he contributed to one of the many requests he received, he usually mentioned that the amount enclosed was much less than he would like to give. Churches, lodges, and schools were among the institutions that received small gifts. In 1943 his tax-deductible contributions were only $268.50; in the late 1940s, he began taking the standard $1,000 deduction.[15]

Russell had a practice of giving a silver pitcher, or some other silver piece, to relatives or staff members who married or had special anniversaries. He usually asked a staff member or spouse to pick out the item. When secretary Margaret Appleby married in 1948, he asked Dorothy Anderson, Leeman's wife, to get the pitcher. It cost $85 and the engraving read: "Margaret Appleby McCormick from Richard Brevard Russell, 1948." Staff members prized these gifts. After Russell attended the wedding and reception of Rachel Styles and Harold Breimyer in December 1941, Rachel thanked him profusely for both his attendance and the lovely wedding gift.[16]

By the early 1940s, Russell's office staff had nearly doubled from what it had been in 1933. Usually there were eight or nine persons on the payroll, full or part-time. Early in 1937, Leeman Anderson and Dorothy Webb, who also worked in Russell's office, were married. Anderson then took a job with the U.S. Department of Agriculture at Harlingen, Texas, in the Bureau of Entomology, which was trying to eradicate the Mexican fruit fly. Gordon Chappell replaced Anderson. At that time, Russell merged some of his personal staff with that of the Immigration Committee, and Chappell worked in both offices. There were rumors at the time that relations between Anderson and Russell had become strained after the 1936 election. Some said it was because Anderson was a friend of defeated Eugene Talmadge for whom he had worked when Talmadge was commissioner of agriculture in the late 1920s. However, that was unfounded gossip. Russell attended Leeman and Dorothy's wedding and gave them the usual silver pitcher. Anderson had not been gone long before he wanted to return to Washington, and in early December 1941 Russell offered him his old job as chief clerk in the senator's office. Anderson was deeply pleased that Russell would take him back, especially since the senator knew his "many limitations and shortcomings," one of which was an alcohol problem.[17]

Although he employed other individuals from time to time, his main secretarial staff in the 1940s consisted of Margaret Appleby, who began in Russell's office in 1937, and Marjorie Warren, who came on board in 1944 and remained in a key position for nearly twenty-five years. Clara Smith, an attorney, joined the office force in 1941 and worked mainly for the Immigration Committee after Russell became chairman in that year. The Russell office was well organized under a system set up by Anderson. Staff members were responsible for carrying out particular assignments. Russell did not see members of his staff very often, except Margaret Appleby who took his dictation. Later Marjorie Warren had that job.

Russell usually arrived at his office about 9 A.M. When Congress was in session, mornings were largely devoted to appointments, committee hearings, and special conferences. In the afternoon, the Senate was in session. If he did not have business on the floor, he would have additional appointments until about four o'clock. By that time, the secretaries would have answered most of the mail and typed up letters ready for his signature. In his private office, Russell would read the day's incoming mail, read and sign the letters that had been written for his signature, and then dictate the letters that needed his personal attention. He would usually work until 6:30 or 7:00 P.M. At least some of the staff remained in the office as long as Russell stayed. They wanted to be there in case the senator "might want something." The Russell staff worked long hours. Some of the office force also was on hand Saturday until noon or later. Staff members often wished that Russell would marry so that he would have to leave the office at a decent hour to get home for dinner. Around seven o'clock, Russell would indicate that he was finished for the day. Then he would open his desk drawer, take out a bottle of Jack Daniels, and pour himself a drink. Sipping his drink, he would listen to the radio, and after he got a television, he watched the news. This may have been the most relaxed part of his day. A half hour or so later, if he did not have an evening engagement, he would go to a nearby restaurant for dinner before returning to his hotel to read.

Russell was rather aloof from his staff. He did not mingle with the secretaries and clerks in their work areas. He was always friendly but somewhat distant and reserved. He deliberately avoided any signs of camaraderie in the office. He was always courteous and referred to the women employees as Miss Margaret or Miss Rachel in the best traditional southern manner. He did not often encourage staff members or give compliments. He believed people should perform their best at all times without having to be pushed or flattered. Yet he had ways of expressing his appreciation to those who worked for him, as well as to close families and friends of long-standing.

The people who worked for Russell had great admiration and respect for their boss, but none of them felt close to him. Indeed, Russell had very few close or intimate friends. He had a host of acquaintances and casual friends and friends who would do almost anything for him. But he was not a man who revealed the depths of his personal feelings to other people, and very few of even his oldest friends really felt near to him. He had warm feelings for individuals, but, outside of his family, he did not express affection for people. He became somewhat more aloof as he grew older, and he had cordial and close relations with only a very few individuals, mostly Senate colleagues. He wrote hundreds of friendly letters to persons he had known for many years, but the relationship did not in most cases extend beyond the writing or brief casual visits.

Russell was known for his calm, objective, and courteous manner. He did not anger easily, was patient, and tried to understand the point of view of others. However, if anyone impugned his character or pushed him too far, he was a ferocious antagonist. An incident involving columnist Joseph Alsop illustrates how dangerous it was to tangle with Russell. In February 1947, David E. Lilienthal, who was accused of being influenced by the private power companies, was being considered for chairman of the Atomic Energy Committee. In speculating on how senators might vote, Alsop wrote that Russell would probably oppose Lilienthal because Georgia was about the "only remaining State where the power people have a real grip on local politics." Alsop added that Russell was also "an avowed enemy of public ownership of power plants." The implication was clear—Russell was under the control of the private power interests. The Alsop story was then broadcast over a Washington radio station by William E. Gold, and Russell heard the Alsop charges repeated on the air.

He was furious. On February 14, he asked to make a personal statement on the Senate floor. Referring to the "All Slop" that the columnist had written, he said that Alsop was among those sensational journalists who had no regard for the truth. He then reviewed his support of the Tennessee Valley Authority, the Rural Electrification Administration, and other public power projects and explained that the Georgia Power Company had supported his opponent in the gubernatorial race of 1930. His record made it clear, he said, that he was not a pawn of any private power interests. He accused Alsop and Gold of vomiting their "putrid falsehood" on those who did not agree with them. He stated that "such miserable characters, such charlatans of the press, such vermin as these, are like unto that animal that is without any pride of parentage or any hope of decent posterity."[18] It is not known whether this tongue-lashing influenced Alsop, but on April 11, he did correct his statements about Russell.

By 1942 Russell's political strength was such that no Georgia politician seriously considered running against him. He had written Ralph McGill as early as July 31, 1941, saying that the political situation looked extremely favorable. As far as his reelection was concerned, Russell stated, "I am most hopeful that I will not have any opposition, but if it must come I think we will be ready."

In writing to other friends, Russell emphasized that his wartime duties in Congress were so demanding that he could not take time to campaign personally. He would leave his welfare in the hands of friends. He did give an account of his work in a number of radio talks and sent advertisements announcing his candidacy to 183 Georgia newspapers. Again he stressed that he could not leave Washington to campaign but that if reelected he would serve the people "honestly, fearlessly, and efficiently during the following term." In a radio talk over WSB in Atlanta on August 29, 1942, he outlined his accomplishments in Washington. Besides supporting wartime legislation and measures to help farmers, he said he believed the federal government should "equalize educational opportunities" for all students. Russell explained that he was "earnestly supporting Federal Aid to Education."[19]

Russell spent only $2,866.07 on his reelection efforts, including the $500 filing fee. The other main expenditures were $523 for postage and mailing and $980 for newspaper advertisements. When one friend whom he had helped to get a position with the Internal Revenue Service in Atlanta sent $100, Russell returned it saying that it was not needed. He treasured such loyal friends, Russell said, and "the first rule of my political creed is to stick to those who are loyal." As usual Russell returned to donors on a pro rata basis all of the surplus campaign funds that were not needed for his election expenses. He wrote, "This will certainly be something new under the sun in Georgia politics."[20]

Russell continued to maintain excellent relations with his constituents. He not only helped them solve their individual problems with government agencies and brought many federal installations to Georgia but also wrote hundreds of letters of sympathy, congratulations, and encouragement. For example, Hubert McDonald was the first young man from Winder to be killed in World War II. On October 22, 1942, he wrote the boy's parents that they could take pride in the fact that their son had died "in fulfillment of the highest call to duty that comes to any man."[21]

Russell was also skillful at handling constituent problems. In 1944, for example, he found himself in the middle of a controversy between two groups of friends. For several years, the Citizens and Southern National Bank of Savannah and the Fulton National Bank of Atlanta had shared the loans to support peanut prices by the Commodity Credit Corporation. When Russell was overseas in 1943, the U.S. Department of Agriculture placed the entire loan with Citizens and Southern. To even things up, Erle Cocke, Sr., one of Russell's closest friends, asked that in 1944 the full loan should be given to Fulton National Bank, of which he was president. The Department of Agriculture, with Russell's recommendation, approved that arrangement. Then friend and supporter William Murphey, chairman of the board of Citizens and Southern, objected. Nevertheless, the Department of Agriculture and Russell gave the entire peanut loan to Fulton National in 1944. This was done with the understanding that in the future the loan would be equally divided between the two financial institutions. Citizens and Southern was not happy over losing any part of the loan in 1944, but President H. Lane Young wrote Russell that, despite the loss of that account, "we have no hard feelings toward you."[22]

At the end of World War II, the United States faced a multitude of difficult problems. These included the reconversion of industry to peaceful purposes, the adjustment of agriculture to nonwar conditions, labor unrest, inflation, the control of atomic power, the emerging cold war, the rebuilding of the shattered Western European economies, and the developing civil rights revolution. It was a time that called for a high level of statesmanship.

Russell was in a position to influence, if not to determine, how at least some of these problems would be approached. He still held membership on the Naval Affairs Committee and had risen to third rank among the Democrats. He was sixth among fifteen Democrats on the Appropriations Committee and remained on the Manufactures Committee. In 1941 Russell had become chairman of the Immigration Committee, and the same year, he asked for and received appointment on the Agriculture and Forestry Committee. He was also appointed to the first Joint Committee on Atomic Energy on August 2, 1946.

Although many important issues were before Congress in 1946, Russell spent most of his efforts trying to protect and enhance the interests of farmers and fighting the FEPC. Except for civil rights, he tended to be a loyal Democrat on most issues, and he supported most of Truman's domestic and foreign policies. By 1948, however, he believed that the president was leading the country down a ruinous path. To halt the direction of the emerging Fair Deal, especially its emphasis on civil rights, Russell sometimes lined up with conservative Republicans to defeat administration bills or to win support for measures not favored by more liberal Democrats. Often economic interests had more to do with the southern Democrat-Republican coalition than any political philosophy. A good example of mutual economic interests was Russell's fight to compute the cost of farm labor in the parity price of farm commodities.

In January 1946, President Truman had recommended an increase in the minimum wage to seventy-five cents an hour over three years. When the minimum wage bill was being considered in March, Russell introduced an amendment requiring that the cost of agricultural labor be included in calculating parity prices. Fellow Georgian, Stephen Pace, carried the fight in the House. The administration, labor groups, and others strongly opposed the Russell amendment, charging that it would be inflationary. Consumers were especially sensitive to rising food costs. Chester Bowles, who headed the nation's economic stabilization program, said it would cost every family $125 a year. Consequently, there was very strong opposition when Russell introduced his amendment in the Senate. Word circulated that Truman would veto the wage bill if it contained the farm labor parity provision.[23]

When critics charged Russell with pushing a measure that the Department of Agriculture opposed and that the major farm organizations were not supporting, he was not in the least deterred. He accused Secretary of Agriculture Clinton Anderson of being a Charlie McCarthy (the well-known ventriloquist's dummy) for Chester Bowles and the Political Action Committee. Taking a swipe at lobbyists, Russell declared that it was a sad day when the Senate could not take up a bill "without having it dinned into our ears that this organization, or that organization . . . is opposed to or is in favor of the measure." Russell charged that the time "has almost arrived" when those without powerful lobby support could not be heard in the Senate. He declared that he was fighting for the farmers, regardless of what any pressure groups said.

Russell did not oppose higher industrial wages and actually favored increasing the minimum wage. He admitted that good wages were necessary to maintain a high national income. But why, he argued, should farmers not be included? What irritated Russell was that higher farm prices were always portrayed as inflationary, while raising industrial prices to meet higher wage costs were not. This was sheer discrimination against the farmer, he insisted. Russell told his colleagues that there were those in the United States who did not care if farmers were forced out of business. If that ever happened, he declared, the "United States is doomed." Launching into a review of the importance of farmers, he said that if farmers were destroyed it "would strike a mortal blow to the soul of America." He concluded "that we cannot save the country and destroy the farmer."

On March 29, Russell's amendment passed the Senate despite widespread and determined opposition. Support came mainly from a Democrat-Republican coalition of cotton and wheat spokesmen whose constituents would have benefited most from the Russell amendment. Senators Arthur Capper of Kansas, Milton Young of North Dakota, Kenneth Wherry of Nebraska, and Chan Gurney of South Dakota, all conservative Republicans, were among those who joined Russell and his cotton-state Democrats to pass the amendment by a vote of 43 to 31. On April 5, a bill to raise the minimum wage to sixty-five cents an hour passed with the Russell amendment still intact. Although the Farm Bloc was strong enough to pass the measure in the Senate, it failed in the House. It took three years for Russell to win his point, but in 1949 Congress included farm labor costs in figuring parity prices.[24]

During the debate over the minimum wage bill, Russell expressed alarm over the growing power of lobbyists in Washington. He believed that senators should make up their own minds on issues without succumbing to the influence of special interests. Pressure groups "are becoming dangerous," he said in April 1946. Then he added: "We must retain the legislator's independence of thought. It is not a good thing when pressure groups elect a man who is forever beholden to them."[25] Russell was especially concerned about such groups as the Political Action Committee that were lobbying for civil rights. But he did not exempt farm organizations from his criticism when he thought it was warranted.

One important measure that Russell did guide through the Senate was the Research and Marketing Act of 1946. He had always looked upon research as an important way to improve the welfare of farmers. The law called for research on new uses for farm products, improvements in marketing, cooperative arrangements for the study of such problems as the mechanization of cotton production, and other possibilities. While Congress did not fund the programs up to the full authorizations, money for agricultural research greatly increased under this law.[26]

The bipartisan Farm Bloc was not a well-organized group, but the senators from major agricultural states could wield a good deal of power on farm issues. The strongest backers of special legislation for farmers were usually senators from the wheat and cotton states. The problem for agricultural legislation was in the House where, as the country became more urbanized, consumer groups were gaining increasing influence. People were very sensitive to rising food prices, and congressmen responded to consumer complaints. This was partly because they ran for office every two years and also because so many of them represented districts with heavy urban populations. Russell could already see the future course of events as the rural population declined and the political power of farmers weakened. He wrote in 1948 that he was trying to get better prices for cotton, "but in view of the attitude of the producers of some other commodities who have joined hands with the representatives of consumers, we have a desperate struggle ahead."[27]

As a result of Republican victories in the midterm elections of 1946, Russell lost his chairmanship of the subcommittee on agricultural appropriations at the beginning of the Eightieth Congress in January 1947. For thirteen years, he had held that important post, and knowledgeable agricultural observers recognized his effective work on behalf of farmers. D. W. Brooks, president of the largest farmer cooperative in the Southeast headquartered in Atlanta, wrote William R. Blake of the National Cotton Council that Russell had done an outstanding job for all farmers, "but has never received the credit to which he is due. An excellent worker," Brooks continued, "but poor publicity man for himself."[28]

Although Russell no longer chaired the subcommittee on agricultural appropriations, he fought as hard as ever in 1947 to raise appropriations for soil conservation, the school lunch program, and the Farmers Home Administration. Price support legislation was not an important legislative issue in 1946 and 1947 because the Emergency Price Control Act of 1942 required that the Commodity Credit Corporation support the prices of wheat, corn, cotton, rice, tobacco, and peanuts at 90 percent of parity for two years after the war ended. The Steagall amendment, pushed by Congressman Henry D. Steagall of Alabama, provided similar supports for a group of other commodities of which the government had asked farmers to increase production during the war. This meant that the government would maintain prices at 90 percent of parity for a sizable list of commodities through the crop year of 1948. The wartime legislation was a marked victory for southern legislators, as four of the South's main commercial crops—cotton, rice, tobacco, and peanuts—were favored with price supports at 90 percent of parity.

The Republican Eightieth Congress sought to reduce federal expenditures by cutting appropriations to a whole list of programs, including some whose funding Russell had worked so hard to increase. As news stories reported the prospect of smaller appropriations for soil conservation, one of Russell's main interests, he received many letters from farmers urging him to preserve the cost-sharing funds needed for payments to farmers.[29] During the war, appropriations for soil conservation had been cut from $500 million to $300 million. Now the Republican House wanted to reduce the figure to what Russell called a "paltry" $150 million. Russell insisted that such a cut would be ruinous. Civilizations had fallen, he argued, because soil fertility had been lost. Moreover, he thought that "we have come to a sorry pass" when Congress quibbled about providing money for soil conservation while sending hundreds of millions of dollars overseas. He urged the Senate to insist that its conferees demand at least $258 million, plus some unexpended funds. After a further tussle, the two legislative bodies agreed on nearly $244 million for soil conservation.[30]

Russell engaged in another bitter fight over appropriations for the school lunch program. In the year ending June 30, 1947, the first full year after passage of the National School Lunch Act, Congress had provided $75 million for school lunches. Russell wanted at least that amount for fiscal 1948. Again, the House shaved the school lunch funds to the disgust of both Russell and Allen J. Ellender. The conference committee finally agreed on $65 million. In reporting to the Senate from the conference committee, Russell expressed regret, but, as he explained, "we had to reach an agreement sometime and we were compelled to make this agreement."[31]

In the case of the Farmers Home Administration in which Russell had such an intense interest, opponents kept him and other supporters from getting substantial appropriations. Poor farmers did not have many spokesmen in Washington. Russell presented evidence of successes among borrowers from the FHA and showed how federal loans had helped tenants become landowners and independent farm operators. But no amount of illustration, argument, or reason could sway budget-conscious lawmakers. Russell talked about veterans needing loans to begin farming and about the "pittance" Congress was considering for all lending purposes, but in vain.[32] Congress provided only $15 million to the FHA for farm purchase loans in 1947. Needy borrowers, including veterans, would have to look elsewhere for farm loans.

Throughout the first half of 1948, Russell was engaged in a fight over permanent farm legislation. The guaranteed price supports of 90 percent of parity enacted during the war would expire at the end of the year. To provide some price protection for farmers beyond 1948, Republican Congressman Clifford Hope of Kansas and Senator George D. Aiken of Vermont introduced new legislation. For some time, the principle of high fixed price supports had been under attack. Such developments as the overproduction of potatoes in 1946 and 1947, when some surplus potatoes were actually burned to get rid of them, produced loud cries against high fixed supports. There was growing demand for the idea of flexible supports based on the level of production rather than on high fixed figures calculated at 90 percent of parity. The flexible price support advocates believed that the way to get farmers to restrict the excessive output that depressed prices was to lower the support level if production rose and raise it if the supply fell. That way farmers could see the practical benefit of not increasing their output beyond market demands.

Despite the backing for flexible supports among farm organizations and within the halls of Congress, in 1948 Congressman Hope, chairman of the House Agriculture Committee, introduced a bill to extend fixed supports at 90 percent of parity through June 30, 1950. The Hope bill passed the House easily on a voice vote. In the Senate, however, the bill sponsored by Senator Aiken provided for flexible supports. Russell strongly favored supporting prices at 90 percent of parity. On June 17, he offered to amend the Senate bill by substituting the House measure. Russell argued that flexible price supports left farmers with too much uncertainty regarding prices and incomes. He declared that heavy demand at home and abroad required high production and that farm prices must be protected as farmers met this worldwide need for food and fiber. He urged the Senate to accept his amendment as a temporary measure until next year when Congress could draw up "a fair and equitable long-range farm program."

Critics argued that high fixed price supports would create surpluses and be costly to taxpayers. Senator Scott Lucas of Illinois declared that consumers might become so angered at costly and wasteful farm programs that the result would be the destruction of all farm legislation. This irritated Russell. Were not farmers also citizens of the United States, he asked. Lucas's argument implied, according to Russell, that the farmer was "a class aside, to himself, and is entitled to scant recognition and should appreciate any crumbs that happen to fall from the congressional table" when laws were passed to benefit other groups.

Russell's pleas failed to win Senate support, and his amendment was defeated by a vote of 55 to 23. With very few exceptions, he was able to get the backing only of southerners and senators from the Southwest. The Republicans and most northern Democrats mounted the flexible support bandwagon. All was not lost, however. When the bill returned from conference committee, some of the Russell principles were intact. The House and Senate agreed to continue price supports of 90 percent of parity until January 1, 1950, only six months less than Russell had suggested.[33]

Russell later explained to his constituents that he had fought as hard as he could for a better law but that the leadership of both parties in the Senate were supporting the Hope-Aiken bill. When he received letters from people blaming inflation on high food prices and social unrest on farm legislation, Russell staunchly defended farmers. He showed how little farmers actually received out of the food dollar and insisted that they were underpaid for their work. He never weakened in his backing for price supports, soil conservation payments, and other farm programs, even when they cost billions.[34]

On postwar foreign policy issues, Russell often found himself out of step with the Truman administration. He believed that the United States was assuming too much responsibility for the economic and military welfare of other countries at a cost that excessively burdened American taxpayers. Russell did not believe that the United States should police the world or try to extend American influence where the country had no demonstrated national interest. He continued, however, to advocate that the United States receive special rights to bases that Americans had helped to build during World War II.

After the war, he pushed for this principle when foreign aid legislation was under consideration. In May 1946, when the Senate was discussing a $3.75 billion loan to Great Britain, Russell told his colleagues that the changing methods of warfare, especially the development of rocketry, required additional overseas bases for defense. He urged, along with a few others, that England should be required to grant American rights to bases in British territories in exchange for the loan. He believed that arrangements could be made without violating the sovereignty of England. Senator Fulbright viewed such a demand as imperialistic, but Russell thought it was just good patriotic common sense. He voted against the final bill because of the large amount of money provided and because of the failure of the administration to insist on any concessions in return. Russell surely did not want England's economic collapse, but he felt that he had to vote against the loan to make his point. He wanted bases strictly for defense, and he never suggested that they could be useful in pushing American trade.[35]

Great Britain's difficulties were not solved by the large American loan made in 1946. Indeed, Russell saw little hope for England's economic future. With the prospective loss of empire, England was a declining nation according to Russell because, as he put it, "Britain's industrial system is not equipped for the modern age." With these ideas in mind, Russell shocked many Americans in March 1947 when he suggested that England, Scotland, Wales, and Ireland should be invited to become American states. He even thought that Canada and Australia also might want to make similar arrangements. Russell told startled listeners that such a political union would create freer world trade and reduce economic competition. Moreover, the resulting political combination would provide a navy of unrivaled power. To some extent, no doubt, his idea of incorporating Great Britain into the United States was encouraged by his reverence for Anglo-Saxon culture and the desire to keep it strong. Although some critics gave Russell credit for being sincere, his proposal gained no support either at home or in England. Reaction varied from the charge that he did not know what he was talking about to the comment that he must be joking.[36]

The question of Soviet-American relations was the central foreign policy issue after 1945. Russell never had any confidence in Russian goodwill or integrity. His attitude had not been softened when the Soviet Union denied him a visa to visit Moscow in June 1945. To him this was a slap in the face of a person who only wanted to promote friendly relations between the two countries. Nevertheless, like most other Americans, he hoped that the United States and the Soviet Union would live together peacefully and cooperatively in the postwar world. Considering the increasingly destructive military power available, he said that the two nations must somehow get along peacefully because "the alternative is too horrible to contemplate." Speaking to the University of Georgia alumni on June 13, 1946, he declared that the United States must exhaust every possibility to reach agreement with the Russians.[37] Russell's attitude soon hardened, however, as the Soviets maintained their position in Eastern Europe and refused such American demands as free elections in Poland.

By the middle of 1946, Russell was becoming increasingly critical of the Soviet Union and believed that no agreements could be reached except from a position of strength. He viewed the Soviet Union as deceptive and untrustworthy and bent on adventurism and expansionism. Consequently, he argued that the United States should not share its atomic secrets and should maintain strong conventional military forces. Over the years, Russell saw the Russians in increasingly unfavorable terms. He referred to them as "evil forces" and described Russian communism as "this godless philosophy."[38]

It is not surprising that he gave strong support to Truman when the president fired Secretary of Commerce Henry A. Wallace in September 1946 for expressing what appeared to many to be pro-Soviet foreign policy views. Russell agreed that Wallace should not be permitted to undercut the policies of Secretary of State James F. Byrnes who was "working his heart out to bring a permanent peace." "The time has come," Russell said, "when the sheep should be separated from the goats in America. The time has arrived when those who want to turn this country over to Stalin should show their true colors and not stick a knife in the back of Byrnes."[39]

In light of his views toward the Soviet Union, it is not surprising that Russell supported the so-called Truman Doctrine in 1947. After the British declared that they could no longer defend Greece and Turkey against Communist encroachments, it appeared that these countries might fall to internal subversion without American help. Although Russell had many reservations about large-scale foreign aid, the possible loss of two countries to communism changed the dimension of the problem. He was willing to help block Soviet expansionism in that part of the world, but before the vote was taken, he stressed that this objective should not be confused with supporting democracy. Russell was careful not to mix idealistic rhetoric with practical opposition to the Soviet Union's aims in the region.[40]

By early 1947, Russell was becoming more vocal against what he considered Soviet imperialism, lack of firmness by the Truman administration, and Americans who supported the Russian position in international affairs. He told a convention of textile manufacturers on May 30 that appeasement would more likely bring war than peace and that strength and power were the only principles understood in Moscow. He was sharply critical of Communist sympathizers. "These pink and fellow travelers working within the United States," he said, "are far more dangerous than any and all threats from abroad." Gratitude was one quality greatly admired by Russell. Consequently, he bitterly denounced Americans who criticized the United States while enjoying the country's blessings. As far as he was concerned, these Soviet sympathizers should go to Russia to live. He once said that he would even contribute from his "modest means" to send some of them there.[41]

Despite his anti-Soviet attitude, Russell had serious doubts about the amount and use of foreign aid to Western Europe in 1946 and 1947. Consequently, he was pleased to have an opportunity to join fifteen other senators to tour the region in the early fall of 1947. The group left on October 8 and returned in mid-November. Russell shared a stateroom with his new friend and colleague, Republican Milton R. Young of North Dakota. Almost exactly the same age, Russell and Young had taken a liking to one another as soon as Young arrived in Washington in 1945. Both men had extensive experience in state government, both had a practical bent, and both were deeply interested in the welfare of agriculture. While Russell was a spokesman for cotton, Young represented the wheat growers. Thus Russell and Young had a mutuality of interest that produced a warm and productive friendship.

Members of the special investigating committee said that their mission was to monitor how the hundreds of millions of dollars of American aid for relief and reconstruction were being spent. The group visited France, Germany, Italy, England, Greece, Turkey, and other countries. They observed the progress of reconstruction, met with military and intelligence officers, and looked at plants in Germany scheduled for dismantling.

Russell returned home with some very definite views about postwar Europe. The economic restoration of Germany, he said, was the key to Western European recovery. He argued that the United States did not have enough resources "to keep Western Europe on her feet while Germany remains prostrate." The dismantling of German factories, therefore, should be "reviewed." Russell was impressed with the German work ethic and added that recovery depended on the willingness of Western Europeans to work hard.[42]

He and the other senators returned home just in time to participate in the discussion of the Marshall Plan then under consideration in Congress. This plan proposed spending around $17 billion over the next four years on European recovery. Russell voted for this massive foreign aid plan but without enthusiasm. He believed that the initial appropriation of $597 million was too much and joined others in an unsuccessful attempt to reduce the figure. Furthermore, Russell maintained that the countries that would receive assistance were not doing enough to help themselves.[43] In 1943 Russell had said that the United States' allies had unreasonable expectations of postwar aid. He was even more convinced of this four years later.

Russell mainly favored short-term humanitarian assistance in contrast to the long-term commitments being pushed by foreign aid advocates in 1947 and 1948. He had a genuine sympathy for American taxpayers, who he believed had sacrificed enough during the war, and he opposed placing additional burdens on them. Russell's resentment against large foreign aid appropriations grew as he discovered that the help was not making many loyal friends in the international community. On military aid, he said he favored supporting "reasonable rearmament" of Western Europe if the arms were used in the "defense of the democracies against Communism." But he had little confidence in some Western European countries. If military aid were given to Italy and there was a clash with the Russians, he wrote, "I think Russia would wind up with most of the arms."44

One of Europe's most serious postwar problems was the desperate condition of more than a million homeless, displaced persons. Deeply sympathetic to the plight of these people, President Truman ordered American officials to speed up immigration to the United States under existing quotas. But that was just the beginning. In January 1947, Truman recommended that some 400,000 displaced persons be admitted to the United States in addition to the regular national quotas. Many senators and congressmen denounced the president's proposal, but perhaps none worked harder to defeat it than Dick Russell. He strongly opposed revising current laws to permit larger numbers of immigrants to reach the United States and did everything he could to resist the Truman plan, including working quietly against it in his Immigration Committee. He believed that the National Origins Act of 1924 was precisely the kind of legislation the country needed to control immigration and to admit the most desirable immigrants.

Russell insisted that granting immigration privileges to additional Europeans would establish a bad precedent. Congress, he said, had "already started the progress of whittling away our immigration laws" enacted in 1924. Quotas had been given to China, India, and other nations whose people had once been excluded. That, Russell believed, was bad policy. Furthermore, if more European refugees were admitted, what about the tens of millions of refugees in India and China who were even worse off than those in Europe, he asked. The next step, Russell argued, would be a demand to admit "tens of thousands of Indians and Moslems from India." Immigrants from Asia and Africa, he believed, would dilute Anglo-Saxon culture and change the very nature and character of the nation. This prospect angered and dismayed him. He believed that the United States should be tightening not loosening its immigration laws. Second, Russell feared that Communist agents would slip into the United States among displaced persons and engage in subversive activities. Although Russell could not defeat the Displaced Persons Act, he and others were able to postpone its passage until 1948 and reduce the figure to 200,000, half the number Truman wanted. But he would not even vote for this compromise measure.[45]

Russell was deeply concerned about the possibility of the Soviet Union building an atom bomb. As a member of the new Joint Committee on Atomic Energy, he stressed secrecy and atomic monopoly. In early September 1947, he and other members of the committee toured the country's nuclear military installations. Russell was especially keen to gain a personal view of the quality of security around the plants. He asserted that the development of the atom bomb had been "a great tragedy of our time" and that it was too bad the emphasis had not been upon using nuclear power for peaceful purposes. He believed that world conditions, however, were such that the United States must maintain the power of the atom bomb to assure peace.[46]

There was a wide variety of public questions in the immediate postwar period in which Russell took only a casual interest. He hardly commented at all on some of the most hotly debated issues of the time. For example, in 1946 he voted against the move to vest the states with control of offshore oil resources, lining up with President Truman who vetoed the resolution. He supported the National Security Act of 1947, which unified the armed forces and established the cabinet-level position of secretary of defense. This measure also provided for the Central Intelligence Agency (CIA). Russell was later appointed to a joint committee for the oversight of the CIA.

One piece of legislation that directly affected Russell and his work in the Senate was the Legislative Reorganization Act of 1946. Among other measures, this law reduced the number of Senate standing committees from thirty-three to fifteen. Immigration was placed in the Judiciary Committee, so Russell lost his only committee chairmanship. The Naval Affairs Committee was incorporated into a new Armed Services Committee. As it turned out, Russell fared well when the reorganization was over. He retained membership on the Appropriations Committee and was appointed to the new Armed Services Committee, giving him membership on the Senate's two most powerful committees. When the Democrats regained control of the Senate in 1949, Russell ranked second in the Armed Services Committee and fourth in the Appropriations Committee.

In the postwar years, Russell did become deeply concerned about the growing power of organized labor. He voted for both the Case Federal Mediation Bill in May 1946 and the Taft-Hartley Act passed the next year. He also voted to override Truman's veto of the Taft-Hartley Act. He did not, however, enter into the debates over this important labor legislation.[47]

Russell did not oppose labor unions or want to restrict them because they fought for higher wages. He told a convention of textile manufacturers around the time the Taft-Hartley Act was being considered that labor unions "have a very definite place in our society today." Unions had brought great benefits to workers, he said, and had helped to build the country. For many years, workers had been at a disadvantage in the economic system, and unions had helped correct that problem. But then legislation in the 1930s had given unions too much power without imposing sufficient restrictions on labor leaders. He declared that a few "greedy labor leaders" had taken a "public-be-damned" attitude that was as bad as that of the monopolists of the late nineteenth century. Russell viewed the Taft-Hartley Act as restoring a balance between labor and industry.

Russell was out of commission during much of April 1947 because of an attack of appendicitis. He entered the U.S. Naval Hospital in Bethesda, Maryland, on April 5 and had surgery on the 11th. He did not, however, recover as quickly as he had anticipated. He wrote his mother on April 18 that he had always thought that he was "so strong and healthy that I could whip anything by merely fighting it," but he added that he now knew this assumption was untrue. He told his mother that he had worried about the surgeon leaving a needle or some instrument inside him but had been assured by his brother, Dr. Alex Russell, who was present, that nothing like that had happened.[48]

In the fall of 1948, Russell was off on another foreign trip, this time to Mexico City. Seven members of the Appropriations Committee wanted a firsthand look at a jointly funded program with Mexico to control hoof-and-mouth disease, which was causing losses of Mexican and American cattle. The group, including Russell's friend, Milton Young, left Washington on November 7 and held hearings in Omaha, Nebraska; Fargo and Bismarck, North Dakota; and Oklahoma City, Oklahoma, before flying on to Mexico City. The senators visited areas involved in the program around Mexico City, talked with Mexican officials, and returned home on the 16th. Russell believed that firsthand observations were useful in determining if this project was successful and if American funds were being properly used.[49]

Russell was not pleased with much of what was happening in the postwar United States. Continued high government expenditures, partly caused by huge amounts of foreign aid, the growing political power of labor, the weakening influence of farmers, tensions within the Democratic party, and the advancing march of civil rights for blacks all disturbed him. Writing his mother on April 9, 1948, he said, "We are living in a very troubled world, and I fear that none of us will again ever see the relative peace and tranquility of the 1930's." Those were tough times, he continued, but problems seem to have grown in magnitude and complexity since the beginning of World War II. But, he added, people should not take a defeatist attitude as the country grappled with apparently insoluble problems. One of the trends that greatly disturbed him was what he considered the Democratic party's and the country's political and social shift leftward from their historic moorings. He was determined to fight this development regardless of how unpleasant the battles might be.

In the midst of national political controversies, it was relaxing and satisfying for Dick to be back in Winder in late August 1947 preparing for the first family reunion to be held since Judge Russell died in 1938. The Russell clan gathered on Monday, September 1, to visit, renew acquaintances, and meet new family members. Ina Russell, now seventy-nine, beamed with pride as all of her thirteen children were back home again, even if only for a day or so. Many of the family stayed to attend the wedding of Sybil Elizabeth Russell, the daughter of Dick's brother Robert, who married Ernest Vandiver, Jr., on Wednesday afternoon, September 3. The entire three or four days were a joyous occasion and one of those times with family that meant so much to Dick Russell.[50]

11

Russell, Truman, and Civil Rights

For about six years after Harry Truman was elected to the U.S. Senate in 1934, he and Dick Russell sat not far from one another in the Senate chamber. Russell viewed his new colleague as a congenial, sincere, hardworking senator but not one of particular distinction. As he said years later, if individuals inside or outside the Senate had been asked to rate senators, Truman would not have been in the top twenty. Russell was impressed with Truman's humility when he assumed office as president, but he later observed that the heady wine of White House power soon destroyed that quality.[1]

Russell sincerely wanted to get along with his old Senate colleague, if for no other reason than his extreme respect for the office of president. This was why, for example, he supported the nomination of Henry A. Wallace as secretary of commerce in 1945 when many southerners strongly opposed the appointment of the former vice president. Critics charged that Wallace was too liberal and not suitable for the position. Although Russell disagreed with many of Wallace's views, he did not accept the arguments of opponents. With such heavy responsibilities devolving on the president, the right of appointment, Russell said, "should be more jealously protected than ever before." To turn down the Wallace nomination, he continued, would "bring joy to the heart of every reactionary and every Roosevelt hater in the United States." Then he added, "I will not be a party to staging a Roman holiday in the Senate at the expense of the President of the United States."[2] When Truman called for party unity in a Jackson Day banquet address in late March 1945, some Democrats boycotted the dinner because Henry Wallace was present. Russell, however, attended the $100 a plate affair.[3] Truman had never been one of Russell's close friends in the Senate, but Russell wished the president well.

Moreover, Russell wanted to heal the growing split that was developing in the Democratic party. He hoped that the major issues dividing members of the party could somehow be compromised. If Russell was anything, he was a loyal and committed Democrat. He had supported Alfred E. Smith in 1928 when many southern Democrats deserted the New Yorker, and he often boasted that Georgia had never faltered in supporting the Democratic party. He believed that the Democrats had been the party of the people, and he was especially proud of the nation's accomplishments since 1933 under the leadership of Franklin D. Roosevelt. This had been a time when the power of southerners had solidified in the party and in Congress, a situation that Russell wished to guard and preserve. In 1946 southerners chaired a majority of the most powerful committees in the Senate, including the Agriculture and Forestry, Appropriations, Commerce, Finance, Foreign Relations, and Immigration committees. As long as the Democrats retained a majority in Congress and the seniority rule prevailed, such senators as Russell, Walter George, Tom Connally, Carter Glass, Kenneth McKellar, and Harry F. Byrd would maintain crucial positions of power.

Russell, however, had become increasingly annoyed at the disparaging comments in the northern press about southern Democrats, who were often portrayed as racist mossbacks who were trying to block the nation's progress. He resented terms like "Southern Tory," "Southern Bourbon," or "Polltaxer." In some quarters, he said, even the term "Southern Democrat" was "often used as one of scorn or odium." Russell declared that he was proud of being a southerner but that he did not always boast very loud about being a Democrat.[4]

Dick Russell refused to accept the conservative label. Indeed, he objected to all such categorizations. He wanted to be judged on the results of his work. He maintained that he and many other southerners had fought for and had helped to win some of the most progressive New Deal reforms. Furthermore, he objected to the practice of some commentators of viewing all southern leaders as the same. "It's a mistake to lump all of us southerners together," he declared, "just as it is wrong to expect people from any one section of the country to think alike." Southern senators differed on many issues. "The only things that we are really united on is the question of racial equality," he explained.[5]

Russell preferred party consensus over confrontation. His nature was to try to find a compromise when differences arose. But the one issue on which he stoutly resisted compromise was, as he said, racial equality. If this issue could somehow be reconciled within the Democratic party, he believed that one of the main sources of conflict could be removed.

Race, of course, was not the only thing that produced strains within

Democratic ranks. The shift of power among groups within the party also created difficulties. Russell and many other Democrats were alarmed at the growing power of organized labor and at the influence of unions in party councils. Many Democrats considered Sidney Hillman, head of the Political Action Committee of the Congress of Industrial Organizations (CIO), as a dangerous and divisive influence. Russell resented that the plumb line against which some Democrats measured liberalism or progressivism was whether a senator or congressman voted for every labor-sponsored bill. A true liberal, he told the University of Georgia alumni on June 13, 1946, was one who supported "the greatest measure of individual freedom for each man . . . so long as he does not impinge on the rights of another individual or threaten the welfare of the whole." This was good Jeffersonian doctrine, nineteenth-century liberalism, but it was out of keeping with the new progressivism characterized by expanding federal powers and responsibilities.[6]

Russell explained the South's past devotion to the Democratic party in terms of its commitment to states' rights and white supremacy. That, he wrote, was why "the southern people have given it their unswerving and devoted support."[7] Russell faced the problem that had been developing ever since he arrived in Washington—the sharp growth of federal power and the relative decline in the position of the states. He had supported most of the legislation that extended national responsibilities in the fields of agriculture, public power, welfare, education, labor relations, and other areas, but now he argued against civil rights on the basis that such legislation would violate states' rights. Here was a contradiction that Russell was unable to reconcile. He favored much of the progressive program of Roosevelt and even a considerable part of the initial Truman recommendations, but the civil rights question forced him to take a strong anti-Truman stance and nudged him into a minority position in the party. Much of Russell's energies were taken up between 1945 and 1948 fighting the proposals by Truman and others for civil rights legislation.

On September 6, 1945, Truman outlined his legislative program to Congress. In general it was a progressive agenda, including a call for a permanent FEPC.[8] While Russell did not immediately comment on Truman's address, he was increasingly concerned about the president's seeming willingness to alienate southern Democrats in exchange for the northern black vote. But Russell hoped that important postwar issues would divert the president and his pro–civil rights supporters away from actual legislation. Surely, Russell thought, recent fights over the FEPC should have sent a message to the president and Congress. Although the southerners had failed to destroy the FEPC by cutting its funding in 1944, in May 1945, they came close to eliminating all money for the agency. As it was, the FEPC's appropriation was cut from $500,000 to $250,000. Funding was to end altogether after June 30, 1946, unless Congress passed new legislation.[9] By enacting a cutoff date, Congress virtually assured that the issue would be taken up again sometime before mid-1946.

In January Senator Dennis Chavez of New Mexico introduced a bill to establish a permanent FEPC that caught the southerners by surprise. Russell moved quickly, however, to organize his anti–civil rights colleagues. He deplored that the issue had been brought up but declared that "we are ready to meet it." Now the acknowledged leader of the Southern Bloc, Russell announced that southerners would fight the bill with everything they had. If the proponents of the legislation rolled in their cots for an extended debate, "we will wheel in ours," he said.[10]

On January 22, Russell delivered a long speech against the FEPC bill. He began by deploring the fact that the Senate was considering such legislation at a time when so many genuine crises faced the nation. He mentioned labor-management conflicts, the rising national debt, and other problems that were "a thousand times more important than this vote-bait measure." Repeating his earlier arguments against the FEPC, he said that passage of the bill would destroy private property, nationalize all jobs, and ruin business and industry. He argued that it would take away the fundamental right of an employer to hire and fire whom he pleased. This was the "entering wedge to complete state socialism and communism," he argued.

Turning to other aspects of the problem, Russell argued that he was fighting for the peoples' right to live as they wished and to employ whomever they wanted without the "blighted hand of federal bureaucracy coming down to harass and annoy them." He declared that the black druggist in Harlem had as much right not to hire a Japanese-American as a white Atlanta druggist had not to employ a black. "That is equality all over the United States," he declared. Under the Constitution, he continued, minorities were entitled to equal rights not special privileges. To establish the FEPC as an independent agency with all of the powers proposed, Russell said, would place excessive and uncontrollable power in the hands of bureaucrats. Worst of all, however, was the measure's threat to "regulate the tastes, the customs, the habits and the manner of life of all the American people." He called it "a fool bill," which would result in miscegenation and amalgamation of the races.

Russell then turned to the concept of discrimination. He explained that the bill did not end discrimination in employment. What about workers who could not get a job because they were not members of a labor union, he asked. The proponents of this measure had nothing to say about that kind of discrimination. What about sex and age discrimination, he inquired again. Russell complained that neither women employees nor older workers had protection under this proposed legislation. It was just a special interest bill for a particular minority. Moreover, most of the states that had considered similar legislation, Russell argued, had rejected it.[11]

Southerners filibustered against the FEPC bill for some three weeks before supporters tried to shut off debate with a cloture vote. On February 9, however, the twenty-one southerners that could always be counted on to fight any civil rights legislation and a few Republicans and northern Democrats defeated the cloture motion 36 to 48, some 16 votes short of the two-thirds necessary to break the filibuster. Southerners had put the FEPC issue to rest in a relatively easy battle.[12]

Although Russell and his southern colleagues had defeated the FEPC measure with comparative ease, growing support for civil rights legislation among both Democrats and Republicans greatly worried him. Some of his constituents reacted with increasing bitterness to the bolder actions of blacks who tried to assert their rights as full citizens. Russell's correspondence reflected deep racial prejudice, bitterness against even token mixing of the races, and opposition to minimum advances of personal rights by blacks. Referring to Primus King of Columbus, Georgia, a black who had won an appeal before the Fifth Circuit Court of Appeals in New Orleans sustaining his right to vote in the white Georgia primary, one Georgian wrote that the South's forefathers would "turn over in their graves from such an obnoxious mess of affairs." Blacks, he wrote, were like any other property, and their role was to "cut wood, plow a mule, or ox and do only laborious work." They had been brought to America to do heavy labor and wait on the white man, he continued, not to vote or ever to be equal with whites.[13]

Russell received letters complaining about the number of black clerks hired in the Atlanta post office and expressing alarm at the lack of separate drinking fountains. Whites, one writer said, sometimes had to wait in line on blacks before they could get a drink of water. Even the partitions between the segregated rest rooms were about to be torn down. Russell also received complaints about the lack of strict segregation in the Atlanta Veteran's Hospital and about other cracks in the walls of segregation. Dr. Walter W. Daniel told Russell that white and black women had even been placed in the same maternity ward at Fort

McPherson, a condition he called "absolutely unbearable." Daniel believed that such actions would justify Russell voting against all army appropriations until the situation was corrected. Russell replied that he would look into that "deplorable situation" at once.[14]

One thing that continued to greatly disturb him was that an increasing number of white southerners were accepting the principle of civil rights legislation. Helen Crotwell, who was associated with the Wesley Foundation at Georgia State College for Women at Milledgeville, wrote him early in 1946 saying that she favored the FEPC and criticizing Georgia's senators for "becoming synonymous" with Theodore Bilbo. Another person, probably a student, wrote that there was no basis to oppose the FEPC "except prejudice." Russell usually refused to reply to black correspondents, but to white writers, he answered in a moderate vein, saying that everyone was entitled to his or her opinions. Russell had difficulty understanding how any genuine southerner did not see things as he did. Even though he knew that most Georgians agreed with him, he viewed the "lassitude of our people in the face of attacks being made upon our institutions" as "most discouraging."[15]

Russell rejected the idea that people in the United States, including some white southerners, opposed segregation on the basis of democratic and Christian principles. He blamed the civil rights movement almost entirely on people he called troublemakers outside of the South. Among these were northern politicians who, he said, were courting the black vote, black organizations, the northern press, which seemed to relish pillorying the South, and left-wingers. He viewed the Southern Conference on Human Welfare as radical and dangerous and said that Malcolm Ross, chairman of the FEPC, was "a wild-eyed radical who has been lionized by the *Daily Worker*." Add to these forces the professional "do-gooders," and the South, according to Russell, had its back against the wall.[16]

When the Fifth Circuit Court of Appeals upheld the right of blacks to vote in Georgia's primary elections early in 1946, the editor of the *Atlanta Journal* believed the people would obey the order. He quoted from several editorials appearing in state papers that expressed the belief that whites and blacks could participate together in local elections. The *Journal's* editor interpreted the comments of "fair-minded and practical rural editors" as a hopeful sign in a situation where "violent language and demagoguery could do a world of mischief."[17] Such black victories as that of Primus King in the white primary case, however, were resisted in every way possible by Russell and his backers. Charles J. Bloch of Macon, one of the senator's closest political friends, helped to prepare the brief for the Fifth Circuit court in Georgia's effort to pre-serve the white primary.

Russell's argument that the South was satisfactorily solving its race problem without any outside interference was dealt a harsh blow on July 20, 1946, by an incident in Monroe, Georgia, only a few miles from his home. A mob of whites stopped a car to apprehend a black man who had been accused of stabbing his employer but was free on bond. The white men dragged Roger Malcolm and a friend from the car with the apparent intent of killing them. When one of the blacks' wives in the car shouted out the name of the white leader, the two black couples were shot in cold blood.[18]

This horrible event received national headlines, and supporters of civil rights legislation discussed the incident in the Senate. Conservative Republican William F. Knowland of California deplored the situation on the Senate floor and declared that "such things must not continue in the United States." Russell quickly came to the defense of the South. Al-though he denounced the crime and emphasized his opposition to mob violence, he reminded his colleagues that murders also occurred in other regions. Stressing a point he had been making for nearly a decade, Russell said, "There seems to be an effort to make political capital out of the crimes in which Negroes are the victims if they are committed in the South and we hear a clamor for Federal intervention which is never raised in the case of similar crimes committed in other sections of the country."[19]

Without doubt, Russell hated such extralegal actions. Not only was a murder revulsive to him personally, but also incidents such as the one that took place in Monroe hurt his fight against federal interference on civil rights issues. One constituent who claimed to be a Sunday school teacher asked Russell how long he would "remain in reticence" at such tragedies. Russell told several correspondents that while he greatly de-plored the murders at Monroe, "I consider it to be a strictly local affair, and our State officers should be unmolested in their efforts to solve the crime."[20]

Despite Russell's best efforts, there was little he could do to slow down the drive for civil rights. Studies done in the postwar years not only revealed the depths of racial discrimination but also pricked the consciences of an increasing number of Americans who believed that change must come. For example, the National Urban League prepared a twenty-seven-page study in 1945 entitled "Racial Aspects of Reconver-sion" and sent it to President Truman on August 27. This document dealt with black employment, education, housing, integration in the armed forces, and other problems. Russell read his copy with great care. He underlined in red the suggestions and recommendations that would weaken or destroy racial segregation.

Although President Truman vacillated somewhat in his support for civil rights, the growing pressure from black organizations, the murders in Georgia, and the move by Republicans to preempt the issue prompted the president to show more support for civil rights principles by 1947. In December 1946, shortly after the Republicans won major congressional victories in the midterm elections, Truman appointed a blue-ribbon committee to study civil rights issues. It was known as the President's Committee on Civil Rights and was chaired by Charles E. Wilson, president of General Electric.[21]

Late in 1947, the committee issued a report entitled *To Secure These Rights*. The recommendations, which received widespread publicity in the popular media, encouraged Congress and the president to support a host of civil rights proposals. On February 2, 1948, the president sent a special message to Congress on civil rights that included several of the major recommendations in the committee report. These included a permanent FEPC, abolition of segregation in the armed forces, and other reforms that would bring about greater equality between the races.

Russell's reaction was predictable. He was both resentful and angry at the president's continual push for civil rights legislation. It would take a great deal to make Russell desert a president or the Democratic party, but Truman's actions on civil rights reached the limits of his tolerance. He wrote a constituent in Atlanta that the president's proposals were the "most outrageous affront to the people of our section that we have had to face since Reconstruction days."[22] He charged that Truman was planning a "gestapo" approach to break down segregation in the South.[23]

Throughout early 1948, Russell wrote and spoke extensively on the civil rights issue. No other domestic question so monopolized his attention. He emphasized the dangers of social integration, of the possible political power of blacks in the South, and of other threats to white supremacy. He told a Florida correspondent that there were forty-three counties in Georgia where blacks outnumbered whites. White people in those counties, he wrote, "can not be expected to turn their children . . . over to schools that are run by negroes, or to live in counties that have negro sheriffs, county school superintendents and other officials." He admitted that whites might be "partly culpable" for conditions in those counties, but he said that the blacks who would be "running things" were "not the type who appear before committees here."[24]

Since there had been such a blitz of publicity over the report of the president's committee and his subsequent message on civil rights, Russell hoped to bring the South's position on these issues before the American people. On March 6, twenty-one southern senators from the eleven former Confederate states met in Senator Harry Byrd's office to plot their anti–civil rights strategy. Only Senator Claude Pepper of Florida was absent. The senators announced that they were placing themselves under the "generalship" of Russell, a position that in practice he had held for some years. They agreed to look to Russell for leadership and organization as they sought to kill civil rights measures. Russell announced after the meeting that the southerners would have a man on the Senate floor at all times in order to deal with any possible "quickie" parliamentary maneuvers designed by civil rights supporters. There would always be someone on hand, Russell said, "just to keep an eye on things" and to "stand guard."[25]

The southern senators also discussed the matter of getting their views before the nation. They had been greatly annoyed at the widespread publicity given to civil rights proposals. The Mutual Broadcasting System (MBS), for example, had broadcast several radio programs by civil rights advocates. Consequently, on March 5, the senators sent a telegram to the president of the Mutual Broadcasting System asking for time to reply and to present the southern viewpoint. The senators reminded MBS that the Federal Communications Commission required networks to grant equal time for discussions of political issues. Robert D. Swezey, vice president of MBS, agreed to make the network available.[26] As their leader, Russell was designated by his colleagues to make the principal address, while others would deal with specific legislative proposals. Senator Burnet Maybank of South Carolina was to discuss the bill to eliminate the poll tax, Senator Clyde R. Hoey of North Carolina the antilynching bill, and Senator Lister Hill of Alabama the FEPC.

On the evening of March 23, 1948, Russell delivered a major address over the MBS radio network. First he wanted his listeners to know that the President's Committee on Civil Rights was not, in his judgment, an objective, fact-finding group. Rather, according to Russell, the members and the hired staff sought information to confirm their preconceived notions. Then he accused the committee of embracing and approving "every suggestion and theory brought forward by professional agitators whose vocation it is to represent the various minority pressure groups here in the National Capitol." If the recommendations of the President's Committee on Civil Rights were implemented, Russell said, not only people in the South but all Americans were in danger of losing their liberties from the extension of federal police powers. He pictured "hoards" of federal bureaucrats who would be running around "as federal policemen to enforce these drastic laws." Russell emphasized that blacks had made remarkable progress since freedom from slavery and that whites had borne heavy taxes to provide separate but equal facilities. Because of the way the South had worked out its racial problem, and the progress of blacks, he declared that southerners were "entitled to better treatment at the hands of our fellow Americans than to be kicked as a political football in every election year, and to have our good name constantly bartered by political auctioneers in bidding for votes."

While Russell warned of violations of states' rights, the expansion of federal powers over southern institutions, and the economic progress of blacks, his main fear was the threat to strict segregation. All people, he said, should be free to choose their associates and not be forced into integrated situations. He declared that southerners believed in "equality of administration of the law" but insisted "upon the right that we regard as sacred and unalienable of choosing our own associates."[27] Russell told a newsman that he had never seen southerners so upset over the racial question. This was because they saw Truman's demand for an end to Jim Crow legislation as "an opening wedge in the fight to stop all segregation," which would mean that blacks and whites would "attend the same schools, swim in the same pools, eat together, and eventually, intermarry."[28]

Russell's position as leader in the Senate of the opponents of civil rights brought him many accolades. The *Atlanta Constitution* editorialized on March 13 that it was a real compliment to Georgia for Russell to be chosen as the South's spokesman "in the continuing effort to defeat President Truman's unwise demands for far-reaching civil rights legislation." The writer referred to Russell as enlightened, articulate, "free from demagoguery," and one who epitomized the New South.[29]

In the middle of his efforts to organize southerners against possible civil rights legislation, Russell received word that his eighty-year-old mother had fallen and broken her hip. He immediately left for Atlanta by train, arriving on March 9. He saw his mother briefly at 1:30 P.M. at the Piedmont Hospital and was relieved to learn that she was getting along fine. That evening he took the train back to Washington to continue his all-out fight against civil rights. As he was about to board the train in Atlanta, he told newsmen that Truman's civil rights proposals would "virtually do away with the states by creating a massive totalitarian centralized government operating from Washington."[30]

There was no time to relax in light of growing pressures for civil rights legislation. In March the poll tax was back before Congress. Russell admitted that of all the civil rights measures, the poll tax was least important. Indeed, Georgia had already eliminated the tax. It was, however, a symbolic issue, and Russell was not about to make any compromises. As he put it, "We are not going to yield an inch without a protest."[31] Poll tax legislation was turned back without difficulty.

During the spring and summer of 1948, Russell and his southern colleagues were faced with another racial issue—integration of the armed forces. President Truman announced in May that he had given instructions to end racial discrimination in the military services. Russell still hoped that something might be done to halt that move. When the Armed Services Committee, of which he was the second ranking minority member, held hearings on a proposal for Universal Military Training in March and April, Russell took that opportunity to show how unwise Truman's goal of an integrated military was. First Senator Leverett Saltonstall of Massachusetts asked General Eisenhower about the situation. Eisenhower admitted that racial prejudice was a problem in integrated units. Some social difficulties arose, he said, "because you always have men that do not like to mingle freely between the races, and therefore if you have a dance for your soldiers, you have a problem." Then Russell began his questioning. More than racial prejudice was at stake, he said. Russell got Eisenhower to admit that crime was higher among black troops and that more blacks than whites had venereal diseases. Russell later inserted statistics on these matters in the *Congressional Record*. While Eisenhower admitted that some problems existed with integration, he concluded that he did not favor the strict segregation he had found when he entered the army many years before.[32]

Russell was determined to block this additional move toward the destruction of segregation if at all possible. On May 12, 1948, joined by Senator Maybank, he introduced an amendment to the Selective Service Act that would permit an inductee into the armed forces to choose whether he wanted to serve in a segregated or integrated unit. Russell argued hard for his amendment. Declaring that he did not like to talk about percentages of crime or venereal diseases, he said that the real issue was the "health and morals of hundreds of thousands of American boys who will be taken from their homes into the services." Integration, he added, "would directly affect the morale and discipline of our services." He then took a swipe at the media, charging that some of his

questions and General Eisenhower's testimony had been "censored."
According to Russell, people had not been permitted to hear the truth
about race mixing. He insisted that integration would greatly reduce
military effectiveness. Although Russell's amendment was rejected by a
voice vote on June 9, he did vote for the Selective Service Act, which
passed by a large majority the next day. On July 26, Truman issued an
executive order banning racial discrimination in the military services.[33]

Much to Russell's disgust, other aspects of the racial issue kept
emerging in 1948. There was further discussion of the poll tax in both
the House and Senate. The Senate dealt with the matter in late July and
early August, just before adjournment. Much of the discussion at that
point revolved around whether to deal with the issue by statute or by
submitting a constitutional amendment forbidding any such tax. Russell had no objection to submitting a constitutional amendment to the
states. He felt reasonably sure that such an amendment would not pass.
But, he said, if the Senate pushed for a statute outlawing the poll tax for
voting in federal elections, the southerners would fight it as long as "we
have the power and the right to do so." The poll tax was not the real
issue, however. "We are fighting," he said, "for the right to control our
own elections in our own states."[34] He wrote Sam J. Ervin, then a
member of the North Carolina Supreme Court, on July 29 that "our
position . . . is desperate for we are hopelessly outnumbered on the civil
rights recommendations here in Congress." He added that he would
fight to defeat the "pernicious proposals and the tormentors of the
South will know that they have been in a battle."[35] The situation in the
Senate was much less dangerous than Russell implied. He won a skirmish on a point of order on August 2, quickly ending the debate on the
poll tax.[36] Legislators were anxious to get home to begin campaigning.

Meanwhile Russell studied proposals to relocate blacks out of the
South as a way to solve racial problems. Since those pressing for civil
rights were mainly in the North and West, proponents of the plan argued that people in those sections should be happy to accept a larger
black population. The idea had been around for several years, although
Russell had never publicly endorsed it. Early in 1948, however, a number of southerners urged him to promote the plan. In February he wrote
a Floridian that he had given much thought to the idea and that the next
time a civil rights bill came up he might introduce an amendment to
"scatter the negroes over the country, somewhat in proportion to population." He accused civil rights advocates of insincerity when they objected to having any more blacks living in their communities. On August 3, after the poll tax fight had ended, he wrote that, while he had

considered this approach seriously during the recent fight, he was not yet willing for any publicity on the matter.[37]

Already, however, the *Atlanta Constitution* had carried on July 28 a front-page article with the headline, "Negro Resettlement Proposal Awaits Russell Introduction." According to this story, the Russell bill would provide federal aid of up to $1,500 for any black family that wanted to move out of the South. Russell declined to comment on this report, saying that the story had been leaked before he was ready. Although he actually had planned the main outlines of such a bill, he said that he was still studying the matter. There the question of relocation rested for the remainder of 1948.

Despite Russell's efforts to block every move toward racial integration, voices of compromise continued to surface throughout the South. In Georgia, Ralph McGill, the distinguished editor of the *Atlanta Constitution*, told his readers in the summer of 1948 that the South must face the fact that civil rights measures were coming one way or another. He wrote that people who loved the South must realize that trends throughout the world were working against a strict segregationist position. McGill was not leading any charge to abolish segregation, but he favored gradual change from the old system of enforced inequality of the races. In Arkansas Congressman Brooks Hays was seeking some compromise on civil rights issues. Segregation, Hays wrote McGill, was the toughest part of the problem, "but we should give ground."[38]

Senator J. William Fulbright, former law professor and president of the University of Arkansas, also struggled with these complex issues. Although he was a reliable member of the Southern Bloc, he repeatedly told constituents that he did not know the correct course to take. He told some correspondents that better education and health care might develop more tolerant feelings in the South but admitted that not much had changed so far. Fulbright concluded that he could only hope that "maybe some way to reconcile the differences may arise." While Fulbright was saying in 1948 that he was uncertain of the right path to take, Russell and most other southern senators never had any such doubts. It was segregation and white supremacy now and always.[39]

Few southerners wanted to think critically about their class and caste system, but Malcolm Bryan, president of the Federal Reserve Bank in Atlanta, shared some of his innermost thoughts with Ralph McGill. Writing in 1947 or 1948, he did not actually send his undated letter to McGill until about a decade later. Comparing the system of segregation in the South to Francisco Franco's government in Spain, Bryan acknowledged the existence of "a government of oligarchy, by an elite" in the

South. He continued, "We also use all the machinery of the state and of society to suppress those who do not believe that our rule quite approaches the heart's desire. We choose our elite, of course, on the basis of the white skin." Bryan concluded that power exerted by a self-chosen elite was just as wrong in the United States as it was in Spain.[40] Such ideas would have been horrifying to Russell, whose paternalistic views toward blacks accepted the white elitist position as both natural and desirable.

During the controversies over civil rights, Russell took every opportunity to prove that segregation worked for the benefit of blacks. In the growing contest for public opinion, he praised blacks who accepted their condition and sought to progress in a segregated society. According to Russell, these were the blacks to be emulated in the black community. Thus he was happy when Davis Lee, publisher of the *Newark Telegram*, a black weekly newspaper, wrote a lengthy article in the summer of 1948 on "The Negro North and South." Lee made an extensive tour of the South, observing both blacks and whites. He concluded that segregation was the better system because both races knew where they stood in the scheme of things. In the South, Lee wrote, it had been clear where he would be accepted, but when he had gone to restaurants in New Jersey, a state with firm civil rights laws, he had been denied service. He declared that blacks spent too much time and energy trying to prove that they were equal to whites. They should convince the world of their talents, he said, "not by propaganda and education but by demonstration." He held up Joe Louis, the great heavy weight prize fighter, as the ideal example. Blacks would be accepted, Lee wrote, when by their living standards and conduct they proved their equality.

The Lee article appeared in a number of southern newspapers. Highly gratified because it expressed his own views, Russell ordered one hundred copies for his personal distribution. The article, he claimed, "should certainly serve to convince those who are willing to be moved by reason and logic."[41]

Other articles written in the summer of 1948 were less pleasing to Russell. Ray Sprigle, a Pulitzer prize-winning writer for the *Pittsburgh Post-Gazette*, wrote a series of twelve articles for the *New York Tribune* after traveling throughout the South. Pretending to be black, Sprigle visited many different kinds of people on a segregated basis. He wrote about murders, sharecroppers, segregation, and other issues. Russell charged that the Sprigle pieces were the most "skillful jobs" of propaganda waged by the NAACP that he had ever seen. Admitting that there was a germ of truth in what Sprigle wrote, he said that most of the articles were "badly overdone." Commenting on sharecropping, Russell denied that all sharecroppers were "terribly imposed on." Indeed, Russell argued that many farmers, both black and white, preferred share-cropping because "they incur no risk." He admitted that the South's social system was not "perfect," but he charged that blacks were much better off in the South than elsewhere. Within their own institutions, they could become college professors, college presidents, doctors, and other professionals, opportunities that were less available to blacks in an integrated society.[42] In any event, everywhere he turned, Russell was faced with new challenges to the South's current social and racial system. Defending this system was becoming a huge burden.

Although the civil rights issue was much on the minds of members of the Eightieth Congress, it also loomed as a major question in the forthcoming presidential campaign. While Russell and Truman were far apart on the civil rights issue, Russell found that he and the president could work together on some other issues. Russell voted for the tax increase over Truman's opposition in March 1948, but he supported the administration's farm program and the president's call for federal aid to education. The latter question badly divided the Southern Bloc, with Byrd, Connally, and A. Willis Robertson of Virginia voting against it. Russell was right in saying that the southern senators were really only united on one major question and that was the racial issue. He would easily have actively supported Truman in 1948 if it had not been for civil rights. Indeed, Russell wrote some years later of his "own high opinion" of Truman and his "sturdy Americanism."[43]

Russell first discussed prospects for the 1948 presidential election when he was home in late July of 1947. He told a writer for the *Atlanta Constitution* that the 1948 election would be between liberal Democrats and conservative Republicans. Without a doubt, he said, President Truman would be renominated, but Russell declared that he would like to see his party name General Dwight D. Eisenhower as its candidate for vice president. According to Russell, however, the Democrats would probably nominate a more liberal vice presidential candidate, and he mentioned Senator Claude Pepper of Florida and former Governor Ellis Arnall of Georgia as "out-standing southern liberals."[44]

By early 1948, Russell was reappraising his earlier views on the election. When he was asked whether he would support Truman's bid for the Democratic presidential nomination in 1948, he at first hedged his reply. On March 16, he told a reporter for the *New York Times* that "as chairman of the Senate group opposing this civil rights stuff, I am unable to comment on those questions." Russell explained that in the

Southern Bloc there were both those who opposed and supported Truman and that his job was to hold the group "together to fight the civil rights program." Many Democrats were already calling for Truman to withdraw as a candidate. Some of his most vocal critics were in the South. Senator John Sparkman of Alabama said that the Democrats would be "cut to ribbons" in November if they nominated the unpopular Truman. Commenting on Sparkman's call for Truman to drop out of the race, Russell said that he would be "very happy to see Truman step out and General . . . Eisenhower step in as Democratic presidential exchange."[45]

When the Georgia State Democratic Convention met in Macon on July 2, only ten days before the beginning of the party's national convention in Philadelphia, it joined in the move to nominate Eisenhower even though the general had made it clear that he was not available. Georgia Democrats also urged Truman to drop out of the race. The convention then endorsed Russell for vice president. But the senator, who was at his home in Winder, said that he would not permit his name to be advanced for the second slot on the ticket.[46]

Meanwhile, extremists among southern states' rights advocates were talking about withholding their electoral votes from Truman if he should be nominated and make the race. The southerners wanted a strong candidate to contest Truman's nomination. Governor J. Strom Thurmond of South Carolina and other leaders of the political states' rights movement approached Russell and urged him to permit his name to be placed before the convention. If they were not successful in getting Russell nominated by the regular Democrats, they wanted him to head a states' rights Democratic party. Russell later recalled that the states' righters were going to raise "almost incredible sums of money . . . if I would run on a third party ticket." He said that he was "taken a way up on the mountain with that one." But Russell rejected the view of the Promised Land and all of the blandishments of his southern colleagues and friends.[47]

The best efforts of Truman's opponents could not force him to step aside. On July 11, the day before the Democratic National Convention opened, a *New York Times* headline read, "Southern Leaders Abandon Drive to Make Truman Quit." They next tried to defeat the rather strong civil rights plank in the platform. Unsuccessful in this effort, the states' righters decided to take the only remaining course and draft a southern leader who would agree to seek the nomination against Truman as a kind of symbolic gesture of opposition to the president and civil rights. The *New York Times* reported on July 12 that the states' rights caucus had so far been unable to produce a candidate to stand against Truman. At that point, Russell, who was then resting at home, reluctantly agreed to let his name be put forward. Explaining his action later, he wrote, "I was very reluctant to permit the use of my name, but decided that those who were opposed to Mr. Truman were entitled to have someone for whom they could vote."[48]

When it came time to nominate candidates, Alabama yielded to Georgia and Charles J. Bloch, longtime friend, Macon attorney, and ardent segregationist, placed Russell's name in nomination. Although conceding that Georgia delegates were not going to bolt the convention, Bloch said that the South "is no longer going to be the whipping boy of the Democratic Party." Nor, he said, could the Democrats take the South for granted any longer. He reminded the delegates that "if it wasn't for the vote of the South four years ago, Henry Wallace would be sitting in the White House today," an abhorrent thought to most Democrats in 1948. Bloch described how Truman's civil rights proposals, if enacted, would revolutionize the relations between blacks and whites in the South. As the civil rights movement had gained headway, Bloch declared, Russell had led the charge to defeat the obnoxious bills. Concluding with a paraphrase of William Jennings Bryan in 1896, Bloch dramatically asserted, "You shall not crucify the South on this cross of civil rights."

When the roll call concluded, Russell received 263 votes to 947.5 for Truman. Russell got votes from Alabama, Arkansas, Florida, Georgia, Louisiana, North Carolina, South Carolina, Tennessee, and Texas. The Mississippi delegates and some of the delegates from Alabama had walked out of the convention before the voting began.[49]

All except four of the Georgia delegates voted for Russell. Only Ralph McGill, George L. Googe, southern director of organization for the AFL, and two other labor representatives stuck by Truman. This was unpleasant for Russell, since McGill and Googe had earlier been good friends and supporters. Googe had worked hard in Russell's gubernatorial and senatorial campaigns to swing the labor vote to him. But as Googe wrote J. Howard McGrath, chairman of the Democratic National Committee, "We refused to parade with the Southern Rebels because 'Dick' had voted for the Taft-Hartley Act."[50]

The convention's nomination of Truman and support of a moderate civil rights plank were enough to force states' rights Democrats to meet in a rump convention in Birmingham, Alabama, on July 17. Since Russell had earlier rejected the possibility of heading a states' rights ticket, the disaffected Democrats, in a highly emotional meeting, nominated South Carolina Governor J. Strom Thurmond and Governor Fielding Wright of Mississippi as candidates for president and vice president of the states' rights party. Better known as the Dixiecrats, these southerners offered little except some outmoded constitutional theory and opposition to civil rights legislation.[51]

Russell had no desire to weaken or destroy the Democratic party. He hoped to reshape it so that southerners would have more influence over policy matters, but he knew that a split among the Democrats at that point would only help Republicans and weaken southern power in the Senate. Believing that Truman would be defeated with the party split into three factions—the regular Democrats, the liberals who supported Henry A. Wallace, and the Dixiecrats—Russell wanted to maintain his party credentials and be available to help modify Democratic policies on such matters as civil rights after the party's projected defeat. Moreover, as mentioned earlier, Russell was intellectually and emotionally attached to the Democratic party. He later declared that he did not like the planks in the 1948 platform any better than those delegates who bolted the convention. But he said that he did not "propose to be driven from the house of my fathers merely because a group of Johnny-come-latelys had taken over its administration temporarily." He added that most Democrats prior to 1948 had always been for states' rights in their basic philosophies.[52] He hoped, he said, that the party would return to the position of its Democratic forebears.

Shortly before the election, Russell announced that he planned to vote for Truman, although he played absolutely no part in the campaign.[53] He spent the period from mid-August, when Congress adjourned, until the beginning of the Eighty-first Congress in January 1949 in Winder resting and visiting family and friends. Actually, the states' rights leaders never tried to pressure Russell to join them. They knew Dick Russell well enough to know that he did not respond to pressure. As Strom Thurmond remarked years later, "We offered him the opportunity to help us and said that we would welcome his support," but that was about all.[54]

Russell himself was up for reelection in 1948. But as had been true six years earlier, he had no opposition. For a time, rumors circulated that Tom Linder, state commissioner of agriculture and a person Russell personally detested, might run against him. But everyone knew, including Linder, that he could not really challenge Russell, and he never pursued the matter. Russell paid his $500 filing fee and sat back to await reelection to his third full term in the U.S. Senate.[55] He also saw his home state again vote the regular Democratic ticket.

Nearly a decade after the 1948 campaign, a student from Texas asked Russell about the use and meaning of the term "Dixiecrat." The senator replied that it had first been used in a "spirit of derision" in connection with southern Democrats during a filibuster in 1947. Then, Russell added, it had been the label given to the third party. But, he continued, "in as much as I am an old-school Jeffersonian Democrat who believes in States' Rights and who has opposed all sectional bills aimed at our beloved Dixie I have never felt any particular resentment when this label was applied to me." Of course, people who knew Russell never labeled him a Dixiecrat. On another occasion, Russell defended the South by writing that "I like to think . . . that our heritage of love of honor, respect for truth, appreciation of our form of government, is still very much alive. While we are prejudiced [in favor of the South], I am sure that no other area has as good manners as our people, and certainly no more spirit of chivalry and respect for womanhood."[56] Ralph McGill had written shortly before the election that it was time for the South to "revalue its thinking and its attitudes."[57] There was no sign, however, that Dick Russell was considering any such reevaluation.

12

Dangers at Home and Abroad

===

The election of Harry Truman and Democratic majorities in both houses of Congress in 1948 was as much of a surprise to Dick Russell as it was to millions of less politically astute Americans. Although he did not relish the idea of having to fight some policies and programs that he knew Truman would continue to push, Russell was pleased that Congress had returned to Democratic control. Southerners would once again become chairmen of a majority of the major Senate committees.

When the Eighty-first Congress opened in January 1949, Russell did not chair any standing committee. He was second only to Millard Tydings of Maryland on the Armed Services Committee and ranked fourth on the Appropriations Committee, chaired by Kenneth McKellar. With Democrats in control of the Senate, Russell again became chairman of the subcommittee on agricultural appropriations, a position that pleased him because of his strong interest in farm legislation. He still served on the Joint Committee on Atomic Energy and on the CIA Oversight Subcommittee. While Russell had a wide range of interests and concerns, he concentrated most of his efforts on blocking civil rights legislation, strengthening the nation's defenses, and helping farmers.

Russell was also a member of the seven-man Democratic Policy Committee, a position he had held since the committee's formation in 1947. This committee discussed issues, and members expressed opinions, but the group generally avoided portraying their ideas or actions as true Democratic policy. Russell was also a member of the Democratic Steering Committee, which made committee assignments. This placed him in a strong position to help his friends get desired committee appointments. For example, John Stennis of Mississippi, elected in 1947, sat on two of the Senate's less important committees, Public Works and Rules and Administration. He wanted to be appointed to either the Appropriations or the Armed Services Committee. Russell told Stennis that there was no place open on Appropriations but that he would do "anything I can to help you with Armed Services."[1] Early in 1951, Stennis was named to the Armed Services Committee.

Russell had become a master at helping colleagues in the Senate with projects of special interest to them. For example, in 1951 Senator William Benton of Connecticut had proposed an amendment to the Mutual Security Act that he feared might lose. Benton wrote Senator Brien McMahon of Connecticut about having the assistant director of the European Cooperation Administration testify before a conference committee in support of his amendment. Benton also sent a copy of the letter to Russell. However, Russell told Benton that he opposed having witnesses appear before conference committees. "I think your amendment will be all right," Russell wrote. "Just sit tight for the time being." The next day, Benton wrote Russell: "You put my amendment through very nicely and I am most grateful to you for it. You gave me just the right advice—to sit tight!—as you always do."[2] It was this kind of favor that had helped Russell to build his reputation for knowing how best to get things done. Such actions also permitted him to build up credit with his colleagues that he could draw on when needed.

Returning to Washington right after Christmas in 1948, Russell found the civil rights issue facing him. In his State of the Union Address in January 1949, President Truman again called for civil rights legislation. Russell reacted strongly against this aspect of the president's Fair Deal. He wrote a constituent that he would fight civil rights measures with all of his power. "They were" he said, "conceived in politics and thrive on the misrepresentation and misunderstanding of the worst sort of propaganda."[3]

Russell viewed this as the time to push the idea of solving the racial problem by redistributing blacks throughout the United States. On January 27, 1949, he introduced a bill that called for setting up a Relocation Commission and appropriating $500 million to provide credit for blacks who wanted to migrate from the South to other parts of the country. Up to $1,500 would be provided for each black family that wished to go elsewhere. He explained that the eleven former Confederate states had only 24 percent of the country's population but contained 75 percent of the black population. He argued that "common fairness" demanded that those who were trying to destroy the South's social order should be glad to "assist in equalizing our racial problem with that of the rest of the Nation." His bill should appeal to all "social-minded people," Russell said, because it would not only redistribute the black population but also raise the living standards of blacks. According to Russell, this was a plan to "assure domestic tranquility and national betterment." Actually, of course, he was trying to prove that many northerners were racists and, in his view, hypocrites.[4]

Hubert H. Humphrey, the new senator from Minnesota, a liberal and an ardent civil rights supporter, was one of the severest critics of relocation. He said that it was borrowed from the Hitler-Stalin school of shifting populations around. Russell, however, received encouragement for his plan from rank-and-file Americans but not enough to have any effect on Congress. A Californian wrote that it would be especially appropriate for Minnesota "with its loud-voiced Humphrey" to relocate the first 100,000 blacks in that state. The editor of the *Commercial Appeal* of Memphis, Tennessee, wrote that the Russell measure would give those criticizing the South an opportunity to descend from their "peaks of theoretical wisdom and virtue" to the "plains where real effort is under way" to solve problems. Russell told Congressman Frank Boykin of Alabama that his bill did not have much chance but that "it will at least enable us to put our finger on the hypocrites."[5] As Russell expected, the Senate refused to give the relocation measure serious consideration. Indeed, some observers could not believe that Russell was serious about such a bill.

Russell also gave some attention early in 1949 to the proposal for relocating blacks to Africa. An old idea and one pushed by Senator Theodore Bilbo of Mississippi before he died in 1946, it was regarded even by some blacks as a practical answer to discrimination and segregation. Benjamin Gibbons, president of the Universal African Nationalist Movement, headquartered in New York, wrote Russell in early 1948 asking for his support in assisting blacks who might want to emigrate to Liberia. Russell replied that he would assist in any way he could, but he did not give Gibbons any encouragement. While Gibbons and Russell had several exchanges of letters, and Gibbons actually visited the senator once in Washington, Russell always answered Gibbons in the most general and noncommittal way.[6]

Southerners were faced with another threat when early in 1949 pro–civil rights forces sought to change the cloture rule in the Senate. The rule, which had been in effect since 1917, required a two-thirds vote of those present to cut off debate. Now, however, there was a move to strip southerners of the protection of unlimited debate. On January 5, Senator Wayne Morse of Oregon introduced a resolution that, if passed, would permit halting debate by a simple majority vote. After such action, the Morse resolution would not permit a senator to speak for more than two hours on a motion or measure before the Senate.

Morse said it was time to begin majority rule in the U.S. Senate. Russell objected at once. He admitted that long speeches had sometimes irritated senators, but he contended that unlimited debate had never damaged national interests. Indeed the Senate stood as "the last citadel of free and full discussion where the rights of the minority can be heard and fully protected."[7]

Some two months later, in a news conference, Truman announced his support for changing the cloture rule. Russell reacted as quickly against the president as he had against Morse. He made it clear that if Truman and his legislative leaders pushed any plan to weaken cloture, the president's entire legislative program might be in jeopardy.[8]

Beginning in late February, the Senate hassled over the cloture issue for more than two weeks. Southerners, under Russell's leadership, were adamant against the possibility of cutting off debate by majority vote. Their most effective way to defeat a civil rights measure was by talking it to death. If anything, they wanted to make it even more difficult to end debate. As the matter turned out, the southerners, with considerable Republican support, did change the cloture rule, but to their own advantage. Instead of requiring a two-thirds vote of senators present, the 1949 rule required a two-thirds vote of all senators, or sixty-four. This made it even more difficult to cut off debate and gave southerners additional power to resist civil rights measures through the filibuster. While Russell was pleased over the rule change, he knew that there would be no lessening of demands for civil rights legislation. However, during the rest of the Truman administration, civil rights legislation made no real headway.[9]

Congress was again confronted with doing something about farm legislation in 1949 since the 1948 law extended farm benefits only to January 1, 1950. Although the fight in 1948 between the supporters of high fixed price supports and those advocating flexible supports still continued, Secretary of Agriculture Charles Brannan proposed a new plan for congressional consideration. The Brannan plan called for maintaining the price of basic commodities at 90 to 100 percent of parity for farmers agreeing to production controls. On perishable commodities, however, there would be no controls and prices would settle wherever the market dictated. Brannan proposed to pay producers of perishable commodities a cash subsidy amounting to the difference between the market price and the parity price. He argued that the plan would provide good incomes for farmers and abundant and cheaper food for consumers.

Strong opposition to the Brannan plan arose quickly. Critics de-

clared that it would cost the government huge sums and involve government too heavily in the agricultural economy. Consequently, the House
defeated the measure in mid-1949. After defeat of the Brannan scheme,
Congress turned to other approaches. Russell had opposed the Brannan
plan because, as he wrote, he doubted that Americans would "stand for
a farm program for many years which might cost as much as $8 billion
per annum." Russell wanted to enact reasonable production controls in
order to avoid situations like the potato scandal and to fix supports
high enough to give the farmer what he called a living wage.[10]

With the Brannan plan out of the way, the Senate turned to a bill
introduced by Senator Clinton Anderson of New Mexico. While the
Anderson measure called for flexible supports, it did contain a provision
that Russell had been pushing for several years—the inclusion of farm
labor costs in figuring the new parity formula. Otherwise, Russell did
not like the Anderson bill. After considerable jockeying, on October 4,
he and his friend Milton Young rallied southerners and westerners behind a move to restore fixed supports at 90 percent of parity in the
Anderson bill. It was a real tug-of-war. On the first vote, the Senate
rejected the Russell-Young amendment by a vote of 37 to 38, but after
reconsidering, it voted a tie, 37 to 37. Vice President Barkley then cast
the tiebreaking vote in favor of the amendment. The Anderson bill was
then recommitted to the Committee on Agriculture, and when it re-
emerged for Senate action, the Russell-Young fixed supports position
was defeated. The 1949 farm bill that was passed later in October
turned out to be another compromise. Supports of 90 percent of parity
were provided for the 1950 crop year, after which the sliding scale
would become effective. Those who opposed the Russell amendment
charged that it would cost an additional $2 billion, an accusation that
Russell firmly denied.[11]

Because of the inflationary impact of the Korean War, farm prices
were relatively good in the early 1950s. The price of several farm commodities actually rose above parity by 1951. Cotton, the South's leading
crop, however, did not enjoy strong prices. A huge crop in 1951 caused
prices to drop, leading Russell to say that farmers were taking "a terrible beating." In mid-August, Senators Russell, Maybank, Ellender, and
other cotton-state spokesmen met with Secretary Brannan to urge some
program that would strengthen cotton prices. About a week later, Brannan announced that large credits would be granted to foreign buyers to
purchase surplus cotton. Increased demand wiped out the surpluses of
most other crops held by the Commodity Credit Corporation, and in
1952 farm production and demand were in fairly good balance. Never-

theless, to protect farmers in the future, in 1952 Russell and other Farm Bloc senators succeeded in extending price supports at 90 percent of parity through 1954. This was a clear victory for agricultural political power in Washington, which continued to reject the principle of flexible supports.[12]

Russell took great pride in his work on behalf of farmers, even though in contemporary evaluations of his career little was usually said about it. In hundreds of letters to constituents he repeated time and again how he got the initial appropriations for parity payments and how he had fought for appropriations for the Rural Electrification Administration and the Farm Security Administration and cost sharing for soil conservation. Writing about his support for the Farmers Home Administration in 1952, he declared, "That is one thing that I know has done a great deal of good." Mentioning that black as well as white farmers had been helped to become independent operators, Russell explained that some of the loudest civil rights advocates had opposed appropriations for the FHA, a program that had "meant more to negroes of Georgia than any of the alleged civil rights bills would."[13]

Although Russell was willing to spend more to prop up agricultural prices, the same was not true of foreign aid. By 1949 he had become a consistent critic of huge expenditures for military and economic aid. The amounts being appropriated, according to Russell, greatly exceeded anything that the United States was getting in security. Russell believed that a much higher defense priority was to strengthen American military might. He saw the large sums going into foreign aid as weakening the American economy. "I am afraid that our program of supporting Europe," he wrote, "if carried on for many years will ruin our economy." Besides, Russell did not think that the United States' European allies would use military equipment very efficiently.[14]

Russell voted to establish the North Atlantic Treaty Organization (NATO) in April 1949, but he opposed the $1.3 billion appropriation requested by the president to support the Western alliance. He argued, along with some conservative Republicans, that such huge outlays for military supplies and other foreign aid would place a dangerous strain on the American economy. Russell believed that federal spending was getting out of control. Just before the Senate voted on the foreign aid package in September 1949, Russell introduced an amendment that would have reduced the amount of aid by $400 million. Explaining the proposed cuts, Russell said that he had earlier voted for every measure to strengthen the nation's defenses. If Russian armies moved against Western Europe, he said, the United States' self-interest would demand striking the Soviet Union "with every means at our command," presumably meaning atom bombs. But, Russell said, this measure would not promote "mutual aid and self help" as it claimed. Rather, it would be the beginning of endless annual appropriations for foreign assistance. His remarks turned out to be quite prophetic.

Russell's position was that the Western European allies could not withstand a Russian land onslaught regardless of how many weapons the United States provided them. It was a delusion to think otherwise, he declared. If a land war erupted in Europe, Russell predicted, as he had earlier, that most of the American military hardware provided to those nations would quickly fall into Russian hands. Apprehensive over deficit financing, Russell said he was greatly alarmed over the "casual manner" in which Congress viewed the large deficit created by spending more money than was taken in. He added that it was unfair to blame the president for the deficit because Congress shared as much or more of the responsibility for the problem. Like Mark Twain said of the weather, Russell declared, Congress talked about economy but did nothing about it. Russell repeated that the worst feature of the whole foreign aid program was making financial commitments that extended so far into the future. The Russell amendment, however, was defeated 46 to 38. Some fellow southerners supported Russell, as did such conservative Republicans as John Bricker of Ohio, Chan Gurney of South Dakota, and Kenneth Wherry of Nebraska.[15]

By 1949 and 1950, Russell had become one of the leading opponents of large outlays for foreign aid. Moreover, he was one of the principal advocates of economy and lower taxes. Yet, he did not want to lower taxes until the budget was balanced. He was far from consistent on this question. Russell continued to get as much federal largess as possible for his state, an effort that paid off handsomely as millions were spent at military bases and other federal facilities.

Whenever Russell and some of his southern colleagues were joined by conservative Republicans in opposing certain liberal programs, critics often commented about this unholy conservative alliance. Russell, however, believed that reporters made too much of a purported conservative coalition. He had supported a good many progressive reforms, and even Hubert Humphrey once said that, except on civil rights, Russell could be considered a "leading progressive." Russell wrote early in 1949 that he wanted to go along with the president when he could in good conscience, but when he thought the president's recommendations would be harmful to the country, he would oppose them and welcome support from any source, "whether it be Republican or Democrat."[16] As mentioned earlier, Russell was not a political theorist but a pragmatist. He was more concerned with results than with theories.

By the second Truman administration, there was considerable talk about political and party realignments in American politics. Russell often commented on such possibilities. Speaking in July 1950, he said that he would like to see "a very strong Republican Party in the South." The one-party system in the South, he declared, had weakened the region's political clout because the national Democratic party simply took the South for granted. Russell even predicted that conservatives who believed in strict constitutional government would eventually get together politically. Furthermore, he thought that if the Republicans would defend the rights of the states, protect business interests (a slap at the FEPC), and nominate strong candidates, people would be surprised how many southerners would vote Republican. At about the same time, he wrote privately that until the two major parties had "to bid for our votes as they do for votes of minority groups in the doubtful states," the South would not "have the influence in our government to which we are entitled."[17]

Russell admitted that he did not know if any new party would emerge or if there would be some restructuring of the old parties. He did, however, see current political alignments in a state of flux. Although he was unhappy with the Democratic party under Truman's control, Russell opposed conservative South Dakota senator Karl Mundt's idea of a more formal alliance between southern Democrats and conservative Republicans. Russell was perfectly willing to work with conservative Republicans, such as Robert A. Taft, to gain certain limited objectives, but he did not want to seriously weaken the Democratic party.[18] Russell's goal was to try to get the Democrats back to what he considered true Democratic principles. But in this he was not very hopeful. He saw both old parties as having "sold their souls to minority groups." As Russell looked at the midcentury political scene, he saw no sure solution to the South's dwindling political power.

Battles over civil rights, agricultural policy, the budget, and foreign aid made the 1949 congressional session a tough one. Also it was a time when major world events shattered the possibility of complacency in Washington. The victory of the Communists in China, the Russian explosion of an atom bomb, and the trial of Alger Hiss stemming from charges of Communist connections alarmed many Americans whose security seemed threatened both at home and abroad. Russell, however, responded to these world-shaking events with balance and reason.

While resting at Winder in late October after Congress adjourned,

Russell visited with Ken Turner of the *Atlanta Constitution*. Looking back at the session, Russell thought that Georgia and the South had fared quite well. Farmers were assured of high price supports for at least another year; millions of federal dollars for public works, flood control, conservation, and military installations were being funneled into Georgia; and the Senate rule on cloture had strengthened the position of southerners who opposed civil rights legislation. Russell was less optimistic about the future and expressed greatest concern over Truman's continued call for civil rights legislation and over the long-range effects of deficit financing.[19]

Although Russell blamed many of the world's problems on Soviet expansionism, he did not agree with many Americans who believed that internal subversion in the United States had been responsible for Russian success in producing an atom bomb. He told Turner that the Russians would have had the bomb sooner or later and added that the United States should be able to "keep well ahead" of the Russians in the development of nuclear weapons.

While the Communist victory in China distressed Russell, he did not think that the United States could have changed the outcome. He had concluded after his visit to China in 1943 that there was no hope of "getting order and decency in the Nationalist Government." When the Republicans were trying to get more funds to "save" the Chiang Kai-shek government in 1949, Russell opposed the move. "I regret to see China going Communist," he explained, "and if there were any way to prevent it, I would be willing to support measures to that end." Admitting that China might be used to communize the rest of Asia, he thought it would do no good to rely on Chiang Kai-shek to stop the Red tide. Russell said that "our experiences have proven that the present Nationalist Government is not worthy of confidence." Once the Nationalists had been forced to flee to Formosa, there was discussion of use of American power to protect the Chiang Kai-shek government from Communist attack. Russell told a friend that his sympathies were with Chiang, but "I am not in favor of going to war with Communist China to defend Formosa." This could bring about a world conflict, he said, and Formosa was not worth that "as much as I should like to have the Nationalists prevail."[20]

Russell had concluded even before the outbreak of the Korean War on June 25, 1950, that it was unwise to build American foreign policy on unreliable allies. Also he opposed inserting American power in areas of the world where the national interest did not clearly demand it. His statement on protecting Formosa was typical of his views. He did see the

Soviet Union as the source of most of the trouble around the world, but he did not believe there was danger of a direct Soviet attack on the United States. The Russian plan to defeat the United States, Russell argued, was to encroach on those countries bordering the Iron Curtain, causing Americans to respond with huge amounts of military and economic aid to resist greater threats. In this way, Russell said, the Soviets would "bleed America white" and weaken the United States by causing deficit spending and inflation.[21]

To Russell the best protection for the United States was an invulnerable defense. He gave strong support to maintaining a sufficiently large military establishment and providing the military with the best weapons that American technology could supply. But even here, Russell believed that savings could be made without loss of effectiveness by adopting Universal Military Training. Writing shortly after the beginning of the Korean War, Russell said that if Universal Military Training had been added to the Selective Service Act of 1948, "we would have had a great deal more national defense today at much less cost." What was needed, Russell said, was "a reservoir of trained manpower." In his view, it was just too expensive to maintain a very large standing army, navy, and air force.[22]

On January 8, 1951, in the midst of the Korean War, Russell introduced a Universal Military Training bill sponsored by nine members of the Armed Services Committee. He had just become chairman of the committee as a result of Senator Millard Tydings's defeat in the 1950 midterm elections. The committee bill required the registration of seventeen-year-old men who would then undergo four months of military training when they reached eighteen or completed high school, whichever came first. The bill had been authored by Lyndon B. Johnson and members of a subcommittee.

In presenting the measure to the Senate, Russell declared, "We stand at a crossroads of history, where the desirability of universal military training is no longer a debatable matter." There were two choices before the nation, he said. One was to maintain a large standing army, which would eventually bankrupt the country, and the other was to adopt Universal Military Training, which would "not impair the national solvency." Russell asserted that implementation of the program would permit the United States to remain both free and financially solvent. It was unfair, he continued, to compel thousands of Americans to fight two wars while others "who are able to do so have never been called on to defend their country in one war." The need to call up veteran reservists was, according to Russell, un-American. Such an injustice would continue, he said, until the country had a "large ready reserve, capable of mobilization upon very short notice, constantly augmented by new trainees from the ranks of those who have performed no military duty."

Calling up veteran reservists for service in Korea while others had never been drafted for military duty was, Russell explained, a perfect example of the unfairness that Americans were "sick and tired of." He rejected the claims that Universal Military Training would militarize and corrupt the morals of the nation's youth. If eighteen year olds could not be trusted away from home for a few months of military training, Russell said, "then our homes, our churches, and our schools have failed." Besides being fair and providing for a system to meet American worldwide military needs, Russell argued, Universal Military Training would "serve notice on the mad masters of communism" that the United States was prepared to see the "struggle through to the bitter end."[23]

During the next few months, Russell skillfully guided the Universal Military Training bill through the Senate. He granted interruptions and time to key supporters, he worked closely with Lyndon Johnson, and from time to time, he politely destroyed the arguments of those opposing the bill. Although the Senate and House passed a Universal Military Training measure that was signed by the president in June 1951, Congress could not agree on how to actually implement the plan in 1952. Consequently, the law never became effective. Russell was greatly disappointed, but support for Universal Military Training dropped quickly as the Korean War wound down.[24]

The outbreak of war in Korea had caught Russell as much by surprise as it had most other Americans. He strongly supported President Truman's decision to make a stand against Communist expansion in Korea. When the Chinese entered the war, however, he advocated pulling all ground troops out of Korea immediately. As he put it later, "I did not want to try to fight a land war with the Chinese." Once American troops were withdrawn, Russell recommended bombing an important target in China every day until Chinese troops left Korea.[25]

The Korean War caused Russell to place even more blame for destabilizing the world on the Soviet Union. His earlier suspicions of the Soviet Union now became hard-line opposition. He traced most evil in international relations directly to the Kremlin. To Russell, like many other Americans, communism was monolithic, and the worldwide movement was controlled from Moscow.

Even though Russell's views on what should be done in Korea were ignored by the administration, Russell followed the president's lead on most matters relating to the conflict. He opposed a formal declaration of war against North Korea, arguing that the United States had never recognized North Korea as an independent nation. Moreover, he opposed dropping an atom bomb on North Korea since military authorities did not think any worthy targets existed to justify such action and since it would endanger American troops. Despite his admiration for General MacArthur, whom he had known for twenty years, Russell opposed bombing targets in China as long as American troops were in Korea. He believed that such bombing would bring the Soviet Union into the war with submarines and air power and threaten the possibility of safely withdrawing American troops from the Korean peninsula. Secondly, he saw bombing China as a first step toward placing American troops on the Asian mainland beyond Korea. In December 1950, he wrote Clarence Poe, editor of the *Progressive Farmer*, that the thought of getting into a land war with China "has been a nightmare to me since our forces have been in Korea." In short, Russell backed, but not with enthusiasm, the administration's idea of a limited police action. He believed that American intervention was necessary because otherwise "we would not have had a friend left in the world in the case Russia had attacked us."[26]

Russell's frustrations at the Soviet Union emerged when he talked about the Russians achieving their goals by using "satellites and trained seals." Writing in late 1950, he declared that undoubtedly "Russia is the source of all our troubles." Responding to a member of the Democratic National Committee in the spring of 1951, he declared: "It is my opinion that the B-36 and our large stockpile of atomic bombs is the thing that has kept Stalin from an overt act. He is willing to take anything he can capture through the military action of his satellites." He explained to an earlier correspondent that "until we are prepared to strike at the heart of Russia with unrelenting blows, they will call the tune in world affairs." But how could this be done? Russell had no answer. He later explained that the United States' hesitancy to use the atom bomb during the Korean War was due to fear of Soviet reprisal. The only way the United States could avoid atomic warfare would be to stay "ahead of Russia in the matter of armed might," he said.[27] He privately criticized the "leadership here in Washington" for not explaining American foreign policy more clearly, and he believed that the State Department and General MacArthur had made serious mistakes in regard to Korea. But whatever the errors, Russell said, no national benefits could be derived from stressing those mistakes. Rather, he argued, it was time for all Americans to unite. He claimed that there was some consolation in the fact that the horror and sacrifices experienced in Korea had the useful purpose of alerting Americans to the "dangers of world communism."[28]

As the Korean War dragged on and negotiations seemed to be getting nowhere, Russell became more militant. He said in August 1951 that if no peace was forthcoming soon, the United Nations might have to institute "vigorous" warfare against Red China.[29] Presumably this meant heavy bombing of some kind. But Russell sometimes purposely used such unclear language.

Meanwhile, the controversy over wartime policy in Korea reached a dramatic climax on April 11, 1951, when President Truman announced his removal of General MacArthur as commander of the United Nations and U.S. troops in the Far East. MacArthur had rejected the police action approach and outlined his prescription for victory. He had called publicly for instituting an economic and naval blockade of China, expanding air power over China, and supporting Chinese troops on Formosa in an attack on the mainland. There was no substitute for victory, he had said. Many Americans agreed with MacArthur, but his policy had been clearly at odds with that of his commander-in-chief. By urging military policies contrary to those of the president, MacArthur had raised a constitutional question of civilian control over military matters. His proposals had been a clear challenge to the president that Truman could not ignore.

The dismissal of a popular military hero in the midst of an unpopular war brought a flood of criticism against Truman. Emotions ran high. Russell and other senators and congressmen were deluged with telegrams and letters complaining about the president's action. F. A. Garrett of Mineral Wells, Texas, wrote Russell, sending copies to several other senators, that people were aroused "to probably a greater degree than they were over the issue of slavery in 1861." Other communications read: "How dumb can a president be. Let's fire Truman and give MacArthur the job"; "Impeach Truman"; "Consider the dismissal of General MacArthur the most disgraceful episode in our national history"; and "This is one of the most dastardly things that has been done in this country in years." One critic wrote that for MacArthur to follow Truman's orders was comparable to "a lion following the orders of a jackal." Still another constituent declared that either Truman was mentally incompetent or "too small a man for the Presidency of the United States." The dismissal of MacArthur released a tremendous amount of anti-Truman sentiment that had been building up throughout the country. To many this act seemed the final proof of the president's incompetence, his softness on communism, and his general bungling.[30]

With emotions riding so high, Russell saw that it would not be easy to maintain calm, rational attitudes in Congress. While Senator Robert S. Kerr of Oklahoma came to Truman's defense in a ringing speech, Russell sought to work more quietly to get over the crisis and minimize any political damage to the Democrats. One way to do this would be to hold well-structured hearings in executive session before his Armed Services Committee. Russell was out of Washington on the day Truman made his announcement, but after he returned, on April 13, he called his committee members into executive session where they voted to conduct an inquiry into MacArthur's dismissal. After the meeting, Russell reported that the committee would invite General MacArthur to testify. Calling MacArthur one of the "great captains of history," Russell said that people were entitled to know the facts.[31]

Although Russell had initially envisioned that the hearings would be held by the Armed Services Committee, on the morning of April 17 he and Tom Connally, chairman of the Foreign Affairs Committee, discussed by telephone the idea of their committees joining forces to conduct the inquiry. Russell and Connally agreed that this would be a good procedure. Although the questions to be considered were primarily military in nature, Russell said, aspects of foreign policy would also be examined. This would justify combining the two groups. The same afternoon, Russell explained the arrangement to his colleagues and said that, as chairman of the Armed Services Committee, he would preside. According to Russell, Connally had suggested that Russell oversee the proceedings. Russell asserted that while he had no "particular desire to do so, I have never shirked any responsibility."[32] Actually, Russell wanted very much to chair the hearings and had always had every intention of doing so. He believed that he had enough power and influence to direct the investigations along the lines that would be most useful to the country.

As plans developed for the hearings to begin on May 3, Russell drew a great deal of attention in the public press. Even though Mac-Arthur's appearance before a joint meeting of Congress on April 19 commanded the center of media attention, newspapers gave Russell liberal billing. His statements and picture appeared in most newspapers throughout the country. On April 15, the *Miami Daily News* announced, "Sen. Russell to Hold Spotlight in Probe," and on the 18th, the *Atlanta Journal* reported, "Russell Calmly Takes Helm in Policy Probe." Some of the leading columnists portrayed Russell as the ideal person to head the inquiry. According to Marquis Childs, he was judicious, calm, and objective. One Washington observer told Childs that if anyone could protect the national interests against those who sought personal or political gain, "Dick Russell can." George E. Reedy, who later served as staff director of the Democratic Policy Committee, once wrote in connection with the MacArthur hearings that Russell had "one of the most astute minds that has ever entered the Senate."[33]

Russell was determined to question witnesses in executive session. In the first meetings with his committee, Russell got unanimous support from Democrats and Republicans for that position. He never talked to Truman about "whether closed or open," as he scribbled on a telephone pad, but he did ask General MacArthur who replied that he preferred closed sessions. Russell argued that military secrets might be revealed in open hearings that could result in the death of American soldiers in Korea.[34] The very thought of open hearings with radio transmitters and television cameras in the room, which might create a "circus atmosphere," greatly disturbed Russell.

Russell's insistence that the hearings be held in executive session brought him considerable criticism. Ralph McGill, however, was one editor who believed that Russell was 100 percent right in that decision. Russell wrote McGill that he *knew* he was right. Despite loud complaints, Russell said that he planned to "stick to my guns." He told McGill that such work was "highly distasteful" to him, "but since it has been thrust upon me I intend to try to do a good job without fear or favor." It was an exaggeration and a degree of false modesty for Russell to say the job had been forced upon him. Indeed Russell had moved quickly after MacArthur's dismissal to assure his leadership of any investigation.[35] Connally believed that Russell had pushed him aside.

When some of the Republican committee members changed their minds and called for open hearings, Russell chastised them for reversing themselves. On the afternoon of May 3, following MacArthur's first appearance before the joint committee, Russell returned to the Senate floor and told his colleagues that his patience was "worn a bit threadbare" over the continued demand for open hearings. He reiterated that "orderly procedure, expeditious handling, [and] objective search for the truth, . . . will be best accomplished in an executive session." He said that open hearings might "pay political dividends," but they would not be in the best interests of the country. The American people might see and hear more, but representatives of *Pravda* and the Kremlin would also gain information.[36] Although Russell won his position for closed hearings, he did arrange at the end of each day to provide to reporters copies of testimony that had been purged of information that would compromise security.

Senator Russell and General Douglas MacArthur shake hands at MacArthur hearings, May 1951. (Photo courtesy of Russell Memorial Library, University of Georgia, Athens.)

The hearings began on May 3. To provide assistance in what he knew would be a long and grueling affair, Russell asked his old friend, attorney Charles J. Bloch of Macon, to help out on a voluntary basis. William H. Darden, Jr., chief clerk of the Armed Services Committee, also worked closely with his boss. In order to try to shift the spotlight away from MacArthur, the official title given to the hearings was the *Military Situation in the Far East*. Nevertheless, almost everyone referred to the investigations as the MacArthur hearings.

Before calling General MacArthur as the first witness, Russell made an opening statement. He said that the "momentous questions" that the committee would examine were "vital to the security of our country and the maintenance of our free government." Facts would be sought, he explained, to help Congress "make proper decisions on the problem of war and peace in the Far East and indeed throughout the world." Hoping to head off any attempts at political maneuverings, he declared that he hoped the hearings would be conducted in the true spirit of "national interest," which transcended "the fortunes of any individual, or group of individuals." The American people, he said, wanted the truth "without the color of prejudice or partisanship, and with no thought of personalities."[37]

Russell himself began the questioning of MacArthur. He presented a series of questions on the cooperation and unification of the armed forces, the use of air power, Chinese and Soviet strength in the region, the quality of American military intelligence, and other crucial matters. Three days and 320 pages later, the committee completed its questioning of the general. Russell praised MacArthur for his "patience, thoroughness and frankness" and said that the hearings had been an example of "democracy at work." During the next seven weeks, committee members queried Secretary of Defense George C. Marshall, General Omar Bradley, Secretary of State Dean Acheson, and other administration advisers and policymakers.[38]

One of Russell's main concerns throughout the hearings was the prevention of security leaks. On May 14, when Marshall testified, Russell said that he was very uneasy that some of the information being revealed might end up in the press. He reminded the committee that it was dealing with military and diplomatic issues vital to the nation's survival. He said that testimony had been sought on some of the most secret plans possessed by the United States. "The committee was entering doors," he emphasized, that had been barred, opening books that had been closed, and unlocking secrets that had been protected by steel safes.[39] Russell was embarrassed when some of Marshall's testimony leaked to the press. Marshall commented that he felt like he was act-ing as an intelligence agent for the Soviet Union. Russell lectured his colleagues and warned them that if American fighting men in Korea were endangered through a committee member's indiscretion or careless statements, neither "our God nor our fellow citizens will ever forgive us nor would we deserve forgiveness." He cautioned his fellow senators about the danger of "a careless word, a slip of the tongue." Russell confessed that at times he possessed information so highly secret that he wished he did not know it. He challenged senators to prove that in a democracy a balance could exist between providing the people enough knowledge on which to make proper decisions and at the same time protecting the nation's security.[40]

One crucial question that arose during the hearings was whether witnesses were protected by executive privilege and could refuse to an-swer certain types of questions. During the questioning of General Omar Bradley, Senator Alexander Wiley of Wisconsin asked Bradley to reveal the content of his conversations with President Truman on April 6, 1950, shortly before the outbreak of the Korean War. Bradley said that he did not feel free to relate anything that the president had said on that occasion. Despite Wiley's complaints, Russell ruled that a "private conversation between the President and the Chief of Staff as to detail can be protected by the witness if he so desires." Russell said that he could be overruled but stood his ground.

Senator Wiley was especially disturbed by Russell's ruling. On May 16, Wiley and some of his Republican colleagues met to discuss at length the principle of executive privilege that Russell was enforcing. Wiley informed the committee that he had been discussing this question "with a group of Republican associates" and that they planned to challenge Russell's ruling in the Bradley case. Seeing the meeting of Republican senators as a move to politicize the investigation, Russell told Wiley that he was disappointed that the senator was "having huddles with just members of his party with respect to this issue." He had hoped, Russell said, that the hearings would not degenerate into a partisan fight in which party members held "huddles." Committee members should not be settling differences as Democrats or Republicans, Russell lectured sternly, but as Americans.[41]

Russell probably overreacted to some members' disagreement on the matter of executive privilege and to what seemed to him to be their Republican partisanship. Also he was still annoyed at the Republicans' call for open hearings after they had agreed to closed meetings in execu-tive session. In any event, Russell had lost patience with the committee.

On the evening of May 16, he wrote a four-page letter of resignation as committee chairman, which he planned to hand members the following morning. He explained that he had tried to keep the hearings on a high nonpartisan plane but that the Republicans had held "rump sessions" and seemed more interested in "some political advantage than a non-partisan investigation." When Republicans injected politics into the hearings, he wrote, he could no longer preside. "I am submitting my resignation and my decision is irrevocable." He added, "I do not propose to act as a ring master of a political circus."[42]

What caused Russell to revoke his irrevocable decision is not clear. Perhaps it was a night's rest. He appeared the next morning, May 17, in his usual place as chairman. The letter was not distributed. As had been true the day before, argument resumed over the question of executive privilege. After more discussion, the chairman's ruling was brought to a vote. No one was surprised that Russell was upheld by a vote of 18 to 8. Russell might be challenged but not defeated. He usually had the votes to control procedural decisions as well as other matters. For example, committee member Lyndon Johnson sent him an undated note saying, "Dick—vote my proxy on any and all matters as you vote." On May 31, Senator Fulbright forwarded Russell a handwritten memo stating that he would be gone after June 1 and that "I authorize you to vote for me on any questions coming before the joint committee during my absence." These proxies were typical of the majority support Russell commanded. Besides the Democrats, he usually had the backing of Republicans Lodge and Saltonstall.[43]

But his problems were not over. On May 18, Senator Wiley wrote Russell a long letter charging that the chairman's failure to require witnesses to answer certain questions and President Truman's refusal to release his staff from executive privilege were placing an "iron curtain" over information leading to MacArthur's dismissal. Moreover, Wiley wrote, committee members were being denied information about "the down fall of Nationalist China, the blunders at Yalta, Teheran, Potsdam, and any other critical issues which our Committee may want to explore." Wiley accused the Democrats of politicizing the investigation in their "frantic desire to cover-up and white-wash."[44]

Wiley's letter infuriated Russell. He considered the suggestion that his motive was anything less than promoting the national interest to be an insult to his integrity. But more important to Russell than the questioning of his motives was his desire to keep the Republicans from using the hearings to criticize Democratic foreign policy from World War II to the Korean conflict. Thus he maintained his calm and did what he could to keep the testimony confined to MacArthur's dismissal and the situation in the Far East. Shortly before the hearings ended, Russell wrote MacArthur asking if he would like to appear before the committee again in light of the fact that other witnesses had access to his testimony but he had not been privileged to theirs. MacArthur replied on June 19 that he did not want to offer further testimony, saying that it would not be in the public interest.[45]

Although Russell believed that the hearings continued too long, he said they could not have been shortened without bringing charges of whitewashing. Finally, however, on June 25 the testimony ended. Russell was greatly relieved. Most of the time during the previous seven weeks he had worked until eight or nine o'clock in the evening trying to keep up with both the hearings and his other Senate business. The fact that he had asked many of the questions himself and had been responsible for seeing that the hearings proceeded smoothly had taxed both his physical and mental resources. The full record of the investigation filled some eight thousand pages and consisted of more than two million words.

Russell's picture appeared on the cover of the *U.S. News and World Report* on June 29, as the magazine carried a story on him and his work on the committee. Russell reviewed what he considered some of the benefits and disadvantages of the investigation. One good result, he believed, was that people now had a better understanding of American foreign policy and how it had developed. He also thought that the investigation had shown the impracticality of neglecting American interests in Asia for the sake of protecting Europe. The most harmful thing that came out of the hearings, he said, was the revelation of certain policy and military decisions. For example, testimony had revealed that Chinese bases in Manchuria might have been bombed if it had not been feared that the Soviet Union would enter the war. This, Russell believed, pushed the Soviet Union and China closer together whereas American policy should have been to try to drive a wedge between them.[46]

Now that the hearings had ended, what next? Should there be a committee report? If so, what form should it take? Russell did not desire any official committee report. More than anything else, he wanted the entire episode to fade from the public consciousness. Not only did he believe that continued discussion of matters raised in the hearings would complicate American actions in the Far East, but also he did not want to provide Republicans any ammunition for the forthcoming presidential election. Moreover, the writing of an official report would be divisive, probably resulting in two reports, one by the Democratic majority and another by the Republican minority. Also Russell could argue that since no legislation was anticipated as a result of the hearings no report was necessary.

While still undecided about writing some kind of official report, the joint committee met on June 27 and unanimously agreed to make a general statement to the American people. According to Russell, the purpose of the statement would be to assure the citizens of the United States that although differences of opinion and policy had been revealed in the testimony Americans were united on fundamentals "which are necessary to enable us to survive as a free people." The thrust of Russell's statement, to which the committee agreed, was to praise the strengths of democracy and to proclaim "devotion to liberty and justice." No "alien aggressor," he declared, should be misled by any apparent differences among Americans. The citizens of the United States were united to defend themselves and to cooperate with other freedom-loving countries, Russell announced. His statement was a call for national unity and a warning to Communist aggressors.

The decision to make a statement to Congress and the American people did not settle the question of whether there would be an official committee report. For a time, Russell did nothing. He was busy with other Senate matters, particularly with completing work on the agricultural appropriations bill in late July. It was not until August 17 that he called a meeting of the committee to determine if members wanted "a detailed report of these hearings." While Russell said that he had no wish to influence any senator, he told his colleagues that he did not consider a detailed report useful. The committee's investigation had received national publicity, and he believed that people had already made up their minds on the issues involved. Nothing the committee might write could change peoples' views, Russell said, so an official report would be an "anti-climax to the hearings." He also reminded his fellow senators that even if they unanimously agreed to restore General MacArthur to command, they could not. Russell also believed that any report that showed a division of opinion might affect truce negotiations in Korea.[47] Senator William Knowland and several other Republicans asserted that they believed there should be a formal report. But when the vote was taken, Russell prevailed by a vote of 18 to 5.

Then the committee passed a resolution simply transmitting the records of the hearings to the Senate. If they chose to do so, members of the committee could include individual statements in the appendix of the record of the hearings. The vote for this procedure was 20 to 3.

Finally, the committee passed a resolution of gratitude to Russell for the "fair and very splendid" way he had conducted the committee work and then adjourned.[48]

That did not quite end the ordeal. Eight of the eleven Republican senators on the committee issued a statement criticizing the conduct of foreign affairs in the Far East. It had been one of the worst failures in the history of American foreign policy, they said. Trying to make some political points, the Republicans declared that American foreign policy since the 1940s had been based on expediency rather than "the principles of liberty and justice." These senators stated that the nation needed more information than Russell or the press had given out. But the Republican complaints were designed to influence public opinion rather than to affect policy.

Russell had skillfully deffused the MacArthur firing. And Truman was grateful. Considering the high emotions aroused by MacArthur's dismissal, the affair could have developed into a most divisive issue at the time when negotiations in Korea were being considered. By acting quickly to investigate MacArthur's removal, Russell gave Americans something to concentrate their attention on. Then by proceeding in a calm and judicious manner, by emphasizing the need for national unity, and by releasing most of the testimony to the public, he encouraged the perception that something was being done to improve the situation in the Far East. Within a few weeks, people tended to forget the affair. William S. White may have summarized the significance of the hearings best when he wrote in his book *Citadel: The Story of the U.S. Senate*: "Without rejecting outright a single MacArthur military policy, without defending at a single point a single Truman policy, without accusing the General of anything whatever, the Senate's investigation had largely ended [MacArthur's] influence on policy-making. It had set in motion, by the nature of the inquiry, an intellectual counterforce to the emotional adulation that for a time had run so strongly through the country."[49]

The hearings also gave Russell a great deal of national publicity. He was much better known throughout the country in June than he had been in April. Richard Strout, writing in the *Christian Science Monitor*, described him early in the hearings as the "most powerful man in the Senate." He went on even further to say that Russell was the Senate's de facto leader, despite the fact that Senator Ernest McFarland of Arizona officially held the majority leader position. Russell always gave the appearance of outward humility, but he relished these flattering comments.

As chairman of the Armed Services Committee, Russell spent more and more of his time on military matters. During the early fall of 1951, the Defense Department and General Eisenhower, who was then commander of the North Atlantic Treaty Organization forces, urged him to visit Western Europe to inspect American bases and the overall military situation. Part of the reason for sending Russell to Europe was the hope that his opposition might be softened to foreign aid. In mid-August, Truman had called congressional leaders including Russell to the White House to make a pitch for his $8.5 billion foreign aid package. After that meeting, Russell had recommended cutting about $1 billion from the president's figure.[50]

Russell agreed to the trip, and upon his return in early December, he was interviewed by a reporter from the *U.S. News and World Report.* He said that he was impressed with the morale and training of American troops, who were "ready for any eventuality." Russell also believed that the Europeans were doing more for themselves than earlier, but he still thought they were contributing less than should be expected by the United States. This was an opinion Russell had expressed many times, and one that General Eisenhower and other American officials did not like to hear from a man in Russell's position. While admitting that foreign aid should be continued for several years, Russell insisted that economic help should be "related to defense purposes." He did not favor pulling U.S. troops out of Western Europe, but he hoped that the number could be greatly reduced before 1955. Russell used this interview to again make a strong pitch for Universal Military Training.[51]

On the matter of waste in the military budget, Russell admitted that it was bound to occur where the Defense Department was spending such huge sums. Nevertheless, Russell said it was the responsibility of military authorities, as well as Congress, to eliminate all waste possible. When constituents complained to him about this matter, he said that he was doing all he could to reduce waste and inefficiency. The Defense Preparedness Subcommittee that had been set up in the Armed Services Committee and was headed by Lyndon Johnson, Russell said, was serving as a kind of watchdog on these matters.[52]

Although Russell devoted much of his time to matters that fell under the purview of the Armed Services Committee in 1950 and 1951, he also carefully nurtured his own power in the Senate. During the fall of 1950 after the defeat of majority leader Scott Lucas of Illinois, many of Russell's friends urged him to accept the leadership post. On November 9, the *New York Times* speculated whether Russell would take the position, but he announced two days later that "he was too much out of line with the Administration to go out" for the majority leadership.

Nevertheless, several of his colleagues persisted. Senators Joseph C. O'Mahoney, Dennis Chavez, Pat McCarran, John Sparkman, and others said that Russell would be an ideal majority leader.[53]

Two things were clear. Russell could have had the job, but he did not want it. He told his friends and supporters that he appreciated their endorsements, but he maintained that he could not compromise his independence. He wanted to be free to support or oppose the administration's programs on the basis of his individual judgment. Russell wrote that he would be happier and would render more service in the Senate if he avoided the "unpleasantness" of the "weekly meetings at the White House" and retained his "absolute independence of thought and action." In their biography of Lyndon Johnson, Rowland Evans and Robert Novak wrote that it was reported that Truman sent Clark Clifford to Winder to convince Russell to accept the majority leader post. This story is interesting but groundless.[54]

Although Russell shunned the Democratic leadership post, no colleague was likely to get it without his approval. By 1950 and 1951, Dick Russell was at the center of the inner circle of Senate power, and he gave the nod to Senator Ernest McFarland of Arizona for majority leader. For majority whip, he supported his young friend from Texas, Lyndon B. Johnson. One of the class of senators elected in 1948 that included Hubert Humphrey, Estes Kefauver of Tennessee, Robert S. Kerr, the oil millionaire from Oklahoma, and a number of others, Johnson had no special claim on the whip position. Moreover, it was not very important at the time. But Johnson wanted it to help him toward his goal of Democratic leadership and political advancement. He got the position because Dick Russell backed him.

By 1950 Russell and Johnson had become good friends. They had known one another casually since the late 1930s when Johnson was elected to the U.S. House of Representatives. Johnson was an ardent supporter of the Rural Electrification Administration, and he had often fought losing battles in the House for larger appropriations. In those cases, he had hoped that Russell, as chairman of the subcommittee on agricultural appropriations, could restore House cuts in the Senate. Russell liked what he saw of this lanky young congressman from the Tenth Congressional District in Texas. Johnson, on the other hand, appreciated Dick Russell and knew that the powerful Georgian could be crucial in advancing his career. When Johnson was elected to the Senate, he sought appointment to the Armed Services Committee. He had been on the Naval Affairs Committee and later the Armed Services Commit-

Senator Russell and Senator Lyndon B. Johnson visit at a meeting in Corpus Christi, Texas, November 1949. (Photo courtesy of Russell Memorial Library, University of Georgia, Athens.)

tee in the House, which, beginning in 1949, was chaired by Carl Vinson of Georgia. Vinson spoke highly of Johnson to Russell, and with the support of two influential Georgians, Johnson was named to the Senate Armed Services Committee over a number of senators who had much more seniority. Johnson was deeply grateful for Russell's support. Although Johnson had a deep interest in defense matters, his main reason for wanting to serve on the Armed Services Committee was to be near Russell. In this way, he would be working naturally with one of the main power brokers in the Senate and doing so without appearing pushy. Johnson knew the difference between the so-called "whales" and the "minnows" in the U.S. Senate. He wanted to be close to one of the whales. Johnson would learn his Senate politics from one of the masters of the game. As he said, "I knew there was only one way to see Russell every day, and that was to get a seat on his committee."[55]

The fact that a close relationship developed between Russell and Johnson seemed unusual, even strange. In both temperament and personality they were not at all alike. It might be said that as opposites they were drawn to one another. Russell was a quiet, thoughtful, introspective man, somewhat aloof, modest, and always a gentleman. In contrast, Johnson was an expansive extrovert, rough, sometimes bombastic and ill-mannered, and one who only slightly disguised his intense political ambitions.[56]

Russell, however, was not turned off by Johnson's evident ambition to gain power and prestige in the Senate. He admired Johnson's abilities, energy, and knowledge of the issues. Russell himself was not devoid of political ambition, a quality to which he frankly confessed as far back as the 1920s. Actually, Russell and Johnson were not as different as they appeared on the surface. Indeed, on the essentials of Senate operations they thought much alike. They greatly revered the Senate as an institution and understood power and how to wield it. Russell liked that about his young Texas friend. Russell was a good mentor, and Johnson was a devoted student. Writing to Russell in October 1949 on some unnamed issue, Johnson declared, "I am young and impressionable, so I just try to do what that Old Master, the junior senator from Georgia, taught me how to do."[57]

Whereas Johnson courted Russell to help advance his prestige and power in the Senate, Russell saw Johnson as one who could bridge the gap between North and South. Coming from Texas, Johnson held many of the southern attitudes on race. Yet, he was not identified with the issue and with other southern senators so firmly that he could not deal with northern moderates and liberals. Johnson established his civil rights credentials with Russell when he spoke up in favor of tightening cloture rules in January 1949. While he maintained his independence by not attending meetings of the southern caucus, he voted consistently with the South on civil rights questions. To Russell, Johnson appeared like a person who might heal the differences between North and South. At least the Texan seemed like the best hope. Thus Russell quietly pushed Johnson ahead in the Senate power structure at every opportunity.[58]

From the time he arrived in the Senate, Johnson courted Russell's friendship and support. He treated the older senator with exaggerated respect and flattered him unmercifully. And Russell was not immune to such attention. Lady Bird and Lyndon Johnson also began to bring Russell into their family circle. Basically a lonely man who drew his main satisfaction in life from his Senate work and quiet reading, Russell appreciated the visits and invitations to dinner at the Johnson home. It was not long before the small Johnson daughters, Lynda Bird and Luci Baines, were calling Russell "Uncle Dick."

In November 1949, the Johnsons invited Russell to their home in Texas. Returning afterward to Winder to spend Thanksgiving with his mother, Russell wrote Johnson that his trip to Texas seemed like a dream. "Everything was so perfect that it is difficult to realize that it could happen in real life. My only regret is that I could not have stayed longer." Johnson replied in his usually flattering manner that Russell need not worry about dreaming because he was "the most wide-awake man in the Senate" and added that the Johnson facilities were available "for Dick Russell to return and enjoy 365 days a year." By mid-1949, Russell and the Johnsons were exchanging gifts. Lady Bird called Russell on July 29 to thank him for the wonderful Georgia peaches he had sent.[59]

Johnson seldom let any opportunity pass to ingratiate himself with Russell. When Russell's mother died on August 30, 1953, Johnson not only sent flowers but also attended the funeral in Winder. Russell was overwhelmed at this act of friendship. He wrote Johnson that only a "true friend" would travel so far to attend his mother's funeral. Johnson replied that it was the least he could do. "Your friendship," Johnson wrote, "has been the most strengthening and inspiring experience of my life." About a month later, Johnson sent Russell birthday greetings, saying that, despite a tight schedule, he could always find time to "send birthday greetings to my dearest and closest friend." Johnson added that his few years in the Senate had brought him many rewarding experiences, but the greatest thing of all "is our friendship and the realization of how much your kindness meant to me when I first entered the Chamber."[60] A firm friendship and alliance had developed between two hardworking and effective senators. For the next several years, it was a combination that carried tremendous influence in the Senate.

13

A Bid for the Presidency, 1952

===

Severe problems faced the Democrats as they looked toward the presidential election of 1952. Divisions within the party were particularly foreboding. Southerners were up in arms over Truman's continued push for civil rights legislation and over the belief that the party had come under the domination of special interests, especially organized labor and minority groups. Moreover, many Democrats outside the South could see little to admire in the Truman administration. The unpopular war in Korea, accusations of administrative corruption, and charges that the administration was soft on communism gave the Democrats an unpopular public image.

Dick Russell took no delight in these Democratic troubles. After all, he considered himself a loyal and true Democrat. Moreover, if Democrats lost control of Congress as they had in 1946, he and several of his southern friends would lose their positions of power and leadership in the Senate. There was, however, one glimpse of hope from Russell's viewpoint. The confusion and divisiveness within Democratic ranks offered an opportunity for the South to regain some of its lost influence in party affairs. If southerners could get organized and help nominate a candidate less confrontational with the South than Truman, southerners would have gained a good deal. The South, Russell insisted, must cease being a source of Democratic votes that actually helped to keep the northern, liberal wing of the party in power. How could this idea be achieved?

One approach was to nominate a candidate from the South. Every careful observer of the Democratic party, however, knew that such a possibility was very remote. Another more practical idea was to organize enough strength so that southerners would have major influence when it came time to nominate a candidate and write a platform for 1952. As southern leaders considered possible candidates from Virginia to Texas, the man who stood out above all others as one who might achieve either of these goals was Richard Russell.

Ever since 1948 when Russell had permitted his name to be placed in nomination for the presidency, some southerners had viewed him as the strongest candidate in the South. Unlike a number of other southern political leaders, Russell, except for civil rights, was fairly close to mainstream Democrats. He had supported the New Deal and much of the Fair Deal. In a survey of votes on twelve leading issues in late 1951, even the liberal Americans for Democratic Action (ADA) listed Russell as voting "right" in seven cases.[1] If he could accept some compromises on civil rights and labor issues, he might make a strong candidate. Reports of his work in connection with the MacArthur hearings in the spring and summer of 1951 had certainly portrayed him as a fair, reasonable, and intelligent leader.

Throughout 1951 there was a good deal of discussion in Georgia about Russell as a presidential candidate. He said that he was flattered by such comments, but he told one correspondent that "the chances of any Southern Democrat residing at 1600 Pennsylvania Avenue during our lifetime [are] very remote." He wrote a friend in Atlanta that a "southern man of my decided views against the modern trend euphoniously labeled 'civil rights' " had no chance for the nomination. Besides, he wrote, he could better serve "our beloved Georgia and Southland in the Senate."[2]

There were even more suggestions that Russell become the Democratic vice presidential nominee. Early in 1951, a number of southerners declared that General Eisenhower and Dick Russell would make an unbeatable ticket for the Democrats. On February 18, Harry M. Ayers, editor of the *Anniston [Alabama] Star*, entitled an editorial, "Eisenhower and Dick Russell." If Eisenhower could be drafted, he wrote, then Russell would make an ideal running mate. Russell consistently and firmly denied that he had any interest whatever in the vice presidential nomination. But he did write Ayers on March 2, "Confidentially, I believe that General Eisenhower can win on either ticket, and I would like very much to see the Democrats get a mortgage on him as soon as possible."[3]

As talk of a Russell candidacy for either president or vice president continued, Russell did his best to discourage such speculation. With most of his time and attention directed toward the MacArthur hearings, he said that it was not a good time to be discussing politics. Wright Bryan, editor of the *Atlanta Journal*, agreed and wrote an editorial on May 3 headlined, "Don't Embarrass Senator Russell." As Russell put it, even if he craved the presidential nomination, "I could not conceive of a more unpropitious time to launch a campaign."[4]

Despite Russell's denial of interest, his name kept emerging as a presidential candidate. By the fall of 1951, he was telling supporters that he appreciated being mentioned but that he was certain that the controlling forces of the Democratic party would not permit the nomination of anyone from a southern state. To a Texas backer, he wrote that he had permitted his name to be put forward in 1948 but now preferred that "some other Democrat represent the South at the next national convention."[5]

By the summer of 1951, the anti-Truman forces were desperately looking for a way to keep Truman, or anyone named by him, from getting the nomination. Senator Harry F. Byrd spoke at the Jefferson-Jackson Day dinner in Atlanta on June 25, where he delivered a scathing attack on the president and his administration. Other southern Democrats also tried to discredit Truman. As criticism of the president mounted, the name of Russell as an alternate kept arising with increasing frequency among southerners. Russell, however, declared on October 20 that he had no desire to be a "front man" for those opposing the president.[6] Commenting further on the political situation, he said that the outlook for the Democrats appeared "pretty dim right now" but that he thought the situation would begin to clarify in January.

Shortly afterward Russell left for his European trip to investigate the American military situation. Upon his arrival home on December 12, he was asked again about his presidential plans. What was his response, reporters asked, to the suggestion by Senator John Stennis that Russell should seek the presidential nomination and lead the effort to block Truman and his backers? Russell replied again, "I'm under no illusions about any southerner being elected President of the United States."[7]

Russell's insistence that no southerner could be nominated or elected as president did not quash the talk of his candidacy. By early 1952, he came under increasing pressure from southern senators and congressmen, including those in Georgia, to become a candidate. The leaders of the move for Russell were Governors Herman Talmadge of Georgia and James Byrnes of South Carolina and Senator Harry Byrd.[8] In late January, Governor Byrnes spent a weekend in Washington conferring with southern senators. A few days later, on January 28, Senator Maybank of South Carolina said that he opposed another term for Truman and that Senator Russell should be the Democratic nominee.[9] At a news conference on February 2, a reporter asked President Truman if he would vote for Senator Russell if the Georgian should head the Democratic ticket in the fall. Truman responded, "Of course I'll vote for him." When asked if he thought there was much likelihood of such a development, the president replied, "You mustn't put me on the spot," a comment that brought laughter from reporters.[10]

Pressure on Russell to become a candidate from colleagues in Congress, as well as from many ordinary citizens, continued to be heavy. On February 6, Governor Byrnes spoke before a joint session of the Georgia General Assembly, making an eloquent appeal to support Russell for president. Russell agonized over his decision. He was caught between his belief that the South needed a strong spokesman and the reality that his chances of getting the nomination were marginal at best. It was becoming increasingly difficult, however, to resist the pressure. On January 30, the Georgia House of Representatives unanimously passed a resolution urging him to seek the nomination. This was backed up by a strong endorsement by the State Democratic Executive Committee. His friend Spence Grayson of Savannah had drawn up the resolution after revising it to eliminate overly strong language about the FEPC and segregation. Russell and Grayson both knew that the civil rights issue must be kept in the context of states' rights rather than blatant racism if Russell was to have a chance. As late as February 18, however, Russell told Grayson that he had not yet arrived at a decision on becoming a candidate.[11]

But just ten days later, on February 28, Russell made a formal announcement that he was a candidate for the Democratic presidential nomination. Dressed in a dark suit, sitting before several microphones, and surrounded by colleagues Russell Long, Burnet Maybank, and John Stennis and numerous reporters, Russell officially threw his hat into the ring. Describing himself as a "Jeffersonian Democrat" who believed in the "greatest practicable degree of local self-government," Russell said that he opposed centralization of authority by the federal government, which threatened individual rights and liberties. He declared that he favored a strong defense, careful public spending, and a government free from "fraud, corruption and divided loyalties." Russell said nothing specifically on civil rights.[12]

Following his formal statement, however, reporters naturally turned to the matter of civil rights. Russell said his views were the same as they had been when he voted against the FEPC and similar legislation. "My idea," he asserted, "is that a good deal of civil rights legislation should be called civil wrongs legislation." Another reporter asked why, in light of Russell's earlier statements that a southerner could not get the nomi-

Senators congratulate Russell at the opening of his presidential campaign head-
quarters in Washington, March 1952. *Left to right*: Burnet R. Maybank, A.
Willis Robertson, Russell, J. William Fulbright, J. Allen Frear, Jr., and John C.
Stennis. (Photo courtesy of Russell Memorial Library, University of Georgia,
Athens.)

nation, he now thought he had a chance. Russell replied that his friends
and well-wishers had changed his mind.[13]

The initial response to Russell's announcement was most encouraging from southerners and from conservatives elsewhere. The day after
Russell made his statement, the South Carolina legislature passed a
concurrent resolution endorsing his candidacy and commended him
to the people of the United States. The senator told Governor Byrnes
that he was swamped with congratulatory letters and telegrams, which
seemed to confirm that there was a great reservoir of goodwill toward
him and his candidacy. Lyndon Johnson wrote that one of his constituents had provided the ideal slogan for the Russell campaign: "Let's
Hussle for Russell." Despite support and encouragement, Russell, always the pragmatist, wondered whether this goodwill could be trans-
lated into delegate strength at the Chicago convention. That was the
crucial question.[14]

Up to the time of Russell's announcement, Senator Estes Kefauver
seemed to be leading the chase for the Democratic nomination. Less
than two weeks later, on March 11, he defeated President Truman in the

New Hampshire primary. Others often mentioned as possible nominees were Senator Robert Kerr and Governor Adlai Stevenson of Illinois. There was widespread speculation that Stevenson was Truman's choice if he did not seek nomination himself. But as yet no one knew what the president intended to do. Russell, however, did not think that Truman would run again and said so on several occasions. Kerr had said that he would run only if Truman did not, but Russell claimed to be a candidate for the nomination regardless of what the president might do. If Truman were nominated, would Russell vote the Democratic ticket, reporters asked. He had never deviated from supporting the Democratic party, Russell replied, and had "no plans for it in the future." He said that he always put country above party, and only if the platform would damage the nation, would he consider abandoning the Democrats.[15]

Did Russell think that he had any real chance to win the nomination? While he did not explicitly comment on that question, in light of his earlier statements about a southerner being unable to gain the nomination, it seems certain that the initial purpose of his announcement was to increase the South's bargaining power in party councils. As time passed, however, he showed some gleam of hope that he might win the nomination.

A few commentators believed that Russell's strength would be nationwide not just regional. Raymond Moley, a member of the early New Deal brain trust, turned conservative, wrote that the "restatement of these Democratic principles by Senator Russell will inspire many more than the citizens of the South. It will be a message of cheer to millions of Northern Democrats who over the past few years have been politically homeless." Russell was not just leading a sectional revolt. "Its significance is national," Moley wrote.[16] This may have been more a statement of hope than of reality.

Most observers, however, did not think that Russell had any chance of winning the Democratic nomination. While acknowledging his personal abilities, editorial writers, columnists, and reporters discounted his chances in Chicago. The reason, they said, was because he was from the South and because of his stand on civil rights. Doris Fleeson told a Rotary Club in St. Louis that Russell would make an "excellent president" if he "were not saddled with the traditional southern attitude on civil rights." Calling him "one of the ablest members of congress," an editorial writer for the *St. Louis Post-Dispatch* wrote that Russell was, however, too "limited in his outlook" and therefore could not be nominated. Referring to him as "the logical candidate of the South," a *Washington Post* editorial said that if it was not for Russell's stand on civil rights, his candidacy would no doubt have received wide approval among northern Democrats. The *Cincinnati Enquirer* said that he had "no chance" even though he was "dignified, articulate and competent." Joseph and Stewart Alsop called him "an able man and a Democrat to his fingertips," but one who was only warning the Democrats about the future course of the party. John Gunther wrote that Russell could not "possibly be president" but that on the basis of ability "he is quite possibly the best Democrat in the race."[17]

Writers portrayed Russell as a loyal, moderate Democrat who had outstanding abilities as a legislator but who was irreparably handicapped by his southern location and attitudes. *Time* magazine reported that all of his supporters knew that Russell had "about as much chance of being nominated as a boll weevil has of winning a popularity contest at a cotton planters' picnic."[18] Perhaps his chances were better than that, but when the Gallup organization polled Democratic voters on their presidential preferences in late April, only 8 percent favored Russell compared to 41 percent for Estes Kefauver.[19] It was widely presumed, however, that Russell's candidacy would strengthen the South's influence in the Democratic party. Even if Russell could not get the nomination for himself, he could be a power broker at the convention with his approximately three hundred delegates. He could have, some observers said, an impact on who got the nomination and on the platform as well.[20]

To become a viable candidate, Russell had to solve several major problems. In the first place, he must prove his leadership of Democrats in the South. From a practical point of view, this meant defeating Kefauver in the upcoming Florida primary on May 6. He really did not want to enter the Florida contest, but the Florida congressional delegation strongly urged him to become a candidate, and Russell now felt that he must carry the state. However, if Kefauver won the Florida primary, it would be a blow to Russell and his supporters who claimed overwhelming backing in the South. Moving quickly, Russell informed the Florida secretary of state that he was designating H. E. Wolfe at the Exchange Bank of St. Augustine as his campaign treasurer for the primary. Dr. Eugene J. Peek, Sr., of Ocala agreed to head the Russell for President Committee in the state. He also wrote numerous friends urging them to begin working on his behalf.

While his supporters were organizing his campaign in Florida, Russell was looking for delegates nationwide. He called on friends and acquaintances wherever they might be. For example, on March 10, he wrote Democrat Herbert Hitchcock of South Dakota with whom he had served in the Senate in the late 1930s. Russell explained that, despite strong backing in the South and in some other agricultural areas, he would face difficulty "in persuading the leaders who control the big states with the large blocs of votes that I can win the nomination." If Hitchcock could get some delegate support for him in the Upper Midwest, Russell said, it would "greatly enhance my chances for the nomination." Although it had been years since they were in the Senate together, Russell declared that he had "grown in ability since then. If you can help me, I shall earnestly endeavor to deserve your confidence."[21] Hitchcock made no promises. However Russell did receive names of prominent Democrats in South Dakota from his Republican Senate colleague Francis Case, who told Russell that the people whose names he was sending were "Jeffersonian Democrats."[22] But significant support from other sections of the country failed to develop.

One unexpected announcement of support came from his close Republican friend in the Senate, Milton Young of North Dakota. Young said that "if the Democrats have sense enough" to nominate Russell, he "would be happy to support him." Young called Russell one of the strongest supporters of agricultural legislation and one of the most "able, conscientious, honest, sincere and likeable personalities in public life today." Those in the Midwest who were concerned about agriculture would be wise to support Russell, Young said. Young's statement caused deep concern among North Dakota Republicans, but Russell said after reading of Young's support that he "would rather deserve the confidence and friendship manifested by the news story I have just read than to be President."[23]

Surely Russell's greatest challenge was to remove his sectional image. That he was intelligent, capable, and in the political mainstream on most major issues except civil rights was widely recognized. Once he had announced his candidacy, he had plenty of opportunities to present his views to national audiences, as news columnists, radio broadcasters, and television commentators eagerly sought him out for interviews. On "Meet the Press" on March 16, Lawrence Spivak asked Russell whether, if elected president, he would place national interests above the special concerns of the southern states. Russell replied that he had always tried to avoid sectionalism, although he believed the South did have some special problems that were misunderstood by the rest of the country. "I hope I'm not sectional," he told Spivak. Then Russell explained that he had supported the national interests in foreign policy, national defense, agricultural legislation, and other areas.

Russell did everything possible to project himself as a middle-of-the-road Democrat who had the best interests of all Americans at heart. When asked if he would be able to give blacks a fair deal, Russell replied that blacks had nothing to fear if he were president. He repeated that he had helped blacks by supporting the Farm Security Administration and other federal programs so that they could buy farms. These actions, he said, had done more for blacks than the FEPC and other special laws. Russell insisted that he had not opposed the FEPC on sectional grounds or on the basis of race but because he could not support legislation that would permit government interference in private business and employment. Moreover, he insisted that he had tried to work out compromises on the FEPC question but that his attempts had been rebuffed by the administration and defeated in Congress. He was referring to his proposal for a voluntary FEPC. Here Russell presented himself as a moderate on race who was searching for compromise solutions that could reconcile differences within the Democratic party. But he could not muster enough moderation to criticize segregation. When reporters pressed him to comment on segregated food counters at drug stores in Washington, Russell said that he was "American enough to believe that, if a drug store owner wants to serve only redheaded people with brown eyes, he can do it."

On other issues, Russell tried to show that he was in tune with majority opinion. In an interview with Edward R. Murrow, he said that the United States must "maintain the social and political gains we have made over the past two decades." He did not favor new and expensive social programs, however, until the country had been adequately rearmed and until Congress could balance the budget and cut taxes. Hold the New Deal and Fair Deal gains, Russell suggested, but do not go further at the present time. Actually Russell's overall philosophy was not very different from that of Eisenhower, which proved to be widely popular in 1952.[24]

On foreign policy, Russell strongly favored the Truman position. While he supported less military and economic aid for the free peoples resisting communism, his differences with Truman were more of degree than of principle. "Basically," he said, "I have favored this policy of resistance to Communism everywhere, and attempting to unify the fight for that purpose." On the stalled negotiations in Korea, Russell declared that if the discussions became hopeless, "we must then apply new means and new methods to secure an end to the Korean War and secure the freedom of South Korea from the Communist domain." As had been true in the past, Russell did not explain what his "new methods" might entail. Overall, however, President Truman's policy of containing communism had Russell's strong support. He just advocated spending less on foreign aid.

More progressive southerners believed that if Russell were to succeed, he must make a larger break with the South's past. One of those was Truman supporter Jonathan Daniels of North Carolina, respected publisher of the *Raleigh News and Observer*. In response to a letter from Russell seeking support, Daniels outlined in some detail what he believed Russell must do to win national acceptance. Explaining that he did not believe Truman would seek the nomination, Daniels suggested that there would be a "reintensified struggle" for control of the Democratic party. It would not be just a North-South struggle, but a progressive-conservative conflict as well. In the midst of this political and party adjustment, Daniels believed that Russell had a great opportunity for creative leadership. First, according to Daniels, Russell must show that his candidacy was not just a "leadership of negation" or "a sort of strategic mobilization of a sectional protest and no more." The *New York Times* had described Russell as one who stood "as the southern symbol of defiance" against the president's civil rights program.[25] Daniels believed that Russell's friends, as well as his enemies, who were portraying his candidacy as a reaction against current trends in the Democratic party and in American life were doing Russell a great disservice.

Daniels urged Russell to assert strong leadership and surmount the idea that his candidacy was only a regional veto. He told Russell that the American people would welcome a statement by such a respected southerner as Russell on the problems that divided the nation. He urged Russell to talk about greater opportunities for all Americans. Admitting that old prejudices did not die easily, Daniels said it was time for new ideas, and Russell was the ideal person to express them. If Russell would speak out on equal opportunity, Daniels said, it would take his candidacy "into the main stream of the American faith to which you are devoted. I am sure the Southern cause has no chance except in that main stream."

Russell replied that he did not consider himself a sectional candidate. He told Daniels that he hoped providence would give him wisdom to follow the proper path, as he wanted to be of genuine service to his party and his country. Russell added that he had tried to work more closely with Truman, but that he had been disappointed in the president's attitude toward "me personally on some comparatively minor matters of local concern and in his completely uncompromising attitude toward all the approaches that I made to him to undertake in good faith to work out some settlement of the so-called Civil Rights proposals."[26] Russell really never caught the vision laid out for him by Daniels, or if he did, the change for him would have been too drastic and the results too unacceptable. Unfortunately for Russell, many people continued to view his candidacy as a tactic to block the nomination of a candidate who might threaten traditional southern attitudes and institutions.

If Russell were to make any headway in the campaign for the presidential nomination, he had to get an organization in place. Immediately after his announcement on February 28, letters and telegrams of support, along with some unsolicited campaign funds, piled up in the senator's office. So, on March 18, he announced that he was setting up campaign headquarters in Washington's Mayflower Hotel. Even though his headquarters was a modest two rooms, Russell was aghast at the cost. He wrote Erle Cocke, Sr., "I shudder when I see the expenses that are involved in an undertaking of this kind." The headquarters, he said, would cost $750 a month and that was without a single employee, a typewriter, or postage stamps. This was "a new league," Russell wrote.[27]

Although Russell did not find it easy to get his campaign organized, he promised that he would carry his message nationwide "in every sense of the word." His Senate responsibilities, however, kept him from leaving Washington as much as he desired. Consequently, two months after his official announcement, all he had accomplished was to open a headquarters, seek national attention through the media, and write letters to prospective delegates and supporters both inside and outside the South. Aaron L. Ford, former Mississippi congressman and friend of Russell's brother-in-law Hugh Peterson, headed a very small staff at the Mayflower headquarters. Actually, Ford was manager only in name. Russell relied mainly on his nephew, Robert L. Russell, Jr. Young Bobby Russell had a keen political sense and was a favorite of his Uncle Dick.[28] Russell employed Thomas D. Blake to handle his publicity. Blake had been an assistant to Stephen Early, Franklin D. Roosevelt's press secretary. He appointed his old friend Erle Cocke, Sr., president of the Fulton National Bank in Atlanta, as his campaign treasurer. Erle Cocke, Jr., a former national commander of the American Legion, also worked in the campaign.

Russell was pleased with the support he received, both personal and financial. So many invitations to speak poured in that he could not accept a fraction of them. In March and April, thousands of dollars for his campaign also arrived. Most of the contributions were less than $25, but he received a few larger amounts. His friends Alexander A. Lawrence and Spence Grayson each mailed in $1,000, and Hughes Spalding and Robert W. Woodruff were among his Atlanta friends who contributed $500 or more each. Spalding also solicited funds from a number of other leading Atlantans. A Los Angeles resident sent $5,000. But scores of checks were for $5, $10, or $25. A number of presidential dinners were held in Georgia that raised several thousand dollars. For example, the small community of Louisville had such a dinner and collected $3,062.[29]

The personal and financial support that he had built up by late March gave Russell a great deal of encouragement. His candidacy, he wrote some friends, might fool the "wise boys" of politics. He told his niece Betty Vandiver and her husband Ernest that while he had an uphill fight, "circumstances seem to be in our favor and much stranger things have happened than that I should be nominated and elected."[30]

Meanwhile other activities were underway as plans were being made for an extensive campaign. Early in March, E. W. Akins wrote the words and music for the song, "Hustle with Russell." It started out, "Come on let's hus-tle, and make Dick Rus-sell, our next President." A sixteen-page brochure entitled "A Human Interest Sketch of Senator Richard B. Russell" was also prepared. This account described the senator's personality and qualities of character, his successes in politics, and his work in state government and in the U.S. Senate. Many of these brochures were distributed to the press and to potential delegates.

In order to gain more favorable attention outside of Dixie, Russell accepted an invitation to speak before the Lions Club in Altoona, Pennsylvania, on April 23. He began by describing the expansionist goals of Russian communism as insatiable. The Russian objective, he claimed, was "dominion over the entire world." According to Russell, the United States was the only "dike holding back the flood tide of Communist Revolution" with its powerful new weapons. Then he discussed the strength of freedom and democracy, but to preserve these, he urged rearmament and strong defenses.

Russell declared that he had no fear of a Communist revolution in the United States but that the country must be awake to "sabotage, espionage treachery" and also watch out for the "well-intentioned but empty-headed" people who would accept peace at any price. He added that there were also dangers from the "professional despairers." The senator then attacked the "hucksters of hysteria" as the most dangerous of all. These were the people, he declared, who played on the emotions of citizens, who deceived and lied, who pitted American against American, and who, by criticizing those who disagreed with them, degraded

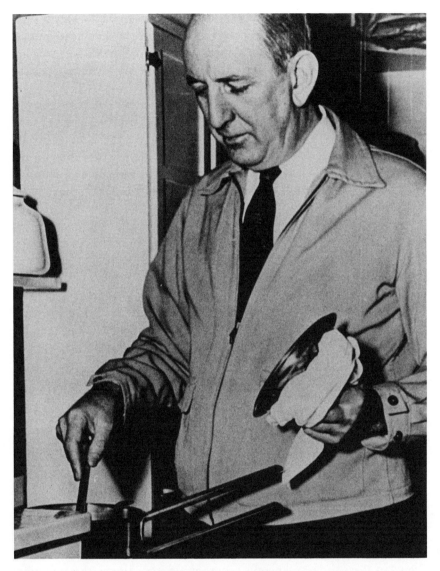

Senator Russell cooking supper in his Washington apartment, March 1952. (Photo courtesy of Russell Memorial Library, University of Georgia, Athens.)

"the American system of fair play." These "salesmen of infamy," he said, would fail because of the good common sense of the American people. This seemed to be an indirect slap at Senator Joseph McCarthy who, since 1950, had been accusing many people of being Communists or sympathetic to radical groups.

Turning to the economy, Russell insisted that foreign aid programs needed to be reassessed. "Dollars can't buy good will," he asserted, and American funds should be spent only where the United States would benefit. The Russians, he claimed, would like nothing better than for the United States to spend itself into bankruptcy in the name of national defense. He believed that military expenses should and could be reduced and that federal domestic programs could also be cut. The Altoona address contained a ringing denunciation of communism, a strong endorsement of freedom and justice, bitter criticism of those attacking American liberties, support for reduced federal expenditures, and a call for national unity. The press, including the *New York Times*, gave his speech considerable attention.[31]

Two days later, on April 25, Russell officially launched his campaign for the Democratic nomination at a $50 a plate dinner at the Biltmore Hotel in Atlanta. He arrived in Winder early that morning by train from Washington. Modine Thomas, the family's black cook, prepared him a hearty southern breakfast of ham, eggs, grits, and toast before he traveled on to Atlanta.[32] The Central Railway Company of Georgia ran a Dick Russell Special from Savannah to Atlanta, helping to produce a good crowd for the kickoff. A large parade preceded the banquet. An enthusiastic crowd greeted Russell as he sat high on the back seat of a convertible with Governor Herman Talmadge on one side and Mayor William B. Hartsfield on the other. The Georgia Tech marching band played the "Ramblin' Wreck," and several high school bands, including the black band from Howard High School, joined in the festivities.

That evening Governor Byrnes introduced Russell to a cheering crowd of three thousand people representing some thirty states. Emphasizing that Russell was not a provincial or regional candidate, Byrnes said that the senator would put an end to the warfare between the White House and Congress. He declared that Russell was sound on both domestic and foreign policy and that he would "put away the termites that sap the structure of our government."

By this time, Russell had pretty well delineated the principles on which he would seek the nomination. He told the enthusiastic crowd that his program included fighting Communist expansionism, building up American defenses without waste, achieving a balanced budget, providing mutual assistance to American allies, cleaning "subversion and dishonesty" out of government, and preserving states' rights. Russell emphasized that he was not a sectional candidate nor was his a symbolic campaign. "My sole objective," he said, "is victory in July; yes, and in November." He promised to carry his campaign to all parts of the country and announced that he would begin winning grass roots support the next day as he opened his campaign in Florida. The crowd cheered and applauded, and Russell spokesmen estimated that $125,000 had been raised for future campaign expenditures.[33]

Russell seemed to be moving slightly in the direction that Jonathan Daniels had urged him to take. Talking about his devotion to constitutional government, he said that the Constitution "enumerated the basic and fundamental rights which are the heritage of every citizen without regard to race or creed." He further stressed that he believed in equality before the law for all Americans. Actually Russell was trying to push the specifics of civil rights into the background and present general principles that could be accepted by everyone.

On Saturday morning, April 26, Russell flew from Atlanta to Gainesville, Florida, where he began his campaign to win the Florida preference primary. Although Kefauver had already been in the state, Russell had the advantage of having the state's political power structure behind him. The leaders supporting Russell included Governor Fuller Warren, Senators Spessard Holland and George A. Smathers, and all of the congressional delegation. Speaking before some 850 people on the courthouse lawn, Russell tore into Kefauver in his best campaign style. He accused his Tennessee colleague of pushing the idea of an Atlantic Union and favoring some type of world government. Trying to picture himself as the underdog, Russell declared that Kefauver headed a "super-political" organization with a large office in Washington staffed by some thirty campaign workers. Then Russell emphasized his stand for states' rights and the other principles that he had been discussing as recently as the night before in Atlanta. He later flew on to Ocala for another talk and ended the day's campaigning in Orlando where he spoke before a large crowd.[34]

During the next nine days, Russell made four to five speeches a day as he traveled to the state's largest cities and many of the smaller towns. While earlier he had soft-pedaled civil rights issues, he returned to the attack on this question during his Florida talks. He accused Kefauver of really being unreliable on the civil rights question after the Tennessean had said he would feel "morally bound" to support a Democrat platform, including an FEPC provision, if he were nominated at Chicago. Russell asserted that if he were the candidate and the convention passed such a platform, he would ignore the FEPC plank. He argued that a good precedent for such action was Alfred E. Smith's refusal to abide by the liquor plank in the Democratic platform of 1928. Russell found that his differing position with Kefauver over civil rights was helping him with Florida voters, but it was spotlighting an issue that would hurt him nationally.[35]

Throughout the ten-day campaign, opponents accused Russell of heading a move supported mainly by Dixiecrats who would bolt the convention. Others said that to back Russell was to waste one's vote because he could not possibly win the nomination. Moreover, critics charged that all Russell really wanted was to arrive at the convention with enough pledged delegates to place him in a strong bargaining position with the more liberal Democrats. Russell, however, sharply denied that he was a stalking-horse for any group or faction. He argued that in light of current political opinion, he was the only Democrat who could beat "a certain military personage," meaning, of course, General Eisenhower, who was expected to be nominated by the Republicans. He asserted that millions of Democrats would vote for him who had been unhappy with the recent trends in the Democratic party. Moreover, time and again he pledged his party loyalty and said that he would not walk out of the Democratic convention over the FEPC issue. Russell was trying to appeal to a broad middle-of-the-road constituency, which he believed would send the next man to the White House.[36] His political sense was accurate, but he would not be that man.

On May 6, over 650,000 Floridians cast their votes in the preference primary. Russell polled 367,980 votes to only 285,357 for Kefauver, winning 56 percent. He wrote Ralph McGill that his majority of 82,622 votes was much larger than he had thought possible. Moreover, his victory had been won with an expenditure of only $28,233.49.[37] Although the Florida outcome was pleasing, in some ways the results were disturbing. Russell did best in the more rural north Florida and did much less well in cities like Miami. It caused observers to wonder whether he could appeal to urban delegates and voters. It was not a matter of Russell's views lacking publicity. He had been followed in the campaign by writers for the *New York Times*, the *Chicago Tribune*, the *Christian Science Monitor*, the *Wall Street Journal*, and other major papers. But he could not shake his regional image. Russell appreciated having his picture appear on the cover of *Time* on May 19, but he wrote William S. Howland, *Time*'s bureau chief in Atlanta, that he disliked the sectional label of the accompanying story.[38]

On May 8, two days after the Florida primary, Russell spoke at a National Press Club luncheon in Washington. He exuded optimism and told reporters that he believed he would be nominated in July and elected president in November. That, he said, would destroy a fable of long standing that "no citizen from the southern part of our nation can be elected president." Russell again emphasized that he was not running as a southerner but as an American.

While the Florida primary retained his leading position as far as southern delegates were concerned, it was necessary for him to build a broader base of delegate support. On May 29, Russell announced that Senator Edwin C. Johnson of Colorado would be his national campaign manager. Accepting the appointment at a press conference in Russell's office, Johnson praised Russell as one of "the ablest men and greatest Democratic leaders in the history of the Senate." He added that Russell was the best-qualified man for the presidency in either major party. Johnson's appointment seemed to be a bid for votes in the farm states of the Midwest and West. It was an obvious move to reverse the idea that Russell was a regional or sectional candidate.[39]

Johnson moved quickly to present Russell as a truly national figure. He solicited endorsements and favorable statements from fellow senators, which were widely publicized. While such senators as Guy M. Gillette of Iowa and Theodore Green of Rhode Island made statements praising Russell highly, they did not endorse him for the nomination. Pat McCarran of Nevada, however, did support Russell and said that his election as president would be the best thing that had happened to the country since 1945. But the civil rights issue continued to plague Russell. Senator John O. Pastore of Rhode Island wrote Edwin Johnson that "if [Russell] agreed with me on the issue of FEPC, I would be one of his staunch supporters for the Presidency."[40]

During June the Russell camp put out a steady stream of press releases stressing Russell's national appeal. Much of the effort was directed toward the midwestern agricultural states. Congressman Stephen Pace of Georgia organized and headed an Agricultural Advisory Committee that sought support for Russell's nomination. This committee had representation from all sections of the country except New England. These agricultural leaders praised Russell's record on behalf of farmers and spotlighted his work on soil conservation, rural electrification, the school lunch program, price supports, farm credit, flood control, and parity prices. This publicity was an obvious appeal for the farm vote.

Shortly after he entered the race for the nomination, Russell seriously considered running in the California primary. But he soon announced that time would not permit him to undertake a vigorous campaign there. Nevertheless, during the latter part of June he did make an extended speaking trip throughout the West in an effort to drum up delegate support. Traveling in a DC-3 airplane, he stopped at Des Moines, Iowa, Omaha, Nebraska, Bismarck, North Dakota, Casper, Wyoming, and other western towns. He talked to civic clubs and other groups as well as to political leaders and individual delegates. His best bet was in Nevada where Senator McCarran provided strong backing for his nomination. Besides talking about adequate defenses, a balanced budget, and other issues that he had been stressing, Russell insisted that he was the only Democrat who could beat General Eisenhower. Time and again, he said that he could "lick" either Eisenhower or Robert Taft.[41] The Gallup poll indicated that he was correct, at least in the South. Before the Republican National Convention, in thirteen southern states, voters were asked if they would vote for Russell if he were the candidate against Eisenhower. Forty-five percent said they favored Russell compared to 38 percent who expressed a preference for Eisenhower. But when Russell's name was mentioned to a cross section of national voters, he was never the preferred candidate of more than 10 percent of Democratic voters.[42]

Russell made a good impression on his western trip, but he could not escape the fact that he was from the South. Preston Wright, a reporter for the *Great Falls Tribune* in Montana, wrote Oliver DeWolfe in the senator's campaign office that he believed Russell would pick up some Montana votes after the delegates were released from the unit rule. However, Wright added, "a lot of the boys the Senator convinced the other night still are working under the theory that no southerner can be elected on the Democratic ticket." Both Robert Kerr of Oklahoma and Averell Harriman of New York had been campaigning for the Democratic nomination in Montana, Wright said, but neither had made as good an impression as Russell. "You have an awful job to sell a Southerner to the nation as a whole," Wright continued, but "when the Mason-Dixon line is obliterated it will be by someone of the caliber of your Senator."[43]

Unfortunately, Russell did not have a strong campaign organization. There was too much suspicion, squabbling, and jockeying for position, which neither Aaron Ford, who opened the campaign office, nor

Senator Edwin Johnson, who was named national campaign director, could straighten out. Consequently, Russell tended to rely more on his relatives, especially his nephew Bobby Russell. While Bobby had keen political instincts and was probably the senator's closest adviser, he had no experience working at the national political level. In the late spring, the senator brought another relative, Ernest Vandiver, to Washington to help with the campaign. Vandiver took a leave of absence from his post as director of Selective Service in Georgia to go to Washington. The senator's brother-in-law, Hugh Peterson, also continued to assist in various ways. An old friend of Russell's, Erle Cocke, Jr., was energetic and loyal in his campaign efforts but lacked experience and judgment on important political matters. In May Senator George Smathers sent a confidential memorandum to Russell's headquarters staff complaining that Russell suffered from poor scheduling and failure to be in contact with state Democratic organizations.[44]

Throughout June Russell had to respond to Kefauver's charge that he had made a deal with Governor Adlai Stevenson of Illinois to accept the vice presidency on a Stevenson-Russell ticket. Kefauver's spokesmen accused Russell of joining Stevenson in order to block the Tennessean's nomination. Russell hotly denied this charge and declared that "machine politicians" would resort to anything "to get publicity and . . . confuse the public." Russell always insisted that he had no interest whatever in the vice presidency. Kefauver himself later wrote to Francis Biddle, chairman of Americans for Democratic Action, that he believed Russell was sincere in saying that he did not want the vice presidency. "While Dick and I have our disagreements, I certainly know that his word is his bond," Kefauver wrote.[45]

At the close of his trip through sixteen western states on June 29, about three weeks before the convention, Russell seemed optimistic about his chances. To Arnold Olsen, Montana's attorney general, he wrote that "my strength is increasing daily," and he added that his position was better than any other Democratic aspirant. If he were nominated, Russell said, "there is no doubt in my mind that I can be elected."[46]

Although Russell solicited support from delegates outside the South both by letter and through personal contact, the results were disappointing. As he put it, backers signed on "slower than I would like."[47] As a matter of fact, the best that he could do was to get some commitments for support on the second ballot. He was not even certain that he would get every vote in the states of the Deep South. Nevertheless, the Russell campaign headquarters prepared delegate booklets, luggage stickers, buttons, posters, and other materials to place in the hands of all Chicago delegates.

At 3:00 P.M. on June 10, Russell had an appointment with President Truman to discuss how to handle the rebellious North Korean prisoners held on Koje-do Island. Before they began their main business, the president said: "Dick, I do wish that you lived in Indiana or Missouri. You would be elected President hands down. We have differed on a great many issues, but we have always understood each other. You are a great Democrat and I respect you. You have always stood by the Party organization." Russell acknowledged their differences but stated that they were both loyal Democrats and that he hoped the two of them could work together to assure a united Democratic party. Truman repeated how much he wished he could help Russell, and the senator declared that he would surely appreciate the president's support. With just a little more help in key places, Russell said, he could win the nomination and be elected. Finally, according to Russell, Truman said that he would very much like to see him president, "but you know that the left-wing groups in Chicago, New York, St. Louis and Kansas City must be kept in the Democratic Party if we are to win and they will not vote for you."[48]

Although Russell knew he could not get Truman's support, he was realistic enough to know that if he was to win the Democratic nomination he must make some accommodation with organized labor. Sometime in June, Russell began to explore whether he could gain any support from labor leaders, despite the fact that in the past he had been critical of them. He asked Philip Murray of the CIO for an appointment, and Murray replied on June 17 that he would be glad to visit with Russell. They were both staying at the Mayflower Hotel so, Murray said, it would be no problem for them to meet. It seems that the two men did not talk, however, mainly because they both had very busy schedules.[49] Early in July, however, Russell did meet with John L. Lewis, head of the United Mine Workers. Over lunch at the Carlton Hotel, they discussed labor issues for more than two hours. Russell had never met Lewis before and found him to be a man "of great intellect and a fine sense of humor." Russell explained to Lewis that he could not compromise on the injunctive provisions of the Taft-Hartley Act unless some other way was found to protect the public interest. Lewis, on the other hand, told Russell that labor had suffered under the Taft-Hartley law and that he strongly opposed the use of injunctions against labor unions. With each man holding such firm views, they parted maintaining their original positions.

The next morning, David Charnay, president of Allied Public Relations, which worked for the United Mine Workers, invited Russell to his office to discuss labor matters. Charnay was one of those personable, persuasive, attractive individuals who occasionally move into the center of a situation and then fade quickly into oblivion. With the support of Erle Cocke, Jr., he had been trying to push himself into the Russell campaign organization for several weeks. Despite the fact that Russell did not believe Charnay could be helpful, by July he was hanging around the campaign headquarters and trying to assist some of Russell's principal workers.

When Russell arrived at Charnay's office, he found Senator Lister Hill, Oliver DeWolfe, and other Russell supporters. Hill had been working on a draft of a law that might be substituted for the Taft-Hartley Act and that Russell might be able to approve. Charnay suggested that he call John L. Lewis who might make some constructive suggestions on Hill's draft. Within a few minutes, Lewis arrived, and for about thirty minutes, he argued strongly for complete repeal of the Taft-Hartley Act. Russell listened carefully but did not commit himself to any position, although it was well known that he opposed repeal of the law. The meeting soon broke up with nothing decided.

On July 16, Russell and DeWolfe left Washington by plane for Chicago and the forthcoming Democratic convention. Also on board was Bartley Crum, a well-known New York labor and civil rights lawyer. Charnay had introduced Crum to Russell during his recent visit to New York. On the way west, Crum talked to Russell at length about labor law and the Taft-Hartley Act. According to Thomas D. Blake who was handling Russell's campaign publicity, Crum told Russell: "You believe that the Wagner Act was too much weighted in favor of labor and that the Taft-Hartley Act is weighted too heavily on the side of management, and you advocate that Taft-Hartley be changed in some respects in order to strike a balance between the Wagner and Taft-Hartley Acts." Russell reportedly replied that this was "a perfect explanation of his position."

After the group arrived at Senator Russell's convention headquarters in the Conrad Hilton Hotel, discussions of the labor issue continued. Lister Hill, Edwin Johnson, John B. Connally of Texas and close friend of Lyndon Johnson, Erle Cocke, Sr., and Jr., Thomas Blake, David Charnay, Spence Grayson, and others were present. The task was to hammer out a position on the Taft-Hartley Act that might reduce labor opposition to Russell as he went into the convention. Russell was going to use the statement in response to a question that would be asked him that night on a Mutual Broadcasting System radio program. His advisers expressed sharp differences of opinion. Charnay, Senators Johnson and Hill, and some others wanted a statement containing the word "repeal." Russell flatly refused. Various other verbs were considered, such as "revise" and "change," but they finally agreed on the word "supplant," as suggested by Spence Grayson. A statement was then prepared for release to the press. The key phrase was that "the Taft-Hartley Act must be supplanted by new legislation in the field of labor relations."

DeWolfe had the responsibility of getting the statement copied and delivered to the press room, but before he got around to it, Charnay had read the release to reporters. Charnay apparently used the term "repeal" because reporters rushed to the telephones with the story headline, "Russell for Repeal of Taft-Hartley." While the official statement never used the word "repeal," most of the newspaper accounts on the morning of July 17 carried the word in headlining the story. Russell was not only stunned by the news stories saying that he favored repeal of the Taft-Hartley Act but was infuriated as well.

What Russell had actually proposed was that if elected president he would appoint a high-level committee representing labor and management to make suggestions for writing new labor legislation that would be fairer to both workers and management. He emphasized that the full play of collective bargaining must be preserved. The Russell statement was a common-sense, practical approach to a very controversial public policy. But the way it was treated by the press angered conservatives who thought Russell favored repeal of the Taft-Hartley Act, and he failed to go far enough to win over any elements of organized labor.[50]

Russell's last-minute attempt to reduce labor opposition to his candidacy had proved not only fruitless but embarrassing. On July 17, he called a press conference and tried to correct the wrong impressions carried in the newspapers by denying that he favored repeal of the Taft-Hartley law. But the damage had been done. James B. Carey, executive secretary of the CIO, declared that labor and minority groups viewed Russell "not as a candidate but as an issue." Although the flurry of publicity on the labor question on the eve of the convention had no effect on Russell's delegate strength, it exemplified the problems candidates had in dealing with such an emotional public issue as Taft-Hartley. It also demonstrated that Russell's convention staff was inexperienced and did not have a firm hold on people and events. Russell and some of his main advisers were later convinced that Charnay had been a mole for the opposition.

In his press conference on July 17, Russell discussed a wide range of issues besides labor relations. He said that he was for equal rights for all people but that some of the civil rights bills "would be like getting a ragweed and wrapping it up in beautiful packaging and calling it an orchid." He believed, however, that the party platform would be satisfactory on civil rights matters. When asked about Eisenhower, Russell said that the general was a "great soldier and a great American" with a "charming personality" but that voters had a "natural aversion" to electing military men as president. When asked if he would welcome Truman's support, Russell replied that he would welcome the endorsement of any "good Democrat, or the support of Republicans, Socialists or anyone who can vote in the election."[51]

Russell settled in Room 906A of the Conrad Hilton with nephew Bobby just across the hall. His convention headquarters occupied two dining rooms on the third floor. Those working on Russell's behalf included some of his oldest and most trusted political friends, such as Hugh Peterson, Charles Bloch, Erle Cocke, Sr., and Jr., Spence Grayson, and Ernest Vandiver. W. J. Primm, an Atlanta businessman, and John B. Connally of Texas also worked hard for the senator. Senate colleagues who pounded the hotel corridors and talked to delegates on Russell's behalf were Lyndon Johnson, Lister Hill, Walter George, and Edwin Johnson. His sister, Ina Stacy, joined him at his convention headquarters to serve as his official hostess.

At noon on July 20, the day before the convention opened, Russell held another press conference. Asked about his strength on the first ballot, he estimated that he would have around 300 votes and if he worked hard enough might get as many as 400. Russell was then questioned about the loyalty pledge being pushed by the Kefauver forces, by which candidates agreed to support the Democratic platform. Kefauver's main concern was support for any civil rights plank that might be adopted by the convention. Russell said that he had not seen the pledge but that it was not necessary to support everything in the platform to be a loyal Democrat. A reporter asked about the accuracy of a statement by a Georgia delegate on the train going to Chicago who reputedly had said, "This is a Democratic train going up, but unless Russell is nominated, it may be a Republican train going back." That situation certainly would not be true, Russell said.[52] Russell had repeatedly stated that he would support the Democratic ticket.

It was not until Thursday noon, July 24, that the convention finally got around to its most important business—nominating a presidential candidate. When the roll call of states began, Alabama yielded to Geor-

Senator Russell and campaign supporters at the Democratic National Convention in Chicago, July 1952. (Photo courtesy of Russell Memorial Library, University of Georgia, Athens.)

gia for the nomination of Russell. Senator George made the principal nominating speech. He reviewed Russell's highly successful political career and praised his ability, honesty, and integrity. Then George catalogued Russell's achievements in the Senate and emphasized that he had served all of the American people. Striving still to remove Russell's sectional image, George declared that he would be president "of all of the United States." He concluded by vowing that Russell favored equal opportunity—educational, economic, and political—for everyone. As George concluded, the southern delegates cheered and applauded and carried on a boisterous twenty-minute demonstration before Chairman Sam Rayburn restored order. Senator Lyndon Johnson was among the most enthusiastic paraders.

Seconding speeches by Senator Pat McCarran and Marguerite Peyton Thompson of Colorado followed. McCarran stressed Russell's patriotism, progressivism, intelligence, and experience. Marguerite Thompson claimed that farm women would welcome a Russell candidacy because of his "fight for cheap light and power which has lifted the drudgery of farm chores" and that "city mothers" would always be grateful for the school lunch program.[53] Later, during "a recess laugh session," comedian Bob Hope said that he was going out for a Russell-burger, which was a barbecued yankee on a bun.[54]

Following Russell's nomination, the names of Senators Kefauver, Kerr, Fulbright, and Barkley, Governors Harriman and Stevenson, and several favorite sons were placed before the convention. On the first ballot, Kefauver led with 340 votes to 273 for Stevenson and 268 for Russell. Russell won all of the votes in Georgia, Louisiana, Mississippi, South Carolina, Texas, and Virginia and lost only half a vote in North Carolina. Kefauver got 8 votes away from Russell in Alabama, 5 in Florida, and several in West Virginia. Outside of the South, Russell picked up 8.5 votes in Colorado, the home of his campaign manager, 8 in McCarran's Nevada, and a few elsewhere.[55]

Unfortunately for Russell, there was no strong shift toward his candidacy on the second ballot as he had hoped. He picked up only 26 votes, a few more than Kefauver but much less than Stevenson. It was clear on the second ballot that the big move was to Stevenson. On the third and last ballot, Stevenson won 617.5 votes, 1.5 more than were necessary for the nomination. On that ballot, Russell dropped back to 261, remaining third behind Stevenson and Kefauver. The delegates then passed a motion making Stevenson's nomination unanimous.[56] Perhaps a writer for the *Washington Star* was correct when he explained the outcome by saying that Kefauver was a lightweight, Barkley and Rayburn were too old, Harriman was too rich, Kerr was too oily, and Russell "was too far South."[57]

Both Russell and Kefauver then made statements supporting Stevenson. Russell congratulated the winner and said the convention "had done much to unify our beloved Democratic Party." He promised to fall into "the ranks of Democracy" and seek party victory in November. Russell concluded by saying that he hoped the Democrats would unite and go forward "not as a party dictated or controlled by any one segment of that party, but the party of all the American people."[58]

Russell accepted the Stevenson nomination with good grace, although he honestly believed that he was better qualified for the presidency than his distant cousin from Illinois. Many others agreed. Calvin W. Rawlings, a member of the Democratic National Committee from Utah, wrote that "if it were not for geography and by the Grace of God," Russell would have been delivering the acceptance speech instead of Stevenson. Russell had told Rawlings that he felt no rancor and believed that Stevenson was fully qualified to serve as president.[59]

Russell could have had the vice presidential nomination if he had been willing to accept it. Frank McKinney, chairman of the Democratic

National Committee, and several Stevenson supporters, approached Russell and urged him to let them place his name in nomination. Russell wrote his old friend Hughes Spalding, "I was carried to the mountain top several times but the vista of V.P. held no allure."[60] He told another friend, "I definitely and unequivocally declined." He had been independent too long, Russell wrote, "to accept any position that would commit me to policies that were the brain child of another man." When he was asked for suggestions, he strongly recommended Senator John Sparkman. "To my amazement," he later wrote Margaret Shannon, a reporter for the *Atlanta Constitution*, the leaders accepted Sparkman, and he won the nomination. Sparkman was also the choice of Truman. Besides not wanting to compromise his independence, Russell loved the Senate and enjoyed his position there too much to even consider the vice presidency.[61]

Would Russell actively join in the Democratic effort to elect Adlai Stevenson, or would he sit out the campaign as he had done in 1948? Initially Russell seemed quite pleased with the Stevenson nomination. He viewed the Illinois governor as a moderate on civil rights and as a man with whom he could work on legislative matters. Russell was further won over to Stevenson when shortly after the convention the governor stated that it would be dangerous to place a limit on Senate debate. Russell interpreted this to mean that Stevenson would not try to use his influence to change the cloture rule.

A few days after the convention, Russell went to Springfield to visit Stevenson. He warmly congratulated the governor for his statement on Senate debate and talked to him about other matters. After dinner at the governor's mansion, Stevenson and Russell were joined on the terrace by Governor Harriman and Senator Blair Moody of Michigan. Moody delivered a message from Governor Mennen Williams strongly urging Stevenson to change his view on the cloture rule. Russell argued vigorously against any modification of Stevenson's position. At times the conversation was heated. Stevenson later admitted that "the long night with Dick Russell, Harriman and Moody" had made him cranky. Nevertheless Russell left Springfield the next morning certain that Stevenson would stand firm on the question of unlimited Senate debate. As far as Russell was concerned, this was a kind of litmus test for the governor.[62]

On August 11, Stevenson wrote to Russell saying that "your visit here heartened me." He was pleased, he said, to have the support of such an experienced and respected leader. "I shall have to rely on your help very much," Stevenson wrote, "and I hope you will never hesitate to tell me if I am making mistakes."[63] Russell needed no such invitation.

He had never been reluctant to advise Democratic political leaders when he thought they were off the track. Stevenson would be no exception.

When Stevenson spoke before the American Legion in New York City on August 27, he indicated that he would not be swayed by pressure groups, regardless of their interests or regions. Stevenson declared that he would even resist pressures from veterans if he believed their demands conflicted with the public interest, which "must always be paramount." This was just what Russell wanted to hear. "When I finished reading this speech," Russell stated, "I stood and saluted." The next day, however, in addressing the New York State Democratic Convention, Stevenson indicated that some change in the Senate rules on unlimited debate might be desirable. Russell viewed this as Stevenson's surrender to minority groups and organized labor—a caving in "to the disciples of Walter Reuther" and the CIO.[64] A few days later, just before embarking on a cruise to Venezuela, Russell told a reporter that Stevenson was drifting to the political left. Stevenson would lose votes in Georgia, he added, if he continued on that course. "A lot of good, conservative Democrats thought Stevenson was a middle-of-the-road candidate," Russell declared. "Now it appears that he is being influenced strongly by the C.I.O. Political Action Committee and the Americans for Democratic Action."[65]

When Stevenson read Russell's remarks, he immediately tried to reach him by telephone, only to find that Russell had already left on his South American trip. Stevenson then wrote Russell saying that he was "disturbed" that the senator felt that he was "reaching to the left." He had not, Stevenson said, compromised any of his views. In any event, he wanted to have "another candid talk" with Russell upon his return. He appealed for Russell's support and again asked him to point out his "mistakes."[66]

After Russell returned from Venezuela, the Stevenson forces placed great pressure on him to participate actively in the campaign. But Russell refused to do more than publicly endorse the party candidates. He had said on October 1 that he would vote for Stevenson but would not campaign for him. On October 21, however, he did release a statement from his Winder office stressing that Stevenson was the superior candidate and predicting the governor's victory in November. Russell said that Eisenhower was confused on some issues and completely unfamiliar with others. The Georgia senator could hardly be sympathetic to a candidate who could not understand the term "farm parity."[67]

Stevenson and leaders in his campaign were reluctant to give up trying to get Russell to make some campaign speeches, especially in

Florida and Texas. They turned for help to Senator Fulbright who was working in Stevenson's campaign headquarters. Fulbright contacted several of Russell's closest political friends, including Erle Cocke, Sr., and Jr., urging them to convince Russell that he should enter actively into the campaign. Erle Cocke, Jr., reported that he had visited with Russell and that he was not at all bitter but would not change his mind. It had been Stevenson's New York speech "that got him," Cocke wrote.[68] The numerous telephone calls and personal contacts had no effect on Russell. About all Russell would say was that Stevenson "was much better qualified for the Presidency than General Eisenhower."[69]

Russell displayed an ambivalence toward the Stevenson candidacy that was out of character with his usual firm positions. He told an Atlanta constituent that while he did not agree with all of Stevenson's positions the governor "had the capacity to make . . . one of the greatest presidents the country ever had." All he needed, Russell wrote, was the toughness to be his own man and follow his own instincts instead of the "demands of the extremists." Despite rather obvious indications to the contrary, Russell kept predicting a Stevenson victory. In mid-October, he told Fulbright that Stevenson was "getting stronger daily" and that by November 4 "it will be a landslide."[70] This was either a careless assessment or an unrealistic expression of hope.

Russell's real reason for giving Stevenson only token support rested on his belief that early in 1953 he would be leading another fight against changing the Senate cloture rule. He would need Republican help for such a battle, and he believed that he would have a better chance of getting it if he did not contribute openly to Stevenson's campaign. "When I open the fight against the drive to Reutherize the Senate next January 3," he wrote, "I think I would be in a stronger position if I do not have to embark on a long explanation for stumping the country for him." Russell's entire action was based on the mistaken assumption that Stevenson would beat Eisenhower. Russell was genuinely surprised and disappointed at Stevenson's defeat. After considering the Eisenhower landslide, however, he regained his political perspective. Following the election, he told friends that he believed he would have won more electoral votes than Stevenson but that he doubted if "any living man could have stemmed the Eisenhower tide."[71]

With time to reflect, what did Russell think of his own effort to get the Democratic nomination? Had anything worthwhile been accomplished? While he saw his campaign as "a great and rewarding experience," he emphasized that he would never again run for president. Nonetheless he told his good friend Frank M. Scarlett of Brunswick that he had fought a good fight and had no regrets. Moreover he thought some good had been achieved. He believed that his influence at the convention had kept the Democrats from nominating "an extreme liberal" and that he had influenced the adoption of a more moderate platform. Senator Stennis wrote that "the South and our cause made distinct gains as compared with four years ago" because opponents of the South could not write Russell off as they had the Dixiecrats. "They knew the conservative wing of the party had a real leader who had to be contended with," Stennis declared. However, Russell and his friend Stennis both overemphasized the senator's influence. The Democrats had never seriously considered nominating a leftist candidate in 1952 anyway, and there was little evidence that Russell's views had any effect on the platform, which contained a strong civil rights plank and a call to repeal the Taft-Hartley law. In short, Russell's candidacy did not have any noticeable influence on the course of Democratic politics. It did greatly enhance his own national image, but his influence was still confined mainly to the South.[72]

Russell was unable, and to some degree unwilling, to become a genuine national leader. Stennis may have made the most revealing statement about Russell's leadership when he said that he was most grateful for Russell's contribution to his state, the South, and the nation—*in that order*. Russell was unable to detach himself from southern interests, which he considered of foremost importance and which commanded his first loyalty.

Did Russell ever think that he had a chance to win the nomination? Not really. At times he expressed optimism and quietly hoped that somehow the course of events might provide a lucky break and the nomination. But Russell was a political realist. He recognized, although he did not like, the fact that the Democratic party had undergone a major transformation since he had gone to the Senate. New and powerful constituencies had to be accommodated, especially minorities and organized labor. These groups had made it plain from the outset that Russell was not acceptable to them. He might hope against hope that the nomination could be his, but he fully realized that the more progressive forces in the party viewed him as a conservative drag on political progress. This, added to his residence in the South, forbade his nomination. In one of his philosophical moments, he said that it was just as well that he did not receive the nomination. "Our wild-eyed friends in other sections," he wrote, "would have pointed to the result as confirmation of their theory that no southerner could be elected."[73]

Russell treasured the flattering letters that he received after the convention from his colleagues in the Senate. Milton Young wrote that he was sorry Russell had not won the Democratic nomination, but even in losing, Russell had "won the respect and admiration of millions of Americans, particularly in the North." Stennis stated that Russell deserved much more credit for "all the good that was done" and urged Dick to get away for a long rest and reflection on the course of events. He had no financial problems resulting from the campaign that might have worried him. He reported on August 12 that his national campaign headquarters had received $235,481 and that expenditures had exceeded that figure by $2,975.[74]

In 1968, some sixteen years after his bid for the presidency, Russell looked back at the events as he answered a letter from Robert A. Bailey, a student at Utah State University who was writing a thesis on the Democratic convention of 1952. It was "not among my most pleasant memories," Russell wrote. He told Bailey that he entered the contest to provide "a holding operation for conservatives" and that he never believed he would get the nomination. Then in his usual frank and straightforward way, Russell advised Bailey that he could get a much better topic for a thesis than Russell's presidential bid, "as interesting as it was to me and to our own people in Georgia."[75]

As the first Republican administration in twenty years was about to take office, Russell indicated that he would fight to keep the Democratic gains of previous years. He made it clear that he would not form any coalition with conservative Republicans to dismantle the New Deal and the Fair Deal. His main objective in the forthcoming Congress, he said, was to protect the measures that had been passed to help farmers. He also stated that he would support Eisenhower in a search for world peace. Russell withheld judgment on Eisenhower and thought some of his fellow Democrats were making a mistake by criticizing the president-elect before they knew more about his program. During December Russell and Stevenson corresponded about the future of the Democratic party, but Russell claimed that little could be done so soon after the disastrous election. Give the Republicans time, Russell counseled, and there would be plenty to criticize. Do not shoot at the Republicans until people can understand "what the shooting is about," he said.[76]

14

Russell in the Eisenhower Years

====

When the Eighty-third Congress opened in January 1953, Russell found the Senate back in Republican hands for only the second time since he arrived in Washington some twenty years earlier. With the Democrats in the minority, Russell's power was somewhat diminished, but because of his long tenure, he still wielded tremendous influence. Many commentators believed that he was the nation's most powerful senator in the early 1950s. Only his colleagues Walter George and Carl Hayden from Arizona had greater seniority. Although now on the minority side, Russell ranked first on the Armed Services Committee and second on the Appropriations Committee. He continued on the Democratic Policy Committee. His increased importance was reflected in his move from Room 410 in the Senate Office Building, where he had been since 1939, to Room 205, a large and spacious suite formerly occupied by Vice President Alben Barkley.

The Democrats were faced with some important organizational decisions. Ernest McFarland, the Democratic majority leader, had been defeated in 1952, leaving that position open. Russell, however, already had McFarland's successor pretty well decided. The new leader would be his friend from Texas, Lyndon Johnson. Despite Johnson's lack of seniority, Russell had been pushing him for a party leadership role for more than two years. He had appointed Johnson to head the Defense Preparedness Subcommittee in 1950. Although this committee in no way compared with the Truman Committee organized to investigate the national defense program during World War II, it did enhance Johnson's image and position in the Senate. Russell had also backed Johnson for majority whip in 1951.

Right after the election of 1952, Russell began to line up support for Johnson. He and several other senators announced on November 10 that they favored the election of Johnson as the next Democratic leader in the Senate. Russell mentioned that he was highly honored that some colleagues had suggested him for the position but said that Johnson was his choice. He added that the Texan was "highly qualified for the job and, in my opinion, he will be chosen for it." This was his public stance. Privately, Russell saw Johnson that same day and wrote on his desk calendar, "Buttoned up leadership for him." Nevertheless, Russell continued his campaign for Johnson through telephone calls and letters. On November 12, he wrote Senator Clyde R. Hoey of North Carolina that he had no desire himself for the leadership position and added, "I think Lyndon is entitled to a promotion, and he will do a good job." Two days later, he told Senator A. Willis Robertson of Virginia, "Lyndon will make us a fine leader," and added that "there is no doubt that he will be chosen."[1]

When the Democratic caucus met on January 2, 1953, Russell nominated Johnson for the minority leader position. Russell's penciled notes jotted down on a sheet of paper indicate the thrust of his pitch for his friend. He stressed that Johnson had courage, character, ability, experience, and tolerance and was a loyal Democrat who had been tested and tried by political fire. Johnson had no peer as a conciliator, he said. Russell continued: "Our leader should be the most able man on the Democratic side of the Senate. My nominee isn't the best parliamentarian, he isn't the most personable, he doesn't have the best mind," but, Russell added, "he is the best combination of all these qualities."[2] With Russell's backing, Johnson was unanimously elected minority leader and chairman of the Democratic Policy Committee.

Johnson and Russell worked closely together on the committee and made appointments that strengthened their control on the Democratic side of the Senate. Johnson occupied the front aisle seat to the vice president's right in the Senate chamber, and Russell moved to the seat directly behind the minority leader. That arrangement continued until Johnson became vice president. During the next seven years, Johnson and Russell were commonly seen whispering and consulting over matters of policy and strategy. They were the center of awesome political power.

The Democratic defeat of 1952 shocked many party members, and during the postmortem, party leaders assessed and reassessed what Russell called "one of our most calamitous defeats." This gave Russell an opportunity to review party affairs and to say things that gained attention after the election but would have been ignored by most leaders before November 1952. He had an opportunity to express his views in some detail when he accepted an invitation to address the Jefferson-Jackson Day dinner in Raleigh, North Carolina, on February 28, 1953.

Russell began his address by declaring that the Democratic party had been founded to serve all of the people. If Democrats were to return to power, he said, the party must be genuinely democratic and "defeat the efforts of all special interest groups to use the party as an instrument to attain selfish ends or special privileges." If special interest groups were allowed to control and direct the party, according to Russell, it would neither enjoy nor deserve future victories. Russell argued that there was room in the Democratic party for "every segment of American political life except the seekers of special privilege or those who would use force or violence to destroy the American way of life." The Democratic party, he declared, had been the party of labor, farmers, and the middle class, but it must never be a labor or a farmer party.

To regain peoples' confidence, Russell said, the party must attack government waste, favor a tax system based on ability to pay, and oppose those who threatened private property. Democrats also needed to resist a federal police state and maintain states' rights. Police powers must continue to reside in the states, he declared, and "we must never desert the principle of home rule and local self-government."

Russell criticized those who labeled members of Congress from the South reactionaries. The social and economic gains of the past twenty years, he said, could not have been achieved without southern support. No doubt thinking of the CIO's Political Action Committee, he attacked the special interest groups who were trying to mold the Democratic party in their image. All these groups had done, according to Russell, was to drive many Democrats out of the party and into the arms of Republicans. Up until then, not many Democrats had been driven from the house of their fathers, but the recent election had indicated a dangerous trend. Without the South, Russell declared, the Democrats could not return to power.

Besides calling for a party in which all elements would be accepted and respected, he warned Democrats against partisanship in matters of foreign policy. Democrats and Republicans alike had "an equal stake in survival," and "partisanship and factionalism must stop at the water's edge." By being constructive critics rather than obstructionists and by acting like statesmen instead of carping complainers, Americans, Russell believed, would regain faith in the Democratic party and return it to power.[3]

Russell's appeal for Democratic unity, his attack on special interests and special privilege, and his call for responsible minority statesmanship produced many favorable reactions. Stephen A. Mitchell, the new chairman of the Democratic National Committee, told young Democrats in North Carolina a few weeks later that Russell's speech included some of the most "thoughtful and constructive comments" on party unity that he had heard. Referring to Russell's statement on inclusiveness, Mitchell declared, "I do not know of a finer statement anywhere of the traditional basic principle of the Democratic Party."[4]

Russell, however, had little time to contemplate his party's future. There were too many critical problems that needed immediate attention. When Congress opened on January 3, 1953, Senator Clinton Anderson of New Mexico introduced a motion to modify the cloture rule to make it easier to limit debate. Charging that the Anderson motion had been inspired by the CIO, Russell gained bipartisan support to table the motion on January 7 by the overwhelming vote of 70 to 21.[5]

With this matter out of the way, Russell turned to the farm problem. By early 1953, overall farm prices had dropped some 10 percent below what they had been in 1951 during the period of high demand created by the Korean War. Cattle prices had declined 30 percent, and in October 1953, cattlemen dramatized their plight by marching on Washington to seek price relief. The outlook was anything but good as surpluses built up again and prices weakened.

On February 5, the new secretary of agriculture, Ezra Taft Benson, sent Russell an advance copy of his statement on the importance of agriculture in a sound national economy. After paying tribute to rural people, Benson outlined the course he believed agricultural policy should take. He recommended a policy less dependent on government and one which would bring "full parity prices in the marketplace, and parity income for farm people." While the secretary favored short-term supports, the main thrust of his statement was toward more freedom for farmers and less government control. Greater freedom, Benson wrote, would encourage farmers to produce for changing consumer demands rather than for government storage.[6]

Russell, Milton Young, who looked after Great Plains wheat growers, and other farm state senators insisted that farmers would suffer greatly if government lowered or removed price supports. Russell, however, found himself in a difficult position. Without federal supports, cotton prices would fall sharply because of overproduction. But if high price supports were continued, acreage limitations would be required. As he put it, prices of 90 percent of parity without production controls would destroy the farm program and "eventually bankrupt the Government."[7] On the other hand, as acreage was reduced, many family farmers raising cotton had so few acres that they could not make a living. It was a problem to which there was no good solution.

Consequently, Russell's farm policy in the 1950s contained little or nothing that was new. He insisted on high fixed supports for basic commodities and at the same time tried to keep the U.S. Department of Agriculture from decreasing cotton acreage to the point where it placed undue suffering on smaller operators. The program was bound to be expensive for the federal government, as indeed it was. After flexible supports were initiated in 1954, Russell saw the agricultural dilemma in political as much as economic terms. As early as the summer of 1953, he wrote constituents and made public statements predicting that the farm issue would help the Democrats regain control of Congress in 1954. Unless the Republicans developed a "common-sense farm program and put it in effect early next year," he wrote in September 1953, "they will lose the House and probably the Senate."[8] Long before the Republicans had a chance to even write a farm bill, Russell charged that the "confusion, uncertainty and lack of direction" of agricultural policy had contributed to falling agricultural prices. Such a statement was pure politics.[9] Farm prices dropped because of heavy surpluses.

On October 9, Secretary Benson announced that cotton acreage for 1954 would be limited to about 18 million acres. Russell promptly urged that the amount be raised to 21 million acres to avert "severe hardships" to cotton growers. Spokesmen for cotton growers in the irrigated West joined those in the Southeast and finally got the figure raised to 22 million acres, which was still well below the 27 million acres grown in 1953 when no restrictions were in effect. Russell was not happy with the figure, but he recognized that it was the best Congress could do.[10]

Russell was also unhappy over the total amount of cotton acreage allocated to the western states. He admitted that the highly mechanized cotton growers of Arizona and California might produce cotton cheaper than the small farmers of the Southeast. Perhaps, he said, the "old cotton states will be forced out of the cotton business." If that occurred as a result of economic forces, he said, nothing could be done. But he did not think that the federal government should accelerate the process by allocating so much acreage to the western states.[11]

Russell also came into conflict with the administration over reorganizing the Department of Agriculture. In 1950 he had been among the leaders who turned back an effort to give the secretary of agriculture the power to dissolve old administrative units and create new ones and to transfer functions from one agency to another. When Department of Agriculture officials made another attempt at reorganization in early 1953, Russell was even more opposed to change because now it would be a Republican secretary of agriculture who would be operating under new authority and guidelines. Russell feared that Benson might weaken some of his favorite action agencies, such as those dealing with soil conservation, rural electrification, and the Farmers Home Administration. He declared that the Department of Agriculture was second in importance only to the Department of Defense and that he did not want to see its effectiveness eroded in any way. As he put it, the welfare of some six million farm families depended on the services and functions of the Department of Agriculture. Russell chided his Republican colleagues who had opposed reorganization in 1950 but were now supporting it, but he failed to garner many votes. The Senate defeated his resolution to disapprove the reorganization plan on May 27 by a vote of 45 to 29.[12]

The Republican emphasis on economy threatened the appropriations for some of Russell's favorite agricultural agencies. Ever since just before World War II, when he had been able to get appropriations up to $500 million for soil conservation, Russell had been trying to stem the reductions. In 1953 he proposed an amendment that would have provided $225 million for fiscal 1954, up from the $195 million approved by the Republicans. This was still less than the $250 million approved for fiscal 1953. Russell argued that the entire nation had a vital stake in soil conservation. To preserve the fertility of the land, he said, was really "a part of the defense effort" because of the importance of food and fiber production. Russell stated that the cuts for farmers in this case went far beyond what was being asked of other groups. The Russell amendment passed by a vote of 39 to 37 on June 15, but then the amendment to which he had added it lost on a tie vote.[13]

Although Russell had always been a strong advocate of agricultural research, he opposed certain additions for that purpose in the 1954 agricultural appropriations bill. He spoke against adding $1.5 million for certain special research purposes, mainly on the grounds that the Department of Agriculture could not find the trained personnel on which to spend the additional money. Russell did not favor spending unless he believed the funds could be wisely and efficiently used.[14]

Russell's real fight for farmers in the Eisenhower years began early in 1954 when the Republicans introduced a new farm bill. The most important aspect of the Eisenhower-Benson legislation was the abandonment of the 90 percent of parity price supports that had been in effect on major commodities since World War II. Secretary Benson recommended flexible supports ranging from 75 to 90 percent of parity to begin January 1, 1955. The level of government price supports would vary with production.

Russell strongly opposed lowering price supports. He believed that farmers were already the most disadvantaged economic group in the United States, and now, he said, the Republicans would strike those "at the bottom of the economic heap" even harder. Restating his agricultural fundamentalism, Russell argued that farming was still the "basis of our economy, and I do not believe that we can maintain prosperity . . . if the farmer is permitted to go to pot." He denied that price supports were a subsidy for farmers, but even if that were the case, why begin to eliminate subsidies for the man "on the bottom," he asked. Many other groups, according to Russell, were being subsidized by the federal government much more heavily than farmers. He cited minimum wages as the most obvious example. The thrust of Russell's arguments was that farmers were of basic importance to the nation, that they were mistreated and gouged by other economic groups, and that they deserved more generous treatment by government. Russell delivered good populist oratory, but he did not change many votes.[15]

Russell was also annoyed with Benson because he believed that the secretary was too sensitive to consumer complaints about high food prices. Benson's job, Russell said, was to concentrate on helping farmers, just as the main task of the secretary of labor was to assist workers. He saw rising consumer resistance to food prices and losses to taxpayers resulting from price supports as ominous signs for farm programs. Despite everything Russell could do, both houses of Congress included flexible price supports at between 82.5 and 90 percent of parity in the Agricultural Act of 1954. The high fixed support crowd had been at least partially defeated. Most of the southern Democrats voted against the Benson program, and they were supported by Democrats such as Gillette of Iowa and Humphrey of Minnesota and by a few Republicans like Young of North Dakota.[16] Russell now became one of Secretary Benson's most severe critics. Admitting to his old friend D. W. Brooks, who often advised him on farm policy, that Benson was an "honorable man," Russell insisted that the secretary's policies would destroy the American farmer.[17]

Russell had predicted that the farm vote would hurt the Republicans in the midterm elections of 1954. The Democrats recaptured control of the Senate by a single vote and gained a majority of twenty-nine in the House, but there is not much evidence that the farmers were

Bipartisan legislative group pictured with President Dwight D. Eisenhower, January 5, 1954. Russell is fourth from left. (Photo courtesy of Russell Memorial Library, University of Georgia, Athens.)

responsible for returning the Democrats to power in Congress. Russell himself was reelected without opposition to a fourth full term.

An issue that greatly agitated the country during 1953 and 1954 involved the unruly and irresponsible actions of Senator Joseph McCarthy of Wisconsin. Beginning in 1950, McCarthy accused the State Department and other government agencies of being infiltrated by Communists and Communist sympathizers. As time passed, he became more reckless and accused not only government employees but also teachers, ministers, and many others of being soft on communism if not actually party members. Early in 1954, McCarthy's Permanent Subcommittee on Investigations, a branch of the Government Operations Committee, held hearings to explore the possibility of Communist infiltration in the army. These hearings were televised nationally in April 1954.

McCarthy's actions were an embarrassment to Russell. He abhorred McCarthy's coarse and extreme language, his heavy-handed treatment of people during committee hearings, and his sensational and unsupported charges. He thought the abuse of witnesses was especially unworthy of a U.S. senator. "McCarthy's methods are very distasteful to me and to many other members of the Senate," he wrote. But when persons contacted him about reining in his Wisconsin colleague by cutting off funds for the committee or taking some other action, Russell refused. He would not interfere with the workings of a legitimate Senate committee, he said, however much he might dislike the way the committee operated.

However, Russell seemed to take some delight in the embarrassment and divisions caused by McCarthy among Republicans. He told several correspondents that McCarthy was a "Republican problem." McCarthy, he wrote with some hint of satisfaction, might be "the secret weapon that will destroy the Republican Party." After Republican senator Ralph Flanders of Vermont indicated that he planned to consider a resolution to censure McCarthy, Johnson called a meeting of the Democratic Policy Committee on July 29, 1954. He asked his colleagues if the Democrats should take an official position on the Flanders resolution. A few additional Democratic senators were invited to give their opinions. Senator Herbert H. Lehman of New York, who was not a committee member, urged Johnson and the committee to lead the charge against McCarthy. However, the members of the Democratic Policy Committee unanimously rejected this plea. Russell argued that the committee had no business trying to commit senators on an issue of this kind. Moreover, he stated that if the Democrats made McCarthy a party issue, the Republicans "will draw closer to McCarthy." Thus the Democratic committee avoided the McCarthy question until December 2, 1954, when all of the Democratic senators voting joined twenty-two Republicans to censure their unpopular colleague.

The McCarthy controversy was not a big issue with Russell except inasmuch as the Wisconsin senator brought disrepute on the institution of the Senate. He wrote on April 30, 1954, that the Army-McCarthy hearings were a reflection upon the Senate and that "everyone who is involved in them will be damaged." Russell also resented McCarthy's unfounded charges against innocent people. He had always believed that a public official should have facts before he spoke, and McCarthy had violated that Russell rule.[18]

When the Eighty-fourth Congress opened in January 1955, Lyndon Johnson assumed the position of majority leader in the Senate and Sam Rayburn again became Speaker of the House. Russell was highly pleased by this turn of events. After becoming minority leader two years before, Johnson's leadership qualities had greatly impressed his mentor. Johnson had achieved something that Russell had talked about, namely, a degree of party unity. At the end of the first session of the Eighty-third Congress in August 1953, Johnson's Democratic colleagues had praised him highly, and Russell was among the most flattering supporters. Russell wrote that he knew all along that Johnson would do a good job but added, "I am frank to say that I did not believe that any man could have achieved as much harmony within the Democratic Party and contributed as much to the operations of the Senate as a whole as you have done." Johnson replied that he was greatly pleased by the remarks of his colleagues on the closing day of the session, but none meant as much as the tribute from Russell, "who I regard as one of the great statesmen of the day." Whatever he had accomplished, Johnson continued, could not have been done without Russell's help and advice.[19]

Johnson's success, in Russell's view, had come from his skillful ability to reconcile and compromise different positions in the Democratic party. One of his main links to the liberal wing was Hubert Humphrey, a senator whose ability Russell respected but whose views on most issues he detested. Johnson was flexible enough, persuasive enough, and wielded enough power to keep Humphrey from pushing his liberal program so hard that the party would be irreparably divided. Thus while Democrats in the Senate did not agree, Johnson displayed a remarkable ability to twist arms, cajole, and compromise the positions of both sides so they could work reasonably well together on most major issues. This was a political talent that Russell deeply admired.

Moreover, Johnson worked carefully so as not to drive southern senators into any permanent legislative alliance with conservative Republicans. As Harry McPherson, who became a staff member of the Democratic Policy Committee in 1956, recalled, Johnson flatly refused to support a particularly liberal policy suggested by McPherson because, Johnson explained, he did not want "Dick Russell to walk across the aisle and embrace Everett Dirksen." Johnson, of course, knew that he had Russell's support in opposing any coalition between southern Democrats and conservative northern Republicans. Russell had often voted with Taft and other Republican conservatives, but he did not favor any formal alliance with Republicans, who he believed wanted to dismantle the New Deal. While the popular press carried a number of articles about Russell as a southern leader in such a coalition, he privately indicated that he never had any intention of formalizing such a group. He would use Republican votes to help him achieve certain limited goals, but his loyalty was to the Democratic party.[20]

During 1955 Russell continued to criticize the Benson farm program and to fight proposals that he believed would be harmful to agriculture. For example, he opposed the idea of raising the minimum wage to $1 an hour because he believed it would increase farm operating costs. In discussing this, he declared that surely if Congress could raise the minimum wage to $1 per hour, the price of agricultural commodities could be maintained at a level high enough to permit farmers to make a decent living. He was alarmed that tens of thousands of farmers were leaving agriculture in the 1950s. Russell envisioned drastic political changes as farmers became a smaller and smaller minority. He wrote one constituent that pressure groups would already control the federal government if it had not been for the balance wheel provided "in our political and economic life of the small independent farmer."[21]

By 1955 Russell was again pushing for his two-price system. High supports for commodities such as cotton had placed them in a disadvantageous position in the export markets. The way to solve this problem, Russell argued, was to maintain a higher price for home consumption and let the exportable portion move into world commerce at world prices. Senator Young and a few other farm-state senators supported this approach, but Congress would not go along. The State Department opposed a two-price system because of the opposition of foreign countries to what they considered the dumping of cheap agricultural commodities on their markets.[22]

Secretary Benson did come up with a pilot program for low-income farmers in 1955, but it consisted mostly of advice and guidance plus some extra credit. Since it only applied to a few counties on an experimental basis, Russell said that by the time it reached the entire nation, "all of the low income farmers now living will be dead." According to Russell, the way a friend in Georgia identified a Republican administration was when he saw two men running across a field chasing a single rabbit so at least one of them would have something for his family to eat.[23]

As the parties squared off for the 1956 presidential election, Russell did everything he could to discount the Republican farm program. As surpluses piled up and storage costs rose, he accused Benson of actually trying to make the price support program look bad so it would lose public and political support. The surpluses could be reduced, Russell argued, if the Department of Agriculture properly administered the program. Actually, Russell offered no viable alternative to a very difficult problem. He could talk eloquently about a general economic decline "if the farmer is permitted to go to pot," but the real problem was how to eliminate the cost-price squeeze that hurt most producers.[24]

Early in 1956, President Eisenhower recommended his soil bank plan as a way to take land out of production and to reduce costly surpluses. In addition to paying farmers to remove a portion of their land from production as in the past, Eisenhower proposed that the government pay farmers to remove entire farms from cultivation. Once the new legislation had been introduced, Russell and his colleagues who favored high price supports passed an amendment raising support prices on basic commodities to 90 percent of parity. But Eisenhower vetoed this measure. Russell wrote that he was "bitterly disappointed at the President's action," but there was nothing he could do. After further congressional wrangling, Congress passed the soil bank bill.[25]

As Russell looked toward the fall elections, he was not encouraged for his party. He admitted that Eisenhower would be very hard to beat and expressed a kind of grudging admiration at the "brazen efforts" to use the soil bank program to win the Midwest farm vote. Moreover, he was not impressed with the probable Democratic candidates.[26]

Russell counted himself out as a candidate as early as May 1955 when a reporter asked him if he might seek the nomination again. "Absolutely not," he replied. He also refused to speculate on other likely nominees, including Stevenson. In October Russell mentioned that Frank J. Lausche, conservative governor of Ohio, would be a strong dark horse candidate. He seemed to be trying to avoid making any public endorsement of Stevenson. On November 6, 1955, however, Russell stated that Stevenson would be the party's "best bet" for 1956. Although he wrote friends that he greatly admired Stevenson as "a scholar and speaker," he believed that the Illinois governor bent too easily before the demands of labor and minority groups.[27]

Although Russell said that he did not plan to take any part in the forthcoming convention or campaign,[28] he later announced that he would support his friend, Lyndon Johnson. To some of Johnson's critics in Texas, Russell explained that Johnson's views were closer to his own than those of any other candidate. Johnson would, according to Russell, make an infinitely better president than any of the active or inactive candidates.[29] Much more was involved, however, than Russell's friend-ship with Johnson. He and other moderate southern leaders believed that Johnson was the best candidate because, as mentioned earlier, they believed he would provide a link between the South and the more conservative Democrats in the West and North. Russell was already working with these senators and believed that the best interests of the South depended on continued cooperation among the more conserva-tive Democrats.[30]

On April 11, 1956, the day after Johnson launched his campaign in Texas, Russell speculated that Johnson would get votes outside of Texas if he were the state's favorite son. A few days later, he again talked favorably about Johnson's candidacy. On June 29, Russell addressed a $50 a plate Democratic dinner in Atlanta. Following the dinner, he held a news conference and endorsed Johnson as the party's "best hope" for victory. He explained that Johnson was "more in sympathy with states' rights than other possible nominees." Other southern senators also endorsed Johnson. Shortly before the Democratic convention, Russell announced that he would do everything he could to advance Johnson's candidacy. He "is the one man we've got," he declared, who could beat the Republicans. The other major candidates, according to Russell, were "a lot of hand-me-downs."[31]

Russell did not plan to attend the Democratic convention. He wanted to go fishing. On August 12, however, the day before the delegates were to gather in Chicago, President Eisenhower summoned congressional leaders back to Washington to brief them on the Suez crisis. As Russell was preparing to return to Winder after the meeting with Eisenhower, Johnson asked him to accompany him to Chicago to help with his campaign for the presidential nomination. Russell did not want to go. He told Johnson that he really could not be of much help, even with the Georgia delegation. But Johnson persisted. He pleaded with Russell and said that he wanted his friend to "sit with me in my headquarters and talk to me and eat with me and be with me." Finally, Russell reluctantly agreed to go for a day and a half, something he considered a great concession to his friendship for Johnson.[32] Johnson had no chance to win the nomination, and Russell knew this as well as anyone. As a Johnson supporter, however, he believed that pushing Johnson in 1956 would strengthen the Texan's claim to party leadership in the future.

The Stevenson forces nominated their candidate on the first ballot. A more exciting fight took place over the vice presidential nomination, which finally went to Kefauver. Russell was again faced with a ticket that he could not enthusiastically support. He refused to campaign for Stevenson, although he did respond to Stevenson's request for suggestions on how to deal with some of the issues. Russell urged Stevenson to stress the need for a strong defense, including selective service, and a high technology military establishment that would strengthen the nation's defenses and lessen the need for so many ground, sea, and air troops.[33] Although he voted for Stevenson in 1956, Russell sat out the presidential campaign as he did so often after 1940. Eisenhower's reelection was no surprise to him nor any great disappointment. That the Senate continued in Democratic hands, although by only a majority of two votes, was of greater concern to him. He had been able to work fairly well with Eisenhower on many issues, probably better than he could have with a liberal Democrat in the White House. The main domestic issue on which he differed sharply with the president was farm policy.

Russell continued to be one of the most vociferous critics of the Eisenhower-Benson program of reducing government involvement in agriculture. He accused the president and his secretary of agriculture of purposely trying to drive the small, family-type farmer off the land. He wrote one constituent that the Republican administration seemed determined to eliminate "the small farmers of this country and the odds against those few of us in the Congress who are endeavoring to combat this trend are heavy indeed." One Georgian wrote early in 1957 that Roosevelt had killed the little pigs, but Benson was in effect "slaughtering small farmers who owned the pigs." Russell replied that he could not understand the "policies of this Administration which are threatening to destroy rural America." Every thread of American history, he continued, demonstrated that small farmers had contributed to "our liberty, welfare and progress."[34]

Russell could do little to change Republican agricultural policy. Early in 1957, he did make another attempt to get special help for cotton farmers. Convinced that the Eisenhower administration was catering to Midwest corn growers in order to hold Republican votes there, he introduced another two-price bill for cotton. With strong opposition from Benson and the Department of Agriculture, as well as processors who feared that higher cotton prices would reduce their competitive position in world markets, Russell's bill did not even come up for a vote.

By the late 1950s, Russell was deeply discouraged over getting any legislation that he believed would be genuinely helpful to farmers. He continued reluctantly to support the soil bank program because, as he said, he did not want to take "this crumb away from the farmers." He also fought the effort to limit government payments to individual producers. A strong move developed in the second Eisenhower administration to legislate a limit on price support loans to not more than $50,000 for a single farmer on any one crop. Despite Russell's opposition, in 1959 Congress finally enacted such a measure.[35]

Russell was not consistent in opposing limits on price supports while pleading the cause of small farmers. The ten- and fifteen-acre cotton growers had never benefited much from the price support programs. Russell, however, opposed limitations because he believed they were just another way to discriminate against farmers in an economy where other economic interests had no limits on their entrance to the government trough. Moreover, by the late 1950s, capitalization and operating expenses had become so high in commercial agriculture that the $50,000 limit would affect many of the larger family farmers not just corporate or plantation operations.

The Republicans were as bothered by farm problems as the Democrats. Internal documents of Republican legislative leadership meetings indicate that Eisenhower and his advisers worried a great deal over farm matters. On March 18, 1958, a group of Republicans met with Eisenhower and Benson at the White House, where they had a long discussion about price supports, the situation of various crops, the dairy program, and other issues. After extended consideration, Eisenhower asked if anyone had "ever stopped to think how much easier these leadership meetings would have been through the years if agriculture never had to be discussed." He thought that Republicans agreed on sound principles but that "application of those principles is not always easy and simple in a society as complex as ours."[36] Neither the Republicans nor the Democrats had any real answers to the complex farm problems. Russell, however, believed that he could develop policies greatly superior to those of the president and Benson, but he did not have the political power to do so.

Russell was discouraged over the continued decline of farm political influence. He saw the divisions within agricultural ranks and despaired of ever getting the "scattered segments of the farm group back together," as he put it. Disunity among cotton senators, he wrote, "left us easy victims to senators from nonfarm states."[37] More important than division among farm spokesmen, however, was the growing urban and consumer influence in Congress.

While overall agricultural policy was outside of Russell's control, he continued to have a great impact on many of the agencies and programs that served farmers, such as the Rural Electrification Administration, the Farmers Home Administration, agricultural research, and soil conservation. He also got increased appropriations for what he called "one of my legislative pets," the school lunch program. Between 1953 and 1960, federal cash payments for school lunches rose from $67.3 to $93.7 million.[38]

Despite Russell's complaint about Republican treatment of farmers, federal expenditures for agricultural programs rose dramatically between 1953 and 1960 as the national government tried to prop up farm prices. Outlays for farm and natural resource services jumped from $2.9 billion in 1953 to $4.2 billion in 1956 and reached $5.6 billion in 1959 before dropping some the next year.[39] While Russell favored these increased expenditures, as well as added military and defense spending, he kept calling for economy. He criticized many of the new domestic programs and charged that both Eisenhower Republicans and liberal Democrats were irresponsible spenders. When his constituents called for some tax relief, Russell usually replied that he could not support revenue reductions until spending had been brought under control. But Russell refused to do the obvious, which was to appropriate less money for government agencies.

Russell tried to correct the misconception that rising national defense costs were responsible for driving up the federal budget. Defense spending was actually less in 1960 than in 1954 right after the Korean War ended. He blamed the deficit on foreign aid and burgeoning social programs. Writing a constituent, he explained that the budget could not be balanced as long as Congress maintained "this monstrous give-away program abroad." Russell explained that he opposed both deficit financing and increased taxes but that if he had to choose, "I would rather see taxes raised."[40]

In April 1959, Russell addressed the Georgia Bankers' Association convention in Augusta. He took that opportunity to talk about the nation's huge debt, excessive spending, and the threat of inflation. Unless the United States put its financial house in order, he said, "we may wake up some morning to find that our system of free enterprise and individual freedom . . . has been transformed into a system of State Socialism." Temporary deficits might be necessary, he continued, but deficit financing should be the exception and not the rule. He added that there could be no tax relief as long as spending continued to rise. He admitted that Eisenhower was trying to balance the budget, and, he added, "that is more than can be said for some of the ultra-liberals in the Democratic Party."

Russell argued that spending must be judged on the basis of national interest. Expenditures failing to meet that test should be abandoned or postponed. The main thing, he said, was to provide for the country's "security and survival." Russell complained about special groups that sought government grants and federally financed programs for local purposes. He declared that these interests "seem to work on the assumption that such programs are financed by sleight of hand rather than by the increasing burden of taxes and inflation." The only solution was for people to forgo new programs and the expansion of old ones.

Russell was surely a committed fiscal conservative—except when it came to spending on federal projects in Georgia. Like other Senate and House members, he violated his own standard for spending—the national interest—when it came to local and state programs. He successfully supported so many federal projects that it was once said that if another one was located in the state, Georgia would drop into the Atlantic Ocean. Russell was a master at getting what he wanted from the Defense Department, the Department of Agriculture, the Bureau of Reclamation, the Corps of Engineers, and other agencies and departments. His position as chairman of the Armed Services Committee and second ranking member of the Appropriations Committee and his chairmanship of the subcommittee on agricultural appropriations and later defense appropriations placed him in a most powerful position to obtain federal installations for Georgia.

The Russell files present a clear picture of the political back scratching, vote trading, special interest pleading, and political favors that were part of the pork barrel activities in Congress. In the area of federally funded projects, politics was the overriding factor. Neither sectionalism, political philosophy, nor national interest played a major role in the decision making. Liberals and conservatives and northerners and southerners worked together almost as kinsmen as they voted money to keep federal projects going from Maine to California and from Florida to Michigan. Many of the local, state, and federal facilities did not involve huge sums of money, but when they were all added together, the totals were significant. It is easy to see why economy was practiced more in word than in deed.

For example, in 1953, Senator John M. Butler of Missouri asked Russell's support for the Anacostia Flood Control Project in his state. Russell replied that he had done everything he could to get the desired $200,000 but without success. However, he told Butler that "we will take care of this next year." When Butler brought up the matter again early in 1954, Russell wrote that "we should be able to put this over." In response to a "Dear Dick" letter from liberal senator Wayne Morse thanking him for putting through the "Oregon projects," Russell said that he was pleased to help. Conservative Republican Homer Capehart of Indiana wrote that he would highly appreciate Russell's support for reservoir projects in his state, and Russell promised to do his very best to convince the House conferees to include them. When Congressman E. L. Forrester of Georgia could not get one of his favorite projects funded by the House, he turned to Russell and asked him to handle it on the Senate side.

William Proxmire, Hubert Humphrey, Lyndon Johnson, Strom Thurmond, and scores of other senators and congressmen turned to "Dear Dick" for help in getting local projects approved and funded. Every dam, flood control project, forest reserve, special road, airport, research center, and military installation and a host of other local facilities were pictured as being vitally important to the nation's welfare. Lyndon Johnson explained that the Canyon Dam and Reservoir on the Guadalupe River was "urgently needed for flood control and water conservation." Referring to water projects, Senator Kerr of Oklahoma said that "these projects are of utmost importance to my state." Kerr also asked Russell to assist him in getting $2.5 million for a hospital and dental clinic at Tinker Air Force Base in Oklahoma City when the Appropriations Committee brought up the supplemental bill in 1956. Russell said that he would support those projects and added, "If any is left over after you and Oklahoma get through with the Treasury, I hope to get a few dollars for Georgia."[41]

Russell had no problems getting a "few dollars" for so-called civil projects in Georgia. He got federal funds not only for water and conservation projects but also for airports and many other purposes. For example, he began working in 1946 to get a Southeast Poultry Research Laboratory built in northeast Georgia in the center of the developing broiler industry. He told President Harmon Caldwell of the University of Georgia that if such a facility were built anywhere in the Southeast, he could "get it for our state." It was subsequently built not far from the university campus in Athens.[42]

Russell began trying to get money for Buford Dam on the Chattahoochee River northeast of Atlanta in 1948. The next year, he managed to get funds added to the army civil functions bill in order to begin the project. However, Clarence Cannon, the powerful chairman of the House Appropriations Committee, opposed and subsequently cut out many such projects, including Buford Dam. At the time the House took this action, Representative Albert J. Engel of Michigan told Russell that he would do whatever he could to get the Buford Dam money restored. Fortunately Engel was still on good terms with Cannon after the chairman had made so many cuts. Engel talked with Cannon and finally convinced him to add the needed $750,000 for Buford Dam. The change was made so quietly in conference that several of the conferees were not even aware of it. This was an example of Russell achieving his goal even against what seemed to be impossible odds.[43]

Russell had less trouble getting the necessary $500,000 for a new airport in Winder, although perhaps it was not as easy as one writer claimed. According to the story, Russell was looking over a list of authorized projects for airport construction. On the spur of the moment, he said, "I might as well put down an airport for Winder." The facility was built to handle jet aircraft, and in later years, army and navy planes landed there to let Russell off or pick him up as he traveled back and forth to Washington.[44]

In its move toward economy, the Eisenhower administration sought to close a number of military installations that were considered unnecessary for national defense. Russell fought hard against any closings in Georgia, while at the same time insisting on greater economy. Although he failed to stop the Defense Department from closing the Augusta Arsenal in 1955, he successfully resisted threats to close Moody Air Force Base in Valdosta, Fort Gordon near Augusta, and Hunter Field near Savannah. In 1957 Fort Gordon became a prime target for closing, but Russell pulled out his big guns to avoid it. When President Eisenhower called him to the White House on August 26, 1957, to discuss the foreign aid bill and other matters, Russell raised the question of maintaining Fort Gordon. According to the staff notes, the president promised "to try to hold on to Fort Gordon, even if it might have to be on a reduced basis." The president spoke favorably of Fort Gordon after Russell said he would back the administration's overall defense program, although he had told Eisenhower that he could not support the foreign aid package. When Fort Gordon again seemed in danger in 1962, Russell advised Governor Carl E. Sanders that the best way to protect the facility was to get additional permanent construction underway at the base. "Without boasting," Russell wrote Sanders in 1962, "I am confident that all three [bases] would have been closed long before this if I had not happened to be the chairman of the Senate Committee on Armed Services and the ranking member of the Appropriations Committee for the Department of Defense." By 1957–58, there were fifteen defense establishments in Georgia, and some $30.2 million was spent on construction alone at military facilities.[45]

Russell also guarded the interests of Lockheed, which built military planes, at Marietta. When the Republicans talked about cutting and restructuring defense efforts early in 1953, Russell declared that he was strongly opposed to closing the Lockheed plant "because of the economic effect it would have on my state." Later he assured Marietta residents that he would see to it that Lockheed "secured its fair share of defense contracts." The United States needed planes, he wrote, and he added that it would be a mistake to rely too much on missiles that were not fully proven.[46]

Although defense facilities brought the most federal money and jobs to the state, Russell also fought hard to get funding for the establishment of various research facilities in Georgia. For years he complained that a disproportionate amount of federal research and develop-

ment money went to Ivy League and West Coast institutions. He refused
to believe, he said, that the nation's brains and intelligence were concentrated in New England, Chicago, California, or Texas. Georgia and
other southern states, he argued, should "share equitably in the intellectual, scientific and economic benefits that flow from our tax dollars that
go to support government research." Over the years, he had considerable success in bringing research funds to Georgia. He wrote Governor
Sanders in 1963 that "it has been a source of great pride to me for the
past several years that I have been able to bring so many scientific and
research facilities to Georgia." Besides the Southeast Poultry Research
Laboratory, he was especially proud of the Forest Research Laboratory
also located at Athens. He saw these and other facilities not only as
providing employment but also as important assets to the state's overall
economic development. Of course, Russell had his limitations in obtaining new federal projects, and he did not hesitate to frankly state his
inability to meet some requests. When Peyton Hawes of Elberton, Georgia, telephoned him on May 16, 1960, asking support for two new
dams on the Savannah River, Russell explained, "I can not help this
year." At about the same time, he told Lyndon Johnson that he could
not offer much hope in getting money for the Great Plains Field Station
at Bushland, Texas.[47] On projects relating to defense, Russell had a
powerful ally in Carl Vinson, chairman of the House Armed Services
Committee. However, he had less powerful allies in pushing other types
of projects.

One of Russell's most interesting and controversial pork-barrel
projects was his long campaign to establish a peanut research laboratory in Dawson, Georgia. In 1961 he managed to get $130,000 appro-
priated to plan and locate a peanut research laboratory. He had carefully tried to cultivate the support of his colleagues from the other main
peanut-producing states, mainly Virginia, North Carolina, Alabama,
Texas, and New Mexico. There seemed to be general agreement that
such a research laboratory was needed, and Russell believed that the
project would move ahead without difficulty. He planned to put additional money in the appropriations bill for agriculture in 1962, and
within a year or two, he hoped that the laboratory would be in operation. It was the usual procedure—get planning money, and then go back
the following year for construction funds.

Several conditions developed to thwart his best-laid plans. Some
senators from peanut-producing states feared that the new facility
might take over research already being done in their states. They could
not tolerate that. Also, while Russell kept the location quiet as long as

he could, the announcement that the laboratory would be in Dawson produced a loud outcry. Some representatives of the peanut industry charged that Russell had acted in bad faith in locating the facility in Dawson, which they portrayed as an educational and cultural wasteland in southwest Georgia. That location would not draw top scientists, the opponents argued.

While Russell replied sharply to his critics, he continued to press ahead with the project. Whatever commitment he had to Dawson, he had no intention of welshing on it. He got $1.6 million approved in the Senate for the laboratory in 1962 and again in 1963, but he was unable to get the House to approve any funds for the Dawson facility. Late in 1964, House conferees nearly agreed to go along with the Senate as agreements were being reached on other agricultural appropriations, but again they rejected the peanut laboratory. At last, however, in 1965 both the Senate and House passed appropriations for the facility that scarcely anyone wanted except Dick Russell. It had been a five-year fight, but he finally prevailed.[48]

In light of Russell's work for his constituents, it is no wonder that the people of Georgia planned a Russell appreciation day to honor the senator. Besides many people from around Georgia, congressmen and senators from other states gathered in Winder on a cold blustery day on October 26, 1957, to pay tribute to Dick Russell. After a long parade that filled the streets of Winder, the participants went to the Lions Clubhouse grounds for barbecued chicken. Then a number of speakers praised Russell and his work in Washington. Senator Strom Thurmond called Russell the greatest senator "this nation has produced" and added that if Russell had been elected president in 1952, "we wouldn't be undergoing the troubles we are today."

Senator Herman Talmadge, elected in 1956 to replace Senator George, delivered the main address. When Russell was Speaker of the House in 1927, he had appointed thirteen-year-old Talmadge as a page in the Georgia legislature. Talmadge praised Russell for his leadership against civil rights legislation earlier in the year and stated that if Russell had become president the country would have a man "in the White House and not out on the golf course."

Russell was overwhelmed by the crowd and by the flattering remarks by his friends and colleagues. He insisted that he did not deserve such generous plaudits. Although Russell presented a humble demeanor, he loved hearing good things about himself. The appreciation day reached its climax when a group presented him with a new deluxe Chrysler automobile and scrolls of appreciation from local residents.[49]

Despite his frequent jibes at the Republicans, Russell found that he could work in reasonable harmony with the Eisenhower administration. He disagreed with the administration on such major issues as agricultural policy and foreign aid, but in general he supported the president more often than some Republican senators. Among many examples of Russell's support for programs and people favored by Eisenhower, Russell strongly supported the Landrum-Griffin Act of 1959 that placed added restrictions on labor unions; he voted to uphold the president's veto of housing legislation in 1959; he backed the nomination of Lewis Strauss as secretary of commerce although Strauss was strongly opposed by many Democrats and ultimately failed to win confirmation; he pushed through the Defense Reorganization Act of 1958, which greatly pleased the president; and he voted to uphold the president's veto of increased federal pay legislation in 1958.

The president was grateful for Russell's support and frequently expressed his thanks to "Dear Dick." On June 19, Eisenhower wrote, "I can not fail to recognize the courage, wisdom and spirit of fairness you demonstrated in the vote of the confirmation of Lewis Strauss. I am grateful." Eisenhower praised Russell for his "excellent job on the defense reorganization bill" and added that both he and Russell would be gratified with the effect it would have "on the readiness and efficiency of our defenses over the months and years ahead."[50]

Russell gained recognition from his colleagues early in 1955 through inadvertence and procrastination. Like other senators and congressmen, he had always provided a short biographical sketch for the *Congressional Directory*. But in 1955 Russell and his staff failed to get the material to the Joint Committee on Printing in time for publication. Consequently, when the 1955 *Congressional Directory* appeared, the senator's entire biography consisted of, "Richard Brevard Russell, Democrat, of Winder, Ga." To his surprise, Russell received so many compliments from his colleagues for what they assumed was a deliberate downplay on self-importance that he never again changed the skimpy listing.

His colleagues, however, were much less brief in eulogizing and praising Russell on the twenty-fifth anniversary of taking his seat in the Senate. On January 13, 1958, one after another of his fellow senators outdid themselves with superlatives about Russell and his work. He was described as a great professional, as a senator's senator, as "the South's most eloquent spokesman," and as a possible presidential candidate for 1960. Russell said he was humbled to "be held in such high regard by those for whom I have so much affection." If there was a better response than "thank you," he claimed, he would use it, but that was the best he could say.[51]

Russell was popular not only with Senate veterans but also with newcomers. He was an excellent teacher of Senate ways, and new senators often looked to him for guidance and counsel. Over the years, scores of first-term senators had turned to Russell for help and advice. He invited them to lunch, counseled them on the ways of the Senate, visited with them in the cloakroom and in his office, and expressed a genuine interest in them and their families. What was one of the best ways to get along in the Senate? When Howard Edmondson of Oklahoma asked this question when he was about to succeed Senator Kerr in 1963, Carter Bradley, Kerr's administrative assistant, told him, "Go see Senator Russell." When Edward Kennedy arrived in the Senate, he said that his older brother, President John Kennedy, gave him valuable advice by telling him to visit with Dick Russell. Kennedy later recalled that Russell was "extremely kind and generous."

Senator Gale McGee of Wyoming, elected in 1958, found Russell most helpful. McGee opposed the nomination of Lewis Strauss as secretary of commerce but did not know if, as a new senator, he should take a leading role against Strauss. So he went to see Russell. McGee said he had heard that certain powerful senators might punish him by voting against Wyoming projects if he opposed Strauss. After several discussions of the matter, Russell said, "Well, Gale I want to say that you ought to go ahead with this cause, and to the best of my ability, I'll see to it that you don't get hurt." McGee always treasured that comment. Other new senators had similar experiences. At the end of the session in 1959, Senator Howard W. Cannon of Nevada wrote Russell expressing his appreciation for "the help and consideration you have given to me as a junior member." Robert C. Byrd of West Virginia wrote that it was a "glorious experience" to have worked with Russell during his first year in Washington.[52]

On questions concerning the institution of the Senate, Russell always held conservative and traditional views. In March 1958, the question arose about installing a public address system in the Senate chamber. Russell wrote Senator Thomas C. Hennings, Jr., chairman of the Committee on Rules and Administration, that he might be considered "old-fashioned, but I am very strongly opposed to the installation of such a system." His reason was that if people in the gallery could hear better they might be noisier. Presently, Russell said, people were reasonably quiet in the gallery "in order to try to hear what is taking place on the floor."[53]

Russell was old-fashioned in other ways. In the 1950s, senators began adding public relations experts to their office staffs. These individuals arranged newspaper and television interviews, produced press releases, wrote news columns, and, as Russell put it, extolled "the activities of the Senator involved." In 1957 he wrote one friend that Senator Talmadge had several people doing publicity work and that "I told him jokingly the other day that it would not be long before the people of Georgia would be asking the name of their other Senator." Russell explained that he never thought it was "appropriate to spend tax money in this way." In the old days, he said, reporters wrote stories from actual coverage of events on the floor of the Senate, but now they wrote from press releases and copies of prepared speeches. Russell did not like the trend but admitted that he might have to hire a "press agent" to "magnify my activities and minimize my failings."

Early in 1959, he finally gave in and employed William M. Bates as his first press secretary. The senator's nephew, Bobby, arranged the interview. A newsman with some ten years experience, Bates received little or no direction from Russell regarding his specific duties or the procedures he should follow. It was clear for some time, Bates said later, that Russell did not really appreciate the work of a press secretary. Gradually, however, Russell permitted himself to rely more heavily on Bates for speech writing, arranging interviews, and other public relations work.[54]

Russell's personal life changed little in the 1950s. He lived at the Mayflower Hotel and had a somewhat more restricted social life than in earlier years. This was because of increasing responsibilities in the Senate and periods of poor health. He accepted fewer and fewer invitations to cocktail parties and dinners, unless fellow Georgians were involved. As invitations came in, Russell would scribble across the written invitation or the telephone message "decline" or "accept." There were many more "declines" than "accepts." For example, when the Averell Harrimans invited him to dinner on April 18, 1951, he wrote "decline," as he did when Senator Mike Monroney of Oklahoma asked him to a dinner in honor of General and Mrs. Omar Bradley a few days later. In a single week during January 1952, he turned down invitations from the ambassadors of Egypt, Cuba, and England, even though Winston Churchill would be at the latter affair. Russell's staff assumed that their boss would turn down most invitations and acted accordingly.

The exceptions were affairs sponsored by his close friends in the Senate. He frequently had dinner with Lyndon and Lady Bird Johnson and sometimes spent a relaxing Sunday afternoon at their place. Russell liked to go down to Virginia occasionally on Sundays to have lunch with the Harry Byrds, to go on a fishing trip with Senator Robertson of Virginia, or to have a steak dinner with Guy Gillette of Iowa. He told Gillette that he never had any doubts about the tenderness of Iowa beef, but he was always willing "to accept additional proof." And to Robertson he wrote that while he was no fisherman, after hearing of Robertson's skill, "I am not afraid of going hungry."[55] During most of the years Russell spent in Washington, some members of his extended family lived there, and he often visited on Sundays with one of what he commonly called the "Washington group" of Russells.

His most constant female companion in the 1950s continued to be Harriet Orr. They often had dinner together and sometimes attended a movie. But as had always been true, most of Dick's evenings were spent with a good book. When he did not have to read official papers and documents, he spent hours reading books on history. Such books might vary from a biography of Doc Holliday, the western gunslinger, to John F. Kennedy's *Profiles in Courage*. But Civil War history was always his first love. He read everything Emory University history professor Bell Wiley wrote on the Civil War, plus the works of scores of other writers on that conflict.[56]

Russell's interest in sports never lagged, although his very busy schedule left him little time to observe sporting events. The *Washington Daily News* published a spoof which supposedly reflected his love of baseball. In an imaginary game between the Washington Senators and the New York Yankees, the score was tied in the fourteenth inning. Both teams had used all their pinch hitters. Charlie Dressen, manager of the Senators, spotted Russell in the crowd, and after Russell agreed to help out, Dressen asked permission for him to play. Despite Yankee manager Casey Stengel's vigorous objections, William Harridge, president of the American League, ruled that Russell could play if he signed a contract with Calvin Griffith, the Senators' owner. This was quickly arranged, and a uniform and shoes were provided. Dressen then sent Russell to the plate. Being a switch hitter, he chose to bat from the left side. He hit a ball that trickled down the first-base line, and the winning run raced to the plate. The huge headline of the article on the game read: "RUSSELL'S HIT WINS FOR SENATORS." Russell also continued to be a loyal follower of the University of Georgia Bulldog football team. Late in 1959, he wrote Dan Magill that the 1959 team had thrilled him "more than any team in history."

In 1955 Russell joined the Alfalfa Club, a rather unique club for men in Washington. Each year the club gave a dinner for its members and then recessed into the national convention of the Alfalfa party. The president of the group would give a brief humorous speech as though he were accepting the nomination for president of the United States on the Alfalfa ticket. It was a delightful affair that Russell thoroughly enjoyed. The club held, as Clark Clifford recalled, "some marvelously entertaining dinners."[57]

The death of his mother on August 30, 1953, was an especially sad occasion for Dick Russell. Over the years, his love, affection, and admiration for Ina Russell had steadily grown. He never ceased being amazed and grateful for all that she had done for her large family of thirteen children. She had "always been the vital core of our family" and was "the greatest person I have ever known and her faith, spirit and courage have been a source of inspiration to all who knew her intimately," he stated. For years before her death, he wrote and telephoned her regularly and sent a monthly check. Sometimes the check was late, and he blamed his procrastination. Following his mother's death, he purchased the old home and the land immediately surrounding it from the other family heirs. Another serious blow was the death from cancer of his brother, Robert, in 1955. Of the six brothers, Dick had been closer to Robert than to any of the others. As he wrote, we "were about as close as brothers could be." The fact that Robert, a U.S. Circuit Court judge, died at the height of his career greatly saddened and distressed Dick.[58]

After Ina Russell died in 1953, the senator continued to employ Modine Thomas as his cook and housekeeper at the family home. Mrs. Thomas had begun working for the Russells in the late 1930s and was almost considered a member of the family. An efficient and strong-minded woman, she took excellent care of Russell when he returned to Winder. She was a good cook and prepared what Russell liked to eat. She also did not hesitate to protect his privacy and health if she believed that was necessary. She might at times tell visitors that the senator was not at home when actually he was upstairs resting. Russell was very fond of Mrs. Thomas, and she was still working for him at the time of his death.

In the early 1950s, there were some changes in Russell's office force. William H. Darden, Jr., a graduate of the University of Georgia, joined the staff in December 1948 shortly after finishing law school. In April 1951, Darden resigned to become chief clerk of the Armed Services Committee, which Russell then chaired. When the Republicans assumed control, Darden stayed on with the committee in a staff position but later became chief of staff of the committee. Marjorie Warren, who had been in the office for nearly a decade, was the backbone of the secretarial staff, and Clara Smith, who had originally worked with Russell on the Immigration Committee, had a variety of office responsibilities, including sorting the mail. By this time, a new technology had arrived at senators' offices: the automatic typewriter. In September 1949, Russell got his first machine, and the next year, the Senate Committee on Rules and Administration permitted each senator to have three "automatic typing machines." This permitted the secretaries to write more letters and to do it quicker than with the older typewriters. The amount of paperwork the office could handle increased dramatically due to the automation of office equipment. This is clearly evident by the growth in volume of Russell's files.

Although Russell left the operation of his office up to Leeman Anderson, he made certain that the actions of his staff were above reproach. On May 15, 1951, a representative of a van company visited Russell's office to talk about getting contracts with government agencies to move men, presumably around military bases. A staff member wrote on the message, "Offers to pay well for our troubles in his behalf." Russell scribbled below the message, "We don't do business that way— hope you told him emphatically."

Unlike many of his colleagues, Russell refused to hit the professional lecture circuit. When he was approached in 1951 by National Lecture Management, which represented Senators Alben Barkley, Paul Douglas, and others, about making professional lecture engagements, Russell turned down the offer. His full commitment was to the business of the Senate. Furthermore, he did not need the additional money. After he spoke at Georgia State University in Atlanta in 1959, he received a check for $200. He endorsed the check over to the school's foundation, saying that he did not accept honorariums from "our state institutions."[59]

As his work load grew, Russell turned down invitations to speak that he normally would have accepted. For example, when he was asked by Oklahoma Democrats to make the Jefferson-Jackson Day speech in that state on November 1, 1951, he reluctantly declined. He said that as soon as Congress recessed he had to get away for some rest. In recent years, he wrote, he found that his energy was not "without limitations and I do have such a thing as nerves."[60]

It was in the mid-1950s that Russell began to have health problems. He had been a heavy smoker since he was a teenager, and the ill results were becoming evident. By 1952 he had a heavy morning cough, and by 1955 he suffered from a definite shortness of breath. Right after the Democratic convention in Chicago in 1952, Russell went to the Mayo Clinic in Rochester, Minnesota, for a complete physical checkup. He was there from August 26 to August 30. He complained of fatigue, pain in his left shoulder, abdominal cramps, and especially morning coughing. After four days of tests, Dr. J. C. Cain reported that overall Russell was in excellent health. His cough was due to excessive smoking. Cain urged Russell to stop the habit for at least ten days to see if the cough would diminish. Then the doctor advised Dick not to smoke more than half a pack of cigarettes a day. This would be difficult for one who had commonly smoked two, three, or even four packs a day.

Russell did not quit smoking, and his cough and shortness of breath got worse. By 1955 he was coughing heavily each morning for thirty minutes to an hour after he arose for the day. His condition was very bad if he caught cold. He returned to the Mayo Clinic in 1956, and Dr. Cain again emphasized that Russell must quit smoking. According to the doctors who examined him, his cough was directly connected to his smoking. Cain and other doctors did not think that Russell's lungs had been irreparably harmed but warned him to quit smoking before worse conditions developed. Russell was in the early stages of emphysema. He did quit smoking for a short time early in 1956, but when his cough continued, he said that he might as well smoke. On days when he was under considerable pressure, he smoked a pack a day.[61]

Fortunately, Russell's health did not yet impair his effectiveness in the Senate. And that was important to him. Throughout the 1950s, he used every bit of stamina and strength he could muster to beat back the growing demand for civil rights legislation. No other issue took so much of Russell's time and attention in the middle years of that decade.

15

Civil Rights: The 1950s

No domestic issue so distressed and alarmed Dick Russell as the persistent demand for civil rights legislation and the gradual breakdown of segregation in federal agencies. Up to 1953, he and his supporters had been able to block legislation designed to extend federal protection to blacks mainly through filibuster tactics. Conservative Republicans and Russell Democrats joined together in January 1953 to defeat overwhelmingly a move to weaken the principle of unlimited debate. So far the power of the filibuster, or threat of a filibuster, had been enough to turn back civil rights advocates who looked to federal legislation to achieve their goals. Why, then, was Russell so deeply worried in 1953? The answer to this question could be found in his inability to stop the presidents from expanding black rights in the federal agencies and in his fear of unfavorable decisions by the Supreme Court. Already the Supreme Court had weakened segregation by ordering that white law and graduate schools in Texas and Oklahoma accept qualified black students.

The move toward equality and integration in military camps and other federal facilities brought cries of protest from Georgians and other southerners. A retired army colonel who lived in Columbus, Georgia, described what he considered terrible conditions at Fort Benning. He wrote that white soldiers were quartered with blacks and nothing could be done about it. Even worse, he stated, black "wenches" were living with white Wacs, using the same rest rooms, showers, and sleeping and eating facilities. Blacks were even going to the Officers' Club and were swimming in the pools with the wives and daughters of white officers. "To be perfectly frank, Dick, it is the most obnoxious thing we have had to stomach." Russell heartily agreed.

Russell received hundreds of letters in the early 1950s objecting to integration at military posts, government hospitals, and elsewhere. These expressions reflected the depth of racism that gripped the minds and emotions of most white southerners and probably most whites elsewhere. As the danger to white supremacy increased, the reaction to that development became more emotional and irrational. A resident of Griffin told Russell about taking a veteran of World War II to the hospital in Dublin. As the veteran approached the ward, he saw black veterans inside and, according to the correspondent, yelled, "Not this. I had rather go back home and die." But he was too sick not to be hospitalized and had to stay.

Russell answered concerned constituents who related such "shocking" and "sickening" incidents by saying that, while he strongly opposed integration, he could do nothing to change the situation. At military installations, Russell explained, he had twice tried without success to enact legislation that would permit men entering the armed forces to choose integrated or segregated units. Eisenhower, he wrote, was simply carrying out the Truman executive orders with all the power of his office, and a senator could not curtail presidential authority.[1]

Creating additional danger to traditional race relations in the South were a growing number of moderates who saw approaching change in the region. Among the most conspicuous and influential of these moderates was Russell's old friend Ralph McGill, editor of the *Atlanta Constitution*. Back in 1936, McGill had been a strong Russell supporter in his campaign against Eugene Talmadge, and he continued to admire and support Russell in the following years. Although he did not favor racial integration, by the late 1940s McGill was beginning to reassess his position on racial matters. He came to believe that the South must extend basic rights to blacks. By 1953 McGill had become a strong voice for moderation and change in Dixie. He also had given up hope on Russell as a southern statesman.

On December 11, 1953, McGill published a front-page editorial on the racial situation. Three days later, *Time* magazine carried his views on its education page. McGill predicted that the Supreme Court would probably declare segregated schools unconstitutional. "All over the world," he wrote, "the tide runs that way." Arguing that the world was in the throes of a social revolution, he stated that segregation by law no longer fit new conditions. In his view, the Supreme Court had no alternative but to interpret the Fourteenth Amendment as it was written. He added that those who insisted that segregation could be preserved were doing the people a "disservice." McGill stated that the Supreme Court was not trying "to force mingling of the races" or to require "people to associate socially," but legal segregation, he said, was definitely on the way out.[2] McGill was not without support for his views, among both blacks and whites. Ray Moore of WSB-TV in Atlanta wrote McGill that he wanted to shout "bravo" for the McGill editorial and added that McGill's admirers would make up a good-sized chorus.[3]

Russell himself foresaw the end of segregation. On November 11, 1953, he spoke at a large Armistice Day gathering in Atlanta, where he commented that he expected the Supreme Court to rule against segregation in the South's public schools. Until recently he had believed that the Court would uphold legal segregation, he said, but appointments of justices during the last few years had caused him to change his mind.[4] Although Russell seemed to be preparing intellectually for the decision in *Brown v. Board of Education* that would be handed down on May 17, 1954, he was not emotionally ready for such an eventuality. He had been a devoted supporter of *Plessy v. Ferguson*, which had established the separate but equal doctrine in 1896. The *Brown* decision overturned *Plessy* and all of the laws and customs that had been built on it.

Southerners bitterly denounced the *Brown* decision and the Supreme Court that delivered it. Russell released a statement in which he called the Court's action "a flagrant abuse of judicial power." He declared that the *Brown* case had struck down the rights of the states, "plainly guaranteed" by the Constitution, "to direct their most vital local affairs." This decision, he continued, made "mere satrapies out of once sovereign states." Russell argued that the *Brown* decision had also clearly violated the constitutional principle of separation of powers because the Supreme Court had become "a mere political arm of the executive branch of the Government." Russell was especially critical of the justices for substituting psychology and social science arguments for law and legal precedents in interpreting the Constitution. He concluded that the decision would create genuine hardship for many people and might even destroy the common school system in some southern states. The following day, Russell repeated on the floor of the Senate that the *Brown* decision violated states' rights and had been politically inspired.[5]

It was his inability to effectively resist the eventual breakdown of segregation that so frustrated Russell. During the rest of 1954 and throughout 1955, he considered a variety of approaches that might somehow mitigate the decisions of the Supreme Court and thwart prospective integration. These included a constitutional amendment giving states the right to decide on segregation, restrictions on the jurisdiction of the Supreme Court, the establishment of private segregated schools, and even outright resistance. But Russell knew that none of these ideas was practical or popular enough to gain national support. He wrote complaining constituents that, while the *Brown* case in his view was

Members of the U.S. Senate's southern caucus, 1953. Senator Russell is seated at center. (Photo courtesy of Wide World Photos, Inc., New York.)

unconstitutional, he could do nothing to change it. Congress would take no action to curb the Supreme Court, he said, and in the case of private schools, there would be numerous obstacles to overcome.[6]

Although Russell resisted school desegregation, he did not become affiliated with any organized effort to maintain the status quo. He sympathized with the white citizens' councils but did not become a member of such a group. In April 1959, the Jackson, Mississippi, Citizens' Council was planning to produce a film and asked Russell to make a statement against school integration. Bill Bates, Russell's new press secretary, left a note for his boss saying, "I have serious reservations about being linked with this Citizens' Council outfit." So did Russell, and he did not participate.[7]

Everywhere Russell looked, the walls of legal segregation seemed to be tumbling down. Despite his best efforts, he could not maintain the principle of white supremacy. The executive branch and the Supreme

Court were both bringing about integration, regardless of what Congress might do. Moreover, sentiment was growing in Congress for broad civil rights legislation. The Eisenhower administration had its civil rights bill, and Democrats such as Hubert Humphrey were pushing their own measures. Those who supported white supremacy also believed that the South's position on racial matters was not getting fair treatment by the media throughout the nation. According to Russell, the northern press was prejudiced against the South and refused to present a fair and accurate picture of conditions. What could be done?

Early in 1956, Senators Strom Thurmond and Harry F. Byrd proposed to Russell that the southern senators draft and publish a statement presenting southern views on recent Supreme Court decisions and on integration. Russell thought this was an excellent idea. Soon an informal committee consisting of Russell, Sam Ervin, and John Stennis was at work on writing a position paper. Russell did the final drafting. However, he found it most difficult to compose a statement that he believed would state the southern case strongly enough and yet would hold the support of a majority of southern senators and congressmen. Writing one friend as he was working on a draft, Russell admitted that some southern senators "actually favor the [*Brown*] decision." Others objected, he said, to any suggestion that the *Brown* decision was unconstitutional. By this time, only twelve or thirteen senators were considered to be completely reliable as protectors of the white South. It was an uphill fight, he wrote, and one that he seriously considered giving up. He was trying desperately "to get something respectable that most of our Southern Senators can sign, but when you run into 5 or 6 who are unwilling to denounce the decision as illegal and unconstitutional it is discouraging." He believed that presenting no statement would be better than making "a feeble, watered-down gesture of protest."[8] Although Russell claimed that the changes he made were mainly cosmetic, he did agree to some substantive modifications before publication.

On March 12, 1956, the text of the Declaration of Constitutional Principles, better known as the Southern Manifesto, was released to the press. Many newspapers carried the complete text and the names of the signers. Nineteen senators and seventy-seven House members signed the manifesto. Neither Estes Kefauver nor Albert Gore of Tennessee would sign it. Otherwise, all of the senators from the former Confederate states, except Lyndon Johnson, placed their signatures on the document. Senator Gore told Ralph McGill that he was tremendously worried about the South's future "because of the intransigent attitudes on race by so many southern leaders." Gore and McGill seemed to agree that the Deep South was blinded to what McGill called "the great historical forces which are at work."

The Southern Manifesto attacked the Supreme Court, calling the *Brown* decision "a clear abuse of judicial power," familiar Russell phraseology. The Court was taking over the powers of Congress by "undertaking to legislate" and was encroaching upon "the reserved rights of the states and the people." Emphasizing that neither the Constitution nor the Fourteenth Amendment mentioned education, Russell wrote that previously the states had governed their school systems as they saw fit. Segregation had been established long before 1896 but was then confirmed in the *Plessy* case. This decision had ratified peoples' "habits, customs, traditions and way of life" in many states. But now, according to the manifesto, the justices had exercised "naked judicial power and substituted their personal political and social ideas for the established law of the land."

Besides being constitutionally in error, the statement insisted, the *Brown* case had produced bad social consequences. According to the document, the decision had destroyed friendly relations between the races and was planting "hatred and suspicion" where before there had only been "friendship and understanding." Outside agitators had created a dangerous and explosive situation by demanding "revolutionary changes" in the public school systems of the South.

Despite the horrible consequences of the *Brown* decision, Russell wrote, southerners reaffirmed their adherence to the Constitution as the basic law of the land. The manifesto commended the states that had announced resistance to "integration by any lawful means." Then the southerners appealed to people throughout the country to consider the time when such judicial power might be used against them. Admitting that they were a minority, framers of the manifesto declared that a majority of Americans believed in the federal system and the division of powers and in time would help fight to preserve states' rights. Finally the document pledged that the South would "use all lawful means" to reverse the decision and "to prevent the use of force in its implementation."[9]

Although the manifesto was widely publicized, it did nothing to change the minds of those working toward broad civil rights legislation. Russell lamented that even some southerners were not unified behind a strong states' rights position. He referred to what he called "Saturday night" states' righters who were not entirely reliable. He and his supporters were a minority, he wrote, which could not even count on all

"The Huddle": Russell, at right, discusses civil rights strategy with Senate colleagues John Stennis of Mississippi, at left, and Lister Hill of Alabama. (Photo courtesy of Wide World Photos, Inc., New York.)

senators and congressmen from the South. But Dick Russell maintained his stance. When a constituent wrote urging him to speak up more forcefully for the South, Russell replied sharply, "I yield to no man in the fight I have made in Congress to protect the South against legislation." He and others had defeated "all repressive legislation aimed at the South," Russell wrote, which had forced the NAACP and "their cohorts" to go to the Supreme Court and the White House for "illegal decisions and Executive orders to accomplish their ends."[10]

Southern senators who signed the manifesto received some sharp criticism. One of J. William Fulbright's constituents in Arkansas asked him how he could defy the Constitution. "Is this the end of the road for a Rhodes scholar?" she remarked. Others who believed that a man as well educated as Fulbright should not take such a position also attacked the Arkansas senator. In defending his support of the manifesto, Fulbright told one correspondent that he considered it "a moderate statement, somewhere between the two extremes advocating nullification on the one hand and the use of troops to enforce the decision on the other."[11]

Lyndon Johnson did not sign the manifesto, and Russell did not urge him to do so. The reason given was that as Senate majority leader Johnson had to work with all elements of the Democratic party, and he should not, therefore, be identified with a sectional position. The real reason, however, was that both Johnson and Russell knew that no one who signed such a document could ever become president of the United States. Russell was much more interested in pushing Johnson for president, which he was then doing, than in having another name on the manifesto.

Although the House passed a civil rights bill on July 23, 1956, before the national political conventions met in August, Russell succeeded in convincing the Senate not to take up the measure. At a Democratic Policy Committee meeting on June 27, Russell told his colleagues that "if we got into civil rights, we will have trouble even recessing over the convention." Senator Thomas Hennings of Missouri explained that in regard to civil rights his situation was "a little more complicated" than that of some of his colleagues because of "the large Negro vote" in his state. There were more than 125,000 black votes in the St. Louis area, he said, and another 50,000 in Kansas City. Nevertheless, Russell and other southern senators warned Majority Leader Johnson that bringing up a civil rights measure would provoke a long filibuster. Such lengthy debate would surely create bitterness that would carry over into the Democratic convention. With that threat, Johnson agreed to drop the matter.[12]

Once the presidential election of 1956 was over, the pressure to enact civil rights legislation became even more intense. Both parties included civil rights planks in their platforms, and Eisenhower had been committed to a civil rights bill since early in his administration. With Republicans strongly backing civil rights, supported by liberal Democrats, the time seemed ripe for passing civil rights legislation that had been before Congress in some form for nearly a decade.

On June 18, 1957, the House passed the administration's civil rights bill by the overwhelming vote of 286 to 126. The measure called for creating a civil rights division within the Department of Justice and establishing a bipartisan commission to investigate civil rights violations. More important, the Republican bill would empower the attorney general to seek court injunctions against those violating any person's civil rights and then to bring civil and criminal contempt proceedings against those disobeying the court order. The bill had both investigative and tough enforcement provisions.

It was now up to the Senate. Republican William F. Knowland of California believed that he had the votes to win Senate approval of the House bill. But he underestimated the raw power and political strategy of Dick Russell and Lyndon Johnson. By 1957 Russell recognized that he and his southern colleagues could not defeat the passage of some kind of civil rights measure. Thus, his strategy was to weaken the bill to such an extent that it would be ineffective and unlikely to disturb racial relations in the South. His first move to achieve this end was to deliver a carefully constructed speech on the Senate floor in hopes of creating doubts in the minds of some senators by pointing out the most objectionable aspects of the bill. One thing was certain—when Dick Russell spoke, senators and members of the Eisenhower administration listened.

On July 2, Russell arrived in the Senate chamber prepared to point out the great dangers that awaited the country if Congress enacted the civil rights bill. He argued that, while propagandists had presented the measure as a way to guarantee all Americans the right to vote, in reality it was a proposal that would give the attorney general legal and even military power "to compel the intermingling of the races in the public schools and in all places of public entertainment in the southern states." It was not a "moderate" bill at all, as the proponents claimed. Part 3, Russell said, would give the attorney general such extreme enforcement powers as to make any such law "a potential instrument of tyranny and persecution." He stated that "injunction suits could result in the jailing of American citizens for an indeterminate period, without the benefit of a jury trial." According to Russell, the omission of jury trials for violators of proposed civil rights legislation was a "gratuitous insult" to every white citizen in the South because it implied that white juries would not be fair in cases that involved blacks.

Passage of such a bill, Russell said, would create "unspeakable confusion, bitterness and bloodshed in a great section of our common country." If the federal government were to move into the South to enforce civil rights as this bill proposed, "the concentration camps may as well be prepared now, because there will not be enough jails to hold the people of the South who will oppose the use of raw federal power forcibly to comingle white and Negro children in the same schools and places of public entertainment."

Russell insisted that the "full implications" of the bill had probably never been explained to President Eisenhower. Then, turning to his colleagues outside the South, he warned that passing legislation to punish the South could become a precedent that might threaten life and society in other sections. Again holding up what he considered the horrors of Reconstruction, Russell stated that the bill under consideration was far worse for the South than anything ever proposed by Thad Stevens or Charles Sumner after the Civil War. Finally, Russell proposed that a national referendum be held to determine what people throughout the United States thought of the civil rights measure.

The heart of Russell's argument was that passage of the civil rights bill would extend federal powers to the point where they would be extremely dangerous to the nation's peace and tranquillity. While the current measure was aimed at the South, he said, uncurbed power in the hands of a reckless and vindictive attorney general could threaten people throughout the United States.

Russell gained much of what he wanted to achieve by his talk. The South's position got widespread publicity as newspapers and magazines gave his address much attention. The *U.S. News and World Report* carried nearly the full text in its July 12 issue. The *New York Times* and other major newspapers published substantial excerpts from it on July 3. Suddenly, too, Russell was in great demand for radio and television appearances. Writing to Charles Bloch on July 30, he said that he had been on so many radio and television programs "that I feel like a member of the Actor's Guild."[13] Congratulatory and supportive messages from all around the country poured into his office.

More important, however, were the doubts that his talk generated about Parts 3 and 4 of the bill in the minds of President Eisenhower and some senators. At a press conference on July 3, the president indicated that he wanted to take a closer look at some provisions of the bill. In reply to a reporter, he said: "I was reading part of the bill this morning and I—there were certain phrases I didn't completely understand. So before I make any more remarks on that I would want to talk to the Attorney General and see exactly what they do mean." To Russell this confirmed his claim that Eisenhower really did not know the bill's full implications. The president also indicated that he was willing to consider some compromise.[14]

Also on July 3, the southern caucus met in Russell's office to develop future strategy. Sitting at the head of the big round table, Russell explained to the fourteen colleagues who were present that he did not think the old filibuster tactic would work in this case. The South was not as solid as it once was. At most there were only eighteen members of the southern caucus, four less than a decade or so earlier. Moreover, conservative Republicans were no longer dependable allies. As Russell had mentioned earlier, he thought the approach should be to amend and weaken the bill so drastically that it could not hurt traditional social relations in the South. A filibuster should be used only as a last resort, he said. Strom Thurmond and Olin Johnston of South Carolina favored more militant action and even suggested marching to the White House to impress the president with the South's determination not to accept the civil rights bill. But Russell convinced his fellow southerners that such action would be unwise, and members of the caucus agreed to follow their leader. That evening he wrote former senator Walter George that the combination "of left-wing Democrats and Conservative Republicans" was forcing "our backs to the wall" but that he was trying "to find some way out . . . and we have no intention to surrender anytime soon."[15]

Dick Russell and Lyndon Johnson were in complete agreement on how to handle the Republican civil rights bill. Once Russell had portrayed the dangers of the proposed legislation, Johnson, as majority leader, would round up the votes to eliminate features of the measure most opposed by the southerners. This meant calling in political IOU's and arranging any necessary voting deals. No one was more skillful at political horse trading than the wily Texan.

Meanwhile, Russell would work on the president. On July 10, he went to the White House for a long visit with Eisenhower on the civil rights bill. For nearly an hour, Russell outlined what he considered the awful consequences if the bill were passed. The power proposed for the attorney general under Part 3, including the use of troops to enforce civil rights, Russell argued, would deny people their constitutional rights and violate American ideals and traditions. He painted the grim picture of federal troops forcing school integration in the South at bayonet point. After their conference, Russell said that the president's mind was "not closed" in regard to civil rights legislation.

It soon became clear that Eisenhower was having second thoughts about his own bill. He said that he was mainly interested in guaranteeing blacks the right to vote and that it might be best to restrict the bill to that issue.[16] When the president was asked at a news conference on July 17 if he believed the attorney general should have the power to bring suits on his own motion against school officials to achieve integration, Eisenhower replied that the request should first come "from local authorities."[17] Since local school boards in the South would not make any such requests, this statement, as Senator Douglas, who supported the bill, said, "pulled the rug out from under us." On July 22, the president wrote his friend E. E. Hazlett in North Carolina that change "must come gradually and with consideration of human feelings." He added that some of the language in the administration bill "has probably been too broad."[18]

Shortly before the Senate debate began on the civil rights bill, Johnson had arranged a political deal that achieved Russell's goal of weakening the measure. In 1956 the Senate had defeated a proposal for building a hydroelectric dam at Hells Canyon, Idaho. Although Russell had historically been a supporter of public power, he and a number of other southern senators voted against the Hells Canyon bill. The issue was again before the Senate in June 1957. Johnson convinced a number of southern senators that with civil rights legislation ready to be considered, they should vote for the Hells Canyon project. On June 21, five southerners—Russell, George Smathers, James Eastland, Sam Ervin, and Russell Long—changed their votes from a year earlier and helped carry the bill by a majority of 45 to 38. If those five senators had voted as they did in 1956, the bill would have been defeated.

Now Johnson concentrated on gathering votes of western senators and others for whom he had done favors to eliminate Part 3 of the Republican civil rights bill. Johnson arranged for Senator Clinton Anderson, a strong civil rights proponent, to present an amendment that would discard the objectionable features of Part 3. Anderson got Republican George Aiken of Vermont to cosponsor his amendment. Johnson had done his work well. On July 24, the Senate defeated Part 3 of the Republican bill by a vote of 52 to 38. A number of western Democratic senators repaid their southern colleagues who had voted for Hells Canyon a month before.

Having eliminated what southerners considered abusive powers in the hands of the attorney general, they turned now to insert a jury trial provision. Russell argued that in order to insure justice, a jury trial was absolutely essential in criminal contempt cases dealing with civil rights violators. On August 2, after a fourteen-hour session that went on beyond midnight, the tired senators finally voted to consider the jury trial amendment. Russell said that it was "very refreshing to see this body rise above sectional differences to guarantee the sacred right of trial by jury."[19] Five days later, the Senate passed the measure by a vote of 72 to 18. Although he had been a major actor in bringing about modification of the bill, Russell preserved his record with the home folks by voting against it. Russell told a reporter on August 3 that the bill was "infinitely less objectionable" than when the House passed it, but it was still unsatisfactory to him. To strong civil rights backers, however, the Senate

Senator Lyndon B. Johnson, center, and others hold 1957 civil rights bill while Senator Russell at left refuses to even look at it. (Photo courtesy of Wide World Photos, Inc., New York.)

bill appeared weak and ineffective. Observing the action of the Senate, Thomas L. Stokes wrote in the *Washington Evening Star* on August 5 that Johnson had nearly compromised the civil rights bill into oblivion. In this case, Stokes said, he was "the errand boy for Senator Richard B. Russell, who put Lyndon Johnson in the post of leadership." Both men shared the overall strategy, Stokes believed, "with most going to Dick Russell."[20]

By the end of August, after hard bargaining, the Senate and House had reconciled the differences in their bills, and on August 29, two days after the House acted, the Senate finally approved the Civil Rights Act of 1957 by a vote of 60 to 15. Russell, of course, voted nay. The final drama did not end, however, before Strom Thurmond, against the wishes of Russell and other southern senators, delivered a record-breaking twenty-four-hour-and-eighteen-minute filibuster against the bill. Thurmond's action was an embarrassment to Russell, although as an advocate of unlimited debate, he could not object.[21]

This law was a clear victory for Lyndon Johnson—and for Dick Russell. The majority leader could say that he pushed through the first general civil rights bill since 1876, something that strengthened him with the liberals in the Democratic party. He had kept the Democrats from angrily splitting over the issue and weakening the party for the next presidential election. Russell could claim that he had so defanged the final bill that it would not really threaten southern race relations. Calling Russell the "Rear-guard Commander," *Time* magazine carried Russell's picture on its cover on August 12, the second time in five years, and described his work on civil rights as "one of the notable performances of Senate History."[22]

Praise for Russell and his work came from many quarters. But he most appreciated compliments from fellow senators. Colleague William Fulbright wrote that he could not leave Washington without letting Russell know "what a wonderful job you did in managing the very difficult Civil Rights battle." Fulbright added that "your restraint and wisdom and good judgment have never been better." Then he concluded, "I am confident you took the right road, and you deserve the gratitude of all of us."[23]

Russell realized, as did Johnson and other political realists, that the compromise worked out by southerners in 1957 was only a temporary victory. Nevertheless, the measure had been weakened far beyond what seemed possible when the fight began. "Looking back over the past month," Russell wrote on August 6, "it appeared that we have almost accomplished the impossible in striking the most vicious provisions from this bill." He was tremendously gratified by the support of "my home folks in Georgia," which, he wrote a friend, was a constant source of strength to him during the legislative battle.[24] When a constituent remarked that he was "just fighting a losing battle," Russell admitted as much. "I am trying to delay [integration] ten years if I'm not lucky, 200 years if I am," Russell explained. As it turned out, effective civil rights legislation passed Congress even before his so-called unlucky ten years had elapsed.[25]

Why did Russell refuse to lead a filibuster against the 1957 civil rights bill as he had done so successfully on earlier occasions? On August 30, the day after the bill's final passage, he rose in the Senate to review the political realities of the previous two months. Although he described the civil rights bill as thoroughly bad, dangerous, and even vicious legislation, he said that southerners did not filibuster because such action could not have been successful. Conditions were much different in 1957 than they had been earlier, he explained. Opponents of the bill simply did not have enough votes to defeat a cloture motion. If southerners had organized a filibuster, a vote would have passed to limit debate and an even more "vicious bill" would have been approved. To have passed the original bill, according to Russell, would have led to "unparalleled disaster" in the South.

Recognizing the overwhelming political support for some kind of civil rights legislation, Russell said that he and his colleagues adopted the policy of appealing to the reason, justice, and fair play of fellow senators. Considering that they only had eighteen absolutely reliable votes, Russell declared, "I can, in all modesty, say for myself, and my associates that the legislative history of the Senate does not reveal as great a victory by so few senators as the one we attained." This would not have been possible, however, except for the "brave and fair minded" senators from other sections who "rallied to the cause of constitutional government" and helped to eliminate the bill's worst features. In the final analysis, southerners, with the help of other colleagues, had kept the "withering hand of the Federal Government out of our schools and social order." That, he said, was "the sweetest victory of my 25 years as a Senator." Then expressing his deepest emotions, Russell concluded that he had enjoyed a full and satisfying life but that he would give up the remainder of it if such a sacrifice would "guarantee the preservation of a civilization of two races of unmixed blood in the land I love."[26] Lives would be given in the racial struggle but not by Russell and the segregationists; the sacrifices would come from those fighting to abolish legal segregation.

Meanwhile, Russell watched sporadic moves toward school desegregation in the South with dismay. By 1957 token integration had occurred in a number of southern towns and cities where historically segregation had prevailed. But up to that time change had been meager. The whole question of school desegregation was dramatized in September in Little Rock, Arkansas. Local and state authorities failed to provide protection for black students who, under court order, were permitted to attend previously all-white Central High School. On September 24, President Eisenhower sent federal troops to Little Rock to enforce the ruling of the federal court and to maintain law and order.[27]

To say that southerners were shocked and bitter at the president's action is an understatement. Probably no one was more angry at Eisenhower's action than Russell. He declared that the situation in Little Rock demonstrated the "folly and danger of politically dictated federal power from Washington" trying to enforce uniform social patterns for the whole country. He admitted that nothing could prevent the president from using "overwhelming military might to take over functions of the state," but he said that did not give him any constitutional right to do so. He added that, while "totalitarian rule" might "put Negro children in white schools in Little Rock," it would "have a calamitous effect on race relations and on the cause of national unity."[28]

On September 26, Russell sent Eisenhower a long telegram protesting what he called the "high-handed and illegal methods" used by the armed forces to compel a mixing of the races in Little Rock. The rights of American citizens were being violated, Russell stated, "by applying tactics which must have been copied from ... the office of Hitler's Storm Troopers." Russell's complaint was in response to the arrest of some white troublemakers in Little Rock. Russell said there was no need for federal troops unless the president was trying to "intimidate and overawe" all those who opposed race mixing.

In reply, Eisenhower explained to Russell that when states sought to frustrate a federal court order or failed to protect people's constitutional rights, the president must act to provide the needed enforcement and protection. To do otherwise would result in "anarchy and the dissolution of the Union." Eisenhower resented Russell's reference to Hitler's storm troopers. He told Russell that in Germany troops had been used to achieve the goals of a "ruthless dictator," while in Little Rock they had served "to preserve the institutions of free government."[29]

Passage of the Civil Rights Act of 1957, the Little Rock crisis, and some token integration of schools in a few areas of the South caused Russell great distress—even pain. He brooded over approaching changes and the gradual disappearance of the southern social and racial structure he knew and loved. He took some comfort in the hundreds of congratulatory letters and telegrams that he received from his constituents. It was satisfying to know that he represented them so accurately. But he knew that segregation could not be preserved. He kept saying that the situation would be different if the masses of people knew the facts, but it is difficult to believe that he was really convinced by his own rhetoric. Russell, however, could not force himself to admit publicly and openly to the reality that conditions were going to change. Late in September 1957, an Atlanta attorney who deplored the *Brown* decision wrote Russell about the facts of national life. "Is not the South faced with the proposition of either complying or else having a civil war?" Then he got to the heart of the issue. "Why don't Southern political leaders frankly state that the segregation cause is lost and advise their constituents that a civil war would be unthinkable" and also hopeless? Russell replied that he abhorred violence and recognized that the race question must be solved in a rational manner. But, he repeated, he could never condone intermingling of the races. On the matter of desegregated schools, Russell stated a year later that the fight "to preserve the white race in Georgia" had hardly begun. There could not be such a thing as "a little integration," he wrote. "If you do this it will not be long until all the doors are open to the integrated flood."[30]

Russell could not have been happy over the support given to the president during the Little Rock crisis. Ralph McGill endorsed Eisenhower's action and encouraged him by assuring the president that there was "a fifth column of decency here in the South which applauds your action." McGill admitted that he did not personally favor desegregation. "I would much have preferred for things to have stayed as they were," he wrote Charles Bloch. The old way, McGill said, was more comfortable, generated less tension, and produced less trouble. But there was a larger issue, McGill insisted; he could not "in conscience or in Christian belief" accept the principle that citizens of the United States should be treated differently under the law.[31]

One of the most frustrating things about trying to work out racial problems in the South, according to McGill, was the lack of sincere and honest political leadership. Although most Deep South senators, congressmen, governors, and state legislators would privately admit that desegregation was coming, "so long as defiance and subterfuge will serve they will make no move toward even token integration." Then, he added, "they put their political careers ahead of their country," something, incidentally, that should not have surprised as keen an observer as McGill.[32]

McGill had correctly concluded that Russell could never play a constructive or positive role in solving racial problems. He and his closest advisers were too intransigent to ever compromise on segregation. Charles Bloch, on whom Russell often depended for legal advice, wrote McGill a long letter in November 1958 concluding that the federal government could "never compel Georgia to operate integrated schools—never, never." Russell himself viewed integration as an evil comparable to communism. He wrote a friend early in 1957 that he would fight both communism and integration "with every power at my command."

In characterizing southern extremists, McGill pictured Russell as a "sick and somewhat broken man [Russell had been quite ill in the fall of 1958], almost frantically trying to be 'right' on the racial question so as to have no opposition in the summer primary of 1960." Senator Herman Talmadge, McGill believed, was acting somewhat more statesmanlike because he did not come up for reelection so soon. McGill told President Eisenhower that he could expect Russell to become "even more frantic than usual" on the race question to discourage political opposition. McGill was right about Russell's paramount concern with opposing civil rights and preserving segregation, but he was wrong in saying that Russell was motivated by political fear. He had no worries about his forthcoming reelection in 1960. However, his civil rights position surely enhanced his standing with voters in Georgia. At a White House conference on August 26, 1957, Russell told Eisenhower that he had gained so much credibility among Georgians as a result of the civil rights fight that he did not need to worry about opposition in the next election.[33]

By the late 1950s, the racial issue was influencing Russell's thinking and actions on a variety of major national questions. For example, he had been an enthusiastic supporter of federal aid to education since arriving in Washington a quarter of a century earlier, but he voted against the National Defense Education Act in 1958. He had explained earlier that if Congress passed such a bill, "I am completely confident that within a year or two at best we will be confronted with provisions on appropriation bills that will deny funds to states that do not integrate their schools." In opposing the National Defense Education Act, he found himself teamed up with a few ultraconservative southern Democrats and Republicans. Several members of the southern caucus, including Fulbright, McClellan, Smathers, Ellender, and Long, were among those who favored the legislation but not Russell. He saw the new law as simply another avenue through which the federal government could intervene in southern schools and destroy segregation.

He also opposed statehood for Hawaii and Alaska partially on racial grounds. His main objection to admitting those territories as states was his belief that the federal government would have to fully control them for purposes of national defense. However, he wrote that admitting noncontiguous Hawaii would surely bring demands from Puerto Rico, Guam, and the Virgin Islands for statehood. He did not think that "we should start admitting states scattered all around the oceans of the earth, particularly in view of the fact that the population of these possessions are very dissimilar to the population of the continental United States."[34]

From Russell's viewpoint, the pressures from civil rights advocates in Washington were never ending. Early in 1959, he wrote his old friend Frank Scarlett in Brunswick that he could not accept an invitation to go hunting because he did not dare leave Washington. The antisouthern attitudes, he wrote, had "almost become a national disease." He had to stay in Washington to protect the South's interests.[35] At that time, Russell was trying to stop the critics of cloture from making it easier to limit debate in the Senate. Despite his opposition, the Senate voted 72 to 22 to change the rule so that debate could be cut off by two-thirds of those present and voting instead of by two-thirds of the entire Senate. Russell admitted that this rule change would not greatly weaken filibuster efforts in light of modern communication and transportation that could bring absent senators to the Capitol quickly. Also, Russell had presented this same rule change as a compromise late in 1958.[36]

In January 1960, President Eisenhower proposed further civil rights legislation, and the majority of Congress seemed more than willing to oblige. The bill called for authorizing the attorney general to send federal representatives to areas where people had been denied the right to vote. Distressed by the possibility of officials from the Department of Justice invading local communities that might have discriminated against black voters, Russell labeled the measure an unconstitutional "force bill." It was aimed strictly at the South, he said, and was reminiscent of "carpetbagger regimes" and "scalawag rule" during Reconstruction.

Russell organized the southern senators for a lengthy filibuster. Lyndon Johnson wanted to pass the bill and announced that starting on February 29 he would keep the Senate continuously in session until a civil rights bill passed. But even Johnson did not realize the determination of his friend from Georgia. Russell was not the least intimidated by Johnson's threat and declared that he would institute "legislative torture" by demanding frequent quorum calls, which would require senators to appear on the floor. A few past-midnight quorum calls, Russell believed, would soon discourage the continuous sessions. Also, Russell said that he would halt all Senate business by objecting to any unanimous-consent agreements.[37]

He divided the southern senators into squads of three to carry on the filibuster. Each squad had an eight-hour shift on the Senate floor. That way, the Senate proceedings could be properly guarded without physically exhausting the eighteen senators. Russell personally kept a close eye on everything that went on in the Senate chamber. After a few days, Johnson and those favoring civil rights were dead tired, and they saw no hope of breaking the filibuster, so the majority leader called off the continuous sessions. Then a cloture vote was taken, but it went down to defeat as Russell rallied every vote he could find. Despite defeating a cloture vote, southerners agreed to let a weak civil rights measure pass. Other than permitting federal judges to appoint "voting referees" in case of racial discrimination, the Civil Rights Act of 1960 achieved very little. It could be said that while Russell and his small band of diehards had not been entirely successful, they had not lost much. After passage of the 1960 law, Senator Harry F. Byrd said that eighteen southern senators, "superbly led by Senator Richard B. Russell," had "demonstrated the effectiveness of courageous massive resistance."[38]

His attempt to hold back the tide of civil rights was an ever-increasing burden. It took an unbelievable amount of Russell's time and energy. Not only did his leadership against civil rights in the Senate require hours of preparation and meetings, but his correspondence was heavy and the requests for talks and public appearances arrived in large numbers. In March 1960, he advised his staff that in correspondence he wanted to avoid using the term "civil rights." He instructed them to use such phrases as "fight for constitutional government" and when the term "civil rights" was used, to always precede it with "misnamed."[39]

Russell's annoyance with the term "civil rights" could, of course, have no effect on the force of the movement. He realized that fundamental changes were coming, but he refused to openly admit their inevitability or to work toward some compromise solution. Although he was known as a great compromiser on most political issues, on legislation that would bring integration he was absolutely unbending.

16

Russell and the Cold War

===

On December 1, 1955, Dick Russell and other members of Georgia's congressional delegation attended the State Chamber of Commerce luncheon in Atlanta. When his turn came to make a few remarks, Russell commented briefly on world affairs. Although the Soviet Union had recently exchanged a frown for a smile, he said, the fundamental aim of the Russians was to conquer the world. He did not believe that the United States and the Soviet Union would become involved in war, however, "so long as we remain strong." To achieve the necessary strength may be expensive and tiring, he concluded, "but bear the burden we must do. We must weary with it until God in His wisdom will send some event to bring the Cold War to a close."[1]

Russell had been espousing similar cold war views since shortly after World War II. The world, he wrote in 1951, was divided into two hostile camps—"Russia and her satellites" and the "United States and some of our allies." According to Russell, the Russians were imperialistic and bent on world domination. Only superior military force by the United States could hold them in check. Although he favored negotiating differences with the Soviet Union whenever possible, he insisted that this must be done "from strength rather than from weakness." Raw power was the only thing the Russians understood, he said time and again. Russell believed that the United Nations served some useful purposes, but he scoffed at the idea that it could ever maintain peace. The only way to assure peace and independence, and America's "blessed freedoms," he declared, was through national military and economic power. From Russell's viewpoint, the country could have no higher priority than strong and invincible military capability.

Russell tried to translate these ideas into concrete policies during the 1950s. In the first place, he gave his unswerving support to a military buildup during the Eisenhower years, including Universal Military

Training. He also insisted on maintaining superiority in nuclear weapons. In order to achieve his defense objectives, Russell was willing to accept deficit spending and to delay tax cuts. National survival, he said, was all important. Russell also continued his opposition to spending large sums on foreign aid because he thought those expenditures drained money away from larger outlays for manpower and military hardware at home. He had little faith in America's NATO allies, or in recipients of American aid, as genuine barriers to expansionism. On one occasion, he suggested taking the whole foreign aid appropriation and transferring it to the U.S. Air Force! Although Russell and President Eisenhower worked closely together on most defense matters, Russell pushed the president to do more than Eisenhower thought was politically and economically prudent. Although Russell once told Eisenhower at a White House conference that he would never quarrel with the president on defense matters, that was not always the case. Russell, however, consistently held that defense was not a partisan issue.[2]

When the Eisenhower administration came into office in January 1953, Republican leaders were determined to revise American postwar foreign policy. John Foster Dulles, the new secretary of state, had been critical both before and during the presidential campaign of the Democratic policy of trying to contain communism from further expansion throughout the world. That policy would exhaust the nation's "economic, political and moral vitals," Dulles said. It was a never-ending and no-win policy, which would leave countless millions of people under the yoke of communism forever.

According to Dulles, the United States should develop a "dynamic" foreign policy that would not be content with containment but look toward helping captive peoples free themselves from Soviet control. On January 15, 1953, he told the Senate Committee on Foreign Relations that the United States must keep "alive the hope of liberation." The way to deal with the Soviets was to develop the means to strike quickly at aggression wherever it might occur. With atom bombs and strategic air and sea power, aggression could be halted before it began. This was dubbed the policy of massive retaliation. But Dulles would not rely on military power alone to liberate enslaved peoples. He believed that moral and psychological force could also be effective in rolling back the outposts of communism.[3]

The Dulles proposals of massive retaliation and liberation of peoples controlled by communism were more rhetoric than policy. As it turned out, the Eisenhower administration followed about the same policies of containment as Truman had pursued. As long as the president took a strong anti-Communist stance, he could count on the support of southern Democrats, including Russell. Believing in a bipartisan foreign policy, and hoping for a national consensus, Russell declared: "My disposition is to try to help General Eisenhower in every possible way. Our big objective now is world peace and times are too perilous to indulge in partisanship for the sake of partisanship."[4]

The Republicans wanted a defense policy for minimum cost so they could keep their campaign promises to cut government expenses and lower taxes. In February 1953, the president talked about maintaining adequate military power "within the limits of endurable strain upon our economy." President Eisenhower submitted a defense budget that was about $5 billion less than Truman had recommended. Most of the reduction was in appropriations for the air force. This greatly alarmed Russell. Speaking on July 23, the same day the Senate voted on defense appropriations, Russell argued vigorously against defense cuts, especially for the air force. He considered air power fundamental to national protection. While admitting that the number of planes would not be cut back immediately by the proposed budget, he expressed deep concern over what he called a drastic decrease in "the rate of growth of the military strength of the United States." It might be acceptable to delay or stretch out the acquisition of some military hardware, he said, but not in the case of airplanes. Advance orders were critical, he continued, because one could not acquire planes "as one buys toys in a dime store." He insisted that the projected expenditures would slow deliveries in 1954, 1955, and 1956.

Then Russell launched into a discussion of the dangers of unpreparedness. He declared that Americans had apparently learned nothing from history. Twice in a single generation, 1918 and 1945, he argued, the United States had dismantled the "mightiest fighting machines ever known on earth" before it had been assured of peace. Moreover, Russell believed that the United States had invited the North Korean attack because American military strength had been permitted to decline. This unpreparedness, he declared, had "brought darkness to thousands of homes" and sorrow to mothers and fathers throughout America. Only greater military strength would save the nation from the "terrors of a third World War."

Some had argued that more defense could be bought with less money if waste were eliminated in the military. Russell frankly admitted that some waste existed and stated that it should be eliminated if possible. But waste, in his view, was not nearly as bad as being thrown into a war unprepared. American military effort, he said, must match or exceed that of the Soviets because they could not be appealed to on the basis of reason or humanitarianism. They understood only one thing, he said—power.[5]

Despite Russell's efforts to maintain higher defense budgets, he knew that he was engaged in a losing battle. As he put it, word had "come down" from the White House and the Defense Department as to what should be appropriated. In calling for greater defense outlays, Russell found himself in a difficult position with Eisenhower as president. People looked to the president, who had spent a lifetime in the military, as an expert in such matters, and they considered him a more reliable authority on defense needs than any senator or group of senators. As Russell told Arthur Godfrey, the radio and television personality, the average person regarded Eisenhower "as the last word in military knowledge" and accepted "his assurances that what he has requested is adequate."[6]

This did not keep Russell from charging that the administration's policy on defense was shortsighted and inadequate. In explaining his position to constituents, Russell said he wanted a balanced budget but would not endanger American security by canceling orders for "planes, tanks or other necessary weapons of war." He wrote that he would not vote for a cut in "a single plane." In September Russell appeared on "Meet the Press" and declared that there was no way the administration could cut $5 billion from the defense budget and still adequately protect the country from a possible Russian atomic attack.[7]

Not all of Russell's close associates on the Armed Services Committee believed that the United States was as unprepared as Russell seemed to think. Senator Stennis visited American military installations in Europe in late 1953 and reported to Russell that he was "tremendously impressed and encouraged at the enormous striking power that we could put into action on many fronts in a matter of hours should we be attacked." The United States, he said, had "overwhelming power of retaliation." Like Russell, though, Stennis wrote that "I think our proper ultimate place in the European defense should be largely confined to air power."[8]

However, not even a favorable report on American defenses by a close friend could convince Russell that the United States had adequate defenses. He especially objected to the Republican policy of setting a figure for defense and then fitting expenditures for military hardware and troop strength within that amount. For example, in late 1953, under pressure from Defense Secretary Charles E. Wilson, the Joint Chiefs of Staff agreed to a gradual reduction of forces and a ceiling on expenditures for defense of $33.8 billion by 1957. New money appropriated at the administration's request dropped even lower, to $28.8 billion for fiscal 1955. To Russell this seemed foolhardy and dangerous to the nation's security. Some of Russell's closest friends occasionally joshed him about his intense concern for greater military strength. Milton Young once remarked that southern political leaders seemed more interested in military preparedness than those from other parts of the country. He asked Russell why this seemed to be the case. Russell replied, "Milt, you'd be more military minded too if Sherman had crossed North Dakota."

Despite the fact that Russell returned to the chairmanship of the Armed Services Committee and ranked second on the Appropriations Committee, in January 1955, he was unable to prevent a variety of cuts in defense appropriations. Although those favoring a smaller military establishment pointed to the death of Stalin in 1953 and the subsequent lessening of tensions between the United States and the Soviet Union, Russell rejected the idea that the Soviets had become more reasonable and cooperative or less imperialistic. Besides, he argued, any effective negotiations must be backed by adequate force. Discussing defense matters shortly before the president left for the Geneva Summit in July 1955, Russell attacked the administration's plan to reduce the number of marines, calling it "tragic."[9]

On May 18, Russell declared that the Armed Services Committee would soon call in high-ranking military officers to question them about all aspects of air defense "from guided missiles on down." Reports that the Russians had large, intercontinental bombers capable of dropping atom bombs on American cities, Russell said, had failed to sufficiently alert the administration to dangers from the Soviets. Although Congress could not create or operate military equipment, he stated, lawmakers were "ready and willing" to supply whatever was needed to assure that "we have an adequate Air Force."[10]

According to Russell, the Strategic Air Command was the principal guarantor of peace in the world. Speaking on the Senate floor in June 1956, he said the knowledge that the United States could deliver an atom bomb anywhere in the world had been the main factor in preserving peace after World War II. Throughout the 1950s, Russell urged the Eisenhower administration to step up spending on the air force. The people of the free world, he said, were depending on American air power. Russell constantly repeated his devotion to economy, but when dealing with the country's security, he said, "I want to see planes first, and then consider the cost in dollars."[11]

Time and again, Russell argued that only the most formidable American striking force could prevent war. Without such air superiority, he envisioned country after country becoming intimidated by the Soviets and either seeking a neutral status or actually shifting over to the Russian orbit. He answered critics who said that fewer B52s should be built because they would become obsolete by arguing that the same was true of other military high technology. So what, he replied. The B36s had become obsolete, but they had kept the Russians behind the Iron Curtain. The fact that they did not have to be used, and that they had to be replaced with newer models to continue deterring the Soviets, just proved his point, Russell said. They had successfully kept the peace, and it was the best money the nation ever spent. Russell urged spending more on defense, even if funds had to be taken away from other government programs. But the opposite was happening. "The policy of increasing the appropriations for foreign aid and for many domestic activities while reducing our armed strength," Russell wrote, "is completely incomprehensible to me."[12]

What dismayed Russell was the Eisenhower administration's continued requests for huge expenditures for military and economic assistance to foreign countries while at the same time reducing funds for the American defense establishment. During 1953–56, the United States spent $12 billion on military assistance and $6.8 billion on economic aid around the world. In 1955, for example, the administration reduced manpower in the marines but requested an additional $300 million for foreign economic aid. This was bad policy, Russell said.[13]

Every year Russell would attack the foreign aid appropriation as being excessive and not in the national interest. He declared repeatedly that the billions being spent on foreign assistance prevented Americans from enjoying some tax reduction. When Congress was considering an emergency aid package for the Middle East early in 1957, shortly after the Suez crisis, Russell objected to what he called throwing money around the world to placate people. He criticized Secretary Dulles for promoting no other solution to international problems than spending more American dollars. At the opening of Congress in 1956, he said that the State Department was "so sterile of ideas that the only answer they have to the Russians is to ask for more money."[14] When U.S. diplomats faced a problem, he stated, their only answer "is to pump a few more millions from the pockets of our taxpayers into the troubled area."[15] This was the easy way, he stated, but it was not very effective or in the nation's best interest.

Russell's objections and complaints, along with those of others, did help to reduce foreign aid expenditures. Combined military and economic assistance dropped from $5.9 billion in 1953 to $4.1 billion in 1955 and to $3.9 billion in 1957. But this was still far in excess of what Russell thought the United States should provide. Moreover, he believed more American aid should be in the form of loans rather than grants. In an interview on May 23, 1957, he told a reporter that the total foreign aid program should be cut to $2.5 billion at most and that all economic assistance should be abolished except for "a reasonable technical program."[16]

Besides the cost, by the late 1950s Russell saw another disturbing aspect of foreign economic aid. It was taking on the character of permanent policy. Initially, American assistance was considered to be temporary. It was offered to help people help themselves, or so Russell believed. But as the years passed and the war-torn countries recovered, foreign economic assistance still flowed worldwide in large quantities. Was there to be no end to this burden on American taxpayers, he asked. As he stated early in 1956, he was opposed to any "permanent foreign aid program."[17]

Russell also believed that foreign economic aid was extremely wasteful. He explained to one constituent that if people could see how their tax money was wasted in the name of foreign aid, "we would have a political revolution in the country." Moreover, it had not won America many friends. The Soviet Union, he said, provided very few economic grants and only modest loans. Even with such meager aid, the Soviets in many cases were able to "undo all of the benefits" supposedly coming from large American grants. Russell feared that the United States would bleed itself economically to the point where the American standard of living would be threatened. When Senator Fulbright appealed to him to support the foreign aid bill in 1959, Russell replied that, despite his personal affection and respect for his Arkansas colleague, he could not vote to increase the appropriation.[18]

Eisenhower used all of his persuasive powers to convince Russell to support foreign aid. The president even solicited advice from Lyndon Johnson on how he should approach Russell. For example, on the morning of August 26, 1957, Johnson had breakfast with Eisenhower at the White House, where they discussed how Russell might be convinced to back a larger foreign aid package. Johnson suggested that Eisenhower visit with Russell off the record and appeal to the senator's patriotism and high regard for the presidency. General Wilton B. Persons, Eisenhower's legislative liaison man, mentioned that in talking to Russell the president might get Russell's attention by casually mentioning the possible closing of some military installations in Georgia. The president acted promptly and called Russell to the White House that same evening at 5:30. Eisenhower and Russell had a pleasant visit, but the president said he did not get far with the senator. Russell told Eisenhower that he had made so many speeches against foreign aid that he could not vote for the appropriations bill. As Doris Fleeson wrote, Russell had become "the leader of a sustained attack on the whole aid concept."[19]

While Russell fought to keep foreign aid expenditures as low as possible, he insisted on providing increased funds for the latest weapons for the Defense Department. Indeed, he saw a direct relation between these two matters. Highly technical weapons were very expensive, and the cost increased as the degree of sophistication grew. There would be sufficient money for the latest planes, missiles, and other military equipment, Russell believed, if expenditures were reduced for overseas economic aid.

In 1958 and 1959, Russell intensified his criticism of foreign aid. He spoke and wrote against it at every opportunity. Referring to it sometimes as "dollar diplomacy," he repeated time and again that it was a losing policy. He said that he hoped to make foreign aid as distasteful and unpopular as he could among the American people. Throwing money at diplomatic problems, Russell argued, could not have a long-term positive effect or enhance America's position in the world. But like so many other policies that Russell opposed, he was unable to block what he considered an unending flow of American money to every nook and cranny of the world. The harder he fought higher appropriations for economic aid, the more expenditures seemed to increase. In 1956 and 1957, economic assistance amounted to about $1.5 billion a year, in 1958 it rose to $1.8 billion, and in 1959 to $3.3 billion.[20]

Outside of foreign aid, Russell usually worked cooperatively with the Eisenhower administration on most national defense and foreign policy issues. He was regularly included in the bipartisan congressional leadership conferences at the White House that Eisenhower called to discuss international affairs. The common format of these meetings, which often lasted two or three hours, was for Secretary Dulles to review the situation around the world followed by remarks by the president. Sometimes Eisenhower would speak first. In any event, the president was not a passive bystander but played a positive leadership role in these meetings. Then the senators and congressmen had an opportunity to ask questions and to make suggestions. Occasionally, Russell would raise a question, but most of the time he would listen instead of talk. Russell was one legislative leader whom the president could count on not to reveal any information that was supposed to be kept secret.[21] When one examines the records of Eisenhower's bipartisan foreign policy meetings, it is clear that Russell was considered a leader among that small congressional group. Yet, the minutes do not reveal that he played a leading part in the discussions or pushed hard for any particular policy, except to resist enlargements of foreign economic aid.

The president also called Russell in from time to time to help solve specific problems. For example, on June 24, 1959, Eisenhower met with Senators Johnson, Fulbright, and Russell to deal with a resolution introduced by Senator Henry Jackson on May 5. This resolution proposed to investigate the "effectiveness of present governmental organization and procedures for the development and execution of national policy for survival in the contest with communism." Eisenhower strongly opposed the resolution because he believed that it was the first step by Congress or a congressional committee to involve itself with the National Security Council.[22] He feared that any inquiry into the National Security Council would create a conflict between the executive and Congress. Since the council advised the president, a crisis could easily develop if a congressional committee decided to investigate the advice the council had been giving Eisenhower since the president believed such advice should be kept confidential.

Neither Johnson nor Russell liked the idea. Johnson had been holding up action on the resolution in the Democratic Steering Committee, and Russell said that he had advised Jackson the previous February not to proceed with any investigation. After some further discussion by the president, Russell came up with the idea of how best to proceed. He suggested that Eisenhower write a letter to Johnson stating that it was a poor time to conduct such a study and that any inquiry of the National Security Council could create serious differences between the president and Congress. Eisenhower liked that approach and said he would have a letter in Johnson's hands the following day.

The president wrote Johnson that any investigation of the National Security Council would invade presidential prerogatives in regard to national security. To pursue such a course in a time of dangerous international crises could only produce "harmful consequences." The council had been very helpful to the president, and he would not like to see any arm of Congress impinge upon the process to the point where members would withhold their "frank and vigorous expression" on critical security matters. He concluded by urging that no further action be taken on Jackson's resolution. The Russell strategy worked, and Jackson's move for an investigation was toned down to the point where the council would just be studied, something to which the president had no objection. When Bryce Harlow, the president's assistant who wrote the letter, sent a copy to Russell, he added a handwritten note: "Dear Dick—hope this is the kind of thing you had in mind as being most effective—*Many, Many* thanks."[23]

Foreign economic assistance was not the only major aspect of foreign policy to which Russell vigorously objected. He was strongly opposed to any direct U.S. involvement in Southeast Asia. While he had supported the Korean War as a reaction to outright aggression by the North Korean Communists, he believed that any further land campaigns in the Far East should be avoided at all costs. By 1954, however, conditions were shaping up in Indochina that threatened to draw Americans into the region.

Following World War II, instead of supporting an independence movement for the people of French Indochina, the United States backed the French as they tried to reassert their colonial authority in the region. Despite some $2 billion worth of American aid, by early 1954 the French were on the verge of defeat. As far as the United States was concerned, the question was whether Americans should become directly involved by providing air power and possibly some maintenance personnel. As the French position became more precarious, President Eisenhower instructed Secretary Dulles to call congressional leaders to the White House on Saturday, April 3, to discuss the matter. Secretary Dulles; Assistant Secretary of State Thruston Morton; Admiral Arthur W. Radford, Chairman of the Joint Chiefs of Staff; and other administrative officials were on hand to present the case for American intervention to eight congressional leaders—five senators and three congressmen.

Secretary Dulles and Admiral Radford feared that defeat of the French would threaten the free world and said they hoped for a congressional resolution supporting American air attacks on the Vietnamese who had surrounded the French at Dien Bien Phu. At first Republican Majority Leader William Knowland seemed sympathetic, but when Lyndon Johnson and Dick Russell finished discussing the matter, none of the legislators expressed support for use of American air power in Vietnam. Johnson, who at that time still relied heavily on Russell for advice on major policy matters, talked first because of his position as minority leader. He stoutly opposed the ideas advanced by Radford and Dulles. Russell was even more vehement against such a move, and, as he recalled later, "the discussion got a bit heated." Russell argued that involving Americans in Indochina could have two disastrous consequences. In the first place, it might bring China into the Vietnam conflict. But, more important, it could well be the first step in sending American ground troops to Vietnam, although Dulles denied any such intention. To Russell, nothing could be more foolhardy. According to Senator Knowland, Russell said that American action probably could not be limited to air strikes. "Once you've committed the flag, you've committed the country. There's no turning back; if you involve the American Air Force, why, you've involved the nation." He told the assembled officials that he "was weary of seeing American soldiers being used as gladiators to be thrown into every arena around the world." Writing an old friend a few days after the White House conference on Vietnam, Russell said that the situation in Indochina "causes me very grave concern."

Strong congressional opposition and Dulles's failure to get other countries to cooperate in any action forced the administration to give up any immediate intervention. In May 1954, the French stronghold of Dien Bien Phu fell to the Vietnamese and France was ready to leave Indochina. In July a conference was called in Geneva to deal with problems in the region. One result was to divide Vietnam at the seventeenth parallel with the Communists in control of North Vietnam.

Later in the summer, there was another move to help the anti-Communist South Vietnamese. Knowing that Russell was vigorously opposed to anything that might lead to American intervention in the area, Thruston Morton called Russell in Winder and said he would like to fly to Georgia and visit with the senator. Over lunch in Atlanta, Morton told Russell that the administration intended to send additional arms and some technicians to Vietnam to assist the South Vietnamese. Morton made it clear that he was not asking for Russell's advice but was simply keeping him informed as to what was being done. Russell was deeply disappointed. He was also frustrated because a few months earlier he had believed that he had played a major role in turning back American involvement. He told Morton that he would support the flag but that he feared intervention could lead to a long, drawn-out conflict that would be very costly in blood and money. But again Russell found himself unable to stop a policy favored by the administration, and over the next few years, the country gradually deepened its involvement in Vietnam.[24]

In considering American defenses, Russell had a keen interest in visiting the nation's military bases in Europe. In the late summer of 1955, he decided to visit American military installations in Western Europe and then take a trip to the Soviet Union. Russell much preferred to travel with one or two companions rather than with a group of senators or other high government officials. He believed that he could learn more when he went alone and that less time would be spent at social affairs. On his 1955 trip, he took Lieutenant Colonel Edward N. Hathaway, a representative from the Office of Legislative Liaison of the Department of the Army. He wrote a constituent that it had been four years since he had visited "our overseas stations, and with the immense amounts of money that we are now spending there I do not feel that I can delay an inspection any longer."

Russell and Hathaway sailed from New York for London on August 19. They visited American air bases in England and then went on to Spain before stopping in Paris on September 5 to see General Alfred Gruenther at the Allied headquarters in Europe. During the next ten days, they went to Wiesbaden, Heidelberg, and Frankfurt visiting American troops and talking to military leaders. They stopped at a number of other cities before arriving at Helsinki on September 19. There Russell and Hathaway were joined by Ruben Efron, a Washington lawyer who would serve as their interpreter in the Soviet Union.

By that time, Russell was tired and had a bad cold. Nevertheless, on September 23, he and Hathaway left by train for Leningrad. It was cold and the train was not heated. Russell wrote that he had never experienced such an uncomfortable day. Efron had to be left behind because of problems with his visa, but he got the matter straightened out and caught an afternoon plane for Leningrad. He checked in at the hotel, had dinner, and later met Russell and Hathaway when the train arrived at 11:30 P.M.

The three travelers spent the next two days enjoying the sights of Leningrad. Life at the Astoria Hotel was less enjoyable. There was no heat, and when they complained, they were informed that the heat was not turned on until October 15! Nevertheless, Russell was happy to have an opportunity to see the historic sites of Leningrad. Then, at midnight on September 25, lodged in one compartment, the travelers took the train for Moscow. The hotel kitchen had prepared sandwiches for the trip, and the porter served tea frequently.

Arriving in Moscow at midmorning the next day, Russell registered at the Hotel National and began making plans for some sight-seeing. His main interest, however, was to visit the battlefields at Borodino, where Napoleon had fought in 1812 and where there had been bloody battles in World War II. The Russians, however, said Borodino was in a restricted area and Russell could not visit that vicinity. Hathaway explained through Efron that Russell was a historian and was traveling as a private citizen. There was no reason, they said, why he should be denied such a visit. While negotiations were going on with the Soviet Intourist officials, Russell met Roswell Garst of Iowa who was in the Soviet Union selling hybrid seed corn.

Russell was thoroughly annoyed at the Russians for denying his request to visit Borodino. He finally told Hathaway and Efron to inform the Intourist people that if he could not go there, he would cancel the remainder of his trip. This, he said, would be a test case "to see how far the Soviets would go in their new 'sweetness and light' policy towards Americans." Finally, after consulting "higher authorities," the Intourist officials informed Russell that an exception was being made in his case and he could go to Borodino the next day.

Early on the morning of September 29, the Russell party left Moscow in a Zis automobile for the Borodino battlefields some 125 kilometers away. They carried a lunch of caviar sandwiches prepared for them by the hotel cook. They visited the museum located in the middle of the battlefields and toured the area with an escort. The guide was surprised at how much Russell knew about the military actions in the area. After a good day of sight-seeing, they returned to Moscow in the late afternoon.

Russell and his companions left Moscow on September 30 and flew to Stalingrad. Subsequently, they visited Baku, Tiflis, Sochi, Rostov, and Kiev. At each stop, they toured the city and visited battlefields and other historic sites, museums and cathedrals, farmers' markets, and collective farms, and they traveled to Stalin's birthplace at Gori. Russell talked to his Russian guides about education, elections, and other subjects and took a degree of devilish satisfaction in embarrassing them by asking about Trotsky. After eighteen days in the Soviet Union, the Russell party left Kiev by train for Prague and then flew on to Zurich and Italy. Russell left Genoa on the USS *Independence* and arrived in New York on October 23. He had been gone for more than two months.

Nothing Russell saw changed his mind about the Soviet Union. People seemed well fed and clothed, he wrote, but living conditions were primitive by American standards. Nevertheless, Russell did not think that the economic and military potential of the Soviets should be underestimated. The trip was an interesting and educational experience, he said later, but "I would not choose Russia as a place to live."[25]

The view that many Americans held that the Soviet Union was a backward country lagging behind the United States in science and technology was shattered on October 4, 1957, when the Russians disclosed that they had placed a 184-pound satellite in orbit. Less than a month later, on November 3, they launched a 1,100-pound satellite that carried a dog into space. In August, well before these two events, the

Soviets had announced that they had successfully tested an intercontinental ballistic missile.

These startling events shocked many Americans out of their notions of scientific superiority. In opening up Senate hearings on the situation a few weeks later, Lyndon Johnson declared, "Our people have believed that in the field of scientific weapons and in technology and science, that we were well ahead of Russia." But, he added, with the launching of Sputniks 1 and 2, not merely American supremacy but equality had been challenged.[26]

Russell was as surprised as anyone over this course of events. However, he claimed that the Armed Services Committee had been deeply concerned for some time about the weaknesses of the American missile program. Russell said that he had been "prodding" the administration to move faster on the nation's missile projects. He blamed the Eisenhower Defense Department for delays and failure to keep up with the Russians. Congress, he said, had offered all of the necessary resources to do whatever was necessary to assure American superiority in space. In regards to funding, Russell said Congress had given the Pentagon "every dollar they asked for."[27]

Senator Stuart Symington of Missouri, also a member of the Armed Services Committee, had been one of the strongest proponents of more air power and a stronger missile program. He believed the situation was so critical that Eisenhower should call a special session of Congress. The United States must make a much greater effort, he wrote the president on October 8, in both research and development. Symington declared that "our people are properly disturbed by the presence of the Russian satellite over our skies."[28] Symington criticized the Defense Department's "creeping strangulation of our programs for obtaining modern missiles and aircraft." The president, however, wrote Symington that he saw no need for a special session.

Symington and other senators were also urging Russell to conduct high-level hearings before the Armed Services Committee to investigate shortcomings in American defense capabilities, especially in the missile program. Stennis wrote Russell that he should handle the investigation himself. "This is so vital a matter that nothing short of your own guidance will give it the necessary prestige and force," Stennis wrote.[29] Russell, however, decided that this issue was the responsibility of the Preparedness Subcommittee chaired by Lyndon Johnson. He authorized Johnson to proceed with an "all out investigation . . . of our missile and satellite programs."[30]

Why did Russell turn this important responsibility over to Johnson rather than undertaking it himself as Stennis urged? Although the Russell correspondence does not reveal the answer to this question, the best explanation seems to be that he hoped that leading the investigation would promote Johnson. Martha Roundtree, writing in the *Atlanta Journal* on November 25, speculated that this was one way for Russell to give Johnson another push toward the presidential nomination in 1960. In any event, as Johnson prepared to open the hearings, Russell was far away in Georgia talking to various constituent groups about the Russian threat.

Speaking at Valdosta on Armistice Day, Russell declared that "there is no use hemming and hawing about the missile and satellite program." The Soviets, he said, "were far ahead of us." He used this opportunity to denounce the administration's stand on the civil rights issue. He argued that in the current missile crisis, the federal government must end its "undeclared war on the South and face the real threat—that of Communist superiority in the ultimate weapons of warfare." He added that it was time to quit training troops to integrate the schools and prepare them to defend the country from aggression.[31]

On November 4, the day after the Russians launched their second satellite, Russell, Johnson, and Senator Styles Bridges of New Hampshire, Republican minority leader, were called to the Pentagon for an extensive briefing. For some seven hours, Secretary of Defense Neil H. McElroy reviewed the American missile and satellite situation with the three senators. While Russell and Johnson commented gingerly after the briefing, they did score the Republicans for complacency in the missile program. Everyone was now emphasizing the need for the United States to act fast.[32]

But there would be more embarrassment before things got better. On December 6, when the United States attempted to launch the Vanguard satellite rocket, it blew up on lift-off. Russell called this event "a grievous blow to our already waning world prestige." Americans were further humiliated when the Soviet delegate to the United Nations asked the American representative if the United States would like to receive aid under the Soviet Union's program of technical assistance to backward nations![33]

Johnson's Preparedness Subcommittee began its hearings on November 25. In opening the inquiry, Johnson said the purpose of the investigation was to inquire into the facts surrounding the nation's security. "Our country is disturbed over the tremendous military and scientific achievement of Russia," he said.

Altogether, the subcommittee held eleven days of hearings, completing its investigation on January 23, 1958. Scores of scientists, military experts, defense administrators, and other authorities testified about the current situation and what the United States must do to get ahead of the Soviets. Dr. Edward Teller, father of the H-bomb, was the first witness, and among others who testified was Admiral Hyman G. Rickover, assistant chief of the Bureau for Nuclear Propulsion and the main force behind developing the nuclear-powered submarine. Witness after witness declared that much larger sums were needed for research and development, that the missile and satellite programs required strong, centralized administration, and that the national will must be strengthened in support of the missile and satellite projects.[34]

Although Russell did not attend any of the subcommittee hearings, leaving Johnson in the limelight, when he returned to Washington in early January 1958 for the second session of the Eighty-fifth Congress, he devoted much of his energy to the missile question. On January 7, he addressed the Democratic conference and declared that Congress could appropriate sufficient money for the missile and satellite programs, but it could not force the administration to act more quickly or more responsibly. Earlier he had praised Eisenhower's appointment of James R. Killian, president of the Massachusetts Institute of Technology, as a special adviser on missiles, but now Russell said it would probably take three or four days for Killian even to get an appointment with Eisenhower. The programs needed more efficient administration and organization, according to Russell. Finally, he stated that "we have the time; we have the means; it is only a question of whether we have the will to assure our survival." His fellow senators broke into applause.[35]

The deep concern over the United States' defense posture resulted in an increase in defense appropriations for fiscal 1959 of around $2 billion. The $41 billion provided for the Defense Department was less than Johnson's subcommittee and some other study groups had recommended, but it was an amount to which Congress readily agreed. Russell urged that the increases needed for the missile program should be taken from foreign aid appropriations, but he was unable to win any significant support for this view. In fact, much to Russell's dismay, foreign economic aid jumped about $1.6 billion from 1958 to 1959. Congress also passed the Defense Reorganization Act of 1958, which tightened up the administration of the Defense Department, including giving the secretary of defense authority to assign the development and operation of new weapons systems.[36]

As chairman of the Armed Services Committee after January 1955, Russell had to deal with many issues. His committee considered such questions as military pay, Universal Military Training, the draft, housing at military bases, waste in military construction, retirement compensation for military personnel, pay for local draft boards, approval of the appointment of high defense officials, and a host of other matters. Chairing the Armed Services Committee was a very demanding job at a time when more than half of the federal budget went directly or indirectly to military and defense programs. Moreover, when his chairmanship of the Armed Services Committee was combined with his second ranking on the Appropriations Committee, he was in a position to wield great power.

Occasionally, Russell would become unduly agitated over some matter related to defense. On the morning of August 14, for example, he was listening to the radio. Suddenly, he said, he could not believe his ears. He heard the commentator announce that the Defense Department was funding a study to determine how and under what circumstances the United States might surrender to an enemy in case of total war. Russell was so upset that he could hardly wait for the Senate to convene. He told his colleagues that he was shocked that the Defense Department would enter into a contract for such an outlandish study. The Armed Services Committee had not approved "a single dime" of taxpayer money "for studies or plans for the surrender of this country and its people to our enemies." Instead, he said, the United States should be preparing to destroy any country that "would attack us, instead of cowardly counting the cost of developing plans for surrender." It was important to assure Americans, he continued, that however remote the possibility of attack, Congress would never place them "at the mercy of the godless forces of communism."

On further investigation, it was found that the Rand Corporation had undertaken a historical study on "Strategic Surrender," which had nothing to do with the surrender of the United States in a modern war. This explanation, however, was not enough for Russell. He said that people needed to be assured in "this very jittery age" that Congress would never tolerate "any study of this Nation's possible surrender." The president referred to the surrender talk as nonsense, but on August 15, the Senate passed a Russell amendment forbidding federal expenditures on surrender studies by a vote of 88 to 2.[37]

Russell also won some headlines in late 1958 when he attacked the State Department for returning to the United States some U.S. soldiers who had been captured by the Chinese in the Korean War and then had renounced the United States. He was fighting mad that American taxpayers would be paying the bill to get these "turncoats" home. "These

men renounced their American citizenship," Russell wired Secretary
Dulles, and "vilified their fellow citizens and our country and spat upon
our flag." Let them stay in Communist China, he insisted. However,
Russell's outburst did not change the State Department's policy.[38]

On September 16, 1959, Russell, along with members of the Foreign Relations Committee, had an interesting meeting with Soviet leader
Nikita Khrushchev, who was visiting in the United States. When Senator
Fulbright introduced Russell to Khrushchev, Russell remarked, "It is
easy to see that our guest would be a most formidable antagonist in any
parliamentary forum anywhere in the world," to which Khrushchev
responded that he would be "not an antagonist but a defender." Then
Russell explained that he was surprised at Khrushchev's belief that the
United States wanted to control or influence the internal affairs of the
Soviet Union. That, Russell said, was just not the case. Khrushchev's
reference to self-determination gave Russell an opportunity to ask the
Soviet leader if he would permit the people of East Germany to vote on
the kind of government they wanted. Khrushchev replied that he would
not discuss other countries. Then Russell asked him if the Russians had
experienced any failures before they successfully launched their first
satellite. Khrushchev replied that he could not answer that question, but
it was subsequently revealed that the Soviets had had some failures.
Russell was glad to have an opportunity to meet the Soviet leader and
referred to him as being "able and quick-witted." Yet Russell thought
Khrushchev was poorly informed on many issues.[39]

Because of his strong backing for the Defense Department and the
individual military services, Russell had a close working relationship
with the nation's military and defense leaders. They could count on him
to support most of their requests for new and more sophisticated weapons, for more manpower, and for military construction. They, in turn,
supplied him with the information he needed to make his case in Congress for stronger defenses. Russell was careful to preserve the right of
individual service secretaries and high military officers to testify and
make proposals directly to Congress without having to funnel everything through the secretary of defense.

An example of the kind of assistance Russell could provide occurred in 1958 when the House placed limitations on expenditures by
the Office of the Secretary of Defense to influence legislation. The Department of Defense considered its liaison with Congress most important and turned to Russell to help out. In the conference committee,
Russell got the restriction eliminated. This was the kind of favor the
defense establishment did not easily forget.

The service secretaries and other administrators of defense policies had high praise for Russell. Indeed, they were often excessive with their flattery. After Thomas Gates was confirmed as secretary of the navy in May 1959, he wrote Russell a longhand note thanking "the unique anchor of the Armed Services Committee" for his support and friendship. "There is much to learn," Gates stated, "and I will continue to rely on your help and guidance." The year before, Secretary of the Army Wilber M. Brucker expressed his appreciation to Russell and his committee for "your distinguished public service in ministering the Army's affairs in the Senate." While still at sea testing the nuclear submarine USS *Theodore Roosevelt*, Admiral Hyman G. Rickover wrote Russell thanking him "for your help and encouragement in building a nuclear powered Navy."[40]

The military services treated Russell not only with respect but almost with awe. He customarily traveled wherever he wanted to go by air force or navy planes. He never purposely tried to take advantage of his position as chairman of the Armed Services Committee, but he did not seem to realize that his slightest wish was considered a command among the military services. For example, on Thursday he might say to a staff member, "I wonder if the Air Force has a plane going to Maxwell Air Base or somewhere else in the Southeast in the next day or two that could drop me off at Winder." The staff member would offer to inquire about the matter, knowing full well that a plane would be going if Russell wanted a ride. Then the staff person would call an air force officer who would usually ask, "When does the senator want to go?" The plane would just "happen" to be going precisely when Russell wished to leave Washington for a weekend at home or to make a talk somewhere. Moreover, at the appropriate time, the air force would have a car present to pick up the senator at his hotel or in front of the Senate Office Building to take him to the plane at Andrews Air Force Base. It was a most convenient arrangement that became increasingly important to Russell as his health deteriorated in the 1960s.

The matter of congressional travel in military aircraft was scarcely ever questioned by reporters, although it would have been the topic of intense discussion and criticism after Watergate. On one occasion in 1959, a reporter did ask Russell's office about a person traveling on the plane with Russell who was presumably the wife of his press secretary, Bill Bates. When it was revealed that the person was not Mrs. Bates but Barboura Raesly, the senator's secretary, nothing more was heard of the matter.[41]

Although the civilian and military leadership treated Russell with great deference, he was not overawed by the military brass. He held firmly to the constitutional principles of civilian control over the armed services. He had demonstrated that clearly when he headed the MacArthur hearings. Harry L. Wingate, Jr., chief clerk of the Armed Services Committee, recalled an incident that illustrates this point in a different way. In the early 1960s, Secretary of Defense Robert S. McNamara was testifying before Russell's committee. The testimony went on longer than anticipated, keeping General Maxwell Taylor, chairman of the Joint Chiefs, waiting for some time. When it became evident that the committee could not hear General Taylor during the morning session, Russell whispered to Wingate to tell him to come back at two o'clock. Taylor, surrounded by his aides, looked at his watch and told Wingate that he had other important appointments and could not return at that hour. Wingate relayed that message to Russell, who said, "Go tell General Taylor that if he can't be here at 2:00 we won't need his testimony." Taylor managed to return at the appointed time.

In connection with the entire defense effort, Russell had almost a phobia for military security and for a high degree of independence by the Central Intelligence Agency. As mentioned before, Russell held a low opinion of colleagues who were given privileged information and then talked about it or leaked it. Russell took great pride in claiming that he had never released, "even to my very best friends in the press," any classified or confidential information. His one and only great disillusionment with the Senate, he said in 1956, was when members were given secret information and "within a couple of days," it "trickled to the press."[42]

Russell was keenly sensitive to the possibility that atomic secrets might leak out. As a member of the Joint Committee on Atomic Energy, he wanted to protect atomic technology for peaceful uses, but he was much more concerned about maintaining absolute secrecy in connection with all nuclear weapons. In 1957 when Eisenhower proposed that the United States share nuclear information with NATO countries, Russell expressed strong reservations. He said that he did not favor sharing "our military secrets just to bolster our friends' morale."[43] He continued to fight the exchange of scientific and technical nuclear information with friendly countries, but he could not stop it. Russell called the policy foolish and shortsighted.

Russell also strongly opposed requiring the Central Intelligence Agency to report to a large committee and staff. In 1955 Senator Mike Mansfield of Montana introduced a concurrent resolution, cosponsored by a number of other senators, to set up a Joint Committee on Central

Intelligence. This committee would study the CIA and handle legislation relating to the agency. Moreover, the CIA was to keep the joint committee "fully and currently informed with respect to its activities." The Rules Committee favorably reported this resolution in February 1956. A new committee, it was argued, would place greater control over the agency and assure Congress that the CIA was doing its job properly.

Russell vigorously objected to the resolution. It was both dangerous and unnecessary, he stated. He said that the oversight subcommittee of the Armed Services and Appropriations committees consisting of Senators Byrd, Johnson, Saltonstall, Bridges, and himself as chairman provided adequate and confidential oversight of the agency. Two or three time a year, Russell explained, the director of the CIA and members of his staff appeared before the subcommittee. They had never failed to answer questions, he said, and had always been "forthright and frank." He also strongly opposed making the CIA's budget public. If the CIA had to submit a detailed budget the way other agencies did, it would give the Soviets a blueprint of the agency's operations, he declared.

In reply to the charge that the oversight subcommittee had never shared its information with the rest of Congress, Russell fully agreed. That was only half of it. He announced that he never intended to tell others what the CIA was doing. Nothing in the United States, he declared, "should be held so sacred behind the curtain of classified matter" as "the activities of this agency." Rather than share the information with members of Congress and their staffs, Russell argued, it would be better to abolish the CIA. He declared that when so many people had classified information, it was sure to leak out and increase the hazards of working for the agency. Russell promised his fellow senators that the subcommittee would keep track of what the CIA was doing and urged them to defeat the Mansfield resolution. He was saying in effect, trust me and my small subcommittee. The Senate fell into line and defeated the Mansfield proposal on April 11 by a vote of 59 to 27.[44]

Being chairman of the Armed Services Committee and of the Subcommittee on Defense Appropriations placed Russell in an unusually influential position on defense matters. The Senate and House Armed Services committees approved major equipment such as planes, ships, and missiles for the Defense Department before appropriations were considered. Senators who were members of both the Armed Services and Appropriations committees, like Russell, heard more testimony than other senators and were better informed than their colleagues. This detailed information gave them greater power and influence.[45]

Russell also had a keen sense of how to get things done without generating unnecessary antagonism. George Reedy, who worked closely with Lyndon Johnson for several years, related how Russell got an anti-Soviet resolution passed at the NATO conference in Paris in the fall of 1956. One of the major issues before that meeting was condemnation of the Soviets for their invasion of Hungary. The State Department had prepared a resolution for the American delegation to introduce. According to Reedy, it bristled with left-wing Socialist phrases condemning the Soviet Union. When the State Department representative read the resolution, Russell remarked that it was a fine effort. But, Russell said, "do you think the American delegation should introduce it?" Taken aback, the American representative asked why not. Would it not have more impact, Russell replied, if it came from a labor or Socialist government?

At that point, Russell launched into what Reedy called "one of the most brilliant discussions of international politics I have ever heard." Others there had no idea that Russell knew so much. Reedy said it was a performance that would have made Harvard proud. Then Russell advised taking the resolution to Paul-Henri Spaak, the Belgian leader, and telling him his friend Richard B. Russell would like his opinion on it. He cautioned the messenger not to tell Spaak that Russell wanted him to introduce it. He said to just say that "I want his opinion on it. He'll know what to do." The next day, the Socialist government of Belgium introduced a resolution condemning the Soviet Union, and it passed without the slightest controversy.[46]

In addressing the graduating class at Georgia State College of Business Administration in Atlanta on June 7, 1959, Russell took the opportunity to present his view of the international Communist threat. He told his student listeners that the "most constant and pressing danger" they would face in the years ahead was the "continuing threat from world communism." Russell said that he could see nothing to indicate that the leaders in the Kremlin had given up their "grand design to achieve world domination." The Soviet threat, he continued, was economic as well as military. But, he insisted, the United States had one great advantage over the "degrading slavish communist system." That was the strength of "free enterprise and individual initiative."[47] So, he said, while the challenge was great on both the military and economic fronts, the United States would prevail. There was nothing to indicate that Russell had changed his cold war stance over the previous fifteen years. If anything, his views had become more firm.

17

Kennedy, Russell, and the New Frontier

════

Richard B. Russell, Jr., reached the height of his power in the U.S. Senate during the 1950s. There is no way to determine precisely when political figures reach the pinnacle of their influence, but surely by John F. Kennedy's election to the presidency in 1960, Russell no longer had the same power over legislative matters that he had during the 1950s. During the last ten years Russell was in the Senate, his image of power was greater than its substance. This, of course, is not to say that Russell was not one of the most powerful senators until his death early in 1971. Seniority and his chairmanship of the Armed Services Committee until 1969 and of the Appropriations Committee after that placed him in an influential and strategic position in the Senate. Presidents Kennedy and Johnson consulted him often, but very seldom did they take his advice on major national and international issues. Few senators were more out of step with the course of events in the 1960s than Dick Russell. He knew this even if others did not recognize the fact. As Russell looked around in the late 1950s and 1960s, he did not approve of much that he saw.

A number of conditions combined to gradually reduce Russell's power. One was his deteriorating health in the 1960s. From 1958 until his death, his breathing problems worsened. Although he stopped smoking in 1958, great damage had already been done to his respiratory system. By that time, his cough was getting worse, and he was increasingly short of breath. His mild-to-moderate case of emphysema that was diagnosed in the mid-1950s gradually became worse. Besides, Russell was becoming something of a hypochondriac, and he worried a great deal about his health. In 1959 he wrote Harry G. Thornton, an old friend and classmate at the University of Georgia, that he was afraid to go to the doctors for fear they would operate on him. He said he had a horror of any further operations.[1]

By 1959 and 1960, Russell was taking an unbelievable variety of medicines and health treatments. His pocket calendars and daybooks were filled with lists of pills and schedules for taking medicine. Intermittently, he took antibiotics, potassium iodide, oral bronchodilators, phenobarbital, Librium, and aspirin and used nasal sprays and other medications. He also used vaporizers and did abdominal breathing exercises. In January 1960, he went to the Bethesda Naval Hospital for a battery of tests. The doctor prescribed additional medicines, but Russell said he did not have much faith in any of the prescriptions. By that time, he was taking four or five medications a day and sometimes more. There were times in 1961 when he took some kind of pill or medicine as many as thirteen times in twenty-four hours.[2]

To what extent his health reduced his effectiveness cannot be definitely known, but it surely began to cut his energy and made it harder to keep up with his vast amount of work. He sometimes performed less ably than in earlier years. After speaking to the Medical Association of Georgia on March 31, 1960, he noted, "Made poor speech to them and left awkwardly."[3] His declining health probably only had a marginal effect on his career until 1965, but from that time onward, it was an important factor in his declining influence. There were times in 1965 and 1967, for example, when he was out of the Senate for several weeks. Moreover, the condition of his health greatly worried Russell and added to his hypochondria. His health also caused him to cut down even more on his social life.

Of much greater influence in reducing his power, however, were the changes that occurred in the Senate after 1958. In that year, sixteen new Democratic senators, mostly liberals, were elected. They included Edmund S. Muskie, Eugene McCarthy, Gale McGee, Frank Moss, and Philip Hart. When Congress opened in January 1959, the Democrats had a majority of thirty compared to a majority of only two in 1957. Moreover, these more liberal Democrats were unhappy with the operation of the Senate, which, they believed, gave southerners like Russell too much power. That power rested on seniority and the Senate rules, as well as on individual abilities.

Joseph Clark of Pennsylvania, elected in 1956, had already been pressing the Senate establishment for changes that would give liberals more influence. Early in 1957, Clark and six other liberals had written all Democratic senators, urging them to support legislation that would implement the 1956 Democratic platform on civil rights, housing, education, help for depressed areas, and other policies. To achieve these goals, they also called for more democratic operations of the Senate.

When Joe Clark looked at the Senate in the late 1950s, he saw

Senator Russell in his office, Room 205 of the Senate Office Building, ca. 1960. (Photo courtesy of Russell Memorial Library, University of Georgia, Athens.)

Russell, the Senate's second most senior member, as "the Commander in Chief of the Senate Establishment." He continued, "As such his duties begin before each Congress convenes and continue throughout each two-year session. He regularly floor manages the opening session fight against changing the filibuster Rule XXII. He masterminds the meetings of the Democratic Steering Committee. He takes an active role in the work of the Policy Committee." Then Clark described Russell's chairmanship of the Armed Services Committee, his service on the Appropriations Committee, and numerous other duties and responsibilities. This amount of responsibility and power, Clark said, was too much for any one man.[4]

The liberals particularly objected to the power exerted by conservative southerners through their chairmanships of standing committees. Russell, Harry F. Byrd, James Eastland, A. Willis Robertson, and others, according to Clark, were able to block most progressive legislation by bottling it up in committee. Clark, as well as other liberals, also complained that the Democratic Policy Committee, chaired by Lyndon Johnson, did not truly represent Democrats in the Senate. The industrial states and the cities, Clark said, were hardly represented at all. On April 14, 1959, the Democratic Policy Committee considered Clark's complaints. Johnson said that his appointment of Senator James Murray of

Montana provided "good liberal representation on this committee." But he added sarcastically, "The point is that we don't have Senator Clark." Russell said he did not think Clark's complaint had been made in good faith, and he opposed any changes. The other members agreed.[5]

Liberal Democratic senators did not give up trying to increase their influence. Nothing symbolized southern power and control as much as the Senate cloture rule, which required a two-thirds vote to cut off debate. But when the liberals tried to change this rule in January 1959, they were decisively batted down again. Senate liberals were clearly frustrated. Senator Clark called the 1959 session of Congress "a sorry one" and said that liberals even lost some ground when Congress passed the Landrum-Griffin Act, a measure placing further restrictions on organized labor.[6]

In 1960 it appeared as though the liberals might gain significant advances in civil rights. However, as mentioned previously, southerners were again able to strip some of the most important features from the civil rights bill before it passed. Clark, probably speaking for several unhappy northern liberals, declared that "in the end, the leadership on both sides of the aisle capitulated to the Southern generalissimo, Richard B. Russell of Georgia." Russell, Clark wrote, did not demand "unconditional surrender." Indeed, he was "a gracious victor" who threw "a few crumbs . . . to the frustrated civil rights advocates." Then, speaking to Russell, Clark said: "Dick, here is my sword. I hope you will give it back to me so that I can beat it into a plowshare for the spring planting." This was a reversal of Lee's surrender to Grant at Appomattox in 1865![7]

Despite meager gains by the liberals in 1959 and 1960, Clark predicted that "we are approaching the end of an era." Changes were coming, the Pennsylvanian declared. No one was more aware of a gradual power shift in the Senate than Dick Russell. He was resisting it at every turn, but the old order of things was under strong pressure. Writing shortly after the Senate elections in 1958, he said that he could not yet assess the influence of the new class of senators but that many of them were obligated to organized labor. This meant, he said, an even stronger push for civil rights and other so-called liberal legislation. Like Senator Clark, Russell saw the end of an era approaching, but unlike Clark who viewed the forthcoming changes as being good for the country, Russell saw them as a great threat to the nation's welfare. Commenting on resolutions dealing with housing, civil rights, immigration, and other matters passed by the National Convention of Young Democratic Clubs in November 1959, Russell wrote, "This is about the most radical and anti-southern document that I have ever seen."[8]

From Russell's viewpoint, the Democratic party continued to drift dangerously to the left. This had been caused, he believed, by special interest groups such as blacks and organized labor pushing for civil rights and a broad spectrum of other social reforms. Russell was aware of the increasing number of liberals in Congress. He realized that he and a few loyal supporters could organize a rear-guard action to block some distasteful measures temporarily, but he knew as well as anyone that eventually a liberal agenda would prevail. How fast Congress would pass reforms would depend not only on the make-up of Congress but on who occupied the White House. The national political arena, however, did not contain any Democratic candidates who would agree with the South's position, but one man possibly offered more hope than any other in Russell's view. He was Lyndon Johnson.

In early January 1959, Russell scribbled a note on a telephone pad: "LBJ for president." Although Russell and Johnson had differed over a number of issues, they had remained strong friends. "For many years," Johnson wrote in 1959, "I have been sensible to the fact that without Dick Russell, Lyndon Johnson would be a man who sorely lacked a trusted and wise counselor." Russell had equal admiration for his Texas friend. He told Rufus G. Harris, the president of Mercer University, that over the years he had known many senators but that "in my opinion Lyndon Johnson is the ablest legislator who has served in congress in the past half century." That was not flattery but a sincere assessment of Johnson's abilities and the view of a close friend.[9]

On November 2, 1959, Governor Price Daniel of Texas wrote Russell a personal and confidential letter regarding the position of the South in the forthcoming presidential election. In order for the South to protect its interests, Daniel said, the region must get organized behind a suitable candidate. "Of course," he wrote, "I think Lyndon is our best bet." Daniel explained that he would be pleased to see Russell assume a leadership role in getting the South organized behind Johnson's candidacy. Daniel had visited with Johnson about a month earlier, and Johnson indicated that he was leaving any campaigning on his behalf to others. Johnson believed that by letting his friends take the lead he would arrive at next year's convention with a strong bloc of delegates from the South and West. Sam Rayburn agreed with this approach. However, Daniel told Russell that he did not think this was good strategy and that he believed Johnson needed commitments before some of the southern governors made promises to other candidates. Daniel wanted Russell's advice and suggestions.

Russell replied that he had talked with Johnson in some detail about the forthcoming nomination of a presidential candidate. But Russell believed that by giving strong and vocal support to a candidate, the southern states would alienate the other states necessary to gain the nomination. Because of this fact of political life, Russell had told reporters that he was not pushing a presidential candidate but that Lyndon Johnson was the strongest man the Democrats could nominate. What should be avoided, Russell said, was "any concerted action that would stamp Lyndon as the 'Southern' candidate." He was sure of this because of his own experience in 1952. Russell concluded by saying that "if I were to start stumping the country" for Johnson, it would do "a great deal more harm than good." The strategy of southerners, then, should be to work as quietly as possible behind the scenes to line up support for Johnson but avoid giving the impression that he was a southern candidate.[10]

A major problem was that Lyndon Johnson could not really decide if he wanted to run for president. Nevertheless, Speaker Sam Rayburn announced on October 17, 1959, that an unofficial Johnson campaign headquarters was being set up in Austin with himself and Governor Price Daniel as cochairmen. But in the succeeding months, the efforts of the Johnson supporters were so clumsy and disorganized that he had little chance to get the nomination. He did not officially announce that he was in the race until July 5, only a few days before the convention. By the time the Democrats met in Los Angeles in July 1960, John F. Kennedy was far out in front and was nominated on the first ballot.[11]

Was the South now out of the picture as far as the national ticket was concerned, or would Johnson accept the vice presidential spot if it were offered to him? Many of his closest friends and supporters, including Russell, urged him not to give up his majority leader post for a largely powerless position of presiding over the Senate. Eugene C. Patterson, a native Georgian, graduate of the University of Georgia, and at the time editor of the *Atlanta Constitution*, recalled that he and Bobby Russell were in Los Angeles having a cup of coffee in a hotel across the street from the convention center. Bobby, the senator's nephew and confidant, was one of the Georgia delegates. While Patterson and Bobby were visiting, Bobby was told that he had a telephone call. He excused himself to answer the call and soon returned highly agitated. "What was wrong?" Patterson asked. Bobby replied, "You're not going to believe this, but Senator Russell just called me from Washington and he said that Senator Johnson is about to take the vice presidential nomination." He explained that Russell had asked him to see Johnson immediately and urge him not to make what he considered a foolish move. Bobby then rushed out the door to deliver Russell's message to Johnson. It was, of course, counsel that Johnson rejected.[12]

On July 19, Johnson called Russell to explain why he had not taken his mentor's advice. He told Russell that Rayburn and other confidants had finally agreed that he should accept the vice presidential nomination and, perhaps more important, that he would have been left out of things if he had refused the nomination. Russell accepted this explanation, but he was nonetheless disappointed to see his old friend on the ticket. This was mainly because Russell was so upset over the Democratic platform.[13]

Russell viewed both the Democratic and Republican platforms as "reprehensible and socialistic." They were reprehensible, he believed, because of strong civil rights planks and socialistic because of the proposals dealing with housing, education, labor legislation, and other matters. The entire trend of affairs, Russell wrote, made him sick at heart and might even be contributing to his "physical indisposition." The Democratic platform promised the horrors of "a second Reconstruction," he wrote. Russell hoped that providence would give him strength and wisdom to save "our Southland from the evil threat of that platform," but he was not optimistic about the outcome. He feared that his beloved South was "in for some very sad and tragic days." Indeed, he could not find "the slightest ray of brightness" in the whole political spectrum.[14]

How could Russell support Lyndon Johnson and the ticket without at least indirectly endorsing the hated platform? That was his predicament. He would be glad to back Johnson "in most any way that would not require me to embrace the worst platform that has ever been suggested by a major political party," he wrote.[15] From Russell's viewpoint, it seemed best to remain as quiet as possible and not participate in the campaign. This would protect his integrity as far as the platform was concerned and also not alienate some Republicans who had helped him block civil rights legislation in the Senate. The fact that he had not been a bitter partisan in recent political campaigns, he wrote, had helped him get those votes.[16]

Therefore Russell had every intention of sitting out the campaign as he had done in every presidential contest since 1944. But it was the platform, not Kennedy and Johnson, that turned Russell off. Personally, he liked Kennedy. They had served together on a special committee in

1956 to select five outstanding senators whose portraits would be placed in the Senate reception room. In 1957 he called Kennedy a "very capable young man" who had an attractive personality and a good sense of public relations. Russell had said that he would not be surprised to see Kennedy on the "National Democratic ticket one of these days." That time had come sooner than Russell had thought likely, but he did not resent his young colleague seeking the nation's highest office.[17] He would not campaign for Kennedy, however, because he could not endorse in public speeches a platform whose implementation he would subsequently oppose in the Senate. He emphasized, however, that Kennedy's religion had nothing to do with his position. He had made speeches for Al Smith in 1928 and was proud of it, he wrote.[18]

Russell made no statement of what he intended to do in the 1960 election until September 24. On that day, he and Senator Talmadge both announced that they would vote the Democratic ticket. Russell tersely declared, "On November 8, I shall vote the straight Democratic ticket as I have always done." He did not mention either Kennedy or Johnson by name or urge anyone to vote for them.[19] Shortly afterward, Russell headed for Europe to inspect American military bases. Leaving October 9, accompanied by William H. Darden, Jr., his former office assistant and now chief clerk of the Armed Services Committee, he visited military leaders and embassy officials in England, Italy, Greece, Turkey, and Spain. This was not the first time he had gone abroad just before a presidential election in which he did not want to become involved.

The best-laid plans, however, do not always work out. Russell returned home on October 30 to find Kennedy and Nixon in a very tight race. There was a serious question whether Kennedy and Johnson would carry Texas. Conservatives in the state had pictured the Democratic candidates as little short of Socialists and the party platform a disaster. What Kennedy-Johnson Democrats in Texas needed was someone with stature to give the party a more conservative appearance. Who could do this better than Dick Russell?

Russell had scarcely settled back in Winder to watch the outcome of the election when his telephone began to ring. It was Lyndon Johnson on the line. Johnson pled with Russell to come to Texas and make some speeches and appearances for the party. Russell flatly declined. Johnson telephoned a second time and told Russell how much the party needed his assistance. Again Russell said no. A short time later, Johnson called again and pleaded with Russell to help out an old friend. "Come for my sake," Johnson said. Russell could not resist this arm-twisting and told Johnson he would go to Texas. "I finally decided on the basis of our personal relations to go out to Texas to do what I could to help him," Russell wrote.[20] Already Russell staff members Bill Bates and Bill Jordan were doing everything they could for Johnson. There was also another factor that may have caused Russell to go to Texas to help his friend. While Russell was close to Johnson, he was also personally very fond of Lady Bird. He had been angered when he read in the newspapers that she had been mistreated by a crowd in Houston. Perhaps he hoped that his going to Texas to help Lyndon and the Democrats would vindicate the abuse anti-Johnson extremists had piled on Lady Bird.

For two days before the election, Russell urged Texas voters to back the Democratic ticket. He made speeches, held press conferences, and advised voters not to forsake the Democrats. He admitted that he did not like major parts of the Democratic platform, but he added that the Republican campaign document was even worse. At a campaign luncheon at the Shamrock Hotel in Houston, Russell declared, "I have *never* been disappointed in Lyndon Johnson."[21] As far as Kennedy and Nixon were concerned, Russell later said that he accepted Kennedy as "the lesser of two evils."[22] When the results were in and the Democrats narrowly won Texas, greatly helping Kennedy and Johnson squeak through to victory, Russell was pleased with his contribution. Some of Johnson's aides believed that Russell had played a key role in carrying Texas and several other southern states. Johnson himself was very grateful and called Russell to express his appreciation.[23]

Following the election, Russell had several conversations with Johnson about the vice president–elect's responsibility to protect the South. This was the reason Russell had pushed him for president and supported him for vice president in the first place. On November 17, he told Johnson that the South was depending on him. In another telephone call the next day, Russell emphasized that the South had elected him and now the region expected him to protect it from the radicals.[24] It is difficult to imagine how Russell could expect Johnson to protect the South, as Russell understood that term. Johnson was angling for national not regional leadership. To achieve that goal, Johnson would have to support policies strongly opposed by most white southerners. At best Russell may have thought Johnson would help him with some delaying strategies. But Russell was too smart a politician to believe that Johnson would be of much help to southern political aims. Johnson was trying to lead the South out of its past; Dick Russell was doing everything he could to hold the region to its historic roots. The room for agreement or even compromise was small.

It was not necessary in 1960 for Russell to worry about his own reelection. Although there had been some complaints in 1959 that he was losing touch with the people at home, this was only wishful thinking on the part of a few critics. There were even some newspaper stories that, because of ill health, Russell would not run again. After the usual rumors and speculation, it turned out that no one wanted to challenge Russell, and he was renominated and elected a sixth time. His only expense was the $1,500 filing fee, which was provided by friends. Some supporters had sent in money in case he did have opposition, but Russell returned it with thanks.[25]

Shortly after the election, the press reported that Russell and Kennedy intended to meet for a discussion of national and international affairs. On December 1 at 11:30 A.M., that meeting took place. Because of Russell's seniority and prestige in the Senate, Kennedy had planned to go to Russell's office for the meeting although other senators were making their way to the president-elect's office for their conferences. However, Russell would not agree to that. He insisted on going to Kennedy's office. "I decided that the proprieties required me to come up here," he told reporters outside Kennedy's office. This gesture was another sign of Russell's deep respect for the office of the president. Although Kennedy was not yet president, he had been elected and that was enough for Russell.[26]

Russell and Kennedy discussed defense matters and agricultural policy for nearly an hour. Russell reminded the president-elect that southern farmers had voted Democratic while those in the West and Midwest had mostly supported Nixon. Kennedy's victory, to a considerable degree, Russell said, could be credited to southern farmers. Therefore, the secretary of agriculture should come from the South. Russell's candidate was D. W. Brooks, founder and head of Gold Kist, the Southeast's largest farmer cooperative. Kennedy admitted the importance of southern farmers to his victory but explained to Russell that during the campaign he had promised to appoint a secretary of agriculture from the Midwest. Kennedy said that he would be glad to appoint Brooks to any other high position in the Department of Agriculture.

Although the two men discussed defense matters, neither indicated what specific issues they covered. Kennedy then brought up the possibility of appointing his brother, Robert, as attorney general. Russell advised him to name Robert to some other responsible position rather than attorney general. Kennedy responded by saying he would not want to alienate the South by such an appointment. Kennedy then mentioned that he might appoint his brother under secretary of defense. When the president did appoint Bobby as attorney general, Russell considered it "most unfortunate." He casually discussed opposing Robert's nomination and talked with members of the southern caucus about blocking it. But those who had worked with Bobby on the McClellan committee investigating labor racketeering believed, Russell wrote, that "they could keep him within bounds." According to Russell, those colleagues later found out how wrong they were.[27]

Kennedy and Russell emerged from their private talk smiling and in good humor. Neither, however, would give any details of their conference. Russell did say that he expected to maintain "very cordial" relations with Kennedy and that he would support the Kennedy administration "as far as I possibly can." When asked if they had discussed civil rights, Russell replied, "We didn't wish to indulge in any futile discussions."[28]

During November and December, Russell was constantly consulted by Kennedy and his associates about appointments in the new administration. The president-elect recognized his political debts to the South, and he wanted to work as harmoniously as possible with the southern leaders. Russell was the key to that relationship. On November 29, for instance, Kennedy called Russell to ask his opinion about appointing Dean Rusk as secretary of state. Russell raised the question as to whether Rusk would be tough enough. He then had a long talk with Johnson about Rusk on December 12 and advised Johnson that Rusk might involve the administration in a war. His two assessments of Rusk seemed completely contradictory. Russell also talked about lesser appointments. After Kennedy appointed Governor Orville Freeman of Minnesota as secretary of agriculture, Russell hoped that his friend D. W. Brooks might get the under secretary position. On December 29, Bobby Russell told Russell that Georgia could have that post. But Brooks turned it down.[29]

Dick Russell was a great admirer of strong oratory, and Kennedy's inaugural speech on January 20, 1961, greatly impressed him. He referred to it as having "a Churchillian touch." The new president's remarks about bearing any burden, paying any price, and opposing any foe "to assure the survival and the success of liberty" moved the aging senator. So did the stirring words, "Ask not what your country can do for you. Ask what you can do for your country." But Russell's quickened emotions soon sagged as Congress received the concrete proposals embraced by the New Frontier.

Russell's disappointment is not surprising in light of the fact that the young president's legislative agenda had practically nothing in common with what Russell thought was best for the country. Just how far apart they were philosophically can be illustrated by an analysis done by the Americans for Democratic Action in the fall of 1960. The ADA, one of the nation's most liberal groups, compared Kennedy's and Russell's records on twelve domestic and foreign policy issues. Russell received a zero and Kennedy 100 percent in the ADA's grading. On January 6, 1961, Russell wrote Bobby Russell that "I greatly fear that you will find that [Kennedy] will not take any step that is really opposed by *The New York Times, The Washington Post* and the ADA."[30] To make matters worse from Russell's viewpoint, the electorate in 1960 had sent more liberals to the Senate, and the Democratic majority continued with 64 Democrats to 36 Republicans. He saw clearly that it was going to be harder and harder to block passage of distasteful legislation.

Kennedy proposed to carry out the Democratic platform by passing civil rights legislation that would wipe out racial discrimination in housing, schools, and other areas of American society. He called for more aid for education, help for cities, medical care for the aged, and other programs of social and economic reform. Although the liberals made only modest gains in 1961, the pressure to allow the federal government to intrude more and more into American life and accept responsibility for peoples' needs greatly disturbed Russell. He also saw proposals for new laws on housing and education as the means to break down segregation and force racial integration.

By the early 1960s, Russell felt more than ever that he was being alienated from the mainstream of the Democratic party and that he was out of step with the trend of major events. This situation, of course, was not new. It had been developing slowly for a decade or more, but the feeling intensified after 1960. Johnson's election as vice president did not give him any assurance or comfort that the erosion of the traditional southern position on racial matters might be slowed. Russell understood Johnson perfectly well. He had said that Johnson was the best prospect for president in 1960 because he would defend traditional white southern attitudes and causes, but in his heart, Russell knew better. His friend Lyndon had great ambitions, and as a national figure, he had to seek black votes. As Russell looked around, he could see nothing but increased pressure for social and economic reform, which included more rights for blacks. From his viewpoint, the future looked bleak.

During the election of 1960, Russell wrote with a tinge of sadness, "My party had deviated from the past and has gone off and left me." On the same day, he wrote another friend that he did not see "the slightest ray of brightness on the whole political horizon." He complained that the rest of the nation was stacking the Senate against the

South by electing "self-styled" liberals. According to Russell, these new senators were subject to the demands of the pressure groups that elected them. He was fighting, he said, to prevent the greatest system of government ever devised from being perverted by selfish interests but was not having much success. Russell often wrote about the "old times" when life was less perplexing. Admitting that the nation had made great technological and other gains, nevertheless he believed that peoples' moral fiber and patriotism had declined. It would be wrong to give the impression that Russell sat around brooding and feeling sorry for himself. He was far too busy and constantly in the middle of high-level decision making to permit that. But in his quieter moments, he revealed a frustration and unhappiness with the course of current events and the prospects for the future.[31]

Occasionally, by 1959 and 1960, self-doubt about his own influence and leadership swept over Russell. During the 1960 civil rights fight, he scribbled a handwritten note that said, "Afraid my leadership has lost inspiration." On another slip of paper he wrote, "I can not inspire you any longer." A year earlier, he had written to a friend that he was experiencing more frustrations than at any time in his long political career.[32]

Some sources of concern came from his own bailiwick. A few leaders in the South were increasingly calling for changed attitudes. Ralph McGill continued his criticism of strict racial segregation. Speaking in Washington in April 1959, McGill talked about a New South, one that would require leaders with different attitudes and outlooks. The New South demanded leadership, he said, that "will not consider the greatest issue to be where a colored man shall sit on a street car, or where his child will go to school."[33]

Russell may have been discouraged at the course of national events, but this only increased his determination to protect southern interests. In January 1961, liberal senators led by Humphrey and Clark again moved to place restrictions on the filibuster. These Senate reformers proposed that the cloture rule be amended to permit cutting off debate by a simple majority vote. Russell not only organized his southern lieutenants but arranged for a block of Republican votes as well. When the Senate voted on January 11, the liberals were defeated 50 to 46. Russell hailed the outcome. It was, he said, "a great victory for sanity, dignity and prerogatives of the Senate."[34]

One incident early in the Kennedy administration produced considerable embarrassment for Russell. The *Atlanta Journal and Constitution* carried a headline on January 2, 1961, that Governor Ernest Vandiver of Georgia, the husband of Russell's niece Betty, had been appointed secretary of the army. Two days later, the *Atlanta Constitution* announced that Kennedy was not going to select Vandiver after all. Columnist W. H. Lawrence wrote that if Vandiver were not chosen, Kennedy would be risking future troubles with Russell and Vinson, chairmen of the Senate and House Armed Services committees. Writers presented the matter as a conflict between Russell and Vinson who favored Vandiver and liberals who opposed the Georgia governor because he favored segregation in the armed forces. Upset by the implication that he was insisting on Vandiver's appointment, Russell wired the president on January 4 saying that someone in the administration had leaked the story and that it was "grossly unfair and wholly untrue." Russell said that he had made it perfectly clear to Kennedy and Johnson in August, shortly after the Democratic convention, that he would seek "no personal favors or national patronage." As he told a constituent, "Neither of them had anything that I would want or expect after their election." Kennedy then denied that he had received any pressure from Russell or Vinson on behalf of Vandiver.[35]

The short Kennedy administration was filled with intermittent international crises and lively agitation for liberal legislation in Congress. The frantic activity in Washington after January 20, 1961, was in sharp contrast to the calmer Eisenhower years. Kennedy had made much of getting the country moving again. Russell had felt much more comfortable in the 1950s with the Eisenhower-type leadership than he did in the 1960s when Kennedy and Johnson produced a kind of legislative frenzy with their demands for large numbers of advanced social and economic reforms. Besides Russell's heavy responsibilities as chairman of the Armed Services Committee, the push by Kennedy and other liberal Democrats for programs that Russell opposed placed him under great pressure.

Russell found himself out of step with most of the Kennedy domestic program except the president's plan for agriculture. The program included legislation for subsidized housing, aid to education, a bill to fund the rebuilding of economically depressed areas, and a proposal broadening the number and kind of workers covered by the minimum wage. Russell did not object to raising the minimum wage to $1.25 an hour, but he strongly opposed placing several million additional workers, especially those in the retail trades, under the law. When the measure was being considered in April 1961, he introduced an amendment that would have prohibited adding any more workers to those covered by the minimum wage. But his amendment was badly defeated 63 to

34.[36] On the matter of federal aid to education, Russell had concluded that education should not be dominated by national policy. He was still fearful that federal aid to education would be used to force further integration in the public schools.[37] By this time, Russell was convinced that there would be an effort to racially integrate any institution or agency receiving federal funds. Moreover, he believed that federal aid to public schools was just a first step. Soon there would be demands for federal support of private and parochial schools as well. That, according to Russell, would be bad.[38]

Russell admitted that the social legislation that he opposed did have some desirable features. However, he believed that the laws were being "driven through largely by pressure group support" and without any plans to fund them. Passage of these measures would only add to the public debt, which would plague all future generations. The depressed areas measure, he insisted, would eventually require billions. But Russell was a pragmatist. When he saw that the bill was going to pass, he urged the Georgia Municipal League to get busy and help depressed communities in Georgia to file applications for federal assistance. He would do all he could in Washington to assist.[39]

Although Russell opposed most of Kennedy's domestic program, he agreed with the president on farm policy. The new administration's plan was one of "supply management," which, it was hoped, would reduce surpluses and cut the costs of storing farm commodities. Russell had been an especially sharp critic of the Eisenhower-Benson farm programs that generally relaxed production controls over wheat and feed-grain producers. Surpluses in these crops had piled up to the point where by 1959 and 1960 storage charges alone cost the federal government some $800 million a year. Moreover, Russell resented that cotton, tobacco, and peanuts had been under production controls for many years, while wheat and corn growers had been free to produce as much as they pleased with no meaningful penalties. Consequently, the $6.5 billion in government inventories held by the Commodity Credit Corporation were mostly corn, grain sorghum, and wheat. Like the president and Secretary Freeman, Russell wanted to place stricter production controls on wheat and feed-grain farmers.

Congress, however, rejected the president's proposals for a long-term farm program that would implement tight control of supplies. After defeating Kennedy's plan, Congress then passed the Emergency Feed Grains Bill of 1961. This law called for reducing feed-grain acreage by about 20 percent in exchange for higher price supports and some direct payments in cash or commodities. Russell voted for this measure, although he did not think it restricted corn production as much as necessary. He told Kennedy that if grain producers did not accept stricter production controls, the government should not try to prop up their prices.[40] Despite support of the president and backing by Russell, those favoring stricter production controls on feed grains and wheat lost out again in 1962. When the administration tried to place marketing quotas on wheat by getting two-thirds of the producers to vote for such restrictions, the referendum in May 1963 went heavily against controls.[41] Considering the bills better than nothing, Russell voted for farm legislation in both 1962 and 1963.

Russell continued to plead for special help for the family farmer and fought for those government programs that he believed would help the smaller operator. If the trend toward bigness continued, he wrote, it would not be long before a few producers and processors would control most of agriculture. He favored rural development programs because he believed this kind of federal help would assist in keeping people on the farm. He reported to his colleague Wallace F. Bennett of Utah in 1962 that during the previous decade ninety Georgia counties had lost population—mostly out of agriculture. "It is sad to see the passing of the family type farm operation," he wrote Bennett.[42]

In 1962 Russell became involved in the famous chicken war with the European Common Market countries. By that time, broilers had become big business in Georgia, and after 1960 the United States forged into first place as an exporter of chicken to Western Europe. In July 1962, the Common Market countries sharply raised the tariff on American poultry, which reduced exports and lowered the price to domestic producers by several cents a pound. The Georgia poultry interests turned to Russell for help. Jesse D. Jewell of Gainesville, the founder of large-scale poultry raising in Georgia, and D. W. Brooks of Gold Kist, which exported millions of pounds of chicken annually, urged Russell to use his influence to reverse the European Common Market tariff policy. Russell pressed the president to take firm action and also called on Secretaries Freeman and Rusk to help fight the battles on behalf of poultrymen. Largely at Russell's insistence, Kennedy sent Rusk to Bonn to negotiate a more favorable import policy with West German chancellor Konrad Adenauer.

When Rusk arrived in Bonn and told Adenauer that he wanted to discuss the import restrictions on American poultry, the German leader was astonished. "Do you mean that the President of the United States sent the Secretary of State to Germany to talk about chickens?" Adenauer exclaimed in amazement. "Indeed, he did, Mr. Chancellor," Rusk replied. Rusk did not explain to Adenauer that the trip had been promoted primarily by Russell, chairman of the Armed Services Committee, and Fulbright, chairman of the Foreign Relations Committee, whose states were the leading poultry producers in the United States.

Rusk's trip, however, achieved nothing, and the United States lost the chicken war. American poultry exports dropped sharply. Unable to preserve the overseas markets, Russell turned to increasing consumption at home. He convinced Secretary Freeman to distribute even more chicken through the school lunch program and through programs to feed needy persons.[43]

If Russell found himself in disagreement with Kennedy on many domestic issues, he admired and supported the president's request for a stronger defense. Russell had been complaining for several years that the Eisenhower administration had failed to do enough to strengthen conventional forces, to say nothing of falling behind in acquiring the proper quality and quantity of missiles and other more sophisticated weapons. He had pushed steadily during the Eisenhower years to spend more and do more for all aspects of defense. Russell was alarmed over what he considered a serious missile gap. Commenting early in 1960, he declared: "I can't accept the statement that there is no missile gap. I think there is." When the Eisenhower Defense Department wanted to hold expenditures to no more than $39.7 billion for fiscal 1961, Russell called for more. This, he said, is no time to "quibble over a couple of billion dollars."[44]

Kennedy's call for heavier expenditures for defense heartened Russell. It also reflected a different approach to defense than the massive retaliation concept of John Foster Dulles. By the mid-1950s, the Russians had a full array of advanced military hardware, including nuclear weapons and the means to deliver them. This meant that massive retaliation on the part of the United States could mean the possible destruction of both countries. Kennedy, McNamara, Rusk, and other administrative leaders saw the best defense in balanced forces and the ability to provide a more flexible response to Russia's international probings. These ideas fit closely with what Russell had been recommending for several years. Not only had he pressed hard for faster development of missiles and long-range manned aircraft, he wanted to modernize the army with new tanks and strengthen all of the military services.[45]

The president's desire to "modernize and augment our ability to resist aggression," then, was precisely the right policy, according to Russell. He believed that the United States should become so strong that "no aggressor will attack us." Peace could best be kept through strength, he argued—a view he had held since 1946. As far as Russell was concerned, the president was surely on the right track. He was also greatly impressed with the new secretary of defense, Robert S. McNamara. He told a reporter that McNamara was one "of the most remarkable men" he had ever known and "one of the greatest cabinet members of history."[46]

Russell not only gave strong support to Kennedy and McNamara on defense matters but also was sometimes out ahead of them when it came to expenditures. He was especially anxious to get additional money for long-range bombers. On Saturday, February 25, 1961, the president called Vice President Johnson, CIA director Allen Dulles, and Russell to the White House to discuss the defense budget. For an hour, they went over Kennedy's request for an increase of $2.1 billion. Russell gave it his enthusiastic support. Most of the increase was to go for bombers and missiles, just what Russell wanted. Russell told reporters afterward that the people would support such increases if they thought they would get their money's worth. Other increases, however, were still to come. In May Russell's Armed Services Committee recommended another $525 million for long-range bombers for 1961–62. Nearly a billion more was added in July. When Congress finally approved the military budget for fiscal 1962 on August 10, all of the increases took the figure for defense to $46.7 billion, some $6.4 billion over what it had been during the last Eisenhower budget.[47]

Much of the desire for greater defense outlays in 1961 resulted from the crisis in Berlin. Kennedy's meeting with Khrushchev in Vienna early in June had convinced him that the Soviets intended to push the Western powers out of Berlin. In press conferences and then in a television address to the nation on July 25, the president called for building up U.S. and NATO strength to block Russian expansionism. It was in this tense atmosphere that Congress greatly increased the defense appropriations. The crisis became most serious in August when the Soviet Union sealed off the border between West and East Berlin by building a concrete and barbed wire wall between the sectors.

During the Berlin crisis, Russell kept emphasizing that the United States would meet the Russian challenge and defend the nation's rights and liberties. He also explained that the cold war would last "into the foreseeable future" and would test American determination for many years to come. Since 1947 and 1948, when Russia revealed her "true character," he said, "we have been moving from one crisis to another." He stressed that Americans should accept the idea that for many, many years "we will test our nerves, our courage and our fiber as a strong people." And Russell believed that the fiber of the American people was still tough. He was convinced, he said, that Americans had the "will to fight and will assemble the means to fight." Russell declared that the Russians would make a "tragic error" if they confused U.S. tolerance with cowardice. "Kaiser Wilhelm and Hitler made that mistake," he said.[48]

One event on which Russell was strangely silent was the embarrassing attempt by some thirteen hundred Cuban refugees to overthrow Fidel Castro in April 1961. He had opposed the action, presumably because he did not think it would succeed with such a limited and poorly trained force. Russell usually opposed military action to implement foreign policy unless overwhelming military power was available to assure success. Probably the main reason, however, that he did not comment much on the Bay of Pigs fiasco was because of the involvement of the CIA. As chairman of the subcommittee that provided congressional oversight of the agency, it would have been both revealing and embarrassing to recognize publicly the agency's poor judgments and nearly independent actions. Russell admitted to President Kennedy in late 1961 that he and his subcommittee had not known of the CIA's plans for the Bay of Pigs.[49]

Kennedy was very upset over the Bay of Pigs venture. He not only ordered a review of CIA operations in September but also replaced Director Allen Dulles with John A. McCone. During the years Dulles ran the agency, it had become very close to an independent unit of government. Allen Dulles, the brother of John Foster Dulles, Eisenhower's secretary of state, had operated pretty much on his own. Although the CIA was responsible by law to the National Security Council, that group had failed to provide much effective supervision. Russell was as secretive as the CIA itself, and his subcommittee, consisting of members of the Armed Services and Appropriations committees, did very little to control or direct the agency. The CIA would develop its budget, which would then be run quickly by the National Security Council and the president. Then Russell would hide the figures in the huge defense budget, and only a very few people knew what was being spent or for what purposes.

Although Russell had beaten back a move led by Mike Mansfield to establish a Joint Committee on Central Intelligence in 1956, the issue of broader congressional surveillance of the CIA would not die. Members of the Foreign Relations Committee and Chairman Fulbright were especially insistent that Russell's watchdog subcommittee be enlarged to include some members from the Foreign Relations Committee. They justified their demand by arguing that the CIA was actually involved in aspects of foreign policy. Moreover, some senators charged that Russell's subcommittee was unnecessarily secretive and placed too many restrictions on access to information relating to CIA activities.

Discussion of this matter continued through the early 1960s, and finally on March 15, 1966, Fulbright wrote to Russell reminding him that there were several proposals in the Senate to create a "special watchdog committee on the CIA." A resolution written by Senator Eugene McCarthy of Minnesota was then being circulated in hopes of achieving that end. Although Fulbright did not specifically mention in his letter what he believed should be done, his real desire was to add three members from the Foreign Relations Committee to the current oversight subcommittee.

Replying on April 30, Russell told Fulbright that he had discussed the proposal for a new watchdog committee with members of his group. They had unanimously rejected the idea. This was a matter, Russell said, clearly under the jurisdiction of the Armed Services Committee, and he saw no need for change. But the matter did not end there. Majority Leader Mike Mansfield wrote Russell on May 25, explaining that a resolution would soon be introduced by the Foreign Relations Committee to form a new intelligence committee to oversee the CIA. Mansfield said that this would probably produce a hot jurisdictional fight between the committees on foreign relations and the armed services, which could embarrass the Democrats and even reflect adversely on the Senate. In order to work out some compromise, Mansfield said he was asking Russell, Senator Carl Hayden, chairman of the Appropriations Committee, and Fulbright to meet with him on June 1. Mansfield made it clear to Russell that he personally favored the resolution and would vote for it.

Despite the majority leader's support for a new committee, he could not sway Russell. Russell knew that he had the votes to defeat any change. All that Mansfield could do at the conference was to reach an agreement that Russell would defeat the resolution by a point of order rather than by a straight-out vote, which would reduce the embarrassment to Fulbright. The plan called for Russell to raise a point of order, saying that any such resolution must first be considered by a proper standing committee, which in this case was his Armed Services Committee. If his point of order was upheld, the resolution would then have to be sent to his committee where it would die.

Meanwhile, there were increasing demands both inside and outside the Senate to broaden the CIA oversight subcommittee. On May 8, the *New York Times* referred to the Russell subcommittee as the "secret-seven" and even suggested that the CIA might have actually approved the subcommittee members before their appointment. Such a silly charge angered Russell, who explained that the members gained their positions on the oversight subcommittee through seniority on the Armed Services and Appropriations committees. Russell argued that there was no need to have representation from the Committee on Foreign Relations because the CIA did not make foreign policy. But his main reason for keeping the subcommittee small, he said, was to prohibit leaks of secret information. Too many of his colleagues, some of whom were on the Foreign Relations Committee, seemed unable to keep confidential information. When the matter was discussed on the Senate floor, other members of the oversight subcommittee, including Leverett Saltonstall, John Stennis, and Milton Young, supported Russell. Fulbright claimed that he did not want to change the subcommittee structure that had been originally proposed but insisted that adding three members to the subcommittee from his Foreign Relations Committee would improve CIA oversight and provide needed information to that committee. Fulbright emphasized that nothing he said or none of the suggested changes reflected in any way unfavorably on his distinguished colleague from Georgia.

Discussion of this matter, which began in May, reached its climax in mid-July 1966. While Russell argued against any change on principle, he also saw the move as a threat to his power. He frankly said that he was trying to keep Fulbright from "muscling in." The CIA, he repeated, had always been under the Armed Services Committee, and any resolution relating to the agency must come from that committee. It was here that he raised his point of order. After hours of debate, part of it in closed session, the Senate upheld Russell's point of order by the hefty vote of 61 to 28. This meant that the resolution to modify the CIA oversight subcommittee must be sent to the Armed Services Committee, where it died. The issue was settled for the time being, and Russell had won the day.

The *New York Times*, which Russell referred to as Fulbright's "Bible," editorialized that "here was the Senate Establishment—the 'Club' at its stuffy worst." *Time* magazine said that Fulbright could not flout Russell, "the uncrowned king of the Senate's inner establishment." Such comments by the eastern establishment press did not bother Russell. He had protected his turf and maintained the oversight subcommittee as he thought it should be. The next year, however, he did agree to add three members from the Foreign Relations Committee to the subcommittee. But it was not until after Russell's death in the 1970s that the CIA was brought under closer congressional surveillance.[50]

During the crisis atmosphere of the early 1960s, Russell saw no hope for peace in disarmament or any slowdown in the development or testing of more destructive weapons. Late in 1961, he called for a resumption of atmospheric testing of nuclear bombs. In both private correspondence and public statements, he outlined the dangers of Russian weapon superiority and what he considered the muddled thinking of the pacifists. Philosophically, he said, he was for disarmament. He would like to concentrate the nation's energy and resources on peaceful pursuits. But he stated repeatedly that he was not willing to build a "better country for Russia to take over and enjoy while enslaving the builders." To let the Soviets gain superiority in nuclear power, he wrote, "would mean our ultimate destruction." Russell viewed the superpower conflict in cataclysmic terms.

Russell simply did not trust the Russians. He continually referred to their constant probing for weaknesses in the Western alliance and their failure to permit free elections in the Eastern European nations. "They broke every promise and made satellites of every one of those countries," he wrote. While Berlin might be the "hot spot" in August 1961, earlier it had been Formosa, Lebanon, or some place else. There could be no slackening of diligence in protecting U.S. interests, according to Russell.[51]

Part of America's defense rested on the ability to keep military secrets, something that Russell believed had been done poorly. He wrote in mid-1961 that conditions had become so bad that the Russians did not need an elaborate espionage network to get secret information. All they had to do, he stated, was read two or three leading American newspapers. Russell had been carrying on a kind of feud with the Defense Department for several years about plugging the leaks of secret information. He had been equally critical of some members of the Armed Services Committee. However, on the second day of hearings by the Armed Services Committee on April 5, 1961, Russell gave Secretary McNamara and his colleagues a strong lecture on plugging leaks.

He told McNamara that the press statement that had been released from the secretary's office dealing with the previous day's testimony had revealed too much strategic detail for the good of the country. It was "utterly ridiculous," Russell said, that the public be told "the most highly secret of our defense plans." He declared that all the average citizen wanted was to know the amount expended on defense and the objectives to be achieved and the assurance that the nation was adequately defended. Not one person in ten thousand, he argued, cared about the number of hydrogen bombs or the fact that Charleston, South Carolina, was the only place Polaris submarines could be loaded. In putting out information on the country's defenses, Russell said, McNamara should "err on the side of not putting out enough, and do not err on the side of telling the Russians every little detail about our plans."

According to Russell, there had been a gradual growth of defense information leaks since World War II. The situation had gotten out of hand, he said, and "we have practically told the Russians in advance where everything is, where every detail to the last bomb, the last missile, is located." Russell offered an apology for his heated comments, but he said that he had been "riled" about defense leaks for several years. He acknowledged that this was not the first time he had "exploded" before the committee on this issue, but he believed that a "monstrous wrong" was being perpetuated on the American people "by letting this information leak out under the guise of the right to know." Senator Saltonstall, the leading Republican on the committee, commented that this was "the biggest explosion I have heard from the Chairman in fifteen years" and that he hoped it would be effective in restricting secret information to where it belonged. Some newsmen accused Russell of threatening freedom of the press, but he denied any desire for censorship.[52]

Although Russell worked closely with Kennedy on most defense matters, he disagreed with several major aspects of the administration's foreign policy. He continued to fight foreign aid appropriations with all of his influence. Russell's arguments against foreign aid were the same as they had been since 1952. The program was wasteful and ineffective in resisting communism or in gaining support in the United Nations. In terms of national interest, he claimed, the returns were too small to warrant such burdens on American taxpayers. Moreover, he saw the program as stretching "into eternity." The apparent open-endedness of the program caused him ever-increasing concern. Foreign aid had become a national "disease," Russell charged. He said that the United States was taking up responsibilities all over the world, including "many emerging nations and tribes in Africa." When, he asked, would Congress consider the needs of the United States first? He blamed the situation on the State Department, which, he wrote, would give "any country on the face of the globe anything that it asked of us that would cost the American taxpayer money." Besides consistently voting against the major foreign aid bills, he supported crippling amendments whenever they were offered. As in the past, however, his efforts failed to curb the program.[53]

Congress finally adjourned on September 27, 1961, following the longest session since 1951. It had been a tiring and to some extent a frustrating nine months. Russell found that things moved at a hectic pace in the Kennedy years, and his work load seemed to increase steadily. His days were filled with appointments with Vice President Johnson, Secretary McNamara, Secretary Freeman, and other administrative leaders. The president also called frequently to discuss defense and other matters. On May 20, Kennedy wrote to ask Russell to take his place on Memorial Day and lay a wreath on the tomb of the unknown soldier in Arlington Cemetery. Kennedy penned an added note saying, "I hope your Confederate grandfathers do not learn of you joining forces with the G.A.R. [Grand Army of the Republic]." Russell replied that he was greatly complimented by the president's request. He observed that he did not believe his forebears would object to his participation in the ceremonies because as a boy he had heard Confederate veterans express "wholesome respect" for the original members of the GAR.[54]

By this time, Russell had drastically reduced his social life. Besides being extremely busy, he needed to conserve his strength. Moreover, he disliked long social affairs that ate up his time. He was more likely to attend a luncheon or dinner from which he could be excused after an hour or so. Most of his social activities were with his closest friends in the Senate, supplemented by events involving Georgians. He usually attended the Lockheed congressional dinner, as he did on April 12, 1961, and he gave high priority to the Georgia Farm Bureau Federation dinner. He was generally present for Senator Byrd's Apple Blossom luncheon. He often had dinner with the Johnsons. Sometimes he and Lyndon would be working on something into the evening, and Johnson would say, "Come and go home with me and Lady Bird will cook up something."[55] Johnson and Russell also often had lunch together, but these were usually working sessions.

But Russell generally turned down invitations to events that took several hours. Kennedy invited him to attend a dinner and program on July 10, 1961, at Mount Vernon in honor of President Ayub Khan of Pakistan. At first Russell accepted but then wrote, "Did not go to Mt. Vernon—begged off at last." When two days later Johnson gave a luncheon for President Khan, however, Russell did attend. At this time, Russell was living at the Woodner Hotel and had an unlisted telephone number. His staff was careful not to give the number to anyone except the senator's closest friends such as Lyndon Johnson.[56]

On November 11, 1961, Georgians held an appreciation dinner for Russell and Vinson in Atlanta. Secretary McNamara was the main speaker. He began by saying that as "the newest pupil in the Russell-Vinson school for Secretaries of Defense," he was honored to be present. He claimed that the United States was strong militarily and should be comforted to know that Russell and Vinson were on hand to provide guidance and counsel in the future. Russell remarked that Georgians were still unashamedly patriotic and would have "no part of the panty-waists who say 'better red than dead.' " About forty blacks picketed the meeting, protesting the fact that it was held in a segregated hotel.[57] Russell was less disturbed by this than he was by the fact that his friend Lyndon Johnson could not attend.

The most serious diplomatic problem in the Kennedy administration was the Cuban missile crisis in October 1962. Although Russell supported the president, he did not agree with the manner in which Kennedy handled the problem. After Castro announced that he was an avowed Marxist-Leninist, many Americans feared that Cuba might become a beachhead for Soviet power in the Western Hemisphere. When it was learned that Soviet arms were flowing into Cuba, concern turned to alarm. At first President Kennedy said that Russian troops and military supplies in Cuba were no threat to the security of the Western Hemisphere. However, congressional leaders, including Russell, did not agree.

On September 17, Russell presided over secret hearings held by a joint committee of the Armed Services and Foreign Relations committees for the purpose of gaining information on the Soviet threat in Cuba. Two days later, the committees passed a joint resolution on the problem "of intrusion of international communism into Cuba." Both houses of Congress quickly passed the resolution, and the president signed it on October 3.

Written mainly by Russell, this resolution reaffirmed the Monroe Doctrine and resolved to prevent "by whatever means may be necessary" the "Marxist-Leninist regime in Cuba" from extending by force or by the threat of force "its aggression and subversive activities to any part of this hemisphere." It also warned Cuba against using any "externally supported military capability" that endangered the United States.

The resolution gave the president authority to use any means he chose to achieve the stated goal of preventing international communism from using Cuba as a base for expansion in the Western Hemisphere.[58]

During the previous weeks, there had been a good deal of discussion about the nature of Soviet arms imported into Cuba. Were they "offensive" or "defensive"? By the week of October 15, however, photographic evidence clearly showed that the missiles and planes being placed in Cuba were offensive and could be a threat to U.S. security. The president ordered a military alert, and on Monday evening, October 22, he went on television to inform the American people of the Soviet danger.

Before going public, however, Kennedy wanted to inform congressional leaders who at the time were scattered all over the country. He sent Air Force One to pick up several senators and congressmen, including Fulbright in Arkansas and Russell and Vinson in Atlanta. As they flew back to Washington in a plane so new that the president himself had not flown in it, Russell and Fulbright speculated on the nature of the crisis. They suspected that it had to do with Cuba.[59]

The congressional leaders met at the White House at 5:00 P.M. with Kennedy and other administration officials. This was not consultation in any meaningful sense. Kennedy already had decided what he would do. He was essentially asking congressional leaders to support him in a time of crisis. Kennedy described what had occurred in Cuba and then explained that he proposed to quarantine Cuba to prevent any additional offensive weapons from reaching there. He would also urge Khrushchev to withdraw the bombers and missiles already in place.

For Russell and most other senators and congressmen, this was not enough. Sitting directly across from the president, Russell argued vigorously for wiping out the Russian planes and missiles with American air power. Fulbright, chairman of the Foreign Relations Committee, heartily supported this approach although he and Russell seldom agreed on major foreign policy issues. According to his handwritten notes of the conference, Russell said that a quarantine would not remove the danger of missiles already placed in Cuba. He believed that these missiles should be destroyed before the quarantine was announced, thereby assuring that none of them could be used against U.S. cities. He declared that Russia and Cuba had been clearly warned that to establish offensive bases in Cuba "would in effect be considered an act of war against this Hemisphere." Russell argued further that a quarantine would probably create incidents that would more likely lead to nuclear war than "the *fait accompli* of having done that which we told them we would do." He later explained that before the meeting broke up after 6:00 P.M., he had insisted to the last that "realistic measures," meaning the use of force, "to eliminate communism, Castro and missiles from Cuba" be implemented. Indeed, the president became impatient at Russell and others who tried to convince him to take stronger action.

After the White House conference ended, a reporter asked Russell about the meeting. He replied that he had never thought it appropriate for a congressional participant to discuss the details of a meeting held with the president. Information on such a meeting, he said, should come from the White House. The next morning, however, Russell issued a press release criticizing Communist "treachery, deceit and falsehood" and urging people to get behind "our Commander-in-Chief." No useful purpose could be served by discussing the White House meeting because the president had decided on a course of action and "the only voice that can speak for the United States" at such a time was the president, he said.[60]

Although the crisis eased after Khrushchev agreed to remove the missiles from Cuba, Russell never believed that Kennedy took the right action. He was convinced that if force had been used against Cuba, it would have given the United States an opportunity to get rid of Castro and provided a much stronger deterrent to Soviet adventurism. Russell did not believe that Russia would have fought a war, either with nuclear or conventional weapons, over Cuba. He admitted, however, that the Soviets might have made trouble nearer to their home. This was what the Kennedy administration feared. Rusk, for example, believed that if the United States had bombed Cuban bases, the Russians would have taken West Berlin. Nevertheless, Russell continued to complain about lack of firmness toward the Soviets.[61]

Russell received a heavy correspondence on the Cuban crisis. Many writers were unhappy with the settlement. Russell always explained that he had urged stronger action but that his approach had been rejected. Despite his disappointment with Kennedy, Russell usually told his correspondent that only the president could speak for the nation in international relations and that he should be supported. By December 1962, Russell's letters had become more moderate in tone. On December 7, he left word with his staff that they should leave out of letters on Cuba the paragraph about "getting the missiles, bombers, Castro, and Russian technicians out of Cuba" in future correspondence.[62]

Russell continued to believe, however, that the president was not tough enough in standing up to the Russians. He viewed Kennedy as being much softer on communism than Eisenhower and Dulles. He considered the administration's actions, or lack of them, as signs of weakness that would not add to the prospects of peace so devoutly desired by the American people. Kennedy and his advisers were not inspired by fear, Russell said, but by "the erroneous belief that they can placate the Soviet authorities."[63]

Although it was an agonizing decision for Russell, he finally voted against the Nuclear Test Ban Treaty in September 1963. He had not indicated what stand he would take until shortly before the vote. On Saturday morning just a few days before the Senate was to decide the matter, he awoke at 2:00 A.M. After two hours of considering all angles of the treaty, he decided that to vote "yea" would endanger the country. He then prepared a lengthy talk against ratification of the treaty.

Addressing his colleagues on the Senate floor on September 17, Russell said that no one wanted peace more ardently than he did. However, he explained that the treaty under consideration was more likely to bring war than peace. His main objection to ratifying the treaty was that it did not contain any method of inspection to guarantee compliance. The Russians, he said, could not be trusted, and to prove his point, he introduced a large number of treaties that the Soviets had violated since 1920. Secondly, he saw the treaty as a first step toward disarmament that would come piecemeal over the next few years. Such action would be dangerous, according to Russell. Also he viewed the treaty as moving toward some kind of world government that would be disastrous for the United States. Russell seemed to be setting up straw men and then knocking them down. However, he was not trying to change the minds of senators. He was speaking to a national audience—something that he did only on rare occasions. Russell believed that through duplicity, deception, and perfidy, the Russians would take advantage of the United States and he wanted to warn the people. Russell, however, had few supporters for his views. The Nuclear Test Ban Treaty was ratified on September 24, 1963, by the overwhelming majority of 80 to 19.[64]

Russell wrote his friend Charles Bloch a few days later that he voted against the treaty because of secret testimony he had heard from the CIA. While he could not disclose what he had heard, he said that it dealt with previous Russian violations of testing agreements. He told Bloch that he hoped he was mistaken about the treaty but that "I greatly fear the future will prove the minority to have been right."[65]

Kennedy praised and flattered Russell at every opportunity as he tried to reduce southern opposition to his domestic programs and hold support for his military buildup. Despite Russell's opposition to the Nuclear Test Ban Treaty, at a news conference a few days before the

Senator Russell and President John F. Kennedy at White House press conference, August 22, 1963, at the time of the rollout of the Lockheed C-141 Star Lifter. Senator Herman Talmadge looks on. (Photo courtesy of Russell Memorial Library, University of Georgia, Athens.)

Senate vote, the president referred to Russell as "probably the most individually respected [person] in the Senate." Kennedy invited Russell to accompany him to the U.S. Air Force Academy graduation exercises on June 5, 1963. In accepting, Russell told a White House staffer that he had handled the legislation to establish the academy and the appropriations to build it but that he had never visited Colorado Springs. He was delighted to attend. On October 12, 1962, at the close of the Eighty-seventh Congress, Lawrence F. O'Brien, special assistant to the president, wrote Russell that "the President is particularly appreciative of your Committee's activities in behalf of the Administration's defense program."[66]

Russell liked the president and enjoyed being with him. Moreover, he was pleased when Kennedy remembered special occasions in his life. On November 2, 1962, Kennedy sent Russell warm birthday greetings. Honored that the president had remembered his birthday, Russell replied that there were getting to be "too many candles on the cake." The fact, however, that he could include the president among his friends and that he was entitled to an additional $600 exemption on his income tax "makes me more philosophical to the rapid passage of the years," he wrote. On January 12, 1963, the thirtieth anniversary of Russell's arrival in the Senate, Kennedy wrote to congratulate the senator, "as your warm friend," on a career that had won people's "admiration and respect."[67]

Despite their personal relations, Russell opposed most aspects of the New Frontier. He consistently voted against about every major domestic program suggested by Kennedy in 1963, except the Mass Transportation Act that provided matching grants to local and state governments for mass transportation. He opposed the Youth Conservation Corps, amendments to the Areas Redevelopment Act, and a National Services Corps.

During 1962 and 1963, Russell and his supporters were able to block any significant civil rights legislation, despite growing demand for action by the president, liberal Democrats, and an increasing number of Republicans. In February 1963, Majority Leader Mansfield tried to push through a revision of the rule governing cloture, but Russell and his backers defeated the move by a vote of 54 to 42. Supporters lacked 12 votes for the necessary two-thirds majority. Although proponents of civil rights legislation saw that they probably could not stop a southern filibuster if the administration fought for new laws, street demonstrations and sit-ins by blacks, beginning in 1960, created a new dimension in the fight over civil rights. The defense of segregation was becoming increasingly difficult.

During late August 1962, some seventy-five ministers were arrested in Albany, Georgia, for marching against segregation and demanding an end to discrimination. Senator Jacob Javits of New York called the arrests "absolutely outrageous and disgusting." Russell quickly came to the defense of Georgia authorities. He accused Javits of playing politics and said the people of Albany should "take pride in their police force" for upholding local laws. Russell added that Javits was hardly one to speak about disturbances in Albany when the streets of his home city of New York were so unsafe. He further accused Javits of discussing conditions about which he knew nothing and of caring only about "the political mileage involved."[68]

A few months later, Russell urged the president not to send troops to integrate the University of Mississippi at Oxford. When troops were dispatched there anyway, he joined Senator Stennis in complaining about the number involved. As race demonstrations and confrontations became more intense in the spring of 1963, Russell grew increasingly bitter over federal interference in local law enforcement. He frequently wrote and spoke about the reserved powers of the states and warned that the people were being "absorbed by force of arms into the central government."[69]

By 1962 and 1963, Russell's uncompromising stand against civil rights legislation was beginning to bring him more criticism than ever before in his long political career. Some blamed him for not doing enough to preserve the ways of the South, while others faulted him for being too rigid and a part of the problem. On October 2, 1962, following racial clashes in Alabama, the *Macon Telegraph* editorialized that most Georgians believed resistance by Governor Ross Barnett in that state to federal authority was futile—but not Russell. The editor charged that Russell was out of touch with reality on this question and that his "intemperate and misguided" statements did nothing to help improve the racial situation in Georgia and elsewhere throughout the South. One Russell supporter, however, scribbled a comment beside the editorial that read, "98% of the people of Ga. are with you."

Several Georgians accused Russell of not doing enough or being sufficiently active in opposition to civil rights. One writer suggested that he get on television more frequently to better advertise the southern position. The *Atlanta Journal* carried a brief editorial on June 17, 1963, which said that the civil rights fight had at least one positive effect for Georgia—"it has brought Senator Russell back to life." The writer complained that recently Russell had been "unavailable and inaccessible." "Welcome back, Senator. Good to know you're still around," the piece concluded.

Russell deeply resented criticism that he was not doing all he could to defeat civil rights laws or that he was not handling his job capably. He replied to the critic who urged him to get more publicity that he was more concerned about "beating these [civil rights] bills than I am in running to the television every few minutes" for the sake of publicity. It was irritating, he told another correspondent, after working fifteen to twenty hours a day fighting for the southern position, to have someone from the sideline tell him how to proceed. To a woman in Atlanta who suggested that he should give up trying to refight the Civil War, Russell replied that he was making no such effort. But, he added, "I did not understand that Appomattox abolished the Constitution."[70]

The editor of the *Atlanta Journal* also got a sharp letter from the senator. Russell accused the editor of not having any idea of what was really going on. He said he had fought "a life and death struggle" in February to defeat a change in the cloture rule and then had been involved with a great deal of important legislation, including looking after federal agencies and military establishments in Georgia. The fact that the editor had implied that Russell had not been doing his job, Russell wrote, showed just how little he knew. It is clear that by 1963 Russell was more short-tempered and less forgiving of criticism than he had been in his earlier career.[71]

During 1963 when Russell was working so hard to resist broader civil rights legislation, his old friend Lyndon Johnson was pressuring the Kennedy White House to provide much more vigorous leadership in this area of national policy. On June 3, 1963, Johnson had an interesting telephone conversation with the president's assistant Theodore Sorensen. Johnson even went beyond being frank in suggesting how the president ought to proceed on this issue. He said that blacks were "tired of this patience stuff" and wanted greater action by Kennedy. Johnson told Sorensen that the president should go to Jackson, New Orleans, or some other southern city and make a high moral statement on civil rights. Then he advised the president to sit down with Russell and answer every argument Russell made against civil rights legislation with responses that carried weight. Make the anti–civil rights crowd "show every card they got," Johnson said. He added that the opponents of civil rights were "experts at fighting this thing and we are not prepared for them." The administration had been using a popgun, but it needed a cannon. "The President is the cannon," Johnson said. Johnson continued that the president needed to line up every Republican, every preacher, and every decent southerner he could find. Get to Everett Dirksen, Johnson advised, and take him away from the Russell camp.[72]

In effect, Johnson told Sorensen that Kennedy had been politically amateurish and not fully committed to the civil rights fight. This was advice from a political pro who knew how to wield power and get results in the Senate. The president, however, either did not have the time or the disposition to develop and implement the Johnson strategy. All possibilities that he would push harder for civil rights ended with that fatal shot in Dallas on November 22. Until then, the resistance of Russell and his supporters had been quite successful. The civil rights bill before the Senate still had a long way to go before passage.

When the news of the president's assassination reached Washington, Russell was reading the Associated Press and United Press news ticker tapes in the Marble Room behind the Senate chamber. Although stunned at the tragedy, his first reaction was to learn if the nation's defenses were ready for any eventuality. He moved quickly to a telephone and called McNamara. Assured on that point, he sat with Mike Mansfield in the radio-TV gallery with tears in his eyes. Kennedy's assassination was a "dastardly crime," he said, "which had stricken a brilliant dedicated statesman at the very height of his powers." But he was not thinking only of the dead president. No doubt he was contemplating the changes that might occur with his friend Lyndon in the White House. During the next few days, however, the thing that most impressed Russell was the demeanor of Jacqueline Kennedy, the president's widow. On November 26, Russell wrote her:

> At the danger of being thought presumptuous, I am writing to express my unbounded admiration of your demeanor and every act indeed during the past four tragic days.
>
> No queen, born of the purple, could have acquitted herself more admirably. Your calm dignity vanished the hysteria which threatened millions of your fellow Americans who followed your every movement on the television screen.
>
> I am so old-fashioned as to believe that those who have departed this earth still know what transpires here, and I therefore believe that President Kennedy was prouder of you then than he has ever been in this life. Only a great lady in the finest traditions of the old school could have displayed such magnificent courage.
>
> Thanking you for what you did to steady our national morale and to improve our nation's image, I am, with assurances of deep respect and esteem, sincerely, Richard B. Russell.[73]

18

Johnson and the Great Society

===

It was reported that Lyndon Johnson was keenly disappointed when his old friend Dick Russell was not at Andrews Air Force Base in Washington to welcome him when he returned from Dallas as president on the evening of November 22. Later that night, however, Johnson called Russell at his apartment, and they talked for ten minutes about the tragic events in Dallas. Russell was one of the first persons to visit the White House the next day. As the two men sat talking over lunch, Russell kept referring to Johnson as "Mr. President." Finally, somewhat impatiently, Johnson said, "call me Lyndon as you used to. After all we've been together all these years." "No, Mr. President," Russell responded, "now you're the President of the United States. You to me are Mr. President." Such was Russell's abiding respect for the office of the presidency.[1]

Dick Russell was happy to see his old friend in the White House. Indeed, he had worked quietly toward that end since the mid-1950s. He believed that Johnson had all of the talents and abilities to be a strong president, and he told Earl T. Leonard, his press secretary, that "old Lyndon is going to enjoy being president, he'll enjoy every minute of it, every hour of it."

At the same time, a Johnson presidency left Russell with mixed feelings and some obvious concerns. One thing that Russell understood perhaps better than anyone else was Johnson's skill and effectiveness as a political leader. Would Congress, which had failed to pass much of Kennedy's liberal agenda, now respond to Johnson's leadership and enact a host of social and economic measures, including civil rights legislation? Unhappily, Russell believed that would be the case. He wrote a friend on November 26, 1963, that Johnson had recently "gone all out, even further in some respects than President Kennedy, on the racial issue" and intended to press for passage of the "iniquitous" civil rights bill. He warned that the shock over Kennedy's death was no reason to pass hasty legislation as a kind of memorial to the late president. Russell said that no amount of sympathy for the dead president or high national emotions changed the Constitution.[2] Russell fully realized, however, that the Kennedy mystique and Johnson's "awesome talent for working the Hill," as writer Meg Greenfield phrased it, would result in the passage of many bills that Russell opposed. Senator William Proxmire recalled that after he had once accused Johnson when he was majority leader of usurping Democratic senatorial power, Russell had told Proxmire in the cloakroom that his position reminded him of the story of the bull who charged a locomotive. "That was the bravest bull I ever saw," Russell said, "but I can't say a lot for his judgment." With a man of such demonstrated political power in the White House, and one who was committed so fully to civil rights, it was folly to think that a strong bill would not be passed. That was not a pleasant prospect for Dick Russell.[3]

The first few days of the Johnson administration were hectic for Russell. Besides all of his regular duties, he was on the telephone with Johnson or at the White House almost daily. He had lunch with the president again on November 26 when presumably they talked about Russell serving on the committee to investigate the Kennedy assassination. This was followed by numerous White House briefings for congressional leaders, including meetings on both December 9 and 10. On December 11, Mrs. Johnson invited Russell to dinner, along with Senator George Smathers, the Talmadges, and "the pretty young wife" of an absent Texas congressman. When Jane McMullan, one of Russell's secretaries, asked Lady Bird if it would be a black tie affair, she replied, "Oh, no honey, you know my husband better than that." It was hard for Russell to find any time for quiet or relaxation. When he went to Winder on December 22 to spend a few days at home over Christmas, his phone was ringing with calls from the White House even before he arrived.[4]

Russell had had his first problem with the president before he left town for Christmas vacation. Johnson had moved quickly to set up a commission to investigate the Kennedy assassination, and he wanted Russell to serve as one of the seven members. The senator politely declined. Johnson pleaded with his friend to accept the appointment by stressing their close friendship and emphasizing how much he needed Russell on the commission. But Russell was adamant. He had a number of reasons for refusing the president's request. One factor was the lack of time. He argued that there would not be enough time to attend to his regular Senate duties and also be present at the commission's hearings.

His current schedule, he explained, bordered "on the impossible." Russell did not like to undertake any task unless he could do it well. Moreover, he did not relish the idea of serving with Chief Justice Earl Warren who would be chairman of the commission. Russell believed that Warren had destroyed the integrity of the Supreme Court, and he had been one of the chief justice's sharpest critics ever since the *Brown* decision nearly a decade earlier. Perhaps more important was the fact that Russell knew his main task in the immediate months ahead would be to fight the impending civil rights legislation. That would take a tremendous amount of time and effort.

Johnson, however, paid no attention to Russell's protests. As Russell explained to his old friend Charles Bloch, the president was "so insistent, I simply could not refuse." When Johnson announced the commission members on Friday afternoon, November 29, Russell's name was included. Russell later told a constituent that he had been "conscripted on the Commission."[5]

Russell attended the commission's organizational meeting and heard the first two witnesses testify. However, he did not have the time to attend many of the meetings. He kept up with the hearings, however, by reading "every line of testimony."[6] Russell made no secret of the fact that serving on the commission was most unpleasant. In February 1964, there were even rumors that he might resign from the commission. The rumors proved correct—at least he tried to resign.

On February 24, he wrote the president a long letter reminding him of his reluctance to serve on the commission and outlining the problems he was experiencing in trying to fulfill his responsibilities as a member of that body. He had been able to devote so little time to those duties, he told Johnson, that he felt like a part-time member. Moreover, Russell was miffed because when Robert Oswald, a witness that Russell particularly wanted to hear, testified, his office had not been notified of the meeting time. Russell said that he could not operate efficiently and allocate his time properly under such conditions. In any event, since Russell could not attend a majority of the sessions and also "discharge my legislative duties," he requested the president to accept his "resignation and relieve me of this assignment." Nevertheless, he assured Johnson that he wanted to serve the country and the president in any way he could.[7] In his customary manner, Johnson ignored Russell's request, and the senator continued to give what time he could to the hearings. He revealed on the television program, "Face the Nation," on March 1 that he no longer had any plans to resign and would do his best to get all of the facts to the American people about the tragedy in Dallas.

However intrigued the American people may have been by the unanswered questions surrounding the assassination of President Kennedy, Russell was concerned in late 1963 and early 1964 with what he considered a much greater issue. That was the intensified pressure for civil rights legislation. By means of the filibuster and skillful parliamentary maneuvering, Russell and his few southern supporters had so far been able to defeat what they believed were the worst features of civil rights measures that had been before Congress almost constantly since 1948. Russell had been a master at defending unlimited debate, which in several cases had succeeded in forcing civil rights advocates to drop their bills or to compromise away the strongest features. This had surely been the case in 1957 and 1960.

Since 1938 there had been 11 votes taken in the Senate on cloture in connection with civil rights measures, and Russell had led successful fights against them all. He had also turned back attempts to change the rule so it would have been easier to shut off debate. The last of these fights had been early in February 1963. Following that contest, Senator John Stennis praised Russell for the way he had "maneuvered us through the perilous seas of parliamentary debate" and brought "final victory over the Philistines."[8] How could the southern group have won with only eighteen senators, Stennis had been asked. "My reply was that we did not have eighteen Senators, but that we have seventeen Senators, plus Senator Russell—and that the plus Russell is the thing which makes the difference."

Flattery from a few close friends and colleagues may have been sweet, but it had no effect on the situation regarding civil rights legislation in the congressional session beginning in January 1964. A few weeks earlier, Russell had experienced one of his short, periodic depressions. He felt like giving up the whole fight. Early in October 1963, he had scribbled on a desk pad, "As of today am completely disassociated from any leadership responsibility of our group."[9] Why? The answer was that he could not keep up with so much work, and more important, he said that "too many hearts are not in it who have same priority." Fading commitments from former anti–civil rights activists had surely become a problem and a great discouragement to Russell. As Stennis described the situation early in 1963, all of the six senators who had died in the previous sixteen months "were on our side, but we got the votes of only two of their replacements."

There was no doubt about it—the Senate had been changing. Attitudes and political realities had shifted. Younger senators had been elected, senators who were not chained so firmly to the old ways by habit, tradition, and custom and who believed in the fight for civil rights. Some of them saw that in time they must also have black votes to remain in office. Moreover, several of the most active and loyal soldiers of the anti–civil rights crusade were old and tiring. Senators Willis Robertson and Harry Byrd of Virginia were 76, and Allen Ellender of Louisiana was 73. Russell himself was past 66 and experienced periods of poor health. Time was ravaging the southern army that Russell had led so effectively for some two decades.

Meanwhile, the civil rights forces in Congress had been growing stronger and much better organized. Lobbying groups included black organizations such as the NAACP, spokesmen for organized labor, Americans for Democratic Action, the American Civil Liberties Union, and many more. Churches and church organizations were also exerting increasing influence by 1963 and 1964. These included the National Council of Churches of Christ and the National Catholic Conference for Interracial Justice. In the Senate, Hubert H. Humphrey, a skilled tactician, was now the majority whip, and he was working to build an alliance between northern and western Democrats and Republicans on the civil rights issue.[10]

To top it all off, just as Russell expected, President Johnson threw the full weight of his personality and office behind civil rights legislation when he addressed Congress on November 27, 1963. This appeared to be the opening shot in the campaign for Johnson's Great Society program. The president declared that "no memorial or oration or eulogy could more eloquently honor President Kennedy's memory than the earliest possible passage of the civil rights bill for which he fought so long. We have talked long enough about equal rights in this country," the president said. "It is time now to write the next chapter and write it in the books of law."[11] As Johnson called for fast action on civil rights legislation, most members of the House and Senate cheered wildly. Russell sat glum and disheartened. He did not applaud his old friend.[12] In this instance, not even his total respect for the office of president could gain his approval of Johnson. The action and reaction of the president and Congress should have been enough to cause even the most devoted disciple of segregation and white supremacy to lose spirit. Nevertheless, Russell was ready for one last fight. While he did not give up his leadership role as he had contemplated a few months earlier, he was not optimistic. As he wrote a constituent on December 2, 1963, "The odds against our small group of southern constitutionalists in the emotional atmosphere which prevails are indeed fearful to contemplate." He added, however, that he and a few other "constitutionalists" would go down fighting "with our boots on at the last ditch." When a friend from Dalton raised the question about Russell's determination, the senator replied that there was as much chance of him surrendering on civil rights as there was of moving Stone Mountain from near Atlanta to Dalton.[13]

A strong and comprehensive civil rights bill passed the House of Representatives on February 10, 1964, by the huge margin of 290 to 130. The bill's main provisions included providing for greater protection of black voters; prohibiting discrimination on the basis of race, religion, or national origin in restaurants, hotels, theaters, sports stadiums, and other public accommodations; extending the life of the Civil Rights Commission; permitting cutting off federal funds from programs where discrimination existed; setting up an Equal Employment Opportunity Commission; and giving the attorney general greater powers to desegregate the public schools. Almost every aspect of the bill was unsatisfactory to Russell.

As had been true since the beginning of the fight over civil rights, Russell denied that he was a racist, that he favored discrimination of any type, or that he held any ill will against blacks. "Every Negro citizen possesses every legal right that is possessed by any white citizen," he declared, "but there is nothing in either the Constitution or Judaeo-Christian principles or common sense which would compel one citizen to share his rights with one of another race at the same place and at the same time." Russell argued that he was for civil rights but that the basic question was where do the other person's rights end and "mine begin"?[14] He strongly opposed the public accommodations section of the bill because he believed that it would deny what he called peoples' "inalienable rights . . . to choose or select their associates." Russell usually avoided extremism on any issue, but on civil rights, he sometimes abandoned moderation. If there was a constitutional basis for requiring a restaurant owner to accept a black in his establishment, Russell argued, "it can be used to sustain the validity of legislation that will compel [a black's] admittance into the living room or bedroom of any citizen."[15]

Russell severely criticized abolishing a person's right to operate a segregated service or business. Equality, he said, was the right of every citizen to own and operate a business as he pleased. The use of federal power to force the owner "to unwillingly accept those of a different race as guests creates a new and special right for Negroes in derogation of the property rights of all of our people to own and control the fruits of their labor and ingenuity." Such a law, he maintained, was a long step toward socialism. He argued that the "outstanding distinction between a government of free men and a socialistic or communistic state is the fact that free men can own and control property, whereas statism denies property rights." He wrote Charles Bloch that "we have indeed come on evil days" if a restaurant owner could not select his customers.[16]

For years Russell had been hostile to equal employment opportunity legislation. He believed that it was an unconstitutional invasion of the fundamental right of an employer to hire whomever he pleased. So Russell strongly opposed both the public accommodations section and the equal employment opportunity provision of the civil rights bill on the basis that they unconstitutionally denied people the right to associate with, and employ, people of their choice. From his standpoint, the bill was unconstitutional because it restricted personal freedom and the right to control one's private property.[17] His opposition to a Civil Rights Commission rested mainly on his belief that the agency was dominated by black activists who would not hesitate to discriminate against whites in order to give blacks special privilege. It can be safely said that the bill contained nothing that Russell liked.[18]

Some segregationists hoped that perhaps Russell's personal relationship with President Johnson might help him in eliminating some of the bill's worst features as viewed by southerners. But Russell knew better. He told people both privately and publicly that this would not be the case. Although Russell and Johnson had worked together on earlier civil rights bills with the result that the bills had been weakened, that would not be the situation again. Russell wrote to several constituents that he and the president had been "close friends for a number of years" but that he did not have the influence over Johnson that so many people attributed to him.[19] He regretfully told an audience at Valdosta, Georgia, in late January 1964, that the president would throw his full power behind the civil rights bill.[20] When Russell appeared on CBS's "Face the Nation" on Sunday afternoon, March 1, he again scotched speculation that the president would make any compromises or deals on civil rights. The president's past positions would make that impossible, Russell explained.[21]

Although public opinion polls showed that a majority of Americans favored civil rights legislation, Russell did not believe that in their hearts most citizens supported such measures. He did admit that there had been increasing sentiment for civil rights in his own state, but even Georgians could be brainwashed, he said.[22] The problem, according to Russell, lay in his inability, and that of other segregationists, to inform and educate people outside of the South about the dire consequences of integration and equal rights legislation. If people only knew how a civil rights law would adversely affect American life and society, and how it violated the Constitution, he explained, Americans North and South would bring enough pressure on Congress to defeat it. He summed up his views by telling one correspondent that if some way could be found to show people the "evils and vices" in the civil rights bill, "they would rise up and demand its total rejection."

According to Russell, it was the media that had poisoned peoples' minds on this issue. He accused newspapers, magazines, radio, and television of slanting the news and creating an "anti-southern feeling throughout the rest of the nation" that amounted to nothing less than "a national disease"—a term he often used. He charged that the media had magnified violence in the South while minimizing it elsewhere in the country, all to the end of generating "bitterness and hatred against southern whites."[23]

Russell was distressed and annoyed at the sympathy of some federal officials for the boycotts, sit-ins, marches, and other manifestations of nonviolent civil rights action. He believed that the protection granted to these groups by federal marshalls and other officials only encouraged more of the undesirable activity. He saw the riots and demonstrations strictly in terms of law and order, and he thought local and state law enforcement agencies could and should handle them. The idea that people could block traffic or close off a storefront without any punishment angered Russell. He argued that citizens did not have the right to select which laws they would obey and which they would ignore. He was especially angered when supporters of civil rights bills used the racial demonstrations to justify quick passage of civil rights legislation. In mid-1963, he sharply criticized Kennedy for "using threats of mass violence to rush his social equality legislation through Congress." Russell believed that local and state officials should deal with demonstrators on a law-and-order basis without federal intervention to protect those he believed to be lawbreakers.[24]

Although the position of Russell and his dwindling band of followers appeared hopeless, he received large numbers of letters from people both inside and outside the South who favored his stand and praised his last-ditch efforts to somehow defeat or modify the legislation. This helped to confirm his undying view that the American people really did not want the bill passed and that it was being pushed by special interest groups and vote-hungry politicians. A grandmother from Minneapolis wrote him early in March 1964 that she shuddered to think of her granddaughter being forced to attend an integrated school. A Presbyterian minister from New Jersey heartily congratulated Russell for his stand. Following his appearance on "Face the Nation," letters of support poured in, and he received requests for his remarks from Wisconsin, New York, Pennsylvania, California, Ohio, and other northern and western states. One of the most encouraging aspects of his work against civil rights legislation, Russell wrote, was the support he received from other sections of the country, which indicated to him that "thinking Americans" in all parts of the nation saw the bill's dangers. This, he wrote, was "a well-spring of strength."[25]

Letters backing Russell's position may have buoyed his spirits, but they had no effect on the practical situation. When the Senate began considering the House bill in late February, Russell got a clear picture of political realities when he lost his first procedural skirmish. Pro–civil rights senators wanted to place the measure directly on the calendar for consideration rather than sending the bill to the Judiciary Committee where southern leadership might bury it. Russell argued that bypassing the proper committee would violate Senate rules and destroy the committee system that had been so important to the Senate's successful operation. He insisted that orderly procedure be followed and raised a point of order. However, Senator Mike Mansfield, the majority leader, appealed to his colleagues "to join the leadership in voting to table the appeal of the Senator from Georgia."[26] The Senate voted 54 to 27 to support Mansfield, and the bill went directly to the calendar. By this time, those favoring civil rights legislation in the Senate were much better organized than they had ever been before. This was largely the work of Humphrey.[27]

The last hope of Russell and his small band of supporters was to win enough votes from conservative Republicans to defeat cloture, which would preserve the practice of unlimited debate. They realized that there was no chance to defeat the measure, but they hoped to possibly win some compromises that would make the bill less distasteful. The key to the conservative Republicans was Minority Leader Everett Dirksen, a friend with whom Russell had often worked in the past. He carefully cultivated Dirksen. Russell even contacted the president of the Georgia Institute of Technology on behalf of a student Dirksen wanted admitted to that institution.[28] But Russell was no match for the blandishments and flattery heaped upon Dirksen by other Republicans who favored the bill, Humphrey, and the liberal Democrats. By April they had brought Dirksen over to their side.[29]

From April until the bill finally passed the Senate on June 19, there was a wide-ranging discussion of the measure. It was a period when senators could make their statements to constituents and to the nation, but no amount of oratory would modify the outcome. There were no new or different arguments. Everything had been heard before. Many amendments were offered, but they were either insignificant or defeated. During the discussions, Russell revived his old idea of relocating blacks out of the South and rewarding them for moving to the North or West.[30] He also introduced an amendment providing for a national referendum on the civil rights bill. Neither of these proposals received any serious consideration.[31]

During the long weeks of debate, barbed exchanges sometimes enlivened the proceedings. Senator Jacob Javits and Russell got into a heated discussion when Javits criticized the jury trial amendment in the bill because, he said, southern juries would not convict whites who violated the rights of blacks. Russell jumped to his feet and challenged Javits's interpretation of southern justice. He said that he was sick and tired of his New York colleague intimating that southern juries would violate their sworn oaths. Russell said that he resented the implication by Javits that there was "something fundamentally evil and sinful about people who lived in the South." After further exchanges, Javits declared that he had the highest regard for people in the South, and the two men shook hands.[32]

Another interesting incident involved one of Russell's relatives. A petition submitted by the Fellowship of Concern, a group of Southern Presbyterians, called for immediate passage of the civil rights bill. Among the names on the petition was that of William D. Russell, a minister who was the senator's nephew. Hoping to embarrass Russell, Senator Humphrey mentioned this in a news conference. Russell simply responded by saying he was sorry that there were some clergymen in his family who had been unable to withstand the specious arguments in favor of legislation that would sap the foundations of constitutional government.[33]

Finally, on June 10, the vote was called on cloture, and it passed 71 to 29. That was 5 more votes than were needed to limit debate. Russell got the support of twenty-two Democrats, but only six Republicans voted against cloture. The power of the Southern Bloc, which had held back any comprehensive civil rights legislation for nearly a quarter of a century, had been broken. Russell once told a reporter that he would "vote to gag the Senate when the shrimp start whistling Dixie." The shrimp were not whistling, and Russell was still opposing cloture, but it made no difference.

On June 18, the day before the final Senate vote on the civil rights bill, Russell made his last major speech against the bill. He opened his remarks by saying that the Senate was moving toward the "final act of the longest debate and the greatest tragedy ever played out in the Senate of the United States." For eighty-two days since March 9, discussion of civil rights had totaled some ten million words and filled about sixty-three hundred pages in the *Congressional Record*. But historians, he said, would not find the length of the debate significant. The true importance of this legislation would be the impact that it had "upon our form of government." "The year 1964," he continued, would mark "a turning point in our history." In Russell's view, the civil rights bill would "profoundly affect the American way of life and the rights and individual liberties of every American."

The central issue, Russell argued, was the unrestrained power being granted in the bill to the executive branch of the federal government, which would permit political persecution of citizens by an ambitious and ruthless attorney general and other bureaucrats. The bill bestowed powers on the central government over affairs that, "under our constitutional concept, have been the sole concern of states and local governments." Those governments under the impending bill would become "mere puppets of the gigantic bureaucracy." More than this, Russell said, the bill granted "plenary powers to bureaucrats to enable them to create a horde of special benefits for a selected group of citizens in defiance of our exalted Jeffersonian doctrine of equal rights to all and special privileges to none." The entire measure, he insisted, "had its genesis in politics. It is punitive in its nature, and it is certain to be sectional in its application." Russell stressed that the bill was aimed primarily at the South. Actually, he said, "the most despised and mistreated minority in the country" was "the white people of the Southern States." Those behind the bill had the same motives as those who prompted Charles Sumner, Thaddeus Stevens, and Benjamin Wade to support the hideous Reconstruction legislation designed to punish the South in the post–Civil War years, he declared.

Before concluding his talk, Russell could not pass up the opportunity to praise those few colleagues who had fought civil rights legislation. They had been loyal and dedicated to the cause, he said. Indeed, Russell went so far as to say that some of the constitutional arguments contained in their speeches were equal to "the debates of Webster and Calhoun." He also expressed pride in his personal part in the fight. "We believe in our heart of hearts that we have held the high ground of principle," he told his colleagues. But nothing more could be done. In conclusion Russell called on "a benevolent providence" to "give us stronger and abler leaders to rally the people before it is too late."[34] The final roll call vote was on the following day, June 19. The result was overwhelmingly for civil rights—73 to 27. The measure then passed the House and was signed by the president on July 2. After the fight was over, Stennis wrote Russell, "You won all the constitutional arguments and lost only when the sole determination lay in sheer numbers."[35]

This was not a happy time for Dick Russell. He was tired and discouraged. Although he had known for months that the civil rights bill would become law, that fact did not make it any more palatable or acceptable to him. "Our little group of constitutionalists fought to the limit of our strength and ability to defeat the federal force bill," he wrote, "but our ranks were too thin and our resources too meager to withstand the tremendous pressures that were brought to bear upon us."[36]

What were those pressures? Russell knew them well. Perhaps most important was the gradual change in national outlook that had been occurring for twenty years or more. Russell had seen this coming. He had become distressed and sometimes impatient when even southerners were not all being as true to segregation as he thought they should be. There had been nothing he could do to keep the changing mood from spilling over into the South. Then there were the lobbies and pressure groups that had been so active. After the law passed, CBS correspondent Roger Mudd and writer William S. White visited with Russell just off the Senate floor. White asked, "Well, the reason you lost Senator was because of the pressure blocs, the lobbies, wasn't it?" Russell replied, "You got it. Now you understand how this government works. That's the secret, pressure blocs."

By 1963 and 1964, the churches had become a significant force in the civil rights fight. Indeed, Russell believed that church groups had a major influence on the final outcome. Explaining the situation, he wrote a friend that "we had been able to hold the line until all the churches joined the civil rights lobby in 1964." Senators, he continued, who had very few members of minority groups in their states and who previously had voted against cloture lost heart when "men of the cloth" began to put pressure on them. Russell believed that church spokesmen had taken what was essentially a political question and made it a moral issue, increasing their power as they did so. Then, of course, there was the arm-twisting of the president. After the successful cloture vote, Russell said that Johnson "had more to do with it than any other man."[37]

About the only satisfaction Russell could gain from his years of resisting civil rights legislation was the knowledge that he had delayed passage of the law. He was proud of that fact. There is no doubt that Congress would have enacted a comprehensive civil rights bill much earlier if it had not been for Russell and the Southern Bloc. Senator Stennis, a strong Russell admirer, wrote shortly after passage of the 1964 bill that "except for you and your fine leadership, a strong civil rights bill would have been passed—at least one with major provisions—as early as 1948 . . . or certainly soon after the unprecedented Supreme Court decision of 1954."[38] This was probably an accurate assessment of Russell's influence.

Once Congress had passed the law, however, Russell urged compliance and counseled against any violence or forcible resistance. "Violence and defiance," he said, "are no substitute for the long campaign of reason and logic we must wage to overcome the prejudices and misconceptions which now influence the majority of the American people." While he said that it would be the "understatement of the year to say that I do not like this statute," it was now on the books and should be obeyed "as long as it is there." The American system, he declared, "could not tolerate the philosophy that obedience to laws rests upon personal likes and dislikes." In this speech at Rome, Georgia, on July 15, he expressed the belief that all good citizens would abide by the new law. The next day, the *Atlanta Constitution* praised Russell in an effusive editorial, declaring that the senator had proven himself a "great American, above and beyond his state and sectional ties."[39]

After reading Russell's remarks, Johnson was unrestrained in praising his old friend. "As the acknowledged leader of the opposition to the civil rights bill," Johnson wrote "Dear Dick," it was very important for him to call for compliance with the law. But, Johnson added, this was entirely "in keeping with your personal code and I am confident it will have a great impact." Russell replied a couple of days later, thanking Johnson for his "very gracious note" and adding that it was "extremely gratifying to receive praise from such a source."[40]

Although there were reports to the contrary, the fight over civil rights in 1964 did not damage or rupture the long and close relationship between Dick Russell and Lyndon Johnson. While they differed sharply over this issue, they completely understood and accepted one another's position. They were just as close personally after Johnson became president as they had been earlier. This actually surprised Russell, who did not expect such a close association, particularly the numerous social occasions, to continue. Moreover, throughout 1964, except for civil rights, the president and Russell worked together on about all aspects of the nation's business. They talked on the telephone, or in person, sometimes on a daily basis but at least several times a week. They were often together on weekends.

For example, Johnson called Russell on January 10, 1964, to discuss the situation in Panama. The president telephoned again the next day, and then Russell spent Sunday, January 12, with the Johnsons at Camp David. He arrived at Camp David about 11:00 A.M. Sitting in the large living room and looking out across a beautiful valley, Dick told Lyndon and Lady Bird the history of the Civil War battle of Antietam. Later they had lunch, took naps, and then did "a little bowling." It was a relaxing, family-type day.

Russell's office records indicate that the president either telephoned him or invited him to the White House on January 15, 16, 27, 28, and 29 and February 3. On February 7, Johnson called Russell on the telephone four times between 8:00 A.M. and 6:30 P.M. In their meetings and telephone conversations, they discussed a wide range of issues, including defense appropriations, national security, Vietnam, domestic legislation, and appointments. On June 10, the day the Senate voted for cloture, Johnson talked with Russell about a replacement for Henry Cabot Lodge, ambassador to South Vietnam. Russell recommended the appointment of General Maxwell Taylor, who was named by Johnson a few days later. On July 26, he had lunch with Lyndon and Lady Bird. The same evening, the Johnsons and Russell were together again at dinner with the Fulbrights. It was a "rare pleasure," Lady Bird wrote, to see Dick twice on the same weekend. Then she recorded in her diary, "I never look at Dick Russell without admiration and without thinking of his great talent." But she added that she wished he would put that talent to better use. Presumably, she meant in the support of Johnson and his programs. She was dismayed by what she called Russell's self-imposed "aloofness," because "nobody can be more charming or express himself more lucidly, and sometimes more humorously."

Late in August 1964, Russell wrote a constituent describing his relations with the president. Johnson and he were still good friends, he explained, and "he is gracious enough to discuss many issues with me." Actually, Russell said, Johnson had called him that morning at Winder to discuss several national questions.[41] On November 22, 1964, he joined the president and a number of his friends for the annual hunting gathering at the Texas ranch. While Russell had quit hunting some years earlier, he had been making that annual pilgrimage to the ranch since the early 1950s. In 1965 Russell wrote that the president fully understood his philosophy and that he "does not expect me to support all of his recommendations." They talked often, Russell said, even though

Johnson knew Russell could not support much of his legislative program. All Johnson would ask, Russell related, was the senator's help to get a particular bill on the calendar. This, Russell said, he always did. "I am honored," he concluded, "that he calls me on the phone and that I am invited to the White House almost weekly for consultation on major issues."

Lyndon Johnson did not like to be alone, and he often called Russell to fill his need for companionship and support. One evening Lady Bird returned to the White House about 9:30 and immediately looked for her husband. She found him, she said, in his small office with Dick Russell. Then Lady Bird added: "I'm always glad to find Dick Russell with Lyndon. Whatever lack of red-hot enthusiasm he may have for the Great Society, when the going is rough and Lyndon needs the advice of an old hand, a wise old hand, Dick Russell will usually be there." On another occasion, Lady Bird recalled that Marvin Watson brought Russell to the White House, and "we had a quiet dinner, just Lyndon, Dick and I." Following the meal, Lyndon and Dick spent two hours discussing "the military future of the country—the Senate and its problems and personalities and new faces." Russell himself recalled that "we'd sit around and have a highball and eat supper and talk about things and people." Johnson was interested in what persons on the Hill were doing and thinking. The two men seldom argued, and Russell said that the president was as kind to him "as a man could have been to his own father." Speaking of his policy differences with Johnson during an interview in January 1965, Russell said, "I fear he has been more tolerant of me than I would have been of him had our positions been reversed." In any event, Russell greatly treasured those occasions with his friend Lyndon because he, too, was often lonely.[42]

Russell also continued to have a warm relationship with the Johnson daughters, Luci and Lynda Bird. On the occasion of Luci's marriage to Patrick Nugent in 1966, Russell sent her a warm and affectionate letter, as well as a gift. He was proud, he wrote, to have had the opportunity to watch her develop from "a lovely little girl into an accomplished and beautiful young lady." He wished that some "kindly genie" would permit him to "give evidence of my devotion to you and your family by sending you ... one of the world's greatest treasures." But short of that, he sent her a copy of Gone with the Wind inscribed, "To Luci—with affection, pride and admiration." Never letting an opportunity pass to call upon history, he reminded Luci that the book's locale was the area where "some of your Johnson forebears lived before moving West." Some weeks later, Luci wrote "Dear Uncle Dick," thanking him for the book not because of its own worth "but most especially because we cherish and love you." She mentioned how much she would miss the family dinners with Russell.[43]

Although Johnson clearly recognized that Russell would not support much of his program, he liked to test out ideas on the senator. After throwing out an idea, he would gauge the character and intensity of Russell's reaction. If Russell rejected the proposal, did he strongly attack it or just mildly oppose it? To know this was useful to Johnson. Russell served as a sounding board for a major constituency in the Democratic party. So the president probably conferred with Russell more than with any other senator, even though he may have been fairly sure how he would respond. But it made a great deal of difference on the Senate floor whether Russell expressed mild opposition or whether he worked the Senate apparatus to defeat a proposal. There was also another plus about visiting with Russell. Every president who ever dealt with him, from Roosevelt to Nixon, knew that Russell would never reveal what they discussed. Refusal to reveal anything specific about a presidential conversation was a cardinal principle with Dick Russell. Even his senior staff members recognized this as a firm and fast rule. They, too, were left out.[44]

Despite his cordial personal relations with the entire Johnson family, Russell was determined not to play any part in the president's reelection campaign. He was telling constituents well before the convention that "I do not intend to take any part in the national campaign."[45] He also said that he would not advise anyone on how to vote in the election. He explained to a number of friends that he felt out of place with leaders of the "new" Democratic party and had little or nothing in common with the liberals and radicals who, as he put it, were advocating placing all powers in the federal government. Nevertheless, he insisted that he would vote the Democratic ticket.[46]

Russell announced in August that he would not campaign for the Democratic ticket. Admitting that this had not been an easy decision, he finally concluded that principle must come before what he called his intimate relationship with the president. Many Georgians urged him to become active on behalf of Johnson and Humphrey, but he steadfastly refused. State senator Jimmy Carter was among those who asked Russell to get out and work for the Democrats, at least in Georgia. But Russell explained that not even Johnson would ask me "to stultify myself by getting out now and supporting a campaign platform endorsing and assuring endorsement of a system which changes the form of government that we have heretofore known in this country." The senator certainly would not support a platform that approved the "Federal Force Bill of 1964" or a party whose vice presidential candidate, Hubert Humphrey, had led the pro–civil rights fight in the Senate that had overwhelmed Russell and his group. In regard to Humphrey, Russell admitted to Carter that he was one of the "most attractive personalities" he had ever known but that the Minnesotan's philosophy of government was diametrically opposed to his own and even bordering on socialism. He once described Humphrey as a shooting star, "brilliant but ready to pick up almost any idea—however bizarre—without much reflection." Russell later referred to Humphrey as having "more solutions than we have problems."[47]

Although there is no evidence that Johnson personally requested help from Russell, when the president campaigned in Georgia, he identified himself with the senator at every opportunity. In Macon he expressed regret that "my long time and dear friend, Senator Dick Russell could not be here with us," and at Augusta he said, "In my days in the Senate, no man was kinder to me or gave me more help than this great Senator."[48]

Johnson may not have asked for Russell's help, but Lady Bird did. She first called him on September 12 to ask if he would travel with her on the train as she campaigned through Georgia in October. Russell told her that he was so unhappy with Humphrey and some aspects of the platform that he could not in good conscience accept her invitation. On October 1, she called again only to get the same reply. Four days later, Lady Bird telephoned with another plea to her friend. Russell scribbled on a note pad, "Nothing by pressure—pressure to ride Lady Bird Special and participate in the Presidential campaign." It was painful to Russell to have to turn down Lady Bird for whom he had deep affection, but no amount of coaxing could change his mind. He sat out another national election.[49]

As it turned out, Georgia was one of the six states that Johnson failed to carry. This fact produced a good deal of criticism of Russell for not having used his influence to win the state for the Democrats. The outcome may have surprised Russell because he had said earlier that Georgia was safely in the Democratic camp. In any event, he received sharp reprovals from a surprising number of constituents. One critic wrote in a letter to the *Atlanta Constitution* that he was no longer a "Dick Russell man." If Russell had stood up and been counted during the campaign in Georgia, the writer said, Johnson would have carried the state. Another anti-Russell voter wrote that Georgia needed a senator in Washington "who lives and thinks in the present and future" and one who would keep Georgia up with the rest of the United States and not "run off to Europe like a sulking school boy."[50]

Some of the more extreme Georgians criticized Russell for not having joined Senator Strom Thurmond who found a new political home in the Republican party. Russell explained that he respected Senator Thurmond but that he had always held office under the Democratic banner and had an obligation to the party. This did not mean, however, that he had to follow every party line. Indeed, Russell had always boasted of his independence. On a more practical note, Russell explained that he could best serve Georgia as a Democrat with his long seniority. He had worked too long and hard, he said, "for valuable public projects and military installations that are now almost vital to the economy of our state to sign them away with one stroke of the pen" by changing parties. He argued that Georgia needed his seniority to protect the state's economic interests.[51]

It was with a kind of stoic resignation that Russell witnessed the landslide victory of Johnson and Humphrey. He blamed most of the more radical tendencies in the party on Humphrey, who, he said, drew all of the "extreme left-wing groups into the Democratic fold." He was still smarting from the drubbing Humphrey and the civil rights forces had given the Southern Bloc a few months earlier. As he put it, "The political wounds inflicted by the overwhelming forces, not only in the Senate, but in the communications media and throughout the land, led by Vice President-Elect Humphrey were still bleeding." And the future looked equally grim. Writing to his close friend and ally, Senator Willis Robertson, shortly after the election, he said that he was not looking forward to the next session of Congress. "They have overtaken and overwhelmed us," he said.[52]

The civil rights fight that demanded so much of Russell's effort between March and June 1964 left him little time for work on the Warren Commission. As mentioned earlier, he did not want to serve, and he resented having to spend time on commission business that he preferred to spend on other matters. Thus he missed many of the hearings, and when he did attend, he seldom asked questions. He was present when John B. Connally testified but was absent when such key figures as J. Edgar Hoover, head of the FBI, and John McCone, head of the CIA, appeared. He continued to read transcripts of the hearings faithfully, however, and his underlining and queries in the margins testify to his careful scrutiny of the testimony. He once said that he had read "until I thought my eyes were going to burn up."[53]

Russell's most active part in the commission's work came in early

September when he presided as chairman of an informal subcommittee from the commission that went to Dallas to interrogate Marina Oswald again. He had missed Marina's testimony on June 11 when she was questioned by commission members. On Sunday afternoon, September 6, Russell, Senator John Sherman Cooper, Representative Hale Boggs, and a staff member questioned Mrs. Oswald at the U.S. Naval Station in Dallas. Most of Russell's questions dealt with her husband's contacts with agents in Russia and Cuba and with Cubans in the United States. The Russell subcommittee learned little that was not already known.

One of the most interesting aspects of the four-hour hearing in Dallas was Russell's discussion with Marina about her hope to profit financially from her experiences. She was writing her memoirs, and she did not want certain material that had been revealed in the hearings to be published. If her testimony was published in the official government record before she could sell her account of events, those experiences would lose most of their commercial value. She asked Russell if the material that would appear in the published hearings could be confined to that part pertaining to the assassination. This would be up to the full commission, Russell explained, but showing a softheartedness that often came to the fore, Russell said, "I was hoping that you had found some means of commercializing on it [her life story] either to the moving picture people or to the publishing world."[54]

During his short stay in Dallas, Russell traced the route of the Kennedy motorcade and with Representative Boggs went to the sixth floor of the Texas School Book Depository Building from which the fatal shot had been fired. Taking a rifle, he leaned out of the window and aimed at the spot where the Kennedy car had been. It would be a difficult hit, Russell said; "Oswald must have been an expert shot." After he returned to Washington, reporters deluged him with requests for interviews and comments. His picture, often with rifle in hand, leaning out of the window, and accompanying stories appeared in newspapers from one end of the country to the other. Russell, however, refused to discuss the substance of Marina's testimony, saying only that "it was nothing startling or shocking."[55]

Despite his lack of strong participation in the whole investigation, Russell had considerable influence on the final report. His main change dealt with whether there was a conspiracy between Oswald, Jack Ruby, and possibly unknown parties to kill the president or whether Oswald acted on his own. An early draft of the final report categorically stated that the evidence "indicates that [Oswald] acted alone." Russell insisted that this be changed to "the Commission has found no evidence" that

Warren Commission submits to President Lyndon B. Johnson its final report on
the assassination of President John F. Kennedy, September 27, 1964. Senator
Russell is third from left. (Photo courtesy of Russell Memorial Library, University of Georgia, Athens.)

any conspiracy existed. The phrase "has found no evidence" was repeated several times. Russell saw considerable difference in saying that
there was no conspiracy, or that Oswald acted alone, and that there was
no *evidence* of those things. He did not believe that the commission had
all of the information that existed. The commission had no access to
evidence that might exist in the Soviet Union or Cuba. Moreover, since
Russell was the principal person in the Senate who had oversight of the
CIA and possessed secret information others did not have, he may have
had reason to suspect some kind of conspiracy. Whatever he knew, if
anything, he carried to his grave.[56]

On September 27, the commission released its final report. At the
same time, Russell finally agreed to a lengthy interview on the commission's work and findings. While emphasizing that the commission had
not turned up any evidence that would establish a conspiracy, Russell
said that there were still many unanswered questions. Much of the evidence, he said, was beyond the commission's reach. Nevertheless, he
explained that he thought the report was "the very best we could have
submitted." He frankly admitted that the debate and speculation over
the circumstances of Kennedy's assassination would "continue for a

hundred years or longer." He continued to get mail on the subject, but he left much of it unanswered. He was glad to have the whole thing behind him. When people wrote to him about reopening the investigation, he either ignored them or explained why he did not favor such action.[57]

Nothing much seemed to be going right for Dick Russell in 1964. As if losing the civil rights fight, serving on the Warren Commission, and seeing Hubert Humphrey elected vice president were not enough, he was faced with a flood of legislative proposals that were supposed to produce a Great Society. As we have seen, Russell was not opposed to all social welfare programs. He had supported a good deal of legislation extending the powers of the central government on behalf of those in need. He did strongly object, however, to setting up programs that he considered unnecessary, unworkable, or wasteful. By the mid-1960s, he believed that Congress was passing too much legislation without proper study or consideration of the cost or the long-term consequences. To Russell, Congress had a knee-jerk response to about every demand from a special interest group.

His first difference with the administration came over the Revenue Act of 1964 that passed the Senate in February. This law reduced both individual and corporate tax rates. Russell believed that spending should be cut before taxes were lowered. Lower taxes and increased spending, he said, could only result in further deficits. This seemed totally irresponsible to him. As he had said earlier, that seemed to be the latest Harvard view of economics, but "not having attended Harvard, I take a dim view of this philosophy." Although the bill passed by the large margin of 77 to 21, Russell joined with twenty colleagues and voted no.

In August Congress passed the Economic Opportunity Act, which included much of the administration's antipoverty program. It was an omnibus measure that provided for a Job Corps on the order of the old Civilian Conservation Corps of New Deal days, work-training programs, loans for low-income farm families, work study for college students, and other help for those in poverty.[58] Russell sympathized with the bill's objectives, but he believed that the legislation was too loosely drawn and would result in huge amounts of waste. His main objection, though, was to the Job Corps. He did not think this program would provide any long-term help to young men and women, and even worse he feared that a large number of northern urban black youth would be sent to southern camps and become a disruptive influence in the region.

When Russell could not eliminate the Job Corps provision, he voted against the entire bill as a protest.[59]

Congress also expanded federal aid to education in 1964 and 1965. Although Russell had been an early supporter of federal assistance to education, by the mid-1960s he had come to oppose many of the educational programs. His main complaint rested on the growing influence and control that the federal government was, in his judgment, gaining over institutions receiving funds from Washington. He wanted to preserve local and state control of education and was especially concerned about what he called "the nationalization of our public school systems." However, Russell did support the higher education act of 1965 as well as some other educational measures.[60]

He had similar reservations about Medicare. Russell had favored some kind of national health care for the elderly for several years, and he wrote in 1962 that the votes were available to pass such legislation. It was a matter of getting agreement on specific aspects of the program. His concern, he said, was passing a bill that was "as sensible as possible." He opposed some of the early Medicare proposals, but when the bill "guaranteed the choice of physician and hospital to the person who had the insurance," he supported it. When the Medicare bill was finally passed in July 1965, Russell was absent on special business and did not vote.[61] On the other hand, when the Appalachian Regional Development Act was considered in 1964, Russell backed it. This measure called for expenditures of over $1 billion on a variety of programs designed to eliminate deep pockets of poverty in an eleven-state region in the southeastern United States. Here was something that would definitely benefit parts of Georgia. When the bill was finally passed on February 1, 1965, he voted for it.[62]

Despite his support for some of the Great Society programs, Russell generally believed that Congress was passing more legislation than was needed or could be administered properly. He believed the nation was gorged with laws and administrative rulings that could not be well digested. There were too many agencies with overlapping and duplicative services. He feared the extensive expansion of federal powers and responsibilities, which he did not believe were in the nation's best interests. And it seemed to Russell that more and more of the power was gravitating toward the executive branch instead of Congress.

In late November 1964, when Russell was at the Johnson ranch he and the president talked over a wide range of domestic issues and foreign policies. When reporters asked how he and the president expected to work together harmoniously in light of their recent differences on civil rights, Russell replied that Johnson would be president for the next four years and he would be chairman of the Armed Services Committee so they must work together for the good of the nation. He said that he and the president must cooperate and work toward that overriding goal of keeping the United States free from "communist enslavement."[63]

An event that caused considerable comment among political observers was the fact that Governor Carl Sanders of Georgia was also a guest at the Johnson ranch. Sanders had strongly supported the president in his successful bid for reelection, while Russell had stayed on the sidelines. Several Georgians wrote open letters to the newspapers suggesting that Sanders would make a better senator. One writer said that Sanders "stands 10 feet taller than Richard Russell and Herman Talmadge put together."[64] The tantalizing question was, could Sanders challenge Russell in 1966?

Long before the 1964 presidential election, a number of Georgians wrote to the senator speculating on what Sanders might do. Some were concerned enough that they sent unsolicited contributions in case a campaign against Russell did develop. However, he returned the money and advised his friends that all he wanted them to do was to act as "minutemen" in their communities and keep him informed of the political situation. Shortly after passage of the civil rights bill, one constituent advised Russell to consider retirement. But the senator replied that he was not yet ready for that. "The people of Georgia," he wrote, as he did many times, "have a sizeable investment in me and my seniority and committee assignments are worth a great deal to the state."[65]

Rumors that Sanders might run against Russell in 1966 continued to surface in the closing days of 1964 and early 1965. Then an unexpected event occurred that agitated the prospect. On February 2, 1965, at about ten o'clock in the morning, Russell was taken to Walter Reed Army Hospital with a severe case of "pulmonary edema," a condition where the lungs fill with fluid, making it very difficult to breathe. He was immediately given oxygen. However, the usual medical treatments could not relieve his situation, and on Saturday morning, February 6, doctors performed a tracheotomy, making an incision to open his windpipe. Within a couple of days, Russell showed improvement, but he was still a very sick man. Bill Bates, the senator's press secretary, announced that Russell would probably be confined to the hospital longer than originally planned. Members of the Russell family were genuinely concerned, and several of them came to Washington to be at his bedside.

Meanwhile, a flood of sympathy messages and letters of encouragement reached the senator. The Johnsons were the first to be notified that Russell had been admitted to the hospital. The president telephoned at 4:30 P.M. and immediately sent flowers with a card on which he wrote, "We are thinking of you and pulling for you." On February 11, Johnson sent a touching and emotion-filled letter to Russell. "Not a day goes by that my thoughts and those of Lady Bird and the girls are not with you," he wrote. The president said that he would like to sit by Russell's bedside and visit but that his presence in the hospital would be too disturbing. Lady Bird sent a message through the president saying that if any of the visiting Russell relatives needed a place to stay, the Johnsons would be glad to care for them. Johnson said that he sorely missed Russell and his "wise counsel." "I lean on you so much, Dick, and not having you where I can talk to you is an unfillable void," he wrote. In a handwritten postscript, Johnson concluded, "We think of you (all 4 of us) many times each day." The Johnsons showered Russell with flowers. Even discounting Johnson's usual flowery and flattering language in situations of this kind, it is clear that he truly missed Russell and was saddened by his illness.[66]

During the rest of February and into early March, Russell experienced a very slow recovery. On February 18, one of the doctors who kept the White House regularly informed on the senator's condition reported that Russell would have a lengthy convalescence. He was then eating unassisted, but he had great difficulty breathing. Lack of lung capacity, the doctor said, would continue indefinitely, "probably for life." Doctors were able to remove the tube from Russell's throat on February 26, a sign of progress, but they reported that "it is going to be quite a long pull."[67]

During Russell's illness, Bill Bates put out information on the senator's condition. Even though he talked on the telephone with the senator about various press releases, he was uneasy over how Russell might react to some of the stories on aspects of his illness. Bates was understandably nervous. Just before Russell left the hospital, Bates told him, "Senator, I had to say some things about your condition while you were ill . . . that you may not like," but went on to explain that the senator's nephew Bobby had concurred in the releases. Before Bates could say more, Russell interrupted and said that he did not see why his press secretary had a problem. "Bill," he continued, "all you had to do was tell the truth. . . . Just state the facts and that was all that was necessary."[68]

While Russell lay in his sick bed, political gossip was bubbling in both Georgia and Washington. On February 11, Ralph McGill of the

Atlanta Constitution talked by telephone with Jack Valenti, one of the president's White House aides. McGill said that Russell's illness was much more serious than had been publicly announced and that the president was surely aware that if Russell could not serve out his term, it would create a crisis in southern political leadership. McGill suggested that if Russell had to step down, there would be a chance to "loosen" the hold of conservatives in the South and that Sanders would "almost certainly" be a candidate for the Senate. On February 20, the *New York Times* and other newspapers speculated on the possibility of Sanders challenging Russell. These stories added grist to the rumor mills.[69]

Russell left the hospital on March 9 after a more than five-week stay and recuperated for several more weeks in Puerto Rico and Florida before returning to Winder for additional rest and recovery. Meanwhile, rumors about his health and political future persisted. In an effort to squelch the speculation, he announced late in April 1965 that he had no plans to retire and would be back at his desk in Washington before the current session ended. However, he did not publicly declare whether or not he would seek reelection in 1966, although he had told close friends that was his intention. A few days before he returned to Washington on May 23 after nearly a four-month absence, he held a news conference in Atlanta and declared that he would seek his sixth full term. Appearing "tanned and trim," he said that he had called the news conference so people could see how well he had recovered. Speaking of politics, he expressed the hope that he would not have opposition in 1966 and, in an effort to appear unconcerned about Sanders, maintained that he knew of no one "likely to oppose me."[70]

On Monday, May 24, Russell returned to the Senate amidst the accolades and praise of his colleagues. Mike Mansfield, Everett Dirksen, Henry Jackson, George D. Aiken, Stuart Symington, Milton Young, and others showered him with tributes and expressions of pleasure at his return. In his response, Russell indicated the seriousness of his illness. There was a time, he told his Senate friends, when he did not think he would be able to "finish out this Congress." But now that he was back, he hoped that he could live up to the tributes, and he would always "treasure as priceless jewels the very kind words" spoken by his colleagues. The senators rose and applauded.[71]

Despite Russell's return to his Senate duties and reports that he was feeling fit, rumors continued about the condition of his health and whether Sanders would challenge him in 1966. Jack Valenti left a memo for President Johnson on July 30 saying that Sanders believed Russell was too ill to wage another campaign and "was very anxious to run."[72]

Senator Russell, at right, confers with President Lyndon B. Johnson on the political situation, May 10, 1966. (Photo courtesy of Russell Memorial Library, University of Georgia, Athens.)

Aware of Sanders's strong interest in the Senate, Russell and his friends moved quickly to discourage him. First, Russell needed to show people that, as he put it, he was not "about to fall to pieces physically." During the summer, he wrote many of his friends explaining that he felt better than at any time in several years and was in a position to do more for Georgia than ever before.[73] Secondly, some of Russell's supporters, among them the most powerful people in the state, let it be known that they would go all-out for Russell if he received opposition. Later, Russell established a campaign finance committee with W. C. Harris of Winder, one of his oldest and closest friends, as chairman. This committee would accept money for advertising and general publicity on behalf of the senator. Finally, Russell needed to get out among the people again.

During the fall of 1965, he traveled extensively around the state seeing friends, renewing old acquaintances, and being very visible. This was a planned effort to counter the idea held by many Georgians that he had lost touch with the people. Some of his friends were concerned that young people did not know him, so he visited several college campuses and courted student groups. Reporting on his travels, Russell wrote that his political prospects looked "almost too good." His only weakness, he said, was among black voters. Even among blacks, he believed that he would get the votes of those working at Lockheed in Marietta, at Warner Robins near Macon, and at other places where "they all know the part I have played in creating the jobs that they are holding. . . . The pocket book is still the most sensitive nerve in the human animal."[74]

For many years, Russell had been critical of politicians who raised large sums of money for campaigning, especially when it came from special interest groups. It had been easy for him to take this stand of principle because he had not had to carry on a campaign for nearly thirty years. He was now greatly surprised at how much more expensive campaigns had become compared to his early years in politics.[75] However, he had no problem raising money as funds poured in from both Georgians and supporters outside the state. But in the end, the efforts proved to be unnecessary.

On March 30, 1966, Governor Sanders announced that he would not be a candidate for the Senate. He explained that his interest had been originally prompted only by the senator's illness. Having become convinced that Russell was in excellent health, Sanders declared that the senator should be sent back to Washington to serve the country in "this tortuous time of uncertain internationalism."[76] Russell was pleased and greatly relieved. He had not wanted to make a statewide campaign, but he was ready to do so if necessary. He was happy that it was not needed. Thus he went on to his fifth nomination and election without opposition.

What finally scared Sanders off were the political polls that showed Russell's strong popularity with his fellow Georgians. A poll taken in August 1965 revealed that 89 percent of voter sentiment was generally favorable to the senator. In a Russell-Sanders race, Russell would get 59 percent of the vote compared to only 25 percent for Sanders, with 16 percent undecided. Russell was clearly the statewide favorite. His main strength was among farmers and people in small towns. Older voters, from fifty to sixty-five years of age, favored him by the hefty margin of 69 percent. He did even better with upper-income groups, polling 76 percent. Thus Russell was impregnable among those over fifty, better-off citizens, and farm and small-town voters. Political attitudes were changing, however, and only 39 percent of those polled in the major urban centers said they would vote for Russell. A mere 14 percent of the blacks favored him. The influence of young urban voters and blacks, however, had not yet made a major difference in the political situation as far as Russell was concerned. He was unbeatable, and Sanders knew it.[77]

In his travels about the state in the fall of 1965, Russell found that many of his old political friends on whom he had relied in his early campaigns had "gone to their final reward." He was discovering that after his long years in Washington, he was no longer close to the political leaders in many counties. But the Russell name still carried enough magic and the benefits he had brought to Georgia were so significant that he could be assured of continued support even if he did not enjoy the same close personal contacts that he had a quarter of a century earlier.[78]

With no campaign ahead, Russell began to return surplus campaign funds that had been contributed in late 1965 and early 1966. After the precampaign expenses had been paid, the balance was given back to contributors on a pro-rata basis. He referred to this as a "dividend" or "rebate" to those who had been so generous to him.[79] His strict standard of ethics and honesty, as mentioned earlier, would never permit him to keep those funds and use them for semipersonal purposes—a practice that became common among politicians later.

Although Russell's own political position was secure, by the mid-1960s he had become increasingly unhappy with the Democratic party and discouraged over the general direction of American political life. He kept hoping against hope that things might change, but he clearly recognized that, as he put it, national developments were passing him by. After Johnson's election in November 1964, Russell expressed the hope that the president might shake off "the domination and control of a little group of left-wing liberals" who he believed dictated Democratic policies and platforms. With such a strong mandate, Johnson was in a position to rid the party of control by "termite left-wingers" and take the country "back to the Jeffersonian principles that have made our country great," he wrote. However, he was not optimistic. He believed that Johnson had "one of the best political minds" that he had ever known but was failing to use his political talents in the country's best interests.[80]

Perhaps due to his long bout with poor health, the growing federal pressure to enforce civil rights statutes, or his declining influence on policy-making in Washington, Russell expressed an unusual degree of frustration and disappointment over conditions as they were unfolding in the 1960s. School integration, the breakdown of segregation, racial violence, decisions of the Supreme Court, the growing national debt, and huge increases in federal powers at the expense of the states all aroused his opposition. These and other developments were enough to make any true Jeffersonian weep, Russell believed.

He wrote many constituents in 1965 that he was deeply concerned about the growing power of liberals in the Senate and their belief "that everything should be directed by Washington bureaucrats." Russell kept repeating what he had said time and again—the American people did "not understand the enormity of the changes in our system that are taking place by executive order." Russell wrote that he had done everything he could to hold back "this total grant of power to minions of the federal government here in Washington" but that there was little prospect of reversing the national direction and restoring "our ancient landmarks." He blamed the Supreme Court for much of what he found wrong. Chief Justice Earl Warren, he wrote, was a "professional reformer," not a competent lawyer or judge. He referred often to the nine justices as "the body that passes as our Supreme Court."[81]

Although Russell objected to many decisions of the Warren Court, the cases of *Baker v. Carr* (1962) and *Reynolds v. Simms* (1964), which required legislative reapportionment and affirmed the one-man, one-vote principle, aroused his strongest protests. He did not believe that any court had the constitutional authority to say how state legislatures should be apportioned. Such decisions were an unconstitutional invasion of states' rights, Russell said. He also objected to reapportionment because it would place greater political power in the hands of urbanites.

He believed that a major decline in the rural vote was unhealthy for American democracy. As a confirmed Jeffersonian, Russell considered that rural people were more solid and politically stable than their city cousins. Under state reapportionment, he wrote, too many rural people would have little representation and would be "completely controlled by a large urban vote." Furthermore, Russell saw a connection between urban votes and heavy federal expenditures. Reapportionment, he said, was "bound to increase public spending at both state and national levels."

In an effort to change the situation, he joined those supporting the constitutional amendment introduced by Senator Dirksen in 1965. This amendment would have permitted a state legislature to apportion one house on the basis of population and the other on a different basis. Russell knew that such an amendment could not get the necessary two-thirds vote in Congress. There were too many "self-styled liberals," he wrote, "to ever permit any modification of the Supreme Court decision."[82]

What frustrated Russell most of all was his inability to do anything about the nation's changing directions. His efforts to delay measures, to resist unwanted legislation, or to amend social welfare bills were meeting with less and less success. He often used the term "overwhelmed" when he discussed his failure to block certain legislation. The entire picture became even more gloomy for the senator as he saw the South's continuing decline in the country's political affairs. He voted for Lester Maddox as governor of Georgia over Ellis Arnall in 1966. Maddox, a vigorous segregationist who earlier had attracted national attention when he used an ax handle to stop integration of his restaurant, was not an ideal candidate from Russell's viewpoint. But Russell preferred him to Arnall who, if elected, Russell feared, would try to make the Georgia Democratic party over more nearly in the national image. To Russell, that would be tragic.

Russell had his ups and downs, his pessimistic days and times when things looked brighter. Occasionally, he was positively optimistic and upbeat. Speaking before the Georgia legislature on January 17, 1966, he first waxed sentimental over his days when he served in that body. Then turning to other matters, he said he felt much better than he had a year earlier, his spirits were high, and "my face is turned full to the future." He saw the times ahead beckoning "as never before with hope and opportunity for all [Georgia's] people." That sounded more like the Dick Russell of the 1930s and 1940s.

Then Russell reviewed his service and stewardship for the home folks. While he had opposed many federal programs, he declared, he had always done everything possible "to see that Georgia gets its full share of whatever benefits may be provided." Although he might vote against a particular measure, if it became law, he said, "I take my tin cup and try to fight my way to the head of the line." There was abundant evidence in the form of military installations, dams, research facilities, and other federal projects that he had arrived at the head of the spending line on many occasions.

Russell described how the federal largess had flooded into the state as a result of his work. There were some sixty thousand Georgians employed at the fifteen military bases located in Georgia, he boasted, and in businesses related to national defense. Federal military and civilian payrolls in the state in 1965 totaled more than $1 billion. Georgia had recently become one of the top ten states in the volume of military and defense contracts. Some $850 million had been spent to harness four of Georgia's rivers—the Savannah, the Coosa, the Flint, and the Chattahoochee. Hundreds of millions of dollars more had poured into the state for agriculture, airport and highway construction, education, and other programs. It was a record of "bringing home the bacon" from Washington that was hard to match. Even Russell's sharpest critics could see the obvious connection between his chairmanship of the Armed Services Committee and of the Subcommittee on Defense Appropriations and the flood of money going to Georgia from the Defense Department.

He told the state legislators that he would continue to support federal programs that were based on federal-state cooperation, but he would oppose measures that permitted the national government "to control and dominate the states." Some, he said, viewed him and his ideas as "old-fashioned and outmoded," but he would never forsake his Jeffersonian principles, which emphasized "a government of divided and defined powers." He would always remain true, he pledged, "to the principles of constitutional government which I hold dear." With that pledge to the voters of Georgia, he headed back to Washington to deal with the most frustrating problem of all—Vietnam.[83]

19

The Frustration of Vietnam

═══

During the 1960s, Russell found himself devoting more and more time and energy to national defense and the United States' growing military involvement in Vietnam. His continued chairmanship of the Armed Services Committee and the Subcommittee on Defense Appropriations gave him a huge range of responsibilities. After 1961 he worked closely with Secretary of Defense McNamara and others in the defense establishment. His days were filled with meetings, appointments, and committee hearings, as well as visits to military installations both at home and abroad. Russell had become recognized by many as the leading spokesman and authority on military affairs in Congress.

As mentioned earlier, Dick Russell sharply disagreed with most aspects of Republican foreign policy in the 1950s. But he was no more impressed with the leadership and policies in the Kennedy and Johnson presidencies. Russell strenuously opposed the idea that the United States should serve as the world's policeman. American power, he believed, was limited. While he agreed that Soviet and Chinese communism and expansionism were the principle sources of international instability, he did not think that the United States should or could respond to every crisis in the world. The best defense against communism, he believed, was to make the United States so strong militarily that no nation would ever be so foolish as to attack the United States or its vital national interests. Moreover, he did not think that American military power should be deployed unless vital strategic or important economic concerns were involved. If military power were required, he believed that maximum force should be used to achieve the objective as quickly as possible.

Russell also held to another important principle. The United States could not help people resist aggression or achieve democracy if they were unwilling or unable to help themselves. Wherever Russell looked around the world, he saw American assistance being squandered on people who, from his viewpoint, seemed unwilling to do anything about their own problems. Laos was a case in point. In the late 1950s, the United States poured nearly $300 million into Laos in an effort to set up an effective anti-Communist government. But after spending millions, Russell wrote, the United States could not find "any Laotian who would do any real fighting." The United States was unable, he continued, to help people or countries "who are not willing to lift their finger or suffer even a pin prick in their own behalf." He saw the same situation in Vietnam, where the government was weak, unstable, and ineffective. "There is a general willingness in Congress to support the Vietnamese to the hilt," he wrote, "if we could ever find the same government in power for long enough to make plans to assist them."[1]

Russell also continued to oppose most foreign aid programs that he believed brought few if any benefits to the United States. He not only stressed the point that foreign aid did not encourage other countries to help the United States resist communism, he charged that generous expenditures on foreign assistance led congressmen and senators to spend excessively on domestic projects. Lawmakers in Washington, he said, were reluctant to oppose spending in their districts and states after appropriating billions for economic and military aid all over the world.[2]

The senator also believed that neither the Republican nor the Democratic administrations had taken a sufficiently firm stand for American interests in the Western Hemisphere. He was a staunch defender of the Monroe Doctrine. Russell always believed that Kennedy had badly muffed the Cuban crisis in 1962. On the other hand, he enthusiastically endorsed Johnson's decision to send troops to the Dominican Republic in 1965. He also opposed any move to give up control of the Panama Canal. To him it was an American canal that must be controlled by the United States permanently. In January 1964, there was rioting in the Panama Canal Zone, and four Americans were killed, creating a crisis that took several weeks to resolve. During the numerous meetings and conferences to consider the problems, Russell urged the president to resist any pressure from the Panamanians to revise the treaty regarding the canal. He telephoned Johnson on January 15 and told him that there should be "no surrender" and no revision of the treaty. He again "spoke his piece" at a White House conference on January 29.[3] Russell feared that the State Department would negotiate away vital U.S. interests in Panama.

It was the increasing involvement of the United States in Vietnam, however, that most concerned Russell. From 1954 onward, he had warned against the United States getting involved in a land war in Asia. He declared that "nearly every military leader I have ever known," including Eisenhower and MacArthur, had advised against any conventional military effort in the Far East that might result in a land war with China. And throughout 1963 and 1964, Russell assumed that if American troops became engaged militarily in Vietnam, China would be drawn into the conflict against the United States. Korea seemed to provide a reliable precedent for that view. The thought of sending American men some eight thousand miles from home to a jungle country that had no unity or effective government where they might eventually be faced with hordes of Chinese was a frightening and haunting prospect for Russell.

Moreover, Russell could not see any possible danger to U.S. interests from North Vietnam or any benefits that could possibly accrue from intervention. On March 31, 1964, when Senator Wayne Morse of Oregon was attempting to learn the administration's plans for sending more Americans to Vietnam, Russell declared on the Senate floor that from the beginning he had opposed extending military training assistance to South Vietnam. "I could not see any strategic, tactical, or economic value in that area," he said. "In the day of long range planes and missiles," he continued, "that area has no significant value as a base for military operations." Morse termed Russell's remark "the most important statement that has been made to date by anyone in this country on the folly of the South Vietnam operations."[4]

Russell viewed South Vietnam as an extremely poor place to confront the Communists. While he claimed that he would never retreat from a Communist threat, he could not see why so many Americans had become excited over Vietnam when they were so complacent about "the military bastion erected by the Communists 90 miles off our shores in Cuba." In May 1964, he strongly opposed sending paratroopers or ground combat forces to Vietnam. "I would rather pull out entirely, with whatever loss of face this might bring," he wrote, "for I am convinced that we would be bogged down in the jungle fighting the Chinese in their kind of war for the next 25 years." As he said many times, he initially believed that the Chinese would move into Vietnam promptly if the United States employed ground forces there.

The American buildup in Vietnam progressed rather steadily, despite the arguments and advice of Russell and others who opposed American intervention there. By the time of President Kennedy's death in late 1963, there were some fifteen thousand Americans in that distant country. During Kennedy's last year in office, the United States spent about $500 million in Vietnam on military and economic aid. All of this had occurred despite Russell's early advice to Kennedy to take a "long hard look" before committing any fighting forces in Vietnam. If the Vietnamese equipped by the United States could not whip the Vietcong, "there was something wrong," he told the president on November 9, 1961. Kennedy, however, replied that he believed it was best to send special American forces to Vietnam to deal with the problems there.[5]

Throughout his first months in office, Johnson was indecisive and somewhat cautious about extending more support to South Vietnam. He was being pushed by his main advisers, McNamara, Rusk, and National Security Adviser McGeorge Bundy, to stand tall and be firm against Communist aggression in Southeast Asia. At the same time, the president was being advised by Russell and others to reassess U.S. involvement and refrain from increasing the nation's presence there. The president steered a middle course. He did not want to appear too hawkish before the fall presidential elections; neither did he want to give the impression of weakness before a Communist threat.

Up until June 1964, Russell's most immediate interest had been the civil rights fight. Nevertheless, during the first half of the year, he had numerous conferences on Vietnam with McNamara, Rusk, some of the nation's top generals, and the president. Then there was a flurry of meetings in the last days of July. Majority Leader Mike Mansfield called a small group of senators together on July 28 to hear briefings from Rusk, McNamara, and General Earle Wheeler, chairman of the Joint Chiefs of Staff. Russell talked with McNamara again three days later. Russell was always very secretive about conversations with high administration officials, but his files reveal that these conferences dealt with providing more military help for the South Vietnamese.[6]

On Sunday evening, August 2, Russell had supper with the Johnsons at the White House. It was not the usual pleasant, relaxed family affair that had occurred so often over the years. Earlier in the day, the president had received word that the USS *Maddox*, an American destroyer, had been attacked in the Gulf of Tonkin by North Vietnamese patrol boats. This action aroused strong reactions from American military and civilian leaders. A hurried meeting of leading senators, including Russell, was called for 3:00 P.M. the next day, at which McNamara, Rusk, and Wheeler reviewed the latest situation in Vietnam. On August 4, Johnson called Russell again, and they discussed the growing crisis and the response that the United States should make against North Vietnam. There is no record of what Russell recommended, but that evening the president went on television to tell the nation that the

United States was in the process of bombing targets in North Vietnam.[7] Meanwhile, some of Johnson's closest advisers had been urging the president to seek a broad congressional resolution that would give him authority to take "all necessary measures to repel any armed attacks against the forces of the United States and to prevent further aggression."

When the Senate met on August 6 to consider the administration's resolution, few voices were raised against it. Russell spoke up quickly on behalf of the resolution. There was plenty of precedent for such action, he said. He mentioned the powers given to President Eisenhower in January 1955 when Congress authorized him "to employ the armed forces of the United States as he deems necessary" to protect Formosa against possible Communist Chinese aggression. Russell said that it was important to send a message to North Vietnam that "any further belligerency toward us or our forces can lead to their destruction."

Russell, however, did not wish to engage in a debate over the "original decision to go into Vietnam." This was not the time nor place for such a discussion, he insisted. Admitting that he had grave doubts about "the wisdom of that decision," he argued that it would serve no useful purpose "to dwell on those doubts here today." Indeed, he declared, whether the United States was involved too little or too much in Vietnam was not the question before the Senate. What was crucial, Russell said, was the right of the United States to operate its vessels in international waters without attack or interference. Then he added what to him was probably more important than anything else. "Our national honor is at stake," he declared. "We cannot and we will not shrink from defending it." No sovereign nation could maintain its self-respect if it did not respond to such attacks, Russell said. He admitted that the "portents of this resolution are great," but he reminded the senators that nothing could be done in international affairs that "does not involve some danger." He considered it more dangerous to ignore "aggressive acts" than to pursue "calculated retaliation."[8]

The Gulf of Tonkin resolution passed overwhelmingly. Before the Senate passed the resolution, however, Russell added an amendment that would permit Congress, if it so chose, to end the extraordinary grant of power to the president. (In February 1967, Russell joined in an effort to revoke the Tonkin Gulf Resolution, but the Democratic leadership tabled the move.) Only Senators Ernest Gruening of Alaska and Wayne Morse of Oregon voted against the resolution. Unlike Russell, they took the opportunity to attack further intervention in Vietnam. Gruening argued that Vietnam was not the United States' war and that the United States was wholly misguided "in picking up the burden abandoned by France." Declaring that the United States' so-called friends and allies were not providing any useful help, he expressed regret that the United States was "going it alone." All of Vietnam, Gruening said, was "not worth the life of a single American boy."[9]

Russell believed as deeply as Gruening and Morse that it had been a great mistake to send American military personnel to South Vietnam. He agreed that supposed friends and allies had left the entire burden in Vietnam to the United States. And like his two outspoken colleagues, Russell did not believe that any U.S. interests in Vietnam were worth the life of one American son.

However, Russell faced an emotional and intellectual dilemma that he was never able to resolve. The presidents of the United States were responsible for the nation's foreign policy, and the president was commander-in-chief of the military forces. In steps reputed to be measured and restrained, both Presidents Kennedy and Johnson had gradually extended American military forces into South Vietnam, and on August 4, 1964, Lyndon Johnson had ordered the first bombing of North Vietnamese targets. While U.S. troops in South Vietnam were still serving mainly as advisers, a growing number of them had been killed. However much Russell opposed the initial commitments of personnel to South Vietnam, Americans were there. They were coming under fire as a result of being sent there by presidential order. As Russell saw it, the American flag and national honor were at stake. Caught in the conflict between what he considered bad policy and national honor, he would opt for national honor. Above all, Russell was an intensely committed patriot and nationalist. He would be glad to support withdrawal from South Vietnam if the president would take the lead, but he would never become an outspoken critic of the war and contribute to weakening the nation's resolve as long as his commander-in-chief chose to involve U.S. troops in Vietnam. Thus Russell could never join the camp of Senators George McGovern and William Fulbright, and many other senators, in their criticism and open opposition to the war.

Thus Russell protested America's growing military involvement in Vietnam, but he could never bring himself to plant his influence firmly and publicly against escalation in 1964 and 1965. Rather, he considered it one of his main responsibilities to make sure that American troops were supplied with an abundance of the best and most effective weapons. He had always had a deep personal concern for American military personnel in the field. He had shown this concern in both World War II and in the Korean conflict. Furthermore, Russell fully realized that, despite his close association with Johnson, he was no match for McNamara and Rusk when it came to influencing the president on Vietnam. As he told one constituent, the president had more confidence in McNamara's advice than that of any other cabinet member. The general public simply did not know, he said, how much Johnson relied on McNamara's judgment. "I know from experience," he wrote, "that when my advice is in conflict with McNamara's, it is no longer considered." According to Russell, McNamara seemed "to exercise some hypnotic influence over the President, just as he did over President Kennedy."[10]

The matter of national prestige constantly haunted Russell as he grappled with the Vietnam issue. The senator opposed any action that would reduce the image of a strong and powerful United States. In writing constituents and others in late 1963 and 1964, he talked about how U.S. prestige would suffer if the country simply walked away from Vietnam. "We cannot afford to pull out unless a new set of circumstances gives us some excuse or reason," he wrote in November 1963. He also believed that withdrawal would shake the confidence of the world in the United States' reliability.[11] Such views closely paralleled those held by Johnson.

Actually, Russell had no solution to the difficult Vietnam problem. Like many other Americans, he opposed further escalation but did not favor withdrawal. To be somewhere between those positions and simply hope that somehow things would improve was no policy at all. In November 1964, he declared that every alternative should be explored before "extending the war," but then he added that the United States would have to get out of Vietnam or do something to help the South Vietnamese. "They won't help themselves. We made a mistake by going in there, but I can't figure any way to get out without scaring the rest of the world." Calling it "the most frustrating and complex situation ever to confront the American people," Russell said, "We are there but don't want to be. We want to get out but can't." Such was Russell's indecision and frustration.[12]

By late 1964, Russell was receiving an increasing amount of correspondence from constituents about American involvement in Vietnam. Some were becoming vocal opponents of escalation. A young man from Thomaston wrote Russell on Veterans Day, November 11, complaining that Americans were "fighting down there for really no reason at all." Not a single Communist had been removed from South Vietnam, he said, "except in a hearse." A Macon attorney, whose son was then in Saigon, wrote, "We don't know how we got there, what we are trying to do there, and how we hope to get out of there."[13] In Russell's replies to the growing number of critics of Vietnam policy, he usually explained that he had opposed the initial military intervention but that now the United States could not "cut and run."

During the latter part of 1964, Russell had an extraordinarily busy schedule, even though, as mentioned earlier, he did not participate in the presidential campaign. In mid-October, accompanied by William H. Darden, Jr., chief of staff of the Armed Services Committee, and Charles B. Kirbow, chief clerk of the Armed Services Committee, he left to visit military installations in Europe. His first stop was Athens, Greece. On October 20, he visited the American ambassador and the next day received extensive military briefings before flying to Spain. After settling in at the Christian Hotel in Seville, the senator had dinner with U.S. Marine Corps general Wallace M. Greene. The following morning, he arose at 4:30 and was driven to near Hulva, some fifty miles from Seville, to observe an amphibious landing by American navy and marine units.

Returning to Winder, Russell rested at home until after the November election. Later in the month, he made several talks and attended special events, including the one honoring Carl Vinson in Milledgeville on November 17. On November 22, he flew to the Johnson ranch but returned to Washington on the afternoon of November 24. Early the next morning, an army car picked him up and took him to the Department of Defense dining room where he had a breakfast conference with Secretary McNamara. He worked in his office the rest of the day and then was flown to Winder early on November 26 so that he could be home for Thanksgiving dinner.[14]

Russell spent the first few days of December in Israel. He, Senator Smathers, and several friends left Washington on November 29, stayed overnight in London, and arrived at the King David Hotel in Jerusalem the next day. Russell thoroughly enjoyed his four-day stay in Israel. He had lunch at Kibbutz Ginossai, visited the Sea of Galilee and other historic places, and went to Tel Aviv and Haifa. High Israeli officials were on hand for conferences. Besides visiting with President Zalmar Shazar, he had dinner with Minister of Defense Shimon Peres. It was a hectic schedule, but Russell called it a most informative trip. He wrote Peres that he was greatly impressed with the "vigor and enthusiasm of your people."[15]

Russell met his increasingly busy schedule by utilizing military aircraft for transportation. He had relied on such service for years, but by the mid-1960s, it had become his main mode of travel. The Lockheed Corporation, which had a large plant in Marietta, also put planes at his disposal. This meant that if the senator had a talk in Georgia or else-where, he could go and return to Washington the same day and often still have time for Senate work. For example, when he needed to get from Macon to Milledgeville for the Carl Vinson affair, Charles Kirbow arranged for an army helicopter to fly the senator from Warner Robins, south of Macon, to Milledgeville. The Lockheed Corporation often placed its Jetstar at the senator's disposal, and one official of the company wrote that he was "delighted" to do so. Charles Kirbow frequently flew the senator on his various jaunts. Occasionally Russell would go by commercial plane, but that became less frequent. For example, he took a commercial flight when he went to Georgia to address the state legislature, but on February 21 when he spoke for Senator Spessard Holland's campaign kickoff at Bartow, Florida, he was flown back to Washington in an air force Sabre jet.[16] No one seemed to raise any objection to the chairman of the Armed Services Committee being jetted around the country on military aircraft or even being flown in a Lockheed-owned plane. Russell himself never considered that any impropriety or conflict of interest was involved. He was about the nation's business, and with his busy schedule, time was important.

During Russell's illness and his absence from Washington between February and late May 1965, the American military effort in Vietnam escalated rapidly. Early in the year, President Johnson authorized additional air attacks against North Vietnamese targets, and in March the first marines arrived in South Vietnam. Regarding the strategic bombing of North Vietnam, Russell said in a telephone interview from Winder in early May that he did not think it would have "much effect one way or another."[17] Throughout 1965 General William C. Westmoreland requested more ground troops, and by the end of the year, there were nearly 200,000 American troops in Vietnam. In January, shortly before entering the hospital and following a conference with John A. McCone, director of the CIA, Russell urged that the entire American position in South Vietnam be reevaluated.[18] But it was clear that this had not been done during his absence.

When Russell got back to a full schedule in June 1965, he was again in the thick of discussions over Vietnam. He had endless conferences with the president, Secretary McNamara, and other high officials. He also had numerous requests for interviews, most of which he turned down. On August 3, Bill Bates left him a note saying that a writer for *Fortune* and a reporter from the *St. Louis Post-Dispatch* had asked for appointments to discuss the Vietnam situation. Russell marked in large letters across the memo, "NO."[19]

His concerns in these months were not entirely with the United States' growing military presence in Vietnam. Always alert to the benefits of military bases in Georgia, Russell pressed McNamara not to reduce personnel at Fort Benning or Hunter Air Base near Savannah. In November 1964, the secretary of defense had announced a plan to close ninety-five military installations, which would save nearly $500 million. But Russell saw that Georgia bases were well protected. On July 30, 1965, McNamara called him and said that there would be no reductions at Fort Benning, and a week later, he informed the senator that plans to move airplanes from Hunter Air Base to Charleston, South Carolina, had been abandoned.[20]

A few months later, Russell succeeded in getting the huge contract for the construction of C-5A transport planes for Lockheed in Marietta. This was a major economic plum for the state. There had been a great deal of speculation over which major defense contractor would land this large contract. But all the while, Russell had pressed the president and McNamara to grant the contract to Lockheed. On the morning of September 23, the president called Russell and asked him to support the Ships Loan Bill. The senator told Johnson that he would see that the bill was reported out from committee but that in return he expected the C-5A contract for Lockheed, calling it "an even trade."[21] A few days later, Secretary McNamara announced that Lockheed had been awarded the contract.[22]

The growing uneasiness over and criticism of U.S. policy in Vietnam placed President Johnson in an increasingly difficult and uncomfortable position. More and more Americans were asking about the nation's interests and goals in that far-away country. On July 28, 1965, the president held a news conference and outlined in some detail what he considered the objectives of U.S. policy. Much of the material was subsequently published in a pamphlet entitled, "Toward Serving with Honor." Johnson explained that the United States was providing a "vital shield" to the non-Communist countries of Southeast Asia and that if the United States was driven from the field of battle, no nation would ever again have "the same confidence in American promises, or in American protection." The United States did not choose to be the guardian against communism, but "there is no one else," he declared. The United States, he said, had a commitment going back over three administrations that must be kept, and Johnson insisted that Americans would not surrender or retreat. Once the enemy knew of American determination, the president believed, a peaceful solution would be "inevitable."[23]

Johnson's talk of solemn pledges, honor, integrity, commitment, and holding back the tide of communism was close to Russell's current view of the situation. Although he had initially opposed sending ground forces to Vietnam, he would not now back down under pressure from the Communists. As he told a friend shortly after Johnson's news conference, it was now too late to debate the wisdom of intervention. "We are in Vietnam," he wrote, "our flag is there—and, above all, American boys are under fire there, and I am supporting all of the President's efforts there to the hilt."[24] Thus the president could count on Russell as a staunch and powerful supporter. But what an anomalous situation! The two Democratic leaders who in 1954 had taken the strongest stand against American involvement in Vietnam were now, a decade later, carrying the burden of that policy—a policy in which neither of them really believed. For old friends Lyndon Johnson and Dick Russell, it was a most painful and tragic experience.

A few days after President Johnson held his press conference on Vietnam, Russell appeared on CBS's "Face the Nation." He expressed deep pessimism about the situation in Southeast Asia. Political conditions in Vietnam, he said, were most disheartening. He declared that, in his judgment, if a plebiscite were held in South Vietnam, most people there would vote for Ho Chi Minh. Unless the South Vietnamese could establish an effective government that would mobilize a strong fighting force in the south, Russell said, the United States should pull out. He explained that the main reason the United States should continue fighting in Vietnam was to redeem its national honor. There was no strategic reason to fight there, he told the viewing audience.[25]

About a month later, Russell gave an extensive interview on the Vietnam situation to the U.S. News and World Report. His tone was somewhat less pessimistic than it had been in the earlier television interview, but he said little that could be considered encouraging. He did not mention again the possibility of pulling out of that quagmire, but he did repeat his belief that the war was going to be a long drawn-out affair, perhaps lasting several years. It could not be settled, he said, until Ho Chi Minh's government was threatened, which would be difficult because "he's almost worshiped by his people." The senator said that the American effort would require more troops, possibly as many as 350,000.

Russell took this opportunity to publicize what he had come to believe was the best solution to the United States' problem in Vietnam. He recommended much more intensive bombing of northern industry, ports, shipping, and transportation facilities. "If I were directing the war," he said, "I would undertake to destroy the docks, and wharves and the harbor facilities" in Haiphong. Although he did not believe the war could be won with air power alone, he thought that the United States had not made the most of its air superiority. It did not make sense, he wrote, to bomb bridges, roads, and trucks when it was possible to put "a stopper in the bottle and cut off the flow of the most important weapons that the Viet Cong and North Vietnamese are using." There were only two ways to win the war, Russell declared: on the battlefield or at the conference table. He believed that any successful negotiations depended on stepping up American military operations to the point where the North Vietnamese would be forced to make a satisfactory settlement. When asked if he believed escalating the war would widen the conflict, Russell said "no." He did not think that either China or Russia would intervene.

Russell said that Ho Chi Minh might have been encouraged in his attacks on South Vietnam by the fact that the United States had not wiped out the Russian missiles in Cuba in 1962. If the United States had bombed those Cuban targets, he explained, "it would have had a very salutary effect all over the world; that would have influenced the course of events everywhere there's a contact between the free world and Communism." Russell called this the "Cuban effect," and it was a theme that he repeated regularly after 1962.

The war was also going to be costly in dollars, Russell told his readers. He did not favor raising taxes to get the needed funds until domestic spending had been cut. There were domestic programs of "doubtful value" that could be trimmed "very substantially," he advised, and the savings could be used to strengthen and rebuild the military forces. While no one was "particularly happy" with the war, according to Russell, "we all realize what it means to our position in world affairs," and he was certain that Congress would appropriate "any sum that's necessary to carry this affair in Vietnam to a successful conclusion."[26]

Like many other Americans, Russell had difficulty outlining a clear and workable policy for the United States in Vietnam. He recognized that the American position was hopeless unless an effective civilian government with popular support could be established. Despite the election of Nguyen Cao Ky as premier in June 1965, Russell was not impressed with South Vietnam's new leadership. The only thing he could suggest was to continue increasing the number of U.S. ground troops and intensify the bombing of vital targets in the north. About the only difference at this time between the president and the chairman of the Armed Services Committee was the degree of punishment that they would deal out to North Vietnam with bombs and missiles.

Contrary to his earlier position, Russell had concluded by 1965 that direct action against the United States by either China or Russia in connection with the Vietnam conflict was most unlikely. Now he seemed to believe that the American nuclear deterrent would be sufficient to place restraints on the two major Communist powers. On many occasions, he had urged Johnson to let the Russians and Chinese know that U.S. nuclear power would be used if needed. For example, on July 21, 1965, he scribbled on an office note pad that the president should tell Russia and China that if they escalated the war, "we use nuclear."[27]

Although Russell recommended using greater force, he was pleased and somewhat encouraged when the president offered North Vietnam opportunities to negotiate the conflict. He explained to constituents that he had consistently urged Johnson to seek an honorable conclusion of the war through negotiations. And he believed that he had much to do with the president's repeated offers "to talk to anyone at any time and at any place about ending this war."[28] The only trouble with this policy was that Ho Chi Minh would not negotiate on any basis that the United States would then accept.

By the end of 1965, Russell was becoming concerned over reports that American troops in Vietnam did not always have the best arms and equipment. If this were true, he said, it was completely intolerable. To meet all of the military needs, he insisted that much more money was required for national defense in 1966. The figure should be at least $60 billion, he argued. Unlike the president, Russell insisted that the country could not have "both guns and butter in unlimited quantities."[29] From 1965 onward, he plugged hard for much greater military spending and cuts in appropriations for domestic programs.[30]

Dick Russell may not have been enthusiastic about the United States' Vietnam venture, but he had absolutely no respect or tolerance for his fellow citizens who talked and demonstrated against the war. In December 1965, he wrote that one of the greatest obstacles to the war's success was the "handful of misguided off-beats" who gave the impression that Americans were not united behind the war. He thought it was shameful to show "Hanoi the spectacle of a divided people," especially since there were nearly 300,000 Americans in Vietnam. Russell said that Ho Chi Minh had based "his whole hopes" on the idea that Americans would tire of the nation's Vietnam effort.[31] When one university professor was quoted in the press as welcoming a Vietcong victory, Russell was livid. To Russell, welcoming victory for the nation's enemy was the worst kind of disloyalty and un-Americanism. It was difficult if not impossible for him to comprehend the thinking of any citizen who did not stand behind the flag wherever it was lifted.[32]

Late in 1965, the war was brought home to Russell in a very personal way. Lt. Col. Walter B. Russell, Jr., a nephew who was an operations officer with the First Air Cavalry Division in Vietnam, was shot and nearly killed. For a time, it appeared that the younger Russell might be permanently paralyzed on one side, but he eventually recovered. Nevertheless, the senator felt the pain of having nearly lost a member of his extended family.[33]

By early 1966, Russell was receiving a huge amount of mail on Vietnam, much of which was increasingly critical of how the war was being conducted. Constituents, as well as others across the country, wrote the senator complaining about the United States' halfhearted military measures, the lack of support from other countries, the fuzziness of U.S. objectives, and Americans dying for no worthy cause.

Russell's standard reply was that he saw only three alternatives in Vietnam. One approach, he said, would be to "hang on and drift along as we now are"; a second course would be to "tuck tail and run"; the third way to deal with the problem, and the one he recommended, was to offer to take any steps toward peace but if these gestures were rejected to "punish the North Vietnamese until they would be compelled to come to the conference table." He always added that he would do everything possible to terminate "this tragic and dirty business in Vietnam."[34] It was clear that Russell had no pat answers to the gnawing questions regarding Vietnam that upset so many of his fellow citizens. As he stated over and over again, nothing in his public career had caused him as much frustration and distress as American involvement in the jungles of Southeast Asia.

By early 1966, however, Russell had concluded that the United States should either undertake an all-out war against North Vietnam or withdraw American forces. He was fed up with the gradualism and measured response that characterized American military policy. He was tired of the administration's failure to punish the North Vietnamese with the full extent of U.S. military power. At a White House conference in early January, he told Johnson and others that "we should either destroy our opponents or get out."[35] He said that the United States had "just about humiliated" itself with its pleas for peace—pleas that, incidentally, Russell himself had strongly urged earlier. It was now time to press the war to a successful military conclusion with whatever force and weapons were necessary to achieve that goal, Russell said.

When Russell talked to the Georgia legislature on January 17, he stated that the president had failed to chart "a clear course for our future action" if the Communists rejected negotiations. But, he declared, the situation in Vietnam must not be permitted to drag on. The time for decision was at hand. The United States must decide, he continued, whether to win the war or pull out. Russell said that he did not believe a majority of Americans favored the latter course.[36] Thus the Russell formula for the Vietnam problem was military victory, which was also the position of the professional military leaders. To Russell it was foolish to show restraint in the bombing of North Vietnamese targets when American troops were being killed in the south by the Vietcong and North Vietnamese.

In another interview published in the *U.S. News and World Report* in May 1966, Russell again expressed his belief that the United States should "go in and win—or get out." Declaring that failure of the South Vietnamese to establish a stable government continued to be a major problem, he proposed that a survey be taken among people in South Vietnamese cities to discover what they thought about American intervention. If it were found that a majority did not want U.S. assistance and were anti-American, Russell said, the United States should withdraw. If such a pullout did occur, would all of Southeast Asia fall to communism, Russell was asked. No, he answered, "I don't buy this so-called domino theory."[37] But his main recommendation was to hit the North Vietnamese with all of American power. A bumper sticker showing up on many cars carried the message that Russell endorsed, "Win or get out."[38] Besides greatly intensifying the bombing of northern industry and harbors, at a leadership conference at the White House on July 12 Russell recommended taking a battleship out of mothballs and preparing it to bombard the North Vietnamese coast.[39]

Russell's widely read statement about winning or getting out of Vietnam brought a great deal of favorable response. Several colleagues dropped by his office to congratulate him, and favorable comments arrived from many Georgians and people elsewhere. An increasing number of Americans were becoming critical of the president's vacillation and failure, as Russell said, to chart a clear and understandable course. When the United States bombed North Vietnamese depots in June 1966, Russell announced his enthusiastic approval.

Russell was surely not impressed with the president's assessment of how the war was going or the reasons he advanced for the American presence in South Vietnam. Upon Johnson's return in late October 1966 from a conference with Vietnamese leaders and a visit to American troops at Cam Ranh Bay, Johnson said he found "a huge reservoir of friendliness toward the United States" in the Pacific region. The countries there, he wrote, realized that the United States would sacrifice "to see them remain free," and there were elements in Southeast Asia that strongly supported American policies. Asians, he added, fully understood that "our firm stand in Viet-Nam and in Southeast Asia" was "buying time for all the nations of that region." Russell knew that Johnson was expressing nothing more than wishful thinking. The war was not going well, and governments in Southeast Asia were not providing any meaningful assistance to the United States in Vietnam.[40]

Russell always had been drawn toward isolationism. The slaughter of thousands of "American boys" in distant Vietnam and the failure of the United States' international allies to help there strengthened that basic inclination. It appeared to him that the rest of the non-Communist world was willing to sit back and let the United States shoulder the full responsibility for resisting communism. He was tired of that. Commenting on the situation in Southeast Asia, Russell said that Japan, Australia, the Philippines, and other countries in the region had a much greater stake in holding back communism in Vietnam than the United States. Yet, neither the countries at hand nor American allies in Europe would do anything substantial to assist in that struggle.

In private Russell was sharply critical of the State Department. He believed that the department was far too anxious to take on burdens in parts of the world that were of little interest to the United States politically, economically, or strategically. He called the department "weak and vacillating" and thought it lacked what he considered a "real foreign policy." About the only policy the State Department had, he said, was that of playing "gladiator, throwing American boys into the pit of battle wherever the Communists may appear without even making a serious effort to get any help from those who are more involved than we are." In a long letter to Gary L. Dodson, a soldier from Winder who was in Vietnam, Russell said that he was doing his best to get the State Department to abandon its "gladiator" role.[41]

Russell believed that officials in the State Department were unable or unwilling to distinguish between genuine American interests around the world and the pax Americana concept. He was especially upset in July 1967 when the United States sent three C-130 cargo planes, with accompanying military personnel, to the Congo. President Joseph Mo-

General William Westmoreland and Senator Russell discuss the situation in Vietnam, April 27, 1967. (Photo courtesy of Wide World Photos, Inc., New York.)

butu had requested American assistance, purportedly to quell a rebellion against the central government. On July 8, shortly before the planes left, Secretary Rusk called Russell, as well as some other political leaders, to inform him of the impending action. According to Russell and Senator Fulbright who also got a call, Rusk gave the impression in his telephone conversation that the purpose of sending the planes was to rescue Americans. The following day, however, Rusk called again and said that the planes would be used to move Mobutu's troops "around the Congo to deal with revolutionary elements."

On July 10, Russell took the Senate floor to sharply criticize this action. The situation in the Congo, he said, was purely an internal conflict and one in which the United States should not become involved. He declared that Americans should keep out of "local rebellions and local wars" where the nation had "no stake and where we have no legal or moral commitment to intervene." Russell had objected privately to the "highest authorities" against an earlier dispatch of planes to the Congo, he said, but his protests had gone unheeded. So now, he explained, "I come to the floor and make this public protest." Russell said that he had spent years building up the military might of the United States in order to properly defend the nation. But, he added, he had not built up the armed forces to send them "all over the world" on missions like that in the Congo. Such an assignment was an abuse of the military forces. Russell said that he could not understand it but that "there is a very strong influence in this country which it seems impossible to satisfy unless we do have a very large military presence almost everywhere." This was poor policy and not in the national interest, he insisted.

Other senators quickly joined Russell in criticizing the administration's action in the Congo. Senator Fulbright declared that he hoped the administration would "take most seriously" Russell's advice, while Senator Stennis praised him for his "wisdom and alertness." It was clear from the Senate discussion that something more was involved than just sending three planes to the Congo. Both Russell and Fulbright were sensitive to the fact that, while they had been informed of the pending action, there had been no genuine consultation with the Senate leadership. Fulbright believed that serious discussion, "not just . . . a telephone call," might "impose some restraint upon this kind of intervention." Russell heartily agreed. Russell resented being consulted *after* decisions had been made. This had happened in the Cuban crisis and in other cases besides the Congo intervention.[42] He believed that in important foreign policy decisions there should be a greater partnership between the White House and Capitol Hill.

In December the president informed Russell that the three aircraft sent to the Congo had returned home without incident. While at home in Winder for the Christmas holidays, he wrote Johnson expressing his pleasure over the return of the troops and planes. But he told the president that he must again object to that action. He said that he would "continue to protest our country rushing in unilaterally to aid the side that we may favor in any African country confronted with domestic disorders and conflicts." He had no faith that African tribes could establish stable, democratic governments and again insisted that the United States had no national interest in the Congo. Some may have attributed a degree of racism to Russell's position, but it was not color but lack of experience in self-government and democracy throughout black Africa that caused him to take the position he did, a position that history later confirmed. In any event, Johnson asked Dean Rusk to answer Russell. Rusk argued that the United States had responded to a request from the Congolese government and that the American response "was perfectly consistent with our past actions in supporting the unity and stability in the Congo." But the secretary did not convince the senator. To Russell, this was the kind of ill-advised move that could easily get the United States into unnecessary trouble. At the same time, however, he blamed Rusk and the State Department for convincing the president that heavier bombing and blockading the coast of North Vietnam were ill advised. "The timid souls in the State Department talked him out of that," he later recalled.[43]

As the fighting intensified in Vietnam both on land and in the air, Russell received many letters from people who criticized American bombings that killed North Vietnamese civilians. Some of that criticism came from colleagues in the Senate. While Russell was in Winder for Christmas in 1966, he received a telegram from Senator Stephen M. Young of Ohio regarding attacks on civilian targets in North Vietnam. Young wanted Russell to appoint a fact-finding subcommittee of the Armed Services Committee to inquire into civilian damage and casualties caused "by our bombing over North Vietnam." Young also suggested that such a subcommittee might determine whether further bombing could be justified or if a thirty-day pause in the attacks might be useful. Russell replied the same day that it "would be a miracle" if American bombing had not inflicted some civilian casualties. He had earlier told other critics that it was remarkable that more civilians had not been killed. In any event, he informed Young that he could not justify the appointment of such a subcommittee. He advised his colleague that the full Armed Services Committee would no doubt be able to best address the Ohio senator's concerns. Russell was not about to launch an investigation that might in any way embarrass or discredit American fighting men.[44]

Although Dick Russell viewed the Johnson-McNamara approach to the war in Vietnam as unwise and foolhardy, he could not change the policy. In his many official conferences with the president and talks over supper at the White House, he was unable to wean his friend from the course of gradualism and vacillation. Russell wanted to concentrate the full energies and power of the nation toward winning the war. Johnson believed that he could carry on quite a substantial war in Southeast Asia and at the same time maintain and enlarge his Great Society at home. Russell sharply disagreed with that view. He believed that the war effort must come first, and if Great Society programs had to be cut back or abandoned, so be it. He did not favor many of those programs anyway. He would not shed any tears if the Great Society stalled. As Senator Stennis put it, the Great Society should be "relegated to the rear."[45]

When Russell talked about the president not charting a clear course, he was also criticizing Johnson's effort to carry on business as usual and refusal to make the war his first priority.

Throughout 1967 Russell continued to advocate heavier bombing of vital targets in North Vietnam. He had been critical of the Christmas holiday cease-fire in 1966 because, he said, it had permitted the North Vietnamese to build up their supplies for more attacks on the south. Russell was fully aware of the growing opposition to the war, but on January 14, 1967, he charged that current U.S. policy was "trading American lives for public opinion." He again strongly urged a blockade of Haiphong and the coast of North Vietnam. Most members of the Armed Services Committee agreed with their chairman. In late February and March, Senator Stennis chaired the Preparedness Investigating Subcommittee, which after extensive hearings concluded that it was time to let the military commanders have a greater say in Vietnam operations.[46]

Despite the administration's unwillingness to follow his advice, Russell loyally supported the war. He served as the congressional point man to get the needed appropriations, and he had no trouble obtaining whatever was needed. In February 1967, he guided a $12.3 billion supplemental appropriations bill through Congress for the military effort in Vietnam. This was a heavy cost, he told his colleagues, but it was not nearly "so dear as the loss of life and the suffering that military conflict causes."

Knowing that he would have no difficulty getting the Senate to vote the extra funds, Russell took the opportunity to speak on specific aspects of the war. He rejected the view that bombing of the north should be selective because of dangers to civilians. Tens of thousands of civilians had been killed in Germany and Japan during World War II as a part of the drive for victory, he said. Russell observed that it was strange that there had been no objection to bombing populations in those Fascist countries but that now there were those who ranted "about the inhumanity or the immorality of accidental civilian deaths from bombing military targets in a country ruled by leftists." He praised the performance of American armed forces and said that Congress "owes them the duty of not exposing them to avoidable risks." Stopping the bombing of North Vietnam, Russell argued, would place American troops in much greater jeopardy. That was wrong, he said. Then he urged, as he had earlier, that a battleship be readied to attack the coastal area of North Vietnam. So far, he admitted, he could not convince the Defense Department to place a battleship, or even a battle cruiser, in action there. Nevertheless, Russell said he would continue to harp on the matter.[47] His harping finally paid off. In late July, some five months later, the navy announced that it was getting the battleship USS *New Jersey* ready for action along the coast of North Vietnam.

In March 1967, Russell easily guided a $21 billion defense authorization bill through the Senate that would raise the final appropriations for the fiscal 1968 defense program to around $75 billion. This was more than half of the entire $144 billion budget. A sizable share of military expenditures could be credited to the Vietnam War, which Russell estimated was costing about $2 billion a month. But, he explained, the military services needed more troops, weapons, ships, and planes. Furthermore, additional strategic weapons, including planes, missiles, and an antimissile defense system, were necessary. While he tended to go along with most recommendations from the Defense Department, that was not always the case. Mainly at his insistence, the Armed Services Committee knocked out one of the department's major new requests for military equipment. The Defense Department had asked to build as many as thirty "fast deployment logistic ships" that would be loaded with equipment and stationed for combat in various areas throughout the world. Under this arrangement, combat troops could be flown quickly to any trouble spot, and the floating arsenals would already be on hand with supplies and heavy equipment. Russell explained that he and his committee concluded that the United States should "not unilaterally assume the function of policing the world" as such deployment would imply. As he put it, "If it is easy for us to go anywhere and do anything we will always be going somewhere and doing something." In his view, the United States had already done too much of that. Neither he nor the committee, Russell said, had any desire "to police the entire world or impose a pax Americana."[48]

By the summer and fall of 1967, Russell's constituent mail contained increasing demands for the United States to withdraw from Vietnam. To more and more people—mothers, young people, businessmen, and other establishment spokesmen—the war had become useless and senseless. Correspondents told how they had read and thought about the matter, how they had searched their souls, and finally how they had arrived at the belief that the United States should withdraw from Vietnam. Also, more and more writers said that saving face was no longer important. A Carrollton resident asked Russell: "Has nobody in Washington the nerve to say, 'the South Vietnamese are hopelessly incapable of holding anything we might win militarily for them?' Let's face up to the facts and admit that we have bet on a bad horse." An Atlanta businessman who had served four years in World War II wrote Russell that the United States should withdraw. "I beg you to come on over" to the side of withdrawal, he pleaded. Another writer declared, "Let's admit that we made a mistake and walk away from it."[49] Others, however, recommended that North Vietnam simply be destroyed. One writer argued that nothing should be off-limits to American destructive power.[50] As his constituents and the country divided over what should be done, Russell's own frustrations grew as he saw no end to the struggle under the Johnson policies.

As if his dissatisfaction with American foreign policy was not distressing enough, Russell, now nearly seventy, experienced serious health problems again in 1967 and early 1968. From August 7 to 29, 1967, he was at Walter Reed Army Hospital. He then felt somewhat better for a short time, but on September 27, he flew home to Winder where he remained for about two weeks. During that time, his breathing was very difficult and he coughed up large amounts of sputum. After he returned to Washington, he had to restrict his schedule. He was able to attend a presidential luncheon on October 17 in Senator Ellender's Capitol Hill office, but when Johnson called him for lunch on October 22, he had to beg off. "Feeling bad," he noted. He was taking a great deal of medicine, including four ampicillin capsules, two Tofranil tablets, and one Titalin tablet each day, to help his breathing and reduce his coughing spells. Some days it was nearly impossible to stop coughing. On November 25, he noted that it was 6:00 P.M. before his cough could be brought under control.[51] Early in December, he had to return to the hospital for a few days and was consequently unable to attend the wedding of Lynda Bird Johnson and Charles S. Robb on December 9. This was a great disappointment to him.

As Russell's health deteriorated after his long illness early in 1965, he had given serious thought to what he might do if he became incapacitated to the extent that he could not perform his senatorial duties. This possibility haunted him during times of his severest illnesses because, as he wrote, he did not want to continue in office as Carter Glass had done and not be able to function effectively. Early in February 1967, he made a decision. He composed letters to be sent to the governor of Georgia and the secretary of the Senate in the event of his failing health, stating that "due to physical disability which makes it impossible for me to fully and actively discharge the duties of Senator of the United States, I herewith submit to you my resignation from the date of this letter." The letters were signed but not dated. In another statement, Russell said that his resignation was not to be dated or sent unless W. C. Harris, an old friend in Winder, Dr. A. B. Russell, his brother, and his nephew

Richard B. Russell III, an attorney, unanimously agreed that he was "permanently disabled and incapable of serving actively as a Senator." Fortunately, his so-called "tentative resignation" never had to be implemented.[52]

Despite poor health and weariness, during 1967 Russell carried on a very heavy work load. In addition to heading the Armed Services Committee, he had extra responsibilities on the Appropriations Committee, the CIA oversight subcommittee, and the Space Sciences Committee. His commitments would have overwhelmed anyone with less knowledge, experience, and ability. In the Armed Services Committee, Russell had pushed through money authorizations for the procurement of new weapons and legislation dealing with military construction, amendments to the draft law, increases in military pay, and much more.[53] It was a trying and hectic year.

As far as Russell was concerned, 1968 began in the same dismal and unsatisfactory way that the previous year had ended. On January 23, the USS *Pueblo* was captured off the coast of North Korea, an embarrassing and humiliating event in the eyes of most Americans. This, Russell said, "was a breach of international law amounting to an act of war." The United States must take "a very strong position in demanding release of the ship and return of the crew," he insisted.[54] It was nearly a year later, however, before that occurred.

A happy exception to his frustrations was the praise heaped upon Russell in recognition of his thirty-fifth anniversary in the Senate. On January 18, 1968, six days after the actual thirty-five years, one after another of his colleagues rose to acclaim his greatness. They praised his integrity, wisdom, judgment, capabilities, leadership, and service. They applauded his efforts in building a strong national defense, his contributions to agriculture, and his devotion to sound government and acclaimed him as one who better than any other senator upheld the traditions and precedents of the Senate. All of them wished him many more years of service, unaware, of course, that he had secretly written letters of resignation contingent on the condition of his health. In response, Russell said that to be the recipient of such praise was a surprising and wonderful way to begin the day. Nothing could please him more than to receive the plaudits of his colleagues. While he admitted having had many disappointments as well as victories in the last thirty-five years, he said that the accolades of his fellow senators helped him to "bury the memories of disappointments and frustrations."[55] Two months later, Russell was widely hailed as the only person in the nation's history who had spent half of his life in the U.S. Senate.

Russell's health was an ever-present problem. During his praise of Russell, Senator Mansfield had commented on how well Russell looked. But looks were deceiving. On January 26, less than ten days later, Russell was again admitted to Walter Reed Army Hospital, where he was confined for several days. He was unable to chair the hearings on the authorization for military procurement for fiscal 1969 conducted by his Armed Services Committee that began February 1 and lasted into March. Stennis took over in Russell's absence. Although he was back in the office by mid-February, he confined his strength for several days to performing the most essential tasks. He often took a nap in his office in the afternoons, and if anyone called, his staff explained that the senator could not be located. By late February and March, however, he was attending numerous White House conferences, briefings, and meetings with military leaders and taking care of Senate business much as usual.[56]

On January 31, 1968, during his hospital stay, the Vietcong and North Vietnamese launched their Tet offensive throughout much of South Vietnam. Besides the military implications, the audacity and temporary success of these attacks further weakened American resolve, even among some Johnson administration officials. Earlier Secretary McNamara had quit his post, and he was to be succeeded by Clark M. Clifford on March 1, 1968. Russell had supported Clifford's appointment, but the new secretary of defense was unwilling to place greater military pressure on the North Vietnamese. While Russell greatly admired his fellow Georgian, Dean Rusk, he criticized the secretary of state for inconsistency and vacillation. Writing from his hospital bed on February 8, he told a Savannah friend, "I believe that some of the things that are happening today would have almost put me in the hospital without the emphysema." He was alluding to Vietnam. Shortly before, Secretary Rusk had proposed a relaxation of the bombing of North Vietnam. "This vacillating uncertainty in the field of international relations is maddening," he wrote. Russell had also become critical of General Westmoreland's military approach in Vietnam. He believed that Westmoreland depended too heavily on conventional tactics used in World War II rather than emphasizing guerrilla warfare. His statement on this matter on the floor of the Senate on March 4, 1968, received widespread attention in the nation's press.[57]

By February 1968, President Johnson was under growing pressure to deescalate the war. Following several weeks of meetings and conferences with his closest advisers, many of whom were losing their enthusiasm for the war, Johnson decided to make another gesture that might encourage negotiations. One aspect of his approach was to cease bombing north of the twentieth parallel in North Vietnam. This would exclude most of the main targets in and around Hanoi and Haiphong. Although Johnson did not specifically mention the twentieth parallel in his talk on March 31, it was understood by those with whom he had discussed the matter. When Russell was called to the White House to react to this proposal, he vigorously opposed it. He told Johnson that there should be no cessation of bombing "unless there was some indication of reciprocity on the part of the North Vietnamese." But in describing the situation to his Senate colleagues, Russell added, "As has often been the case in the past, the President did not take my advice or suggestions." Russell predicted that no fruitful conference or negotiations would result from Johnson's show of military restraint. Then he added, "I say, with equal frankness, I have no solution of my own to bring the war to a successful conclusion without considerable escalation."[58]

Although Russell knew the major thrust of the president's speech on Vietnam ahead of time, he was "greatly surprised" by Johnson's announcement that he would not seek another term. Russell did get fifteen minutes advance notice when Barefoot Sanders called him from the White House and told him of the president's intention. But that was all. While many other senators praised Johnson for his statesmanship and courage and for placing the nation's interests above his own political ambitions, Russell was more restrained. He said the president's action was "a very noble individual sacrifice in an effort to secure peace" but added that he did not think it would have any effect on Hanoi. Any bombing pause was dangerous, he believed. There is no evidence that Russell was disappointed with Johnson's decision not to run again.[59]

Despite their many policy differences, Russell and Johnson remained close personal friends. On April 3, only three days after the president's dramatic announcement, Russell and Senator Smathers had dinner with Lyndon, Luci, and Lynda Bird. It was a most pleasant evening for Russell. When he arrived at the White House, both women greeted him with a kiss, and he also received a good-night kiss when he left at 1:00 A.M. As usual, they called him "Uncle Dick," he noted.[60]

One of Russell's great interests in 1968 was pushing ahead with a proposal for the establishment of an antiballistic missile (ABM) system. He had opposed the original authorization for such a system in 1963 because he did not think that research had advanced far enough to warrant procurement of an ABM system. By 1966, however, he had concluded that it was time to actually develop the system. He had secured funding of some $291 million for both fiscal 1967 and 1968 to proceed with procurement, but none of the funds had been spent. In June 1968, Russell insisted that around $500 million be made available for that aspect of the nation's defense. He argued that research had gone on for twelve years and that the time had come to build and deploy a so-called "thin" ABM system.

A number of senators, however, wished to eliminate or at least delay procurement. They argued that no ABM system was ready for deployment, that such expenditures would be wasteful when the country needed to economize, and that the initiation of such a system would hurt the chances of any U.S.–Soviet arms control agreement. Senator George McGovern declared that the Senate should at least wait until after the next presidential election before taking any action. Russell, however, firmly rejected all of these arguments. He admitted that no one knew how effective such a system would be, but he insisted that if it saved several million American lives in case of nuclear war, it would be worth it. He also reminded his colleagues that the Russians were developing such a system and that the United States should not lag behind. It was illogical, he declared, to build offensive weapons to be used against Russia, the only nation that posed a threat to the United States, and not "at the same time undertake to build a defensive system."

Russell saw opposition to an ABM system as muddled thinking by people who really favored "unilateral disarmament" and who naively trusted the Russians. He told his fellow senators that he could not assure them, as he had in the past, that the United States was superior to the Soviet Union in strategic missiles. Indeed, he said, "I think there is a very grave doubt about it." In light of this condition, Russell wanted to reduce his country's vulnerability in any way he could. He was able to defeat the amendment that would have delayed procurement for an ABM system by a vote of 45 to 34.[61]

On October 1, Russell was back on the Senate floor pushing toward passing the largest single appropriations bill ever passed by Congress up to that time—$71.8 billion. Explaining that he regretted more than anyone the necessity for such huge defense appropriations, he insisted that the nation's security demanded the amount requested. The Soviets had not changed, he said, and there was the ever-present threat from Red China. Russell argued that "peaceful coexistence can be maintained only by a strong national defense as a deterrent." Furthermore, he took this opportunity to warn his fellow senators that the Vietnam War had used up the supply of defense materials to a dangerous point, and they needed to be replaced. "We are scraping the bottom of available surpluses," he said, and any "further reductions would . . . jeopardize

our defense potential in the event of an outbreak of large-scale hostil-
ities." He did not want to tell "a scare story," Russell said, but "we have
drawn down too long from the pantry shelf of military hardware."
Large amounts of money were required to deal with this problem.

Russell insisted that aging and obsolete equipment, including ships
and planes, must be replaced and modernized. Also he said the missile
program should be expanded. "We must match our potential enemies
missile for missile, and our missile defense system must be made as
impenetrable as is humanly possible," he declared. The United States
could not afford to "invite aggression . . . through weakness." Opponents of the Sentinel ABM system attempted to cut $387 million from
$700 million included to start building the system, but the Senate fol-
lowed Russell's lead and defeated the amendment. As had been true in
the past, after extended debate the huge appropriations bill passed overwhelmingly and provided funds to begin development of the ABM system. During the debates over missiles, defensive systems, and degrees of
possible destruction, Russell declared that if civilization had to be re-
started after a nuclear holocaust, he wanted the new Adam and Eve to
be Americans—Americans, he might have added, of Anglo-Saxon heritage. His statement aroused a good deal of comment, including notice in
Pravda on January 12, 1969. The Soviet writer charged that Russell was
faithfully serving the imperialists. He was accused of being a most dangerous man to whom lives meant nothing. That, of course, was rubbish,
but Russell did insist that the United States spare nothing to build up its
defenses.

During the discussion of the military appropriations bill, Russell
could not refrain from again expressing his displeasure at the way the
Vietnam War had been and was still being fought. If, he said, "we had
forgotten about world opinion," and, "instead of quivering and quaking
everytime somebody mentioned Russia or China," had used unrestricted
bombing on all northern targets and had blockaded the coast, the war
could have been ended three years before. Not all American troops
could have yet been brought home, he believed, but the attacks by the
North Vietnamese could have been stopped. Russell argued that the
greatest tragedy of the war was that "we have fought it altogether on
terms dictated by the enemy." It was time to follow the advice of people
who had been trained in military tactics and strategy, he declared. Russell added that he did not believe anything useful would come from the
Paris peace talks, which had begun in May 1968. He thought the North
Vietnamese were using the talks to gain time to "recoup, rearm, and
restore the hopes and confidence of their people."[62]

Despite his deep dissatisfaction with the way the United States was conducting the Vietnam War, Russell never flagged in providing the military needs for that conflict or in backing the president. He believed firmly in the constitutional role of the president as commander-in-chief of the armed forces and saw himself as a loyal soldier. He would argue policy in private and public, but when the decision was made, he always supported his commander-in-chief.

There had been a time when Russell felt that same sense of loyalty to the Democratic party, but no more. During the last two decades, he had become increasingly disillusioned with the course of his party. As the presidential campaign of 1968 approached, he again found himself far out of step with the majority of Democrats. When it was suggested that Georgia Democrats might nominate Russell at the Democratic convention as a favorite son, he advised James Gray, chairman of the state Democratic Executive Committee, to discourage such talk. But despite his displeasure with the Democrats, he would not bolt his party. As he said, he had "lived up to my neck in sheer and complete frustration for the past several years," but he planned to vote the Humphrey-Muskie ticket. He was doing it, however, "completely without enthusiasm." His main objection to Humphrey, he wrote, was the fear that if elected president, he would pursue "unilateral disarmament." When rumors surfaced that Russell might not be unhappy if Nixon won, Charles Pou, a political writer for the *Atlanta Journal*, tried to confirm the reports. He contacted Wayne P. Kelley, another writer and correspondent who had good relations with Russell, and asked Kelley to call the senator at Winder to see if the rumors contained any truth. Kelley made the call, but when asked about his favoring Nixon, Russell said the idea was "ridiculous" and too outrageous to discuss. He did not give permission to quote him directly but agreed that Pou could say that "according to reliable sources," the rumors were false.[63]

There is little doubt, however, that Russell quietly favored Richard Nixon over Humphrey as the next occupant of the White House. Of course, he would have preferred to elect what he considered the right kind of Democrat, but Russell had given up on that possibility. Thus he was not disappointed with Richard Nixon's election. And Nixon began courting Russell at once. He telephoned the senator on November 13, and they had an extended conversation. Russell later thought that he may have "responded too warmly" as he assured the president-elect that he would cooperate wholeheartedly with him in the field of national defense. He also congratulated Nixon for supporting stronger defense capabilities. A month later, Russell gave his blessing to the appointment of Melvin R. Laird as secretary of defense and told Laird that he "should make a good man" in the job. From his office in Winder during the Christmas recess, he said that most southerners were pleased with the prospect of a Nixon administration. Speaking of the president-elect, Russell added that "he and I are in accord on a great deal of philosophy" and that their personal relations had been good. He later told his new press secretary, Powell A. Moore, "You'll never get me to say anything unkind about Dick Nixon as long as I have to consider the Democratic alternatives."[64]

Besides the change in administration in January 1969, a shift also occurred in Russell's leadership responsibilities. After Carl Hayden announced his retirement on May 6, 1968, Russell had decided to assume the chairmanship of the Appropriations Committee. He had served on the committee ever since arriving in Washington nearly thirty-six years earlier. In taking on the chairmanship, Russell said that it would permit him "to get a lot done." This move, however, meant that he had to give up the chairmanship of the Senate Armed Services Committee. But that was not a problem, because he had groomed his close friend and admirer, John Stennis, for that job. In Russell's view, the Armed Services Committee would be in good hands with Stennis as chairman. However, Russell retained his chairmanship of the Subcommittee on Defense Appropriations. In addition to increasing his influence in the Senate, Russell believed that becoming chairman of the Appropriations Committee might reduce his work load somewhat. Previously, he had not only chaired the Armed Services Committee, but, because of Hayden's age and periodic ill health, had often been the de facto chairman of the Appropriations Committee. Thus, as second ranking member on the Appropriations Committee, he had frequently carried most of the leadership responsibilities. Comparing it with the corporate world, one observer had called Russell the president and Hayden the chairman of the board. So in January 1969, Russell took over the chairmanship of the Appropriations Committee.

Many people did not realize that Russell had given up his leadership position on the Armed Services Committee, and throughout 1969 he continued to receive many letters on military matters, especially on Vietnam. His standard reply, usually written by staff members, explained that he was no longer chairman of the committee and that he did not have major responsibilities for military matters in the Senate. In response to those who thought that the United States should exert greater military power in Vietnam, he expressed agreement but stated that he could not compel the commander-in-chief to accept his advice.

His correspondence reflected a sense of relief that he no longer had responsibility in the Senate for military matters.[65]

This did not mean, however, that Russell was silent on Vietnam or other matters of national security. During 1969 he continued his criticism of U.S. strategy in Vietnam and scoffed at the idea of successful negotiations, except those based on a complete American withdrawal, which he opposed. He also pressed for a more elaborate antiballistic missile system. Russell's main concern, as it had been for at least twenty years, was to build and maintain such a strong national defense that no nation would ever threaten the United States or its vital interests. He favored developing both the latest and most sophisticated offensive weapons and the best defensive shield that American science could construct against incoming missiles.

Between 1961, when the military buildup in Vietnam began, and the end of 1968, except for the president and the secretary of defense, Russell may have carried the heaviest burden for the war of any official in Washington. His work and responsibilities were heavy, but he was most bothered by the pain of supporting a war that he had advised against. His distress intensified as he opposed the way Johnson fought the war and as opponents of the war at home became more vocal and influential. Furthermore, he was humiliated by the country's failure to complete a military task to which he believed it was committed right or wrong and which it could accomplish if the war was fought in the right way. His old friend Lyndon consulted with him often, but his advice was largely ignored. It is no wonder that Russell stated that the Vietnam War was the most unpleasant and frustrating experience of his long career in the Senate.

20

The End of a Long Career

═══

On Friday, January 3, 1969, Dick Russell reached the height of his career when he was elected president pro tem of the U.S. Senate. He replaced Carl Hayden who had ended forty-one years in the upper chamber. Now Russell was that body's most senior member, having completed thirty-six years of service. As president pro tem, he was third in line of succession to the presidency. Besides presiding over the Senate, his new position provided some of the trappings of prestige. The most obvious sign of influence was the large black Lincoln Continental limousine in which Russell was chauffeured about town. Did he feel more powerful than he had earlier, Russell was asked. "Well," he replied, "I get that big automobile now," and the doorman at his apartment, who had previously paid little attention to him, was "really impressed." He called Floyd M. Riddick, the Senate parliamentarian, and said that he wanted to take the oath of office before the Senate convened the following Monday. When Riddick asked him why he was in such a hurry, Russell explained that he wanted to make sure that no one took his black limousine away from him![1]

In that elite club known as the U.S. Senate, no one was more admired or respected than Dick Russell. Many of his colleagues did not agree with him on issues, but they all had a genuine affection for this Georgia patrician. In a group that often acted like a mutual admiration society, fellow senators characteristically flattered and praised one another. But somehow Russell seemed special. He was held in great esteem for his fairness, integrity, wisdom, help to colleagues on special projects, and steadfastness in protecting the traditions of the Senate.

Respect and affection were one thing; power was something else. In writing about Russell, reporters and columnists often talked about his great power. In fact, however, he had passed the zenith of his ability to influence the course of national events several years earlier. By the late 1960s, he was so far out of tune with the main thrusts of American domestic and foreign policies that little of what he favored or fought for ever became policy or law. Changes in the Democratic party, general acceptance of the Great Society and continued expansion of federal powers by whatever name, changes in the Senate itself, declining political influence of the South in national affairs, and his intermittent bad health combined to reduce his power. Russell, of course, was extremely influential in matters related to appropriations, national defense, and other issues and in behind-the-scenes compromises and conference committees. But his power to determine the outcome of major Senate actions had measurably declined.

In January 1969, Russell finally gave up his leadership of the Southern Bloc. The bloc was no longer a strong influence in the Senate. Its ranks had been thinned by death and retirement, and it had suffered defeat on most civil rights issues. Russell said that he could no longer serve as leader of the southern group because of his position as president pro tem. Since he would preside over the Senate, he said, he must be "blind on the issues" and "rule fairly and impartially without any conflict of interest."[2]

Russell's failure to actively support Senator Russell Long of Louisiana as majority whip indicated further that he was tiring of the old fights. While he announced that he would vote for Long, a fellow southerner, he indicated to Senator Edward Kennedy of Massachusetts who was also seeking the post that he would not place any barriers in his path. Russell did not speak up for Long in the Democratic caucus, which added to the impression that southerners were supporting Long more as a matter of appearance than out of deep conviction. Kennedy was elected.[3]

By the late 1960s, Russell showed less interest in issues that had been very important to him earlier. Agriculture, for example, no longer received the attention that it had during his first twenty-five or thirty years in the Senate. His belief in the virtues of a strong and prosperous agriculture had not weakened, but he simply did not have time to deal with farm questions as he had in previous years. He did not like the trend he saw developing. Speaking at the laying of the cornerstone for the Russell Research Laboratory in Athens on October 19, 1968, he lamented the declining position of agriculture in the nation's life. He stressed that "every great civilization has derived its basic strength and wealth from the soil" and declared that the cities had attracted too many people. It was essential, he declared, "that we start moving from the cities to the farms" and change what he called the population imbalance.[4] Moreover, Russell had given up the chairmanship of the subcom-

Senator Russell receiving the National Association of State Foresters Award, October 1968. (Photo courtesy of Russell Memorial Library, University of Georgia, Athens.)

mittee on agricultural appropriations in the early 1960s, so he was no longer in a position to determine events relating to agricultural policy as he had been from the 1930s through the 1950s.

His strong interest in conserving the nation's land, forest, and water resources continued, and he received widespread recognition for his work in that field. In 1964 the *Progressive Farmer* gave Russell one of its outstanding service awards for his work on behalf of agriculture and conservation. The nation's natural resources, he maintained, should be "developed for the benefit of our people." Spending money on conservation was not "pork-barrel" legislation, he insisted, but an investment in the country's future. Russell called himself a fanatic when it came to the importance of research for conserving the nation's natural resources. His pride was so great over the federal research facilities he had brought to Georgia, he wrote, that he was "almost immodest."[5]

Russell's opposition to racial integration never lagged, but by the last half of the 1960s, his resistance to new civil rights bills had lost much of the old fire. He fought what the administration termed fair housing measures but not with the same vigor and results as he had before 1964 and 1965. He unhappily accepted the inevitable. He argued, however, that if the federal government enforced racial integration in the South, it should do the same in northern cities.[6]

Russell became increasingly remote and isolated by the late 1960s. His ill health and heavy work load contributed to his unwillingness to see very many ordinary callers and to his more restricted social life. When possible, he continued to show up for affairs involving Georgia and Georgians, but beyond that his social life ranged mainly between the Senate and the White House. As mentioned earlier, he sometimes even turned down Johnson's invitations to supper, noting on one occasion that he had "begged off."[7] He and Harriet Orr continued to have dinner together sometimes on Friday or Saturday evenings, but those occasions became less frequent. He maintained his keen interest in sports, but the pressure of work and his health kept him from attending many baseball or football games as had been common in earlier years. He wrote a friend on March 23, 1966, that he could not attend the opening baseball game in Washington for the "first time in many years."[8] He liked to return to Winder as often as possible, where Modine Thomas cooked his favorite food—black-eyed peas, onion casserole, and roast beef—and where he could relax among old friends. When returning to Winder, he usually took one staff member with him so he could keep up with his correspondence.

Russell's schedule in the 1960s remained much as it had been earlier. He usually arrived on Capitol Hill about 8:30 or 9:00 A.M. and had breakfast in the Senate dining room. He commonly had grapefruit, soft scrambled eggs, white toast with honey, and hot chocolate.[9] He spent the mornings in committee meetings and with important appointments. In the afternoon, he was on the Senate floor or attending more meetings. By four or five o'clock, he would return to his office to begin working on the day's mail. He read the more important incoming letters of the day and signed letters that had been prepared by members of his staff. He often changed the contents of a letter if it did not say precisely what he wanted to convey or if it did not sound like Dick Russell. He would either direct how he wanted the letter changed in his inscrutable handwriting or call in a secretary and dictate an entirely new letter.

By 6:30 or 7:00 P.M., Russell would finish working on his mail and sit back to watch the evening television news while he sipped two drinks of Jack Daniels and water and nibbled on Georgia peanuts. Members of his senior staff often remained during those early evening hours, but he did not usually offer them a drink. During that time, the senator was

Senator Russell relaxing at home in Winder, Georgia, June 1970. (Photo courtesy of Russell Memorial Library, University of Georgia, Athens.)

relaxed and easier to talk with. After he had finished his drinks and the news was over, he would head for O'Donnell's Sea Food Grill, his favorite eating place. Occasionally, he would invite members of his senior staff to accompany him, but he usually went alone and sat at the bar to eat his supper. During the rest of the evening, back at his apartment he would review official documents for the next day's hearings or appointments if necessary, but most of the time, he followed his lifelong practice of reading history. His apartment was littered with books. They were stacked on the floor and in chairs. Some of them would be half open, and others had memos inserted.[10]

As had been true for many years, Russell paid little attention to the day-to-day operation of his office. Since he always entered and left his private office directly from the corridor, weeks sometimes went by without him seeing some members of his staff. Barboura Raesly, who began working for Russell in June 1956 and later became his personal secretary and took care of his personal finances, recalled that during her first six months in the office, she saw Russell only three times. In November 1965, he had three employees whom he had not met, and one of them had been there a month. He seldom went into his outer offices, and most of his contacts in later years were with Raesly and two or three members of his senior staff.[11]

If staff problems arose, Russell tended to ignore them. Leeman Anderson, who had been Russell's administrative assistant since he had arrived in Washington except for one short interlude, had by around 1960 become a kind of figurehead in the office. A tougher boss would probably have replaced Anderson. However, Russell did not consider such action. The Senator's innate kindness and his friendship with Anderson outweighed any desire for increased efficiency. When Anderson finally died in August 1969 following problems with alcohol and other difficulties, Russell was deeply saddened. Anderson's death, he said, was a great personal loss to him.[12]

For several years before Anderson's death, William H. Jordan, Jr., really ran the senator's office. But after thirteen years with Russell, Jordan resigned in April 1968 to work for the Senate Appropriations Committee. A few months later, Charles E. Campbell, a young attorney who began working as Russell's first legislative assistant in 1966, became his administrative assistant. Marjorie Warren, who had been with Russell since 1944 and had become a dominant force in the office, left early in 1969 after some difficulties among the office staff. Proctor Jones first worked for Russell in 1961. After a stint in the U.S. Marine Corps in the mid-1960s, he returned to the office on April 1, 1968. Besides his regular work as clerk, Jones helped Russell personally in many ways, especially during times of his frail health. During his last years in office, Russell relied most heavily on Charles Campbell, Powell A. Moore, his press secretary, Proctor Jones, and Barboura Raesly. Russell's senior staff members and secretaries were always very solicitous of Russell's needs and desires. For example, Jane McMullan, one of Russell's secretaries, left a note on the senator's desk in May 1969 saying that she had put some custard in the refrigerator for him. His note of response was, "Excellent custard. Certainly enjoyed."[13]

Although Russell had been initially reluctant to hire a press secretary, several men eventually held that important position. William Bates, the first person employed for the post in December 1958, left in 1961 and was replaced by Earl T. Leonard, a young University of Georgia graduate who had just completed his law degree. Leonard had first met the senator at a Russell appreciation day in Winder. Shortly after finishing law school, Leonard received a telephone call one morning before he was up. A voice came over the line, "Earl, this is Dick Russell. How are you today?" Believing this to be a call from a friend who often facetiously introduced himself as some famous person, Leonard replied, "Well, hello Senator. What in hell are you doing up so early?" Russell explained that because of daylight savings time it was then 9:00 A.M. in Washington. By that time, Leonard realized that he was indeed talking with the senator and apologized profusely. Russell then asked him to take the position of press secretary.[14] When Leonard resigned in 1964, Bill Bates again took over the job, which he held until 1967 when Powell Moore arrived. Moore was a University of Georgia graduate who had edited a Milledgeville newspaper and worked in public affairs for the Southern Natural Gas Company.

It was not easy to be a press secretary for Dick Russell. He tended to shun the press, except for a few favored reporters and writers such as William S. White and Margaret Shannon of the *Atlanta Journal*. Even Miss Margaret, as he called her, did not find it easy to get an appointment. Russell press secretaries often left notes for their boss asking what they should do in response to a particular request from a reporter, only to have the senator ignore the inquiry. When the reporter called back, the press secretary had no answer and had to stall. During Russell's last two or three years in the Senate, he was a little more generous and cooperative with reporters. He once gave correspondent Wayne Kelley permission to tape an hour-long interview, something that was most unusual. Powell Moore, who was then Russell's press secretary, thought it was one of the best presentations he had ever heard the senator make. After the interview, he suggested that Kelley play some of it back. Kelley turned on the machine only to discover that absolutely nothing had been recorded. Russell was not the least bit miffed or angry. He just said, "There goes one hour down the river in a busy life."[15]

It was not easy to judge how Russell would react to a speech or news release prepared for him by his press secretary. For example, when Ralph McGill died, reporters asked Russell for a comment. The senator had known McGill since 1936 when McGill had covered the Russell-Talmadge race. Moore prepared a statement and took it to the senator who was eating lunch in the Senate dining room. Russell read it, looked up, and said, "We should say kind things about the dead, but that is going too far."[16]

Most of Russell's senior staff members over the years were graduates of the University of Georgia. He always maintained a very close relationship with the university and never tired of singing its praises and expressing appreciation for what that institution had done for him and so many other Georgians. In 1967 Leonard wrote an article on Russell and his family entitled, "The Russells in Our Flock, Alumni Family of the Year," which was published in the *Georgia Alumni Record*. It was a flattering portrait of the family, which had had a long and close association with the University, and Russell wrote that it "meant a great deal to me." Once after attending a football staff luncheon, Russell was called on to say a few words. He expressed his great enthusiasm for the university's football team and spoke of his love for his alma mater. He worked hard and successfully to get research facilities for the university, kept close ties with the athletic department, and was finally admitted as an honorary member of Phi Beta Kappa. The venerable Dean William Tate and other faculty members traveled to Winder in December 1969 to perform the initiation ceremony. When Russell learned in 1967 that the university was going to name a residence hall after his dead nephew, Judge Robert Russell, Jr., he wrote President A. C. Aderhold that "all of our family have been tied to the University. We have gloried in its progress and undertaken to fight its battles." He added that the university had been responsible for the success of several members of the Russell family.[17]

Russell always had a deep interest in youth, and over the years, he helped a good many worthy young people. He had an especially warm place in his heart for farm and rural youth. In 1960 Russell, Bill Jordan, and Dr. Tommy L. Walton, a Georgia 4-H leader, planned a patronage program to provide part-time jobs in Washington to help young Georgians go to college. It was known as the Russell 4-H Patronage Program. These students worked a few hours a day and took some college courses. At first Russell relied on the Georgia 4-H Council to select the recipients who had jobs as doorkeepers, elevator operators, and aides in Russell's office. In this way, Russell directly helped a number of young people along the road to success. These individuals became avid devotees of the senator and in later years treasured the fact that they had known Russell and benefited from the relationship. G. W. "Buddy" Darden III was one of the interns and was later elected to Congress. Another intern, Norman Underwood, became a judge. Russell did not counsel these young people on a career, but he influenced them by serving as an example.[18]

As Russell aged, developed poor health, and found himself in disagreement with so many government policies, he became somewhat more irritable and occasionally short-tempered. Seemingly small things would arouse his ire. For example, he complained about the heat and air-conditioning in his office and in 1963 threatened to get the person fired who was responsible for turning off his office radiator. He also criticized some operations of the Senate Office Building. The policy of locking the building at 8:00 P.M. outraged him because he often stayed later than that and found himself locked in. Then he complained about the Saturday food service in the "little cafeteria in the Old Senate Building." He had had to stand in line on two occasions, he wrote, to get "some of the meager choices."[19]

Despite exasperating circumstances, Russell retained his sense of humor. Once when he was in the hospital there were five or six doctors present, including Surgeon General Leonard Dudley Heaton. All of the medics had expressed an opinion on his condition except one young captain. Turning to him, Russell asked, "Young man, what do you think?" Without hesitation, the young officer replied, "I agree with General Heaton." Russell's quick retort was, "I predict a long and brilliant future for you in the Army Medical Corps." On another occasion, Senator Thomas J. McIntyre of New Hampshire, a junior member of the Armed Services Committee, wanted to have his picture taken with Russell. As they stood for the photographer, McIntyre asked to change positions so that his receding hairline would be less noticeable. "Mr. Chairman," he said, "would you mind if I shifted and stood on your other side so that my better side will be photographed?" With a twinkle in his eye, Russell remarked, "You are lucky to still have a better side."[20]

All of the pressures and responsibilities never reduced his innate kindness and concern for people. He remembered those who had served him, as well as others, and recognized their triumphs and tragedies. He continued the practice of giving a silver piece to individuals and couples on special occasions. For instance, when Earl Leonard, his former press secretary, was married in 1965, Russell presented the couple with a sterling silver wine bucket as a wedding gift. He wrote many letters of sympathy to people who had problems, had lost a loved one, or had met some other ill fate. When Evelyn Gordon, a waitress in the Senate dining room, was hospitalized, he wrote her a most gracious letter, telling her how much she was missed and to "hurry back." His letters to old friends and associates in Georgia dripped with sentiment and even affection. Writing a letter of condolence to the widow of a longtime friend, he declared that her husband had never failed the senator and "I tried never to fail him. It was a fine, sweet friendship, and I shall miss him greatly," he concluded.[21]

In his later years, formal religion played little or no part in Russell's life. He seldom attended church services, preferring to relax on Sunday morning either in his apartment or at home in Winder. He sometimes mentioned to constituents that he was a member of the Methodist church, but ties to the church of his youth had become disconnected for all practical purposes. He was religious in the broad meaning of that term, and he believed deeply in basic Christian principles. Yet he had no feeling of need for the organized church in his personal life.

One thing was certain about Dick Russell: he never abandoned his conservative stance on financial matters. Long after he had any need to conserve money, he found ways to save pennies and nickels. For a time, he bought crackers from a vending machine for five cents. Then he discovered that he could get more than twice as many crackers for a dime. He remarked that if he had realized this earlier, he could have saved money over many years. When he moved from the Woodner to the Potomac Plaza in 1962, intern Norman Underwood assisted with the packing. When young Underwood came across a ball of string saved from laundry packages, he asked the senator if he wanted to take the string. Russell replied, "I certainly do. I've been saving that string, and I fully intend to take it."[22] Once just before leaving on a trip overseas, the senator remarked to his brother Fielding that he would like to have a pair of binoculars to take with him, "but they are just too expensive." Fielding's son William asked, "Well, Uncle Dick, what are you saving your money for?" Russell replied, "For my damn nieces and nephews, I guess." However, he did finally break down and buy the binoculars.[23]

His contributions to charitable and religious institutions were usually small, mostly in the $2 to $10 range as late as the 1960s. His records do not reveal any standard or pattern for his giving. Almost without exception, his larger contributions were honoraria he received from speaking. For example, in 1964 he gave $250 to the Southern Christian Home for Children, an amount he had received for speaking at the Peachtree Christian Church in Atlanta. As mentioned previously, Russell treated campaign contributions as a sacred trust. Whenever he could, he returned any unused funds to the donors. However, there were leftover monies that had been donated at Russell dinners in 1952 by people who could not later be identified. Since those funds could not be returned, Russell provided in his will that they should be used to finance a chair in political science at the University of Georgia.

Russell always complained about things being too expensive. He seldom purchased anything—a quart of milk, a shirt, or a suit of clothes—without mentioning that it cost too much. This attitude made him especially sensitive to inflation and helped to harden his position against deficit financing by Congress.

He was equally tight with salaries for members of his office staff. It was well recognized that working in Russell's office meant receiving lower pay than working for most other senators. And Russell was proud of his conservative approach. Early in 1963, he had a study done to show how much he had saved the government in office expenses. From January 1, 1941, to December 31, 1962, the study revealed that he had spent $230,057 less than had been allowed for his office.[24]

Although Russell voted for pay increases for members of the armed services, and sometimes guided the appropriate legislation through Congress, he strongly opposed most increases for regular federal employees in the 1960s. Early in 1969 when President Nixon proposed pay increases for federal workers, Russell stoutly resisted the move. He called the president's recommendations excessive and poorly timed and added that he did not want a raise in his own pay. He had hoped, he said, that this would be "an austerity congress that would reduce federal spending." Later in the year, he voted against general salary increases for federal employees.[25]

Despite having achieved preeminence among his colleagues, Russell was a lonely man in his later years. Not often did he seem genuinely happy. Part of this was associated with his ill health, but even more important was the fact that he had never nourished many close personal friendships. He had a host of admirers and long acquaintances, but only with a few old Georgia friends like Charles Bloch and Frank Scarlett did he have anything bordering on an intimate friendship. In the Senate, of course, there was Harry Byrd and Willis Robertson, and in the White House was his old friend Lyndon Johnson. He probably spent more time with the Johnsons socially than with any individual or family other than his own. But in 1968, a rift with his old friend Lyndon only added to his isolation and loneliness. The break between Russell and Johnson destroyed a close friendship of two decades. The saddest part of the rupture was that Russell's bitterness did not come over any great issue or principle but over a seemingly minor question of appointing a federal district judge in Georgia.

Russell and Johnson had developed a close friendship, but one which contained some strange qualities. For instance, they kept lists of favors that they had done for one another with the idea that a time would come when they might want to call in those obligations. Johnson's office kept a list of "favors granted" to members of Congress, and the list on Russell was several pages long. On the other hand, Russell carried a small pink slip of paper in his wallet with the heading, "Johnson obligations to me," on which he had listed his trip to Texas to campaign in 1960 and his support of bills that the president favored. This may have been rather standard Washington behavior, but Russell himself had once told Senator Gale McGee that friends "did not keep books on such matters," referring to congressional favors. Russell may have been correct when he later said that his relationship with Johnson was one of the "most peculiar in American history."[26]

The two men often got on one another's nerves, but those occasional irritations quickly passed. One instance will illustrate the point. One Saturday morning when Johnson was vice president, he appeared outside the Senate Office Building in his chauffeur-driven limousine where he spotted G. W. "Buddy" Darden, then a student on Russell's patronage, about to enter the building. "Hey, boy, is Dick in?" Johnson shouted out of the car window. Darden, who could see the light in Russell's office, replied, "Yes, sir." "Well, tell him I'm out here in the car and want to see him," Johnson said. Darden hastened to the senator's office and gave him the vice president's message. Obviously annoyed, Russell said, "Well, you just tell the son-of-a-bitch I'm not here. I don't want to fool with him today." Young Darden was on the spot. It seemed best to do nothing, so he just waited in the outer office. Shortly, Johnson came bounding into Russell's office, and they had a most cordial conversation with no sign of irritation on the part of either man.[27]

On February 13, 1968, Russell wrote the president that he was nominating Alexander A. Lawrence of Savannah for a federal judgeship in the Southern District of Georgia. Senator Talmadge also endorsed the nomination. Ten years younger than Russell, Lawrence was a magna cum laude graduate of the University of Georgia and had practiced law since 1931 in Savannah. He had been president of the Georgia Bar Association and was currently president of the Georgia Historical Society and the author of several books. Russell called him an outstanding and dedicated attorney. Besides that, Lawrence was a personal friend. Indeed, the Lawrence and Russell families had been friends for three generations. Russell sent a copy of his letter of nomination to Attorney General Ramsey Clark and to Lawrence. He expected prompt action on the appointment.

To Russell's dismay and surprise, however, opposition to Lawrence developed among civil rights groups who dug up an old Lawrence speech in which he had sharply attacked the U.S. Supreme Court. On November 12, 1958, nearly a decade earlier, Lawrence had addressed the Magna Charta Dames, and in the context of constitutional history from the Magna Charta to the present, he discussed threats to liberty. Entitling his talk, "The Modern Garb of Tyranny," Lawrence argued that the current Supreme Court had usurped power and was as dangerous to liberty and as despotic as the early kings of England. Justices, he said, were zealots who acted on "whim" rather than "law," which had resulted in judicial tyranny. This was strong language, but it did not differ much from what other southern lawyers and political leaders were saying at the time.

When Russell received a copy of the talk, he had it inserted in the *Congressional Record* on February 2, 1959. He regarded the address, he said, as "one of the ablest deliverances on the situation which prevails in the United States today." And well he might have been proud of Lawrence. The views expressed coincided with Russell's own assessment of the Supreme Court. In one of his later speeches critical of the Court, Lawrence said that he had patterned his remarks on a talk delivered earlier by Russell.[28]

Using Lawrence's speeches as ammunition, some white civil rights advocates in Georgia and a number of black groups protested his appointment as district judge. They claimed that he could not be depended upon to enforce decisions of the Supreme Court in civil rights cases. On March 28, Reverend James L. Hooten, president of the Chatham County Council on Human Relations and a former minister of the Savannah Christian Church, wrote the president objecting to Lawrence's appointment. The Georgia Human Relations Council also opposed Lawrence, as did the Georgia NAACP and many individual blacks. He was accused of being prejudiced, bigoted, and racist. Late in March, the newspapers were publicizing this opposition to Lawrence.[29] At the same time, however, a flood of endorsements reached the offices of the president and the attorney general. Former presidents of the Georgia Bar Association and other prominent members of the legal profession in the state strongly supported Lawrence. Even Ralph McGill, who had become critical of Russell, said that even though Lawrence was an old-time segregationist he would rule fairly.[30]

If Russell believed that Lawrence's appointment would breeze through, he was mistaken. Ramsey Clark did not favor the nomination, and he convinced the president that a full investigation of Lawrence should be made in light of the criticism leveled against him by black and other civil rights groups. Russell expected the usual checking with the Federal Bureau of Investigation and the American Bar Association, but after reports from those organizations were favorable in April, he thought the nomination should be sent forward promptly. However, this was not the case. Writing a friend on April 4, Russell said that "there has been a little flair-up by some of the extremists who are protesting his nomination, but I intend to see this through and have him confirmed." A little later, he wrote that it would be "a national shame to have such a pack of wolves and mongrels defeat so fine a man."[31]

Russell did not press the matter personally with Johnson until early in May. By that time, he was getting irritated at the delay. On Saturday, May 4, he called the White House and told Jim Jones, a presidential aide, that he wanted to see the president for five minutes on the Lawrence matter. Later that afternoon, he visited with Johnson and explained his personal interest in Lawrence who, he said, was eminently qualified for the position. He urged the president to forward Lawrence's name for confirmation soon. Johnson asked for and reviewed the Lawrence file while Russell was still in the office. To keep the pressure on the White House, Charles Campbell left a message for Jim Jones on May 7, saying that the senator was "very anxious for Alex Lawrence to be appointed federal judge" and felt "quite strongly about the matter."[32]

When Johnson and Russell visited on May 4, the president said that he did not then know what position Ramsey Clark would take on the Lawrence nomination. Nevertheless, Johnson said he would talk to Clark about the matter. It was not until a conference on May 11 that Clark told Russell he could not support Lawrence. Russell was furious, but he only told the president that he was disappointed and distressed.[33] Thus the appointment remained unresolved.

Unfortunately, the Lawrence appointment got entangled with the naming of Johnson's choice, Abe Fortas, as chief justice of the Supreme Court and with the appointment of Homer Thornberry, a Johnson friend from Texas, to a vacancy on the Court. Russell had indicated to Johnson that he would probably support both of these nominations. But he wanted to maintain his independence and did not want any connection, or even appearance of connection, between his support of Fortas and Thornberry and the administration's appointment of Lawrence. While Johnson denied any such connection, the delay in moving Lawrence's nomination forward convinced Russell that the president did indeed perceive such a relationship and was not playing straight with him. Members of the White House staff and senior Russell assistants Charles Campbell and Bill Jordan tried to work out the matter but without success. It had become a matter strictly between the president and the senator.

Ramsey Clark's opposition to Lawrence placed Johnson in a difficult position. He wanted to do this favor for Russell, but if he ordered Clark to approve the appointment, the attorney general might resign. That might ignite more street demonstrations by young people and others who viewed Clark as the administration's leading spokesman for civil rights and broad social reform. The president did not want that. Johnson explained to Clark that he wanted to make the appointment and that "Dick Russell was the dearest friend he had in the Senate," who had promoted him for every position and honor he had achieved in Washington. Would not Clark agree to the nomination? Clark simply said no. It was an agonizing situation for the president, and he hoped that in time new reports and support for Lawrence would change his attorney general's position. Meanwhile, Russell believed that the president should overrule Clark and order the appointment.

Usually a man of patience and calm demeanor, Russell finally became angry at what he believed was an inordinate delay on the part of the president. His tolerance of his old friend snapped, and on July 1, he wrote Johnson a stinging letter. He declared that "innumerable conversations and communications" had been held in connection with the Lawrence appointment and that it was the first personal appeal he had ever made "to any President of the United States." Even after all of his years in the Senate, Russell declared, he had been naive to not suspect that the Lawrence nomination was being held up "until after you sent in the nominations of Fortas and Thornberry while still holding the recommendations for the nomination of Mr. Lawrence either in your office or in the Department of Justice." Russell continued that, despite Johnson's intentions, this placed the senator in a position in which if he voted for Fortas and Thornberry, it would appear that "I have done so out of my fears that you would not nominate Mr. Lawrence." He resented being "treated as a child or a patronage-seeking ward heeler," Russell wrote. He said that when he had come to the Senate he had nothing but his self-respect and that when he retired or was "carried out in a box," he intended to take that self-respect back to Georgia with him. Thus he was advising Johnson that, because of the long delay on the Lawrence appointment and the "juggling of the nomination," he considered himself "released from any statements that I may have made to you" regarding the Supreme Court appointments. Then Russell told the president that he could deal with the Lawrence matter in any way he saw fit but that as a senator, he would never again make a recommendation for a judicial appointment in his state. On the Supreme Court nominations, he added, he would deal with them on their merits, but he wanted the president to understand that "it is not done with any expectation that I am buying or insuring the nomination of Mr. Lawrence." Russell let Johnson know in no uncertain terms that he resented what he considered shabby treatment. In the parlance of the 1960s, he was saying, take the appointment and shove it.

Johnson was taken aback by the harshness of his old friend's letter. He told staff members that he did not even want the letter in his files. In any event, the president's staff immediately went to work to draft a reply that Tom Johnson delivered in person to Russell the next day. The president reminded Russell that on the previous Thursday he had told the senator that he intended to appoint Lawrence and emphasized that no relationship whatever existed between that appointment and the Supreme Court vacancies. There never had been and there was not now, Johnson wrote. The president said that he was "frankly surprised and deeply disappointed" that Russell had inferred otherwise. "Both my standards of public administration, and my knowledge of your character would deny such an inference," Johnson explained.[34]

Johnson's denial that there was any connection between the appointment of Lawrence and the confirmation of Fortas and Thornberry did not satisfy Russell. When a constituent wrote that it appeared Johnson was holding up the Lawrence appointment to assure the senator's support for Johnson's Supreme Court nominees, Russell replied that he did not know what the president was thinking but that if "he believes his disposition of the former will in any way effect my vote on the latter he is badly mistaken."[35]

There is every indication that in Johnson's mind there was no connection between Lawrence's appointment and the senator's vote for Fortas and Thornberry. But the delay caused Russell to perceive that there was. And perceptions are often as important as facts in human relationships. Johnson stalled in hopes of finding a way to make the appointment and still satisfy his attorney general. Russell seemed unable or unwilling to understand this.

A few weeks later, Lawrence was named judge for the Southern District of Georgia, but Russell did not forgive Johnson for what he considered his temporizing with the appointment. He resented the delay and embarrassment to him personally and what he believed was at least temporary humiliation to Lawrence and his family, caused, he wrote, by a "motley collection of fanatics, mystics and publicity seekers."[36]

There was more to the controversy between Russell and Johnson than met the eye. One might ask why, after knowing that Lawrence was going to be appointed, Russell reacted so strongly. It boiled down to a kind of contest of influence. Russell often referred to those opposing Lawrence as mongrels, zealots, and fanatics. He had no respect for them nor for Ramsey Clark, whom he believed paid too much attention to Lawrence's critics. By delaying the appointment, the president seemed to be listening more carefully to Clark and to Lawrence's detractors than to the senator. Even though Russell knew Lawrence would get the appointment, he was humiliated by the delay and angered that the administration would give so much attention to Lawrence's critics whose views he detested.

The Lawrence affair was responsible for destroying a long and close relationship between two proud and independent friends. On July 1, the very day Russell wrote his hot letter to Johnson, the White House called and asked him to attend an award ceremony. He declined.[37] Except for official business, mostly related to defense and Vietnam, Russell never again had any significant contacts with Johnson. It was not long before newsmen began to notice that Johnson and Russell were no longer seeing one another socially. During October many newspapers carried stories with such headlines as "Johnson-Russell Ties Broken Off," "LBJ Cools to Russell," and "Johnson-Russell Rift Cuts Communications." When asked by reporters about the problem, Russell would only say that there had been a disagreement that had not been resolved to his liking. When invitations no longer came from the White House, Russell accepted the situation, in the words of one writer, "philosophically and silently."[38] No longer was Johnson telling people who had problems with legislation, as he had for years, to "check it with Dick."

When Johnson delivered his last State of the Union Address on January 14, 1969, Russell was one of the congressional leaders who escorted him into the chamber. At the end of his talk, Johnson mentioned several individuals on whom he had depended and relied during his presidency. He was sure, he said, that "I have avoided many pitfalls by the good common sense counsel of the President Pro Tempore of the Senate, Senator Richard B. Russell." Russell told a friend that he was surprised the president had recognized him but was "deeply gratified and flattered when he did so."[39]

Johnson seemed more interested than Russell in repairing their friendship. On November 2, 1968, he wrote Russell the usual warm and flattering birthday message. Referring to his and Lady Bird's years of friendship with Russell as "rich ones for us," the president added that Russell's long service had greatly benefited the country. As the Johnsons were getting ready to leave the White House in January 1969, Johnson wrote that he was proud to call Russell "my friend—a good friend, a stedfast friend, a loyal friend." Then he added that Dick had lightened his load as president and that "you have enriched my life."[40]

Russell, however, did not respond to these friendly overtures. He refused to talk with Professor Joe Frantz who was interviewing Johnson associates to gather oral history for the Lyndon Baines Johnson Library in Austin. Frantz reported that Russell was one of the very few individuals who declined to participate in the Johnson oral history program. Russell gave as an excuse that he would probably write his own memoirs.[41] Moreover, as Johnson left Washington, congressmen and senators delivered glowing tributes to the president. Many of these statements were to be published in a book. The volume was about to go to press when Powell Moore got a call saying that Russell had not submitted anything. Moore mentioned this to Russell and suggested that the senator include a statement. However, Russell replied that he did not want to make any tribute to Johnson. It was only after several urgings by Moore that Russell reluctantly agreed that his press secretary should prepare something. The senator accepted what Moore wrote but added a few sentences on watching baseball games with Johnson and his friendship with the Johnson family.[42]

Russell's deepest resentment in connection with the Lawrence appointment was against Ramsey Clark. As the affair was finally being resolved, he wrote that "I will never forgive the Attorney General for his inexplicable and vicious opposition to Alex."[43] He believed that Johnson should have directed Clark to proceed with the appointment with dispatch. Russell once sarcastically raised the question as to whether Johnson or Clark was president. As Johnson and Russell discussed getting an indictment against Rap Brown, a radical civil rights leader, Johnson said that he could not do so because Clark opposed such action. Russell blurted out, "Are you the president or is Ramsey Clark president?"[44] Incidentally, Russell voted against cloture in the Fortas case, which was really a vote against his nomination. He thought about the matter at length but finally decided that Fortas tended "to substitute political philosophy for law," making it impossible to support him.[45]

Russell's health worsened during 1968 and early 1969. By late December 1968, he was coughing up blood when he tried to clear his lungs. He had lost considerable weight and looked thin and worn.[46] On March 17, 1969, he went to Walter Reed Army Hospital to undergo a routine examination of his respiratory system, and in the course of the tests, doctors found a tumor in his left lung. Three days later, he left the hospital and returned to his office where reporters awaited him. What about the tumor, he was asked. "It is fair to assume that it is malignant," he replied. This proved to be the case. Afternoon newspapers gave wide publicity to this disturbing news. To deal with this added health problem, doctors prescribed a five-day-a-week series of cobalt-radiation treatments. However, they advised Russell to continue his usual schedule. Actually, he looked somewhat better in the spring of 1969 than he had several months earlier.[47]

President Lyndon B. Johnson visiting with Senator Russell at Walter Reed Army Hospital in Washington, June 11, 1968. President Johnson inscribed the photograph, "To Dick, with respect." (Photo courtesy of Russell Memorial Library, University of Georgia, Athens.)

The senator received a flood of letters and cards expressing sympathy over his condition and wishing him a speedy recovery. John A. Sibley, a longtime friend in Atlanta, wrote that he joined thousands in the state in "thanksgiving for your service and in prayer that it may continue for many years." "Touched" by Sibley's words, Russell replied that he would "fight to lick this problem and hope for the best." He wrote to another friend that he had a tough fight on his hands but that "I am giving it all that I have and intend to lick my problem." "By the grace of the almighty," he would see it through, he wrote on another occasion.[48] His colleagues in the Senate spoke movingly of their concern. On March 24, one after another took to the floor to express hope and prayer for his speedy recovery.[49]

On May 6, Russell called in reporters to announce some good news. X rays taken on April 25, he said, had disclosed that the treatments had been successful and that no sign of a tumor remained. The radiation had been "effective beyond anything I ever expected. The response had been fantastic," he said. Whether he was entirely cured, Russell explained, only time would tell. But at least he could now "fall back and worry about the emphysema." It was clear that he retained his sense of humor during the ordeal. He told reporters that he regretted that his illness had "started anticipation in the hearts of a number of persons down in Georgia" who wanted to succeed him. However, looking a little mischievous, he added, "I don't regret it too much."[50]

Although Russell had weathered another serious health crisis, his overall condition continued to worsen. The radiation had destroyed the cancer, but it had reduced the air capacity of the treated lung. His breathing was more difficult than ever. It was necessary for him to restrain his physical movements and to keep oxygen handy. By this time, he had oxygen with him almost constantly, both in his office and at the apartment. He told Dr. Herbert A. Saltzman of the Duke Medical School that as long as he had oxygen, he could get along fine. In any event, his bout with cancer had been a scary experience. He wrote Jack and Mary Valenti that his recent crisis had convinced him "totally and completely of the power of prayer, however unworthy the recipient." He said that he could claim no special relationship with the Almighty himself but expressed gratitude that so many of his friends had strong lines of communication to "a benign Providence."[51]

Despite his health problems, Russell maintained an active schedule in the spring of 1969. He was a hard man to slow down. The evening of March 20, the same day he returned from the hospital, he was presented the first James Forrestal Memorial Award by the National Security Industrial Association. This organization represented major defense contractors. Acceptance of the award gave Russell an opportunity to advance some of his views on the state of the nation, especially on national defense.

The most important national goal, he said, was for the United States to maintain a strong defensive posture. Some people seemed to believe, he continued, that peace could be achieved by weakening American defenses and making the nation's first priorities domestic programs. That was wrong, he said. Then there were those who feared "a gigantic industrial-military complex." Russell said that he did not believe there was any danger in such a relationship. Indeed, he argued that defense contractors had made an outstanding contribution to the nation's security. There was nothing wrong, he said, "in close coordination" between defense agencies and industry. Only by depending on the defense industries, Russell explained, could the country be provided with the highly complicated and sophisticated weapons and equipment needed by the modern military. But, Russell insisted, industry must be responsible and accountable. However, he would not depend entirely on corporate responsibility. "The government must continue to maintain close supervision and control over operations involving the military and defense oriented industry." Russell also took this opportunity to again criticize activists who were against the Vietnam War, and he expressed his disapproval of how the war was being conducted. He sharply disagreed with those who wanted to reduce government expenses by cutting military costs.[52]

Russell was reacting to growing public criticism of the industrial-military complex and to the demand that Congress reduce military spending. There were also serious charges of waste and mismanagement in military procurement. Senator William Proxmire of Wisconsin, chairman of the Subcommittee on Economy in Government, wanted to investigate the huge cost overruns at Lockheed, which was building the C-5A transport plane at Marietta. It appeared as though those overruns might total some $2 billion. Russell quickly came to Lockheed's defense. He stoutly resisted any investigation directed just at Lockheed that might possibly result in reducing defense contracts with the company. He was strongly protective of the jobs provided for Georgians by that huge firm. Russell insisted that Lockheed was a good defense contractor and that cost overruns on the C-5A were no higher than those of other big defense contractors. He blamed much of the increases on inflation. Russell was much concerned about the "wave of anti-military spending sentiment in congress" and saw the attack on Lockheed as part of a pattern to discredit the military and its suppliers. He considered this a serious threat to the nation's defenses.

Russell did not deny that waste existed in defense procurement, and he said that cutting unnecessary expenses should always be a matter of congressional scrutiny. However, he was deeply annoyed when critics of military waste seemed tolerant of waste in other agencies. He pointed out that when it was found that the Office of Economic Opportunity had about a hundred nonexistent people on the payroll, the agency's supporters defended the program and excused the matter as an "isolated incident." In other words, he objected to what he considered a double standard of fiscal responsibility—one for the military and another for the social agencies. He vigorously defended the military against its critics, who, he believed, were shortsighted and directly or indirectly favored "unilateral disarmament." On defense costs, Russell claimed that he had been one of the nation's leading cost cutters. He stated that from 1963 to 1969 he had reduced some $9 billion from the military requests.[53]

As Russell had predicted after the election, he found it easy to work with Richard Nixon. He attended numerous White House leadership conferences in 1969 and supported the president on several major issues. He backed the Safeguard ABM System that Nixon favored and defended going ahead with the system against considerable opposition. After being at the White House on July 22 with other Senate leaders to discuss the ABM, he noted that he was ready to fight to the finish for it. He was a major influence in winning that battle for the president.[54] He also continued to support taking stronger military action in Vietnam and applauded the president's policy in March 1969 of bombing North Vietnamese sanctuaries in Cambodia. Nixon had actually called Russell before he ordered the bombing to commence. The next year, Russell opposed the Cooper-Church amendment that would have set a time limit for withdrawal of American troops from Cambodia. He wrote that he was against the amendment and "any other proposal" that would "tie the hands of the President as Commander-in-Chief." Nixon was grateful to Russell for his support.[55]

Russell, like Nixon, also changed his mind about relations between Red China and the United States. He had consistently criticized the idea of giving any recognition to the Communist government and had also expressed strong opposition to the recognition of Red China by the United Nations. But in early 1969, he stated that it was time to develop better relations between the two countries. He had reevaluated his position, he said, and had concluded that the United States and Communist China should have some kind of official diplomatic exchange.[56]

This was a major step for Russell in light of his long friendship with Madame Chiang Kai-shek. Madame Chiang had been a student at Wesleyan College in Macon from 1909 to 1914, part of which time Russell was at Gordon Institute at Barnesville some thirty miles away. Russell had visited her and General Chiang during his trip to American military installations in 1943. From time to time, they exchanged letters and occasionally met in Washington.

In October 1965, Wesleyan College invited Madame Chiang back to the campus to speak at the fall convocation. The logical person to introduce her was Dick Russell. She and Russell flew to Warner Robins in a military aircraft on October 20 and were then driven to the college. In his introduction of Madame Chiang, Russell said that she had "made as great a contribution to freedom as any human in the last 30 years." Some people may have thought this statement was effusive and excessively flattering, but the senator was genuinely fond of Madame Chiang, who had strongly opposed the Communists in her country. Friendship, however, would not deter his reassessment of what he believed was in the national interest. Russell's revised position on this important issue indicated that he could be flexible in light of changing times and circumstances.[57]

Russell gave enthusiastic support to Nixon's nominees to the Supreme Court. He voted for Clement F. Haynsworth, Jr., in November 1969 and for G. Harrold Carswell in April 1970. He actually left his hospital bed to be present for the vote on Carswell. He had earlier hailed Carswell as one who would help get "the court back in its proper function as a judicial body." Both of these nominations were rejected by the Senate, but Russell stuck by the president because he thought Nixon was right. In each instance, after the vote Nixon wrote "Dear Dick" to thank him for standing by his nominees.[58]

Beginning in 1968, Russell's thirty-fifth year in the Senate, an increasing number of newspaper articles appeared on him and his career. These generally dealt less with specific achievements in the Senate than with his overall influence and prestige. Writers presented him as the Senate's senior statesman, which he was, who better than anyone else symbolized the strength and virtues of that legislative body.

Also, several publishers approached Russell about writing his autobiography or perhaps some other type of book. As early as 1964, Evan Thomas, executive vice president of Harper and Row, suggested to William S. White, one of Russell's favorite writers, that his company would be interested in publishing a book by Russell. White later discussed the matter with Russell, and then Thomas wrote Russell suggesting that he should write a book that would educate northern liberals and intellectuals on the southern point of view. Russell denied that the southern viewpoint was much different from "national thinking" but said he did not then have time to undertake such a project. He added that he would be glad to discuss the matter later.[59]

Ashbel Green, managing editor of Alfred A. Knopf, wrote Russell on March 7, 1969, saying that he had read that the senator planned to write a book. This report had appeared in the *New York Times* after Russell refused to hold an interview with Joe Frantz. If this were true, Green added, Knopf would like a chance to publish it. Russell replied that he did not know if he would ever get around to "assembling my experiences, in the most thrilling fifty years in the life of the human family." If he did, however, he would contact Green. A representative of Doubleday also approached him about publishing his memoirs.[60]

In May 1970, Curtis E. Tate, Jr., of Biographical Publishers in Athens, Georgia, suggested to Russell that the Georgia Alumni Association should sponsor a Russell biography. He mentioned that Emory Thomas of the university's history department would be an ideal author for such a book. Replying for Russell, Barboura Raesly said that the senator was flattered at the suggestion but added that he could not make his files and papers available to Thomas, as Thomas had requested, without opening them to other scholars. Raesly wrote that Russell was too busy to visit with Professor Thomas.[61] It is clear that Russell was not yet ready to open his official files and papers to historians. The main reason was that such action would be to him symbolic of the end of a career, which, despite serious health problems, he was unready to accept.

Meanwhile, a move was underway to establish the Russell Library at the University of Georgia in Athens. For several years, administrators at the university had been urging the senator to place his official papers in the university library. Although he was receptive to the proposal, Russell had postponed taking any action on the suggestion. He told one friend that he feared his materials would become lost or invisible in the mass of books and manuscripts in the main library. The question was how to get the senator to release his official papers so they would be preserved for the use of historians and other writers. Finally, early in 1970, Russell approved the idea of setting up a private foundation that would raise money for the Russell Library. Headed by his colleague, Herman Talmadge, trustees for the newly formed foundation were approved by Russell in May 1970. They were among the state's outstanding leaders in law, business, politics, and the media, plus university president Fred C. Davison. By the end of 1970, the trustees had accepted President Davison's offer to locate the Russell Library on a separate floor of a new addition to the university library, which would have a separate entrance. This meant that no funds had to be raised for a building. The trustees had also laid plans to raise about $2 million, mainly to fund a Russell chair in American history. Russell was pleased and proud of these developments, but by that time, he was too ill to appreciate fully what would eventually be the scope of operations at the library that would bear his name.[62]

Although Russell was quite active throughout much of 1969, at least up until December, he continued to be plagued with deteriorating health. He was in and out of Walter Reed Army Hospital where, he explained in October, he had undergone "every test in the books." The slightest exertion made his breathing extremely difficult. Also in October, he developed severe back pains. Doctors discovered that a cracked vertebra was pinching a nerve and causing his discomfort. It became necessary for him to wear a back brace. He spent several days in the hospital in early October, and after he was discharged, he was able to go to his office only a few hours a day.[63] His increasing battle against ill health brought many letters of concern, support, and sympathy. Even Hubert Humphrey wrote on October 7 that he wanted Russell to know that as "an old friend I have been thinking of you."[64]

In an effort to deal with his various ailments, the senator took an astounding number and variety of medicines. By early 1970, he was taking at least thirteen pills daily, plus Librium as needed every one to six hours.[65] Yet, despite his medicines, frequent hospital stays, and generally weakening condition, he always seemed to recover enough to carry on his work and meet much of his busy schedule. For example, on February 8, 1970, he joined President and Mrs. Nixon for Sunday worship in the East Room of the White House, where his brother, Henry Edward Russell, conducted the service. A large number of Russell family members were present. Two days later, he attended a big reception held for him at a Washington hotel. The occasion was to recognize Russell and his long career in the Senate. This was reflected in a three-part filmed interview produced by the Cox Broadcasting Company for Atlanta television station WSB. The eight hundred persons in attendance saw a shortened version of the film, which was entitled "Georgia Giant." President Nixon attended the gathering and praised Russell as "a great leader," "a man of integrity," and "a fine human being." It was a great evening for Russell, and he did not deny that he loved the attention.[66]

Time, however, was running out for Dick Russell. Although he had said in November 1969 that he would be a candidate for reelection in 1972 if his health permitted, there were rumors and speculation that the senator would not be able to serve out his term. During the spring of 1970, Russell's staff regularly reported to correspondents and visitors that the senator was out of the office or temporarily away from Washington. This was a way to protect Russell and limit his access to the public. In an effort to put at rest rumors that he might retire or resign, Russell said in early September 1970 that he was not considering retirement because of his health. "I've been a little off stride," he said, "but my health is good." He surely had no intention of resigning, he added.[67]

Despite such optimistic public statements, Russell fully realized just how sick he was. When Senator Talmadge saw him after one of his bouts in the hospital in 1970, Talmadge said, "Dick, you're looking good," to which Russell replied, "Well, Herman, I don't feel good. I don't breathe too well. I'm not going to be around much longer."[68]

By mid-1970, it had become very difficult for Russell to perform his duties because the slightest exertion made it hard to breathe. In

Senator Russell and President Richard M. Nixon at a reception given for Russell in Washington, February 10, 1970. (Photo courtesy of the Bettmann Archive.)

September he acquired a three-wheeled motorized vehicle that he could drive around the Senate Office Building and the Capitol to reduce his physical activity to a minimum.[69] By then, too, one of his sisters, either Ina or Patience, was staying with him much of the time.

On October 24, Russell fell at his apartment causing bruises and pain. During the following days, he suffered from dizzy spells and was even irrational for short periods. He could eat very little, usually a small amount of custard or some other bland food. November 2, his seventy-third birthday and the fiftieth anniversary of his election to public office, was a most difficult day. A staff member wrote that the "Senator felt bad and miserable."[70] Most of the calls coming to Russell's office by late 1970 were not about Senate business but inquiries about the senator's health. On December 7, Proctor Jones left a note for the senator saying he would come to his apartment and help "him get ready to go down to the Capitol tomorrow."[71] However, instead of going to his office the next day, Russell was admitted to Walter Reed Army Hospital—for the last time.

Arriving at the hospital, he was met by Dr. Andre Ognibene at the back elevator of Ward 8 and taken to his suite. Dr. Ognibene recalled that the senator "looked extremely thin and drawn" and "was markedly short of breath." His weight during the last two years had dropped from a normal 170 to 180 pounds to about 140 pounds. Russell realized the extreme seriousness of his condition. "I think this is the last time," he told Ognibene.

The doctors changed his antibiotics and used intravenous medications in an effort to help Russell recover. At first he showed some mild improvement. On December 19, President Nixon stopped by, telling Russell that he wanted "to come out and wish you all the best for Christmas." The president's visit buoyed Russell's spirits temporarily, but that was all.

No medication or treatment seemed able to bring him any relief. Russell's attitude varied between deep depression and the belief that he might make it. In the past when he had been in the hospital, he took telephone calls, saw visitors, and even carried on some Senate business. This time, however, he was too ill to think about affairs of state. His last official act was to sign a proxy in support of his friend, Robert C. Byrd, for majority whip. Byrd was so proud and grateful that he had the proxy framed and hung in his office.

By mid-January 1971, Russell's condition was critical. His breath became shorter and shorter, and he was too weak to get out of bed. Members of his family had gathered to support and encourage him, and the doctors sought to make him comfortable. There was nothing more they could do. He drifted in and out of consciousness. Finally, about 2:25 P.M. on January 21, he died quietly. In his own pajamas, in a neat bed, and with his family around him, he passed away with dignity and without elaborate life-support systems. The official cause of death was pulmonary emphysema.[72]

Richard B. Russell, Jr., had told members of his family that when he died he wished to be returned to Georgia as promptly as possible. There would be no lying in state in the national capital. Thus, on Friday morning, January 22, at 10:15 A.M., six soldiers carried his casket from the funeral home and placed it in a hearse, which, accompanied by a few cars for family and staff members, followed a motorcycle police escort down Constitution Avenue toward Capitol Hill. The cortege slowly passed the Senate Office Building and the east front of the Capitol. Members of the Senate stood solemnly and respectfully on the Capitol steps viewing the hearse as it stopped momentarily before moving on to the House wing. The procession then drove to Andrews Air Force Base where the casket was loaded into Air Force One, which quickly took off for Atlanta.

After the casket was met at the airport by Governor and Mrs. Jimmy Carter and other dignitaries, a twenty-eight-car procession headed toward the Georgia state capitol where Russell's body would lie in state for twenty-four hours in the rotunda. At 3 P.M., the capitol doors opened and mourners began passing by the casket to view their departed senator. By noon the next day, Saturday, an estimated ten thousand people had filed through the rotunda to pay their final respects.

Meanwhile, on Friday morning, President Nixon had announced that he planned to fly to Georgia to extend his sympathy to Russell's family and to honor the dead senator. That same evening, while delivering his State of the Union Address to Congress, Nixon paused and asked for a moment of silent prayer for Russell. President and Mrs. Nixon arrived in Atlanta on Saturday afternoon about three o'clock. They proceeded immediately to the capitol where the president spoke to members of the Russell family and laid a wreath of red, white, and blue carnations at the foot of the senator's casket. Calling Russell a "tower of strength and a President's senator," Nixon praised Russell as a leader of highest ability and character. He also described for the gathering his visit with Russell at Walter Reed Army Hospital only a few days before his death. As ill as he was, Nixon said, Russell was still expressing a desire to help the president and the nation with difficult problems. Then the Nixons returned to the airport and left for Washington. They had been in Atlanta a little more than an hour.

Shortly after President Nixon left the capitol, arrangements were made to take Russell's body to Winder. An entourage of some forty cars headed toward Winder late Saturday afternoon, arriving about dusk. The casket was placed in the old family home to await visitors and burial the next day.

One troubling element in the funeral arrangements was the weather. There had been several days of intermittent rain, heavy clouds, and fog, which interrupted air traffic. Would the weather clear up by Sunday when most of the dignitaries from Washington planned to arrive for the funeral? Rather than improving, Sunday's weather in North Georgia turned out to be even worse—more rain, clouds, and fog. The Washington contingent was headed by Vice President Spiro Agnew who would be accompanied by fifty-five senators and others from the nation's capital. Leaving in three planes on Sunday morning, the group planned to land at Dobbins Air Force Base near Marietta and then motor to Winder for the 2:15 P.M. service. However, visibility was so poor that the planes could not land. The closest place to land safely was Charleston, South Carolina, where the planes put down about 12:30 P.M.

The question now arose as to how the vice president and senators could deliver their eulogies at a funeral scheduled in less than two hours. J. Leonard Reinch, president of Cox Broadcasting Company in Atlanta, suggested that direct television communication could be set up between Charleston and Winder so that those who planned to speak but were unable to get to Winder could participate. Their remarks would be transmitted to television monitors at the cemetery.

At about 2:15 P.M., Russell's gray metal casket was taken out the front door of the Russell house and transported a few hundred yards up a slight hill behind the family home to Russell Park and the family cemetery. Nine of Russell's nephews served as pallbearers, and more than a hundred family members and hundreds of friends followed along through the mud and rain. Although the official Washington contingent had been diverted by foul weather, many distinguished government leaders were present. They included former vice president Hubert Humphrey, three cabinet secretaries, General William Westmoreland, Admiral Thomas Moorer, chairman of the Joint Chiefs of Staff, and Dean Rusk, former secretary of state.

After the casket was placed under a tent containing lecterns and two television monitors, the final service began. Reverend Henry E. Russell, the senator's brother, led in prayer and Bible reading, and then from Charleston Senator John Stennis delivered the principal eulogy over television. Stennis praised his departed friend for his many contributions but especially for his efforts to guarantee the nation's security. Russell was a man, Stennis said, whom the nation's youth should emulate. He mentioned the senator's integrity, courage, high standards of public and personal conduct, willingness to serve his country, and common sense. Some observers were heard to whisper how ironic it was that Stennis, one of Russell's closest friends, was unable to attend the funeral, while Humphrey, his main opponent on civil rights, was there! Governor Jimmy Carter gave the last eulogy at the cemetery, a brief three-minute talk, after which the marine band played, "Eternal Father Strong to Save." Following the benediction, mourners slowly departed. Then the casket was lowered in a grave close to Russell's parents. Dick Russell was now back in the red hills of his beloved Georgia forever.[73]

21

Summing Up

R ichard Brevard Russell, Jr., the Georgia Giant, was gone, but he had made an indelible mark on his state and nation. An entire generation of Georgians could not even remember when he did not represent them in Atlanta or Washington. He had been in the Senate for thirty-eight years, which was longer than any other sitting senator and more than half of his entire lifetime. Add to this number his legislative career that began in 1921 and his governorship, and Russell had devoted half a century to public service. He may have been the only individual in American history who had spent more than two-thirds of his life in elective office. He had surely earned the title "dean of the Senate." Russell had worked with, and been an adviser to, six presidents. While Franklin D. Roosevelt, Harry S Truman, Dwight D. Eisenhower, John F. Kennedy, and Lyndon B. Johnson came and went and Richard M. Nixon settled into the White House, Russell was at the same place in Room 205 of the Senate Office Building. Many had called him a senator's senator, but he was, as Nixon said, a president's senator as well.

Russell would be remembered for much more than just longevity in office. His large and extended family would remember him as a loving brother or brother-in-law, a concerned uncle or great uncle, and one who held deep family values. The family reunions in Winder where Uncle Dick presided as the patriarch after the death of his parents were treasured memories for the large Russell clan. Older friends recalled his youthful exuberance, his popularity with girls, the hunting trips to South Georgia, and the evenings spent talking politics and swapping stories. Politicians could not forget his phenomenal vote-getting ability as he had beaten the state's best in his campaigns for governor and senator. Local, county, and state officials reflected on the economic impact on the state of the many federal facilities Russell had brought to Georgia. Friends in the Senate would miss his integrity, intelligence, strength of character, and ability to get things done in a quiet, unobtrusive way. They would also miss his guardianship of the Senate as a political institution. Professional military leaders would not forget his support for a strong defense establishment. Blacks and white civil rights reformers would remember him as an intractable foe of civil rights legislation and racial equality and as the man who had been most responsible for delaying enactment of an effective federal civil rights law. Yes, Dick Russell would be remembered. His name, moreover, would become enshrined on numerous buildings and other public facilities, and most important of all, his place in history would be symbolized by the Russell Senate Office Building, one of those marble monuments on Capitol Hill in Washington.

Russell's thought and actions in his long public life had been determined by a set of deeply held principles. He was at heart an agrarian, a Jeffersonian, who believed in the basic importance of agriculture in the economy and the special place of rural people in society. The family farm was to Russell one of the nation's most prized institutions. Secondly, Russell viewed Anglo-Saxon laws, traditions, and institutions as superior to all others, and Northern European peoples as the makers and purveyors of the highest and most worthy culture. In this connection, he saw the white South as the part of the United States that was truest to that culture. He once boasted that Georgians were the purest Anglo-Saxon stock and that less than 1 percent of the state's population was foreign born. As a result of this view, he looked with great alarm at any revision or weakening of the immigration laws that would admit more Asians or Africans to the United States.

Except under what he considered unusual circumstances such as depression or war, he believed that the federal government should not infringe on the specific rights and responsibilities of the states. While most contemporaries considered Russell a conservative, he was in fact a nineteenth-century liberal who believed in maximum personal and economic freedom. When the term liberal began to be defined as one who favored greatly expanded powers and functions of the central government, he believed that the term's true meaning had been profaned. Russell recognized, as he put it, that government was "never static." During the Great Depression when millions suffered, he supported the expansion of federal power and responsibilities in ways that would help care for people and get the economy moving again. Indeed, he was one of the New Deal's most ardent backers. But, he insisted, he did not favor change just for the sake of change nor what he called expensive federal innovations for which in his judgment there was no genuine need.

Russell considered the U.S. Senate the nation's most important political institution. He held what he called "an almost sublime faith in the Senate . . . as an instrumentality of government and as the last protection and bulwark of the rights of the American people." He saw the practice of unlimited debate as the country's strongest bastion of freedom. He carefully guarded the precedents, traditions, and practices of the Senate and viewed any attack on the Senate as a threat to freedom and democracy. No other senator knew the rules and precedents as well as Dick Russell. When Senator Stennis first arrived in the Senate, he approached Alben Barkley, the floor leader, and got a copy of the formal Senate rules. But Barkley hastily explained that this book did not contain everything a senator should know. Where could he get a book on the precedents and practices not spelled out in writing here, Stennis asked. "You can't get a book," Barkley replied. "The rest of them are in Senator Russell's head."

Another powerful motivating principle with Russell was his nationalism and his deep sense of patriotism. Best reflected in his support for the Vietnam War, which he opposed, he gave full backing to Presidents Kennedy and Johnson because when the flag was committed, Russell was likewise committed. This attitude of "my country right or wrong" caused Russell much frustration and kept him from developing and pushing harder for alternative foreign policies that he believed were more nearly in the true national interest.

Underlying almost everything else was Russell's dedication to the South and its historic social values. Early in his political career, he talked warmly about Georgians being "nurtured at the . . . warm breast of the Mother South." White supremacy and racial segregation were to him cardinal principles for good and workable human relationships. He had a deep emotional commitment to preserving the kind of South in which his ancestors and he had lived. No sacrifice was too great for him to make if it would prevent the extension of full equality to blacks. When Senator Stennis once remarked that Russell would make a great president, he replied, "I wouldn't give up my heritage of the South to be president of the United States." Such was his unshakable commitment to the Old South—a South that industry, military bases, executive orders, education, and common sense were combining to destroy.

Indeed, Russell's thoughts and actions were strongly influenced by his understanding of history. Probably no other senator was as widely read in American and world history as Dick Russell. He believed that history taught specific lessons and that it could be a reliable guide to policy-making. Any society that disregarded its history would suffer dire consequences. Look to the past, he said, as a guide to the future. It was his understanding of history, particularly developments in the South after the abolition of slavery, that caused him to oppose equality for blacks. Rather than a guide to the future, Russell's history chained him to the past—a past that he could not preserve.

Between the time Russell went to the Georgia General Assembly in 1921 and when he became president pro tem of the U.S. Senate in 1969, the United States experienced vast changes. His long career coincided with such momentous developments in American life and society as the Great Depression, World War II, the introduction of nuclear power, the great expansion of federal powers and responsibilities, exploration of outer space, the Vietnam War, and the drive for civil rights. Politics and the nature and operations of the Senate also underwent change. By 1970 the nation and the world were vastly different places than when Russell went to the Senate in 1933.

Of fundamental importance during Russell's public career was the dramatic shift from a nation that was heavily influenced by farm-rural ideology and values to one in which urban standards and influences tended to control the thinking and actions of Americans. This shift was especially noticeable in the South where the number of farmers declined drastically. As a Jeffersonian, Russell viewed the family farm as a national bulwark against radicalism and disorder, and he was deeply disturbed by the rapid trend toward urbanization. He wrote a constituent in 1961 that he had done everything he could "to assure our family-size farmers" an equitable share of the nation's bounty. They were the "veritable backbone of our country," he said, and he wanted to improve agriculture so young farmers would remain on the farm.

In keeping with his basic philosophy, Russell supported a whole range of measures designed to help farmers. He not only backed the Agricultural Adjustment Act with its emphasis on parity prices, but he was enthusiastic in his support of the Rural Electrification Administration, the Tennessee Valley Authority, the Resettlement Administration, the Farm Security Administration, and the Farmers Home Administration. These were agencies designed to help poorer farmers. There was a trace of agrarian populism in his makeup. Russell was also a strong conservationist who made a great contribution by getting needed funds to help conserve the nation's soil, wood, and water. He was one of the leading sponsors of the Agricultural Research and Marketing Act of 1946 and took special pride in the number of agricultural research facilities that were established during his time in Washington. Although Russell received less recognition for his work on behalf of agriculture and conservation than for some other achievements, nothing gave him more pride of accomplishment than doing something to help farmers and trying to strengthen the rural United States.

Closely connected to agricultural issues was his desire to use farm surpluses to assist the needy and to provide improved nutrition for millions of Americans. He was an early supporter of the school lunch and food stamp programs, as well as of the distribution of surplus food through welfare agencies. He authored the School Lunch Act of 1946 and fought successfully to increase funding for that program.

Although Russell devoted more attention to agricultural matters than any other question during his early years in the Senate, he was, as mentioned earlier, a strong supporter of Franklin D. Roosevelt and other aspects of the New Deal. By the 1940s, however, like the rest of the nation, he turned mainly to wartime issues. In 1943 Russell won widespread recognition when he headed a Senate team that investigated the American war effort by visiting military installations throughout many parts of the world. Such postwar issues as foreign aid, economic reconversion, maintaining American military strength, admission of refugees, control of nuclear power, and other questions occupied him and his colleagues in Congress after 1945.

By the late 1940s, after some fifteen years in the Senate, Russell had achieved a strong position of leadership. His increasing power and influence came from service on two powerful committees—the Appropriations and Armed Services committees—membership on the Democratic Policy and Democratic Steering committees, his hard day-to-day work and careful attention to his Senate duties, his knowledge of the issues, and his detailed understanding of Senate rules and procedures. He was generally recognized as the Senate's best parliamentarian. For the most part, Russell worked quietly and exerted his influence behind the scenes. He was more interested in results than in publicity or national attention. His colleagues recognized and appreciated his intelligence, energy, integrity, and fairness. It was the confidence that other senators had in him that gradually strengthened his position in the Senate.

By 1950 Russell had achieved such a position of respect and admiration among his colleagues that he could have had any position of leadership that the Senate had to offer. He could have become majority leader in 1951, minority leader in 1953, or majority leader in 1955. He turned down suggestions by fellow senators that he assume a central leadership role because acceptance would compromise his independence. Russell guarded his independence with a kind of religious intensity. He did not want to be beholden to any person or group. In turning down a leadership post in 1953, he said that he was "more concerned with my own thinking than with the Democratic Party." Moreover, he did not want to be responsible for supporting party policies that he personally opposed. Thus he stayed in the background and pushed his friend Lyndon Johnson into the majority leader spot. Meanwhile, in 1951 his seniority gave him the chairmanship of the Armed Services Committee, which along with his position on the Appropriations Committee gave him tremendous power over national security matters, including funding for new weapons and maintaining strong defense forces.

Russell's power and prestige reached a high point in 1951 when he chaired the committee that investigated General Douglas MacArthur's dismissal. The firing of a popular military hero by an unpopular president who was conducting an unpopular war caused national emotions to run high. The Korean War was already a divisive issue, and MacArthur's firing could easily deepen the country's divisions. Russell promptly stepped into the situation and took charge. Possessing what George Reedy called "one of the most astute minds that has ever entered the Senate," Russell directed the inquiry with a firm hand but in a spirit of fairness and objectivity. He so skillfully deffused the crisis that by the end of the summer the MacArthur issue was scarcely in the public consciousness at all. Many contemporaries believed that this was Russell's finest hour.

During the 1950s, Russell began devoting more and more time to questions relating to national defense and security. By the time John F. Kennedy became president, Russell was widely recognized as the most knowledgeable military authority in Congress. One of his main goals was to make the nation so strong militarily that no power would consider attacking it or its vital interests. By the 1960s, his power was such that he could obtain almost any amount of money for military purposes that he thought necessary. Critics sometimes accused him of being too close to the military-industrial establishment, but he carefully scrutinized military requests and sometimes killed proposals that he thought were unwise.

Although Russell wielded great power in the Senate during the 1950s and 1960s, he found himself increasingly out of tune with the direction of national and international policies. He opposed foreign aid after 1952, but expenditures for that purpose grew substantially; he warned against committing American military forces in Vietnam but could not stop three presidents from expanding the war there; he opposed many of Kennedy's domestic policies and most of Johnson's Great

Society program, but numerous new federal programs were started and old ones expanded. He fought to the last ditch against civil rights legislation but could not block the laws of 1964 and 1965. Presidents Eisenhower, Kennedy, and Johnson often called on him for advice—perhaps no senator was at the White House as much as Russell in those years—but they ignored his counsel on most major national and international issues. Unlike earlier, when, except for civil rights, he had been close to the majority positions, by the 1960s Russell was far outside the mainstream of American political life. No one realized this better than he did.

It was the racial issue that was at the heart of his increasing alienation. In the late 1930s and 1940s, he and a few supporters successfully defeated moves to gain equal rights for blacks. By midcentury, however, the Democratic party had embraced a strong civil rights position. But as a party leader in the Senate, Russell resisted every step toward racial equality. Not only did he believe that whites were superior to blacks and that mixing of the races would weaken the nation, but he saw demands for civil rights as an attack on his beloved South and all that the region stood for. The South with its rigid caste and class system never had a stronger supporter than Dick Russell. As has been emphasized elsewhere, he did not possess a bit of demagoguery in his makeup, nor did he wish ill for blacks. In his view, blacks had made great progress since the end of slavery, and the relationship between whites and blacks should not be disturbed. According to Russell, the races should remain separate and unequal.

Russell's unchangeable views on race kept him from becoming a truly national leader, perhaps even president of the United States. It was clear by the time he sought the Democratic nomination in 1952 that no person could be nominated and elected president who held his racial attitudes and so vigorously opposed civil rights. But he refused to make any compromises or concessions even if by making them he might have become president. He rejected the advice of Jonathan Daniels in 1952 to embrace equal opportunity and take his candidacy into the mainstream of the American faith. Consequently, his presidential support was confined mainly to the South. This was the case even though many contemporaries believed that he was the best-qualified man to be president at the time. Lyndon Johnson once told correspondent Samuel Shaffer, "If the membership of the Senate were to cast a secret vote on the man they believed best qualified to be president of the United States, they would choose Richard Russell."

Russell, however, would not become a national leader unless he could lead the entire nation along the southern road. That, he knew, was impossible. So he settled for regional leadership. Knowing that he could not accept some of the requirements demanded to lead the nation, he chose Lyndon Johnson to become the political bridge between the South and the rest of the country. It was Johnson who provided what one writer called the link "between the South that [Russell] had understood and served and the South as it was going to become." Russell remained what Margaret Shannon called "a symbol of sectionalism." By pushing Johnson into leadership positions, Russell helped do indirectly what he could not do directly—that is, reconstruct the South.

Russell adjusted to most of the modern social and economic trends of his time, but he could not accept one of the most important demands for change—racial equality. He was unable to construct a new path for the South and the nation to follow on this issue. He was a prisoner of history as he understood it, and on the race question, he never left the nineteenth century. He explained his position by saying that he was representing the views of his constituents. He was defending the way of life that both he and most of his constituents had been reared in and still believed in. Unable to modify his racial views, he wasted his great talents and an enormous amount of time and energy fighting unsuccessfully against programs for racial justice. He sought to defend a social system that was indefensible. That was the tragedy of Richard Brevard Russell, Jr.

But Russell left a long list of positive achievements. He served his constituents loyally and effectively, he warned against the growing power of lobbyists and special interest groups and their effect on good government, and he educated a generation of senators in the ways of the Senate. Senator Edward Kennedy declared that Russell "established a code of conduct that captured the essence of what this Senate is." Jack Valenti wrote that Russell was the "embodiment of the Senate's classic constitutional tradition. . . . He knows its moods and its dignity. He guards its honor. He nourishes its heritage." Russell set an example of honesty, integrity, dignity, rectitude, and honor—ancient values that many Americans took too lightly. He presented the image of a statesman instead of that of a self-seeking politician. As a parliamentarian, he broke many legislative logjams, and through skillful legislative maneuvering, he modified and improved hundreds of bills. Moreover, Russell was largely responsible for shaping military budgets during the cold war years, and he warned that only through strength could the United States carry on successful negotiations with the Russians. By opposing foreign aid, resisting liberal immigration laws, and pointing out the failures of overlapping and ineffective federal agencies, he helped to focus on important national problems that many Americans believed should be reconsidered by Congress.

Russell did not achieve as much as he could have if he had modified his racial views. Furthermore, he might have been more influential if he had used the media more liberally. In looking back at Russell's career, Richard Nixon said that Russell did not project himself very well. He was too deferential and self-effacing for a media generation, according to Nixon. In a period when so many people were beginning to rely on television for their information, Russell did not utilize that means of communication very much. Indeed, he complained about his colleagues who were rushing here and there to television studios instead of staying on Capitol Hill and attending to their Senate business. To have sought more publicity and self-aggrandizement, however, would have been completely out of keeping with Russell's personality and character.

On April 1, 1969, Senator Margaret Chase Smith, whom Russell fondly called "Sis" and who had served with him on the Appropriations and Armed Services committees for seventeen years, rose to introduce one of Russell's talks into the *Congressional Record*. She said that there had been several great leaders in the history of the Senate but that there had been only a very few "truly giants of integrity, wisdom, achievement and dedication . . . the giants who really inspire their colleagues." Richard Russell from Georgia, she said, was "one of the rare few giants of the Senate" during her tenure. She continued that Russell should have been president because he "was eminently qualified" for the office and because "our nation would be a better nation had he been President." The country had not agreed with this flattering assessment, but the tribute did indicate what people who worked most closely with Russell thought of him. All things considered, he was, indeed, one of the few Senate giants in the twentieth century.

Notes

CHAPTER 1

1 Richard B. Russell to Richard B. Russell, Jr. (RBR, Jr.), November 2, 1912, Russell Collection, School Years, Correspondence with Parents, 1911–13, Russell Memorial Library, University of Georgia, Athens. See also Ralph McGill, *Atlanta Constitution*, May 2, 1951.

2 Robert Paul Turbeville, *Eminent Georgians* (Atlanta: Southern Society for Research and History, 1937), p. 12.

3 For an excellent discussion of the Russell family background, see Karen K. Kelly, "Richard B. Russell: Democrat from Georgia" (Ph.D. dissertation, University of North Carolina, 1979), chapter 1.

4 "Richard Brevard Russell," in *Dictionary of Georgia Biography*, ed. Kenneth Coleman and Stephen Gurr (Athens: University of Georgia Press, 1983), 2:859–60; Kelly, "Richard B. Russell," p. 15.

5 Undated newspaper clipping, Mrs. Ina Russell's Scrapbook, 1898–1932, Russell Collection.

6 Earl T. Leonard, "The Russells of Our Flock," University of Georgia, *Alumni Record* 46 (May 1967): 8.

7 Marion H. Allen, "Memorial to Chief Justice Richard Brevard Russell," in Georgia Bar Association, *Report of Proceedings* (Macon, Ga.: J. W. Burke Co., 1939), pp. 171–77.

8 Personal, Genealogical, 1, Russell Collection; John B. Harris, ed., *A History of the Supreme Court of Georgia: A Centennial Volume* (Atlanta: Georgia Bar Association, 1948), pp. 219–40.

9 Kelly, "Richard B. Russell," p. 19.

10 Athens City Council, Minutes, 1891–96, Athens, Georgia, p. 314.

11 Athens School Board, Minutes, May 28 and August 6, 1894, Athens, Georgia; Russell family author interviews, 1978–86.

12 C. Fred Ingram, ed., *Beadland to Barrow: A History of Barrow County, Georgia* (Atlanta: Cherokee Publishing Co., 1978), pp. 25, 36, 44, 46.

13 *Twelfth Census of the United States*, 1900, Agriculture (Washington: Government Printing Office, 1902), pt. 1, pp. 7, 158–59, 431.

14 Jackson County Deed Records, Jefferson, Georgia, pertinent years; author interview with Ina Russell Stacy, July 1, 1985.

15 "Richard Russell, Georgia Giant," manuscript for three-part documentary, Cox Broadcasting Company, Atlanta, Georgia, 1970, pt. 1, pp. 4–5.

16 *Jackson Economist* (Jefferson, Ga.), January 26, 1899; *Georgia State Journal* (Atlanta: Franklin Printing and Publishing Co., 1898); Turbeville, *Eminent Georgians*, p. 14.

17 RBR, Jr., Diary, entry for January 17, 1910, Russell Collection, Early Years, 1905–11.

18 E. R. Noderer, *Washington Times-Herald*, June 23, 1952; author interviews with Ina Russell Stacy, June 10, 1981; Patience Russell Peterson, November 30, 1981; and Fielding Russell, September 10, 1980. See also RBR, Jr., Diary, Russell Collection, Early Years, 1905–11.

19 "Richard Russell, Georgia Giant," pt. 1, pp. 6, 7; *Winder News*, February 10, 1910; author interview with Ina Russell Stacy, July 1, 1985.

20 RBR, Jr., Diary, entry for August 23, 1908, Russell Collection, Early Years, 1905–11.

21 See pertinent entries in RBR, Jr., Diary, ibid.

22 RBR, Jr., to Mrs. Ina Russell, March 17 and 19, 1908, ibid.

23 RBR, Jr., Diary entries for January 5 and March 25, 1907, ibid.

24 Memorandum Book, 1910, ibid.

25 *Atlanta Journal*, September 2, 1947.

26 Judge Richard B. Russell to RBR, Jr., November 2, 1912, Russell Collection, School Years, Correspondence with Parents, 1911–13.

CHAPTER 2

1 Gordon Military Institute, Barnesville, Georgia, catalogs for 1911, 1912, and 1913.

2 Mrs. Ina Russell to RBR, Jr., November 15, 1911, Russell Collection, School Years, Correspondence with Parents, 1911–13, Russell Memorial Library, University of Georgia, Athens.

3 Mrs. Ina Russell to RBR, Jr., October 27, September 25, and November 15, 1911, ibid.

4 Robert Russell to RBR, Jr., October 20, 1911, and Mary Willie Russell to RBR, Jr., November 17, 1911, Russell Collection, Family Correspondence, Early Years, 1911.

5 Richard B. Russell to RBR, Jr., October 16 and 21 and November 5 and 26, 1911, Russell Collection, School Years, Correspondence with Parents, 1911–13.

6 RBR, Jr., to Mrs. Ina Russell, October 30, 1911, ibid.

7 *Atlanta Constitution*, February 26, March 31, and April 24, 1904.

8 Mrs. Ina Russell to RBR, Jr., February 11, 1913, Russell Collection, School Years, Correspondence with Parents, 1911–13.

9 Dewey W. Grantham, *Hoke Smith and the Politics of the New South* (Baton Rouge: Louisiana State University Press, 1958), p. 143; *Atlanta Journal*, August 23 and 24, 1906.

10 *Atlanta Journal*, October 12, 1930.

11 Marion H. Allen, "Memorial to Chief Justice Richard Brevard Russell," in Georgia Bar Association, *Report of Proceedings* (Macon, Ga.: J. W. Burke Co., 1939), pp. 171–77.

12 RBR, Jr., to Mrs. Ina Russell, November 1911, Russell Collection, School Years, Correspondence with Parents, 1911–13.

13 Mrs. Ina Russell to RBR, Jr., December 9, 1911; Richard B. Russell to RBR, Jr., December 8, 1911; and RBR, Jr., to Richard B. Russell, December 8, 1911, ibid.

14 Mrs. Ina Russell to RBR, Jr., September 27 and 29, 1911, and RBR, Jr., to Mrs. Ina Russell, October 13, 1911, ibid.

15 Richard B. Russell to RBR, Jr., February 9 and March 4, 1912, and Mrs. Ina Russell to RBR, Jr., February 19, 1912, ibid.

16 Mrs. Ina Russell to RBR, Jr., April 2 and May 29, 1912, ibid.

17 Richard B. Russell to RBR, Jr., September 28, 1912, ibid.

18 Richard B. Russell to RBR, Jr., November 2, 1912, ibid.

19 Mrs. Ina Russell to RBR, Jr., December 8, 1912, ibid.

20 Richard B. Russell to RBR, Jr., May 12, November 29, and December 12 and 16, 1912, ibid.

21 Mrs. Ina Russell to RBR, Jr., May 11, 1912, ibid; *Winder News*, August 13, 1913.

22 Mrs. Ina Russell to RBJ, Jr., February 19, 1913.

23 Ibid., March 31, 1913.

24 See RBR, Jr., Class Work Diary, and letters for 1913 in Russell Collection, School Years, Personal Correspondence, 1911–18.

25 RBR, Jr., Class Work Diary, ibid.

26 Mrs. Ina Russell to RBR, Jr., April 12 and May 1 and 13, 1913, ibid.

27 Gordon Military Institute, Student Record, 1912–13, Barnesville, Georgia; E. T. Holmes to RBR, Jr., August 18, 1913, Russell Collection, School Years, Personal Correspondence, 1911–18.

28 Richard B. Russell to RBR, Jr., May 29, 1913, Russell Collection, School Years, Correspondence with Parents, 1911–13.

29 Ibid.; Russell Collection, School Years, Class Notes.

30 Jamie Stanton to RBR, Jr., October 18, 1913, Russell Collection, School Years, Personal Correspondence, 1911–18.

31 RBR, Jr., to Richard B. Russell, September 16 and 18, 1913, Russell Collection, School Years, Correspondence with Parents, 1911–13.

32 RBR, Jr., Diary, entry for September 29, 1913, Russell Collection, School Years, Diaries.

33 Richard B. Russell to RBR, Jr., May 21 and April 23, 1914, Russell Collection, School Years, Correspondence with Parents, 1914–18.

34 Richard B. Russell to RBR, Jr., February 2 and March 2, 1914, ibid.

35 University of Georgia, Athens, Student Record, 1915–18; Mrs. Ina Russell to RBR, Jr., July 13, 1914, Russell Collection, School Years, Correspondence with Parents, 1914–18.

36 RBR, Jr., to Richard B. Russell, February 8, 1915, and Russell to RBR, Jr., January 24, 1915, Russell Collection, School Years, Correspondence with Parents, 1914–18.

37 Richard B. Russell to RBR, Jr., February 5 and 24, March 8, and April 8, 1915, ibid.

38 Mrs. Ina Russell to RBR, Jr., April 19, 1915, ibid.; Gordon Military Institute, Student Record, 1915. Russell spoke at Barnesville on November 11, 1928.

39 *Barnesville News-Gazette*, January 14, 1915.

40 RBR, Jr.'s, debate arguments are found in Russell Collection, School Years, Illness, Notes, etc. *Taps*, Gordon Military Institute yearbook, 1915.

41 RBR, Jr., student transcripts, 1915–16, University of Georgia, Athens; *Pandora*, University of Georgia yearbook, 1915.

42 RBR, Jr., to Cody Laird, October 29, 1953, Russell Collection, Personal, 1952–53.

43 Medical Record, Russell Collection, School Years, Illness, December 1915 to February 1916.

44 William Quarterman to RBR, Jr., January 26, 1916; Rebecca Hill to RBR, Jr., January 7, 1916; and Melissa E. Hood to RBR, Jr., May 31, 1916, ibid.

45 RBR, Jr., to Mrs. Ina Russell, January 5 and February 18, 1917, Russell Collection, School Years, Correspondence with Parents, 1917.

46 Mrs. Ina Russell to RBR, Jr., March 5, 1917, and RBR, Jr., to Mrs. Ina Russell, March 11, 1917, ibid.

47 Mrs. Ina Russell to RBR, Jr., February 2 and March 27, 1917, and RBR, Jr., to Mrs. Ina Russell, April 3, 1917, ibid.

48 Richard B. Russell to RBR, Jr., April 5, 1917, and RBR, Jr., to Richard B. Russell, April 11, 1917, ibid.

49 "Laurie" to RBR, Jr., May 1918, Russell Collection, School Years, Correspondence with Parents, 1914–18.

50 RBR, Jr., to Mrs. Ina Russell, May 6, 1918, ibid.

51 E. R. Noderer, *Washington Times-Herald*, June 25, 1952.

52 RBR, Jr., to Mrs. Ina Russell, October 4, 11, 17, and 28 and November 8, 1918, Russell Collection, Personal Correspondence, 1918–20.

CHAPTER 3

1 *Fourteenth Census of the United States*, 1920, Population (Washington: Government Printing Office, 1922), pt. 2, p. 1333, pt. 3, p. 207.

2 C. Fred Ingram, ed., *Beadland to Barrow: A History of Barrow County, Georgia* (Atlanta: Cherokee Publishing Co., 1978), pp. 138–42; *Atlanta Journal*, October 24, 1909.

3 "Richard Russell, Georgia Giant," manuscript for three-part documentary, Cox Broadcasting Company, Atlanta, Georgia, 1970, pt. 1, pp. 13–14.

4 Ibid.

5 *Winder News*, September 9, 1920.

6 *Journal of the House of Representatives of the State of Georgia* (Atlanta: Foote and Davies, 1921), p. 276; *Journal of the House of Representatives of the State of Georgia* (Atlanta: Foote and Davies, 1923), p. 245.

7 *Winder News*, July 14, 1921.

8 Author interview with Roy V. Harris, June 4, 1982.

9 J. H. Ennis to RBR, Jr., May 23, 1921; RBR, Jr., to Ennis, May 24, 1921; and RBR, Jr., to Thomas E. Watson, June 8, 1921, Russell Collection, Pre and Georgia Legislative Years, Correspondence, 1920–22, Russell Memorial Library, University of Georgia, Athens.

10 *Journal of the House* (1921), pp. 102–4.

11 Mary Ann Doess, "A Study of Gubernatorial Platforms and Resulting Statutes in Georgia during the Decade of the 1920s" (M.A. thesis, University of Georgia, 1947), pp. 10–11.

12 *Journal of the House* (1921), pp. 131–33.

13 *Macon News*, August 10, 1921.

14 *Winder News*, April 27, July 6, and August 17, 1922.

15 See material on this campaign in Russell Collection, Pre and Georgia Legislative Years, Legislative and Political Correspondence, 1922.

16 Roy V. Harris to Hugh Peterson, June 8, 1922, and Peterson to Harris, June 15, 1922, Peterson Papers, privately held by Mrs. Hugh Peterson, Ailey, Georgia.

17 *Journal of the House* (1923), pp. 16–17; *Winder News*, June 28 and July 12, 1923.

18 Alma R. Hughes to RBR, Jr., February 20, 1923; Maxie T. Summerlin to RBR, Jr., May 7, 1923; McGregor's to RBR, Jr., May 24, 1923; R. J. Smith to RBR, Jr., September 21, 1923; F. C. Neu to RBR, Jr., April 1, 1921; J. Sanford to RBR, Jr., November 25, 1921; and F. P. Stary to RBR, Jr., December 28, 1921, Russell Collection, Pre and Georgia Legislative Years, Personal Correspondence, 1921–26.

19 Albert B. Saye, *A Constitutional History of Georgia, 1732–1945* (Athens: University of Georgia Press, 1948), p. 369. The amendment was approved by voters on November 4, 1924.

20 *Winder News*, March 13, 1924.

21 Reprinted in ibid., May 15, 1924.

22 *Journal of the House of Representatives of the State of Georgia* (Atlanta: Byrd Printing Co., 1925), pp. 57–67.

23 Clifford M. Walker to Hugh Peterson, November 5, 1925, and Peterson to Walker, November 10, 1925, Peterson Papers.

24 Hugh Peterson to Jud P. Wilhoit, January 1, 1926; Peterson to J. S. Burgin, January 19, 1926; and Raymond W. Martin to Peterson, February 8, 1926, ibid.

25 RBR, Jr., to Hugh Peterson, September 20, 1926, ibid.

26 Jud P. Wilhoit to Hugh Peterson, September 10 and 16, 1926, and Peterson to Wilhoit, September 13 and 20, 1926, ibid.

27 Hugh Peterson to J. S. Burgin, September 20, 1926; Peterson to Paul H. Doyal, September 20, 1926; and Peterson to James C. Davis, September 13, 1926, ibid.

28 Marion H. Allen to Frank A. Hooper, Jr., September 21, 1926; unsigned letter to Allen, September 22, 1926; and Paul H. Doyal to Hooper, September 29, 1926, ibid.

29 *Atlanta Journal*, July 4, 1926; *Waycross Journal-Herald*, July 1, 1926.

30 Quoted in *Millen News*, July 1, 1926.

31 Reprinted in *Vienna News*, July 26, 1926.

32 *Georgia's Official Register* (Atlanta: Stein Printing Co., 1927), p. 308.

33 RBR, Jr., to Hugh Peterson, June 10, 1927, and Peterson to RBR, Jr., June 14, 1927, Peterson Papers. On the Harris candidacy, see Roy V. Harris, Oral History, February 24, 1981, Russell Collection.

34 Hugh Peterson, Speech, June 10, 1927, Peterson Papers.

35 *Atlanta Journal*, June 21 and 22, 1927; *Winder News*, June 23 and 30, 1927.

36 *Atlanta Journal*, June 23 and 26, 1927.

37 Ibid., June 22, 26, and 28, 1927.

38 Newspaper clipping, June 26, 1927, Clippings, Russell Collection.

39 *Atlanta Journal*, August 10, 1927.

40 *Journal of the House of Representatives of the State of Georgia* (Atlanta: Byrd Printing Co., 1927), p. 216.

41 *Atlanta Journal*, August 11, 12, 15, and 16, 1927.

42 Ibid., August 11, 1927.

43 Ibid., August 8 and 21, 1927.

44 Ibid., August 18, 1927.

45 Ibid., August 21, 1927; *Atlanta Constitution*, August 22, 1927.

46 RBR, Jr., to Hugh Peterson, May 1, 1927, Peterson Papers.

47 RBR, Jr., to Mrs. Ina Russell, September 13, 15, 21, 24, and 29 and October 6, 23, and 30, 1927, Russell Collection, Legislative Years, Personal Correspondence, 1922–30; *Winder News*, December 1, 1927.

48 *Winder News*, October 4, 1927.

49 Ibid., September 6, 1928.

50 Ibid., September 13, 1928; RBR, Jr., to Hugh Peterson, September 17, 1928, Peterson Papers.

51 RBR, Jr., to Hugh Peterson, June 18, 1927, Peterson Papers; RBR, Jr., to Cecil Neill, April 10, 1925, Russell Collection, Pre and Georgia Legislative Years, Correspondence, Legislative and Political, 1923–30.

52 See letters in Russell Collection, Pre and Georgia Legislative Years, Personal Correspondence, 1921–26, 1927–30.

53 Robert Mark Dunahoo, Oral History, February 19, 1971, Russell Collection.

54 Conditional Sales Contract, August 14, 1929, Governor's Collection, Georgia State Archives, Atlanta.

55 Barrow County Deed Records, Winder, Georgia, books G, H, and J.

56 *Journal of the House of Representatives of the State of Georgia* (Atlanta: Stein Printing Co., 1929), pp. 203–10; *Atlanta Journal*, June 23, 1929.

57 *Atlanta Journal*, June 26, 1929.

58 Ibid., June 27, 1929.

59 Ibid., July 10 and 11, 1929.

60 Ibid., July 12, 13, 17, 24, and 29 and August 5, 6, 14, 15, 16, 20, and 22, 1929. On the tax legislation, see *Acts and Resolutions of the General Assembly of the State of Georgia* (Atlanta: Stein Printing Co., 1929), pp. 93, 101.

61 Hugh Peterson to RBR, Jr., February 14, 1929, Peterson Papers.

62 *Atlanta Journal*, August 20, 1929.

63 *Augusta Chronicle*, September 30, 1930.

64 *Winder News*, July 11, 1929.

CHAPTER 4

1 *Atlanta Constitution*, March 23 and April 6 and 13, 1930.

2 See Russell Collection, Governor's Collection, 1930–32, Clippings, Russell Memorial Library, University of Georgia, Athens.

3 *Valdosta Daily Times*, April 9, 1930.

4 "Richard Russell, Georgia Giant," manuscript for three-part documentary, Cox Broadcasting Company, Atlanta, Georgia, 1970, pt. 1, p. 19.

5 *Savannah Press*, April 28, 1930.

6   *Atlanta Constitution*, May 9, 1930; *Savannah Press*, June 23, 1930; "Richard Russell, Georgia Giant," pt. 1, p. 21.

7   *Savannah Press*, September 24, 1930.

8   For RBR, Jr.'s, speaking schedule, see *Atlanta Constitution*, July 2 and July 16, 1930.

9   RBR, Jr., interview with Edward R. Murrow, April 24, 1952, Russell Collection, Presidential, Political.

10 *Atlanta Constitution*, May 18 and 19, 1930.

11 *Savannah Press*, September 24, 1930.

12 *Atlanta Constitution*, July 27, 1930.

13 See handbills and fliers in Mrs. Ina Russell's Scrapbook, 1935–41, Russell Collection.

14 RBR, Jr., to Station WRHA, March 1, 1950, Russell Collection, Dictation Series.

15 *Atlanta Constitution*, August 24, 1930.

16 Ibid., August 4, 1930.

17 Ibid., August 6 and September 7, 1930.

18 Ibid., August 5 and 7, 1930.

19 *Macon Telegraph*, August 9 and September 13, 1930.

20 *Augusta Chronicle*, August 13, 1930; *Atlanta Constitution*, August 29 and 30, 1930.

21 *Atlanta Constitution*, August 1 and 3, 1930.

22 Ibid., July 17 and August 17, 1930.

23 Ibid., October 2, 1930.

24 Ibid., June 9 and 10 and August 24, 1930.

25 Ibid., August 17, 1930.

26 Ibid., July 20, 1930; *Savannah Press*, September 8 and 12, 1930. See also Joseph L. Bernd, *Grass Roots Politics in Georgia* (Atlanta: Emory University Research Committee, 1960), p. 37.

27 *Atlanta Constitution*, June 16 and October 2, 1930; *Savannah Press*, August 5, 1930.

28 *Savannah Press*, September 9 and 19, 1930.

29 Ibid., September 5, 1930.

30 Lawrence Camp to Hugh Peterson, August 21, 1930, and Peterson to Camp, August 26, 1930, Peterson Papers, privately held by Mrs. Hugh Peterson, Ailey, Georgia.

31 See undated clippings in Russell Collection, Governor's Collection, 1931–32.

32 *Atlanta Constitution*, July 5 and 31, 1930.

33 *Savannah Press*, September 11 and 15, 1930; *Augusta Chronicle*, September 5, 1930.

34 *Savannah Press*, September 11, 1930; *Atlanta Constitution*, October 2, 1930.

35 *Atlanta Constitution*, September 7, 1930.

36 Ibid., September 10, 1930; *Savannah Press*, September 8, 1930.

37 *Georgia's Official Register* (Atlanta: Stein Printing Co., 1931), p. 636.

38 *Atlanta Journal*, October 1, 1930.

39 *Augusta Chronicle*, September 12, 1930; *Atlanta Journal*, September 11, 1930.

40 *Atlanta Constitution*, September 14 and 15, 1930; *Savannah Morning News*, September 14, 1930; E. D. Rivers to J. A. Kitchen, September 18, 1930, Peterson Papers.

41 *Atlanta Constitution*, September 14, 15, and 16, 1930.

42 *Valdosta Daily Times*, September 11, 1930; *Atlanta Journal*, September 15, 1930.

43 *Atlanta Constitution*, September 25, 1930.

44 Lewis Russell to Hugh Peterson, September 29, 1930, Peterson Papers.

45 Lewis Russell to Hugh Peterson, September 26, 1930, ibid.

46 *Savannah Press*, September 27 and 29, 1930.

47 *Macon Telegraph*, September 17–21, 1930; Carswell Flier, Mrs. Ina Russell's Scrapbook, 1935–41, Russell Collection.

48 *Macon Telegraph*, October 3, 1930.

49 See *Atlanta Journal*, October 3, 1930; *Vienna News*, October 2, 1930; and *Georgia's Official Register* (1931), p. 695.

50 *Atlanta Constitution*, October 2 and 3, 1930.

51 Ibid., October 2, 1930; *Atlanta Journal*, September 15, 1930; Harold Gilbert to RBR, Jr., September 28, 1930, Russell Collection, Gubernatorial Years, 1930.

52 *Columbus Enquirer-Sun*, June 27, 1931; *Valdosta Daily Times*, September 13, 1930; *Macon Telegraph*, October 3, 1930.

53 *Atlanta Journal*, October 2, 1930.

54 *Augusta Chronicle*, September 21 and 28, 1930; *Atlanta Journal*, October 2, 1930.

55 *Atlanta Journal*, October 3, 1930.

56 Ibid.

CHAPTER 5

1 *Journal of the House of Representatives of the State of Georgia*, Extraordinary Session, January 6, 1931 (Atlanta: Stein Printing Co., 1931), p. 21. See also *Atlanta Journal*, January 6, 1931.

2 *Atlanta Journal*, March 27, 1931; Amanda Johnson, *Georgia as Colony and State* (Atlanta: Walter W. Brown, 1938), p. 760.

3 *Atlanta Constitution*, June 28, 1931.

4 Russell's inaugural address appeared in full in the *Atlanta Constitution*, June 28, 1931, p. 8.

5 *Atlanta Journal*, June 28, 1931; *Atlanta Constitution*, June 28, 1931; *Griffin Daily News*, June 26, 1931.

6 *Augusta Chronicle*, June 27, 1931; *Savannah Evening Press*, June 27, 1931; *New York Times*, June 26, 1931, p. 22.

7 *Journal of the House of Representatives of the State of Georgia* (Atlanta: Stein Printing Co., 1931), pp. 229–46.

8 *Atlanta Journal*, September 15, 1931; *Atlanta Constitution*, June 28, 1931.

9 *Report of the State Auditor of Georgia* (Atlanta, 1931), p. 263; *Atlanta Constitution*, June 28, 1931.

10 RBR, Jr., Federal Income Tax Return, 1931, Russell Collection, Governor's Collection, 2, Russell Memorial Library, University of Georgia, Athens; *Report of the State Auditor*, p. 27.

11 "Richard Russell, Georgia Giant," manuscript for three-part documentary, Cox Broadcasting Company, Atlanta, Georgia, 1970, pt. 1, p. 24; Mrs. Armeta Reeves to RBR, Jr., September 29, 1932, Russell Collection, Senatorial Campaigns.

12 John H. Willey, "A Study of the Political Mind of Richard B. Russell, Jr., 1930–1936" (M.A. thesis, Vanderbilt University, 1974), pp. 37–40.

13 L. G. Hardman to Hugh Peterson, April 3, 1929, and Peterson to Hardman, April 4, 1929, Peterson Papers, privately held by Mrs. Hugh Peterson, Ailey, Georgia.

14 Hugh Peterson to RBR, Jr., February 14, 1929, ibid.

15 Hugh Peterson to RBR, Jr., March 30, 1931, and RBR, Jr., to Peterson, April 9, 1931, ibid.

16 James T. Colson to Hugh Peterson, March 31, 1931, ibid.

17 RBR, Jr., Address to the Reorganization Committee, April 28, 1931, Russell Collection, Governor's Collection, Speeches.

18 Hugh Peterson to RBR, Jr., September 11, 1931, and Peterson to Philip Weltner, September 11, 1931, Peterson Papers. See also Cullen B. Gosnell, "Reorganization of the State Government of Georgia," *National Municipal Review* 20 (January 1931): 117–18; Gosnell, "Georgia Consolidates Its Administration," *National Municipal Review* 20 (November 1931): 681–82; and Gosnell, "Georgia Cuts State Government Costs," *National Municipal Review* 23 (August 1934): 420–23.

19 "Governor's Messages and the Legislative Product in 1932," *American Political Science Review* 26 (December 26, 1932): 1060.

20 *Journal of the Senate of the State of Georgia* (Atlanta: Ruralist Press, 1933), pp. 24–46.

21 *Atlanta Journal*, August 30, 1931.

22 RBR, Jr., Speech, January 19, 1932, Russell Collection, Governor's Collection, Speeches.

23 *Atlanta Journal*, August 28, 1931.

24 Robert E. Snyder, *Cotton Crisis* (Chapel Hill: University of North Carolina Press, 1984), pp. 40–43.

25 RBR, Jr., to Hugh Peterson, September 1, 1931, Peterson Papers; *Atlanta Journal*, September 12, 1931.

26 J. E. McDonald to RBR, Jr., September 14, 1931, and RBR, Jr., to McDonald, September 19, 1931, Russell Collection, Early Office Files, 1931–32.

27 J. Emory Wood to Hugh Peterson, September 9, 1931; Peterson Papers.

28 *Atlanta Georgian*, September 16, 1931; J. W. Whitley to Hugh Peterson, September 21, 1931, Peterson Papers.

29 *Atlanta Constitution*, September 19, 1931.

30 *Atlanta Journal*, September 20, 1931.

31 RBR, Jr., statement, [1932], in defense of Georgia's penal system, Russell Collection, Governor's Collection. See also "Two Governors Battle for a Chain-Gang Fugitive," *Literary Digest* 115 (January 7, 1933): 9–10.

32 *Journal of the Senate* (1933), pp. 42–43; Statement in Russell Collection, Personal, Genealogical 5, 1967.

33 Hugh Peterson to RBR, Jr., October 1 and 3, 1931, and RBR, Jr., to Peterson, October 2 and 6, 1931, Peterson Papers.

34 Frank A. Hooper, Oral History, March 17, 1971, Russell Collection.

35 *Atlanta Georgian*, December 20, 1931; *Atlanta Journal*, November 24, 1931.

36 *Atlanta Georgian*, November 18, 1932. See also *Atlanta Journal*, November 13, 1932.

37 *Macon Telegraph*, November 7, 1931.

38 *Atlanta Journal,* March 19, 1932.

39 Isaac K. Hay, Oral History, April 13, 1971, Russell Collection.

40 *Atlanta Georgian,* January 3 and November 2, 1932.

41 *Boston Globe,* September 27, 1931.

42 *New York Times,* October 5, 1931, sec. 1, p. 6.

43 Nathan Miller, *An Intimate History* (New York: Doubleday, 1983), p. 247; Hugh Peterson to J. E. Whitley, December 5, 1931, and Peterson to R. W. Martin, December 5, 1931, Peterson Papers.

CHAPTER 6

1 *Atlanta Constitution,* April 22, 1932.

2 Ibid., April 20, 1932.

3 *Atlanta Journal,* April 20, 1932.

4 See *Atlanta Journal* and *Atlanta Constitution,* April 21–26, 1932.

5 *Macon Telegraph,* April 27, 1932; *Atlanta Constitution,* April 27, 1932.

6 Edward L. Reagan to Robert Russell, April 26, 1932, Peterson Papers, privately held by Mrs. Hugh Peterson, Ailey, Georgia.

7 J. L. Storey to RBR, Jr., April 18, 1932, and J. Scott Davis to RBR, Jr., April 25, 1932, Russell Collection, Senatorial Campaigns, Russell Memorial Library, University of Georgia, Athens.

8 Quoted in F. Sheffield Hale, "Richard B. Russell's Election to the Senate: The Watershed of Two Careers," *Atlanta Historical Journal* 28 (Spring 1984): 10.

9 *Atlanta Constitution,* April 27, 1932; *Atlanta Georgian,* April 27, 1932.

10 *Albany Herald,* April 28, 1932.

11 *New York Times,* May 15, 1932, sec. 3, p. 5.

12 RBR, Jr., undated campaign speech, Russell Collection, Senatorial Campaigns.

13 C. E. Gregory, writing for the *Atlanta Constitution,* followed the Russell campaign closely. See his article in the paper's September 15, 1932, issue.

14 RBR, Jr., to Israel Manheim, May 2, 1932, and Manheim to RBR, Jr., May 24, 1932, Russell Collection, Senatorial Campaigns.

15 Charles R. Crisp to R. G. Duncan, July 7, 1932, ibid. It is not clear how this letter got in Russell's files.

16 Hale, "Richard B. Russell's Election," p. 12.

17 Ibid.; *Atlanta Constitution,* August 3, 1932.

18 *Savannah Morning News,* August 7, 1932.

19 RBR, Jr., to State Judges, August 17, 1932, Russell Collection, Senatorial Campaigns.

20 RBR, Jr., to County Officials, June 25, 1932, ibid.

21 *Southern Cultivator* 90 (September 1, 1932): 7.

22 L. A. Whipple to RBR, Jr., August 22, 1932, and B. W. Hendricks to RBR, Jr., August 23, 1932, Russell Collection, Senatorial Campaigns.

23 *Atlanta Journal,* May 31, 1932.

24 Ibid., September 15, 1932.

25 Richard M. Dillard to RBR, Jr., July 27, 1932, and RBR, Jr., to Dillard, August 8, 1932, Russell Collection, Senatorial Campaigns.

26 RBR, Jr., to J. C. Palmer, August 8, 1932, ibid.

27 *Atlanta Journal*, August 12, 1932.

28 *Valdosta Daily Times*, September 8, 1932; *Atlanta Constitution*, August 10 and September 10 and 11, 1932.

29 A. C. Dorsey to RBR, Jr., August 12, 1932; RBR, Jr., to Dorsey, August 15, 1932; and RBR, Jr., to James D. Davidson, August 22, 1932, Russell Collection, Senatorial Campaigns.

30 Hale, "Richard B. Russell's Election," p. 17.

31 *Atlanta Journal*, August 20 and 31, 1932; *Macon Evening News*, August 27, 1932.

32 *New York Times*, May 14, 1932, sec. 1, p. 5, and June 29, 1932, sec. 1, p. 1.

33 *Atlanta Journal*, June 29 and July 1, 1932.

34 *Atlanta Constitution*, September 4, 1932.

35 *Atlanta Journal*, August 27, 1932.

36 Ibid., September 11 and August 14 and 21, 1932.

37 Ibid., August 2, 1932; *Savannah Morning News*, August 3, 1932; *Macon Telegraph*, August 7, 1932.

38 *Macon Telegraph*, September 1 and 16, 1932; *Atlanta Journal*, August 8, 1932.

39 *Hawkeye* (Savannah, Ga.), May 20, 1932.

40 *Atlanta Journal*, August 25 and September 1, 1932.

41 George L. Googe to RBR, Jr., August 10, 1930, Russell Collection, Senatorial Campaigns.

42 *Atlanta Journal*, August 21, 1932; *Atlanta Constitution*, August 20 and 21, 1932.

43 RBR, Jr., to James Eaton, August 31, 1932, and RBR, Jr., to A. Jacodowitz, August 8, 1932, Russell Collection, Senatorial Campaigns; *Atlanta Journal*, August 10, 1932.

44 *Augusta Chronicle*, August 21, 1932; *Atlanta Constitution*, August 21, 1932.

45 *Atlanta Journal*, September 10, 1932.

46 *Atlanta Constitution*, August 30 and 31 and September 7, 1932; *Macon Telegraph*, August 27, 1932; *New York Times*, August 28, 1932, sec. 2, p. 7; *Savannah Morning News*, September 9, 1932; *Macon Evening News*, September 13, 1932.

47 *Atlanta Constitution*, August 23, 1932.

48 Ibid., September 7, 1932.

49 Ibid., September 14, 1932.

50 John A. Sibley, Speech, September 12, 1932, Sibley Papers, Atlanta, Georgia.

51 *Georgia's Official Register* (Atlanta: State Historian, 1933, 1935, 1937), p. 540.

52 See the article by C. E. Gregory in *Atlanta Journal*, September 15, 1932.

53 Hale, "Richard B. Russell's Election," p. 10.

54 *Atlanta Constitution*, September 15, 1932; *Columbus Ledger*, September 15, 1932.

55 *Columbus Ledger*, April 21, 1932; *Carroll County Times*, June 2, 1932.

56 Hale, "Richard B. Russell's Election," p. 19.

57 *New York Times*, September 16, 1932, sec. 1, p. 20.

58 Newspaper clipping, Mrs. Ina Russell's Scrapbook, 1929–33, Russell Collection.

59 Ibid.

60 William Anderson, *The Wild Man from Sugar Creek: The Political Career of Eugene Talmadge* (Baton Rouge: Louisiana State University Press, 1975), p. 82.

61 Newspaper clipping, Mrs. Ina Russell's Scrapbook, 1929–33, Russell Collection. See also Russell Collection, Personal, Finance/Business, 1933–70.

62 *Journal of the Senate of the State of Georgia* (Atlanta: Ruralist Press, 1933), pp. 24–46.

CHAPTER 7

1 *Atlanta Journal*, January 11 and 12, 1933.

2 *Report of the Secretary of the Senate*, 73d Cong., 2d sess., Doc. 83, p. 51.

3 "Richard Russell, Georgia Giant," manuscript for a three-part documentary, Cox Broadcasting Company, Atlanta, Georgia, 1970, pt. 1, pp. 28–29.

4 Ibid., p. 29.

5 Russell Collection, Personal, 1928–32, Russell Memorial Library, University of Georgia, Athens; RBR, Jr., to Mrs. Ina Russell, February 4, 1933, Russell Collection, Senatorial Years, Personal Correspondence with Parents, 1933–40.

6 William S. White, *Citadel: The Story of the U.S. Senate* (New York: Harper and Brothers, 1957), pp. 87–88.

7 "Richard Russell, Georgia Giant," pt. 2, pp. 1–2.

8 RBR, Jr., to Ervin Sibley, March 8, 1933, and RBR, Jr., to George S. Jones, April 8, 1933, Russell Collection, Early Office Files, Banking; RBR, Jr., to Mrs. Ina Russell, March 19, 1933, Russell Collection, Senatorial Years, Personal Correspondence with Parents, 1933–40.

9 *Congressional Record*, 73d Cong., 1st sess., March 16, 1933, p. 539.

10 Gilbert C. Fite, *Peter Norbeck, Prairie Statesman* (Columbia: University of Missouri Studies, 1948), p. 192.

11 "Richard Russell, Georgia Giant," pt. 1, pp. 30–31. See also Russell Collection, Speeches, 1933–44.

12 Hugh Peterson to RBR, Jr., February 27, 1933, Peterson Papers, privately held by Mrs. Hugh Peterson, Ailey, Georgia; Lawrence Camp to RBR, Jr., June 2, 1933, Russell Collection, Early Office Files; RBR, Jr., to Mrs. Ina Russell, April 22 and May 14, 1933, Russell Collection, Senatorial Years, Personal Correspondence with Parents, 1933–40.

13 See Russell Collection, Early Office Files, War and Navy, 1934.

14 *Congressional Record*, 73d Cong., 1st sess., April 20, 1933, pp. 1968–69.

15 Ibid., pp. 1968–70.

16 Ibid., May 25, 1933, pp. 445–56.

17 Ibid., June 15, 1933, pp. 6118–19; RBR, Jr., to Mrs. Ina Russell, March 19, 1933, Russell Collection, Senatorial Years, Personal Correspondence with Parents, 1933–40.

18 *Atlanta Journal*, June 24 and July 1, 1934.

19 Ibid., August 31 and October 2, 1933; RBR, Jr., to Joseph P. Adams, January 15, 1934, Russell Collection, Early Office Files; RBR, Jr., to Mrs. Ina Russell, October 13 and 15, 1933, Russell Collection, Senatorial Years, Personal Correspondence with Parents, 1933–40.

20 *Atlanta Journal*, November 5, 18, and 21, 1933.

21 H. W. Nelson to RBR, Jr., March 1, 1934; T. M. Brumby to RBR, Jr., February 20, 1934; A. D. Hughes to RBR, Jr., February 28, 1934; and RBR, Jr., to Gay B. Shepperson, March 16, 1934, Russell Collection, Early Office Files.

22 John H. Wiley, "A Study of the Political Mind of Richard B. Russell, Jr., 1930–1936" (M.A. thesis, Vanderbilt University, 1974), p. 68.

23 Ibid., p. 77; *Congressional Record*, 74th Cong., 1st sess., May 16, 1935, p. 7681.

24 *New York Times*, February 14, 1935, sec. 1, pp. 1, 82; March 16, 1935, sec. 1, p. 1; and March 17, 1935, sec. 4, p. 1; *Congressional Record*, 74th Cong., 1st sess., February 19, 1935, pp. 2192–94, and February 20, 1935, pp. 2288–94.

25 *Congressional Record*, 75th Cong., 1st sess., July 31, 1937, p. 7956.

26 RBR, Jr., to Dutch Wilkes, June 24, 1937, Russell Collection, Early Office Files.

27 *Atlanta Journal*, April 25, July 4 and 5, and November 17, 1934.

28 Ibid., June 10 and July 5, 1935.

29 William Anderson, *The Wild Man from Sugar Creek: The Political Career of Eugene Talmadge* (Baton Rouge: Louisiana State University Press, 1975), p. 83; *Atlanta Constitution*, January 21, 1933.

30 *New York Times*, September 11, 1936, sec. 1, p. 26.

31 *Atlanta Journal*, October 5, 1934; Anderson, *Wild Man*, chapter 11.

32 *Washington Herald*, May 8, 1935; RBR, Jr., to Mrs. Ina Russell, January 21, 1934, Russell Collection, Senatorial Years, Personal Correspondence with Parents, 1933–40.

33 *Atlanta Journal*, November 30, 1935.

34 RBR, Jr., to Henry C. Walthour, December 31, 1935; RBR, Jr., to C. W. Varn, September 20, 1935; RBR, Jr., to Harry G. Thornton, November 4, 1935; and RBR, Jr., to T. L. Huston, November 13, 1935, Russell Collection, Personal.

35 Anderson, *Wild Man*, pp. 156–67.

36 J. M. Jones to RBR, Jr., July 8, 1936, and Anonymous to RBR, Jr., July 8, 1936, Russell Collection, Senatorial Campaigns.

37 *New York Times*, September 8, 1936, sec. 1, p. 2; RBR, Jr., Speech, July 8, 1936, Russell Collection, Senatorial Campaigns.

38 *Macon Telegraph*, August 19, 1938. For fliers and advertisements, see Russell Collection, Senatorial Campaigns.

39 Thomas J. Hamilton to Marion Allen, July 20, 1936, and "Charles" to RBR, Jr., August 4, 1936, Russell Collection, Senatorial Campaigns.

40 James H. Bowden to RBR, Jr., July 6, 1936, and Miles Dillard to RBR, Jr., August 15, 1936, ibid.

41 RBR, Jr., to Charles C. McGehee, July 11, 1936; D. N. Stafford to RBR, Jr., July 16, 1936; and Edmund H. Worthy to RBR, Jr., July 8, 1936, ibid.

42 See Russell Collection, Political, Senate Race, 1936.

43 Anderson, *Wild Man*, p. 159; *Atlanta Journal*, August 1, 1936.

44 *Atlanta Constitution*, August 6 and 7, 1936.

45 Ibid., August 7, 1936; Anderson, *Wild Man*, p. 162.

46 Anderson, *Wild Man*, p. 163; *Atlanta Constitution*, August 26 and 27, 1936.

47 *Georgia Woman's World*, August 14 and September 5, 1936.

48 *Atlanta Constitution*, July 24 and August 9, 1936. See also RBR, Jr., undated speech, Russell Collection, Senatorial Campaigns, 1936.

49 Karen K. Kelly, "Richard B. Russell: Democrat from Georgia" (Ph.D. dissertation, University of North Carolina, 1979), pp. 267–70.

50 "Richard Russell, Georgia Giant," pt. 2, p. 14.

51 *Georgia's Official Register* (Atlanta: State Historian, 1933, 1935, 1937), pp. 536–40.

52 Franklin D. Roosevelt to RBR, Jr., September 12, 1936, Roosevelt Papers, PPF, 3869, Roosevelt Library, Hyde Park, New York.

53 *Newsweek* 8 (September 19, 1936): 11–12.

54 Anderson, *Wild Man*, pp. 160–61.

55 "Richard Russell, Georgia Giant," pt. 2, p. 17.

56 *Atlanta Journal*, September 11, 1936.

CHAPTER 8

1 *New York Times*, September 11, 1936, sec. 1, pp. 3, 24; RBR, Jr., to Mr. and Mrs. Clyde W. Barge, November 13, 1936, Russell Collection, Personal, 1935–37, Russell Memorial Library, University of Georgia, Athens.

2 RBR, Jr., interview with Edward R. Murrow, April 24, 1952, and RBR, Jr., to William J. Akins, April 14, 1959, Russell Collection, Dictation Series, Presidential, Political.

3 Ibid. See also RBR, Jr., to Roger Newsome, November 21, 1958, Russell Collection, Dictation Series.

4 RBR, Jr., interview with Edward R. Murrow, April 24, 1952, Russell Collection, Presidential, Political.

5 RBR, Jr., to William J. Akins, April 14, 1959, ibid.

6 *New York Times*, March 15, 1935, sec. 1, p. 1.

7 *Atlanta Journal*, September 2, 1933.

8 Wilma Dykeman and James Stokely, *Seeds of Change: The Life of Will Alexander* (Chicago: University of Chicago Press, 1962), p. 243.

9 Sidney Baldwin, *Poverty and Politics* (Chapel Hill: University of North Carolina Press, 1968), pp. 70–71.

10 Fred W. Will to RBR, Jr., March 12, 1935, Russell Collection, Early Office Files.

11 *Atlanta Journal*, March 13, 1935.

12 *U.S. Statutes at Large, 1936*, vol. 49, pt. 1, p. 117.

13 *Atlanta Journal*, April 7, 1935.

14 Baldwin, *Poverty and Politics*, pp. 103–23.

15 Author interview with D. W. Brooks, July 20, 1981.

16 *Congressional Record*, 76th Cong., 1st sess., May 8, 1939, pp. 5209–10; Baldwin, *Poverty and Politics*, p. 223.

17 Will W. Alexander to RBR, Jr., June 26, 1939, Russell Collection, Legislation, Agriculture; Michael L. Hammett, "Senator Richard B. Russell and New Deal Farm Policies, 1933–1941" (M.A. thesis, University of Georgia, 1985).

18 *Congressional Record*, 76th Cong., 1st sess., March 16, 1939, p. 2804, and July 6, 1939, p. 8678; *New York Times*, February 8, 1938, sec. 1, p. 39.

19 *Congressional Record*, 75th Cong., 3d sess., June 1, 1938, pp. 7867–74; *American Cotton Grower* 5 (April 1940): 3.

20 On parity payments up to 1940, see statement by C. G. Garman of the USDA, Russell Collection, Legislation, Agriculture.

21 *Congressional Record*, 75th Cong., 1st sess., May 13, 1937, p. 4483.

22 Russell Collection, Speeches, 1940.

23 *Congressional Record*, 76th Cong., 3d sess., February 13, 1940, pp. 1385–86; *New York Times*, February 14, 1940, sec. 1, p. 1.

24 *Congressional Record*, 76th Cong., 3d sess., March 18, 1940, pp. 2989–93.

25 See statement by C. G. Garman of the USDA, Russell Collection, Legislation, Agriculture.

26 *Congressional Record*, 77th Cong., 2d sess., May 18, 1942, p. 4267.

27 Franklin D. Roosevelt to RBR, Jr., April 20, 1942, Russell Collection, Red Line File.

28 *Congressional Record*, 77th Cong., 2d sess., May 18, 1942, p. 4269.

29 Ibid., p. 4270.

30 Baldwin, *Poverty and Politics*, pp. 352–63.

31 Franklin D. Roosevelt to RBR, Jr., July 18, 1942, and RBR, Jr., to Roosevelt, July 22, 1942, Roosevelt Papers, PPF, 3869, Roosevelt Library, Hyde Park, New York.

32 *New York Times*, May 11, 1939, sec. 1, p. 6.

33 *Agricultural Appropriation Bill for 1941: Hearings before the Subcommittee of the Committee on Appropriations, U.S. Senate*, 76th Cong., 3d sess., February 28, 1940, pp. 392–93.

34 Ibid., pp. 401–3; Gilbert C. Fite, *American Farmers: The New Minority* (Bloomington: University of Indiana Press, 1981), p. 170; *Congressional Record*, 76th Cong., 3d sess., June 30, 1941, pp. 5746–47.

35 *Congressional Record*, 75th Cong., 3d sess., April 9, 1938, pp. 5133, 5441–42.

36 Ibid., 77th Cong., 2d sess., January 27, 1942, p. 4381.

37 Ibid., 75th Cong., 1st sess., April 5, 1937, p. 3120; RBR, Jr., to Eugene Talmadge, January 11, 1934, Russell Collection, Senatorial Campaigns.

38 RBR, Jr., to Lee Olive, December 5, 1935, Russell Collection, Early Office Files; *Atlanta Georgian*, March 13, 1935. On Russell's views, see Russell Collection, Gubernatorial Years, 1930 Campaign, Speeches.

39 *Congressional Record*, 76th Cong., 1st sess., January 28, 1939, p. 10; *New York Times*, January 29, 1939, sec. 1, p. 1.

40 "Richard Russell, Georgia Giant," manuscript for a three-part documentary, Cox Broadcasting Company, Atlanta, Georgia, 1970, pt. 2, p. 19.

41 Ibid.; *New York Times*, February 17, 1937, sec. 1, p. 2; RBR, Jr., to Mrs. Ina Russell, Russell Collection, Senatorial Years, Personal Correspondence with Parents, 1933–40; Alexander A. Lawrence, Oral History, February 26, 1971, Russell Collection.

42 RBR, Jr., to W. F. Hollingsworth, June 24, 1937, Russell Collection, Early Office Files.

43 *Congressional Record*, 75th Cong., 1st sess., July 22, 1937, p. 7381.

44 Charles G. McGhee to Sims Bray, July 21, 1937, and RBR, Jr., to J. H. Skelton, July 26,

1937, Russell Collection, Early Office Files.

45 James A. Farley, *Jim Farley's Story: The Roosevelt Years* (New York: McGraw-Hill, 1948), p. 122.

46 "Richard Russell, Georgia Giant," pt. 2, pp. 18–19.

47 Marvin H. McIntyre to Franklin D. Roosevelt, August 6, 1938, Roosevelt Papers, PPF, 3869.

48 Undated newspaper clipping, Mrs. Ina Russell's Scrapbook, 1933–47, Russell Collection; *New York Times*, August 20, 1938, sec. 1, p. 3; *Atlanta Journal*, August 30, 1938.

49 *Atlanta Journal*, August 12, 1938; *Atlanta Constitution*, August 12, 1938; *Macon Telegraph*, August 12, 1938.

50 RBR, Jr., to Charles A. Ewing, September 12, 1952, Russell Collection, Dictation Series, Political Intraoffice File, Calendars.

51 *Time* 37 (April 27, 1936), pp. 10–11.

52 RBR, Jr., to C. H. Linsey, January 20, 1936, Russell Collection, Early Office Files, Negro File.

53 Thomas J. Crittenden to RBR, Jr., March 27, 1936; RBR, Jr., to Crittenden, March 30, 1936; George Slover to RBR, Jr., May 11, 1936; RBR, Jr., to Slover, May 13, 1936; and RBR, Jr., to C. H. Linsey, January 20, 1936, ibid.

54 Joseph O'Mahoney to RBR, Jr., April 25, 1936, and RBR, Jr., to O'Mahoney, April 29, 1936, ibid.

55 For an excellent discussion of Russell and civil rights, see David D. Potenziani, "Look to the Past: Richard B. Russell and the Defense of Southern White Supremacy" (Ph.D. dissertation, University of Georgia, 1981).

56 Ibid., chapter 2; *Congressional Record*, 75th Cong., 3d sess., January 12, 1938, pp. 374–75, and January 26, 1938, pp. 1098–1115; George C. Rable, "The South and the Politics of Anti-Lynching Legislation, 1920–1940," *Journal of Southern History* 51 (May 1985): 201–20.

57 *Congressional Record*, 76th Cong., 3d sess., January 26, 1938, p. 1108; February 21, 1938, p. 2210; and February 22, 1938, pp. 2265–84.

58 "Richard Russell, Georgia Giant," pt. 2, p. 12.

59 John A. Salmond, *A Southern Rebel: The Life and Times of Aubry Willis Williams, 1890–1965* (Chapel Hill: University of North Carolina Press, 1983), pp. 189–90.

60 "Richard Russell, Georgia Giant," pt. 1, p. 36.

61 Patricia Collins Dwinnell to author, August 10 and September 20, 1985, and October 25, 1988; author interviews with Ina Russell Stacy, July 1, 1985; Patience Russell Peterson, November 30, 1981; and Mary Willie Green, June 10, 1981; article by Eugene C. Patterson, *Atlanta Constitution*, January 25, 1971; RBR, Jr., notes for letter, March 30, 1948, and "Pat" to "Dear Dick," April 2, 1948, Russell Collection, Senatorial Years, Personal Correspondence, 1941–70.

62 *Atlanta Journal*, July 10, 1938.

CHAPTER 9

1 RBR, Jr., to Donald F. Bean, February 23, 1966, Russell Collection, Foreign Affairs, Russell Memorial Library, University of Georgia, Athens.

2 RBR, Jr., Speech, November 11, 1928, Russell Collection, Speeches.

3 *Atlanta Journal*, October 28, 1933, and October 25, 1934.

4 RBR, Jr., to H. L. Roosevelt, January 18, 1934, Russell Collection, Early Office Files.

5 *Congressional Record*, 74th Cong., 1st sess., January 29, 1935, pp. 1054, 1147.

6 Ibid., 74th Cong., 2d sess., March 18, 1936, pp. 3914–15.

7 Ibid., 76th Cong., 1st sess., March 7, 1939, p. 2371, and May 18, 1939, p. 5702; 76th Cong., 2d sess., November 3, 1939, p. 1024; 76th Cong., 3d sess., August 28, 1940, p. 11142; 77th Cong., 1st sess., November 7, 1941, p. 8680, and March 8, 1941, p. 2097; and 76th Cong., 3d sess., May 15, 1940, p. 6142; RBR, Jr., to Mrs. Ina Russell, February 15, 1941, Russell Collection, Senatorial Years, Personal Correspondence with Parents, 1941–53.

8 RBR, Jr., Speech, 1940, Russell Collection, Speeches, 4-H Clubs.

9 *Congressional Record*, 76th Cong., 3d sess., August 28, 1940, pp. 11090–142.

10 *New York Times*, August 29, 1940, sec. 1, pp. 10, 18; September 1, 1940, sec. 1, p. 1; September 2, 1940, sec. 1, p. 14; September 3, 1940, sec. 1, pp. 1, 9, 12, 16; September 4, 1940, sec. 1, pp. 10, 17, 22; and October 20, 1940, sec. 1, p. 17; David L. Porter, *The Seventy-Sixth Congress and World War II, 1939–1940* (Columbia: University of Missouri Press, 1979), pp. 168–69; *Congressional Record*, 76th Cong., 3d sess., September 13, 1940, pp. 12088–113.

11 Russell Collection, Speeches, Wendell Willkie, 1940.

12 *Congressional Record*, 76th Cong., 1st sess., August 1, 1939, p. 10650; 76th Cong., 3d sess., January 8, 1940, p. 92, and May 24, 1940, pp. 6790–92; 77th Cong., 1st sess., June 5, 1941, p. 4757.

13 See David D. Potenziani, "Look to the Past: Richard B. Russell and the Defense of Southern White Supremacy" (Ph.D. dissertation, University of Georgia, 1981), pp. 41–45.

14 RBR, Jr., to John L. Cabell, October 19, 1942, and RBR, Jr., to Mrs. C. R. Harris, October 19, 1942, Russell Collection, Civil Rights, Poll Tax Correspondence.

15 *Atlanta Journal*, November 15, 1942.

16 *Congressional Record*, 77th Cong., 2d sess., November 23, 1942, p. 9065.

17 RBR, Jr., to R. B. Dreeser, May 15, 1944, Russell Collection, Civil Rights, Correspondence, 1944–45.

18 *National War Agencies Appropriations Bill for 1945: Hearings before a Subcommittee of the Committee on Appropriations, U.S. Senate*, 78th Cong., 2d sess., H.R. 4879, June 1944.

19 *Congressional Record*, 78th Cong., 2d sess., June 16, 1944, pp. 6023–38.

20 RBR, Jr., to John M. Slaton, August 17, 1944, Russell Collection, Civil Rights, August–December 1944.

21 *New York Times*, August 10, 1944, p. 30; *Congressional Record*, 78th Cong., 2d sess., August 9, 1944, pp. 6803–9.

22 Margaret Mitchell to RBR, Jr., October 21, 1944, and William S. Fogg to RBR, Jr.,

September 18, 1944, Russell Collection, Civil Rights, August–December 1944.

23 RBR, Jr., to Cobb C. Torrance, May 31, 1944, ibid.

24 Ibid. See also Malcolm Ross, *All Manner of Men* (New York: Reynal and Hitchcock, 1948), p. 35.

25 Material from Senator's Desk, Russell Collection, Civil Rights, FEPC, 1944–49.

26 Josephine Wilkins to RBR, Jr., June 27, 1945, and RBR, Jr., to Wilkins, July 21, 1945, ibid.

27 See Todd L. Butler, "The Vicious Circle of Training and Employment: Black Employment in Defense Industries in Georgia, 1941–1945" (M.A. thesis, University of Georgia, 1985).

28 *Congressional Record*, 78th Cong., 1st sess., June 11, 1943, pp. 5703–4, and 78th Cong., 2d sess., March 28, 1944, p. 3162, and May 2, 1944, p. 3845.

29 Ibid., 79th Cong., 1st sess., May 7, 1945, p. 4225; *New York Times*, June 20, 1945, sec. 1, p. 20; *Congressional Record*, 79th Cong., 2d sess., February 26, 1946, pp. 1623–24, and May 24, 1946, pp. 5602–3.

30 *U.S. Statutes at Large*, vol. 60, pt. 1, p. 231.

31 Ray Schafer, "Legislative History of the School Lunch Program," 1966, Russell Collection, Speeches, School Lunch Program; "The Department of Agriculture's School Lunch Program: A Factual Summary," 1949, Russell Collection, Legislation, Agriculture.

32 *Congressional Record*, 78th Cong., 1st sess., June 30, 1943, pp. 6832–34.

33 Ibid.

34 Thomas R. Austin to RBR, Jr., July 3, 1943, and J. H. Webb to RBR, Jr., July 6, 1943, Russell Collection, Personal, Trips, 1943.

35 RBR, Jr., to Clark Howell, July 6, 1943, ibid.

36 Robert P. Patterson to Franklin D. Roosevelt, July 26, 1943, ibid.

37 Ira C. Eaker to RBR, Jr., August 3, 1943, ibid.

38 Dwight D. Eisenhower to RBR, Jr., July 29, 1943, ibid.

39 RBR, Jr., to Mrs. Ina Russell, August 13, 1943, ibid.

40 RBR, Jr., to Marion Allen, October 2, 1943, ibid.; *Atlanta Journal*, September 29, 1943.

41 RBR, Jr., to J. N. Pyle, October 1, 1943, Russell Collection, Personal, Trips, 1943.

42 Leeman Anderson to RBR, Jr., September 3, 1943, ibid.; RBR, Jr., to Mrs. Ina Russell, August 24, 1943, Russell Collection, Senatorial Years, Personal Correspondence with Parents, 1941–53.

43 *Congressional Record*, 78th Cong., 1st sess., September 30, 1943, pp. 7919–24.

44 *Atlanta Journal*, October 8, 1943.

45 *Congressional Record*, 78th Cong., 1st sess., October 11, 1943, pp. 8189–90.

46 Ibid., October 28, 1943, pp. 8859–66.

47 *New Republic* 109 (October 18, 1943): 503; *Nation* 157 (October 23, 1943): 459; *New Statesman and Nation* 26 (October 23, 1943): 266.

48 RBR, Jr., to Cordell Hull, February 28, 1944, and Edward R. Stettinius to RBR, Jr., March 8, 1944, Russell Collection, Personal, Overseas Trips.

49 RBR, Jr., to Secretary of War Henry L. Stimson, May 14, 1945, ibid.; *Congressional Record*, 79th Cong., 1st sess., May 24, 1945, p. 4943.

50 Log of the Military and Naval Subcommittee to European and Mediterranean Theaters of Operations beginning May 25, 1945, mimeograph copy; and RBR, Jr., to Jefferson

Caffrey, July 11, 1945, Russell Collection, Personal, Trips, 1945; *New York Times*, June 17, 1945, p. 7.

51   RBR, Jr., to Harry Truman, August 7, 1945, and Truman to RBR, Jr., August 9, 1945, Truman Papers, White House File, Official File, box 685, Miscellaneous, 1945–46, Truman Library, Independence, Missouri.

52   *Congressional Record*, 79th Cong., 1st sess., September 18, 1945, pp. 8671–80.

CHAPTER 10

1   Author interview with Harold Davis, July 20, 1981.

2   "Kitty" to RBR, Jr., February 27, 1947; "Kibbie" to RBR, Jr., November 24, 1947; and "Ruby" to RBR, Jr., July 6, 1949, Russell Collection, Senatorial Years, Personal Correspondence, Miscellaneous, 1941–70, Russell Memorial Library, University of Georgia, Athens; Russell Collection, Intraoffice File, Desk Calendars, 1939–49.

3   RBR, Jr., to Roy V. Harris, August 12, 1960, Russell Collection, Senatorial Years, Personal Correspondence, Miscellaneous, 1941–70; Russell Collection, Dictation Series, Political; Russell Collection, Intraoffice File, Desk Diaries, 1941–44, and Calendars, 1939.

4   RBR, Jr., to Robert J. Marshburn, December 8, 1941, Russell Collection, Personal, Miscellaneous, 1940–42; RBR, Jr., to Wallace Butts, August 24, 1949, Russell Collection, General File; author interview with Charlie Trippi, June 7, 1986.

5   Mack Barnes to RBR, Jr., November 6, 1942, Russell Collection, Personal, 1940–42; RBR, Jr., to Kirk Sutlive, September 11, 1953, Russell Collection, Dictation Series.

6   RBR, Jr., to J. William Fulbright, September 29, 1945, Fulbright papers, BCN 32, folder 44, University of Arkansas Library, Fayetteville.

7   RBR, Jr., to W. W. Darden, September 17, 1941; RBR, Jr., to Mary Cash, October 31, 1941; RBR, Jr., to Hugh C. Haynesworth, August 30, 1941; RBR, Jr., to Theodore Ehreu, October 17, 1942; RBR, Jr., to W. L. McElmurray, September 22, 1942; and RBR, Jr., to Mrs. C. R. Rowles, November 24, 1942, Russell Collection, Personal, 1940–42; *Atlanta Journal*, April 14, 1946.

8   RBR, Jr., application for gasoline coupons, October 27, 1942, Russell Collection, Personal, 1940–42; RBR, Jr., to Harry G. Thornton, October 15, 1942, Russell Collection, Political, Senatorial Campaigns.

9   RBR, Jr., to Mr. and Mrs. Marion H. Allen, December 29, 1936, and RBR, Jr., to Harley Langdale, December 29, 1936, Russell Collection, Personal, 1935–37; RBR, Jr., to Mr. and Mrs. Woo Pon Sing, January 3, 1952, Russell Collection, Personal, 1952.

10   RBR, Jr., to Hamilton Hotel, September 15, 1941, Russell Collection, Personal, Miscellaneous, 1940–42; Meg Greenfield, "The Man Who Leads the Southern Senators," *Reporter*, May 21, 1964, pp. 17–21.

11   RBR, Jr., income tax returns and other financial data, Russell Collection, Personal, Finance/Business, 1933–70.

12   Russell Collection, Intraoffice File, Communications and Memoranda, January–June 1962.

13   T. M. Forbes to RBR, Jr., June 8, 1942, ibid. See also correspondence in Russell Collection, Dictation Series, Armed Services, 1961.

14 *Atlanta Constitution*, February 26, 1981. On staff salaries, see *Annual Report of the secretary of the Senate* (Washington: Government Printing Office, 1933–43).

15 William D. Russell, "Remembering 'Uncle Dick' Russell," *Atlanta Constitution*, February 26, 1981; RBR, Jr., to R. L. Watford, July 1, 1947; RBR, Jr., to Mrs. George Massey, October 1, 1947; and RBR, Jr., to J. J. Tullis, September 5, 1947, Russell Collection, Personal, 1947.

16 Rachel Styles Breimyer to RBR, Jr., December 16, 1941, Russell Collection, Senatorial Years, Personal Correspondence, Miscellaneous, 1941–70.

17 Dorothy Anderson to RBR, Jr., February 11, 1937, and Leeman Anderson to RBR, Jr., March 23, 1937, and December 13, 1941, ibid., 1933–40.

18 *Congressional Record*, 80th Cong., 1st sess., February 14, 1947, pp. 1036–38.

19 RBR, Jr., to Ralph McGill, July 31, 1941, Russell Collection, Political, Tom Linder.

20 RBR, Jr., to Kate Sikes, September 3, 1942; RBR, Jr., to J. K. Elliott, August 10, 1942; and RBR, Jr., to Homer C. Parker, September 26, 1942, Russell Collection, Political, Senatorial Campaigns, 1942.

21 RBR, Jr., to Mr. and Mrs. McDonald, October 22, 1942, Russell Collection, Personal, 1940–42.

22 William Murphey to RBR, Jr., June 1, 1944; RBR, Jr., to Murphey, June 5, 1944; H. Lane Young to RBR, Jr., June 19, 1944; Erle Cocke, Sr., to RBR, Jr., January 25, 1945; and RBR, Jr., to Cocke, February 20, 1945, Russell Collection, Legislation, Agriculture.

23 *Atlanta Journal*, April 1, 1946; *Washington Post*, March 31, 1946.

24 *Congressional Record*, 79th Cong., 2d sess., March 27, 1946, pp. 2661–67, and March 29, 1946, p. 2815.

25 *Atlanta Journal*, April 14, 1946.

26 Murray R. Benedict, *Farm Policies of the United States, 1790–1950* (New York: Twentieth Century Fund, 1953), pp. 496–97.

27 RBR, Jr., to Nesbit Baker, July 13, 1948, Russell Collection, Legislation, Agriculture.

28 D. W. Brooks to William R. Blake, August 31, 1946, ibid.

29 Fred Lee to RBR, Jr., April 26, 1947, ibid.

30 *Congressional Record*, 80th Cong., 1st sess., July 21, 1947, pp. 9483–85, 9512–13; *Agricultural Statistics, 1962* (Washington: Government Printing Office, 1963), p. 640.

31 *Congressional Record*, 80th Cong., 1st sess., July 26, 1947, p. 10324.

32 Ibid., July 21, 1947, p. 9513.

33 Ibid., 80th Cong., 2d sess., June 17, 1948, pp. 8567–98, and June 19, 1948, p. 9157. For a discussion of the Hope-Aiken bill, see Allen J. Matusow, *Farm Policies and Politics of the Truman Years* (Cambridge: Harvard University Press, 1967), pp. 137–44.

34 Milton Bryant to RBR, Jr., November 23, 1947; RBR, Jr., to Bryant, November 27, 1947; G. D. Dunlap to RBR, Jr., September 18, 1949; and RBR, Jr., to Dunlap, October 26, 1949; Russell Collection, Legislation, Agriculture.

35 *Congressional Record*, 79th Cong., 2d sess., May 8, 1946, pp. 4590–91, 4601, 4803, 4806.

36 *U.S. News and World Report* 22 (March 14, 1947): 68, 70.

37 *Atlanta Constitution*, June 14, 1946.

38 RBR, Jr., to John T. Flynn, March 30, 1949; RBR, Jr., to W. H. Knight, January 22, 1953;

and RBR, Jr., to John T. Cocutz, February 9, 1951, Russell Collection, Dictation Series.

39 Undated newspaper clipping, Mrs. Ina Russell's Scrapbook, 1933–47, Russell Collection.

40 *Congressional Record*, 80th Cong., 1st sess., April 22, 1947, p. 3793.

41 RBR, Jr., Speech before Tufted Textile Manufacturers, May 30, 1947, Russell Collection, Speeches, 1947.

42 Russell Collection, Trips, 1947, and Personal, 1947; *Atlanta Constitution*, August 20, 1947; *New York Times*, November 14, 1947, sec. 1, p. 6.

43 *Congressional Record*, 80th Cong., 1st sess., November 27, 1947, p. 10907, and December 1, 1947, p. 10980.

44 RBR, Jr., to C. H. Livsey, July 25, 1949, Russell Collection, Dictation Series.

45 *Congressional Record*, 80th Cong., 2d sess., May 26, 1948, pp. 6459–60, and June 2, 1948, p. 6864.

46 *Atlanta Constitution*, September 12 and October 2, 1947.

47 *Congressional Record*, 79th Cong., 2d sess., May 31, 1946, p. 6073, and July 22, 1946, p. 964; 80th Cong., 1st sess., May 13, 1947, pp. 5117, 7538.

48 RBR, Jr., to Mrs. Ina Russell, April 18, 1947, Mrs. Ina Russell's Scrapbook, 1933–47, Russell Collection.

49 *New York Times*, November 8, 1948, sec. 1, p. 22, and November 13, 1948, sec. 1, p. 2; RBR, Jr., to Mrs. Ina Russell, November 8, 1948, Russell Collection, Senatorial Years, Personal Correspondence with Parents, 1941–53.

50 *Atlanta Constitution*, September 2, 1947; *Winder News*, September 4 and 11, 1947.

CHAPTER 11

1 "Richard Russell, Georgia Giant," manuscript for a three-part documentary, Cox Broadcasting Company, Atlanta, Georgia, 1970, pt. 2, pp. 29–30.

2 Russell Collection, Speeches, 1945, Russell Memorial Library, University of Georgia, Athens.

3 *Atlanta Constitution*, March 25, 1946.

4 *Congressional Record*, 79th Cong., 1st sess., January 29, 1945, p. 559.

5 *Philadelphia Record*, April 28, 1946.

6 *Atlanta Journal*, June 14, 1946.

7 David D. Potenziani, "Look to the Past: Richard B. Russell and the Defense of Southern White Supremacy" (Ph.D. dissertation, University of Georgia, 1981), p. 75.

8 Alonzo L. Hamby, *Beyond the New Deal: Harry S Truman and American Liberalism* (New York: Columbia University Press, 1973), pp. 61–62.

9 *Congress and the Nation, 1945–1964* (Washington: Congressional Quarterly Service, 1965), p. 1615.

10 Potenziani, "Look to the Past," pp. 52–53.

11 *Congressional Record*, 79th Cong., 2d sess., January 22, 1946, pp. 178–91.

12 Ibid., February 9, 1946, p. 1219.

13 A. H. Freeman to RBR, Jr., September 23, 1946, Russell Collection, Dictation Series, Civil Rights; *Atlanta Journal*, March 8, 1946.

14 Homer W. Smith to RBR, Jr., April 1, 1942; Walter W. Daniel to RBR, Jr., March 11,

1947; RBR, Jr., to Daniel, March 15, 1947; and Noah M. Brinson to RBR, Jr., April 15, 1947, Russell Collection, Dictation Series, Civil Rights.

15 Helen Crotwell to RBR, Jr., January 25, 1946; Rachel Henry to RBR, Jr., February 7, 1946; RBR, Jr., to Jerry Mabry, February 14, 1946; and RBR, Jr., to Chester E. Martin, March 28, 1946, ibid.

16 RBR, Jr., to Charles J. Bloch, February 13, 1946; Chester E. Martin to RBR, Jr., March 26, 1946; RBR, Jr., to Cecil B. Dickson, January 31, 1946; and Leeman Anderson for RBR, Jr., to A. H. Freeman, September 26, 1946, ibid.

17 *Atlanta Journal*, March 8, 1946.

18 *New York Herald-Tribune*, July 27, 1946; *Atlanta Constitution*, July 26, 1946.

19 *Congressional Record*, 79th Cong., 2d sess., July 27, 1946, pp. 10258–60.

20 H. S. Bynes to RBR, Jr., July 29, 1946; RBR, Jr., to B. L. Betts, July 31, 1946; and RBR, Jr., to Albert C. Keith, June 2, 1947, Russell Collection, Dictation Series, Civil Rights.

21 Potenziani, "Look to the Past," p. 65.

22 RBR, Jr., to O'Hardy, February 10, 1948, Russell Collection, Civil Rights, FEPC Correspondence, 1948.

23 See southern reaction to Truman's message in *Newsweek*, February 16, 1948, pp. 24–25. *Atlanta Journal*, January 8, 1948.

24 RBR, Jr., to Lemuel S. J. Smith, February 20, 1948, Russell Collection, Civil Rights, Relocation, 1948.

25 *Washington Times-Herald*, March 7, 1948; *Atlanta Journal*, March 6, 1948.

26 *Congressional Record*, 80th Cong., 2d sess., pt. 10, appendix, p. A1863.

27 Ibid.

28 Undated newspaper clipping, Mrs. Ina Russell's Scrapbook, 1947–48, Russell Collection.

29 *Atlanta Constitution*, March 13, 1948.

30 Ibid., March 9, 1948; *Savannah Morning News*, March 10, 1948.

31 *Atlanta Constitution*, March 10, 1948.

32 *Universal Military Training, Hearings before the Committee on Armed Services, U.S. Senate*, 80th Cong., 2d sess., March and April 1948, pp. 995–97.

33 *Congressional Record*, 80th Cong., 2d sess., May 12, 1948, pp. 5665–67, and June 10, 1948, p. 7681.

34 Ibid., July 28, 1948, pp. 9463–64.

35 RBR, Jr., to Sam J. Ervin, July 29, 1948, Russell Collection, Dictation Series, Civil Rights.

36 *Congressional Record*, 80th Cong., 2d sess., August 2, 1948, p. 9463; *New York Times*, July 30, 1948, sec. 1, p. 1, and July 31, 1948, sec. 1, p. 14.

37 RBR, Jr., to Lemuel S. J. Smith, February 20, 1948, and RBR, Jr., to Fred R. Splawn, February 20, 1948, Russell Collection, Civil Rights, Relocation, 1948.

38 *Atlanta Constitution*, July 18, 1948; Brooks Hays to Ralph McGill, November 10, 1948, McGill Papers, ser. 2, box 3, folder 13, Emory University Library, Atlanta, Georgia.

39 J. William Fulbright to W. W. Shaver III, February 26, 1948; Shaver to Fulbright, February 22, 1948; Fulbright to A. B. Pribby, February 28, 1948; Fulbright to Herbert L. Thomas, March 15, 1948; and Fulbright to Mrs. Suzanne Chalfont Lighton, February 28, 1948, Fulbright Papers, BCN 48, folder 1, University of Arkansas Library, Fayetteville.

40 Malcolm Bryan to Ralph McGill, August 1, 1958, McGill Papers, ser. 2, box 7, folder 3.

41 RBR, Jr., to Millard Reese, August 23, 1948, Russell Collection, Political, Davis Lee.

42 RBR, Jr., to Elizabeth Caldwallader-Noyes, August 31, 1948, Russell Collection, Civil Rights, Sprigle articles.

43 *Congressional Record*, 80th Cong., 2d sess., March 22, 1948, p. 3233, and April 1, 1948, p. 3958; RBR, Jr., to Paul M. Butler, March 12, 1959, Russell Collection, Dictation Series, Political.

44 *Atlanta Constitution*, August 1, 1947.

45 *New York Times*, March 20, 1948, sec. 1, p. 11. See also Jules Abels, *Out of the Jaws of Victory* (New York: Henry Holt and Co., 1959), p. 73, and John F. Martin, *Civil Rights and the Crisis of Liberalism: The Democratic Party, 1945–1976* (Boulder, Colo.: Westview Press, 1979), p. 81.

46 *New York Times*, July 3, 1948, sec. 1, p. 6.

47 "Richard Russell, Georgia Giant," pt. 2, p. 34; Ann M. McLaurin, "The Role of the Dixiecrats in the 1948 Election" (Ph.D. dissertation, University of Oklahoma, 1972), pp. 106–8; *New York Times*, July 3, 1948, sec. 1, p. 6.

48 RBR, Jr., to Mrs. Elizabeth Caldwallader-Noyes, August 31, 1948, Russell Collection, Civil Rights, Sprigle articles.

49 *Atlanta Constitution*, July 13, 14, and 15, 1948; Martin, *Civil Rights*, p. 87; Irvin Ross, *The Loneliest Campaign: The Truman Victory of 1948* (New York: New American Library, 1968), pp. 127–29.

50 George L. Googe to J. Howard McGrath, November 10, 1948, McGill Papers, ser. 2, box 3, folder 13.

51 *New York Times*, July 18, 1948, sec. 1, pp. 1, 4; McLaurin, "Role of the Dixiecrats," chapter 6.

52 RBR, Jr., to David I. Wells, January 3, 1951, Russell Collection, Dictation Series, Political; Abels, *Out of the Jaws of Victory*, p. 97.

53 *New York Times*, October 29, 1948, sec. 1, p. 4.

54 Author interview with J. Strom Thurmond, June 8, 1983.

55 *Moultrie Observer*, February 20, 1948; *Atlanta Constitution*, February 16, 1948.

56 RBR, Jr., to Skeed Poer, February 15, 1957, and RBR, Jr., to Walter B. Jones, September 4, 1945, Russell Collection, Dictation Series, Political.

57 Ralph McGill to Hardy Lott, August 26, 1946, McGill Papers, ser. 2, box 3, folder 12.

CHAPTER 12

1 RBR, Jr., to John Stennis, November 21, 1950, Russell Collection, Dictation Series, Political, Russell Memorial Library, University of Georgia, Athens.

2 RBR, Jr., to William Benton, September 20, 1951, and Benton to RBR, Jr., September 21, 1951, Russell Collection, Legislation, Armed Services.

3 David D. Potenziani, "Look to the Past: Richard B. Russell and the Defense of Southern White Supremacy" (Ph.D. dissertation, University of Georgia, 1981), pp. 85–86; RBR, Jr., to Foster Bolin, January 6, 1949, Russell Collection, Civil Rights, Negro Repatriation, 1939–49.

4 *Congressional Record*, 81st Cong., 1st sess., January 27, 1949, pp. 570–72.

5   *Commercial Appeal* (Memphis, Tenn.), January 29, 1949; John L. Wells to RBR, Jr., July 5, 1949, and RBR, Jr., to Frank Boykin, February 8, 1949, Russell Collection, Civil Rights, Relocation, 1948–49, and Negro Repatriation, 1939–49.

6   Benjamin Gibbons to RBR, Jr., March 10, 1948, and RBR, Jr., to Gibbons, February 13, 1948, and December 19, 1949, Russell Collection, Civil Rights, Gibbons and Jones.

7   *Congressional Record*, 81st Cong., 1st sess., January 5, 1949, p. 73.

8   *New York Times*, February 1, 1949, sec. 1, p. 28; March 4, 1949, sec. 1, p. 1; and March 6, 1949, p. 1.

9   *Congressional Record*, 81st Cong., 1st sess., March 17, 1949, p. 2721.

10   Gilbert C. Fite, *American Farmers: The New Minority* (Bloomington: University of Indiana Press, 1981), pp. 96–98; RBR, Jr., to C. O. Maddox, April 21, 1949, and RBR, Jr., to Carol C. Head, February 2, 1950, Russell Collection, Legislation, Agriculture; RBR, Jr., to Thomas J. Barrett, June 2, 1949, Russell Collection, Dictation Series, Legislation.

11   *New York Times*, October 5, 1949, sec. 1, p. 1, and October 7, 1949, sec. 1, p. 31; *Congress and the Nation, 1945–1964* (Washington: Congressional Quarterly Service, 1965), pp. 690–91.

12   RBR, Jr., to Charles C. Hertwig, September 13, 1951, Russell Collection, Dictation Series, Agriculture; *New York Times*, August 15, 1951, sec. 1, p. 37, and August 22, 1951, sec. 1, p. 31; Fite, *American Farmers*, p. 99.

13   RBR, Jr., to Cullene Gosnell, September 26, 1949, Russell Collection, Dictation Series, Political Patronage, Judgeships, 1949.

14   RBR, Jr., to W. R. Hendrix, September 13, 1949, Russell Collection, Dictation Series, China.

15   *Congressional Record*, 81st Cong., 1st sess., September 22, 1949, pp. 19163–65.

16   Quoted by Ralph McGill in *Atlanta Constitution*, May 2, 1951; RBR, Jr., to C. H. Pittard, April 9, 1949, Russell Collection, Dictation Series, Political.

17   *New York Times*, July 3, 1950, sec. 1, p. 13; RBR, Jr., to Robert W. Johnson, July 12, 1950, Russell Collection, Dictation Series, Political.

18   See Mundt's proposal in *Congressional Record*, 82d Cong., 1st sess., 1951, pp. A6240–41.

19   *Atlanta Constitution*, October 25, 1949.

20   RBR, Jr., to Colonel Joseph J. Twitty, September 21, 1949, and RBR, Jr., to Mrs. Morris Bryan, June 13, 1950, Russell Collection, Dictation Series, China.

21   RBR, Jr., to Henry W. Grady, July 28, 1950, ibid.

22   RBR, Jr., to Robert Joiner, September 5, 1950, and RBR, Jr., to General George Moseley, October 17, 1950, Russell Collection, Dictation Series, Legislative, Armed Services.

23   *New York Times*, January 9, 1951, sec. 1, p. 11; *Congressional Record*, 82d Cong., 2d sess., January 16, 1952, pp. 232–42.

24   *Congressional Record*, 82d Cong., 1st sess., January 8, 1951, p. 86, and March 9, 1951, p. 2207.

25   *U.S. News and World Report* 32 (February 1, 1952): 30; RBR, Jr., to John B. Foster, [1950], Russell Collection, Dictation Series, China.

26   RBR, Jr., to Clarence Poe, December 6, 1950; RBR, Jr., to Milton Bryant, July 10, 1950; RBR, Jr., to Zack D. Cravey, July 12, 1950; RBR, Jr., to C. F. Morgan, July 15, 1950;

RBR, Jr., to R. H. Brown, July 15, 1950; and RBR, Jr., to Dr. H. C. McCracken, July 19, 1950, Russell Collection, Dictation Series, General International.

27 RBR, Jr., to Wright Morrow, May 22, 1951, Russell Collection, MacArthur Hearings, Correspondence, 1951; RBR, Jr., to Frank Troutman, December 5, 1950, and RBR, Jr., to J. M. Morgan, December 1, 1952, Russell Collection, General, Atomic Energy Committee.

28 RBR, Jr., to Dora Barker, November 20, 1950, and RBR, Jr., to Frank Troutman, February 22, 1951, Russell Collection, MacArthur Hearings, Correspondence, 1951.

29 *New York Times*, August 19, 1951, sec. 1, p. 2.

30 See letters and telegrams in Russell Collection, Personal, Special, 1951, and in Fulbright Papers, BCN 38, folder 13, University of Arkansas Library, Fayetteville.

31 *New York Times*, April 14, 1951, sec. 1, p. 1; *Atlanta Journal*, April 13, 1951; "Richard Russell, Georgia Giant," manuscript for a three-part documentary, Cox Broadcasting Company, Atlanta, Georgia, 1970, pt. 2, pp. 31–32.

32 *Congressional Record*, 82d Cong., 1st sess., April 17, 1951, p. 3946. A great deal has been written on the MacArthur hearings. See John W. Spanier, *The Truman-MacArthur Controversy and the Korean War* (New York: W. W. Norton, 1959); Richard H. Rovere and Arthur M. Schlesinger, Jr., *The MacArthur Controversy and American Foreign Policy* (New York: Farrar, Straus, and Giroux, 1951), chapter 4; Burton I. Kaufman, *The Korean War: Challenges in Crisis, Credibility, and Command* (New York: Alfred A. Knopf, 1986), chapter 5; and D. Clayton James, *The Years of MacArthur*, vol. 3 (Boston: Houghton Mifflin, 1985), chapter 19.

33 George E. Reedy, *Lyndon B. Johnson: A Memoir* (New York: Andrews and McMeel, 1982), p. 91; *Atlanta Journal*, April 25, 1951; Doris Fleeson, *Washington Evening Star*, April 24, 1951.

34 *Congressional Record*, 82d Cong., 1st sess., April 30, 1951, p. 4535, and May 3, 1951, p. 4772; *New York Times*, April 14, 1951, sec. 1, p. 1, and April 15, 1951, sec. 1, p. 1.

35 Ralph McGill to RBR, Jr., April 26, 1951, and RBR, Jr., to McGill, April 26, 1951, Russell Collection, MacArthur Hearings.

36 *Congressional Record*, 82d Cong., 1st sess., May 3, 1951, pp. 4472–75.

37 *Military Situation in the Far East: Hearings before the Committee on Armed Services and the Committee on Foreign Relations, U.S. Senate*, 5 vols. (Washington: Government Printing Office, 1951), 82d Cong., 1st sess.

38 Ibid., 1:318; James, *The Years of MacArthur*, vol. 3, chapter 19; William Manchester, *American Caesar: Douglas MacArthur, 1880–1964* (Boston: Little, Brown, 1978), pp. 664–77.

39 *Military Situation in the Far East*, 2:681.

40 Ibid., pp. 682–83.

41 Ibid., pp. 784–829.

42 RBR, Jr., to Members of Armed Services and Foreign Relations committees, May 16, 1951, Russell Collection, MacArthur Hearings.

43 *Military Situation in the Far East*, 2:765, 784, 829, 870–72. See also Russell Collection, Personal, Notebook, 1951.

44 Alexander Wiley to RBR, Jr., May 18, 1951, Russell Collection, MacArthur Hearings.

45 *Military Situation in the Far East*, 4:2826.

46 *Congressional Record*, 82d Cong., 1st sess., June 18, 1951, p. 7302.

47 *Military Situation in the Far East*, 5:3139; *New York Times*, August 18, 1951, p. 1.

48 *Military Situation in the Far East*, 5:3139–44, 3155, 3161.

49 William S. White, *Citadel: The Story of the U.S. Senate* (New York: Harper and Brothers, 1957), p. 251.

50 RBR, Jr., to J. Dane Watson, October 19, 1951, Russell Collection, Dictation Series, Armed Services; *Atlanta Journal*, August 17, 1951.

51 *U.S. News and World Report* 32 (February 1, 1952): 28–33.

52 RBR, Jr., to Leonard Blanchard, Jr., February 18, 1952, Russell Collection, Legislation, Preparedness, 1956.

53 *New York Times*, November 9, 1950, sec. 1, p. 36, and November 12, 1950, sec. 1, p. 59.

54 RBR, Jr., to Pat McCarran, November 13, 1950; RBR, Jr., to Dennis Chavez, November 14, 1950; RBR, Jr., to G. P. Martin, January 9, 1951; RBR, Jr., to Virgil Chapman, November 21, 1950; and RBR, Jr., to Earnest H. Broughton, November 15, 1950, Russell Collection, Dictation Series, Political; Clark Clifford to author, August 21, 1985; Rowland Evans and Robert Novak, *Lyndon B. Johnson: The Exercise of Power* (New York: New American Library, 1966), p. 42.

55 Quoted in Doris Kearns, *Lyndon Johnson and the American Dream* (New York: Harper and Row, 1976), p. 103.

56 Ibid., pp. 102–8; Evans and Novak, *Lyndon B. Johnson*, pp. 31–45.

57 Lyndon B. Johnson to RBR, Jr., October 17, 1949, Congressional File, Richard B. Russell, Lyndon B. Johnson Library, Austin, Texas.

58 Reedy, *Lyndon B. Johnson: A Memoir*, p. 43.

59 RBR, Jr., to Lyndon B. Johnson, November 25, 1949, and Johnson to RBR, Jr., November 30, 1949, Congressional File, Richard B. Russell, Johnson Library; Russell Collection, Intraoffice File, July 1949, Communications and Memos.

60 RBR, Jr., to Lyndon B. Johnson, September 12, 1953, and Johnson to RBR, Jr., October 1 and 30, 1953, Austin Office, General File, 1953, Re-Ry, Johnson Library.

CHAPTER 13

1 *Washington Evening Star*, November 20, 1951.

2 RBR, Jr., to Frank Loftin, March 30, 1949, and RBR, Jr., to T. H. Harrison, August 15, 1950, Russell Collection, Dictation Series, Political, Russell Memorial Library, University of Georgia, Athens.

3 RBR, Jr., to Harry M. Ayers, March 2, 1951, ibid.

4 RBR, Jr., to Wright Bryan, May 5, 1951, ibid.

5 RBR, Jr., to W. R. Hughes, October 9, 1951, ibid.; Richard Wilson, "Presidential Puzzle: Democratic Senators Wish Truman Would Retire Graciously—and Launch a Boom for General Ike," *Look*, July 3, 1951.

6 *Savannah Morning News*, October 21, 1951. For the fullest account of the presidential election of 1952, see John Robert Greene, *The Crusade: The Presidential Election of 1952* (Lanham, N.Y.: University Press of America, 1985).

7   *New York Times*, December 12, 1951, sec. 1, p. 23.

8   Ibid., February 4, 1952, sec. 1, p. 11.

9   Ibid., January 28, 1952, sec. 1, p. 11, and January 29, 1952, sec. 1, p. 24.

10 *Public Papers of the Presidents of the United States: Harry S Truman, 1952–1953* (Washington: Government Printing Office, 1954), p. 41.

11 Spence Grayson to RBR, Jr., February 9 and 18, 1952, Russell Collection, Dictation Series, Political, Presidential Campaign, 1952; *New York Times*, February 25, 1952, sec. 1, p. 1; February 26, 1952, sec. 1, p. 16; and February 27, 1952, sec. 1, p. 20.

12 Russell's statement was placed in the *Congressional Record*, 82d Cong., 2d sess., February 28, 1952, sec. 1, p. 1587; *New York Times*, February 29, 1952, sec. 1, pp. 1, 22, and March 2, 1952, sec. 4, p. 2; *Atlanta Journal*, February 28, 1952.

13 *New York Times*, February 29, 1952, sec. 1, p. 1.

14 Lyndon B. Johnson to RBR, Jr., March 18, 1952; James Byrnes to RBR, Jr., March 1, 1952; and RBR, Jr., to Byrnes, March 4, 1952, Russell Collection, Political, Presidential Campaign, 1952.

15 *New York Times*, March 3, 1952, sec. 1, p. 14, and March 2, 1952, sec. 1, p. 67.

16 *Newsweek* 39 (March 10, 1952): 108.

17 *St. Louis Post-Dispatch*, February 29, 1952; *Hartford Times*, March 1, 1952; *Washington Post*, March 1, 1952; *New York Herald-Tribune*, March 16, 1952; newspaper clippings, February and March 1952, Clippings, Russell Collection.

18 *Time* 59 (March 10, 1952): 23–24.

19 *The Gallup Poll: Public Opinion, 1935–1971*, vol. 2 (New York: Random House, 1972), p. 1061.

20 *U.S. News and World Report* 32 (March 7, 1952): 24–25; *Newsweek* 39 (March 10, 1952): 27–28; *Nation* 174 (March 29, 1952): 294–95.

21 RBR, Jr., to Herbert Hitchcock, March 10, 1952, Russell Collection, Dictation Series, Political.

22 Francis Case to RBR, Jr., March 4, 1952, and RBR, Jr., to Case, March 11, 1952, ibid.

23 *New York Times*, March 2, 1952, sec. 1, p. 67.

24 Manuscript of questions and answers, "Meet the Press," March 10, 1952; RBR, Jr., interview with Edward R. Murrow, April 24, 1952; and RBR, Jr., to William Randolph Hearst, April 2, 1952, Russell Collection, Presidential, Political, 1952.

25 *New York Times*, March 31, 1952, sec. 1, p. 13.

26 Jonathan Daniels to RBR, Jr., March 25, 1952, and RBR, Jr., to Daniels, March 28, 1952, Russell Collection, Political, Presidential Campaign, 1952.

27 RBR, Jr., to Erle Cocke, Sr., March 14, 1952, ibid.; *New York Times*, March 19, 1952, sec. 1, p. 16.

28 *Atlanta Journal*, March 18, 1952.

29 R. W. Woodruff to B. D. Murphy, July 3, 1952; Hughes Spalding to RBR, Jr., February 29, 1952; and Spalding to Erle Cocke, Sr., July 7, 1952, Spalding Papers, Special Collections, Business Division, box 47, University of Georgia Library, Athens.

30 RBR, Jr., to Herman H. Ross, March 25, 1952, and RBR, Jr., to Ernest and Betty Vandiver, March 22, 1952, Russell Collection, Dictation Series, Political.

31 *New York Times*, April 24, 1952, sec. 1, p. 35.

32 *Atlanta Journal and Constitution*, June 1, 1952, magazine, pp. 10–11.

33 *Atlanta Constitution*, April 26, 1952; *New York Times*, April 26, 1952, sec. 1, p. 17.

34 *New York Times*, April 27, 1952, sec. 1, p. 35.

35 Ibid., April 29, 1952, sec. 1, p. 18.

36 *Newsweek* 39 (May 12, 1952): 28–29; *New York Times* and *Atlanta Constitution*, April 29–May 6, 1952; *Time* 59 (May 19, 1952): 29–32.

37 RBR, Jr., to Senator Guy M. Gillette, August 12, 1952, Russell Collection, Presidential, Political, 1952; RBR, Jr., to Ralph McGill, May 21, 1952, Russell Collection, Dictation Series, Political.

38 RBR, Jr., to William S. Howland, May 19, 1952, Russell Collection, Dictation Series, Political. See also Joseph Bruce Gorman, *Kefauver: A Political Biography* (New York: Oxford University Press, 1971), pp. 136–40.

39 *Atlanta Journal*, May 29, 1952.

40 John O. Pastore to Edwin Johnson, June 25, 1952, Russell Collection, Political, Presidential Campaign, 1952.

41 *New York Times*, June 3, 1952, sec. 1, p. 21.

42 *The Gallup Poll*, pp. 1069, 1075–76.

43 Preston Wright to Oliver DeWolfe, June 21, 1952, Russell Collection, Political, Presidential Campaign, 1952.

44 George Smathers to RBR, Jr., May 12, 1952, ibid.

45 Estes Kefauver to Francis Biddle, July 12, 1952, ibid.; *New York Times*, June 22, 1952, sec. 1, p. 38.

46 RBR, Jr., to Arnold Olsen, July 1, 1952; RBR, Jr., to Frank W. Boykin, July 1, 1952; and RBR, Jr., to William B. Umstead, July 1, 1952, Russell Collection, Dictation Series, Political.

47 RBR, Jr., to Charles Bloch, June 6, 1952, ibid.

48 RBR, Jr., Memo for the File, June 10, 1952, Russell Collection, Political, Presidential Campaign, 1952.

49 Philip Murray to RBR, Jr., June 17, 1952, ibid.

50 Statements and recollections of persons dealing with Senator Russell's discussion of the labor issue, 1952; George E. Stringfellow to RBR, Jr., July 18, 1952; R. E. Abernathy to RBR, Jr., July 19, 1952; and RBR, Jr., Memo for the File, July 28, 1952, Russell Collection, Political, Presidential Campaign, 1952. See also Russell Collection, Political, Presidential Campaign, 1952, Tom Blake, and *Atlanta Constitution*, June 17, 1952.

51 RBR, Jr., Statement at Press Conference, July 17, 1952, Russell Collection, Political, Presidential Campaign, 1952.

52 Press Release, July 20, 1952, ibid.

53 *Official Report of the Proceedings of the Democratic National Convention, Chicago, Illinois, July 21 to July 26, 1952* (M. Kallis, 1952), pp. 280–86.

54 *Atlanta Constitution*, July 25, 1952.

55 *Proceedings of the Democratic National Convention* (1952).

56 Ibid., pp. 538–39.

57 *Washington Star*, July 27, 1952.

58 *Proceedings of the Democratic National Convention* (1952), p. 537.

59 Calvin W. Rawlings to RBR, Jr., July 31, 1952, Russell Collection, Political, Presidential Campaign, 1952.

60 RBR, Jr., to Hughes Spalding, July 29, 1952, Spalding Papers, Special Collections, Business Division, box 47.

61 RBR, Jr., to Margaret Shannon, December 13, 1966, Russell Collection, Personal, Historical, 1966; Greene, *The Crusade*, pp. 165–67.

62 Adlai E. Stevenson to Mrs. Edison Dick, in Walter Johnson, ed., *The Papers of Adlai E. Stevenson*, vol. 4 (Boston: Houghton Mifflin, 1974), p. 37.

63 Ibid., p. 41.

64 Adlai E. Stevenson, *Major Campaign Speeches, 1952* (New York: Random House, 1953), pp. 19, 26; RBR, Jr., to Joe Parham, October 10, 1952, Russell Collection, Dictation Series, Political.

65 *New York Times*, September 14, 1952, sec. 1, p. 79.

66 Adlai E. Stevenson to RBR, Jr., September 16, 1952, Russell Collection, Political, Stevenson, 1952.

67 *New York Times*, October 2, 1952, sec. 1, p. 22; Press Release, October 21, 1952, Russell Collection, Political, Presidential Campaign, 1952.

68 Notes and comments, October 15 and 17, 1952, Fulbright Papers, BCN 78, folders 13, 16, University of Arkansas Library, Fayetteville.

69 J. William Fulbright to RBR, Jr., October 16, 1952, and RBR, Jr., to Wilson Wyatt, October 23, 1952, ibid.

70 RBR, Jr., to Carolyn Cobb, October 16, 1952, Russell Collection, Dictation Series, Political; RBR, Jr., to J. William Fulbright, October 16, 1952, Fulbright Papers, BCN 78, folder 16.

71 RBR, Jr., to Joe Parham, October 10, 1952; RBR, Jr., to D. W. Brooks, November 15, 1952; and RBR, Jr., to Lloyd Griffin, November 14, 1952, Russell Collection, Dictation Series, Political.

72 RBR, Jr., to Leon F. Hobby, August 22, 1952; RBR, Jr., to Harry D. Boivin, August 22, 1952; and RBR, Jr., to Frank M. Scarlett, August 9, 1952, ibid.

73 RBR, Jr., to Lloyd Griffin, November 14, 1952, ibid.

74 Milton Young to RBR, Jr., August 4, 1952; John Stennis to RBR, Jr., August 9, 1952; and RBR, Jr., to Senator Guy M. Gillette, August 12, 1952, ibid. Gillette was chairman of the Senate Subcommittee on Privileges and Elections. The fact that the original copy of Russell's letter to Gillette about his campaign expenses is in Russell's files indicates that it was never mailed.

75 RBR, Jr., to Robert A. Bailey, September 27, 1968, ibid.

76 RBR, Jr., to Lloyd Griffin, November 14, 1952; RBR, Jr., to Mrs. L. C. Buzzett, November 15, 1952; and RBR, Jr., to Adlai E. Stevenson, December 6, 1952, ibid.

CHAPTER 14

1   RBR, Jr., to Clyde R. Hoey, November 12, 1952, and RBR, Jr., to A. Willis Robertson, November 14, 1952, Russell Collection, Dictation Series, Political, Intraoffice File, Calendars, 1952, Russell Memorial Library, University of Georgia, Athens; *New York Times,* November 11, 1952, sec. 1, p. 1.

2   Russell Notes, Subject File, Senate Leadership, Memo, Container 118, Lyndon B. Johnson Library, Austin, Texas; *Atlanta Journal and Constitution,* June 30, 1968.

3   *Congressional Record,* 83d Cong., 1st sess., 1953, appendix, pp. A1007–8. See also John F. Martin, *Civil Rights and the Crisis of Liberalism: The Democratic Party, 1945–1976* (Boulder, Colo.: Westview Press, 1979), pp. 117–23.

4   Stephen A. Mitchell, Speech, May 2, 1953, Fulbright Papers, BCN 77, folder 43, University of Arkansas Library, Fayetteville.

5   *New York Times,* January 6, 1953, sec. 1, p. 1; *Congress and the Nation, 1945–1964* (Washington: Congressional Quarterly Service, 1965), p. 62a.

6   See Gilbert C. Fite, *American Farmers: The New Minority* (Bloomington: University of Indiana Press, 1981), pp. 102–4; Ezra Taft Benson, Statement, February 5, 1953, Russell Collection, Legislation, Agriculture.

7   RBR, Jr., to Thomas J. Barrett, May 5, 1963, Russell Collection, Dictation Series, Legislation.

8   RBR, Jr., to A. M. Bennett, June 10 and 22, 1953, and RBR, Jr., to Franklin G. Murphy, September 26, 1953, Russell Collection, Dictation Series, Political.

9   *New York Times,* September 20, 1953, sec. 1, p. 54.

10 Telegram, RBR, Jr., to Ezra Taft Benson, November 27, 1953, and True D. Morse to RBR, Jr., December 8, 1953, Russell Collection, Legislation, Agriculture.

11 *Congressional Record,* 83d Cong., 2d sess., January 12, 1954, pp. 184–86.

12 Ibid., 83d Cong., 1st sess., May 27, 1953, pp. 5641–53.

13 Ibid., June 15, 1953, pp. 6476–94.

14 Ibid., 83d Cong., 2d sess., June 1, 1954, pp. 7397–98.

15 Ibid., August 9, 1954, pp. 13686–90; RBR, Jr., to Charles W. Hubbard, July 15, 1954; RBR, Jr., to Mrs. R. S. Moore, February 13, 1953; and RBR, Jr., to Hafleigh and Company, March 3, 1953, Russell Collection, Dictation Series, Legislation, Agriculture.

16 *Congress and the Nation, 1945–1964,* p. 63a.

17 RBR, Jr., to D. W. Brooks, April 22, 1955, Russell Collection, Dictation Series, Legislation, Agriculture.

18 Robert Griffith, *The Politics of Fear: Joseph R. McCarthy and the Senate* (New York: Hayden, 1970); Democratic Policy Committee, Minutes, July 29, 1954, and Papers of Democratic Leaders, U.S. Senate, 1949–61, Johnson Library; RBR, Jr., to Roberta Hodgson, July 21, 1953, and RBR, Jr., to Ray L. Miller, July 28, 1953, Russell Collection, Dictation Series, Political; RBR, Jr., to C. W. McKinnon, February 14, 1954, and RBR, Jr., to Samuel J. Boykin, April 30, 1954, Russell Collection, Dictation Series, Legislation; RBR, Jr., to I. E. Morris, February 27, 1954, Russell Collection, Dictation Series, General.

19 RBR, Jr., to Lyndon B. Johnson, August 5, 1953, and Johnson to RBR, Jr., August 18,

1953, Congressional File, Richard B. Russell, Johnson Library; *Congressional Record*, 83d Cong., 1st sess., August 3, 1953, p. 11042.

20 Harry McPherson, Oral History, December 5, 1968, Johnson Library.

21 RBR, Jr., to Nancy Fletcher, November 18, 1955; RBR, Jr., to Ed S. Grant, December 31, 1955; RBR, Jr., to Frank Rogers, May 7, 1955; and RBR, Jr., to D. W. Brooks, April 22, 1955, Russell Collection, Dictation Series, Legislation, Agriculture.

22 RBR, Jr., to J. M. Gloer, December 9, 1955, and February 9, 1956, ibid.

23 RBR, Jr., to C. E. Tollison, May 3, 1955, and RBR, Jr., to E. J. Hancock, November 2, 1955, ibid. See also Gilbert C. Fite, *Cotton Fields No More: Southern Agriculture, 1865–1980* (Lexington: University of Kentucky Press, 1984), pp. 215–17. *Congressional Record*, 84th Cong., 1st sess., April 26, 1955, p. 5095.

24 RBR, Jr., to D. F. Martin, April 13, 1956, Russell Collection, Legislation, Agriculture.

25 RBR, Jr., to G. E. Finch, April 19, 1956, ibid.; Fite, *American Farmers*, pp. 108–9.

26 RBR, Jr., to A. M. Bennett, May 23, 1956, Russell Collection, Legislation, Agriculture.

27 *New York Times*, May 23, 1955, sec. 1, p. 19; October 27, 1955, sec. 1, p. 21; and November 7, 1955, sec. 1, p. 23; RBR, Jr., to J. T. McBrayer, November 21, 1955, and RBR, Jr., to Thomas Blake, November 16, 1955, Russell Collection, Dictation Series, Political.

28 RBR, Jr., to R. A. Craighead, April 30, 1956, and RBR, Jr., to Harold Cooley, May 12, 1956, Russell Collection, Dictation Series, Political.

29 RBR, Jr., to Mrs. W. H. Bridges, April 27, 1956, and RBR, Jr., to Arch H. Rowan, April 25, 1956, Russell Collection, Political, Lyndon B. Johnson, 1956–60.

30 RBR, Jr., to Charles J. Bloch, October 17, 1957, Russell Collection, Dictation Series, Political; George E. Reedy, Oral History, August 17, 1983, p. 36, Johnson Library.

31 *New York Times*, April 12, 1956, sec. 1, p. 18; April 22, 1956, sec. 1, p. 56; June 30, 1956, sec. 1, p. 9; and August 14, 1956, sec. 1, p. 13.

32 Rowland Evans and Robert Novak, *Lyndon B. Johnson: The Exercise of Power* (New York: New American Library, 1966), pp. 234–37.

33 RBR, Jr., to Adlai E. Stevenson, September 20, 1956, Russell Collection, Dictation Series, Political.

34 RBR, Jr., to Joe Salter, April 9, 1959; Erwin Sibley to RBR, Jr., May 2, 1957; and RBR, Jr., to Sibley, May 6, 1957, Russell Collection, Legislation, Political.

35 RBR, Jr., to J. M. Gloer, May 21, 1957, Russell Collection, Dictation Series, Legislation; *Congress and the Nation, 1945–1964*, p. 709; *New York Times*, May 27, 1959, sec. 1, p. 20.

36 Dwight D. Eisenhower Diary Series, Staff Notes, January 1, February 20, and March 25 and 26, 1957, Legislative Leadership Meetings, Eisenhower Library, Abilene, Kansas.

37 RBR, Jr., to B. F. Smith, September 27, 1957, and RBR, Jr., to D. W. Lawson, March 16, 1956, Russell Collection, Dictation Series, Legislation.

38 *Agricultural Statistics, 1962* (Washington: Government Printing Office, 1963), p. 679; RBR, Jr., to Frank A. Smith, April 4, 1950, and RBR, Jr., to H. P. Womack, April 29, 1955, Russell Collection, Dictation Series, Legislation.

39 *Congress and the Nation, 1945–1964*, p. 390.

40 RBR, Jr., to W. D. Shartzer, February 14, 1959, Russell Collection, General, 1957.

41 *Congressional Record*, 86th Cong., 1st sess., April 15, 1959, pp. 5970–71; John M. Butler to RBR, Jr., August 5, 1953, and January 21, 1954; RBR, Jr., to Butler, August 5, 1953, and January 22, 1954; Wayne Morse to RBR, Jr., July 8, 1955; RBR, Jr., to Morse, July 15, 1955; E. L. Forrester to RBR, Jr., June 5, 1958; RBR, Jr., to Forrester, June 6, 1958; Homer Capehart to RBR, Jr., July 17, 1958; RBR, Jr., to Capehart, July 18, 1958; Robert S. Kerr to RBR, Jr., May 22, 1952, and July 10, 1956; RBR, Jr., to Kerr, July 16, 1956; and Lyndon B. Johnson to RBR, Jr., June 6, 1955, Russell Collection, Legislation, Appropriations.

42 Harmon Caldwell to RBR, Jr., December 10, 1946, and RBR, Jr., to Caldwell, January 7, 1947, Russell Collection, Legislation, Agriculture.

43 *Gainesville Daily Times*, March 1, 1950.

44 *Atlanta Journal*, September 14, 1949; *Atlanta Constitution*, January 22, 1981.

45 Dwight D. Eisenhower, interview with RBR, Jr., August 26, 1957, Ann C. Whitman Diary Series, box 9, Eisenhower Library; RBR, Jr., to Carl Sanders, October 3, 1962, Russell Collection, Dictation Series, Political; *Atlanta Journal*, September 16, 1963.

46 RBR, Jr., to Edwin W. Steele, April 17, 1953, Russell Collection, Dictation Series, Legislation; RBR, Jr., to Mrs. Roy Allred, April 17, 1958, Russell Collection, General, 1958.

47 Russell Collection, Intraoffice File, 1960; Lyndon Johnson to RBR, Jr., February 18, 1960, and RBR, Jr., to Johnson, February 22, 1960, Russell Collection, Legislation, Appropriations.

48 RBR, Jr., Note to Staff, Russell Collection, Intraoffice File, 1960; RBR, Jr., to Sylvester Smith, July 31, 1961; RBR, Jr., to Mrs. Nora L. Smith, August 4, 1961; RBR, Jr., to Stephen Pace, March 3 and August 17, 1962; RBR, Jr., to Carl Rountree, August 29, 1962; and RBR, Jr., to Harry F. Byrd, September 17, 1962, Russell Collection, Dictation Series, Legislation; *Atlanta Journal and Constitution*, October 3 and 6, 1963; *New York Times*, October 13, 1963, sec. 1, p. 80, and November 7, 1963, sec. 1, p. 23. Russell spoke on the question of a wider distribution of federal research funds at Jekyll Island on July 9, 1965.

49 *Macon Telegraph and News*, October 27, 1957.

50 Dwight D. Eisenhower to RBR, Jr., July 24, 1958, and June 19, 1959, Russell Collection, Red Line File.

51 *New York Times*, January 14, 1958, sec. 1, p. 24.

52 Howard W. Cannon to RBR, Jr., September 14, 1959, and Robert C. Byrd to RBR, Jr., September 9, 1959, Russell Collection, Personal; author interview with Carter Bradley, May 17, 1982; Gale McGee to author, September 29, 1984; *Congressional Record*, 91st Cong., 1st sess., March 24, 1969, p. 7176.

53 RBR, Jr., to Thomas C. Hennings, Jr., March 22, 1958, Russell Collection, Dictation Series, Legislation.

54 RBR, Jr., to William P. Congdon, June 10, 1957, Russell Collection, Dictation Series, Political; author interview with William M. Bates, July 9, 1986; William Bates, Oral History, February 25, 1971, Russell Collection.

55 RBR, Jr., to Harry F. Byrd, May 5, 1949; RBR, Jr., to A. Willis Robertson, April 15,

1949; and RBR, Jr., to Guy Gillette, April 29, 1949, Russell Collection, Dictation Series.

56 RBR, Jr., to John F. Kennedy, January 11, 1956, and RBR, Jr., to Bell Wiley, March 17, 1958, Russell Collection, General File, Gift Books, 1953–58.

57 *Washington Daily News*, April 16, 1956; RBR, Jr., to Dan Magill, December 2, 1959, Russell Collection, Dictation Series, Legislation; Clark Clifford, Oral History, March 17, 1969, Johnson Library.

58 RBR, Jr., to Mrs. Lilita Bizzelle, February 1, 1955, Russell Collection, Personal Greetings, 1955; RBR, Jr., to Reverend George Scotchmer, December 29, 1953, Russell Collection, Personal, 1953.

59 Joseph C. Duke to RBR, Jr., September 15, 1949, and January 1, 1951, Russell Collection, General, Personal Office Matters; Russell Collection, Intraoffice File, May 1951; John G. Metcalfe to RBR, Jr., August 13, 1951, and RBR, Jr., to Metcalfe, August 15, 1951, Russell Collection, Personal, Miscellaneous, 1951.

60 RBR, Jr., to William C. Doenges, August 16, 1951, Russell Collection, Dictation Series, Political.

61 Dr. J. C. Cain to RBR, Jr., September 3 and October 31, 1952, Russell Collection, Senatorial Years, Personal Correspondence, Illness; Cain to RBR, Jr., March 23 and May 10, 1956, and RBR, Jr., to Cain, April 9, 1956, Russell Collection, Red Line File, 1955–57.

CHAPTER 15

1 Robert J. Whatley to RBR, Jr., [August 1952]; W. H. Darden to Whatley, August 28, 1952; H. G. Daniel to RBR, Jr., June 15, 1954; RBR, Jr., to Daniel, June 21, 1954; Jere N. Moore to RBR, Jr., October 26, 1954; and RBR, Jr., to Moore, October 30, 1954, Russell Collection, Civil Rights, Armed Services, 1952–53, Russell Memorial Library, University of Georgia, Athens.

2 *Atlanta Constitution*, December 11, 1953; *Time* 62 (December 14, 1953): 51.

3 Ray Moore to Ralph McGill, [December 1953], McGill Papers, ser. 2, box 5, folder 10, Emory University Library, Atlanta, Georgia.

4 *Griffin [Ga.] Daily News*, November 12, 1953.

5 *Congressional Record*, 83d Cong., 2d sess., May 18, 1954, pp. 6748–50.

6 RBR, Jr., to H. O. Brooks, June 10, 1954; RBR, Jr., to Floyd Laird, June 30, 1954; and RBR, Jr., to T. E. Hembree, October 20, 1954, Russell Collection, Civil Rights, School Segregation, 1954; David D. Potenziani, "Look to the Past: Richard B. Russell and the Defense of Southern White Supremacy" (Ph.D. dissertation, University of Georgia, 1981), chapter 5.

7 Russell Collection, Intraoffice File, April 1959.

8 Quoted in Potenziani, "Look to the Past," pp. 132–33.

9 *Washington Evening Star*, March 12, 1956; Ralph McGill to Dwight D. Eisenhower, August 21, 1958, Official File, 142–A5(2), Eisenhower Library, Abilene, Kansas.

10 RBR, Jr., to George B. Timmerman, Jr., June 14, 1956, and RBR, Jr., to Ted G. Kelly, August 30, 1956, Russell Collection, Dictation Series, Political.

11 Aleatha Swensen to J. William Fulbright, March 16, 1956, and Fulbright to Thad N. Marsh, March 17, 1956, Fulbright Papers, BCN 10, folder 1, University of Arkansas Library, Fayetteville.

12 Democratic Policy Committee, Minutes, June 27, 1956, Lyndon B. Johnson Library, Austin, Texas; *New York Times,* July 30, 1956, sec. 1, p. 8.

13 *Congressional Record,* 85th Cong., 1st sess., July 10, 1957, pp. 92–94; RBR, Jr., to Charles Bloch, July 30, 1957, Russell Collection, Personal.

14 *New York Times,* July 4, 1957, sec. 1, p. 1.

15 RBR, Jr., to Walter George, July 3, 1957, Russell Collection, Red Line File. On Russell's views, see Sam M. Jones, "Voice of the South," *National Review* 4 (July 27, 1957): 105–6.

16 *New York Times,* July 11, 1957, sec. 1, p. 1; *Congress and the Nation, 1945–1964* (Washington: Congressional Quarterly Service, 1965), p. 1623.

17 *Atlanta Journal,* July 18, 1957, sec. 1, pp. 1, 12; *Washington Daily News,* July 17, 1957.

18 Dwight D. Eisenhower to E. E. Hazlett, July 22, 1957, Dwight D. Eisenhower Diary Series, Dictation, Eisenhower Library. See also Rowland Evans and Robert Novak, *Lyndon B. Johnson: The Exercise of Power* (New York: New American Library, 1966), chapter 7.

19 *Atlanta Constitution,* August 2, 1957.

20 *New York Times,* August 4, 1957, sec. 1, p. 1; Evans and Novak, *Lyndon B. Johnson,* pp. 136–39.

21 *New York Times,* August 30, 1957, sec. 1, p. 1.

22 *Time* 70 (August 12, 1957): 13; Tris Coffin, "How Lyndon Johnson Engineered Compromise on Civil Rights Bill," *New Leader* 40 (August 5, 1957): 3–4; Alfred Steinberg, *Sam Johnson's Boy: A Close-up of the President from Texas* (New York: Macmillan, 1968), pp. 468–71.

23 J. William Fulbright to RBR, Jr., August 30, 1957, Fulbright Papers, BCN 96, folder 11.

24 RBR, Jr., to Milton G. Farris, August 6, 1957, Russell Collection, General File, 1957; RBR, Jr., to Ernest Brazill, Jr., August 23, 1957, Russell Collection, Dictation Series, Political.

25 *Time* 70 (August 12, 1957): 16.

26 *Congressional Record,* 85th Cong., 1st sess., August 30, 1957, pp. 16659–61.

27 See Numan V. Bartley, *The Rise of Massive Resistance* (Baton Rouge: Louisiana State University Press, 1969), chapter 14.

28 *Washington Post,* September 25, 1957; *U.S. News and World Report* 43 (October 4, 1957): 58.

29 RBR, Jr., to Dwight D. Eisenhower, September 26, 1957, and Eisenhower to RBR, Jr., September 27, 1957, Official File, 142–A5(1), Eisenhower Library. For Johnson's role in the 1957 civil rights fight, see Doris Kearns, *Lyndon Johnson and the American Dream* (New York: Harper and Row, 1976), pp. 147–52.

30 Granger Hansell to RBR, Jr., September 27 and October 10, 1957, and RBR, Jr., to Hansell, September 30, 1957, Russell Collection, Civil Rights, Little Rock; *New York Times,* November 22, 1958, sec. 1, p. 43.

31 Ralph McGill to Dwight D. Eisenhower, September 24, 1957, McGill Papers, ser. 2, box

6, folder 1; McGill to Charles J. Bloch, February 24, 1958, McGill Papers, ser. 2, box 7, folder 2.

32 Ralph McGill to Dwight D. Eisenhower, September 20, 1957, McGill Papers, ser. 2, box 6, folder 10.

33 Charles J. Bloch to Ralph McGill, November 13, 1958, McGill Papers, ser. 2, box 7, folder 6; McGill to Dwight D. Eisenhower, February 23, 1959, Presidential Name Series, Ralph McGill and Southern Politics, and notes on a meeting between Eisenhower and RBR, Jr., August 26, 1957, Ann C. Whitman Diary Series, August 1957, Eisenhower Library; RBR, Jr., to T. B. Alexander, February 18, 1957, Russell Collection, Dictation Series.

34 RBR, Jr., to Jack Conort, April 2, 1957; RBR, Jr., to Calvin Usher, September 9, 1958; RBR, Jr., to Robert Rushton, March 13, 1958; and RBR, Jr., to Gene Ingels, June 25, 1958, Russell Collection, Dictation Series, General.

35 RBR, Jr., to Frank Scarlett, January 6, 1959, Russell Collection, Dictation Series, Political.

36 *New York Times*, November 18, 1958, sec. 1, p. 31; Potenziani, "Look to the Past," pp. 183–84.

37 *New York Times*, February 25, 1960, sec. 1, p. 1.

38 Potenziani, "Look to the Past," pp. 188–92; *Congressional Record*, 86th Cong., 2d sess., April 8, 1960, p. 7814.

39 William H. Jordan, Memo to Staff, March 2, 1960, Russell Collection, Intraoffice File.

CHAPTER 16

1 *Atlanta Constitution*, December 2, 1955.

2 RBR, Jr., to Roy S. Salter, April 17, 1953, and RBR, Jr., to Beverly Howard, June 30, 1953, Russell Collection, Legislation, Appropriations, Russell Memorial Library, University of Georgia, Athens; RBR, Jr., to J. A. Simpson, March 17, 1953, Russell Collection, Dictation Series, Legislation; RBR, Jr., Speech to American Society of Newspaper Editors, April 17, 1953, Russell Collection, Speeches.

3 Norman A. Graebner, ed., *Ideas and Diplomacy* (New York: Oxford University Press, 1964), pp. 780–806. See Dulles statement, ibid., pp. 801–6.

4 Quoted in Norman A. Graebner, *The New Isolationism* (New York: Ronad Press, 1956), p. 115.

5 *Congressional Record*, 83d Cong., 1st sess., July 23, 1953, pp. 9586–87.

6 RBR, Jr., to Arthur Godfrey, April 11, 1956, Russell Collection, Dictation Series, Legislation.

7 RBR, Jr., to Roy S. Salter, April 17, 1953, and RBR, Jr., to Beverly Howard, June 30, 1953, Russell Collection, Legislation, Appropriations. See also *New York Times*, May 11, 1953, sec. 1, p. 18, and September 28, 1953, sec. 1, p. 3.

8 John Stennis to RBR, Jr., December 30, 1953, Russell Collection, Legislation, Armed Services Committee.

9 *Congressional Record*, 84th Cong., 1st sess., June 10, 1955, p. 8703; *New York Times*, June 21, 1955, p. 7.

10 *New York Times*, May 18, 1955, sec. 1, p. 1, and May 24, 1955, sec. 1, p. 1; *U.S. News*

and World Report 38 (May 27, 1955): 16.

11 *Congressional Record*, 84th Cong., 1st sess., June 26, 1956, p. 10973.

12 Ibid., pp. 10971–75; RBR, Jr., to Josiah Sibley, March 2, 1956, Russell Collection, Legislation, Armed Services Committee.

13 *Congress and the Nation, 1945–1964* (Washington: Congressional Quarterly Service, 1965), p. 390; *Congressional Record*, 84th Cong., 1st sess., June 20, 1955, p. 8703.

14 *New York Times*, January 4, 1956, sec. 1, p. 1.

15 RBR, Jr., to J. J. Bunch, February 2, 1957, and RBR, Jr., to Kenneth McKellar, February 18, 1957, Russell Collection, Dictation Series, General, International; *Congressional Record*, 85th Cong., 1st sess., February 27, 1957, pp. 2678–83.

16 *New York Times*, May 24, 1957, sec. 1, p. 1.

17 Ibid., January 8, 1956, sec. 1, p. 80, and June 10, 1956, sec. 1, p. 1.

18 RBR, Jr., to Mrs. Roger D. Johnson, Jr., August 30, 1961; RBR, Jr., to J. H. Hines, May 21, 1957; RBR, Jr., to Eugene W. Castle, January 22, 1958; and RBR, Jr., to J. William Fulbright, July 2, 1959, Russell Collection, Dictation Series, Political.

19 Dwight D. Eisenhower, Notes on meeting with RBR, Jr., August 26, 1957, Dwight D. Eisenhower Diary Series, Memo of Appointments, August 1957, Eisenhower Library, Abilene, Kansas; *Atlanta Journal*, March 10, 1957.

20 *Congress and the Nation, 1945–1964*, p. 390; RBR, Jr., to George Todt, May 16, 1958; RBR, Jr., to Louis E. Wolfson, August 28, 1959; RBR, Jr., to Otto E. Passman, May 15, 1959; and RBR, Jr., to G. O. Mabry, June 9, 1960, Russell Collection, Legislation, Foreign Relations.

21 See notes on bipartisan congressional leadership conferences in Legislative Meeting Series, boxes 1 and 2, 1953–57, Eisenhower Library, for examples of the issues discussed at these White House conferences.

22 *Congressional Record*, 86th Cong., 1st sess., July 14, 1959, pp. 13337–39.

23 Dwight D. Eisenhower, Memorandum for the Record, June 29, 1959, Dwight D. Eisenhower Diary Series, box 42, Staff Notes, June 16–30, 1959, and Eisenhower to Lyndon B. Johnson, June 25, 1959, Dwight D. Eisenhower, Dictation, June 1959, Eisenhower Library; Bryce Harlow to RBR, Jr., June 26, 1959, Russell Collection, Red Line File, June–July 1959.

24 For Russell's views, see Chalmers M. Roberts, "The Day We Didn't Go to War," *Reporter* 2 (September 14, 1954): 31–35; Wayne Kelley, *Atlanta Journal and Constitution*, February 4, 1968; and Bernard B. Fall to RBR, Jr., May 23, 1966, and RBR, Jr., to Fall, June 7, 1966, Russell Collection, International, June 1966. See also RBR, Jr., to Reed Sarratt, February 20, 1954; RBR, Jr., to J. D. Koelbel, February 16, 1954; RBR, Jr., to Theodore L. Bailey, February 22, 1954; RBR, Jr., to Granger Hansell, April 22, 1954; RBR, Jr., to Frank Mathews, May 20, 1954; and RBR, Jr., to Zack D. Cravey, April 14, 1954, Russell Collection, Dictation Series, International; and interview with William F. Knowland, June 22, 1967, Columbia Oral History Research Office, New York, New York, copy in Eisenhower Library.

25 Ruben Efron wrote a detailed account of this trip to the Soviet Union, [1955]. The account was classified for several years. See also RBR, Jr., to Joe W. Finley, October 27, 1955; RBR, Jr., to Col. Avery M. Cochran, November 3, 1955; and RBR, Jr., to Charles

W. Shepard, November 17, 1955, Russell Collection, Personal, European Trip, 1955.

26 *Inquiry into Satellite and Missile Programs: Hearings before the Preparedness Investigating Subcommittee of the Committee on Armed Services, U.S. Senate*, 2 vols. (Washington, 1958), 85th Cong., 1st and 2d sess., November 25, 1957, to January 23, 1958, 1:1–2.

27 RBR, Jr., to John Stennis, October 17, 1957, Russell Collection, General, Missile File, 1957; *Savannah Evening Press*, December 3, 1957.

28 Stuart Symington to Dwight D. Eisenhower, October 8, 1957, copy in Russell Collection, General, Missile File, 1957.

29 John Stennis to RBR, Jr., October 17, 1957, and Stuart Symington to RBR, Jr., October 11, 1957, ibid.

30 RBR, Jr., to Charles T. Waite, December 12, 1957, ibid.

31 *Valdosta Daily Times*, November 11, 1957.

32 *Atlanta Constitution*, November 5, 1957.

33 *New York Times*, December 7, 1957, sec. 1, p. 1.

34 *Inquiry into Satellite and Missile Programs*, Hearings, November 25, 26, and 27, and December 13, 14, 15, and 17, 1957, and January 17, 20, 21, and 23, 1958.

35 Democratic Conference, Minutes, January 7, 1958, Papers of Democratic Leaders, U.S. Senate, 1941–61, Lyndon B. Johnson Library, Austin, Texas.

36 *Congress and the Nation, 1945–1964*, p. 390; *Augusta Chronicle*, January 5, 1958; *Washington Post*, December 4, 1957.

37 *Congressional Record*, 85th Cong., 2d sess., August 15, 1958, pp. 17516–18, 17737–43.

38 RBR, Jr., to John Foster Dulles, December 19, 1958, Russell Collection, Dictation Series, General.

39 RBR, Jr., to John J. Rhodes, September 30, 1959, and RBR, Jr., to Carl Marcy, September 24, 1959, Russell Collection, Dictation Series, Foreign Relations.

40 C. J. Hauck to RBR, Jr., August 7, 1958, Russell Collection, Legislation, Appropriations, Defense Correspondence, 1958; Thomas Gates to RBR, Jr., May 21, 1959, Russell Collection, General File, January–May, 1959; H. G. Rickover to RBR, Jr., December 12, 1960, Russell Collection, Legislation, Joint Committee on Atomic Energy, 1957–60.

41 See day sheets, memos, phone calls, etc., 1959 and 1960, Russell Collection, Intraoffice File. Also author interview with Harry L. Wingate, Jr., chief clerk of the Armed Services Committee, February 25, 1982.

42 *Congressional Record*, 84th Cong., 2d sess., April 11, 1956, p. 6048.

43 *New York Times*, December 4, 1957, sec. 1, p. 3; RBR, Jr., to Leslie R. Groves, June 28, 1958, Russell Collection, Legislation, Joint Committee on Atomic Energy, 1957–60.

44 *New York Times*, February 4, 1955, sec. 1, p. 7, and April 12, 1956, p. 1; *Congressional Record*, 84th Cong., 2d sess., April 11, 1956, pp. 6048–50, 6068. See also Harry Howe Ransom, *Central Intelligence and National Security* (Cambridge: Harvard University Press, 1958), chapter 7.

45 Leverett Saltonstall, Oral History, January 17, 1967, Eisenhower Library.

46 George Reedy, Oral History, August 17, 1983, Johnson Library.

47 *Congressional Record*, 86th Cong., 1st sess., June 8, 1959, pp. 10129–30.

CHAPTER 17

1   RBR, Jr., to Harry G. Thornton, May 22, 1959, Russell Collection, Dictation Series, Russell Memorial Library, University of Georgia, Athens.

2   For data on Russell's medication, see Russell Collection, Intraoffice File, Daybooks, Calendars, and Notebooks, 1960 and 1961.

3   Ibid.

4   Joseph S. Clark, *The Sapless Branch* (New York: Harper and Row, 1964), p. 186.

5   Democratic Policy Committee, Minutes, April 14, 1959, U.S. Senate, Papers of Democratic Leaders, 1949–61, box 364, Lyndon B. Johnson Library, Austin, Texas.

6   Clark, *The Sapless Branch*, pp. 1, 7, 9, 11, 14; Michael Foley, *The New Senate: Liberal Influence on a Conservative Institution, 1959–1972* (New Haven: Yale University Press, 1980), pp. 3, 22, 27, 29.

7   Clark, *The Sapless Branch*, p. 14.

8   Ibid.; RBR, Jr., to Walter Hawkins, November 15, 1958, and RBR, Jr., to Frank Rossiter, January 15, 1958, Russell Collection, Dictation Series, Political; RBR, Jr., notes on resolutions, Russell Collection, General, August–November 1959, Red Line File.

9   Lyndon B. Johnson to RBR, Jr., September 15, 1959, Russell Collection, General, Red Line File; RBR, Jr., to Rufus G. Harris, October 7, 1960, Russell Collection, Dictation Series, Political.

10 Price Daniel to RBR, Jr., November 2, 1959, and RBR, Jr., to Daniel, November 8, 1959, Russell Collection, Political.

11 Theodore H. White, *The Making of the President, 1960* (New York: Atheneum, 1961), pp. 43, 169–70.

12 Eugene C. Patterson, Oral History, March 11, 1969, Johnson Library; Arthur M. Schlesinger, Jr., *A Thousand Days: John F. Kennedy in the White House* (Boston: Houghton Mifflin, 1965), pp. 50–57.

13 Russell Collection, Intraoffice File, July 1960.

14 RBR, Jr., to Gus C. Edwards, July 21, 1960; RBR, Jr., to Billy F. Bennett, July 25, 1960; RBR, Jr., to John J. Jones, September 29, 1960; and RBR, Jr., to James B. Polhill, August 24, 1960, Russell Collection, Dictation Series, Political.

15 RBR, Jr., to Harvey J. Kennedy, September 29, 1960, ibid.

16 RBR, Jr., to Harvey J. Kennedy, November 17, 1960, ibid.

17 RBR, Jr., to William P. Kennedy, May 28, 1957, Russell Collection, Political, Correspondence, 1960.

18 RBR, Jr., to Reverend Thomas E. Lee, September 29, 1960, Russell Collection, Dictation Series, Political.

19 *Atlanta Journal and Constitution*, September 25, 1960.

20 RBR, Jr., to James B. Burch, November 9, 1960, Russell Collection, Dictation Series, Political.

21 *New York Times*, November 8, 1960, sec. 1, p. 17.

22 RBR, Jr., to Edwin C. Smith, April 5, 1963, Russell Collection, Dictation Series, Political.

23 *New York Times*, November 10, 1960, sec. 1, p. 1.

24 RBR, Jr., to Mrs. Wright Morrow, November 14, 1960, Russell Collection, Dictation Series, Political, Intraoffice File, Calendar, Memo Sheets, November 1960.

25 R. J. Travis to James L. Gillis, September 22, 1957; RBR, Jr., to Gillis, December 10, 1957; RBR, Jr., to Milton P. Thompson, April 1, 1960; and clipping from *Georgia Recorder*, April 22, 1959, Russell Collection, Political, Personal, Campaign, 1960.

26 *Savannah Evening Press*, December 2, 1960.

27 RBR, Jr., to Joe Hornsby, July 31, 1963, Russell Collection, Dictation Series, Political.

28 RBR, Jr., Statement for the File, December 15, 1960, ibid.; *Savannah Evening Press*, December 2, 1960; *Atlanta Constitution*, December 2, 1960.

29 Russell Collection, Intraoffice File, November and December, 1960.

30 *Augusta Chronicle*, September 23, 1960; RBR, Jr., to Robert L. Russell, January 6, 1961, Russell Collection, Dictation Series, Political.

31 RBR, Jr., to Thomas E. Lee, September 29, 1960, and RBR, Jr., to John J. Jones, September 29, 1960, Russell Collection, Dictation Series, Political; RBR, Jr., to O. D. Johnson, June 12, 1961, Russell Collection, Dictation Series, General, International, America's Welfare, 1961–62; RBR, Jr., to William A. Lufburrow, February 12, 1962, and RBR, Jr., to Carl C. Head, March 21, 1956, Russell Collection, Dictation Series, General, International.

32 RBR, Jr., undated notes, Russell Collection, Personal, Personal History, 1960; RBR, Jr., to E. Smythe Gambrel, September 28, 1961, Russell Collection, Dictation Series, Legislative, Foreign Relations, 1958–63.

33 *Washington Evening Star*, April 22, 1959; *AFL-CIO News*, June 4, 1960.

34 *Waycross [Ga.] Journal-Herald*, January 12, 1961.

35 RBR, Jr., to John F. Kennedy, January 4, 1961, and RBR, Jr., to John W. Turner, September 1, 1961, Russell Collection, Dictation Series, Political; *Athens Banner-Herald*, January 4, 1961.

36 *New York Times*, April 24, 1961, sec. 1, p. 32; *Atlanta Journal*, April 19, 1961.

37 RBR, Jr., to Mrs. Gloria Davis Syabo, February 22, 1961, Russell Collection, Dictation Series, General.

38 Russell wrote a form letter dated June 21, 1961, on the issue of federal aid to education that was sent out to many constituents. See letter in Russell Collection, Dictation Series, General.

39 RBR, Jr., to Elmer George, April 10, 1961, Russell Collection, Dictation Series, Political.

40 Telephone conversation between President Kennedy and RBR, Jr., November 9, 1961, Russell Collection, General, Office Matters, Red Line File, Special Presidential, 1941–67.

41 *Congress and the Nation, 1945–1964* (Washington: Congressional Quarterly Service, 1965), pp. 712–24.

42 Wallace F. Bennett to RBR, Jr., June 1, 1962, and RBR, Jr., to Bennett, June 7, 1962, Russell Collection, Legislative, Appropriations Committee, June–August 1962; RBR, Jr., to Cliff Gregg, June 27, 1962, Russell Collection, Dictation Series, Political.

43 Author interview with Dean Rusk, July 16, 1986; Jesse D. Jewell to RBR, Jr., May 3, 1962, and RBR, Jr., to S. H. Gray, May 9, 1962, Russell Collection, Legislative, Agriculture.

44 *New York Times*, January 27, 1960, sec. 1, p. 13, and May 19, 1960, p. 13.

45 Author interview with Dean Rusk, July 16, 1986; RBR, Jr., to Joseph B. Newcomer, September 1, 1961, Russell Collection, Dictation Series, Legislative, Armed Services.

46 *New York Times*, August 14, 1961, sec. 1, p. 15.

47 *Macon Telegraph and News*, February 28, 1961; *Congress and the Nation, 1945–1964*, pp. 311–13.

48 *Atlanta Constitution*, July 29, 1961; *Savannah News*, August 6, 1961; *New York Times*, July 29, 1961, sec. 1, p. 1.

49 Telephone conversation between President Kennedy and RBR, Jr., November 9, 1961, Russell Collection, General, Office Matters, Red Line File, Special Presidential, 1941–67.

50 Author interview with Dean Rusk, July 16, 1986; J. William Fulbright to RBR, Jr., March 15, 1966; RBR, Jr., to Fulbright, April 30, 1966; and Mike Mansfield to RBR, Jr., May 25, 1966, Russell Collection, Foreign Relations, Correspondence, 1966. For debate on the issue, see *Congressional Record*, 89th Cong., 2d sess., May 16, 1966, pp. 10618–23, and July 14, 1966, pp. 15674–93; *New York Times*, May 3, 1966, sec. 1, p. 14, and July 16, 1966, sec. 1, p. 24. This question of oversight of the CIA has also been discussed by Harry Howe Ransom, *The Intelligence Establishment* (Cambridge: Harvard University Press, 1970), pp. 172–79.

51 RBR, Jr., to R. H. Smith, November 9, 1961, Russell Collection, Dictation Series, Legislative, Armed Services; RBR, Jr., to Mrs. George Hayes, November 9, 1961, and RBR, Jr., to W. V. Flowers, August 30, 1961, Russell Collection, Dictation Series, General, International.

52 *Military Procurement Authorization, Fiscal Year 1962: Hearings before the Committee on Armed Services, U.S. Senate*, 87th Cong., 1st sess., April 5, 1961, pp. 108–15.

53 RBR, Jr., to Mrs. Roger D. Johnson, August 30, 1961, Russell Collection, Legislative, Foreign Relations, 1961; RBR, Jr., to Harry H. McNeal, June 16, 1962, Russell Collection, Dictation Series, Armed Services, 1962; "Entire Voting Record of Senator Richard B. Russell, from March 4, 1933, to October 13, 1962," Russell Collection.

54 John F. Kennedy to RBR, Jr., May 20, 1961, and RBR, Jr., to Kennedy, May 23, 1961, Russell Collection, Red Line File.

55 Mrs. Lyndon B. Johnson, Oral History, June 28, 1977, Russell Collection. See also the article by social columnist Betty Beale in the *St. Petersburg Times*, December 1, 1963.

56 Russell Collection, Intraoffice File, Personal, 1961.

57 See newspaper clippings in Russell Scrapbook, 1961, Russell Collection.

58 *Congressional Record*, 87th Cong., 1st sess., September 20, 1962, pp. 22026, 20058.

59 J. William Fulbright, Oral History, April 19, 1971, Russell Collection.

60 RBR, Jr., notes on White House Conference, October 23, 1962, Russell Collection, Personal, Red Line File, Special Presidential, 1954–65; RBR, Jr., Press Release, Russell Collection, International, Cuba, 1962.

61 Author interview with Dean Rusk, July 16, 1986; RBR, Jr., to E. R. Russell, October 26, 1962; RBR, Jr., to E. Smythe Gambrell, October 30, 1962; and RBR, Jr., to Robert C. Daniel, February 25, 1963, Russell Collection, International, Cuba, 1962 and 1963. See also RBR, Jr., to Maynard R. Ashworth, October 31, 1962, Russell Collection, Dictation Series, General, International, Cuba, 1962.

62 Russell Collection, Intraoffice File, November–December, 1962, RBR, Jr., to Morgan McNeel, December 10, 1962, Russell Collection, International, Cuba, 1962. See also *U.S. News and World Report* 53 (December 17, 1962): 6, and Theodore C. Sorensen, *Kennedy* (New York: Harper and Row, 1965), pp. 702–3.

63 RBR, Jr., to Reverend James B. Sherwood, October 25, 1963, Russell Collection, Legislative, Foreign Affairs, 1963.

64 *Congressional Record*, 88th Cong., 1st sess., September 17, 1963, pp. 17154–166; *Congress and the Nation, 1945–1964*, p. 92a.

65 RBR, Jr., to Charles J. Bloch, October 4, 1963, Russell Collection, Political, Charles Bloch, Special Name File.

66 *Public Papers of the Presidents of the United States: John F. Kennedy, 1963* (Washington: Government Printing Office, 1964), p. 678; Mike Manatos, Office Files, box 14 (1295), Johnson Library; Lawrence O'Brien to RBR, Jr., October 12, 1962, Russell Collection, Legislative, 1961–63.

67 John F. Kennedy to RBR, Jr., November 2, 1962, and January 12, 1963, and RBR, Jr., to Kennedy, November 2, 1962, Russell Collection, Personal, Red Line File, 1962–64.

68 *New York Times*, August 30, 1962, sec. 1, p. 17.

69 *Congressional Record*, 87th Cong., 2d sess., October 8, 1963, p. 22772; RBR, Jr., to L. L. Crager, October 9, 1962, and RBR, Jr., to Mrs. John Cox, October 11, 1962, Russell Collection, Civil Rights, Racial, Mississippi, October 7–9, 1962. For the best account of Russell's resistance to civil rights legislation during the Kennedy administration, see David D. Potenziani, "Look to the Past: Richard B. Russell and the Defense of Southern White Supremacy" (Ph.D. dissertation, University of Georgia, 1981), pp. 193–206.

70 RBR, Jr., to L. H. Mons, September 3, 1963; RBR, Jr., to George B. Inabinet, August 22, 1963; and RBR, Jr., to Mrs. Thomas E. Blackburn, August 12, 1963, Russell Collection, Dictation Series, Political.

71 RBR, Jr., to Editor, *Atlanta Journal*, June 24, 1963, ibid.

72 Telephone conversation between Theodore Sorensen and Lyndon B. Johnson, June 3, 1963, George Reedy, Office Files, Johnson Library.

73 RBR, Jr., to Mrs. John F. Kennedy, November 26, 1963, Russell Collection, Dictation Series.

CHAPTER 18

1 Floyd M. Riddick, Oral History, June 26, 1978–February 15, 1979, Senate Historical Office, Washington, D.C. See also Margaret Shannon, *Atlanta Journal and Constitution*, November 24, 1963.

2 RBR, Jr., to W. E. Aycock, November 26, 1963, Russell Collection, Dictation Series, Political, Russell Memorial Library, University of Georgia, Athens; RBR, Jr., to A. E. Hurst, December 5, 1963, and RBR, Jr., to Albert D. Thomson, December 4, 1963, Russell Collection, Kennedy Assassination; Earl T. Leonard, Oral History, February 15, 1971, Russell Collection.

3 Meg Greenfield, "The Man Who Leads the Southern Senators," *Reporter* 30 (May 21, 1964): 21.

4   Russell Collection, Intraoffice File, December 1–11 and 12–31, 1963.

5   RBR, Jr., to Jay D. Whiting, January 6, 1964; RBR, Jr., to Henry H. Wilson, Jr., March 3, 1964; and RBR, Jr., to Charles Bloch, December 3, 1963, Russell Collection, Kennedy Assassination.

6   RBR, Jr., to Mrs. Henry H. Wilson, Jr., March 3, 1964, ibid.

7   RBR, Jr., to Lyndon B. Johnson, February 24, 1964, ibid.

8   *Congress and the Nation, 1945–1964* (Washington: Congressional Quarterly Service, 1965), p. 1637; John Stennis to RBR, Jr., February 11, 1963, Russell Collection, Red Line File, 1962–64.

9   RBR, Jr., Office Notes, Russell Collection, Intraoffice File, October 1–11, 1963.

10 Theodore H. White, *The Making of the President, 1964* (New York: Atheneum, 1965), pp. 174–76; John Stennis to RBR, Jr., February 11, 1963, Russell Collection, Red Line File, 1962–64.

11 Quoted in Doris Kearns, *Lyndon Johnson and the American Dream* (New York: Harper and Row, 1976), p. 174.

12 *New York Times*, November 28, 1963, sec. 1, p. 20.

13 RBR, Jr., to J. M. Gloer, December 2, 1963, Russell Collection, Kennedy Assassination; RBR, Jr., to Mrs. C. N. Long, February 25, 1964, Russell Collection, Civil Rights; RBR, Jr., to Carter Pittman, April 28, 1964, Russell Collection, Political; *U.S. News and World Report* 56 (February 3, 1964): 8.

14 RBR, Jr., interview with Roger Mudd, June 27, 1963, Russell Collection, Personal, 1963.

15 *Congressional Record*, 88th Cong., 1st sess., June 17, 1963, p. 10937.

16 RBR, Jr., to Charles Bloch, May 21, 1963, Russell Collection, Political, Special Name File.

17 RBR, Jr., interview with Roger Mudd, June 27, 1963, Russell Collection, Personal, 1963.

18 *Congressional Record*, 88th Cong., 1st sess., June 17, 1963, p. 10937.

19 RBR, Jr., to Frank F. Faulk, Jr., December 2, 1963, and RBR, Jr., to W. E. Aycock, November 26, 1963, Russell Collection, Dictation Series, Political, 1963; RBR, Jr., to Mr. and Mrs. Perry C. Bay, December 11, 1964, Russell Collection, Kennedy Assassination.

20 *U.S. News and World Report* 56 (February 3, 1964): 8.

21 *New York Times*, March 2, 1964, sec. 1, p. 12; *Congressional Record*, 88th Cong., 2d sess., March 2, 1964, p. 4069.

22 *Congressional Record*, 88th Cong., 2d sess., March 2, 1964, p. 4071.

23 Ibid., 88th Cong., 1st sess., June 17, 1963, p. 10937; RBR, Jr., to Stephen A. Crump, October 28, 1963, Russell Collection, Civil Rights, 1963.

24 *Congressional Record*, 88th Cong., 1st sess., June 17, 1963, p. 10937.

25 A. L. Garnass to RBR, Jr., March 2, 1964; Laura E. Pomper to RBR, Jr., March [3], 1964; Carl McIntire to RBR, Jr., March 3, 1964; and RBR, Jr., to William R. Geisinger, March 13, 1964, Russell Collection, Civil Rights, 1964.

26 *Congressional Record*, 88th Cong., 2d sess., February 26, 1964, pp. 3718–19.

27 See Hubert H. Humphrey, *The Education of a Public Man* (Garden City, N.Y.: Doubleday, 1976), chapter 19.

28 RBR, Jr., to Edwin D. Harrison, April 17, 1964, Russell Collection, Dictation Series, General Endorsements, 1964.

29 Humphrey, *Education of a Public Man*, p. 278.

30 "One Plan to End Race Troubles: Pay People to Move," *U.S. News and World Report* 56 (March 30, 1964): 36–37.

31 *Congressional Record*, 88th Cong., 2d sess., March 16, 1964, pp. 5338–51; *New York Times*, June 13, 1964, sec. 1, p. 1.

32 *New York Times*, May 2, 1964, sec. 1, p. 1. For a full account of Russell's involvement in the civil rights fight, see David D. Potenziani, "Look to the Past: Richard B. Russell and the Defense of Southern White Supremacy" (Ph.D. dissertation, University of Georgia, 1981), especially chapter 8. See also Charles Whalen and Barbara Whalen, *The Longest Debate: A Legislative History of the Civil Rights Act* (Cabin John, Md./Washington: Seven Locks Press, 1985).

33 *New York Times*, May 8, 1964, sec. 1, p. 37. See also Russell Collection, Civil Rights, Presbyterian Petition, 1964.

34 *Congressional Record*, 88th Cong., 2d sess., June 18, 1964, pp. 14299–302.

35 John Stennis to RBR, Jr., June 22, 1964, Russell Collection, Red Line File, 1962–64.

36 RBR, Jr., to Erwin S. Clark, August 18, 1964, Russell Collection, Civil Rights, 1964.

37 RBR, Jr., to Buford W. McRae, April 22, 1966, Russell Collection, Dictation Series, General, Miscellaneous, 1963; *Atlanta Journal*, June 11, 1964; Roger Mudd, Oral History, March 14, 1971, Russell Collection.

38 John Stennis to RBR, Jr., June 24, 1964, Russell Collection, Red Line File, 1962–64.

39 *Atlanta Constitution*, July 16, 1964; *New York Times*, July 16, 1964, sec. 1, p. 3.

40 Lyndon B. Johnson to RBR, Jr., July 23, 1964, and RBR, Jr., to Johnson, July 25, 1964, Name File, Richard B. Russell, White House Central File, Johnson Library, Austin, Texas.

41 Russell Collection, Intraoffice File, 1964; RBR, Jr., to Mrs. Virginia Polhill, August 25, 1964, Russell Collection, Dictation Series, Political; Lady Bird Johnson, *A White House Diary* (New York: Holt, Rinehart, and Winston, 1970), pp. 185–86.

42 RBR, Jr., to Harvey J. Kennedy, August 13, 1965, Russell Collection, Dictation Series, Political. Russell talks about his relations with Johnson in "Richard Russell, Georgia Giant," manuscript for a three-part documentary, Cox Broadcasting Company, Atlanta, Georgia, 1970, pt. 3, pp. 18–27. See also Lady Bird Johnson, *A White House Diary*, pp. 42, 366, and *Atlanta Journal and Constitution*, January 5, 1969, which mentions Max Cleland's interview with Russell on January 21, 1965.

43 RBR, Jr., to Luci Baines Johnson, August 1, 1966, Russell Collection, Dictation Series, General, International, Special Name File, 1964–66; Luci Johnson Nugent to RBR, Jr., November 22, 1966, Russell Collection, Red Line File, 1966–67; "Richard Russell, Georgia Giant," pt. 3, pp. 25–26.

44 Earl T. Leonard, Oral History, February 15, 1971, Russell Collection.

45 RBR, Jr., to Ed W. Hiles, July 2, 1964; RBR, Jr., to Mrs. B. W. Jones, July 27, 1964; and RBR, Jr., to Edward M. Vinson, July 25, 1964, Russell Collection, Dictation Series, Political, 1964.

46 *New York Times*, August 9, 1964, sec. 1, p. 53.

47 RBR, Jr., to Jimmy Carter, September 1, 1964; RBR, Jr., to Walter D. Sanders, September 29, 1964; and RBR, Jr., to John H. Dillard, October 30, 1968, Russell Collection, Dictation Series, Political; RBR, Jr., to Comer O. Fowler, November 6, 1964, Russell Collec-

tion, Political, Campaign, 1966.

48 *Public Papers of the Presidents of the United States: Lyndon B. Johnson, 1964*, vol. 2 (Washington: Government Printing Office, 1965), pp. 716, 718.

49 RBR, Jr., Desk Note, September 12, 1964, and RBR, Jr., Memos, October 1 and 5, 1964, Russell Collection, Intraoffice File, September 1–14, and October 1964.

50 *Atlanta Constitution*, November 7 and 11, 1964; *Atlanta Journal*, November 12, 1964.

51 RBR, Jr., to Robert E. Fokes, Jr., September 26, 1964, and RBR, Jr., to John Woolfolk, September 26, 1964, Russell Collection, Dictation Series, Political.

52 RBR, Jr., to Mrs. J. Chester Smith, November 16, 1964, Russell Collection, Political; RBR, Jr., to Willis Robertson, November 18, 1964, Russell Collection, Dictation Series, Armed Services Committee, 1964.

53 *Atlanta Constitution*, September 28, 1964.

54 *Hearings before the President's Commission on the Assassination of President Kennedy*, vol. 5 (Washington: Government Printing Office, 1964), p. 600.

55 *Dallas Morning News*, September 7, 1964.

56 Margaret Shannon, *Atlanta Journal and Constitution*, magazine, September 11, 1977; *The Official Warren Commission Report on the Assassination of President John F. Kennedy* (New York: Doubleday, 1964), pp. 20–21.

57 *Atlanta Constitution*, September 28, 1964; *Atlanta Times*, September 29, 1964; *Long Island Press*, October 2, 1964; RBR, Jr., to Julian W. Collins, March 10, 1966, Russell Collection, Dictation Series, Armed Services, June–December, 1966.

58 *Congress and the Nation, 1945–1964*, pp. 1326–29.

59 Telephone Memo from Bill Jordan, July 23, 1964, Russell Collection, Intraoffice File, 1964; *Congressional Record*, 88th Cong., 2d sess., July 23, 1964, p. 16786; RBR, Jr., to George D. Head III, August 5, 1964, Russell Collection, Dictation Series; RBR, Jr., to Herbert Kaiser, July 21, 1962, Russell Collection, Dictation Series, Government Expenditures, General; *Congressional Record*, 88th Cong., 2d sess., July 23, 1964, p. 16786, and September 25, 1964, p. 22921; and 89th Cong., 1st sess., February 1, 1965, p. 1715.

60 RBR, Jr., to Calvin N. Poss, January 15, 1965, Russell Collection, Dictation Series, General.

61 RBR, Jr., to Ed G. Barham, July 7, 1962, and RBR, Jr., to W. C. Harris, August 5, 1965, ibid.; *Congressional Record*, 88th Cong., 1st sess., September 3, 1964, p. 21553, and 89th Cong., 1st sess., July 9, 1965, p. 16157.

62 *Congressional Record*, 89th Cong., 1st sess., February 1, 1965, p. 1715.

63 Office Memo, November 9, 1964, Russell Collection, Intraoffice File, November 1964.

64 *Atlanta Constitution*, November 13, 1964.

65 William F. Buchanan to RBR, Jr., March 30, 1964; RBR, Jr., to Clarence R. McLanahan, May 21, 1964; RBR, Jr., to Ernest D. Key, June 25, 1964; and RBR, Jr., to A. M. Bennett, June 26, 1964, Russell Collection, Dictation Series, Political.

66 *Atlanta Journal*, February 8, 1965; Dr. Burkley, telephone message to White House, February 8, 1965; Johnson family to RBR, Jr., February 2, 1964; and Lyndon B. Johnson to RBR, Jr., February 11, 1964, Name File, Richard B. Russell, White House Central File, Johnson Library; RBR, Jr., notes in appointment book, January and February 2, 1964, Russell Collection, Intraoffice File.

67 C. V. Clifton, Memo for the President, February 26, 1965, Name File, Richard B. Russell, White House Central File, Johnson Library.

68 William M. Bates, Oral History, March 17, 1971, Russell Collection.

69 Telephone conversation between Ralph McGill and Jack Valenti, February 11, 1965, Name File, Richard B. Russell, White House Central File, Johnson Library.

70 *New York Times*, April 29, 1965, sec. 1, p. 20, and May 21, 1965, sec. 1, p. 16.

71 *Congressional Record*, 89th Cong., 1st sess., May 24, 1965, pp. 11326–28.

72 Jack Valenti, Memo for the President, July 30, 1965, Name File, Richard B. Russell, White House Central File, Johnson Library.

73 RBR, Jr., to James V. Carmichael, August 20, 1965, Russell Collection, Dictation Series, Political.

74 RBR, Jr., to R. E. Gormley, October 5, 1965, ibid.

75 RBR, Jr., to Robert W. Johnston, October 16, 1965, ibid.

76 *New York Times*, March 31, 1966, sec. 1, p. 25.

77 John F. Kraft, "A Study of Attitudes of Georgia," Russell Collection, Personal, Political.

78 RBR, Jr., to R. M. Barton, June 26, 1961, Russell Collection, Dictation Series, Political.

79 RBR, Jr., to Price Gilbert, Jr., August 12, 1966, ibid.

80 RBR, Jr., to Clayton Brown, Jr., November 11, 1964, ibid.

81 RBR, Jr., to J. S. Malone, July 29, 1965, and RBR, Jr., to F. W. Kerr, October 5, 1965, ibid.; RBR, Jr., to Sandy Beaver, June 9, 1965, Russell Collection, Dictation Series, Armed Services.

82 RBR, Jr., to Gail Stanley, January 12, 1963; RBR, Jr., to Roy Hemming, September 23, 1964; and RBR, Jr., to W. E. Laitte, Jr., August 5, 1964, Russell Collection, Dictation Series, Reapportionment.

83 *Congressional Record*, 89th Cong., 2d sess., January 24, 1966, pp. 964–66.

CHAPTER 19

1 RBR, Jr., to C. Alex Sears, Jr., May 14, 1962, and RBR, Jr., to Mrs. J. L. Sarbacker, March 4, 1965, Russell Collection, Dictation Series, General, International, Russell Memorial Library, University of Georgia, Athens.

2 RBR, Jr., to Mrs. Roger D. Johnson, August 30, 1961, Russell Collection, Dictation Series, Foreign Relations.

3 Russell Collection, Intraoffice File, 1964.

4 *Congressional Record*, 88th Cong., 2d sess., March 31, 1964, pp. 6629–30.

5 RBR, Jr., to Mrs. J. L. Sarbacker, March 4, 1965, Russell Collection, International; Telephone conversation between John F. Kennedy and RBR, Jr., November 9, 1961, Russell Collection, Office Matters, Red Line File, Special Presidential, 1941–67.

6 Russell Collection, Intraoffice File, 1964.

7 Ibid.

8 *Congressional Record*, 88th Cong., 2d sess., August 6, 1964, pp. 18410–13.

9 Ibid., p. 18413. See also ibid., 90th Cong., 1st sess., February 28, 1967, pp. 4715–17.

10 RBR, Jr., to M. G. Roberts, November 5, 1965, and RBR, Jr., to Carl T. Sutherland, November 5, 1965, Russell Collection, Dictation Series, Armed Services; RBR, Jr., to

Louis E. Wolfson, January 4, 1966, Russell Collection, Dictation Series, General, International.

11 RBR, Jr., to Mrs. W. K. Zeiss, November 6, 1963, and RBR, Jr., to Mrs. J. L. Sarbacker, March 4, 1965, Russell Collection, Dictation Series, General, International.

12 *New York Times*, November 27, 1964, sec. 1, p. 17; RBR, Jr., interview with Max Cleland, July 21, 1965, in *Atlanta Journal and Constitution*, January 5, 1969.

13 Bob Young to RBR, Jr., November 11, 1964, and William C. Turpin to RBR, Jr., January 15, 1965, Russell Collection, International. The books on Vietnam are legion. See Stanley Karnow, *Vietnam: A History* (New York: Viking, 1983); George C. Herring, *America's Longest War: The United States and Vietnam, 1950–1975* (New York: John Wiley and Sons, 1979); Herbert Y. Schandler, *The Unmaking of a President: Lyndon Johnson and Vietnam* (Princeton: Princeton University Press, 1977); and David Halberstam, *The Best and the Brightest* (New York: Random House, 1969).

14 Russell Collection, Personal, Trips, Spain, 1964; Intraoffice File, 1964.

15 RBR, Jr., to Shimon Peres, December 18, 1964, and RBR, Jr., to Zalman Shazar, December 18, 1964, Russell Collection, Trips, Spain, 1964.

16 Russell Collection, Intraoffice File, 1964.

17 *New York Times*, May 1, 1965, sec. 1, p. 16.

18 Ibid., January 12, 1965, sec. 1, p. 1.

19 Russell Collection, Intraoffice File, August 1965.

20 Ibid., July 1965.

21 Ibid., September 1965.

22 Joe Califano, Memo for President Johnson, October 1, 1965, Name File, Richard B. Russell, White House Central File, Lyndon B. Johnson Library, Austin, Texas.

23 Johnson pamphlet, 1965, Russell Collection, International.

24 RBR, Jr., to Harvey J. Kennedy, August 13, 1965, Russell Collection, Dictation Series, Political.

25 *New York Times*, August 2, 1965, sec. 1, p. 3.

26 "What It Will Take to Win in Vietnam," *U.S. News and World Report* 59 (September 6, 1965): 56–60.

27 Russell Collection, Intraoffice File, July 1965.

28 RBR, Jr., to Mr. and Mrs. S. H. Neff, December 1, 1965, Russell Collection, Dictation Series, General, International.

29 *New York Times*, December 31, 1965, sec. 1, p. 3.

30 RBR, Jr., to Dr. Terrell Tanner, December 22, 1965, Russell Collection, Legislative, Armed Services Committee.

31 RBR, Jr., to Donald F. Bean, February 23, 1966, Russell Collection, International, 1966.

32 RBR, Jr., to Douglas M. Audsley, October 14, 1965, ibid.

33 RBR, Jr., to A. J. Bruyere, February 26, 1966, Russell Collection, Dictation Series, Armed Services.

34 RBR, Jr., to Mrs. Rachel Parker, January 6, 1966, Russell Collection, International.

35 Russell Collection, Intraoffice File, January 1966.

36 *Congressional Record*, 89th Cong., 2d sess., January 24, 1966, p. 964; *New York Times*, January 21, 1966, 1:7.

37 *U.S. News and World Report* 60 (May 2, 1966): 56–57.

38 Karnow, *Vietnam*, p. 510. See also *New York Times*, April 27, 1966, sec. 1, p. 5, and May 1, 1966, sec. 4, p. 3.

39 Russell Collection, Intraoffice File, July 1966.

40 *New York Times*, June 30, 1966, sec. 1, p. 1; Lyndon B. Johnson to RBR, Jr., November 3, 1966, Name File, Richard B. Russell, White House Central File, Johnson Library.

41 RBR, Jr., to Gary L. Dodson, October 25, 1966, Russell Collection, International. See also "Richard Russell, Georgia Giant," manuscript for a three-part documentary, Cox Broadcasting Company, Atlanta, Georgia, 1970, pt. 3, p. 25.

42 *Congressional Record*, 90th Cong., 1st sess., July 10, 1967, pp. 18093–97; Wayne Kelley, *Atlanta Journal and Constitution*, magazine, February 4, 1968.

43 RBR, Jr., to Lyndon B. Johnson, December 21, 1967, and Dean Rusk to RBR, Jr., January 29, 1968, Russell Collection, Red Line File, 1969; "Richard Russell, Georgia Giant," pt. 3, p. 25.

44 Stephen M. Young to RBR, Jr., December 29, 1966, and RBR, Jr., to Young, December 29, 1966, Russell Collection, Legislative, Armed Services Committee, 1966.

45 Karnow, *Vietnam*, p. 507.

46 *U.S. News and World Report* 62 (January 16, 1967): 11; *New York Times*, February 14, 1967, sec. 1, p. 10; *World-Wide Military Commitments: Hearings before the Preparedness Investigating Subcommittee, U.S. Senate*, 90th Cong., 1st sess., February 21 and 23 and March 1 and 2, 1967, pt. 2, 116.

47 *Congressional Record*, 90th Cong., 1st sess., February 23, 1967, pp. 4276–78.

48 Ibid., March 21, 1967, pp. 7509–12; *New York Times*, March 22, 1967, sec. 1, p. 13.

49 L. A. Paine to RBR, Jr., August 31, 1967; copy of L. C. Stuart to Lyndon B. Johnson, September 12, 1967; C. W. Hodgson to RBR, Jr., November 17, 1967; Marion Blackwell to RBR, Jr., November 20, 1967; George W. West to RBR, Jr., December 1, 1967; J. H. Griffin to RBR, Jr., December 15, 1967; E. W. Klein to RBR, Jr., August 24, 1967; and John G. Barnett to RBR, Jr., [August 1967], Russell Collection, International.

50 Ben S. Shippen to RBR, Jr., August 23, 1967, ibid.

51 Russell Collection, Intraoffice File, 1967, Office Calendar, 1967.

52 RBR, Jr., Statement on How to Implement Resignation, February 8, 1967, Russell Collection, Senatorial Years, Personal Correspondence, Illness.

53 *Congressional Record*, 90th Cong., 1st sess., December 15, 1967, p. 37424.

54 *New York Times*, January 24, 1968, sec. 1, p. 1, and December 31, 1968, sec. 1, p. 1.

55 *Congressional Record*, 90th Cong., 2d sess., January 18, 1968, pp. 202–5.

56 Russell Collection, Intraoffice File, February–March 1968.

57 RBR, Jr., to Owen H. Page, February 8, 1968, Russell Collection, Personal, Personal Condolence, 1968; *Congressional Record*, 90th Cong., 2d sess., March 4, 1968, p. 4963. See also *Atlanta Journal*, March 3, 1968.

58 *Congressional Record*, 90th Cong., 2d sess., April 2, 1968, pp. 8570–72.

59 Powell Moore, Oral History, March 6, 1971, Russell Collection; *Congressional Record*, 90th Cong., 2d sess., April 1, 1968, pp. 8410–18, 8437–42; *Washington Post*, April 2, 1968.

60 Russell Collection, Intraoffice File, Memoranda, Daysheets, and Notes, 1953–70.

61 *Congressional Record*, 90th Cong., 2d sess., June 24, 1968, pp. 18398–402, 18411.

62 Ibid., October 1, 1968, pp. 28936–42; *U.S. News and World Report* 65 (October 14, 1968): 14–15.

63 RBR, Jr., to John H. Dillard, October 30, 1968, Dictation Series, Political; Wayne P. Kelley, Oral History, March 6, 1971, Russell Collection; *Augusta Chronicle*, April 25, 1968.

64 Russell Collection, Intraoffice File, November–December, 1968; *Atlanta Constitution*, December 11, 1968; Powell Moore, Oral History, March 6, 1971, Russell Collection.

65 RBR, Jr., to Marion T. Wood, July 17, 1969, Russell Collection, Legislative, Armed Services Committee.

CHAPTER 20

1 See Jude Wanniski, "Senator Russell: A One-Man Court over the Nation's Defense Policies," *National Observer*, February 17, 1969, reprinted in *Congressional Record*, 91st Cong., 1st sess., March 4, 1969, pp. 5206–7, and Floyd M. Riddick, Oral History, March 5, 1971, Russell Collection, Russell Memorial Library, University of Georgia, Athens.

2 *Savannah Morning News*, January 9, 1969.

3 Rowland Evans and Robert Novak, *Atlanta Journal*, January 1, 1969.

4 *Athens Banner-Herald*, October 20, 1968.

5 RBR, Jr., Speech before the Georgia General Assembly, February 13, 1964, and Carters Dam Speech, November 14, 1964, Russell Collection, Speeches. See also *Congressional Record*, 88th Cong., 2d sess., January 10, 1964, p. 2434.

6 *Macon Telegraph*, February 8, 1970.

7 Russell Collection, Intraoffice File, Memorandum, January 10, 1965.

8 RBR, Jr., to Lowell B. Mason, March 23, 1966, Russell Collection, Dictation Series.

9 Tina Pannetta, Oral History, March 4, 1971, Russell Collection.

10 Author's interview with Charles E. Campbell, June 9, 1981; Joel Cash Williams, Oral History, November 19, 1979, Russell Collection.

11 Barboura Raesly, Oral History, June 16, 1975, Russell Collection; Russell Collection, Intraoffice File, November 15, 1965.

12 *Pike County [Ga.] Journal*, September 4, 1969.

13 Russell Collection, Intraoffice File, May 1969.

14 Earl T. Leonard, Oral History, February 15, 1971, Russell Collection.

15 Wayne Kelley, Oral History, March 6, 1971, Russell Collection.

16 Powell A. Moore, Oral History, March 6, 1971, Russell Collection.

17 RBR, Jr., to Louis E. Wolfson, June 7, 1967, Russell Collection, Personal, Personal Historical; H. Grady Hutcherson to RBR, Jr., May 3 and July 26, 1969; Charles Campbell to Hutcherson, May 16 and August 13, 1969; and William Tate to RBR, Jr., November 25, 1969, and January 6, 1970, Russell Collection, Personal, Personal Miscellaneous; Vince Dooley, Oral History, March 11, 1971, Russell Collection; RBR, Jr., to A. C. Aderhold, February 18, 1967, Russell Collection, Dictation Series.

18 Norman Underwood, Oral History, February 12, 1971, and G. W. "Buddy" Darden III, Oral History, February 12, 1971, Russell Collection.

19 RBR, Jr., to "Cleaning Help," January 21, 1963, and RBR, Jr., to George Stewart, April 24, 1961, Russell Collection, Dictation Series, General; RBR, Jr., to Ralph W. Yarborough, January 11, 1969, Russell Collection, Dictation Series, Steering Committee, 1964–69.

20 William H. Darden, Oral History, March 5, 1971, and Thomas J. McIntyre, Oral History, April 21, 1971, Russell Collection.

21 RBR, Jr., to Mrs. Robert S. Elrod, July 30, 1961, Russell Collection, Dictation Series, Personal.

22 Norman Underwood, Oral History, February 12, 1971, and Ronald B. Ginn, Oral History, March 2, 1971, Russell Collection.

23 Fielding Russell, Oral History, September 5, 1974, Russell Collection.

24 Statement, 1963, Russell Collection, General, Office Matters, Staff, 1960–66.

25 RBR, Jr., to Jim Dillard, March 12, 1969, Russell Collection, Personal, Family, 1969.

26 Congressional Favors File, White House Central File, Lyndon B. Johnson Library, Austin, Texas; Russell Collection, Intraoffice File, Daybooks, Calendars, 1966; "Richard Russell, Georgia Giant," manuscript for a three-part documentary, Cox Broadcasting Company, Atlanta, Georgia, 1970, pt. 3, p. 16.

27 G. W. "Buddy" Darden III, Oral History, February 12, 1971, Russell Collection. See also Gilbert C. Fite, "Richard B. Russell and Lyndon B. Johnson: The Story of a Strange Friendship," *Missouri Historical Review* 83 (January 1989): 125–38.

28 *Congressional Record*, 86th Cong., 1st sess., February 2, 1959, pp. 1539–41; RBR, Jr., to Alexander A. Lawrence, September 18, 1959, and Lawrence to RBR, Jr., September 21, 1959, Russell Collection, Personal, Personal Miscellaneous; RBR, Jr., to Carter Pittman, February 17, 1959, Russell Collection, Political, Carter Pittman, 1957–60.

29 James L. Hooten to Lyndon B. Johnson, March 28, 1968; Mrs. Ida S. Matz to Johnson, April 1, 1968; C. S. Hamilton to Johnson, May 3, 1968; and Sherman L. Roberson to Johnson, April 3, 1968, Name File, Alexander A. Lawrence, White House Central File, Johnson Library.

30 Tom Johnson, Memo for the President, June 11, 1968, ibid.

31 RBR, Jr., to J. D. Mattox, April 4, 1968, and RBR, Jr., to Carl Espy, April 19, 1968, Russell Collection, Dictation Series, Political Patronage, 1968.

32 James R. Jones recalled this meeting in a memo to Juanita Roberts, July 2, 1968, and Tom Johnson, Memo for Jim Jones, May 7 and 24, 1968, Name File, Richard B. Russell, White House Central File, Johnson Library.

33 RBR, Jr., to Lyndon B. Johnson, May 20, 1968, Russell Collection, Dictation Series, Political Patronage, Judgeships, Southern District. See also Russell Collection, Intraoffice File, April 1968.

34 RBR, Jr., to Lyndon B. Johnson, July 1, 1968, and Johnson to RBR, Jr., July 2, 1968, Office File, Larry Temple, White House Central File, Johnson Library.

35 Jack J. Helms to RBR, Jr., July 5, 1968, and RBR, Jr., to Helms, July 11, 1968, Russell Collection, Political Patronage, Judgeships, Southern District.

36 RBR, Jr., to Lyndon B. Johnson, July 1, 1968, Office File, Larry Temple, White House Central File, Johnson Library. The best account of the Johnson-Russell conflict over the Lawrence appointment is in Bruce Allen Murphy's *Fortas: The Rise and Ruin of a Su-*

preme Court Justice (New York: William Morrow, 1988), chapter 14.

37 Russell Collection, Intraoffice File, July 1–16, 1968.

38 *Atlanta Constitution*, October 11, 1968; *Augusta Chronicle*, October 11, 1968; *Washington Evening Star*, October 11, 1968; *New York Times*, October 11, 1968, sec. 1, p. 23.

39 *Congressional Record*, 91st Cong., 1st sess., January 14, 1969, pp. 648–50; RBR, Jr., to Frank Scarlett, January 23, 1969, Russell Collection, Personal, Commendatory, 1969.

40 Lyndon B. Johnson to RBR, Jr., November 2, 1968, Name File, Richard B. Russell, White House Central File, Johnson Library; Johnson to RBR, Jr., January 17, 1969, Russell Collection, Red Line File, Special Presidential.

41 *New York Times*, March 5, 1969, sec. 1, p. 49.

42 Powell A. Moore, Oral History, March 6, 1971, Russell Collection; *Tributes to the President and Mrs. Lyndon Baines Johnson* (Washington: Government Printing Office, 1969), pp. 53–54.

43 RBR, Jr., to Charles L. Cowan, July 31, 1968, Russell Collection, Political Patronage, Judgeships, Southern District.

44 Wayne Kelley, Oral History, March 6, 1971, Russell Collection.

45 *Atlanta Constitution*, September 27, 1968.

46 RBR, Jr., to Dr. Herbert A. Saltzman, December 28, 1968, Russell Collection, Dictation Series.

47 *Atlanta Journal*, March 20 and 21, 1969.

48 John A. Sibley to RBR, Jr., April 3, 1969, and RBR, Jr., to Sibley, April 10, 1969, Sibley Papers, Atlanta, Georgia; RBR, Jr., to George C. Griffin, April 8, 1969, and RBR, Jr., to Spence Grayson, March 29, 1969, Russell Collection, Dictation Series.

49 *Congressional Record*, 91st Cong., 1st sess., March 24, 1969, pp. 7175–77.

50 *U.S. News and World Report* 66 (May 19, 1969): 22; *New York Times*, May 7, 1969, sec. 1, p. 93.

51 RBR, Jr., to Dr. Herbert A. Saltzman, July 31, 1969, and RBR, Jr., to Dr. J. Willis Hurst, May 19, 1969, Russell Collection, Dictation Series, Health, Education, and Welfare, 1964–65; RBR, Jr., to Jack and Mary Valenti, May 8, 1969, Russell Collection, Dictation Series, 1969.

52 *Congressional Record*, 91st Cong., 1st sess., April 1, 1969, pp. 8249–50.

53 *Marietta [Ga.] Daily Journal*, September 10 and December 19, 1969; *Atlanta Constitution*, June 3 and 10, 1969.

54 *New York Times*, July 22, 1969, sec. 1, p. 30; Russell Collection, Intraoffice File, July 15–31, 1969.

55 RBR, Jr., to Fred L. Young, May 25, 1970, Russell Collection, International, 1970.

56 RBR, Jr., to W. D. S. Sanday, February 4, 1962, Russell Collection, Dictation Series, Political; *Savannah Morning News*, January 1, 1969.

57 Bill Bates, Memo to RBR, Jr., October 8, 1965, Russell Collection, Intraoffice File, October 1–13, 1965; *Atlanta Journal*, October 21, 1965.

58 Richard M. Nixon to RBR, Jr., November 21, 1969, and April 11, 1970, Russell Collection, Red Line File, Special Presidential; *New York Times*, January 20, 1970, sec. 1, p. 1.

59 Evan Thomas to RBR, Jr., April 3, 1964, and RBR, Jr., to Thomas, April 15, 1964, Russell Collection, Personal, Book.

60 Ashbel Green to RBR, Jr., March 7, 1969; RBR, Jr., to Green, March 17, 1969; and Evelyn P. Metzger to Proctor Jones, April 1, 1968, ibid.

61 Curtis E. Tate, Jr., to RBR, Jr., May 18, 1970, and Barboura Raesly to Tate, May 24, 1970, Russell Collection, Personal Autobiography File.

62 Gilbert C. Fite, "The Richard B. Russell Library: From Idea to Working Collection," *Georgia Historical Quarterly* 64 (Spring 1980): 22–34.

63 *Winder News*, October 1, 1969; *Augusta Herald*, October 10, 1969; RBR, Jr., to W. B. Thompson, October 7, 1969, and RBR, Jr., to Clark Cole, September 18, 1969, Russell Collection, Dictation Series.

64 Hubert H. Humphrey to RBR, Jr., October 7, 1969, Russell Collection, Red Line File, Personal.

65 See data in Russell Collection, Personal Correspondence, Senatorial Years.

66 *U.S. News and World Report* 68 (February 23, 1970): 18.

67 *Augusta Chronicle*, September 14, 1970.

68 Herman Talmadge, Oral History, April 21, 1971, Russell Collection.

69 *Washington Evening Star*, September 17, 1970. See also Russell Collection, Intraoffice File, Memoranda, Daysheets, and Notes, 1953–70.

70 Russell Collection, Calendars, 1970.

71 Russell Collection, Intraoffice File, Memoranda, Daysheets, and Notes, 1953–70.

72 Russell's illness has been described by the following medical people in oral histories in the Russell Collection: Dr. Andre Ognibene, Dr. R. J. Pearson, Dr. Robert Zurek, and Major Suzanne Phillips, Army Nurse Corps. See also *Atlanta Journal*, January 21, 1971, and *New York Times*, January 22, 1971, sec. 1, p. 1.

73 *Atlanta Constitution*, January 22, 23, 24, and 25, 1971.

Index

Note: Richard B. Russell, Jr., will be referred to throughout the index as RBR.

Library of Congress Cataloging-in-Publication Data

Fite, Gilbert Courtland, 1918–
   Richard B. Russell, Jr., senator from Georgia / by Gilbert C.
Fite.
      p.   cm.—(The Fred W. Morrison series in Southern studies)
   Includes bibliographical references and index.
   ISBN 0-8078-1937-9 (cloth, alk. paper)
      1. Russell, Richard B. (Richard Brevard), 1897–1971.
2. Legislators—United States—Biography.   3. United States.
Congress. Senate—Biography.   4. Governors—Georgia—Biography.
5. Georgia—Politics and government—1865–1950.   6. United States—
Politics and government—1933–1945.   7. United States—Politics and
government—1945–   I. Title.   II. Series.
E748.R944F57   1991
328.73'092—dc20   90-40277
[B]   CIP